# ARINACCHI GALLERY



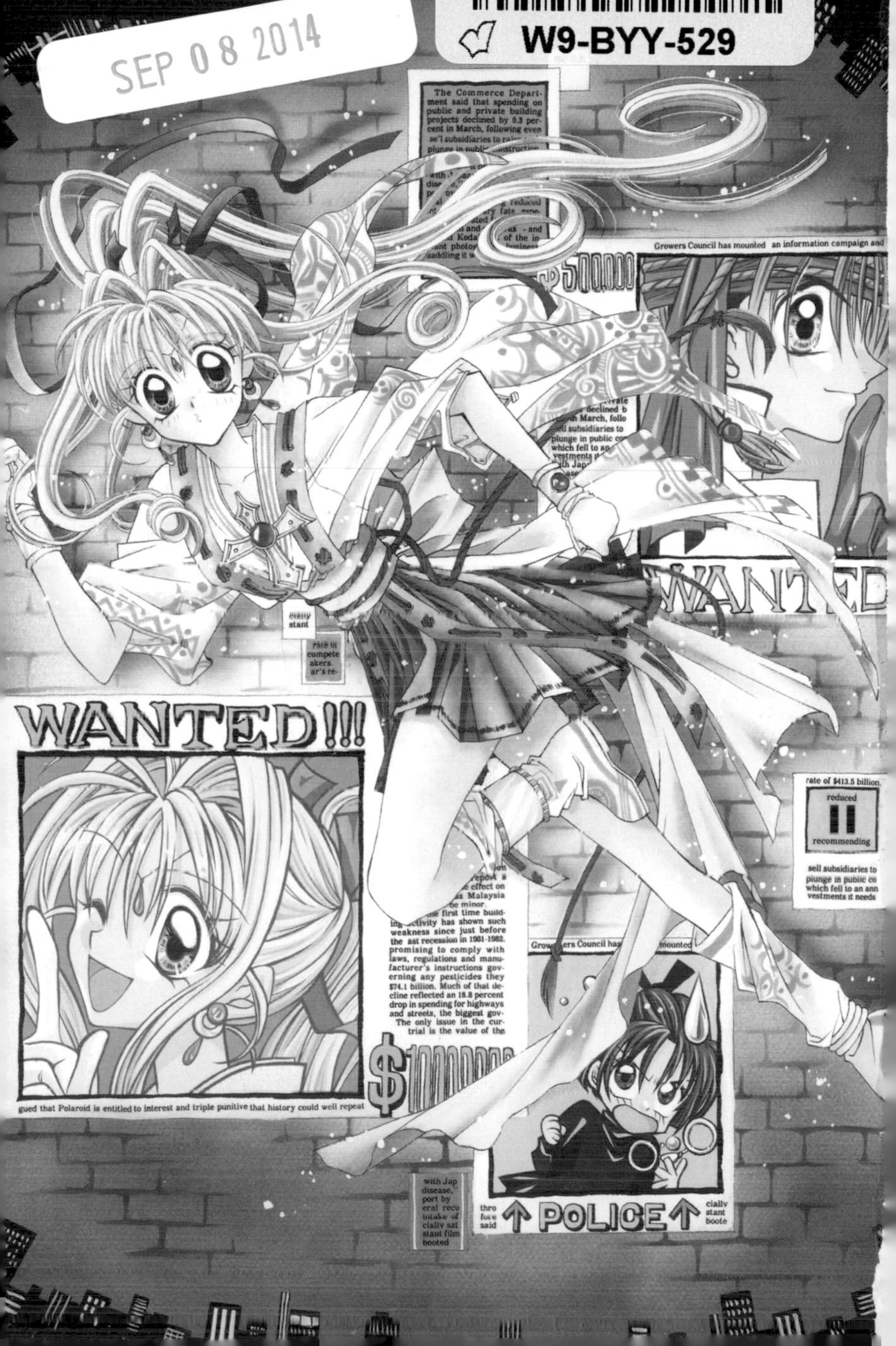
The Commerce Department said that spending on public and private building projects declined by 0.3 percent in March, following even
Growers Council has mounted an information campaign and
WANTED
WANTED!!!
rate of $413.5 billion.
reduced
recommending
sell subsidiaries to plunge in public co which fell to an ann vestments it needs
promising to comply with laws, regulations and manufacturer's instructions governing any pesticides they $74.1 billion. Much of that decline reflected an 18.8 percent drop in spending for highways and streets, the biggest gov-
The only issue in the curtrial is the value of the
gued that Polaroid is entitled to interest and triple punitive that history could well repeat
POLICE

COMMENT FROM **CURATOR ARINACCHI**

This is an illustration I drew for a poster that came with the magazine. I drew it with the image in mind of the police shining a spotlight on Jeanne. You can see the illustration is a bit fancy with the patterns on Jeanne's outfit.

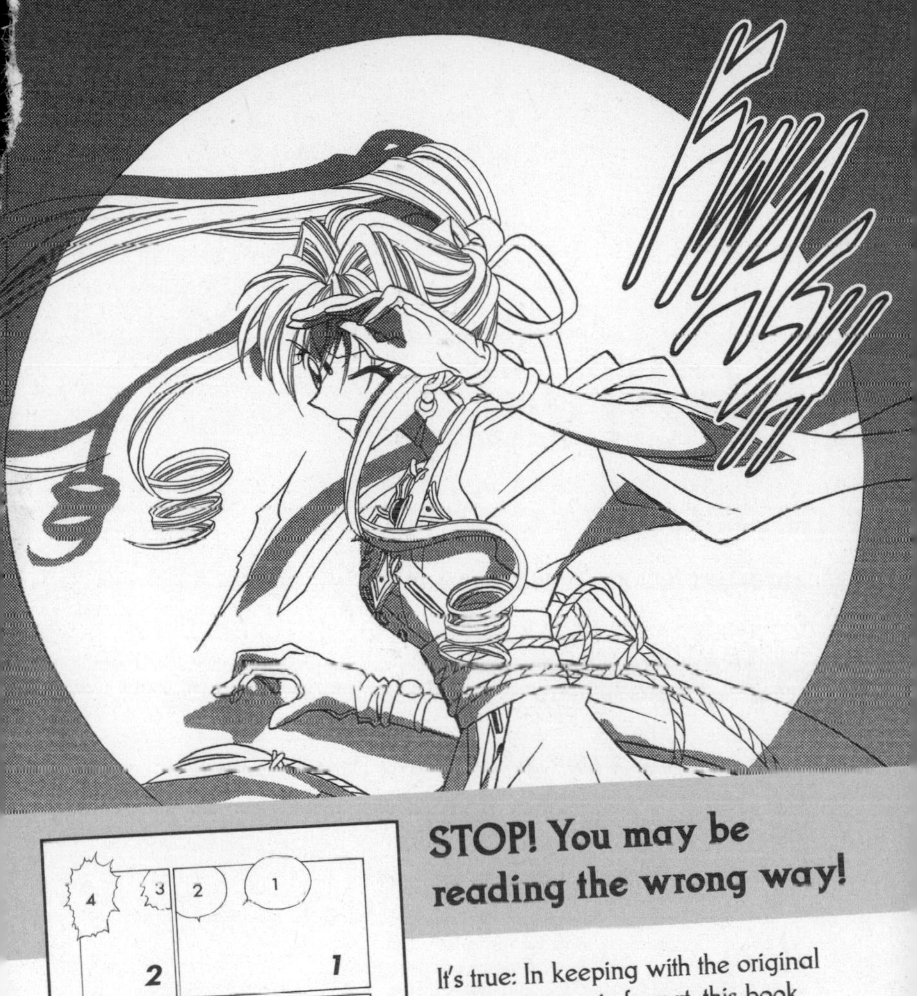

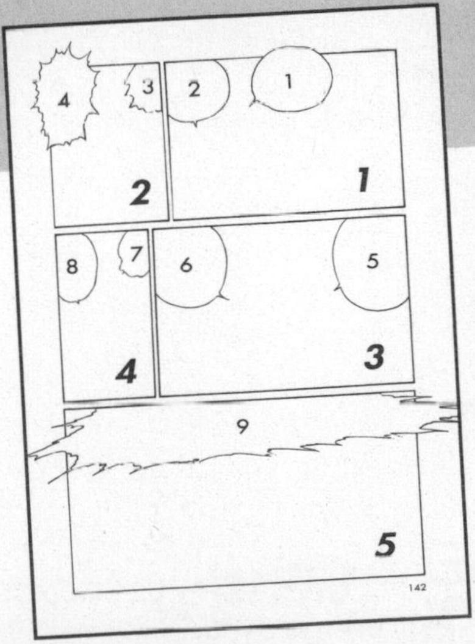

1
2
3
4
1
2
5
6
7
8
3
4
9
5
142


## STOP! You may be reading the wrong way!

It's true: In keeping with the original Japanese comic format, this book reads from right to left—so action, sound effects, and word balloons are completely reversed. This preserves the orientation of the original artwork—plus, it's fun! Check out the diagram shown here to get the hang of things, and then turn to the other side of the book to get started!

## PHANTOM THIEF
# Jeanne

**VOLUME 3**
**SHOJO BEAT EDITION**

**STORY AND ART BY** Arina Tanemura

**TRANSLATION** Tetsuichiro Miyaki
**TOUCH-UP ART & LETTERING** Inori Fukuda Trant
**DESIGN** Shawn Carrico
**EDITOR** Nancy Thistlethwaite

KAMIKAZE KAITO JEANNE © 1998 by Arina Tanemura
All rights reserved.
First published in Japan in 1998 by SHUEISHA Inc., Tokyo.
English translation rights arranged by SHUEISHA Inc.

The stories, characters and incidents mentioned
in this publication are entirely fictional.

No portion of this book may be reproduced or
transmitted in any form or by any means without
written permission from the copyright holders.

Printed in the U.S.A.

Published by VIZ Media, LLC
P.O. Box 77010
San Francisco, CA 94107

10 9 8 7 6 5 4 3 2 1
First printing, July 2014

**PARENTAL ADVISORY**
PHANTOM THIEF JEANNE is rated
T for Teen and is recommended for
ages 13 and up.
ratings.viz.com

www.viz.com

www.shojobeat.com

# ARINA TANEMURA

Arina Tanemura began her manga
career in 1996 when her short stories
debuted in *Ribon* magazine. She gained
fame with the 1997 publication of *I·O·N*,
and ever since her debut Tanemura
has been a major force in shojo manga
with popular series *Phantom Thief
Jeanne, Time Stranger Kyoko, Full Moon,*
and *The Gentlemen's Alliance †*. Both
*Phantom Thief Jeanne* and *Full Moon*
have been adapted into
animated TV series.

*Jeanne* Special Illustrations

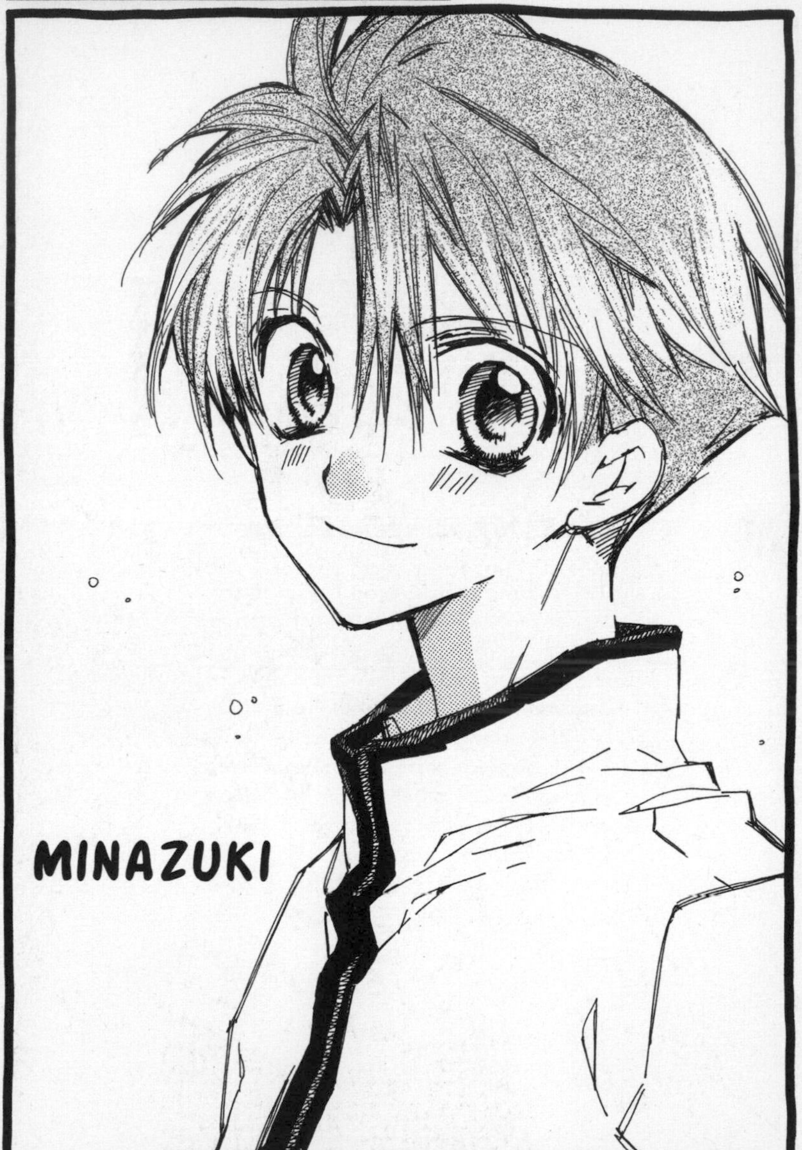
MINAZUKI

Jeanne Special Illustrations

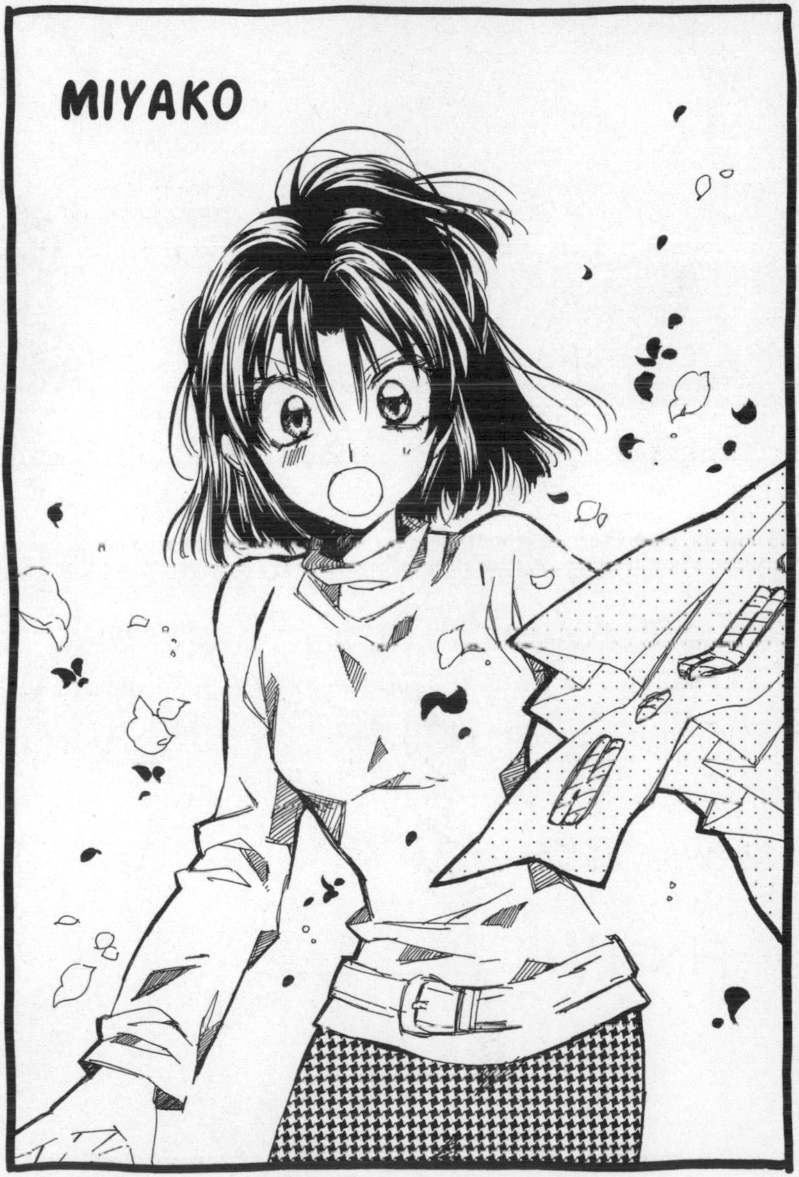
MIYAKO

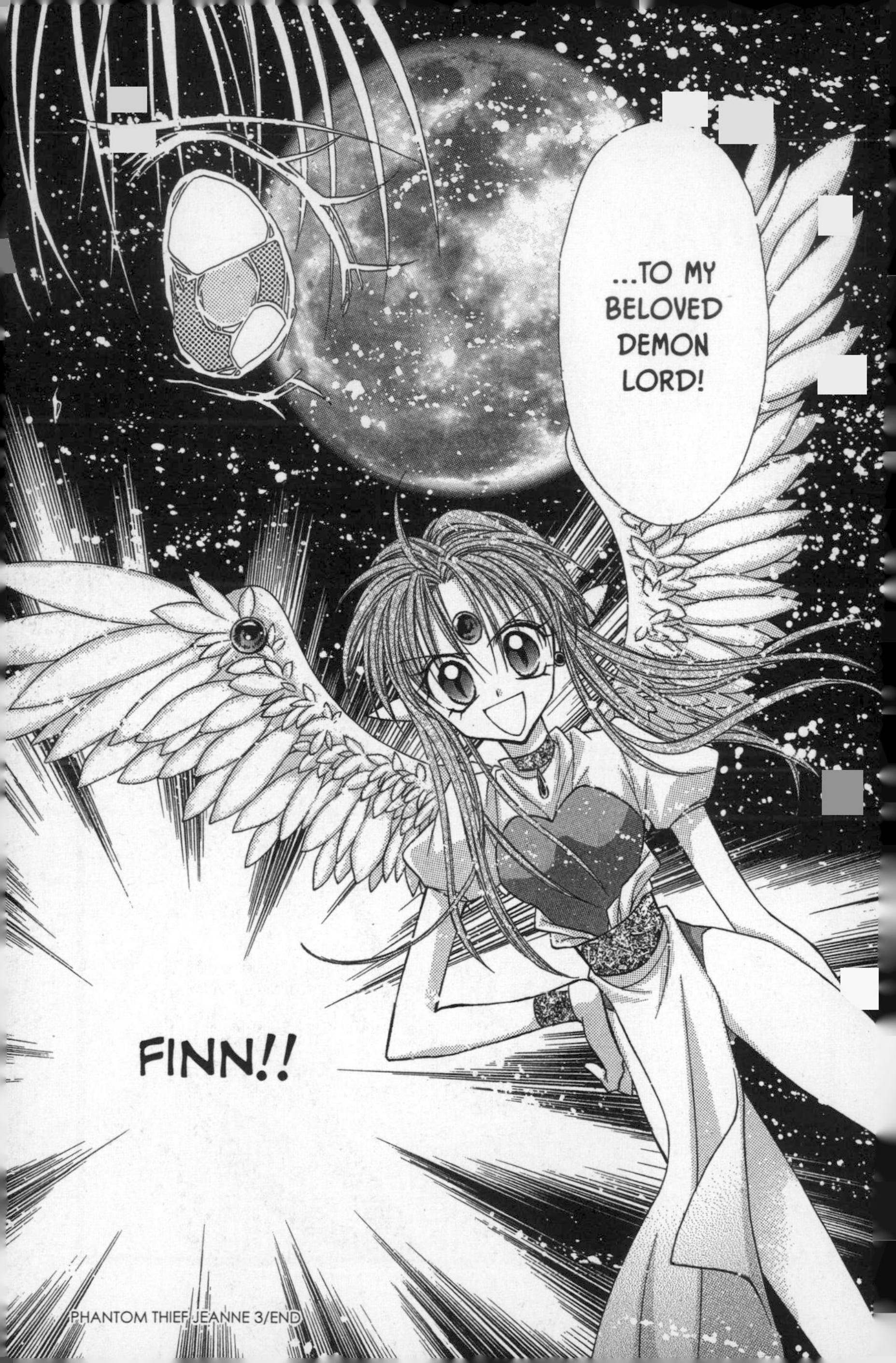
...TO MY BELOVED DEMON LORD!
FINN!!
PHANTOM THIEF JEANNE 3/END

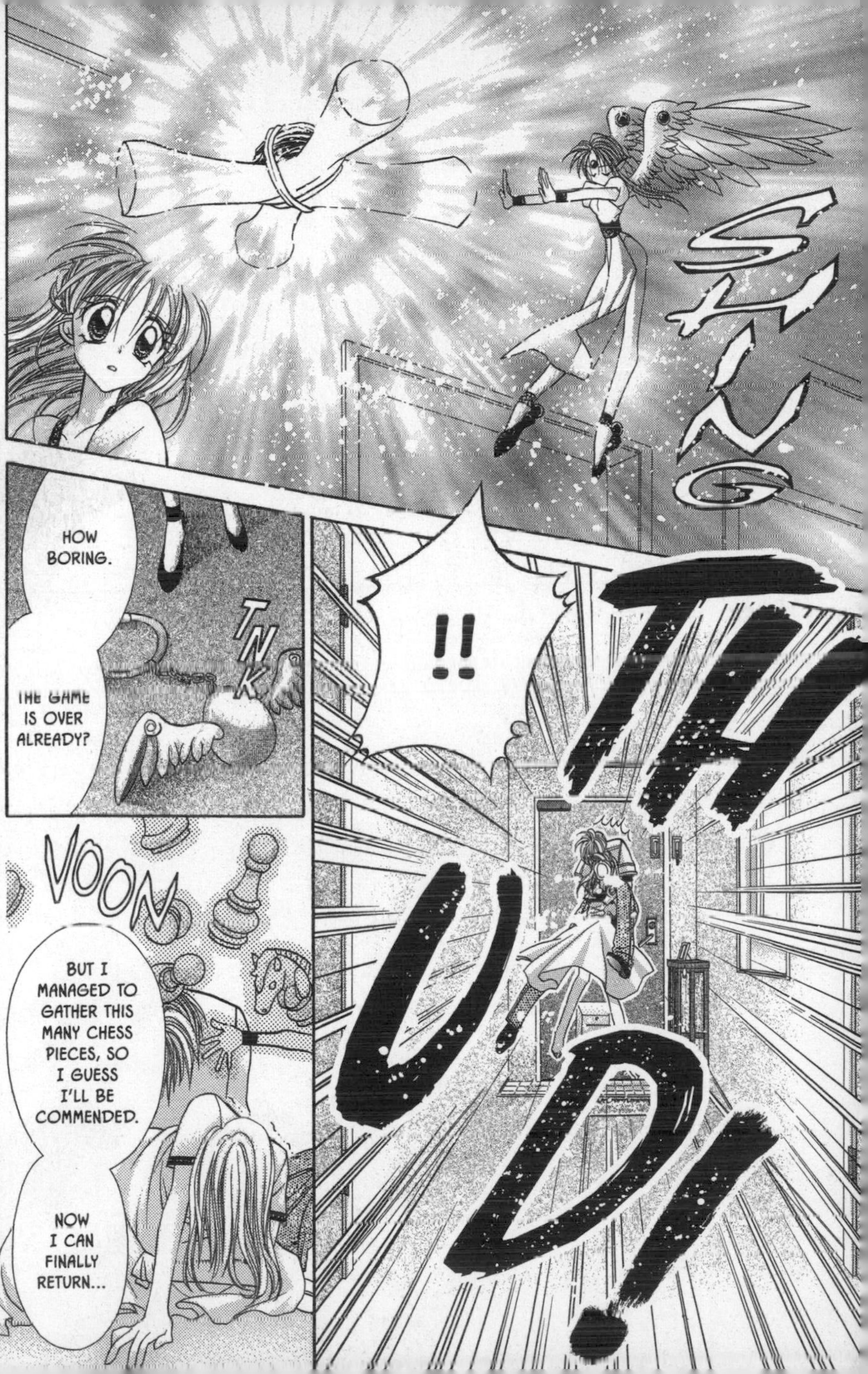
SHING
!!
THUD!
HOW BORING.
TNK
THE GAME IS OVER ALREADY?
VOON
BUT I MANAGED TO GATHER THIS MANY CHESS PIECES, SO I GUESS I'LL BE COMMENDED.
NOW I CAN FINALLY RETURN...

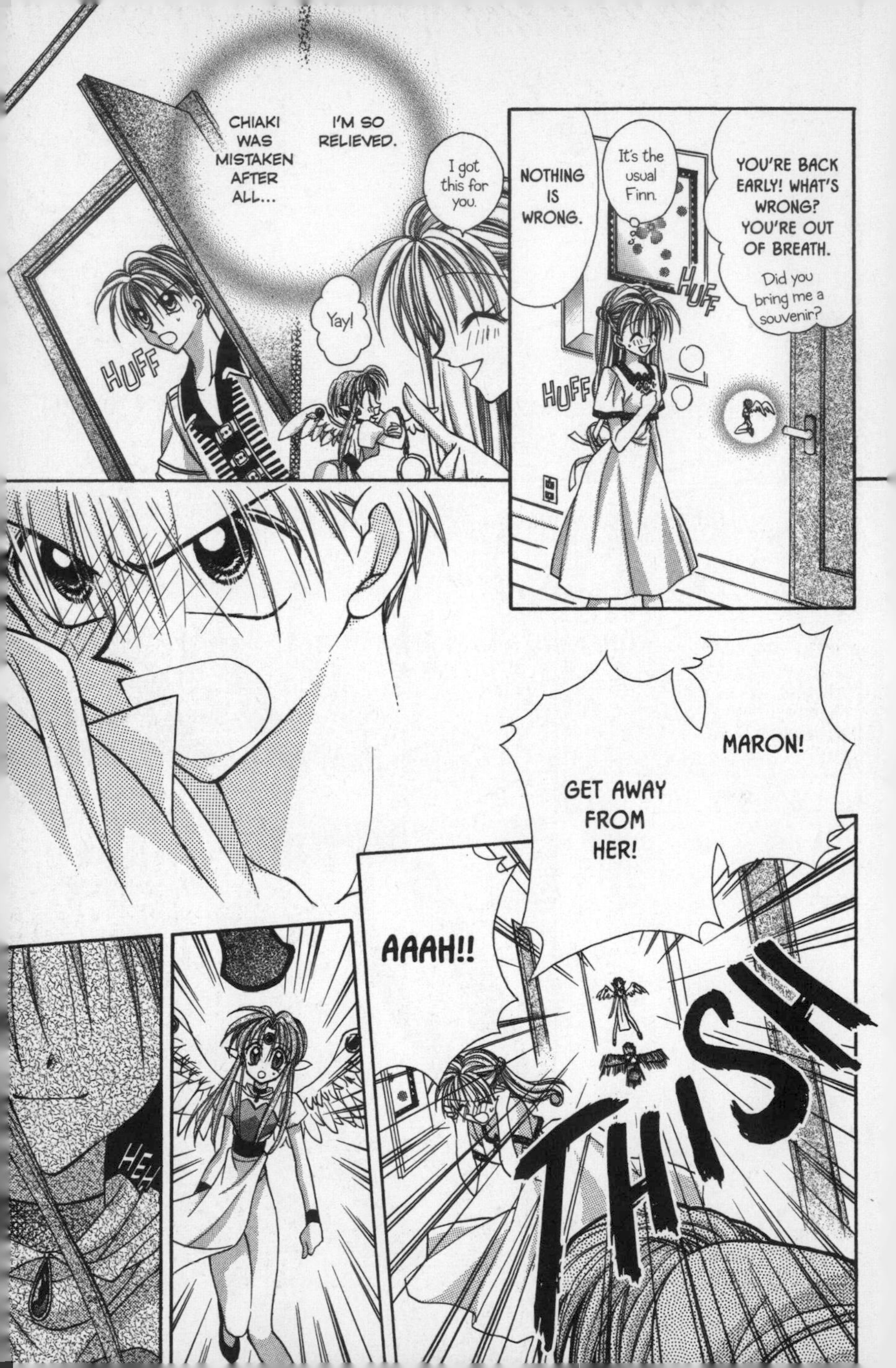
YOU'RE BACK EARLY! WHAT'S WRONG? YOU'RE OUT OF BREATH.
Did you bring me a souvenir?
HUFF
It's the usual Finn.
NOTHING IS WRONG.
HUFF
I got this for you.
Yay!
I'M SO RELIEVED.
CHIAKI WAS MISTAKEN AFTER ALL...
HUFF
MARON!
GET AWAY FROM HER!
THISH
AAAH!!
HEH

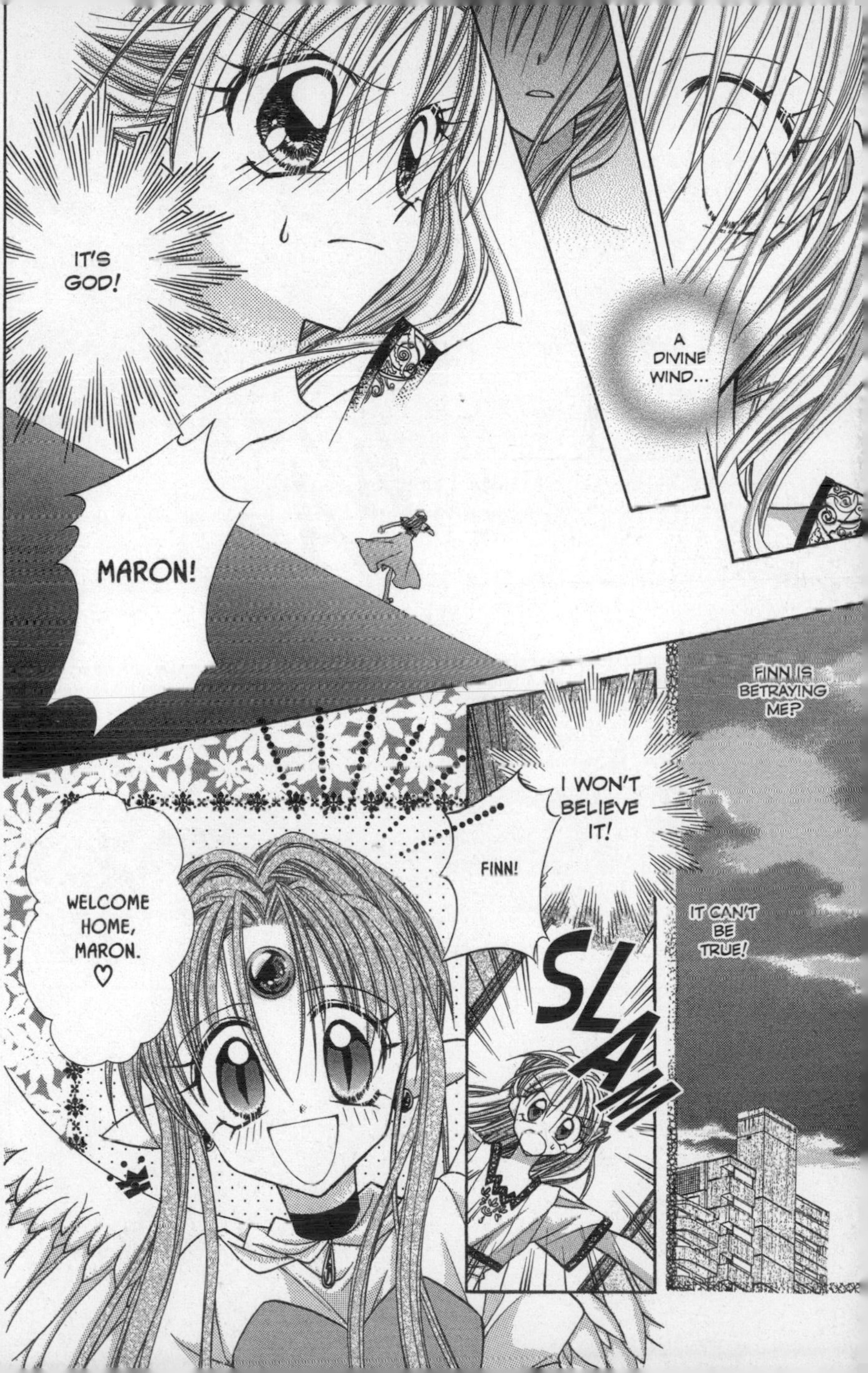
A DIVINE WIND...
IT'S GOD!
MARON!
FINN IS BETRAYING ME?
IT CAN'T BE TRUE!
I WON'T BELIEVE IT!
SLAM
FINN!
WELCOME HOME, MARON. ♡

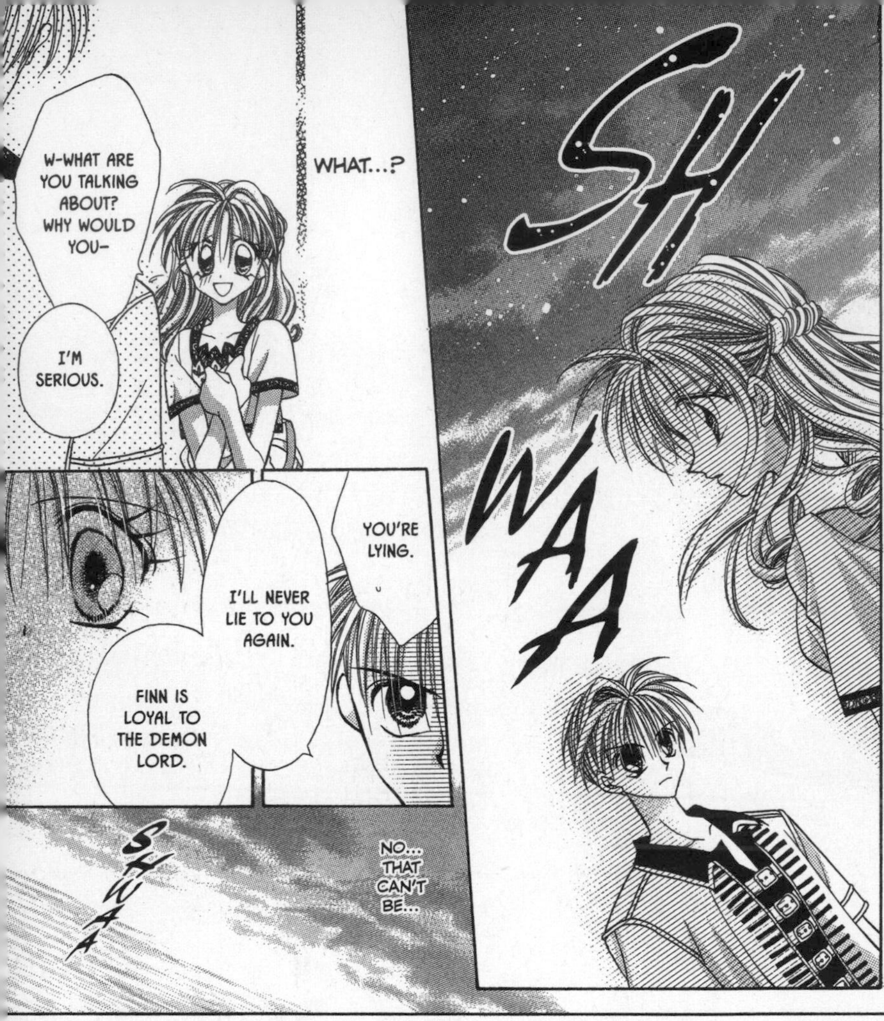
SH
WAA
WHAT...?
W-WHAT ARE YOU TALKING ABOUT? WHY WOULD YOU–
I'M SERIOUS.
YOU'RE LYING.
I'LL NEVER LIE TO YOU AGAIN.
FINN IS LOYAL TO THE DEMON LORD.
NO... THAT CAN'T BE...
SHWAA

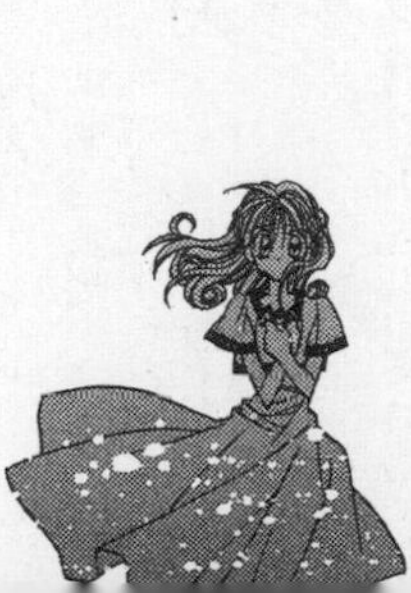

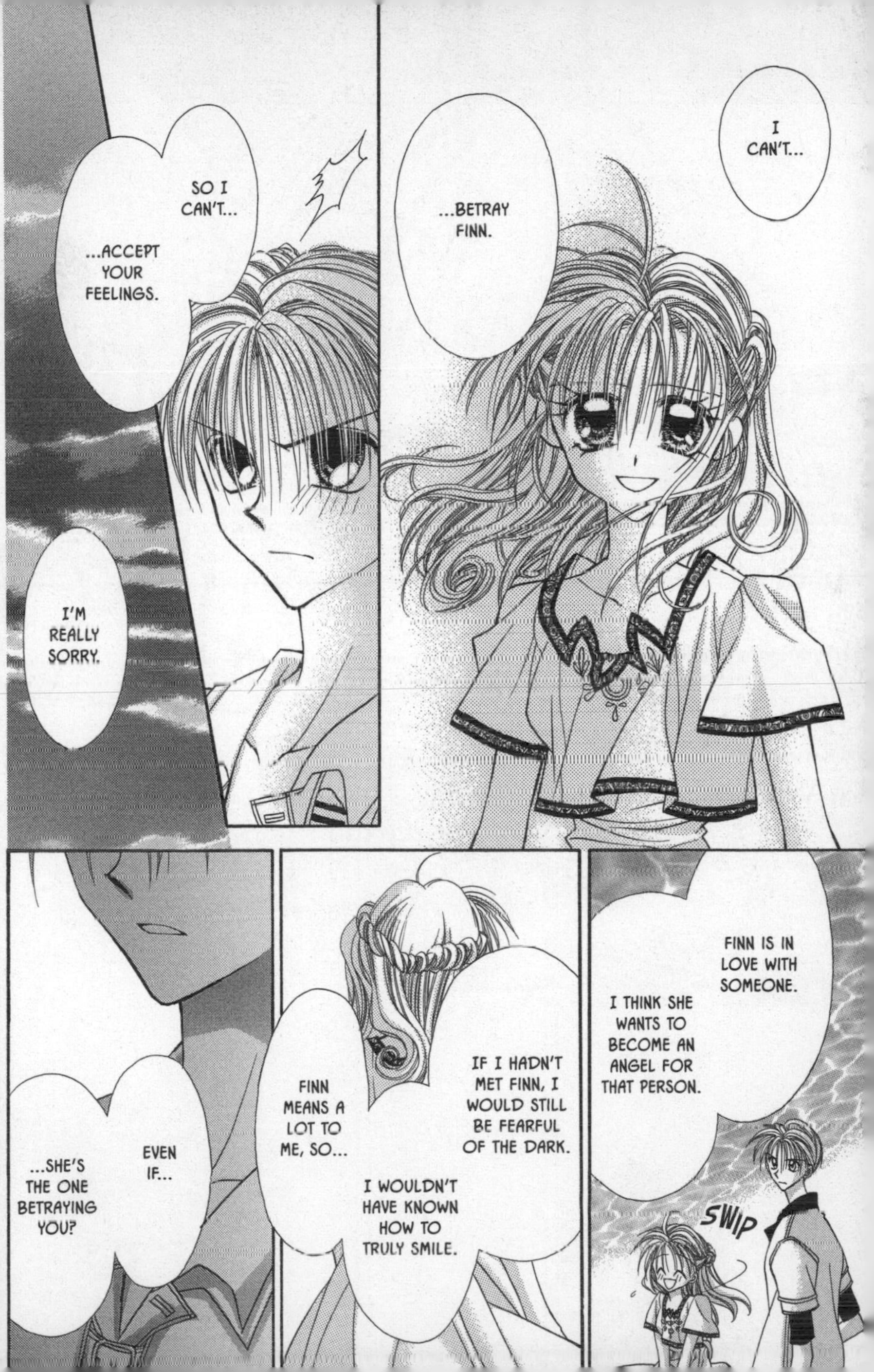
I CAN'T...
...BETRAY FINN.
SO I CAN'T...
...ACCEPT YOUR FEELINGS.
I'M REALLY SORRY.
FINN IS IN LOVE WITH SOMEONE.
I THINK SHE WANTS TO BECOME AN ANGEL FOR THAT PERSON.
SWIP
IF I HADN'T MET FINN, I WOULD STILL BE FEARFUL OF THE DARK.
I WOULDN'T HAVE KNOWN HOW TO TRULY SMILE.
FINN MEANS A LOT TO ME, SO...
EVEN IF...
...SHE'S THE ONE BETRAYING YOU?

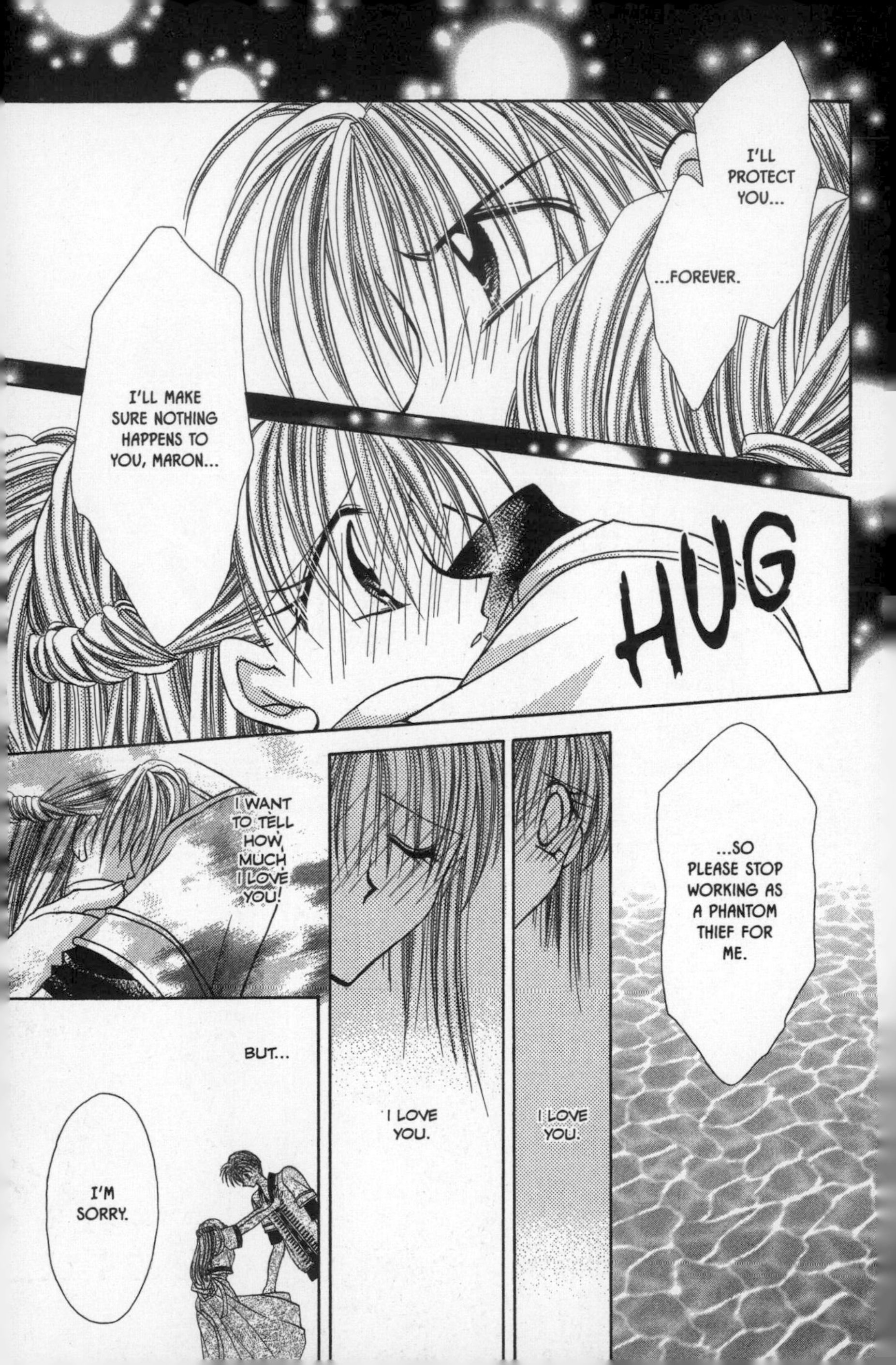
I'LL PROTECT YOU...
...FOREVER.
I'LL MAKE SURE NOTHING HAPPENS TO YOU, MARON...
HUG
...SO PLEASE STOP WORKING AS A PHANTOM THIEF FOR ME.
I LOVE YOU.
I LOVE YOU.
I WANT TO TELL HOW MUCH I LOVE YOU!
BUT...
I'M SORRY.

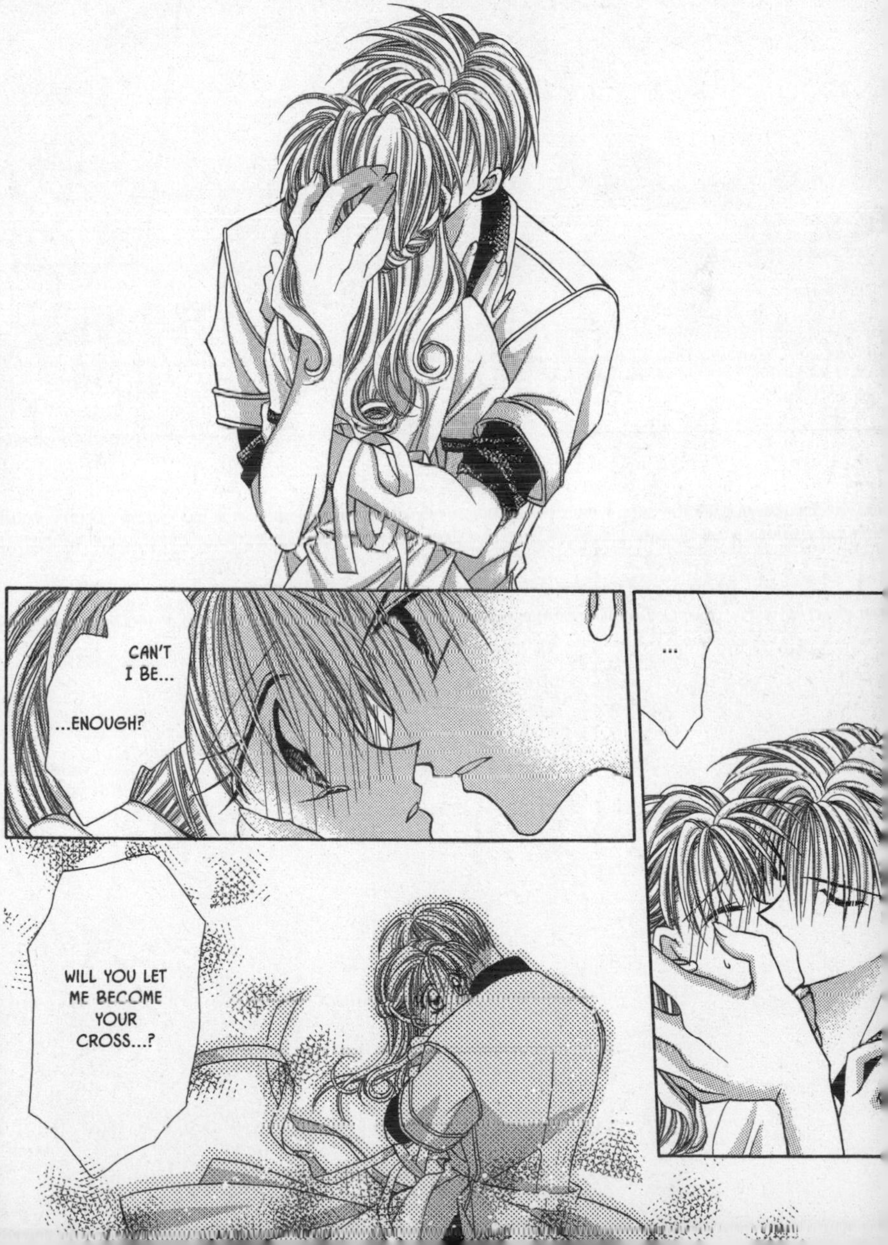
...
CAN'T I BE...
...ENOUGH?
WILL YOU LET ME BECOME YOUR CROSS...?

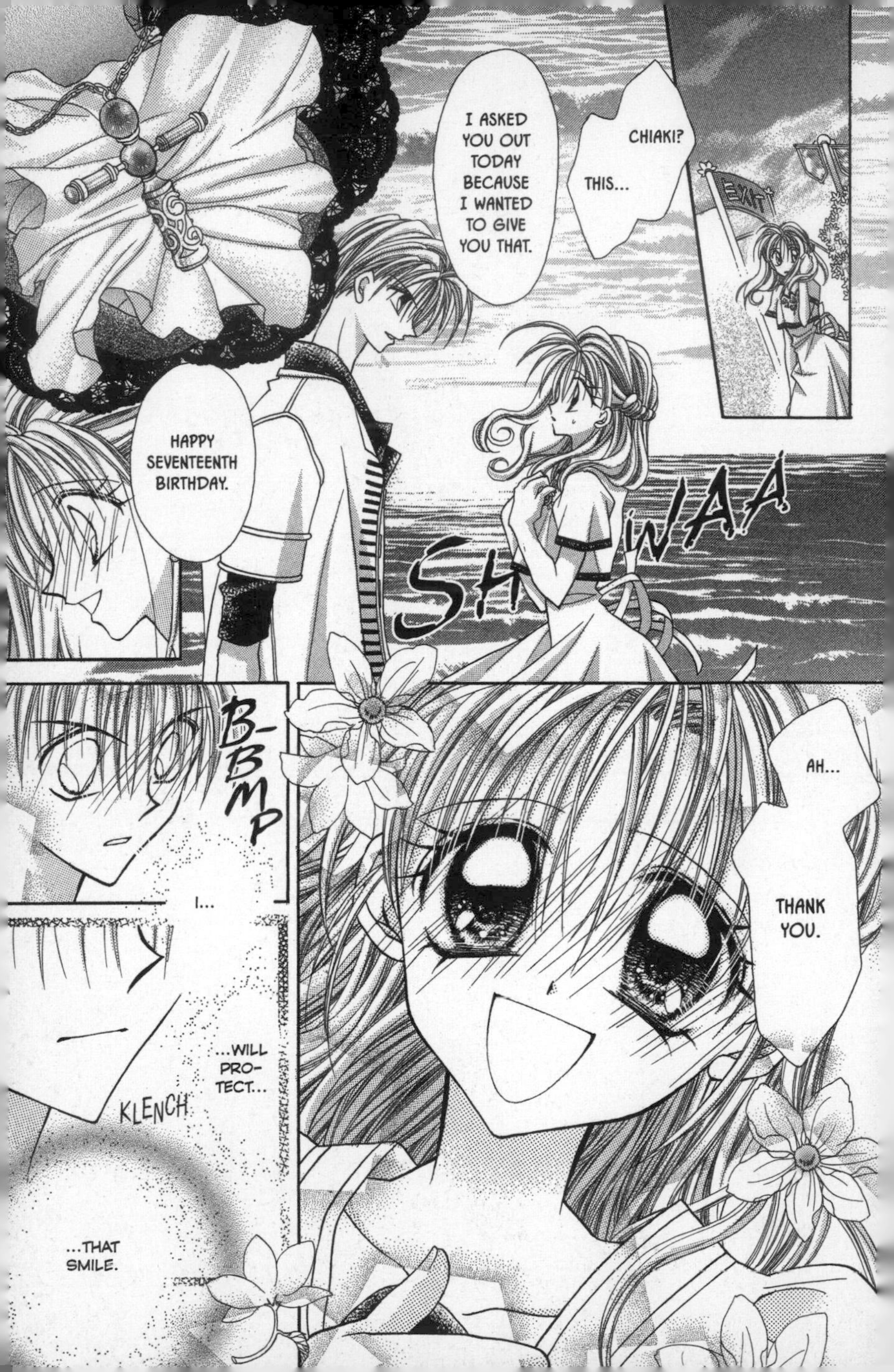
EXIT
CHIAKI?
THIS...
I ASKED YOU OUT TODAY BECAUSE I WANTED TO GIVE YOU THAT.
HAPPY SEVENTEENTH BIRTHDAY.
SHWAAA
AH...
THANK YOU.
B-BMP
I...
...WILL PROTECT...
KLENCH
...THAT SMILE.

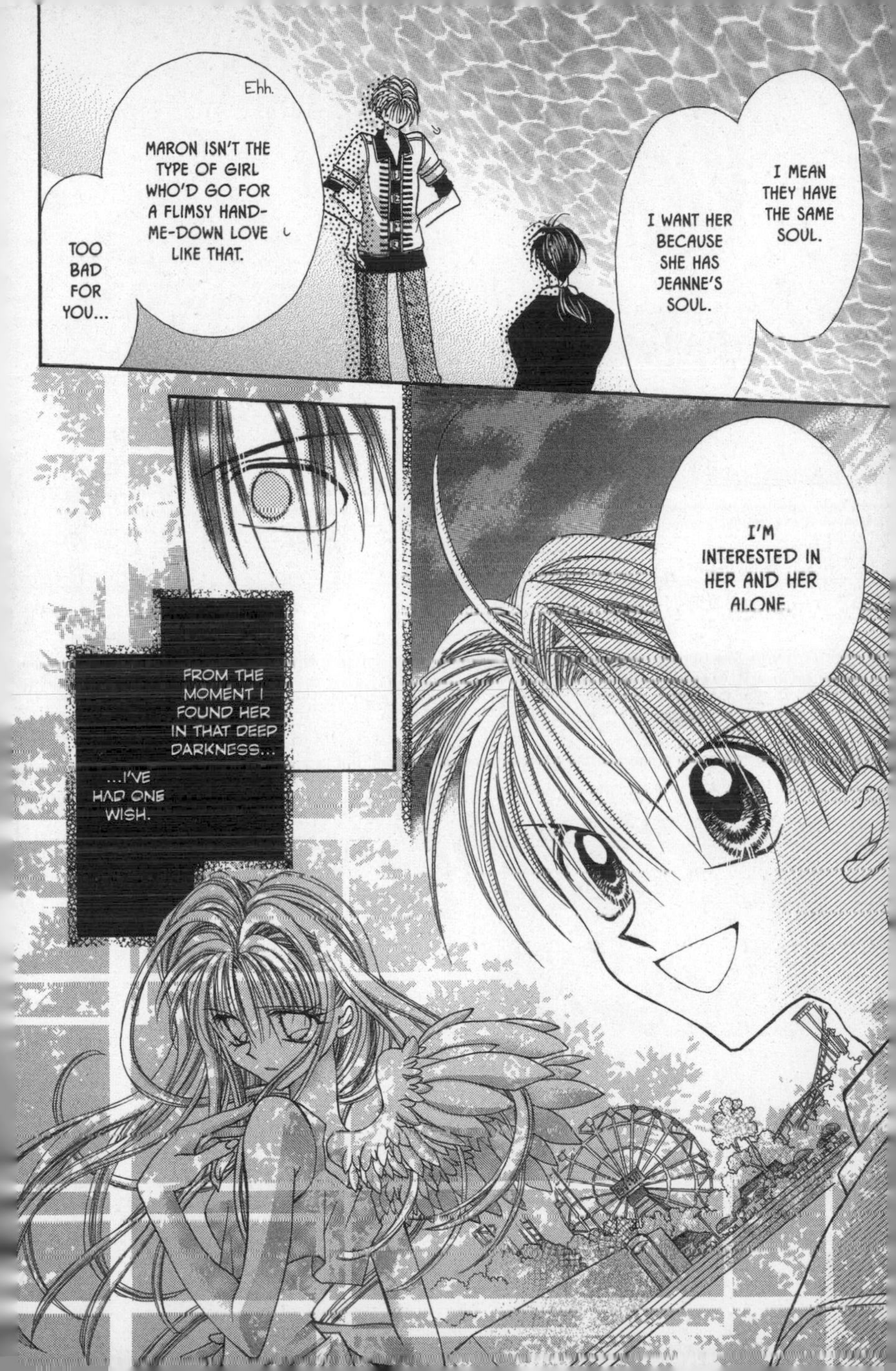
I MEAN THEY HAVE THE SAME SOUL.
I WANT HER BECAUSE SHE HAS JEANNE'S SOUL.
Ehh.
MARON ISN'T THE TYPE OF GIRL WHO'D GO FOR A FLIMSY HAND-ME-DOWN LOVE LIKE THAT.
TOO BAD FOR YOU...
I'M INTERESTED IN HER AND HER ALONE.
FROM THE MOMENT I FOUND HER IN THAT DEEP DARKNESS...
...I'VE HAD ONE WISH.

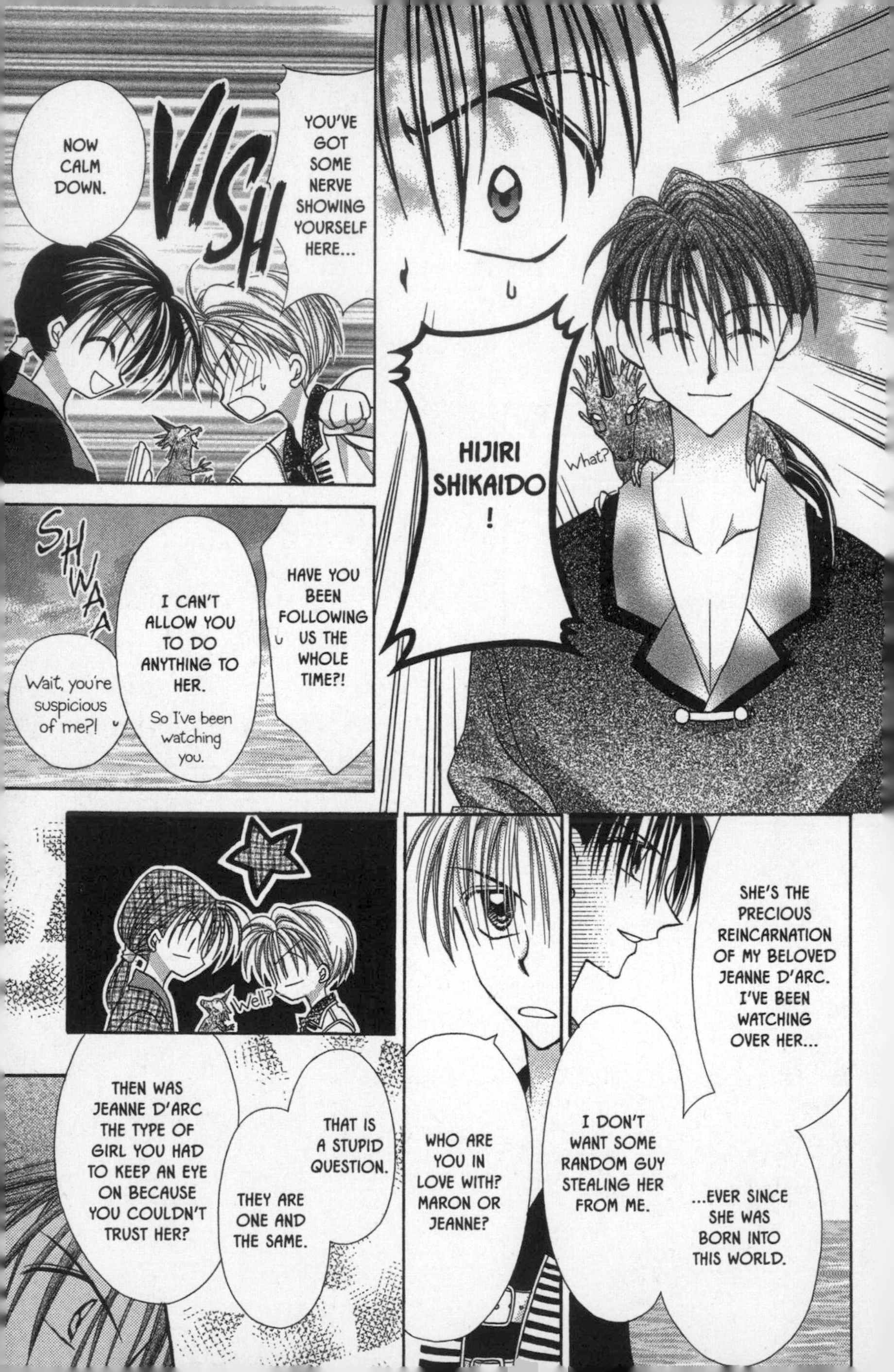
HIJIRI SHIKAIDO!
What?
YOU'VE GOT SOME NERVE SHOWING YOURSELF HERE...
VISH
NOW CALM DOWN.
HAVE YOU BEEN FOLLOWING US THE WHOLE TIME?!
SHWAA
I CAN'T ALLOW YOU TO DO ANYTHING TO HER.
So I've been watching you.
Wait, you're suspicious of me?!
SHE'S THE PRECIOUS REINCARNATION OF MY BELOVED JEANNE D'ARC. I'VE BEEN WATCHING OVER HER...
...EVER SINCE SHE WAS BORN INTO THIS WORLD.
I DON'T WANT SOME RANDOM GUY STEALING HER FROM ME.
WHO ARE YOU IN LOVE WITH? MARON OR JEANNE?
Well?
THAT IS A STUPID QUESTION.
THEY ARE ONE AND THE SAME.
THEN WAS JEANNE D'ARC THE TYPE OF GIRL YOU HAD TO KEEP AN EYE ON BECAUSE YOU COULDN'T TRUST HER?

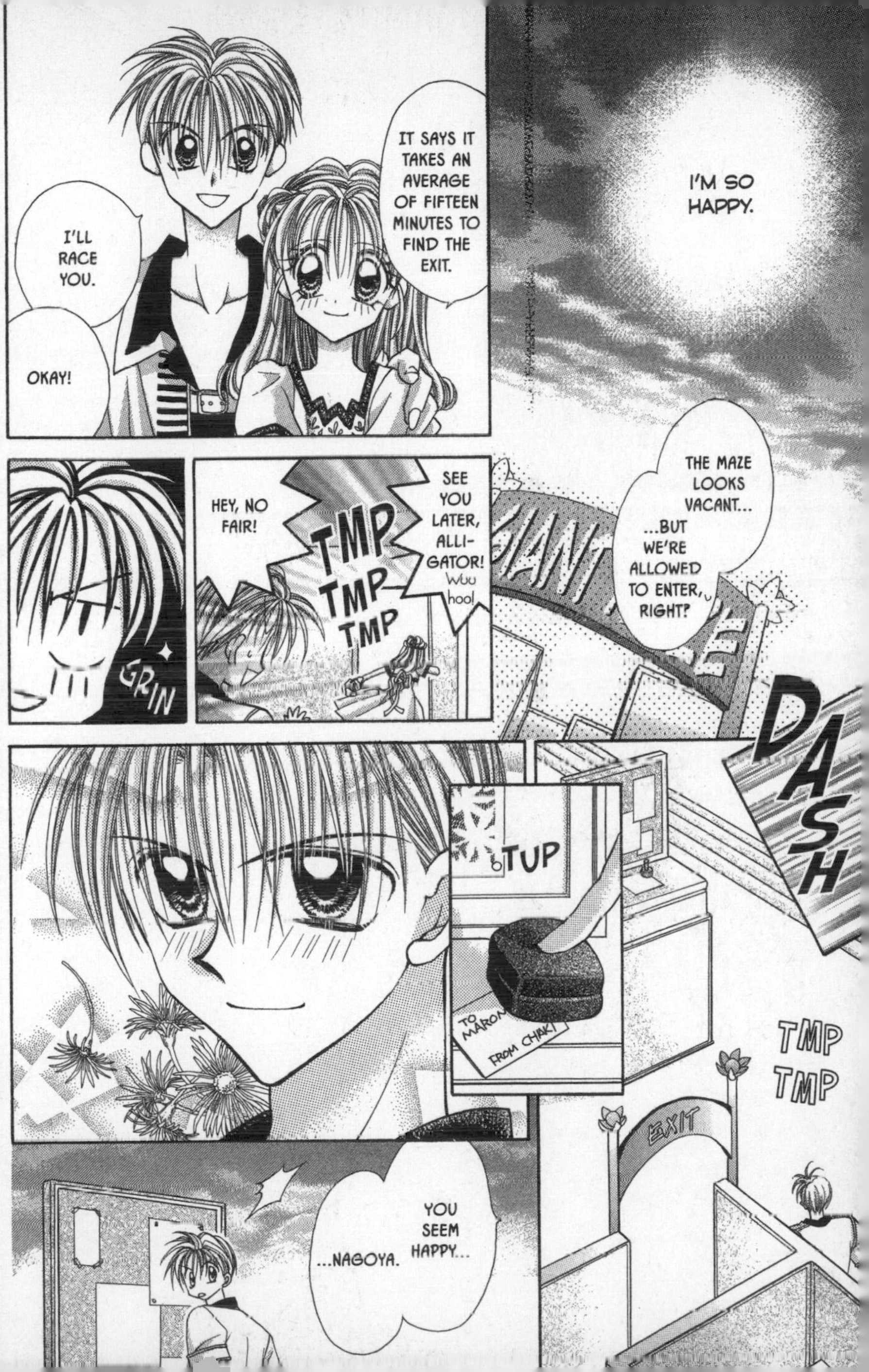
I'M SO HAPPY.
THE MAZE LOOKS VACANT...
...BUT WE'RE ALLOWED TO ENTER, RIGHT?
DASH
TMP TMP
EXIT
IT SAYS IT TAKES AN AVERAGE OF FIFTEEN MINUTES TO FIND THE EXIT.
I'LL RACE YOU.
OKAY!
SEE YOU LATER, ALLI-GATOR!
Wuu hoo!
HEY, NO FAIR!
TMP TMP TMP
GRIN
TUP
TO MARON
FROM CHAKI
YOU SEEM HAPPY...
...NAGOYA.

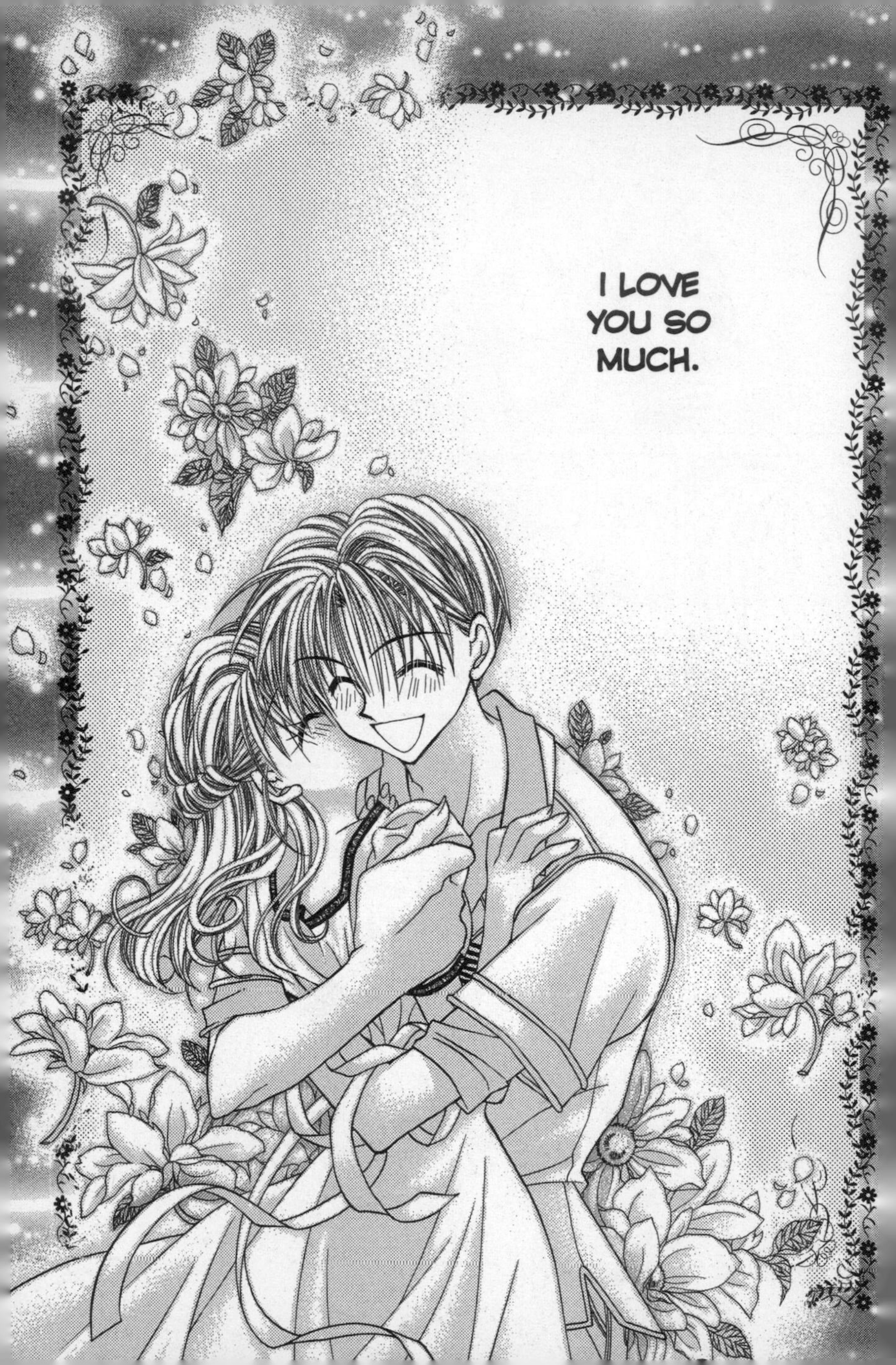
I LOVE YOU SO MUCH.

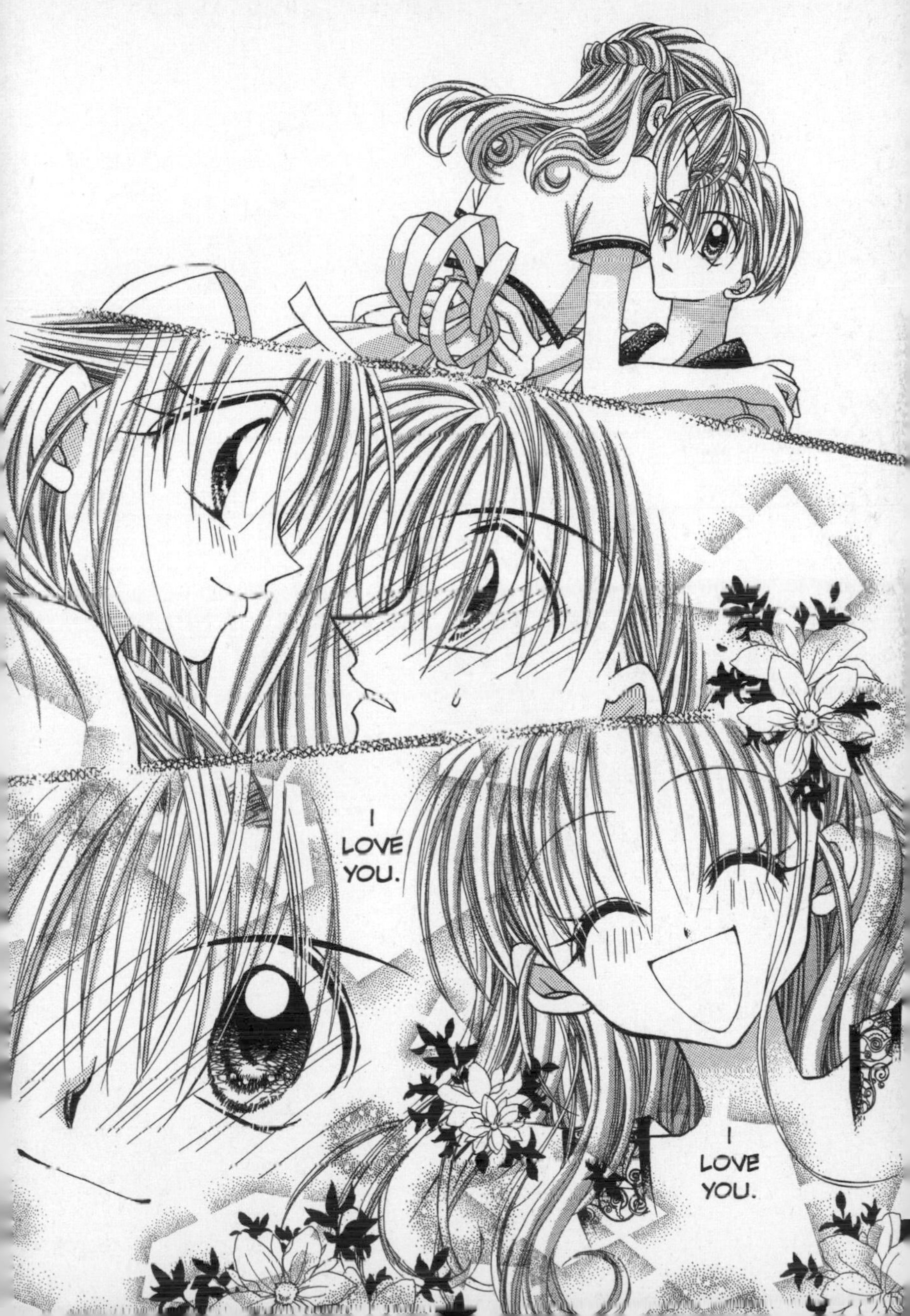
I LOVE YOU.
I LOVE YOU.

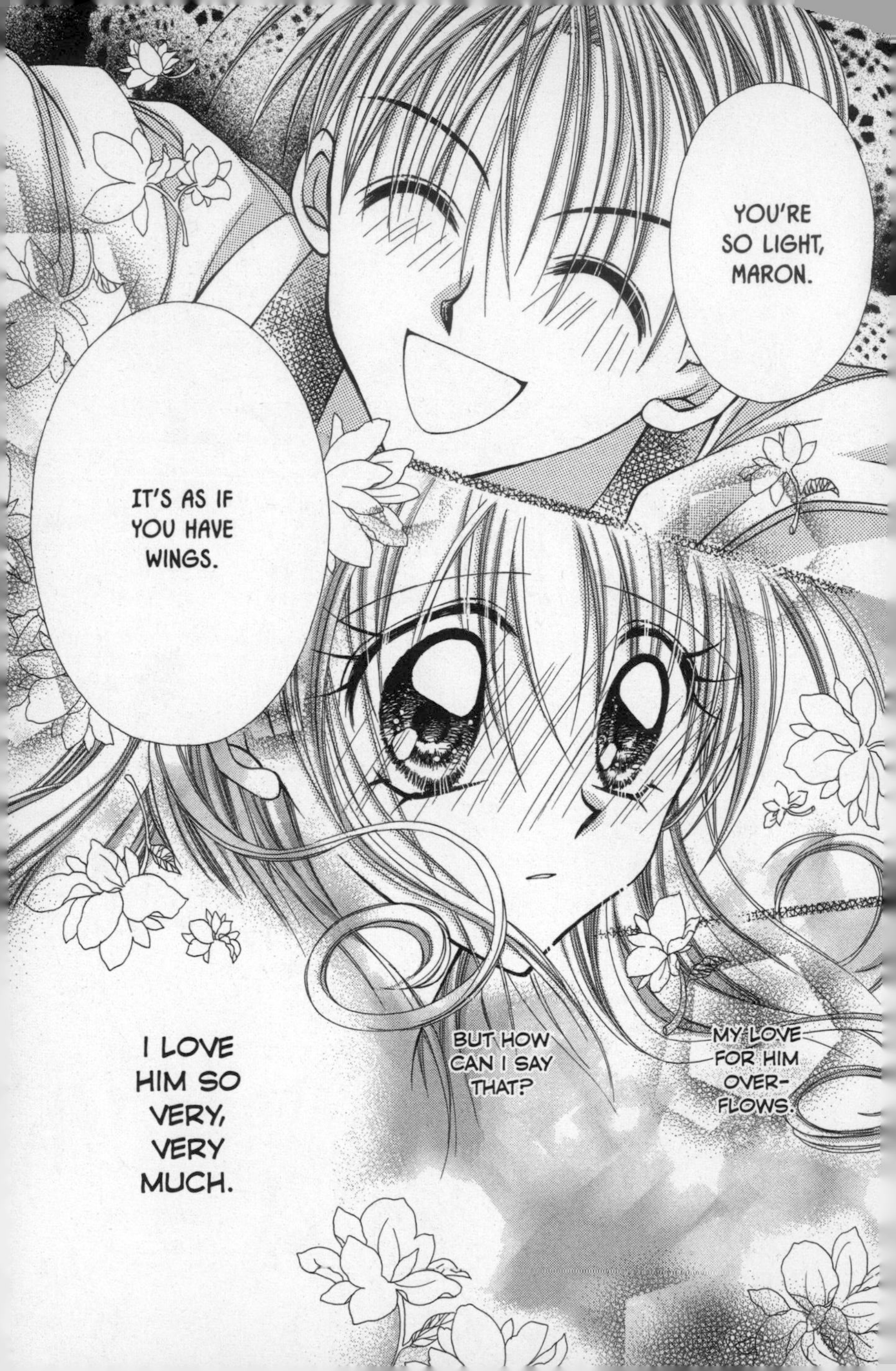
YOU'RE SO LIGHT, MARON.
IT'S AS IF YOU HAVE WINGS.
MY LOVE FOR HIM OVER-FLOWS.
BUT HOW CAN I SAY THAT?
I LOVE HIM SO VERY, VERY MUCH.

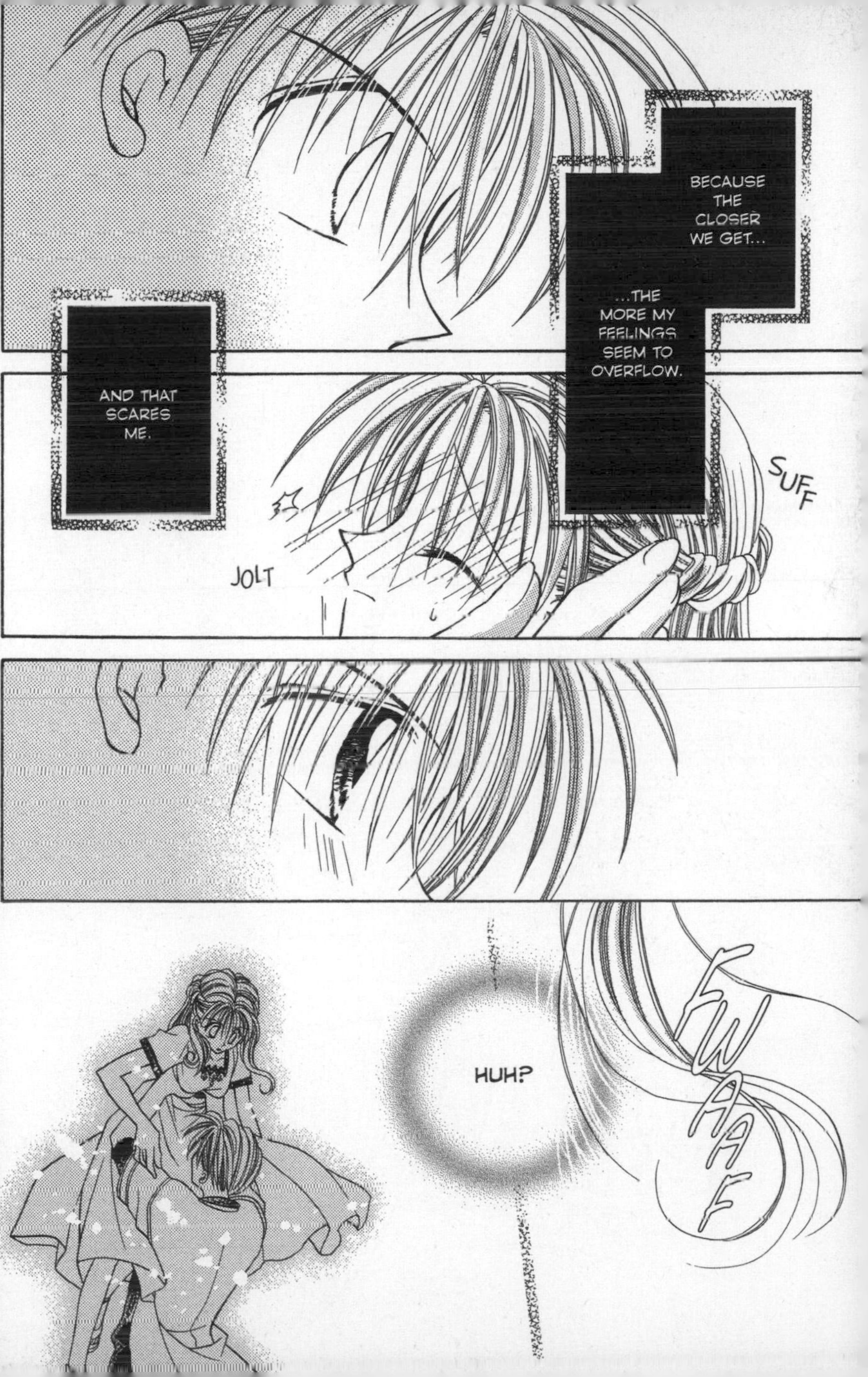
BECAUSE THE CLOSER WE GET...
...THE MORE MY FEELINGS SEEM TO OVERFLOW.
AND THAT SCARES ME.
SUFF
JOLT
KWAAF
HUH?

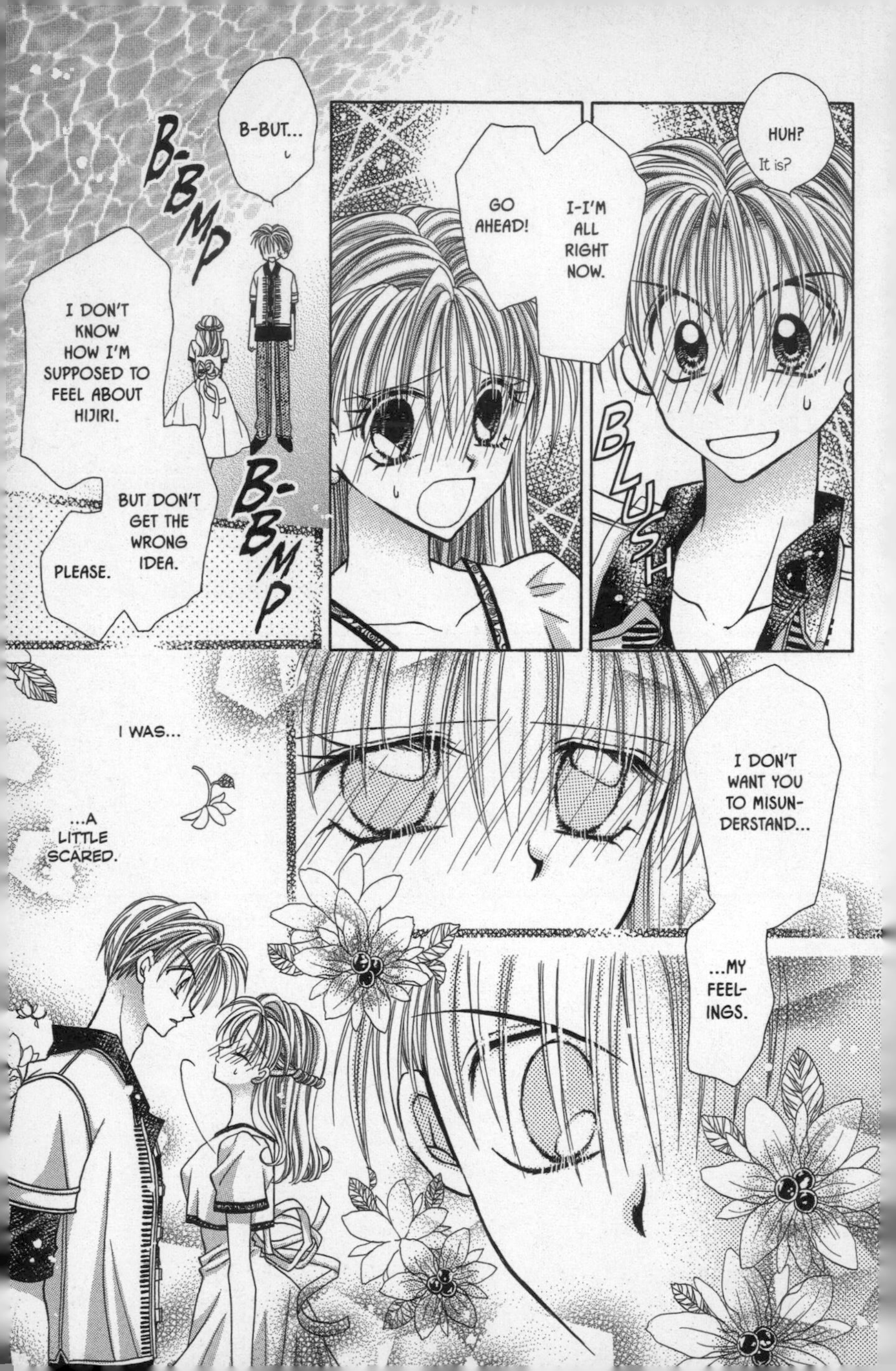
HUH?
It is?
I-I'M ALL RIGHT NOW.
GO AHEAD!
BLUSH
B-BUT...
B-BMP
I DON'T KNOW HOW I'M SUPPOSED TO FEEL ABOUT HIJIRI.
BUT DON'T GET THE WRONG IDEA.
PLEASE.
B-BMP
I DON'T WANT YOU TO MISUNDERSTAND...
...MY FEELINGS.
I WAS...
...A LITTLE SCARED.

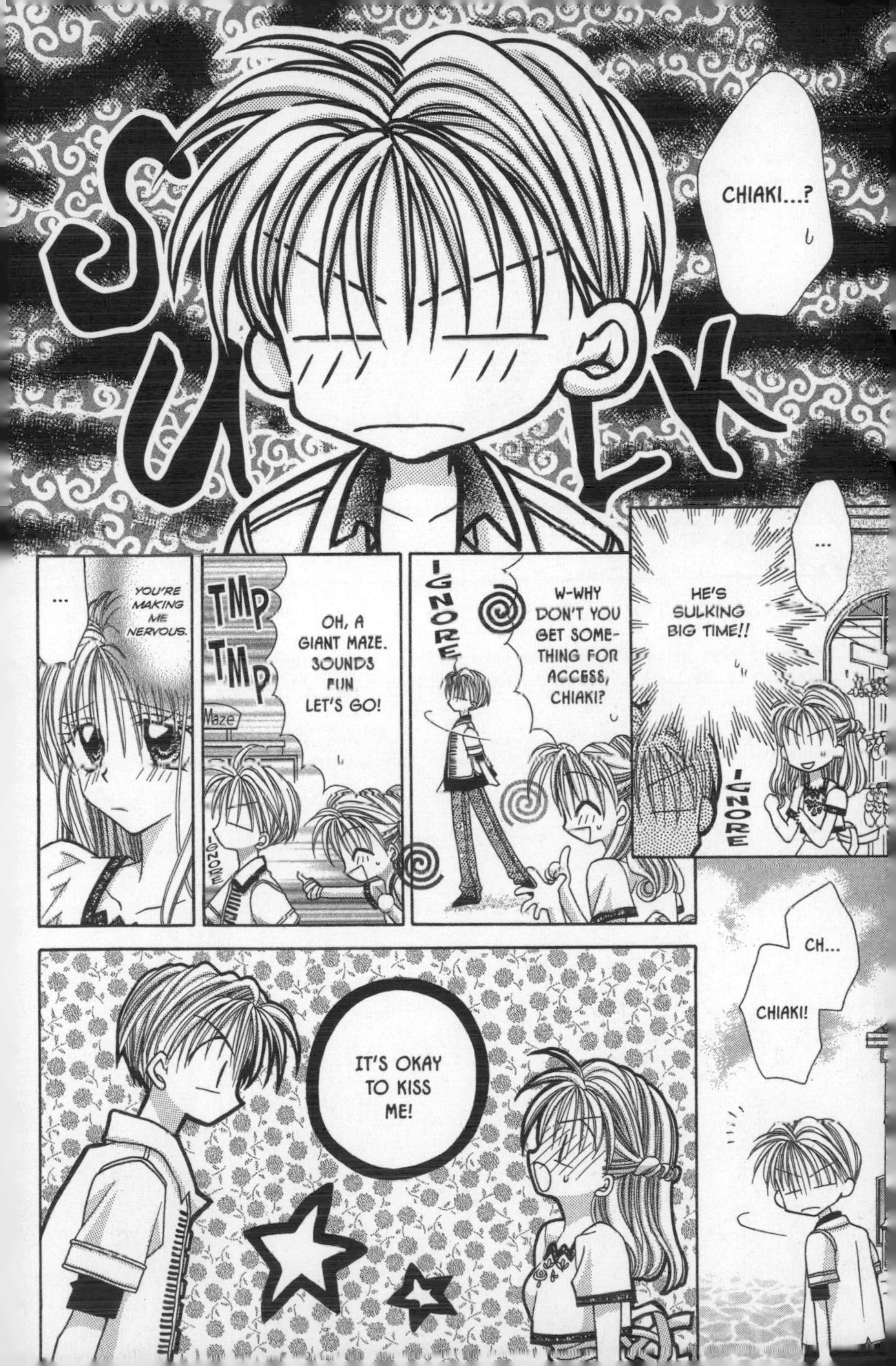
SULK
CHIAKI...?
...
HE'S SULKING BIG TIME!!
IGNORE
W-WHY DON'T YOU GET SOME-THING FOR ACCESS, CHIAKI?
IGNORE
OH, A GIANT MAZE. SOUNDS FUN LET'S GO!
TMP TMP
Maze
IGNORE
...
YOU'RE MAKING ME NERVOUS.
CH...
CHIAKI!
IT'S OKAY TO KISS ME!

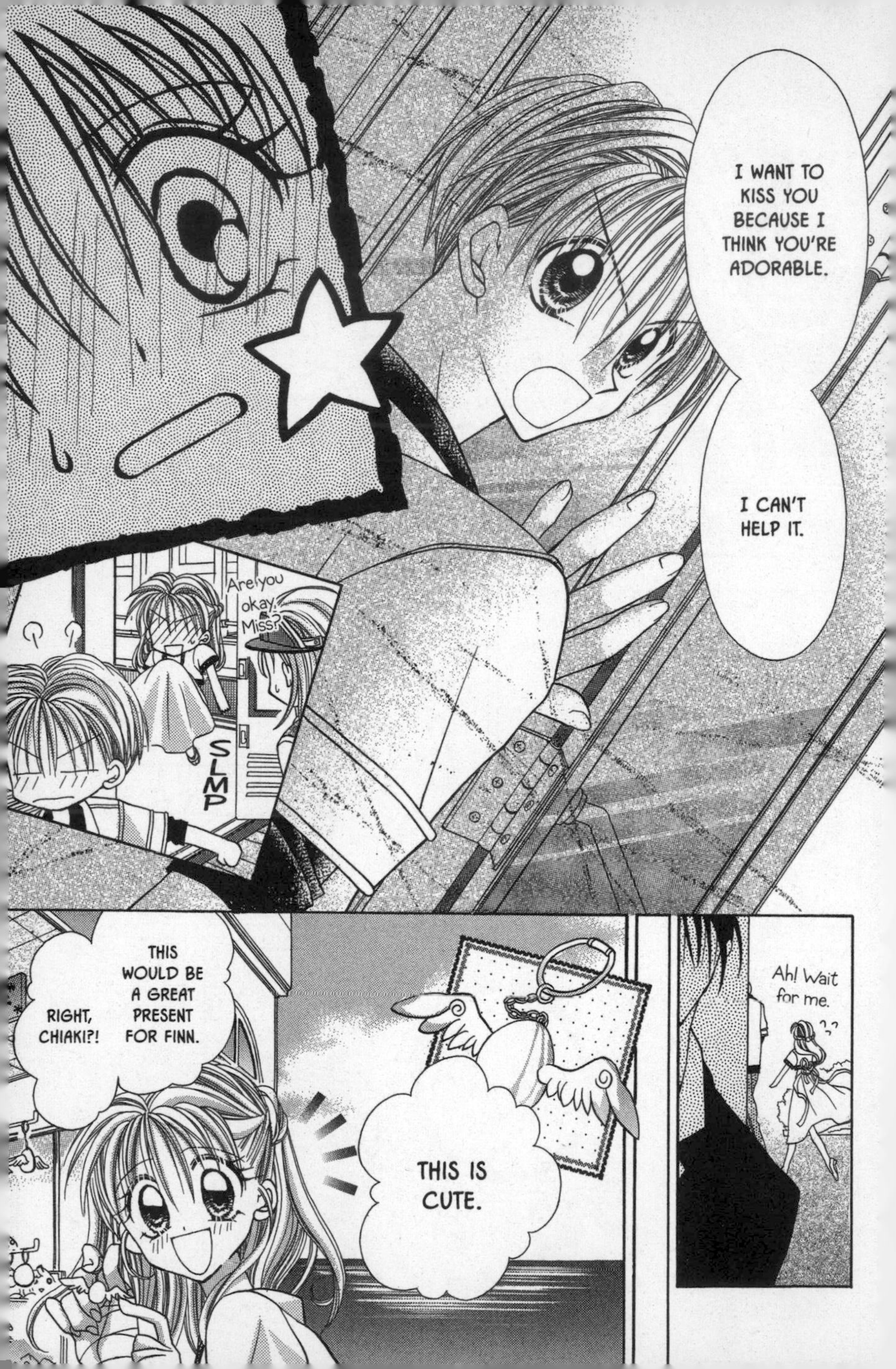
I WANT TO KISS YOU BECAUSE I THINK YOU'RE ADORABLE.
I CAN'T HELP IT.
Are you okay, Miss?
SLMP
Ah! Wait for me.
THIS IS CUTE.
THIS WOULD BE A GREAT PRESENT FOR FINN.
RIGHT, CHIAKI?!

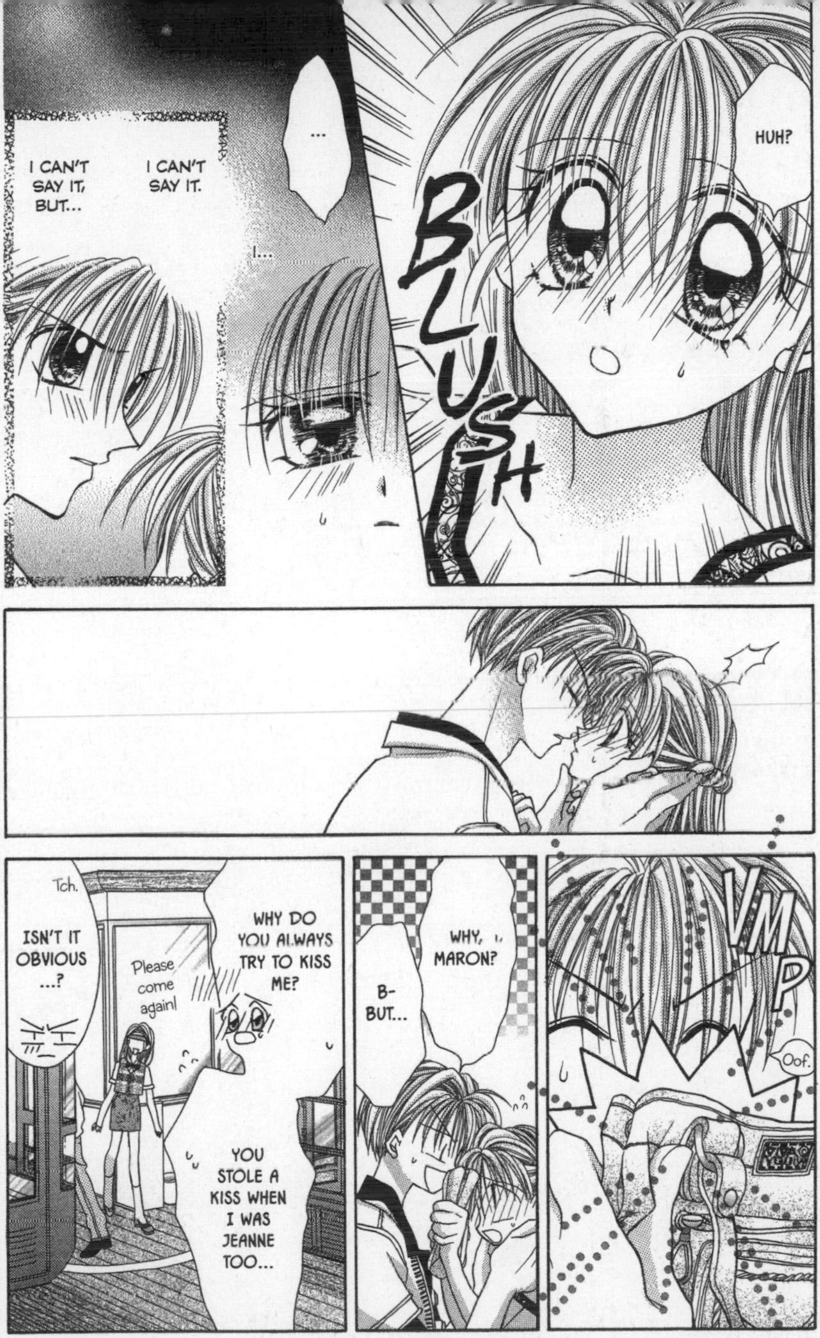
HUH?
BLUSH
...
I...
I CAN'T SAY IT.
I CAN'T SAY IT, BUT...
VMP
Oof.
WHY, MARON?
B-BUT...
WHY DO YOU ALWAYS TRY TO KISS ME?
Please come again!
Tch.
ISN'T IT OBVIOUS ...?
YOU STOLE A KISS WHEN I WAS JEANNE TOO...

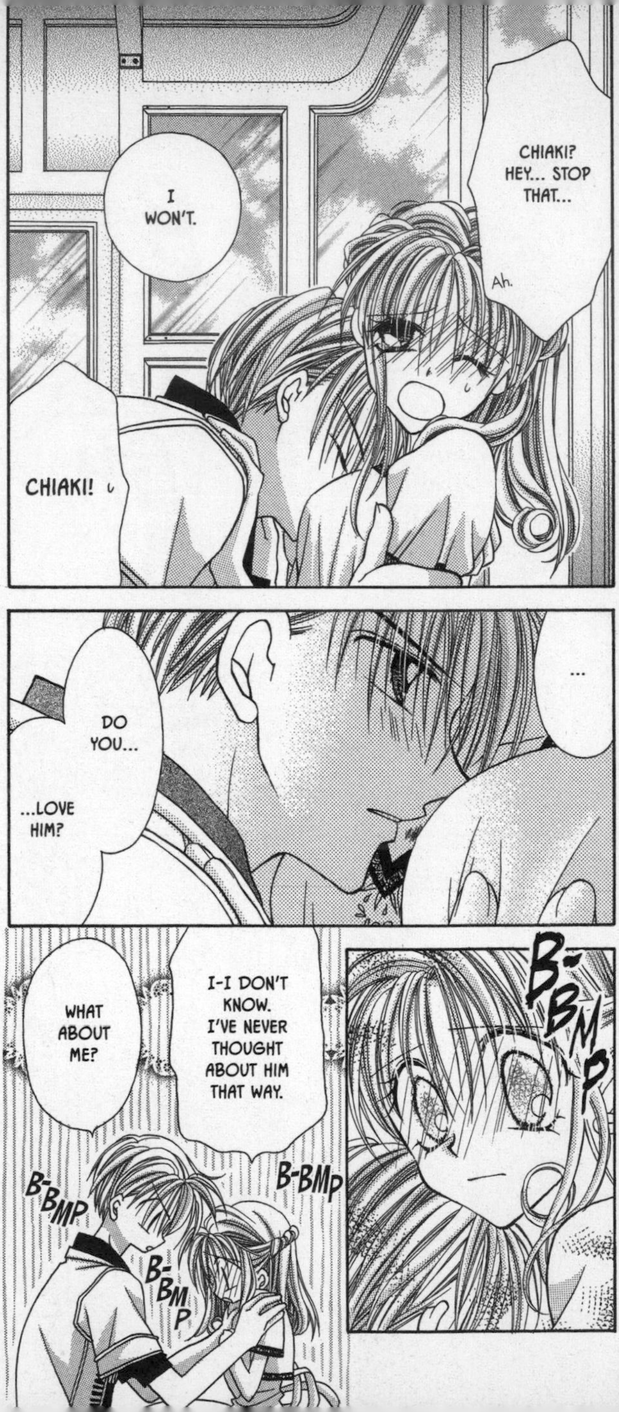
CHIAKI? HEY... STOP THAT...
Ah.
I WON'T.
CHIAKI!
...
DO YOU...
...LOVE HIM?
B-BMP
I-I DON'T KNOW. I'VE NEVER THOUGHT ABOUT HIM THAT WAY.
WHAT ABOUT ME?
B-BMP
B-BMP
B-BMP

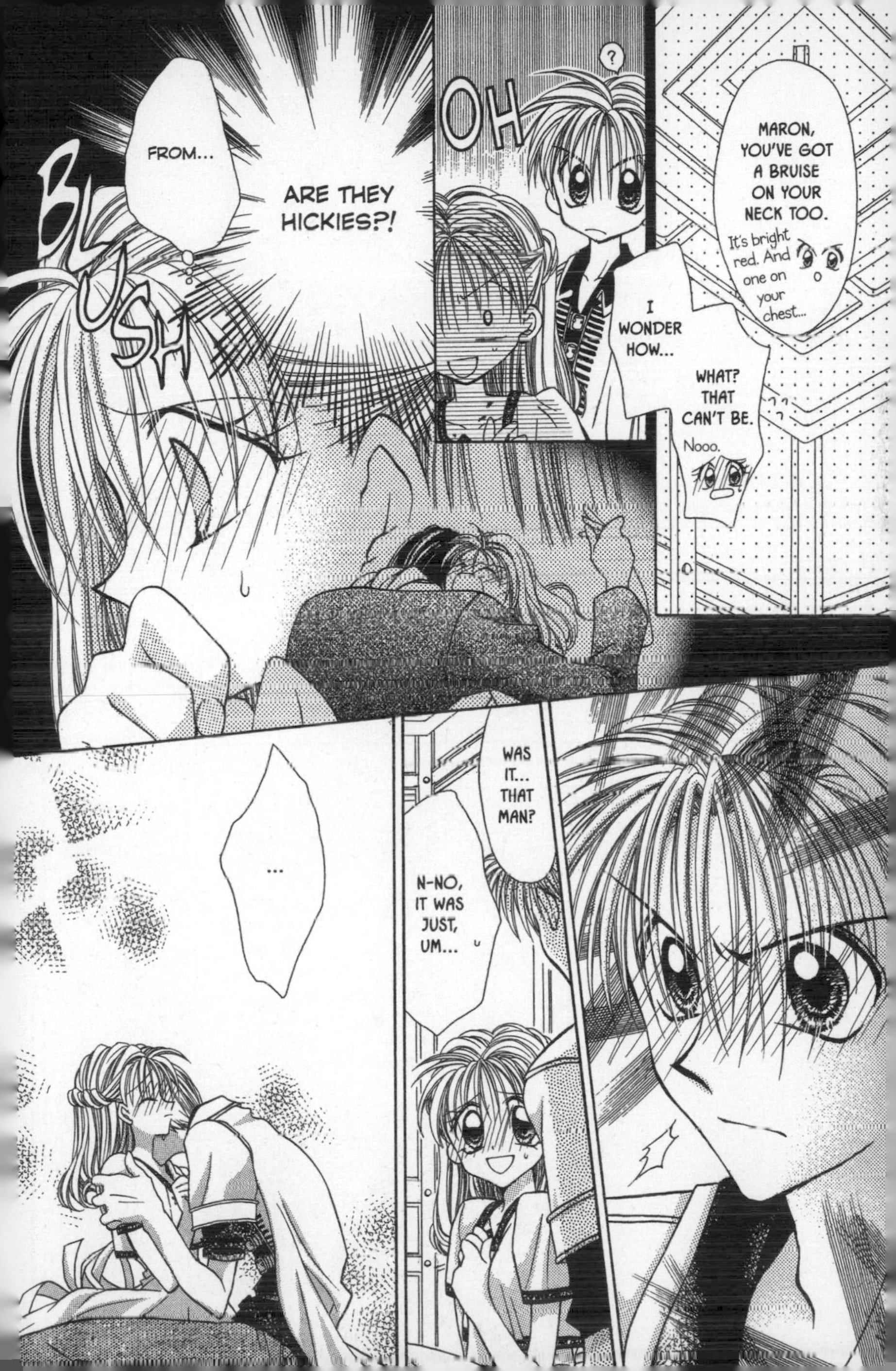
MARON, YOU'VE GOT A BRUISE ON YOUR NECK TOO.
It's bright red. And one on your chest...
WHAT? THAT CAN'T BE.
Nooo.
?
OH
I WONDER HOW...
ARE THEY HICKIES?!
FROM...
BLUSH
WAS IT... THAT MAN?
N-NO, IT WAS JUST, UM...
...

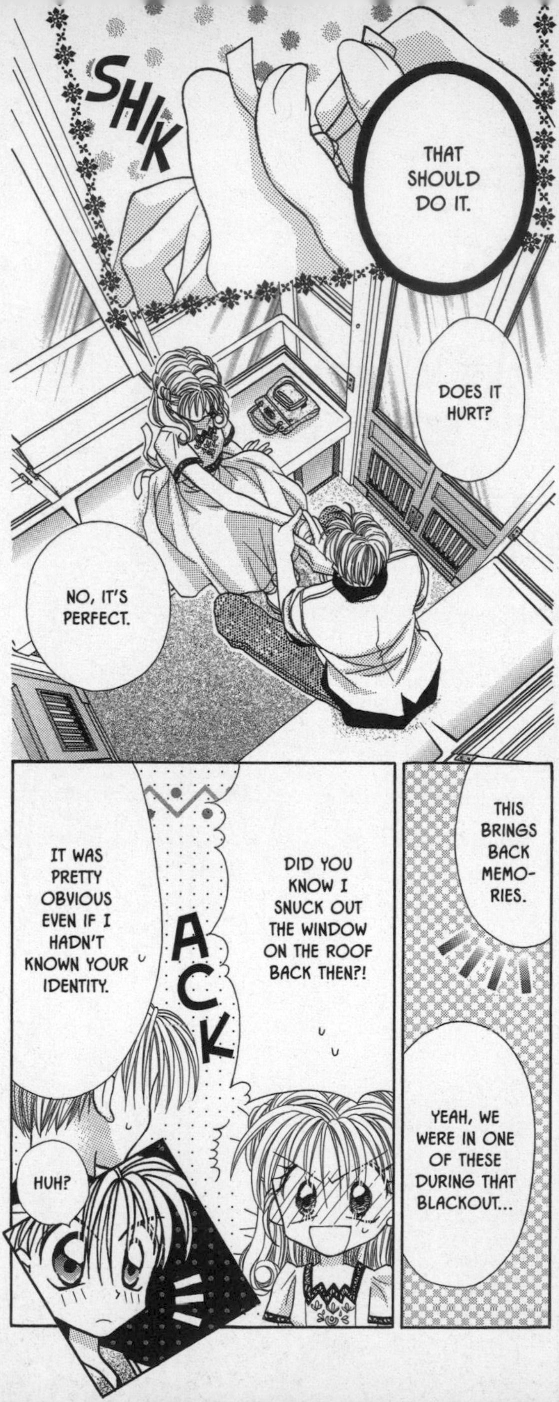
SHIK
THAT SHOULD DO IT.
DOES IT HURT?
NO, IT'S PERFECT.
THIS BRINGS BACK MEMORIES.
YEAH, WE WERE IN ONE OF THESE DURING THAT BLACKOUT...
DID YOU KNOW I SNUCK OUT THE WINDOW ON THE ROOF BACK THEN?!
IT WAS PRETTY OBVIOUS EVEN IF I HADN'T KNOWN YOUR IDENTITY.
ACK
HUH?

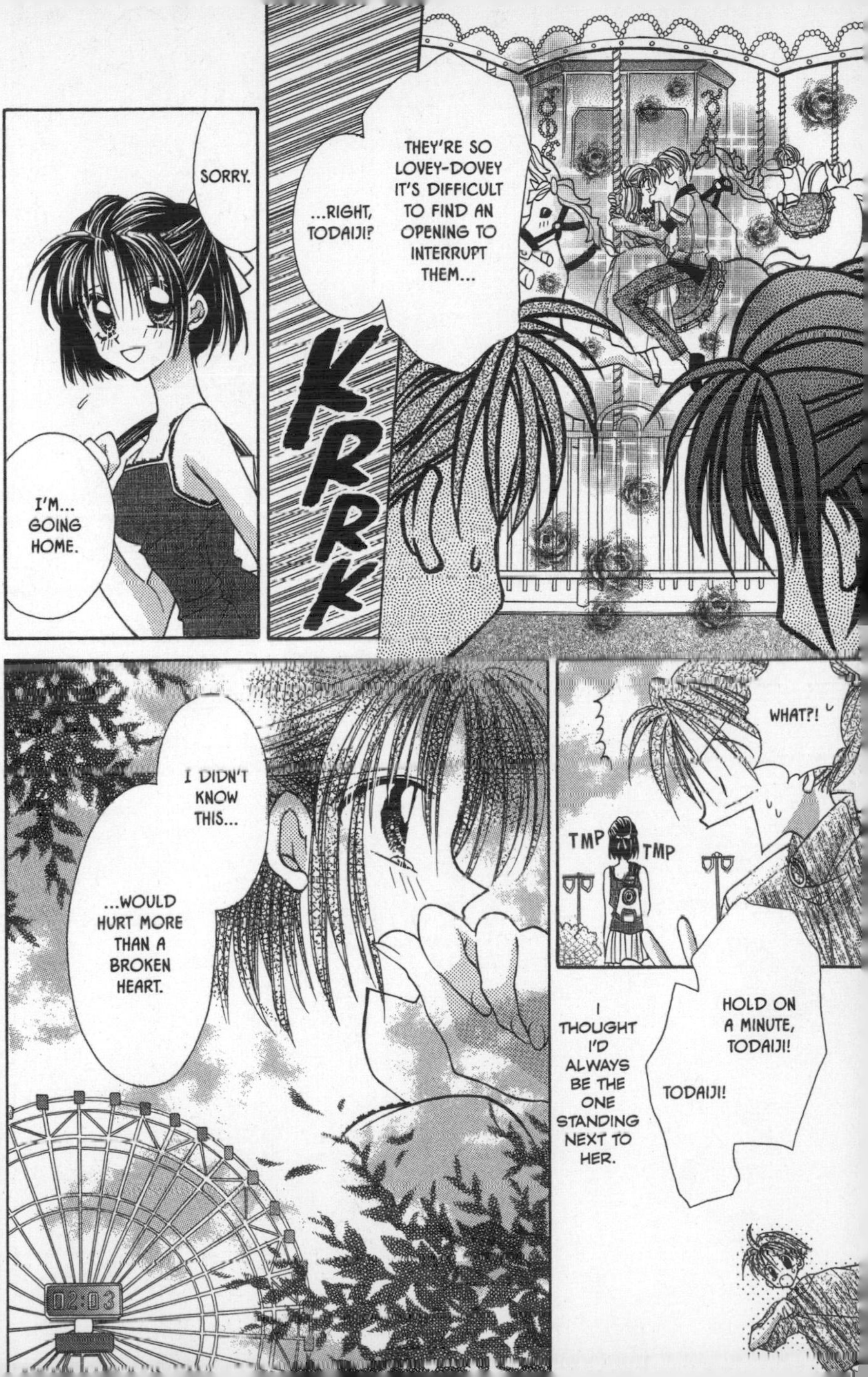
THEY'RE SO LOVEY-DOVEY IT'S DIFFICULT TO FIND AN OPENING TO INTERRUPT THEM...
...RIGHT, TODAIJI?
KRRK
SORRY.
I'M... GOING HOME.
WHAT?!
TMP
TMP
HOLD ON A MINUTE, TODAIJI!
TODAIJI!
I THOUGHT I'D ALWAYS BE THE ONE STANDING NEXT TO HER.
I DIDN'T KNOW THIS...
...WOULD HURT MORE THAN A BROKEN HEART.
02:03

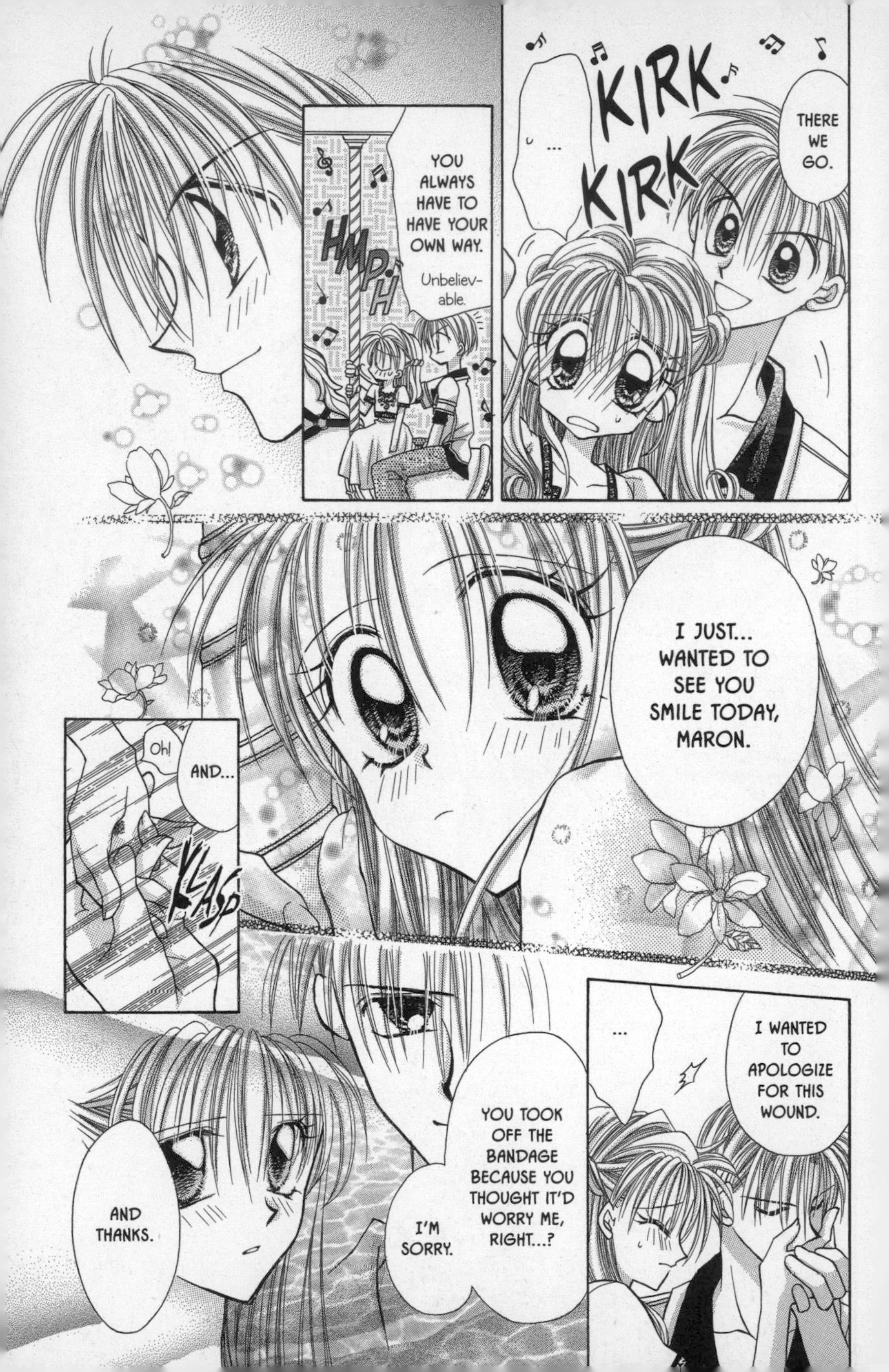
THERE WE GO.
KIRK KIRK
...
YOU ALWAYS HAVE TO HAVE YOUR OWN WAY.
Unbelievable.
HMPH
I JUST... WANTED TO SEE YOU SMILE TODAY, MARON.
Oh!
AND...
KLASP
I WANTED TO APOLOGIZE FOR THIS WOUND.
...
YOU TOOK OFF THE BANDAGE BECAUSE YOU THOUGHT IT'D WORRY ME, RIGHT...?
I'M SORRY.
AND THANKS.

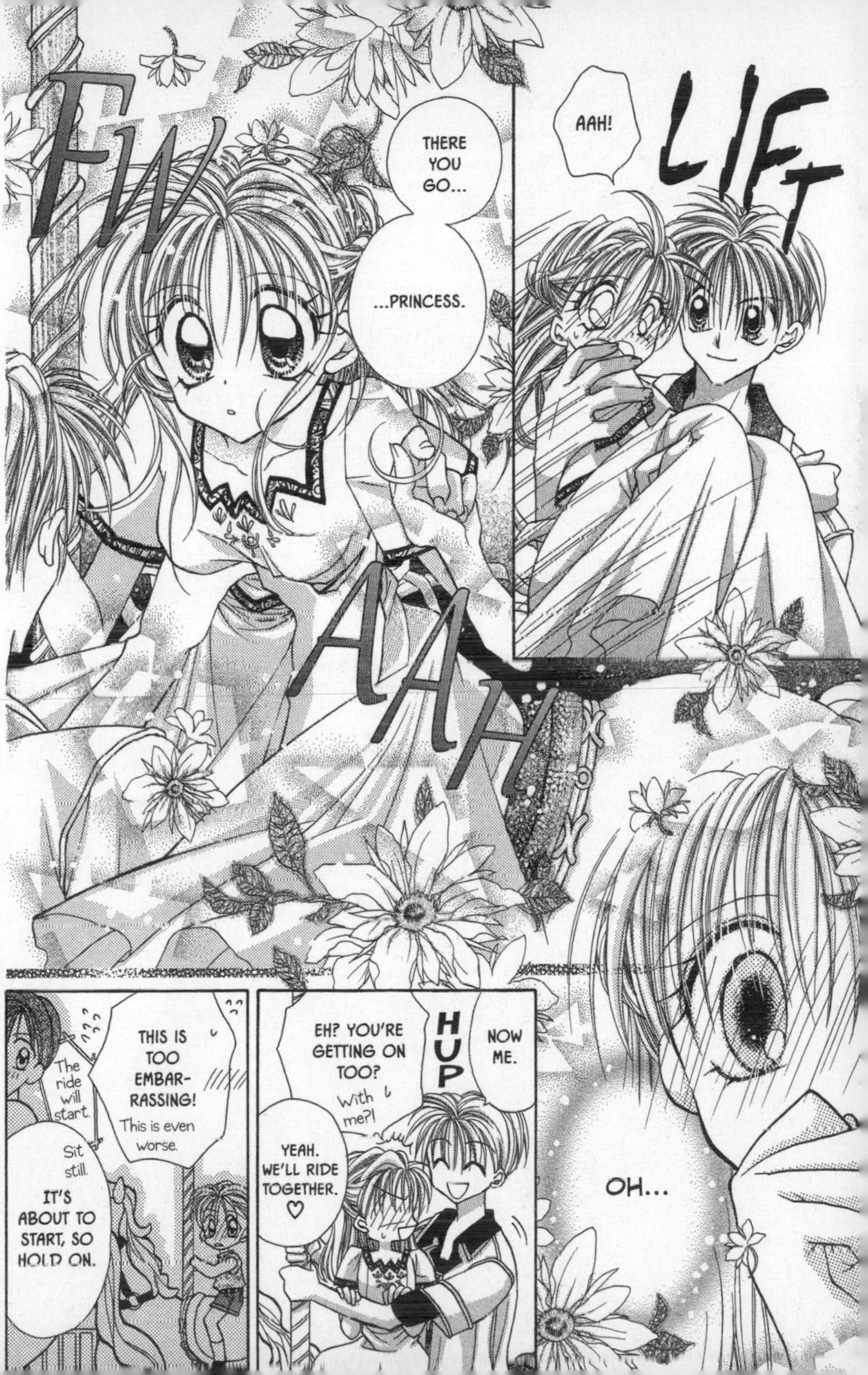

LIFT
AAH!
FW
THERE YOU GO...
...PRINCESS.
AAH
OH...
NOW ME.
HUP
EH? YOU'RE GETTING ON TOO?
With me?!
YEAH. WE'LL RIDE TOGETHER. ♡
THIS IS TOO EMBARRASSING!
This is even worse.
The ride will start.
Sit still.
IT'S ABOUT TO START, SO HOLD ON.

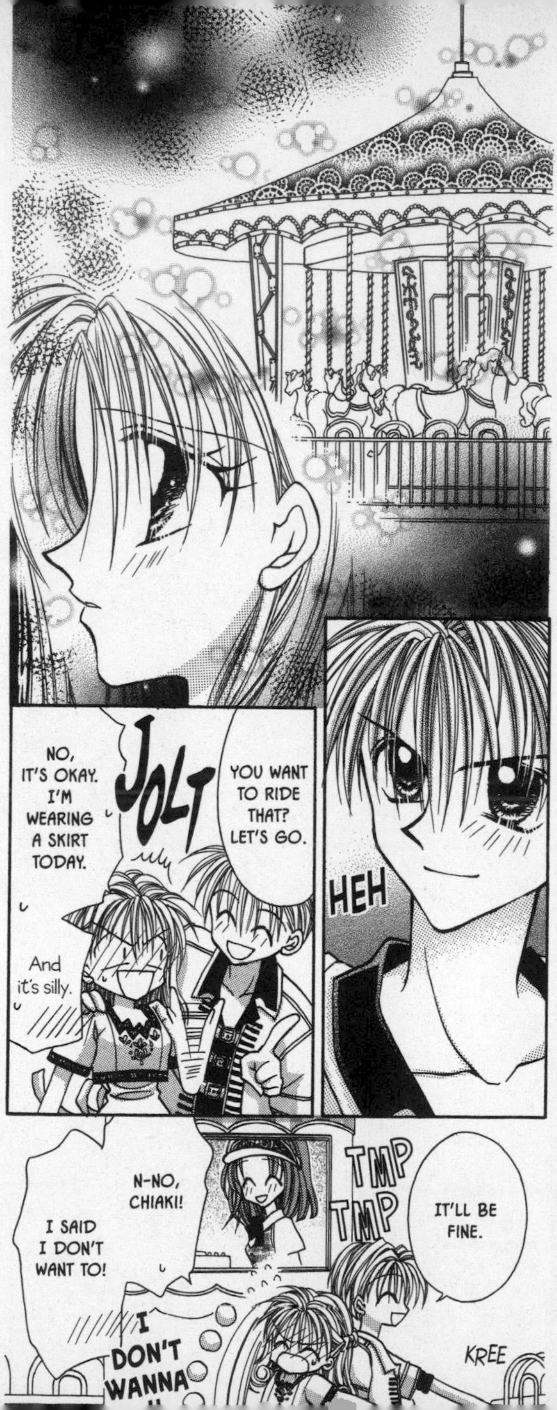
HEH
YOU WANT TO RIDE THAT? LET'S GO.
JOLT
NO, IT'S OKAY. I'M WEARING A SKIRT TODAY.
And it's silly.
IT'LL BE FINE.
TMP TMP
N-NO, CHIAKI!
I SAID I DON'T WANT TO!
KREE
I DON'T WANNA

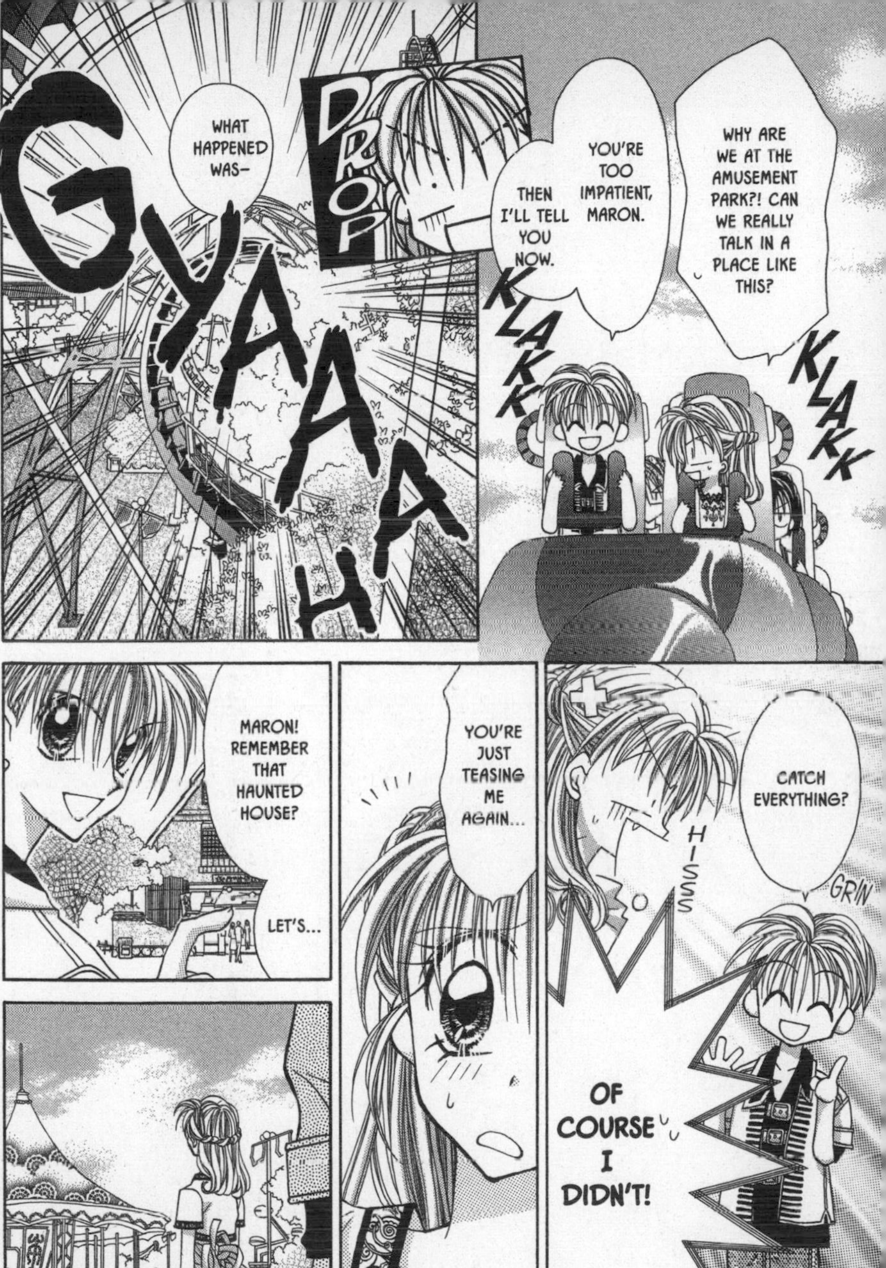
WHY ARE WE AT THE AMUSEMENT PARK?! CAN WE REALLY TALK IN A PLACE LIKE THIS?
KLAKK
YOU'RE TOO IMPATIENT, MARON.
THEN I'LL TELL YOU NOW.
KLAKK
DROP
WHAT HAPPENED WAS–
GYAAAAH
CATCH EVERYTHING?
GRIN
HISSS
OF COURSE I DIDN'T!
YOU'RE JUST TEASING ME AGAIN...
MARON! REMEMBER THAT HAUNTED HOUSE?
LET'S...

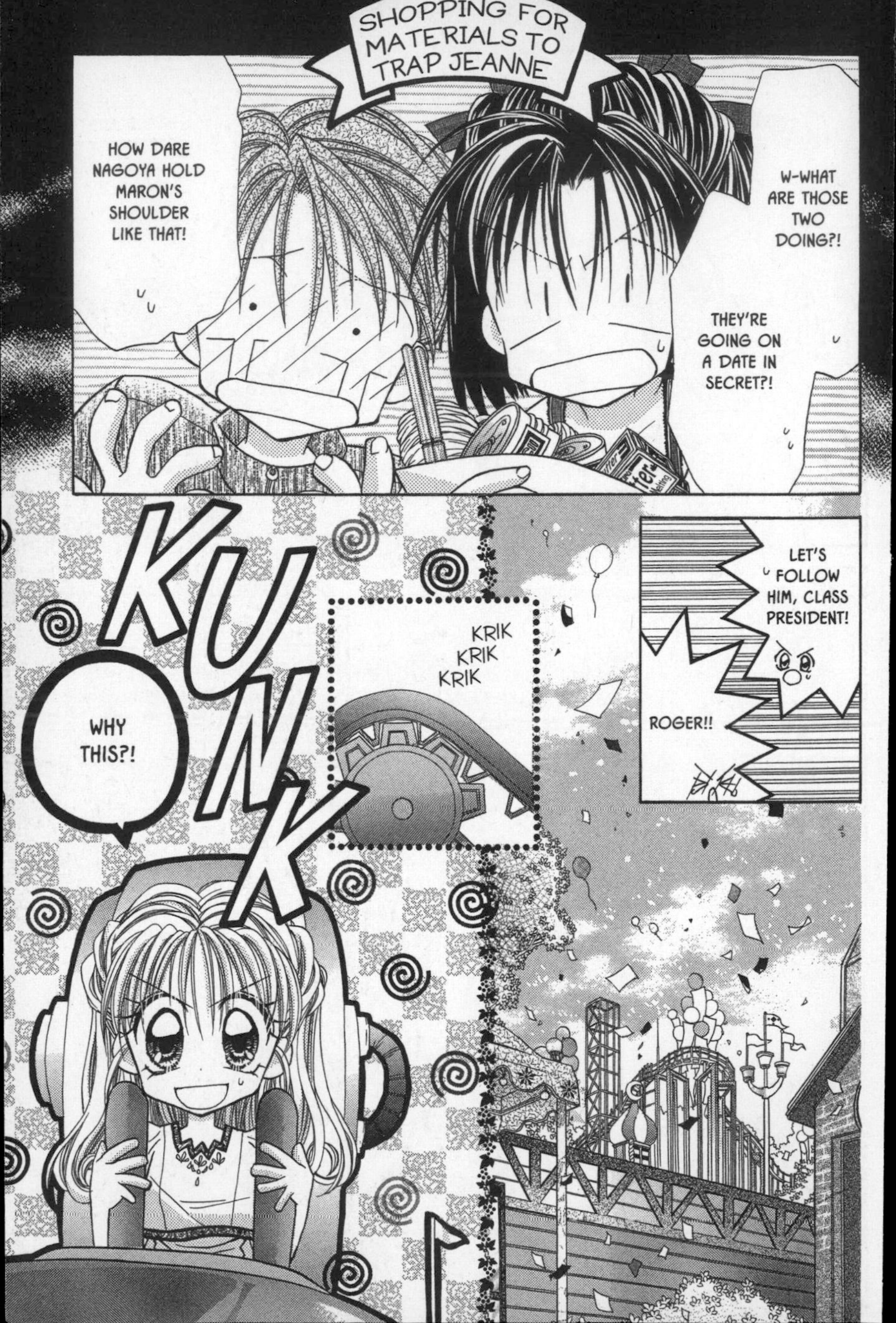
SHOPPING FOR MATERIALS TO TRAP JEANNE
W-WHAT ARE THOSE TWO DOING?!
THEY'RE GOING ON A DATE IN SECRET?!
HOW DARE NAGOYA HOLD MARON'S SHOULDER LIKE THAT!
LET'S FOLLOW HIM, CLASS PRESIDENT!
ROGER!!
KRIK KRIK KRIK
KUNK
WHY THIS?!

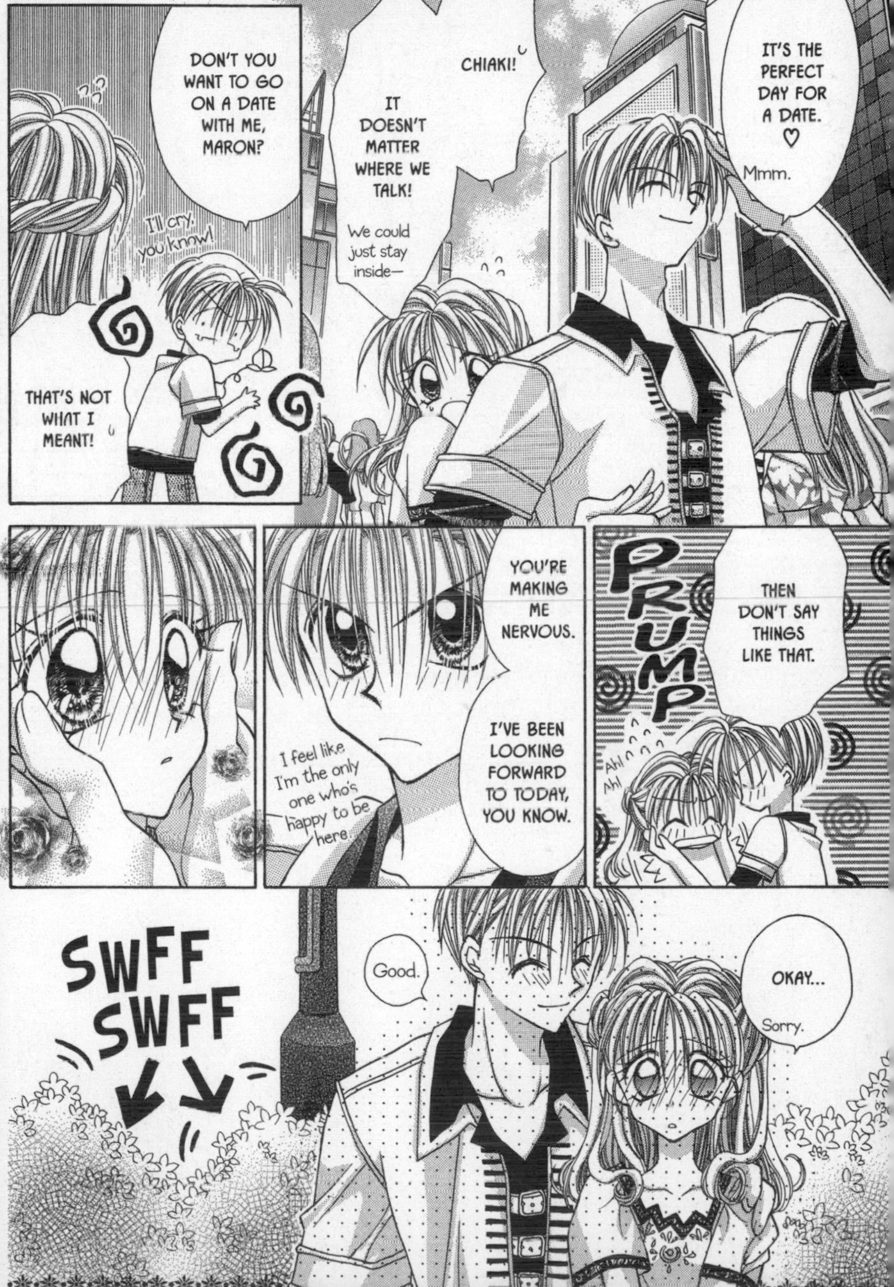
IT'S THE PERFECT DAY FOR A DATE. ♡
Mmm.
CHIAKI!
IT DOESN'T MATTER WHERE WE TALK!
We could just stay inside—
DON'T YOU WANT TO GO ON A DATE WITH ME, MARON?
I'll cry, you know!
THAT'S NOT WHAT I MEANT!
PRUMP
THEN DON'T SAY THINGS LIKE THAT.
Ah! Ah!
YOU'RE MAKING ME NERVOUS.
I'VE BEEN LOOKING FORWARD TO TODAY, YOU KNOW.
I feel like I'm the only one who's happy to be here
OKAY...
Sorry.
Good.
SWFF SWFF

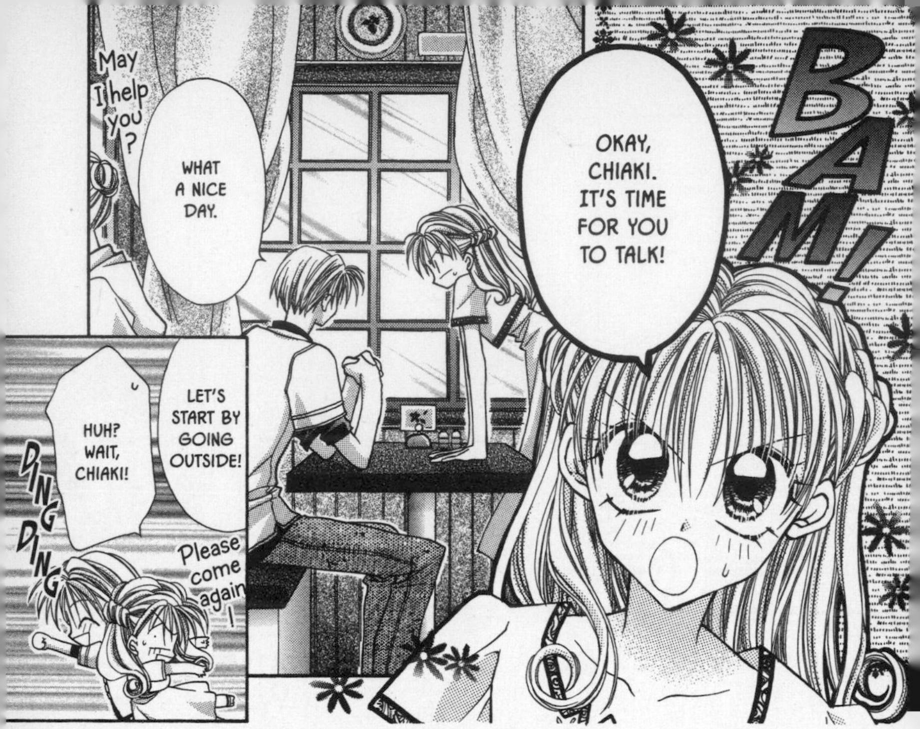
BAM!
OKAY, CHIAKI. IT'S TIME FOR YOU TO TALK!
WHAT A NICE DAY.
May I help you?
LET'S START BY GOING OUTSIDE!
HUH? WAIT, CHIAKI!
DING DING
Please come again!

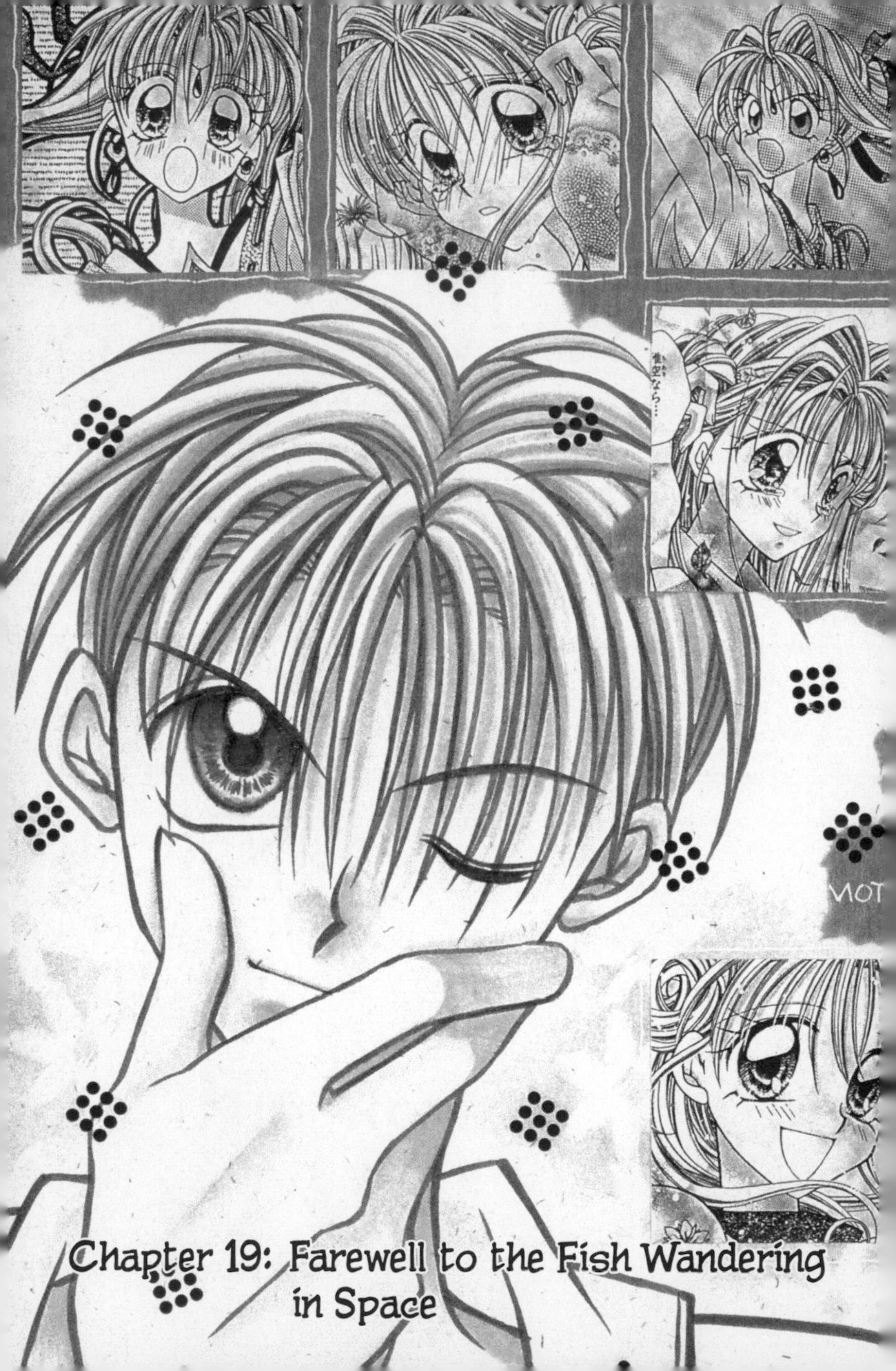

# Chapter 19: Farewell to the Fish Wandering in Space

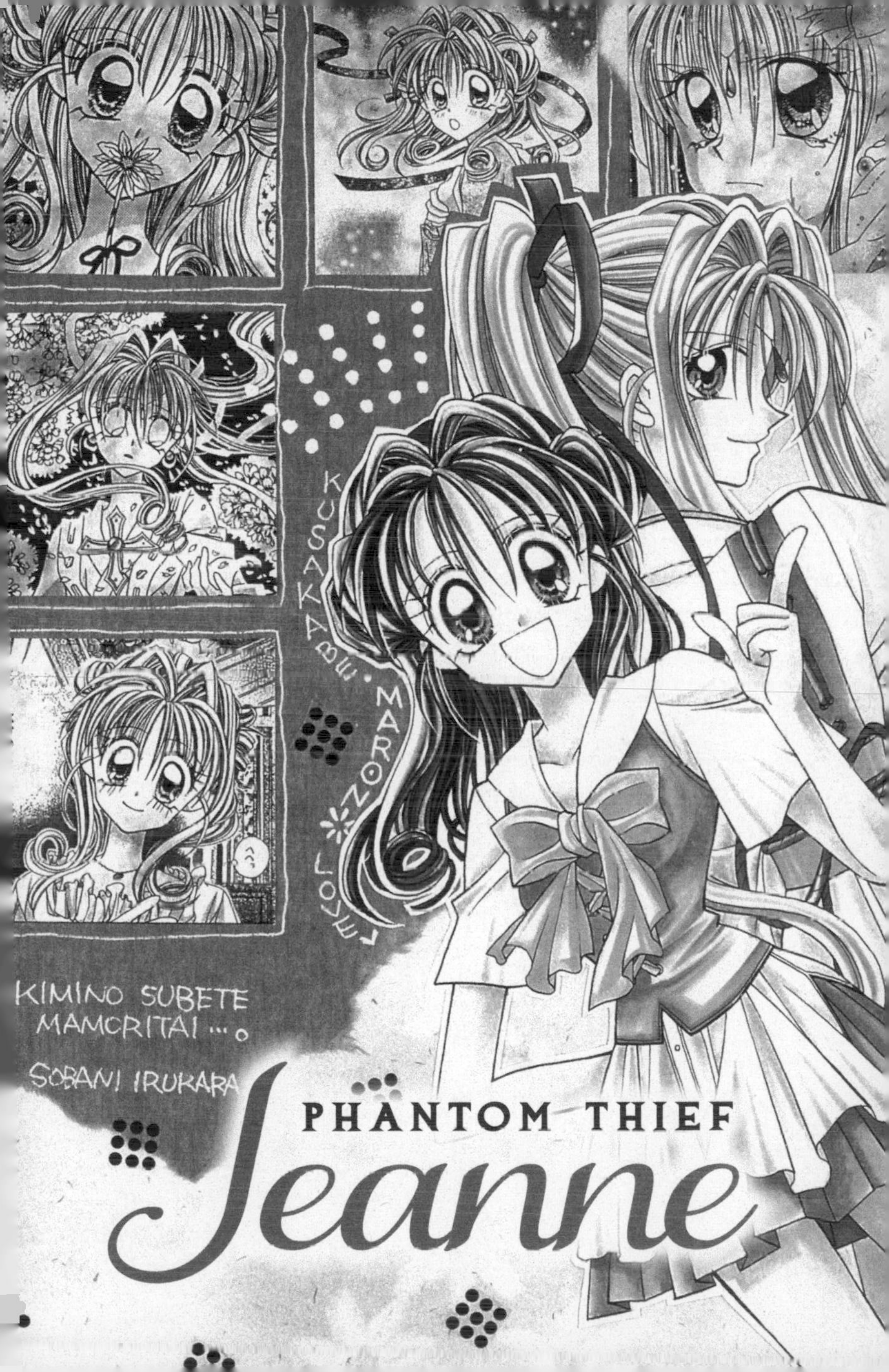
KUSAKABE • MARON ※「LOVE」
KIMINO SUBETE MAMORITAI …。
SOBANI IRUKARA
PHANTOM THIEF
Jeanne

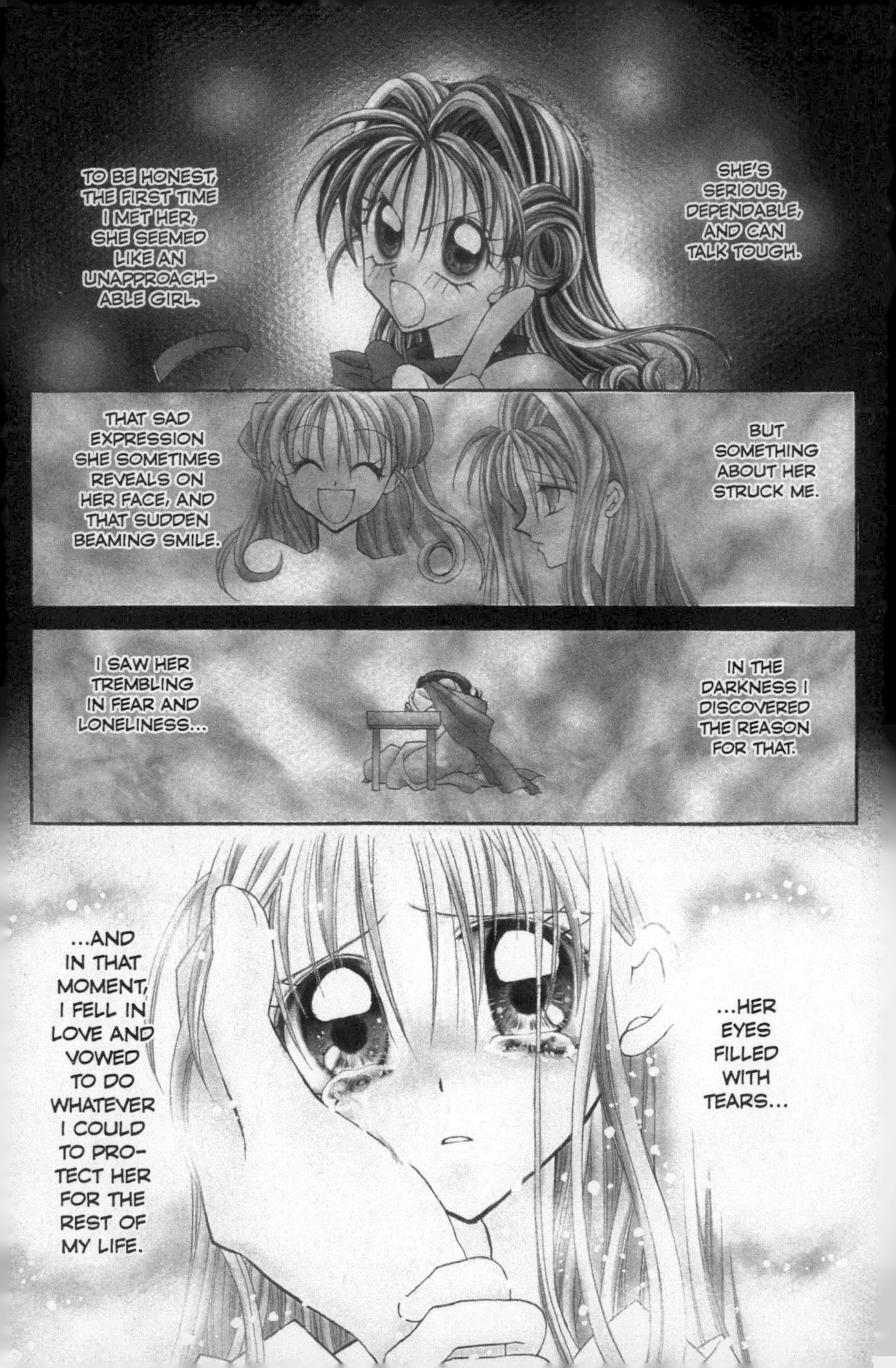
SHE'S SERIOUS, DEPENDABLE, AND CAN TALK TOUGH.
TO BE HONEST, THE FIRST TIME I MET HER, SHE SEEMED LIKE AN UNAPPROACH-ABLE GIRL.
BUT SOMETHING ABOUT HER STRUCK ME.
THAT SAD EXPRESSION SHE SOMETIMES REVEALS ON HER FACE, AND THAT SUDDEN BEAMING SMILE.
IN THE DARKNESS I DISCOVERED THE REASON FOR THAT.
I SAW HER TREMBLING IN FEAR AND LONELINESS...
...HER EYES FILLED WITH TEARS...
...AND IN THAT MOMENT, I FELL IN LOVE AND VOWED TO DO WHATEVER I COULD TO PRO-TECT HER FOR THE REST OF MY LIFE.

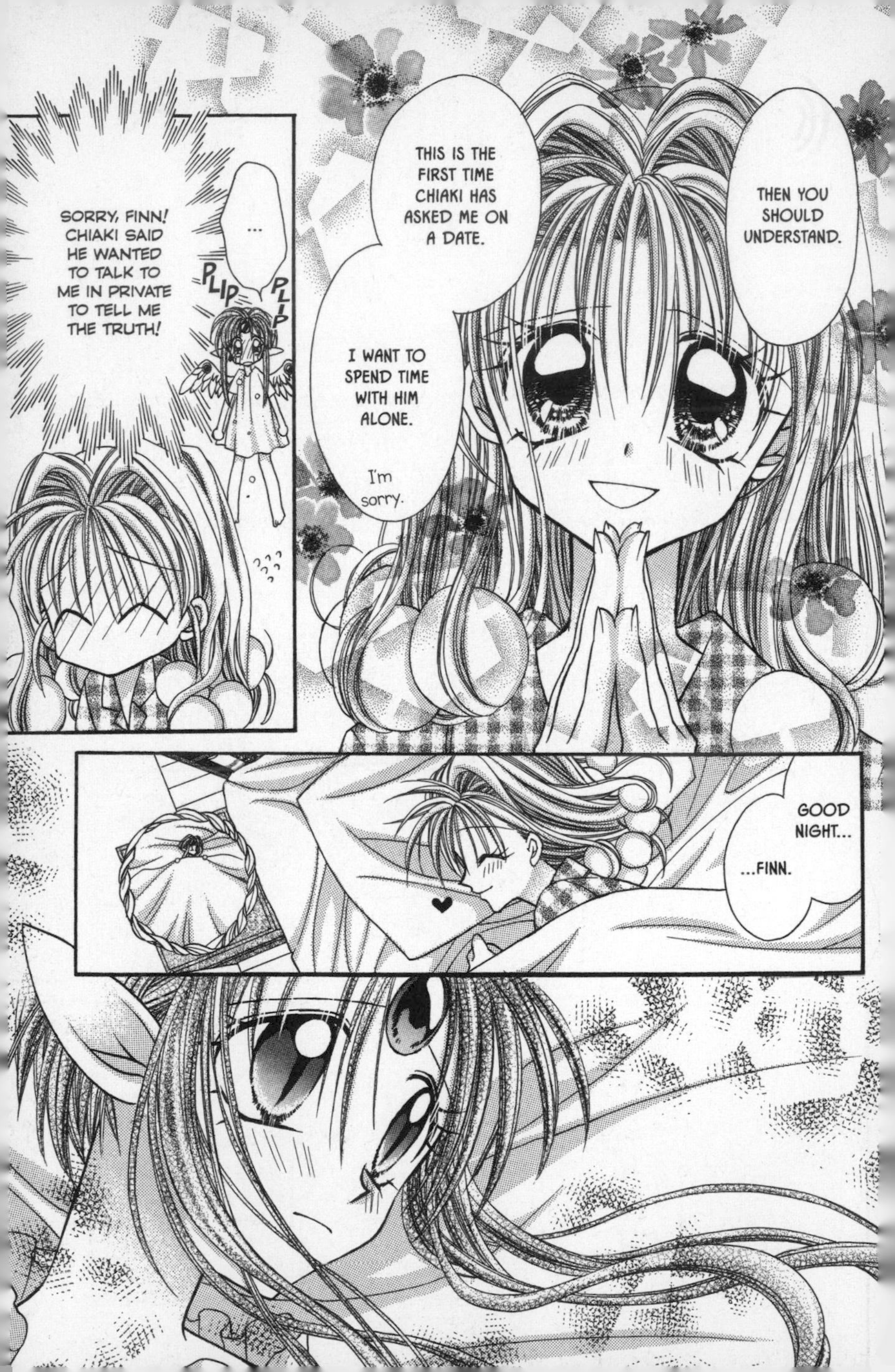
THEN YOU SHOULD UNDERSTAND.
THIS IS THE FIRST TIME CHIAKI HAS ASKED ME ON A DATE.
I WANT TO SPEND TIME WITH HIM ALONE.
I'm sorry.
...
PLIP PLIP
SORRY, FINN! CHIAKI SAID HE WANTED TO TALK TO ME IN PRIVATE TO TELL ME THE TRUTH!
GOOD NIGHT...
...FINN.

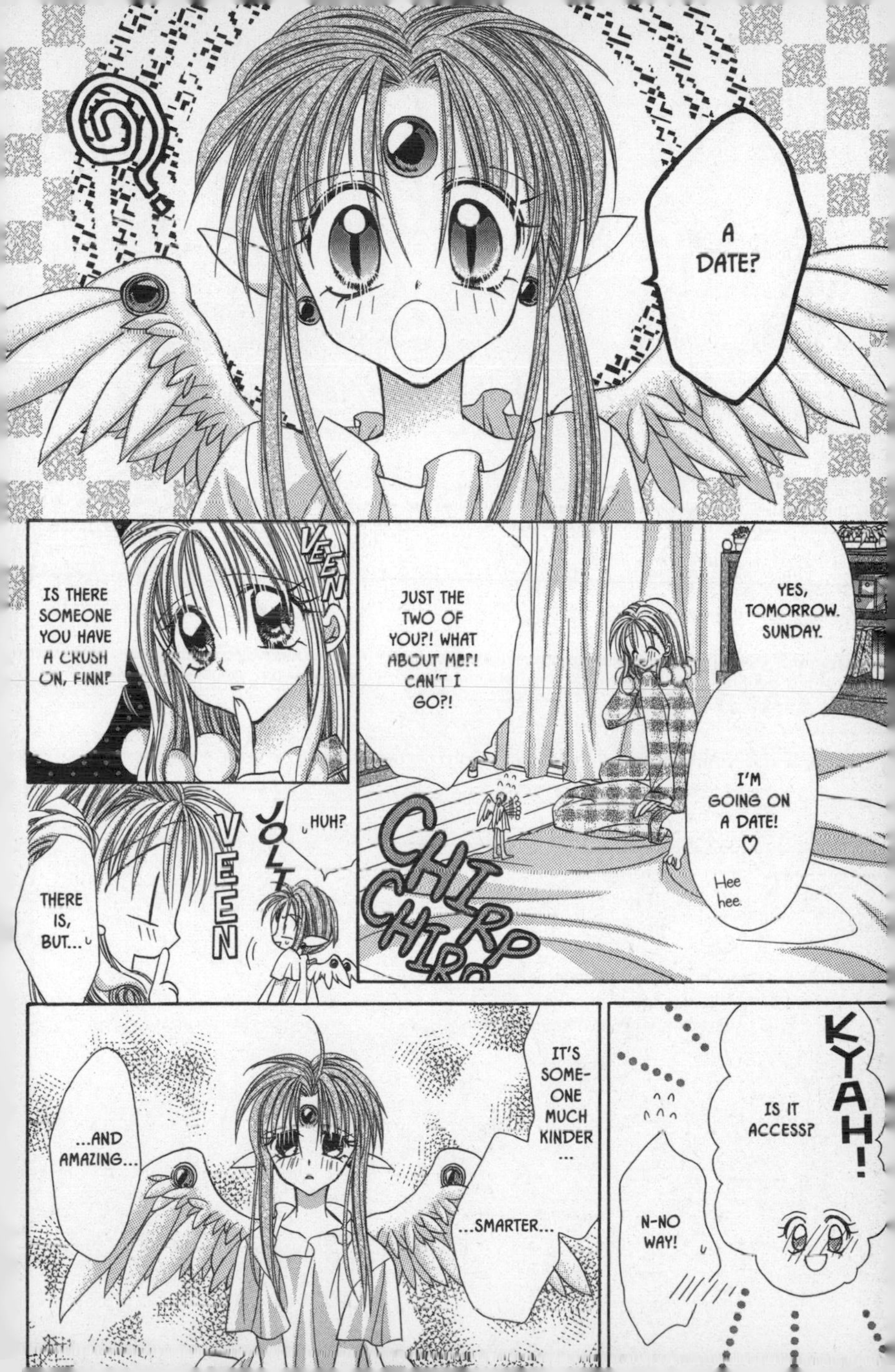

A DATE?
YES, TOMORROW. SUNDAY.
I'M GOING ON A DATE! ♡
Hee hee.
JUST THE TWO OF YOU?! WHAT ABOUT ME?! CAN'T I GO?!
CHIRP
CHIR
VEEN
IS THERE SOMEONE YOU HAVE A CRUSH ON, FINN?
JOLT
HUH?
VEEN
THERE IS, BUT...
KYAH!
IS IT ACCESS?
N-NO WAY!
IT'S SOME-ONE MUCH KINDER ...
...SMARTER...
...AND AMAZING...

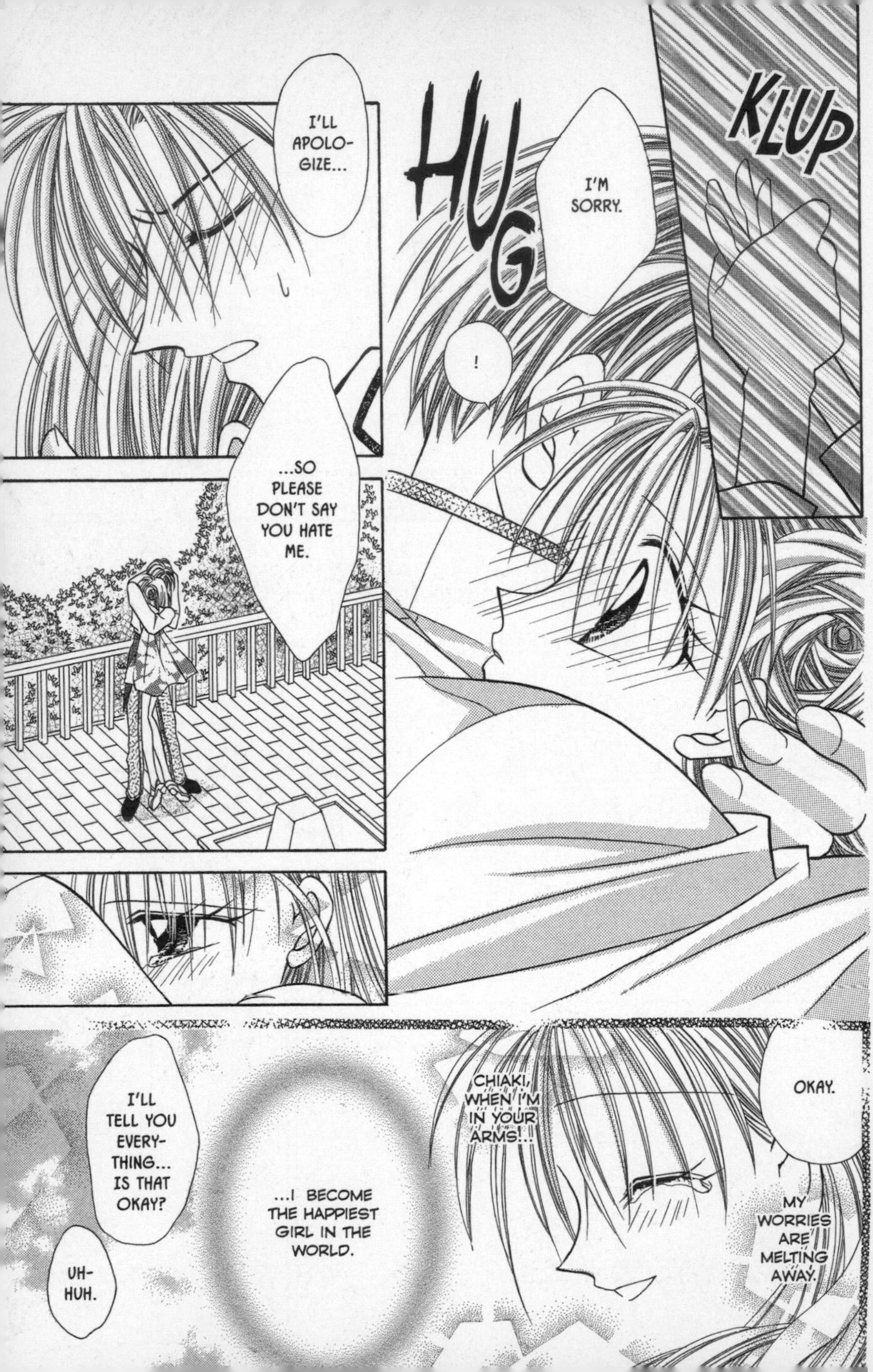
KLUP
HUG
I'M SORRY.
!
I'LL APOLOGIZE...
...SO PLEASE DON'T SAY YOU HATE ME.
OKAY.
CHIAKI, WHEN I'M IN YOUR ARMS...
MY WORRIES ARE MELTING AWAY.
...I BECOME THE HAPPIEST GIRL IN THE WORLD.
I'LL TELL YOU EVERYTHING... IS THAT OKAY?
UH-HUH.

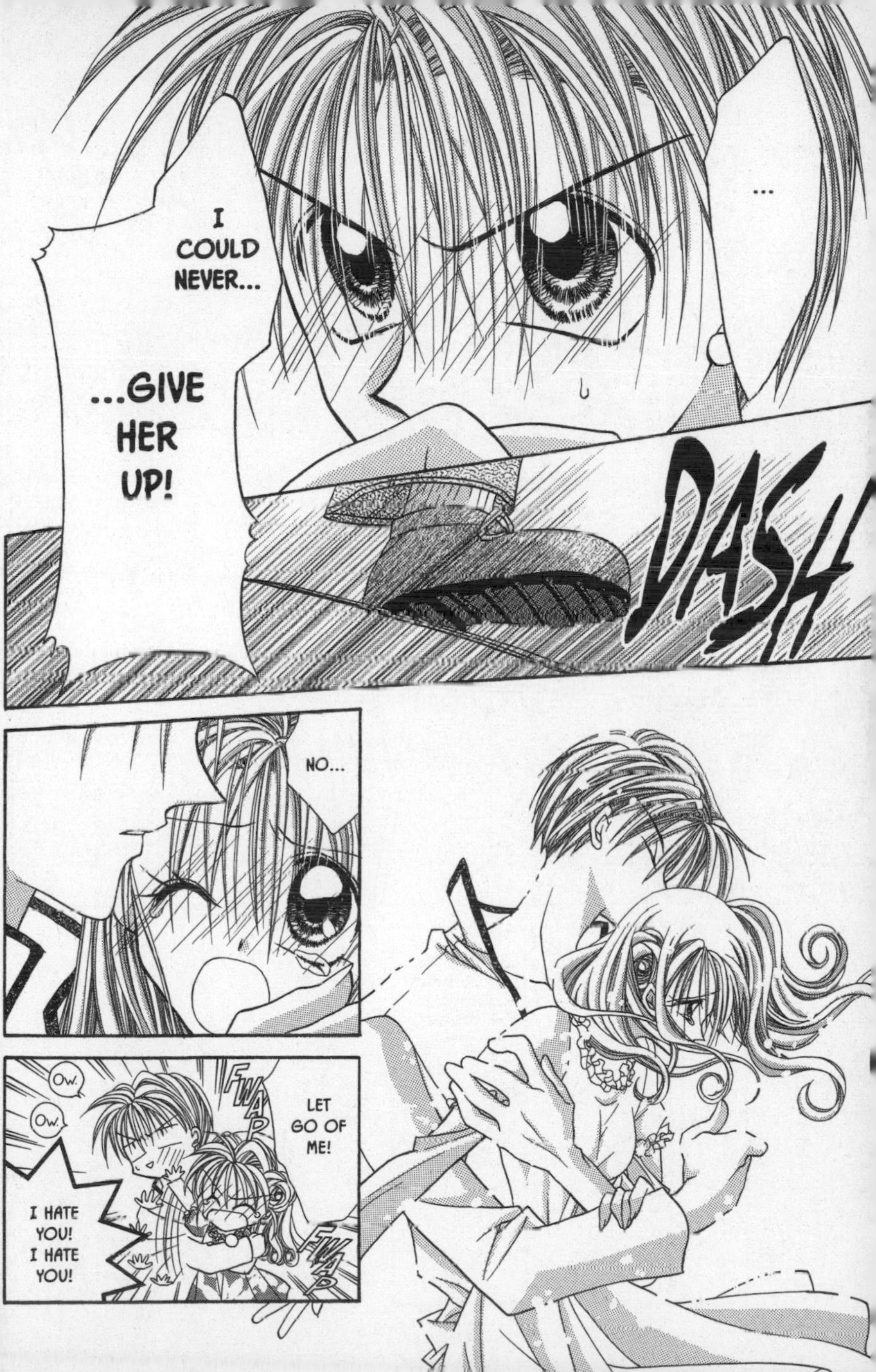
...
I COULD NEVER...
...GIVE HER UP!
DASH
NO...
FWAP
LET GO OF ME!
Ow.
Ow.
I HATE YOU! I HATE YOU!
FWAP

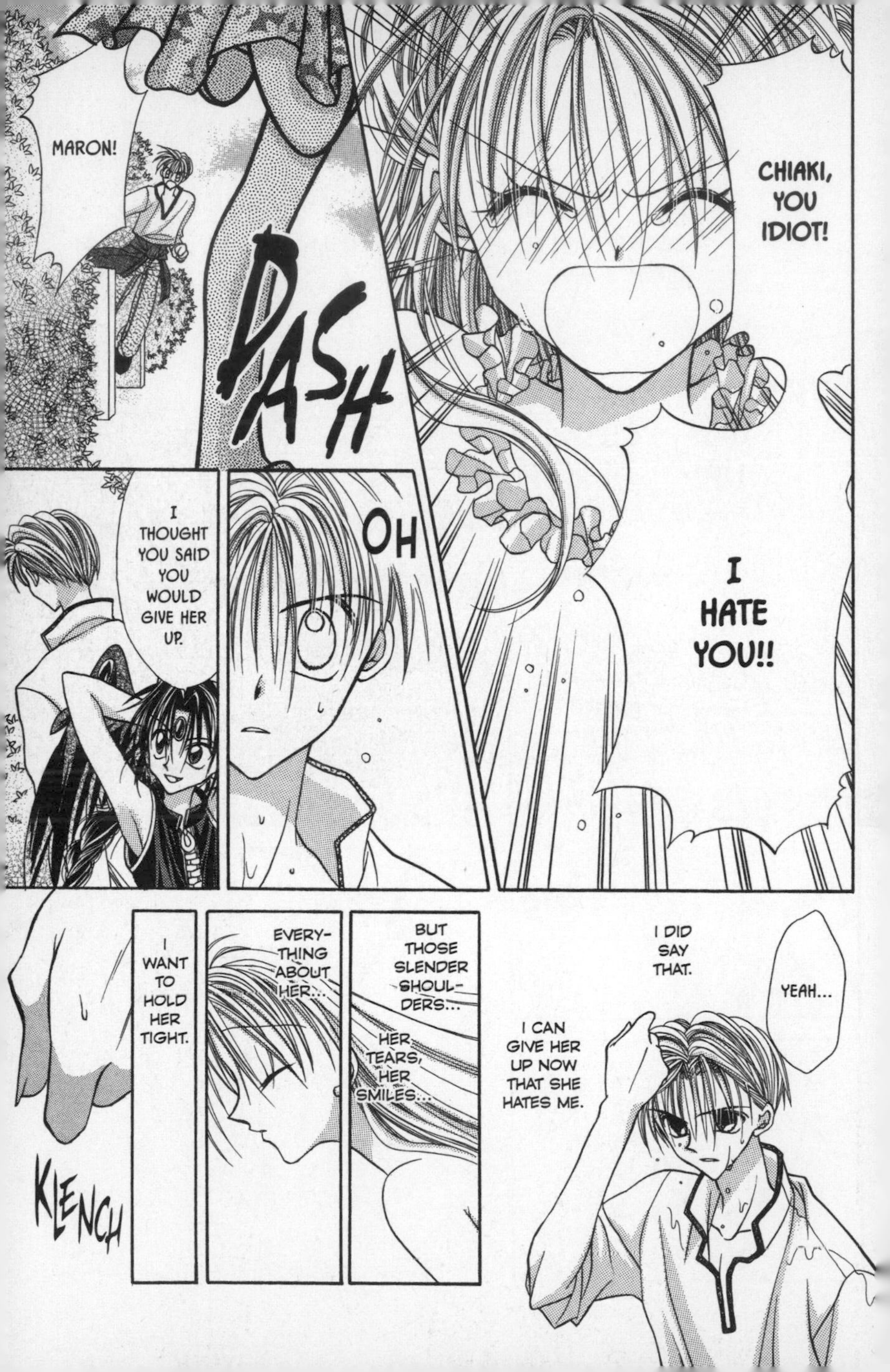
CHIAKI, YOU IDIOT!
I HATE YOU!!
DASH
MARON!
OH
I THOUGHT YOU SAID YOU WOULD GIVE HER UP.
YEAH...
I DID SAY THAT.
I CAN GIVE HER UP NOW THAT SHE HATES ME.
BUT THOSE SLENDER SHOULDERS...
HER TEARS, HER SMILES...
EVERYTHING ABOUT HER...
I WANT TO HOLD HER TIGHT.
KLENCH

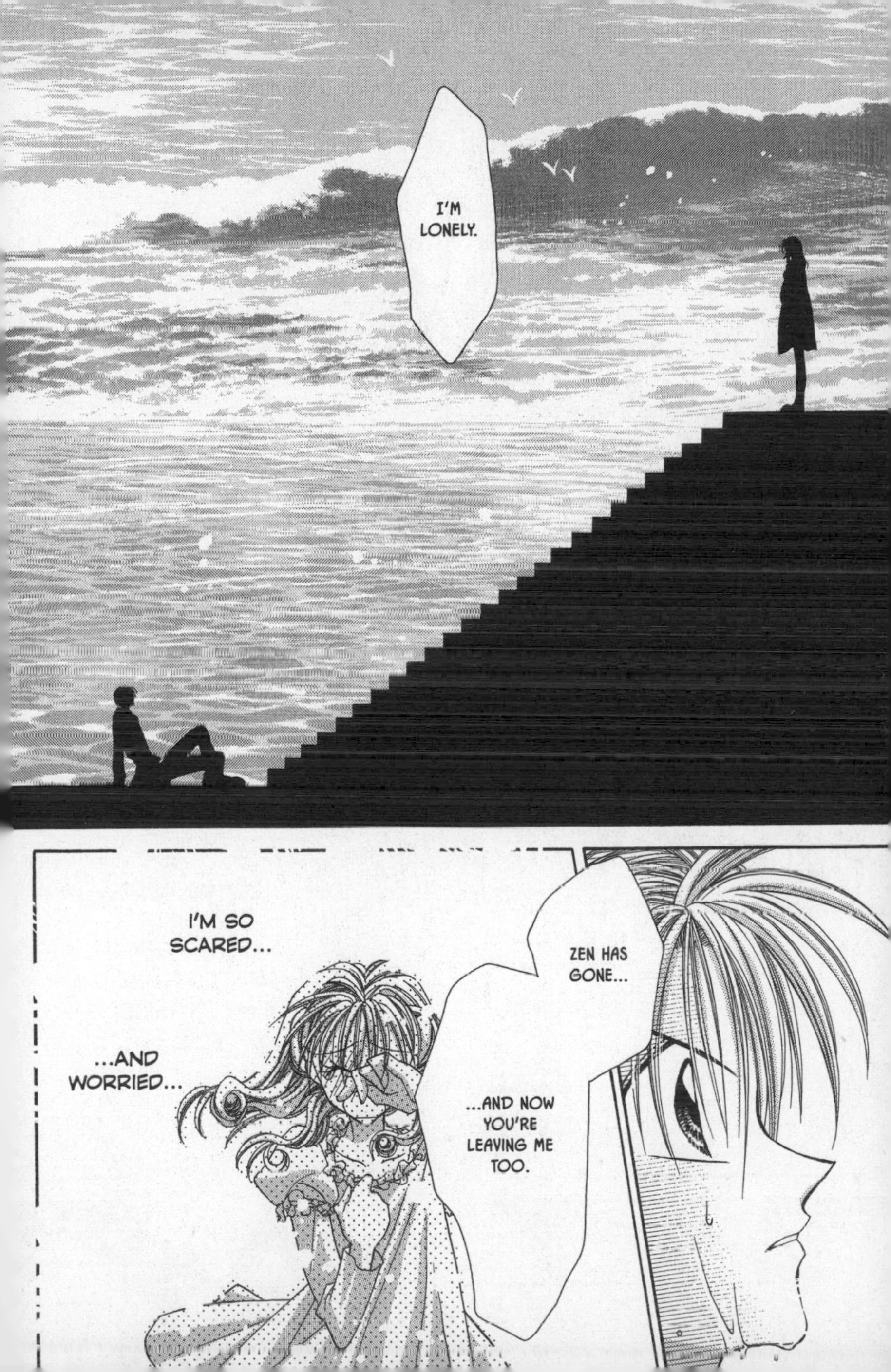
I'M LONELY.
ZEN HAS GONE...
...AND NOW YOU'RE LEAVING ME TOO.
I'M SO SCARED...
...AND WORRIED...

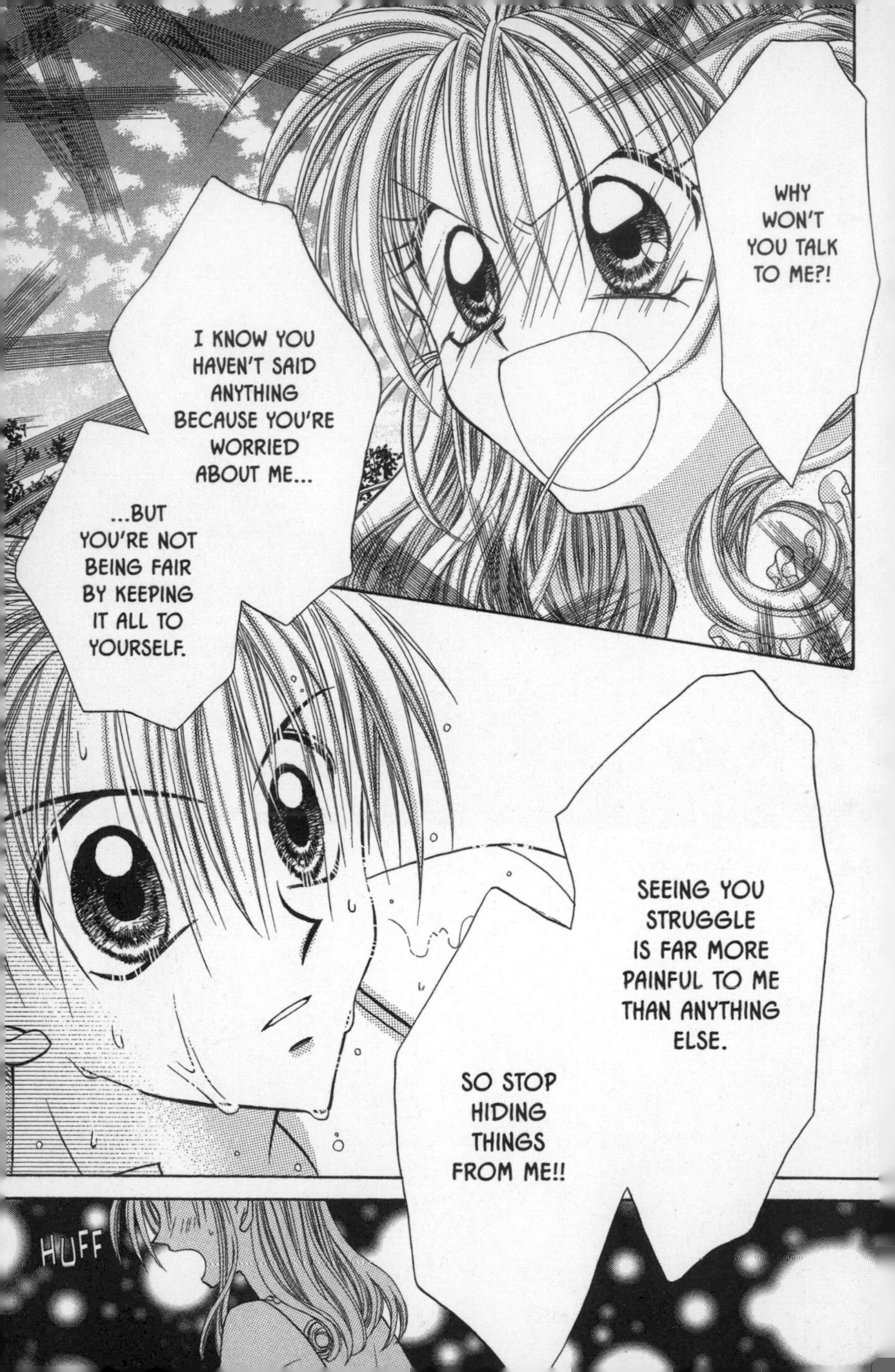
WHY WON'T YOU TALK TO ME?!
I KNOW YOU HAVEN'T SAID ANYTHING BECAUSE YOU'RE WORRIED ABOUT ME...
...BUT YOU'RE NOT BEING FAIR BY KEEPING IT ALL TO YOURSELF.
SEEING YOU STRUGGLE IS FAR MORE PAINFUL TO ME THAN ANYTHING ELSE.
SO STOP HIDING THINGS FROM ME!!
HUFF

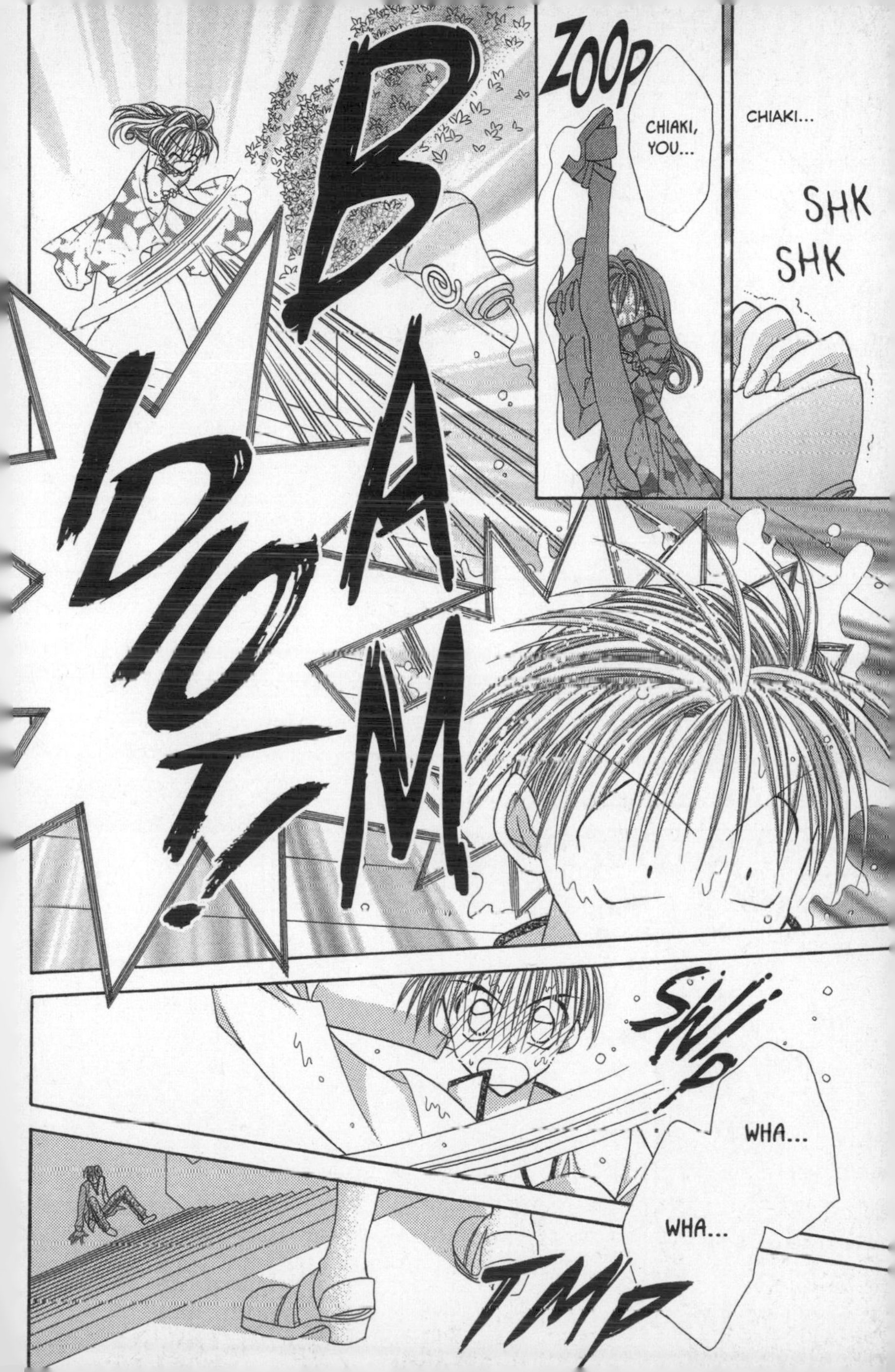
CHIAKI...
SHK
SHK
ZOOP
CHIAKI, YOU...
BAM
DOOT!
SWIP
WHA...
WHA...
TMP

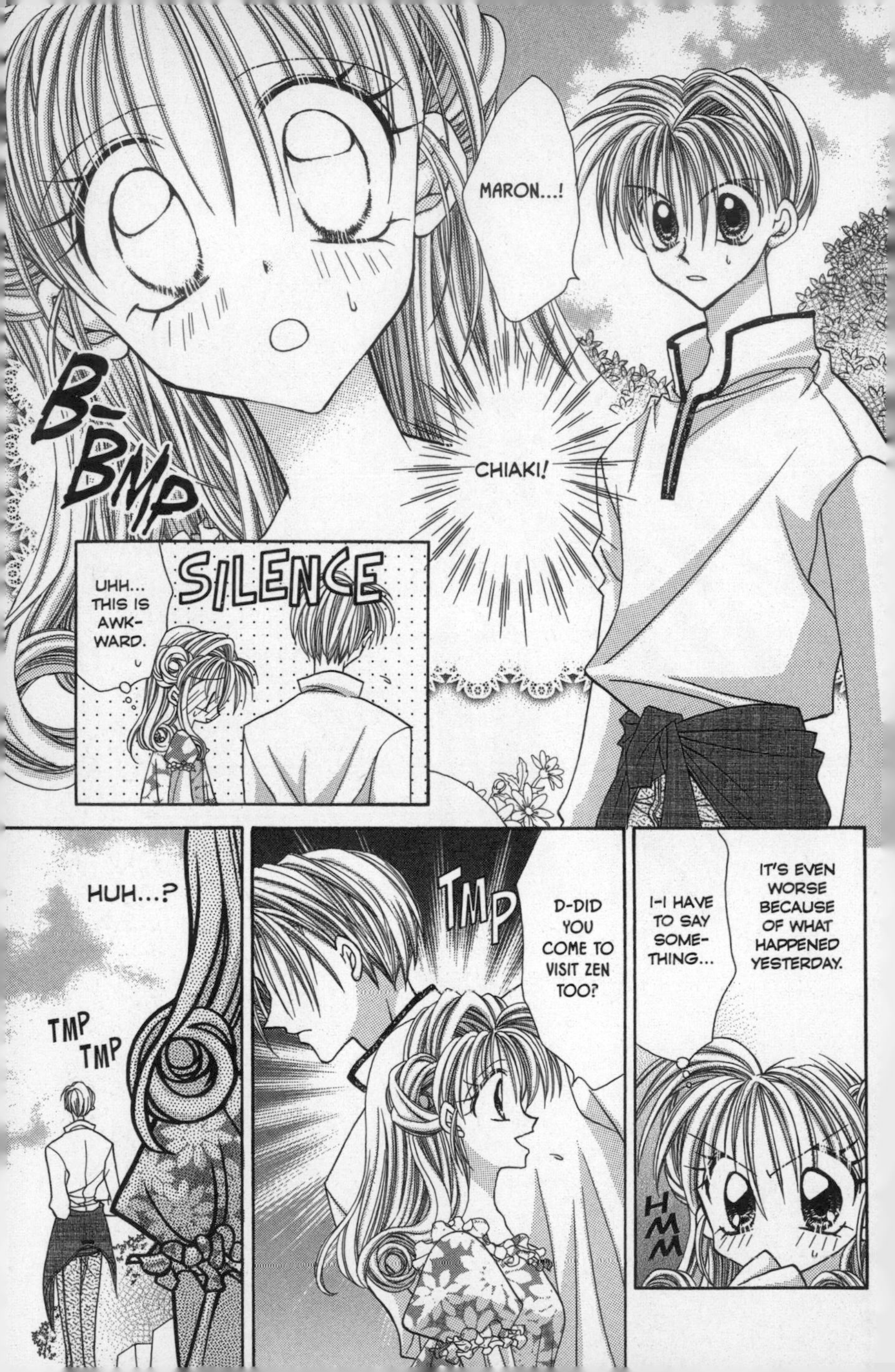
MARON...!
CHIAKI!
B-BMP
SILENCE
UHH... THIS IS AWK-WARD.
IT'S EVEN WORSE BECAUSE OF WHAT HAPPENED YESTERDAY.
I-I HAVE TO SAY SOME-THING...
HMM
D-DID YOU COME TO VISIT ZEN TOO?
TMP
HUH...?
TMP TMP

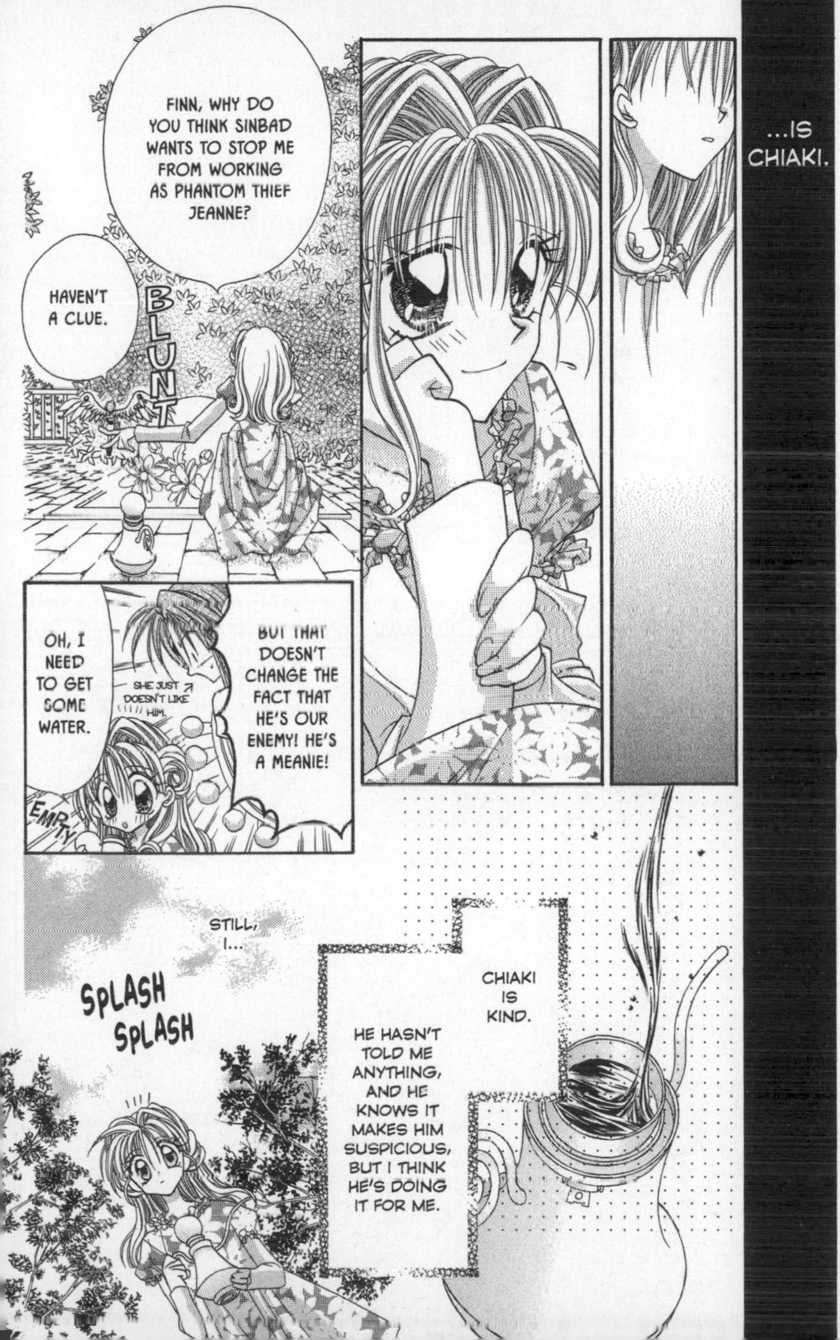
...IS CHIAKI.
FINN, WHY DO YOU THINK SINBAD WANTS TO STOP ME FROM WORKING AS PHANTOM THIEF JEANNE?
HAVEN'T A CLUE.
BLUNT
BUT THAT DOESN'T CHANGE THE FACT THAT HE'S OUR ENEMY! HE'S A MEANIE!
SHE JUST DOESN'T LIKE HIM.
OH, I NEED TO GET SOME WATER.
EMPTY
STILL, I...
CHIAKI IS KIND.
HE HASN'T TOLD ME ANYTHING, AND HE KNOWS IT MAKES HIM SUSPICIOUS, BUT I THINK HE'S DOING IT FOR ME.
SPLASH SPLASH

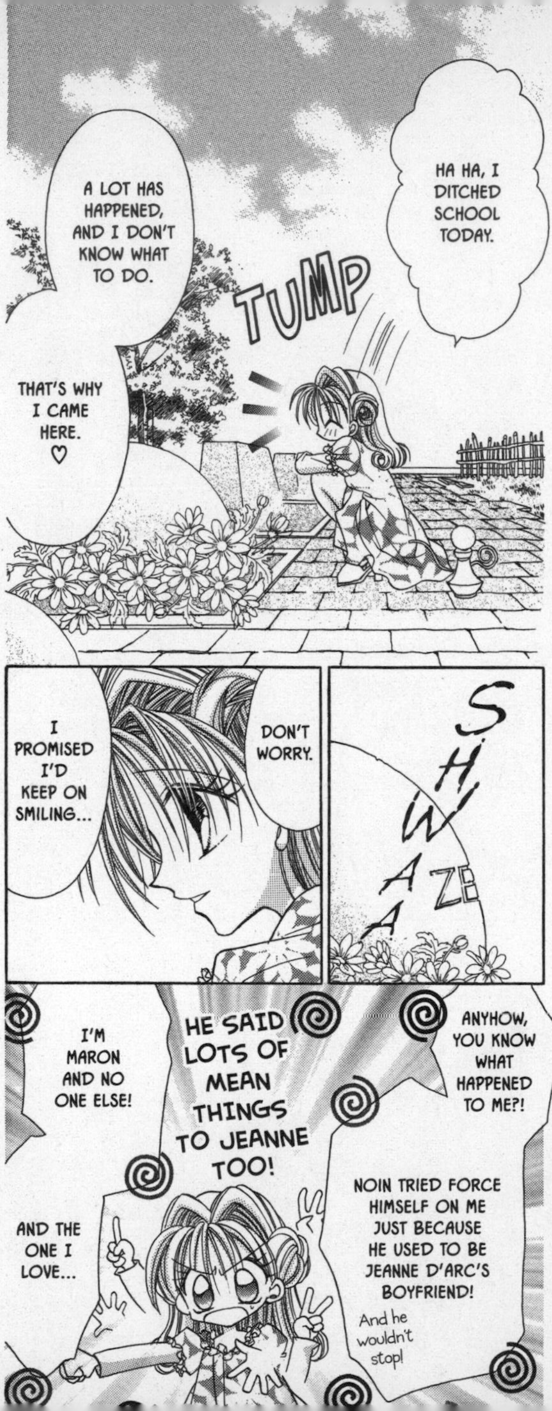
HA HA, I DITCHED SCHOOL TODAY.
TUMP
A LOT HAS HAPPENED, AND I DON'T KNOW WHAT TO DO.
THAT'S WHY I CAME HERE. ♡
SHWAA
ZE
DON'T WORRY.
I PROMISED I'D KEEP ON SMILING...
ANYHOW, YOU KNOW WHAT HAPPENED TO ME?!
HE SAID LOTS OF MEAN THINGS TO JEANNE TOO!
I'M MARON AND NO ONE ELSE!
NOIN TRIED FORCE HIMSELF ON ME JUST BECAUSE HE USED TO BE JEANNE D'ARC'S BOYFRIEND!
And he wouldn't stop!
AND THE ONE I LOVE...

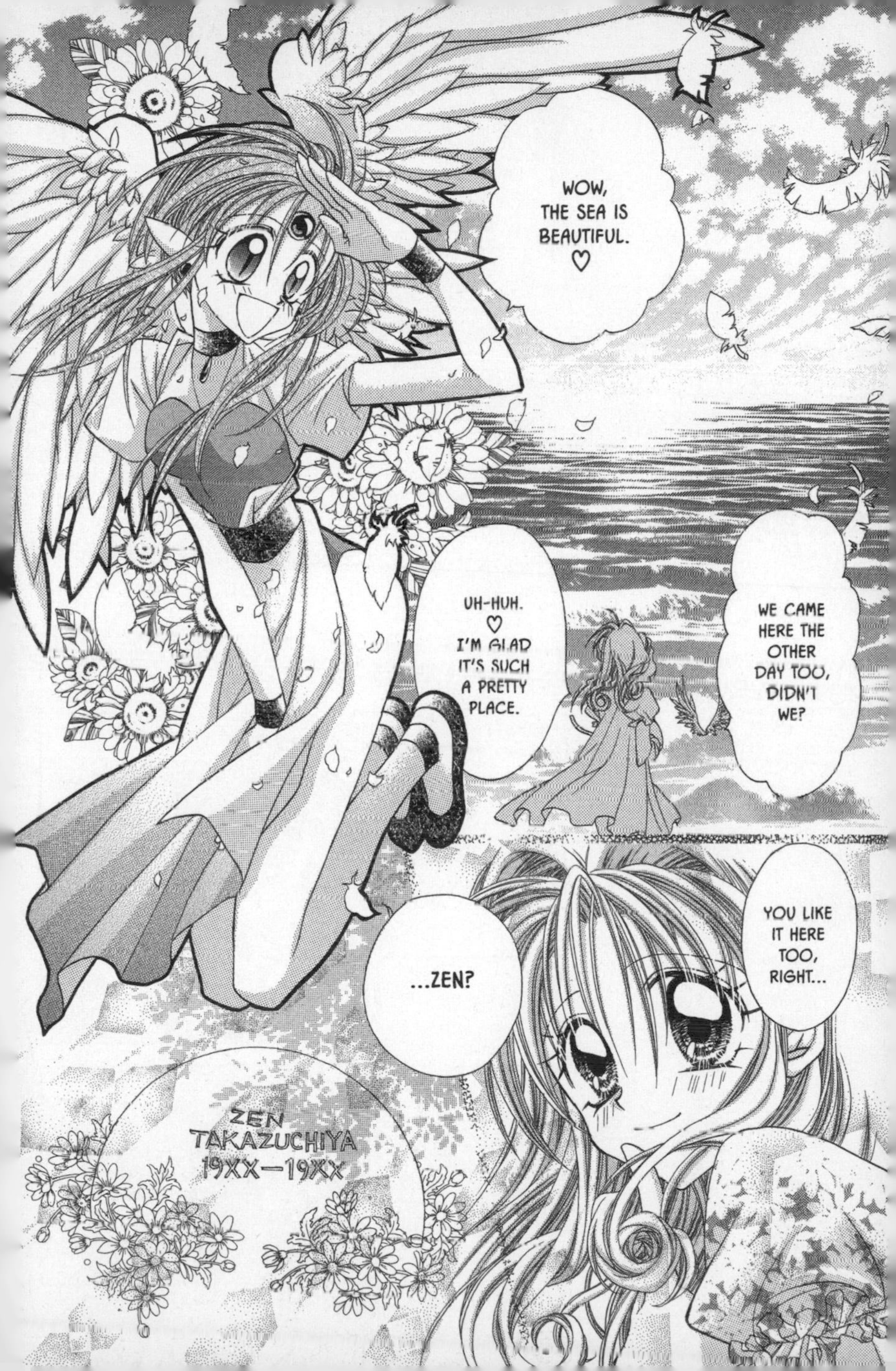

WOW, THE SEA IS BEAUTIFUL. ♡
WE CAME HERE THE OTHER DAY TOO, DIDN'T WE?
UH-HUH. ♡ I'M GLAD IT'S SUCH A PRETTY PLACE.
YOU LIKE IT HERE TOO, RIGHT...
...ZEN?
ZEN TAKAZUCHIYA 19XX–19XX

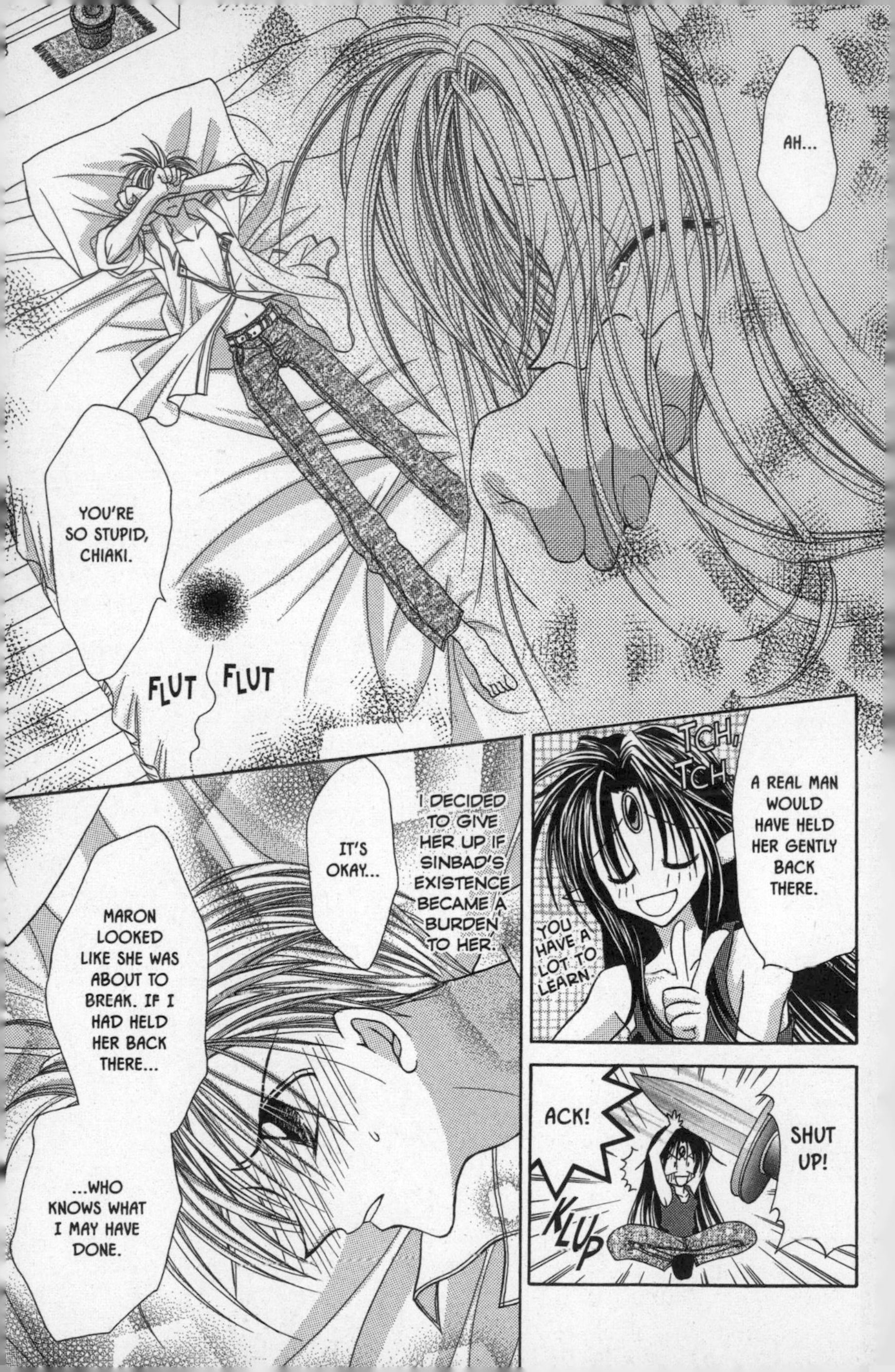
AH...
YOU'RE SO STUPID, CHIAKI.
FLUT FLUT
TCH, TCH
A REAL MAN WOULD HAVE HELD HER GENTLY BACK THERE.
YOU HAVE A LOT TO LEARN.
SHUT UP!
ACK!
KLUP
I DECIDED TO GIVE HER UP IF SINBAD'S EXISTENCE BECAME A BURDEN TO HER.
IT'S OKAY...
MARON LOOKED LIKE SHE WAS ABOUT TO BREAK. IF I HAD HELD HER BACK THERE...
...WHO KNOWS WHAT I MAY HAVE DONE.

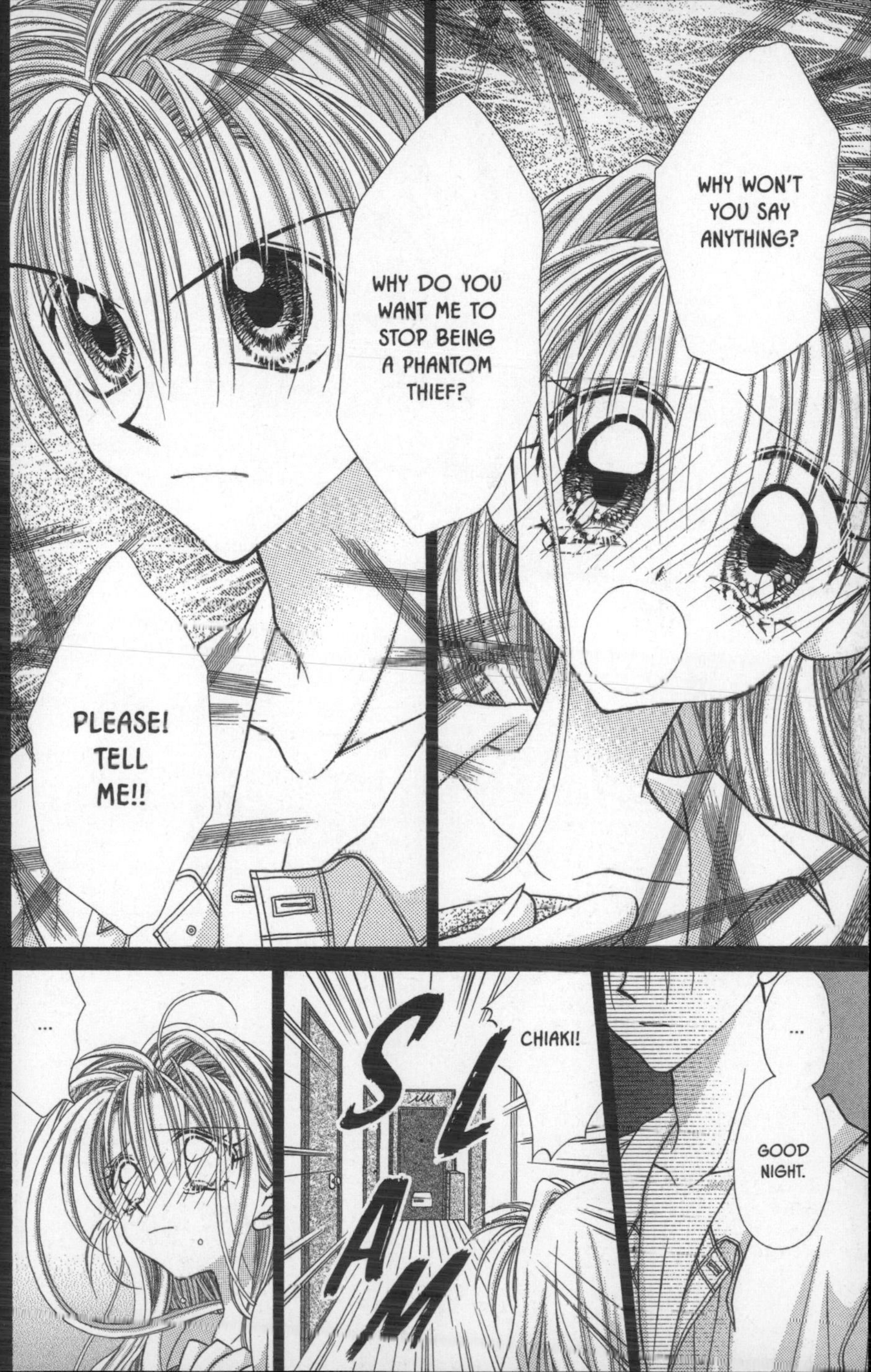
WHY WON'T YOU SAY ANYTHING?
WHY DO YOU WANT ME TO STOP BEING A PHANTOM THIEF?
PLEASE! TELL ME!!
...
GOOD NIGHT.
CHIAKI!
SLAM
...

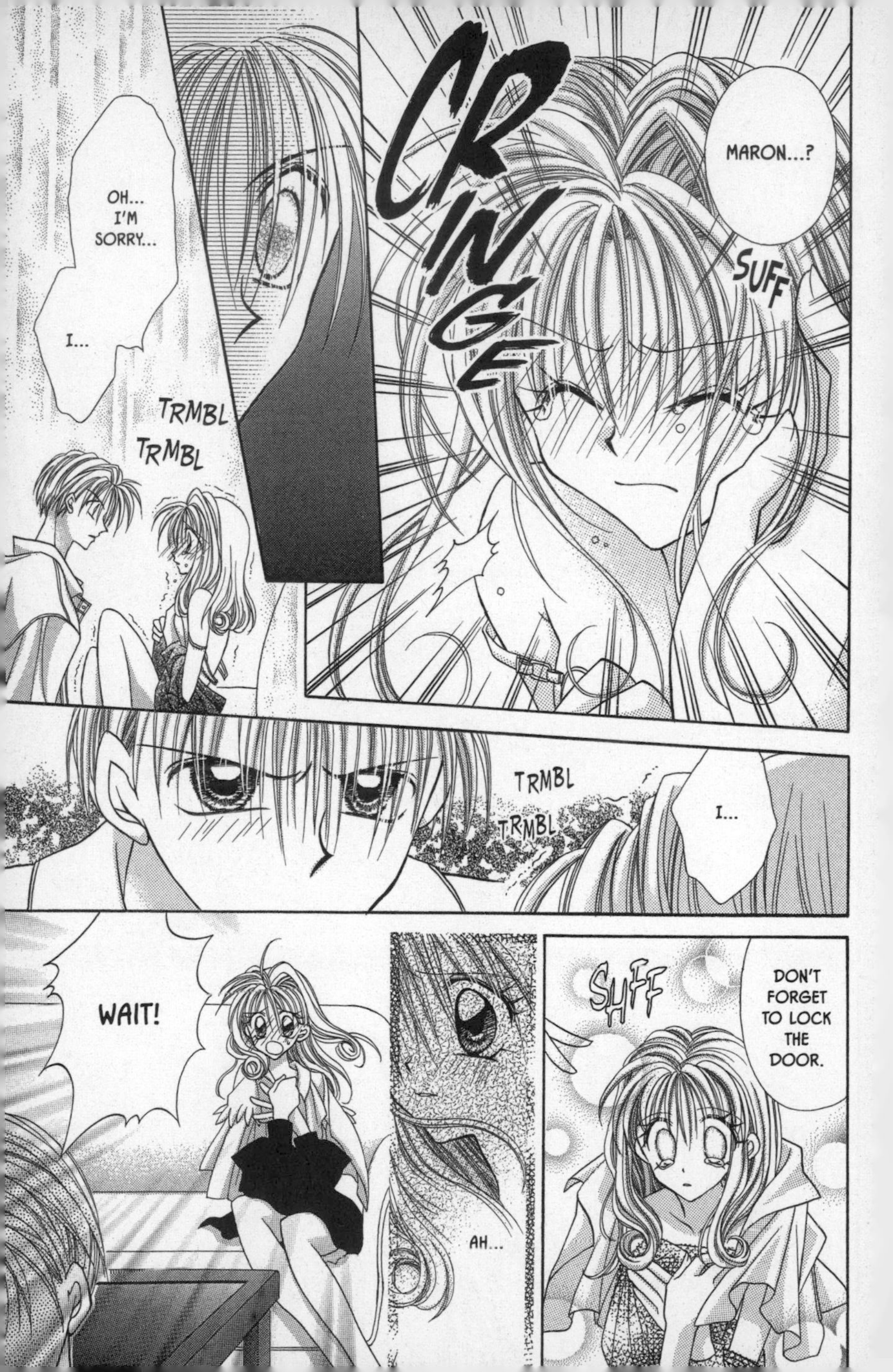
MARON...?
CRINGE
SUFF
OH... I'M SORRY...
I...
TRMBL
TRMBL
I...
TRMBL
TRMBL
DON'T FORGET TO LOCK THE DOOR.
SUFF
AH...
WAIT!

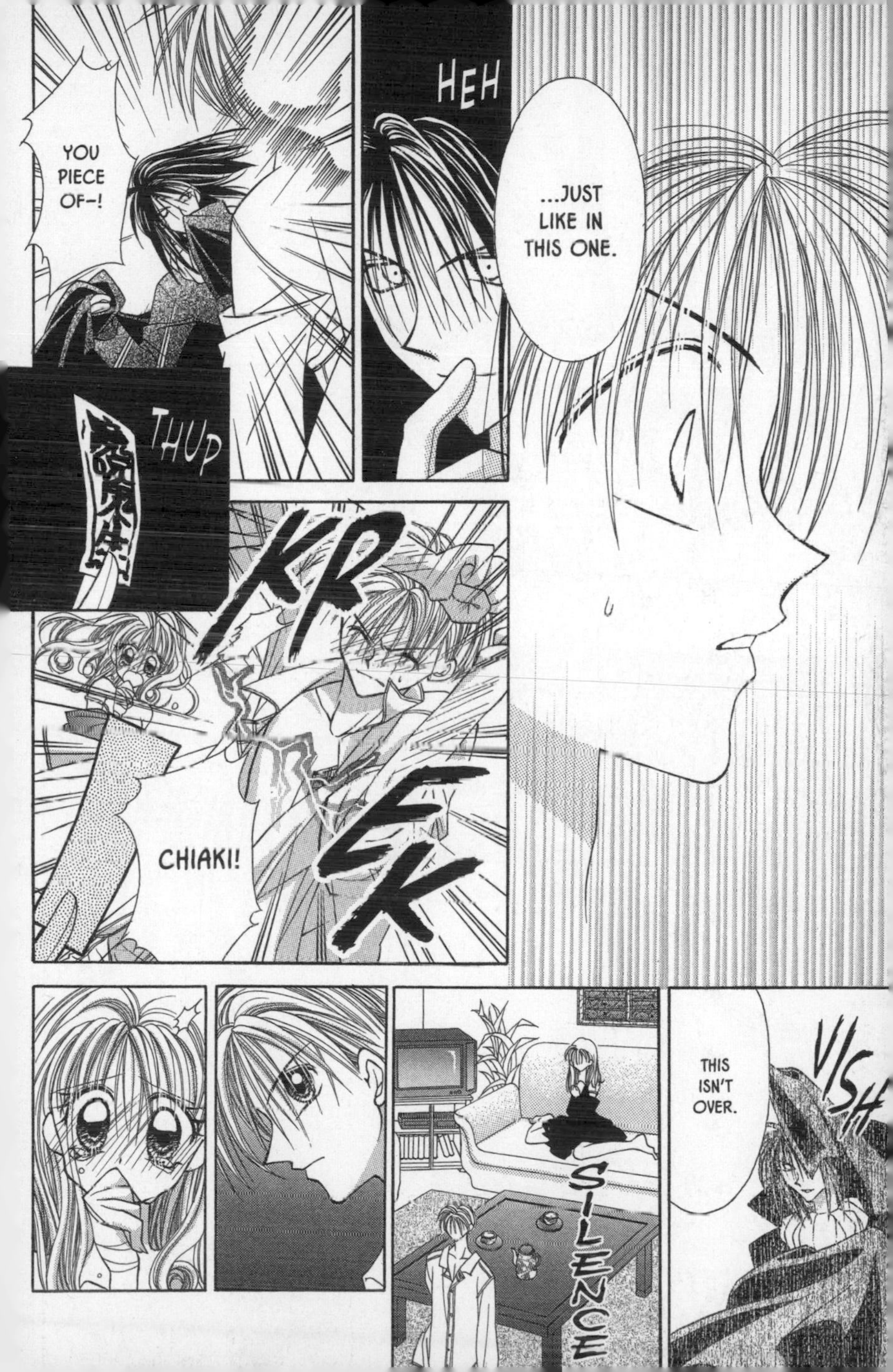
...JUST LIKE IN THIS ONE.
HEH
YOU PIECE OF-!
THUP
CHIAKI!
VISH
THIS ISN'T OVER.
SILENCE

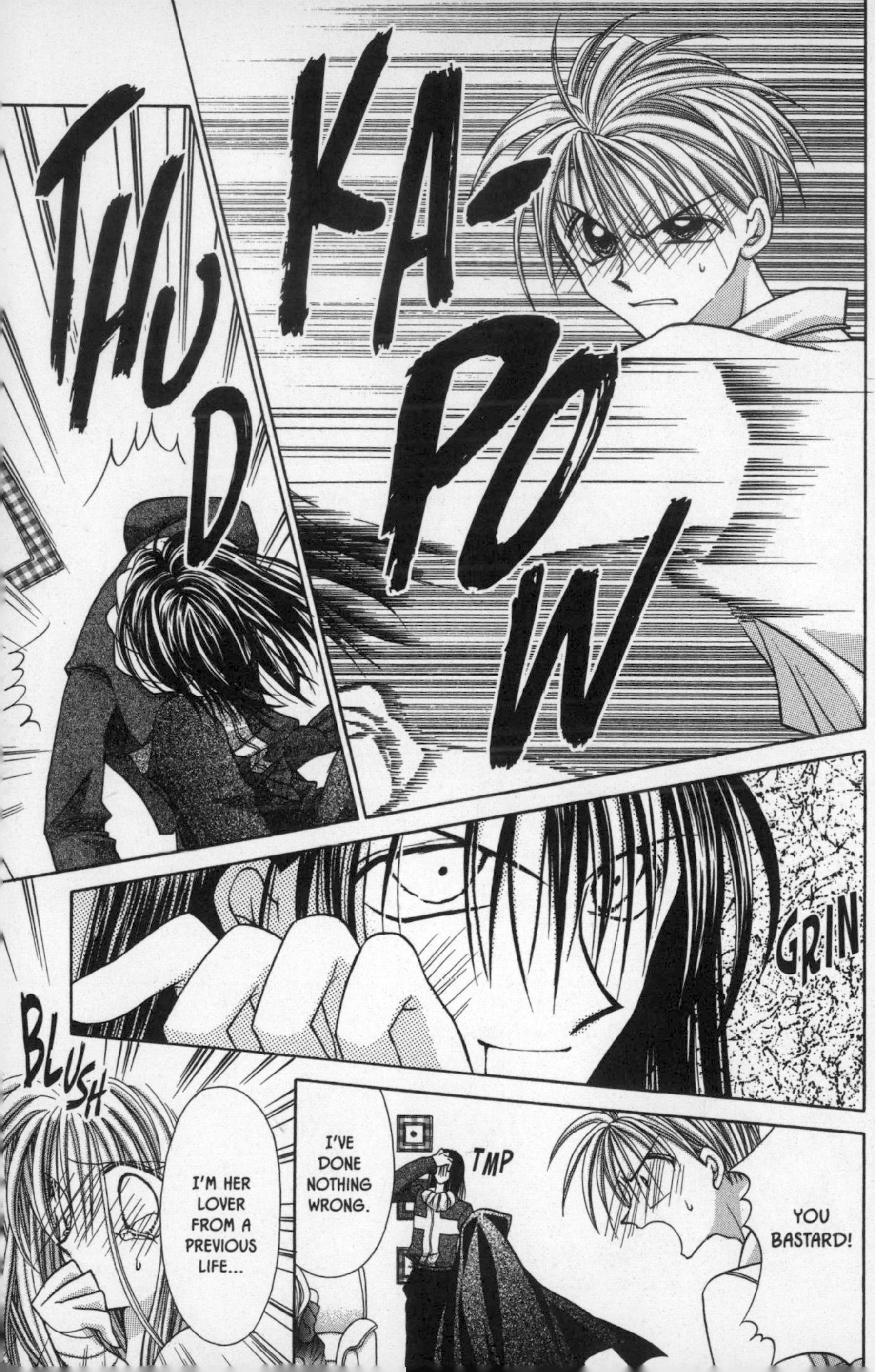
KA-POW
THUD
GRIN
YOU BASTARD!
TMP
I'VE DONE NOTHING WRONG.
BLUSH
I'M HER LOVER FROM A PREVIOUS LIFE...

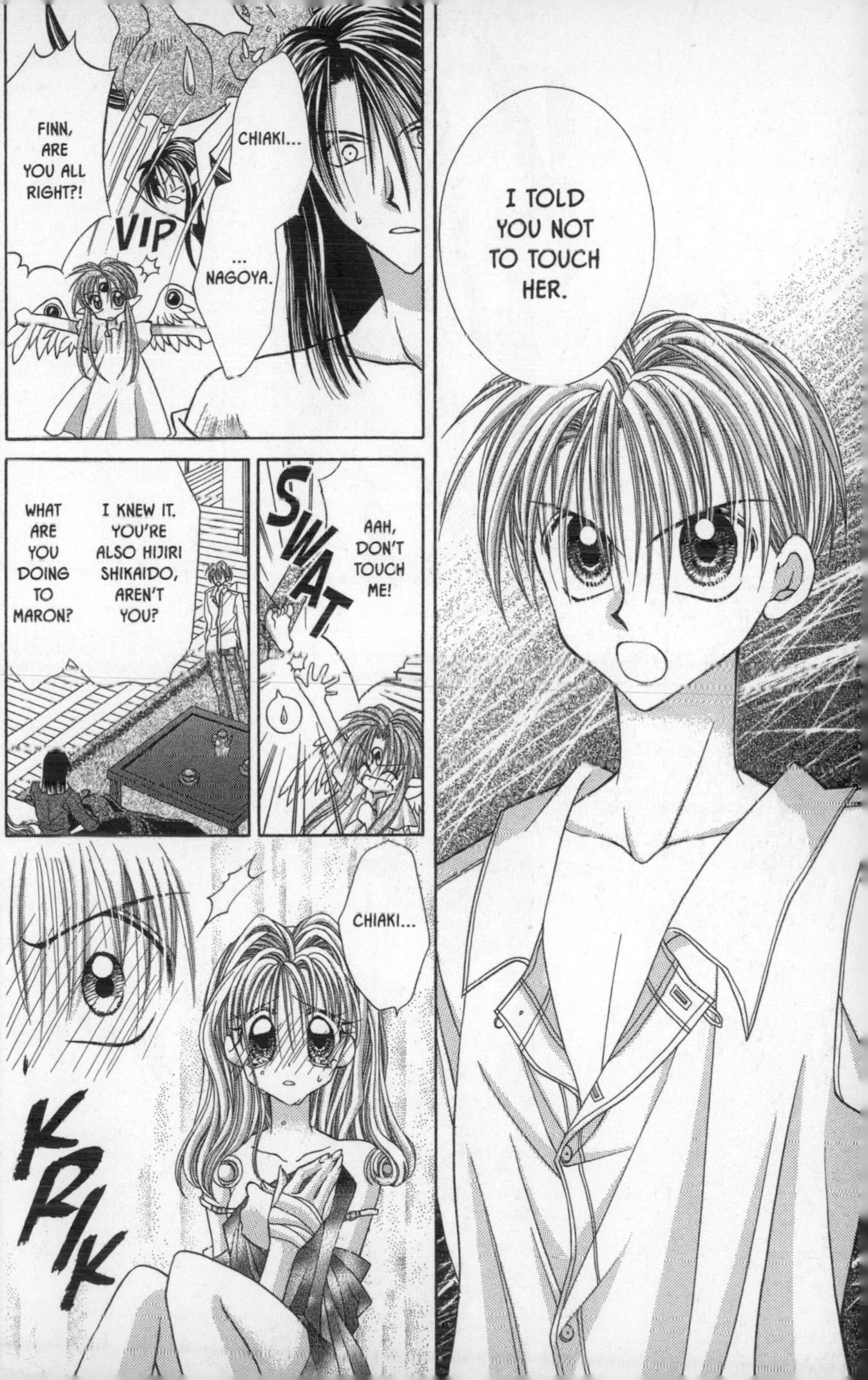
I TOLD YOU NOT TO TOUCH HER.
CHIAKI...
... NAGOYA.
FINN, ARE YOU ALL RIGHT?!
VIP
SWAT
AAH, DON'T TOUCH ME!
I KNEW IT. YOU'RE ALSO HIJIRI SHIKAIDO, AREN'T YOU?
WHAT ARE YOU DOING TO MARON?
CHIAKI...
KRIK

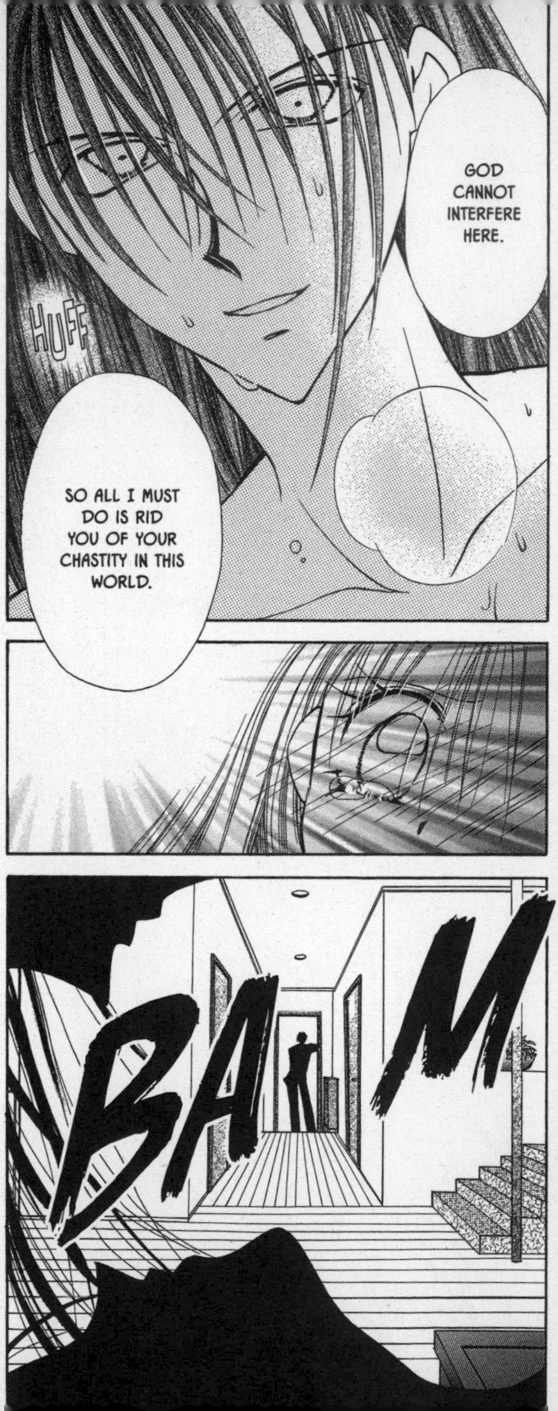
GOD CANNOT INTERFERE HERE.
HUFF
SO ALL I MUST DO IS RID YOU OF YOUR CHASTITY IN THIS WORLD.
BAM

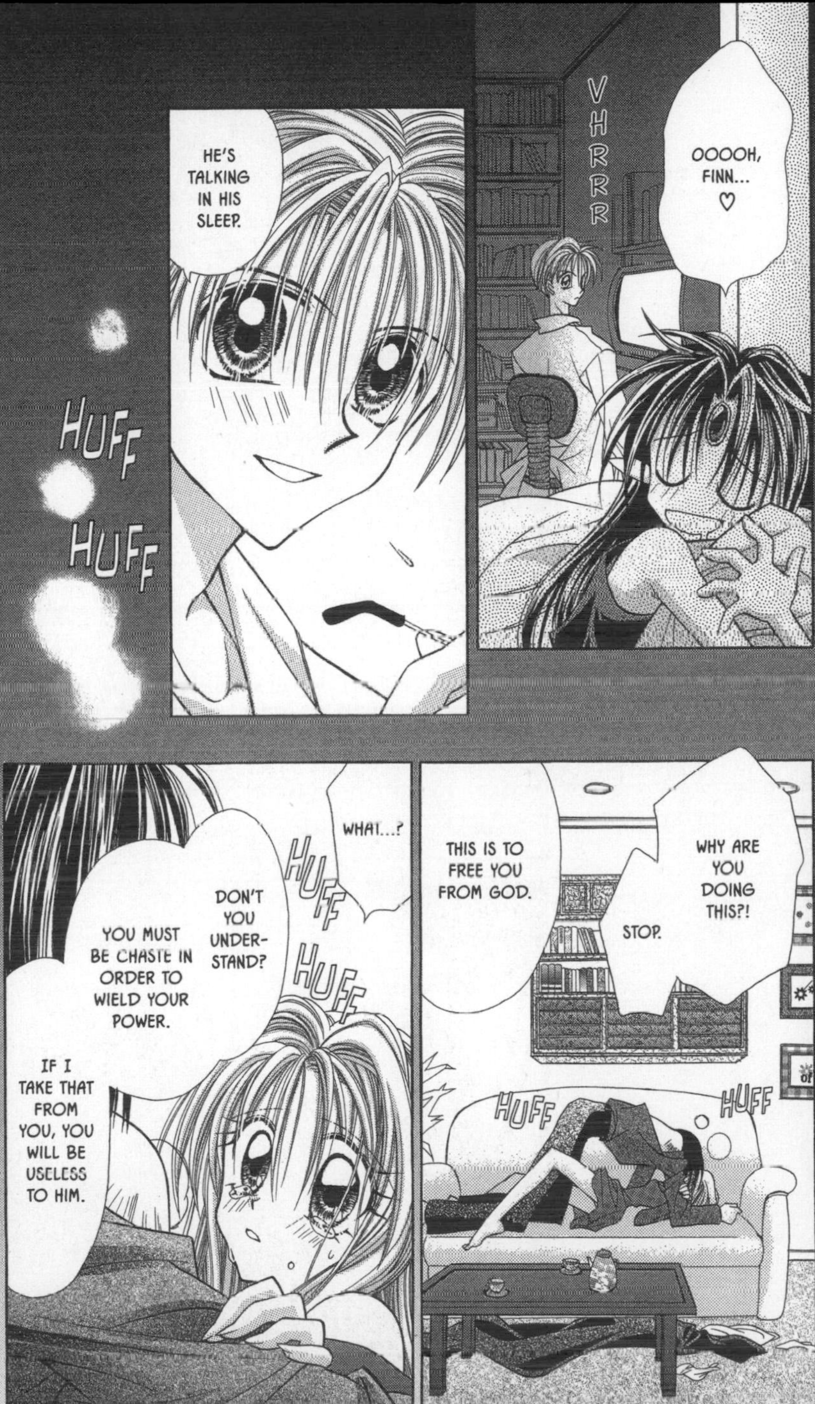
VHRRR
OOOOH, FINN... ♡
HE'S TALKING IN HIS SLEEP.
HUFF
HUFF
WHY ARE YOU DOING THIS?!
STOP.
THIS IS TO FREE YOU FROM GOD.
HUFF
HUFF
WHAT...?
HUFF
HUFF
DON'T YOU UNDER-STAND?
YOU MUST BE CHASTE IN ORDER TO WIELD YOUR POWER.
IF I TAKE THAT FROM YOU, YOU WILL BE USELESS TO HIM.

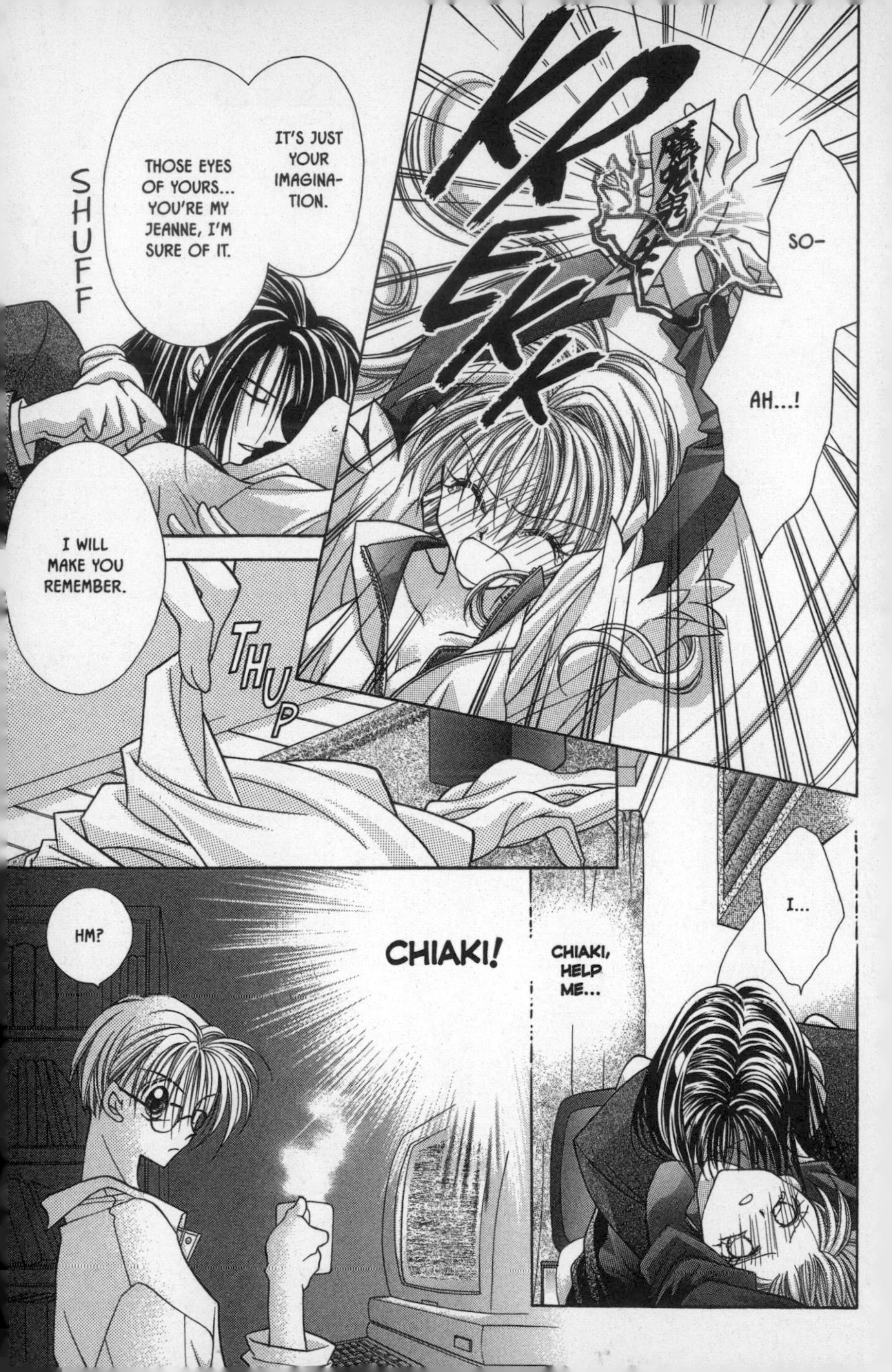
KRSKK
SO-
AH...!
IT'S JUST YOUR IMAGINATION.
THOSE EYES OF YOURS... YOU'RE MY JEANNE, I'M SURE OF IT.
SHUFF
I WILL MAKE YOU REMEMBER.
THUP
I...
CHIAKI, HELP ME...
CHIAKI!
HM?

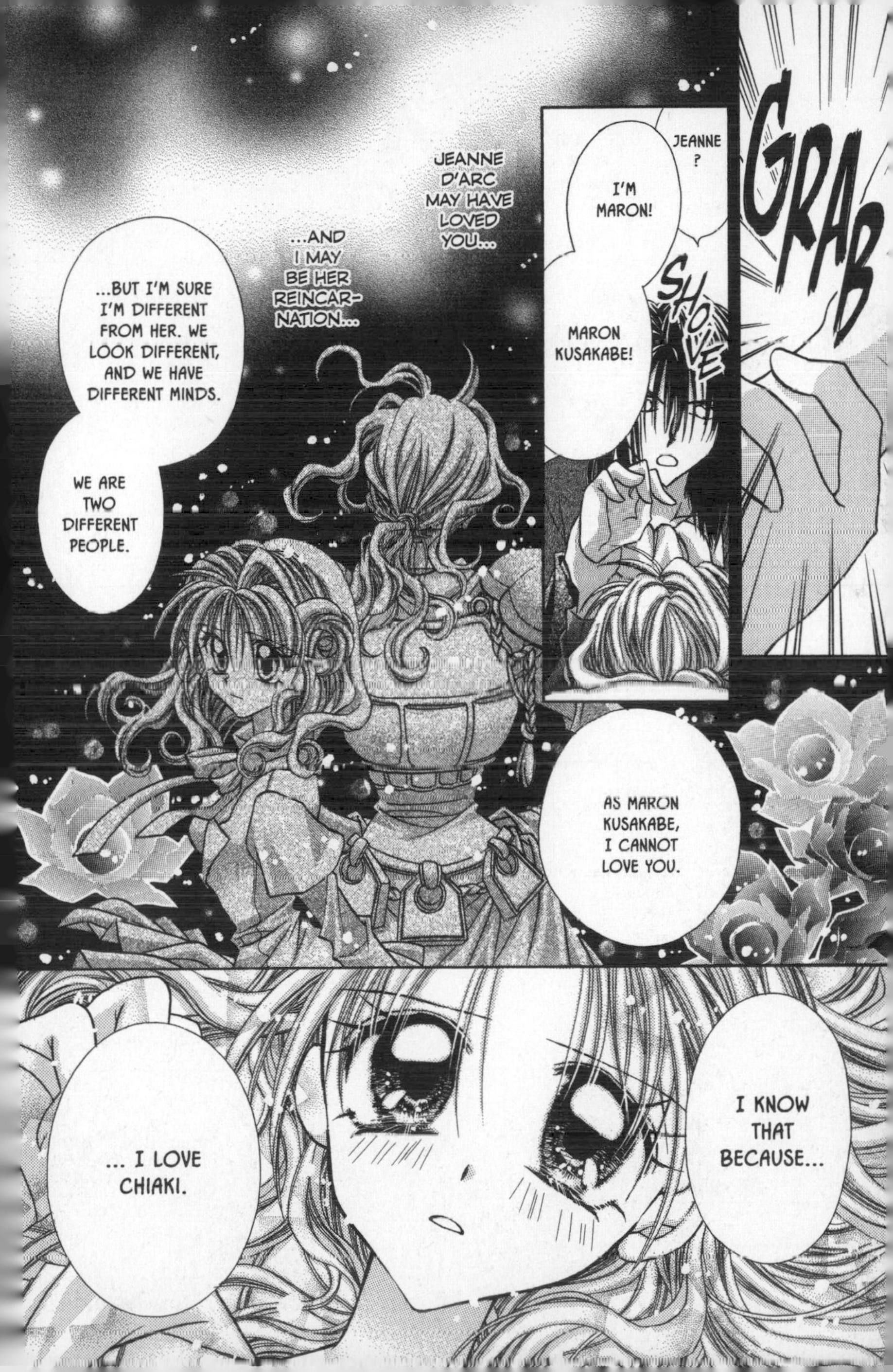
GRAB
JEANNE ?
I'M MARON!
SHOVE
MARON KUSAKABE!
JEANNE D'ARC MAY HAVE LOVED YOU...
...AND I MAY BE HER REINCAR-NATION...
...BUT I'M SURE I'M DIFFERENT FROM HER. WE LOOK DIFFERENT, AND WE HAVE DIFFERENT MINDS.
WE ARE TWO DIFFERENT PEOPLE.
AS MARON KUSAKABE, I CANNOT LOVE YOU.
I KNOW THAT BECAUSE...
... I LOVE CHIAKI.

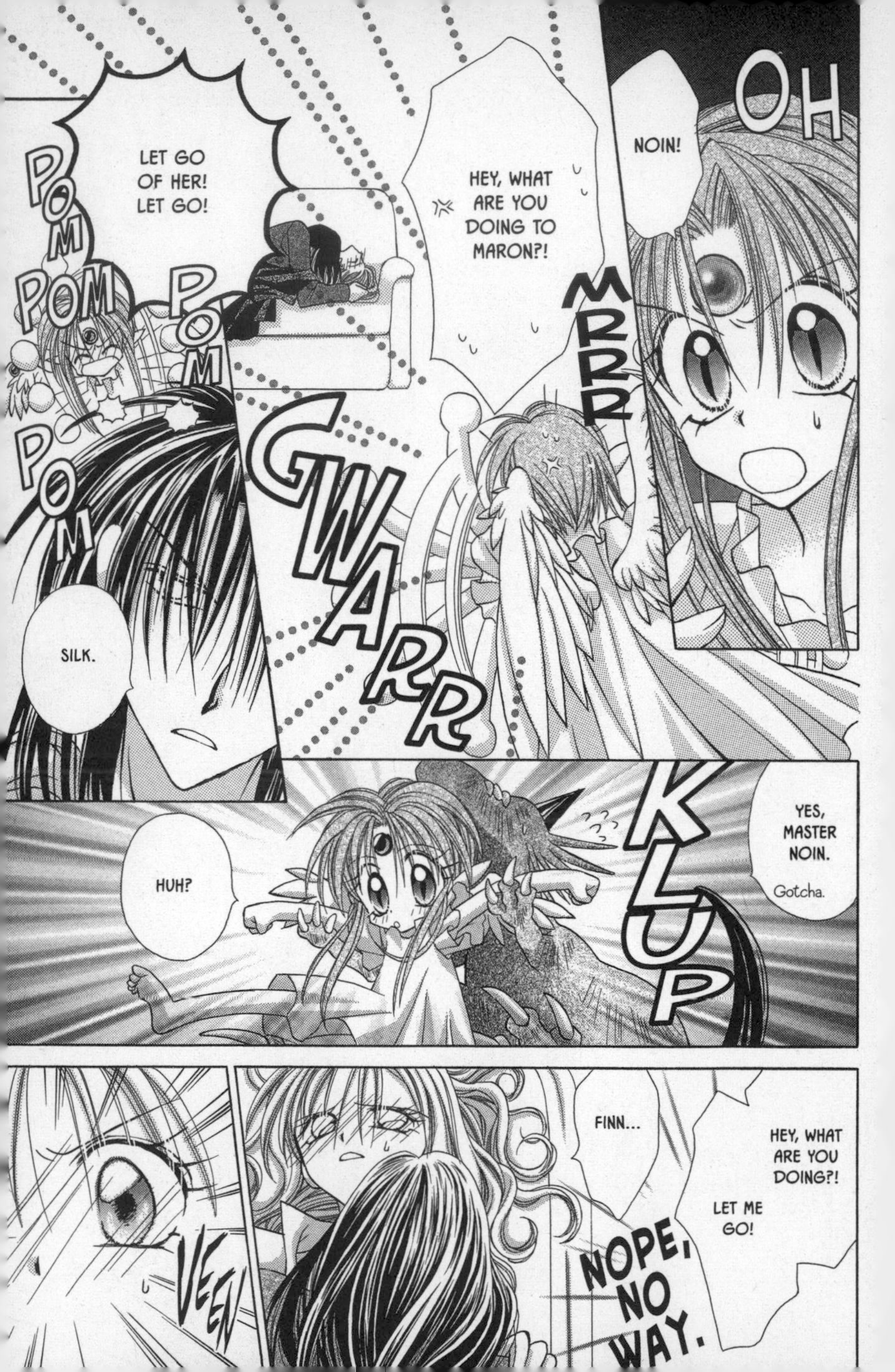
OH
NOIN!
MRRR
HEY, WHAT ARE YOU DOING TO MARON?!
GWARRR
LET GO OF HER! LET GO!
POM POM POM POM
SILK.
YES, MASTER NOIN.
Gotcha.
KLUP
HUH?
HEY, WHAT ARE YOU DOING?!
LET ME GO!
NOPE, NO WAY.
FINN...
VEEN

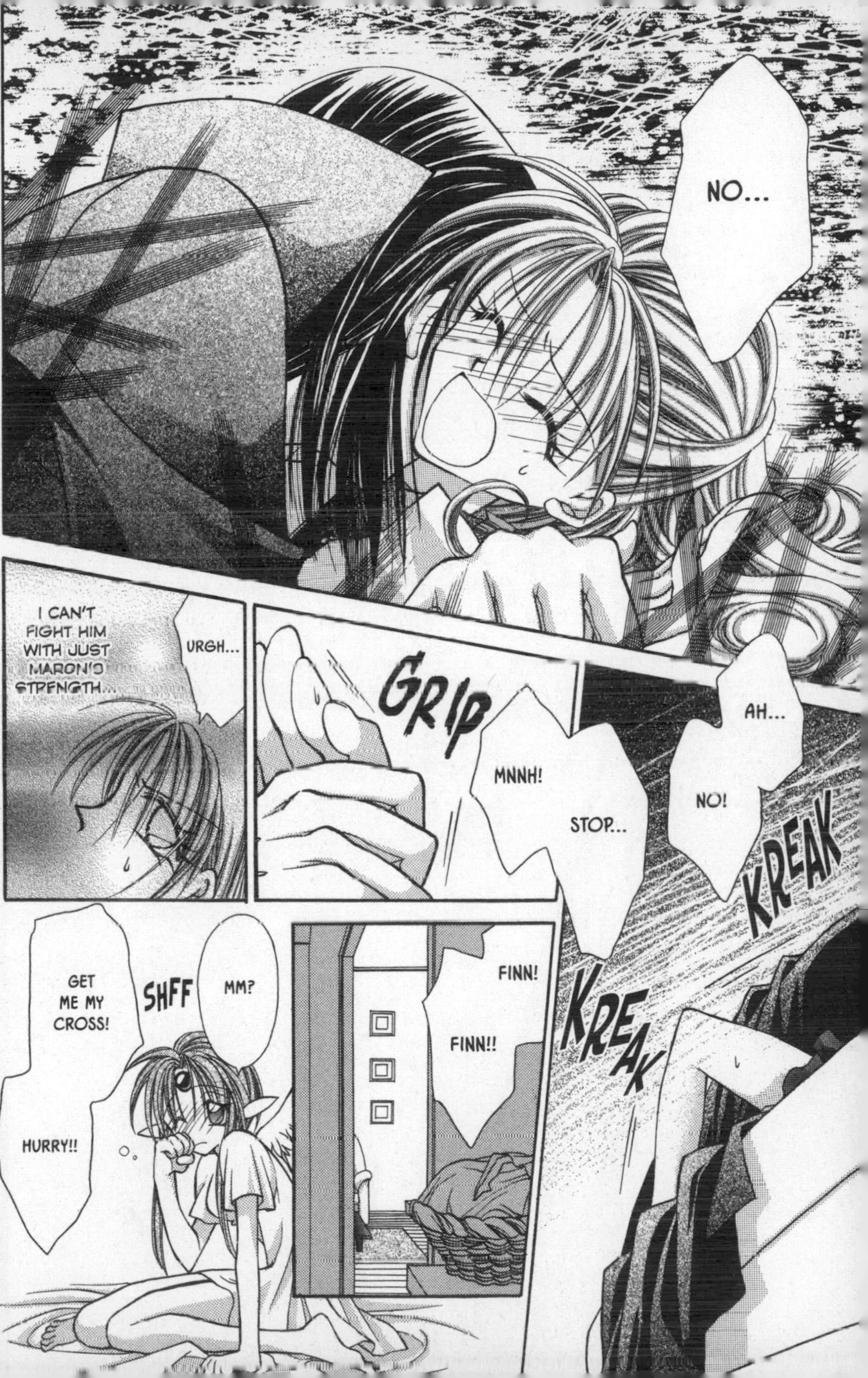
NO...
AH...
NO!
KREAK
KREAK
STOP...
MNNH!
GRIP
URGH...
I CAN'T FIGHT HIM WITH JUST MARON'S STRENGTH...
FINN!
FINN!!
MM?
SHFF
GET ME MY CROSS!
HURRY!!

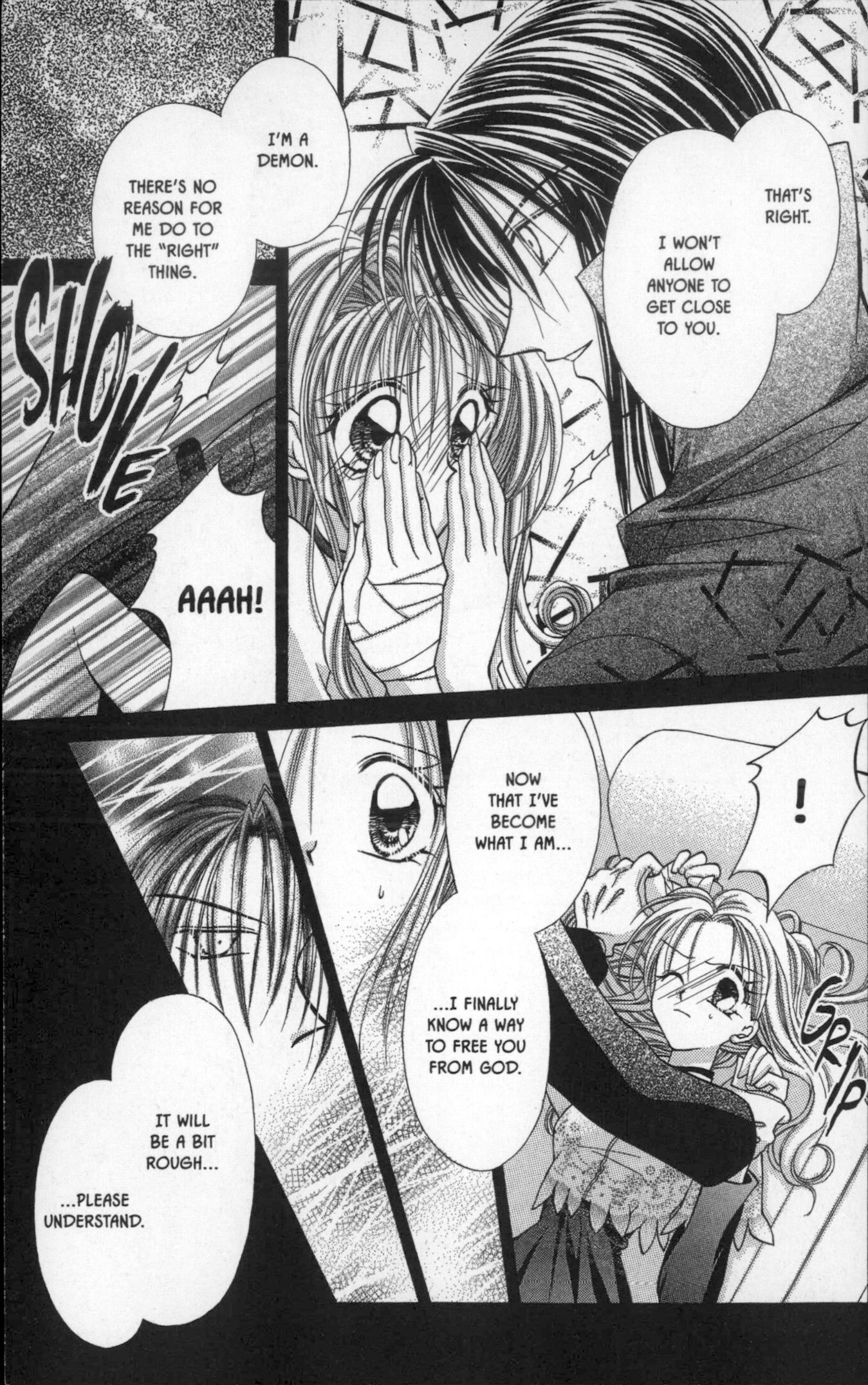
THAT'S RIGHT.
I WON'T ALLOW ANYONE TO GET CLOSE TO YOU.
I'M A DEMON.
THERE'S NO REASON FOR ME DO TO THE "RIGHT" THING.
SHOVE
AAAH!
!
GRIP
NOW THAT I'VE BECOME WHAT I AM...
...I FINALLY KNOW A WAY TO FREE YOU FROM GOD.
IT WILL BE A BIT ROUGH...
...PLEASE UNDERSTAND.

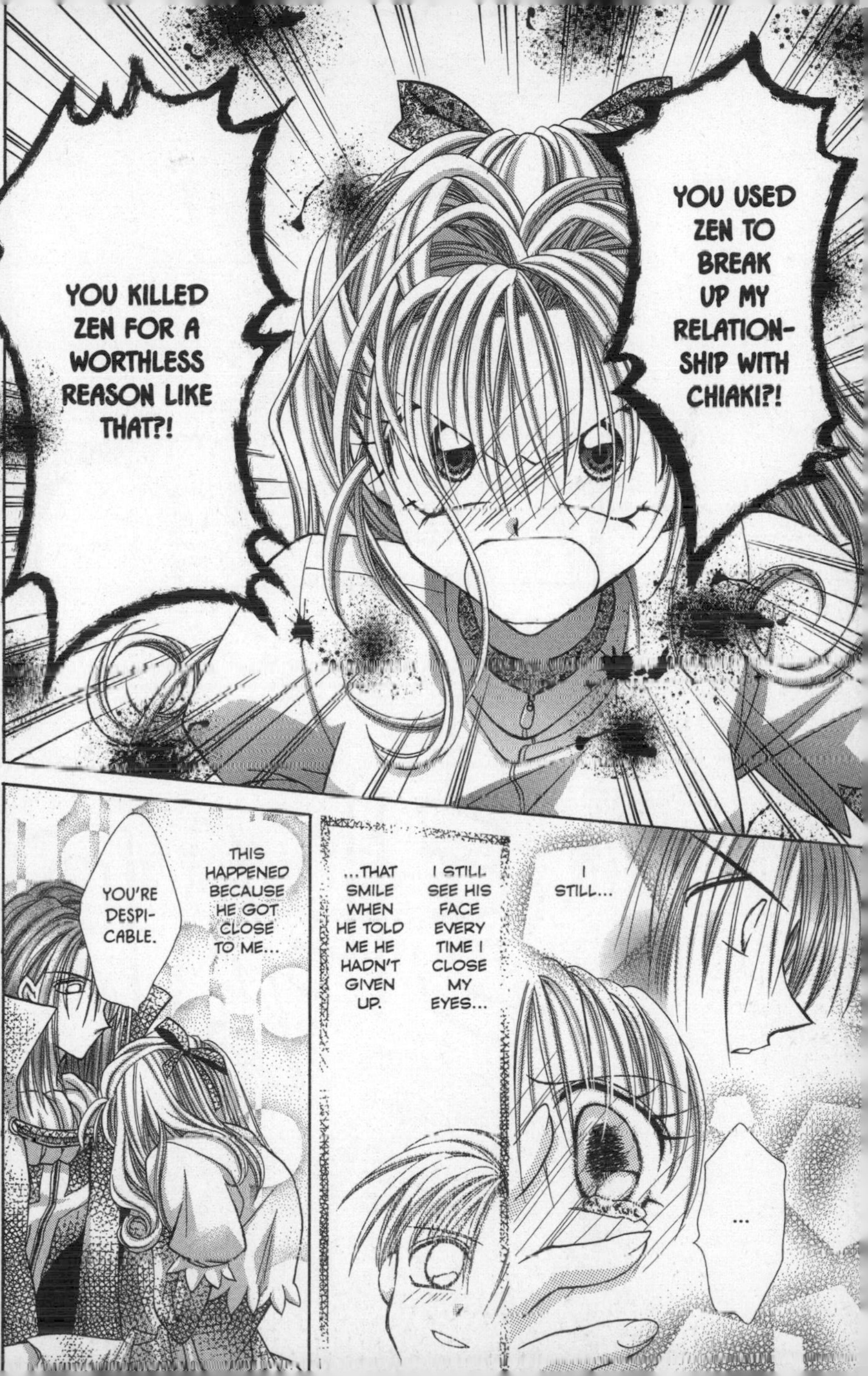
YOU USED ZEN TO BREAK UP MY RELATION-SHIP WITH CHIAKI?!
YOU KILLED ZEN FOR A WORTHLESS REASON LIKE THAT?!
I STILL...
I STILL SEE HIS FACE EVERY TIME I CLOSE MY EYES...
...THAT SMILE WHEN HE TOLD ME HE HADN'T GIVEN UP.
...
THIS HAPPENED BECAUSE HE GOT CLOSE TO ME...
YOU'RE DESPI-CABLE.

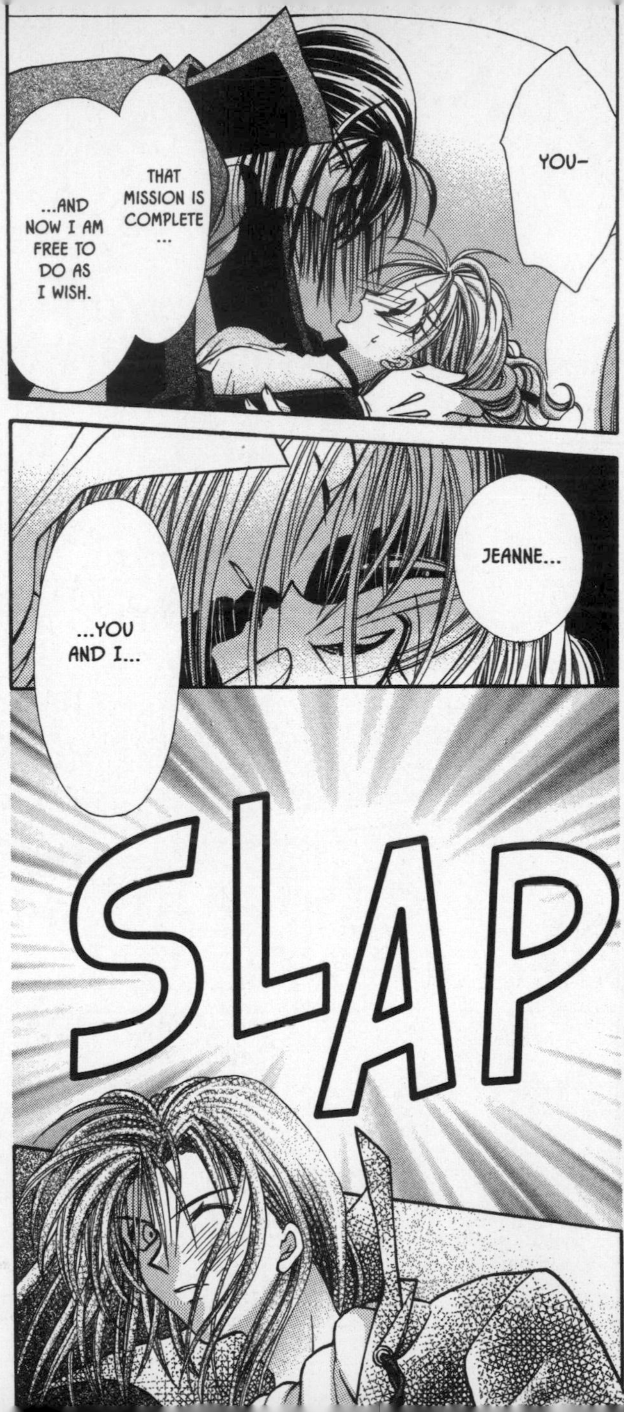
YOU–
THAT MISSION IS COMPLETE...
...AND NOW I AM FREE TO DO AS I WISH.
JEANNE...
...YOU AND I...
SLAP

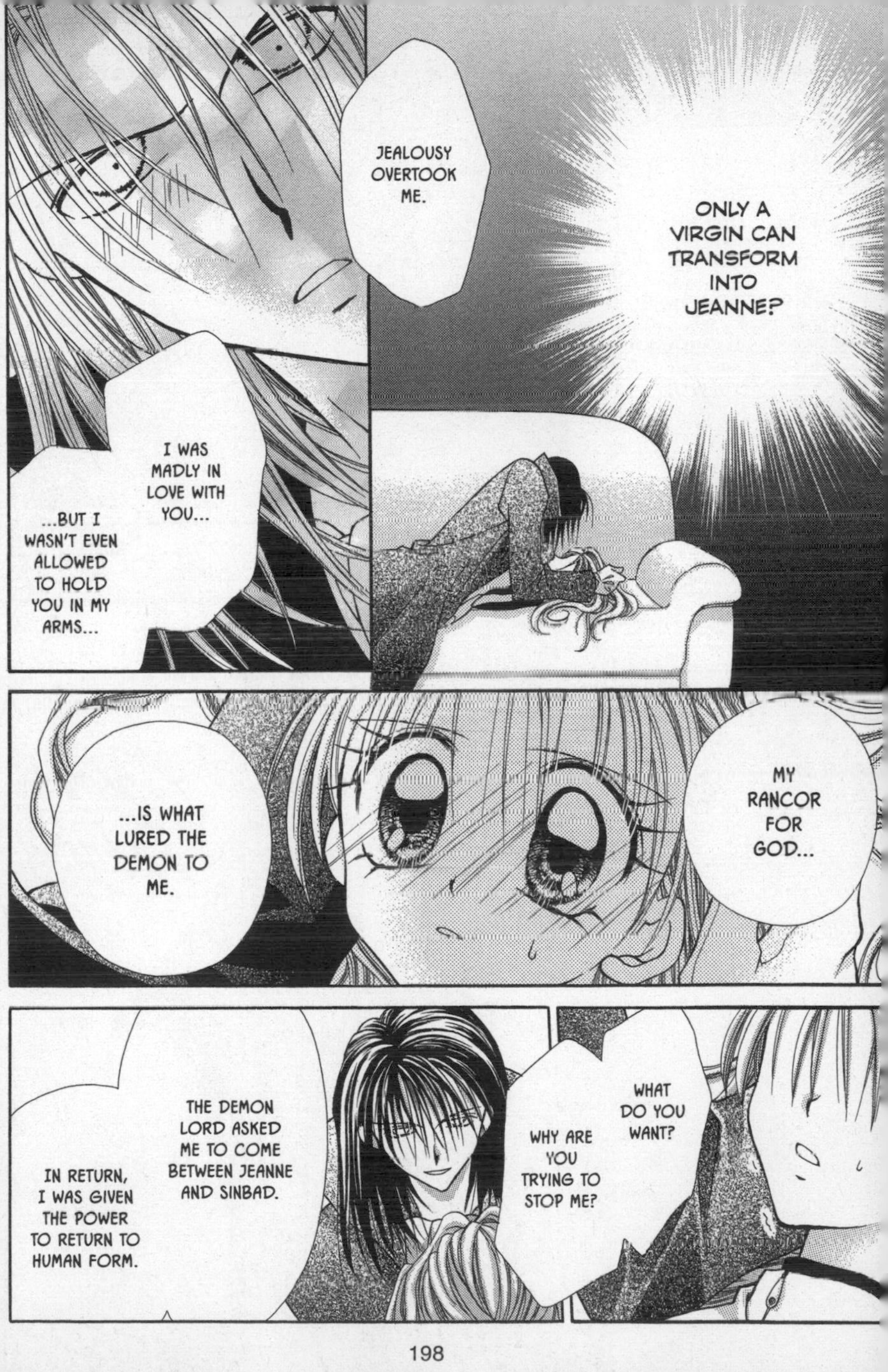
ONLY A VIRGIN CAN TRANSFORM INTO JEANNE?
JEALOUSY OVERTOOK ME.
I WAS MADLY IN LOVE WITH YOU...
...BUT I WASN'T EVEN ALLOWED TO HOLD YOU IN MY ARMS...
MY RANCOR FOR GOD...
...IS WHAT LURED THE DEMON TO ME.
WHAT DO YOU WANT?
WHY ARE YOU TRYING TO STOP ME?
THE DEMON LORD ASKED ME TO COME BETWEEN JEANNE AND SINBAD.
IN RETURN, I WAS GIVEN THE POWER TO RETURN TO HUMAN FORM.

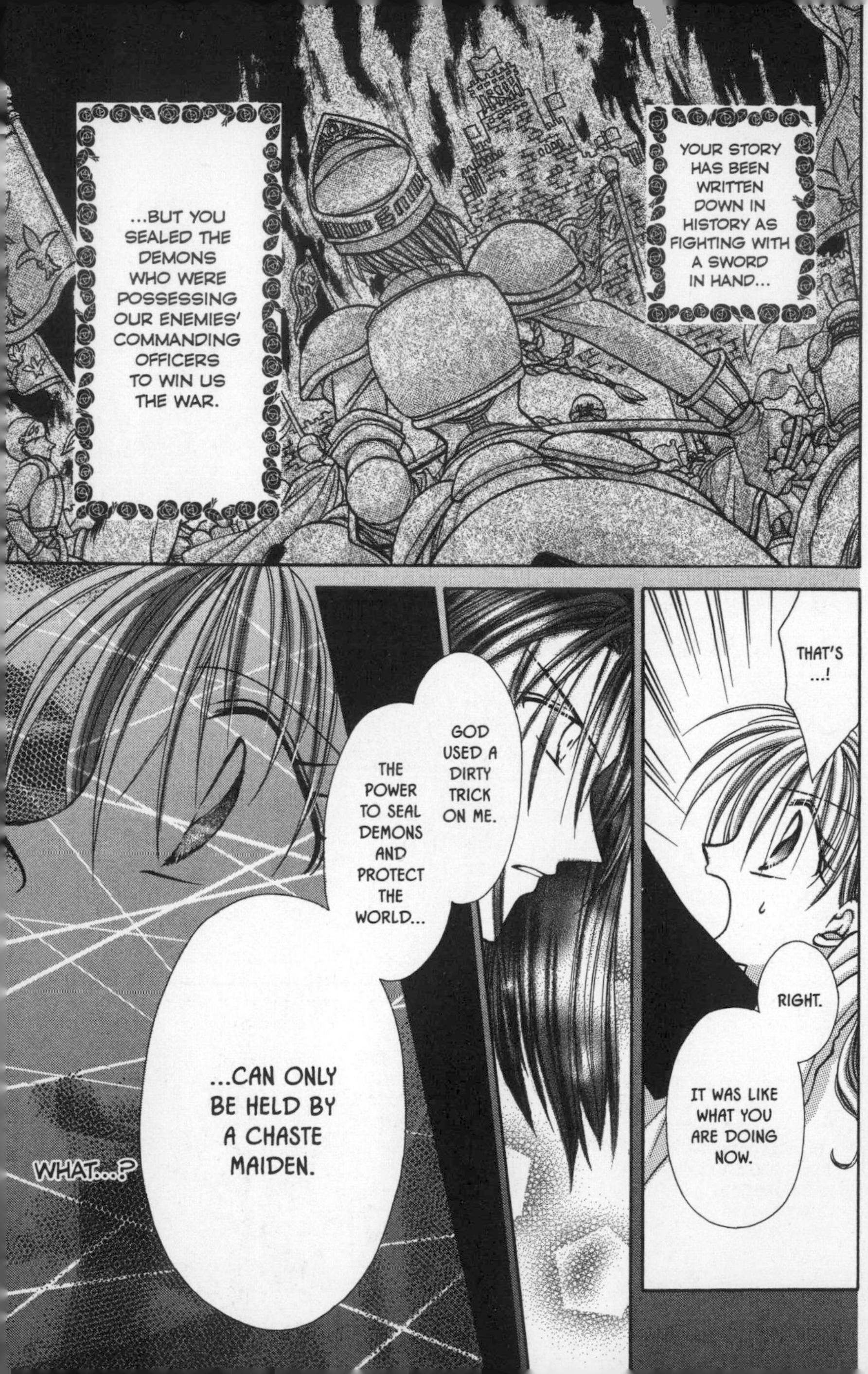
YOUR STORY HAS BEEN WRITTEN DOWN IN HISTORY AS FIGHTING WITH A SWORD IN HAND...
...BUT YOU SEALED THE DEMONS WHO WERE POSSESSING OUR ENEMIES' COMMANDING OFFICERS TO WIN US THE WAR.
THAT'S ...!
RIGHT.
IT WAS LIKE WHAT YOU ARE DOING NOW.
GOD USED A DIRTY TRICK ON ME.
THE POWER TO SEAL DEMONS AND PROTECT THE WORLD...
...CAN ONLY BE HELD BY A CHASTE MAIDEN.
WHAT...?

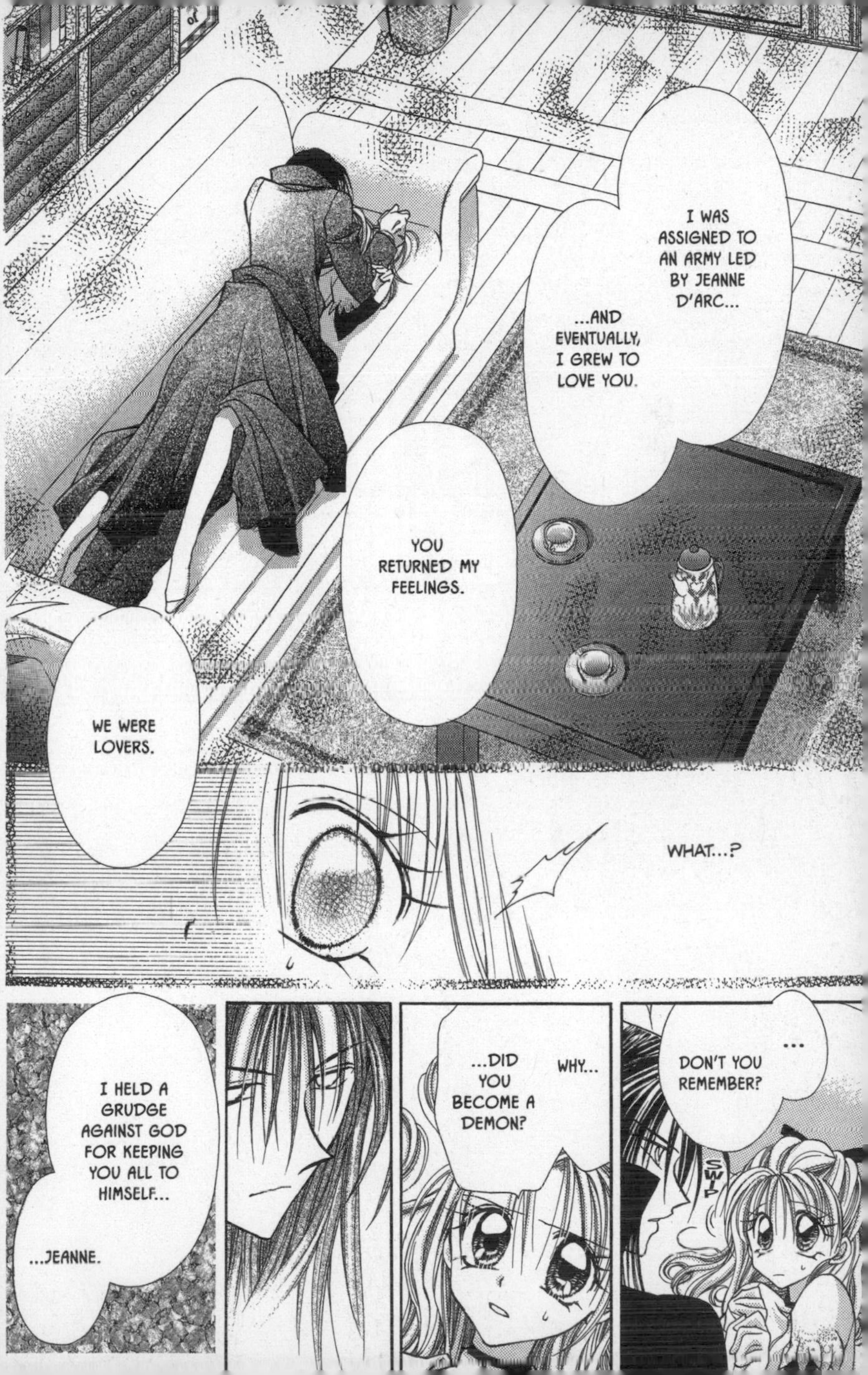
I WAS ASSIGNED TO AN ARMY LED BY JEANNE D'ARC...
...AND EVENTUALLY, I GREW TO LOVE YOU.
YOU RETURNED MY FEELINGS.
WE WERE LOVERS.
WHAT...?
...
DON'T YOU REMEMBER?
SWIP
WHY...
...DID YOU BECOME A DEMON?
I HELD A GRUDGE AGAINST GOD FOR KEEPING YOU ALL TO HIMSELF...
...JEANNE.

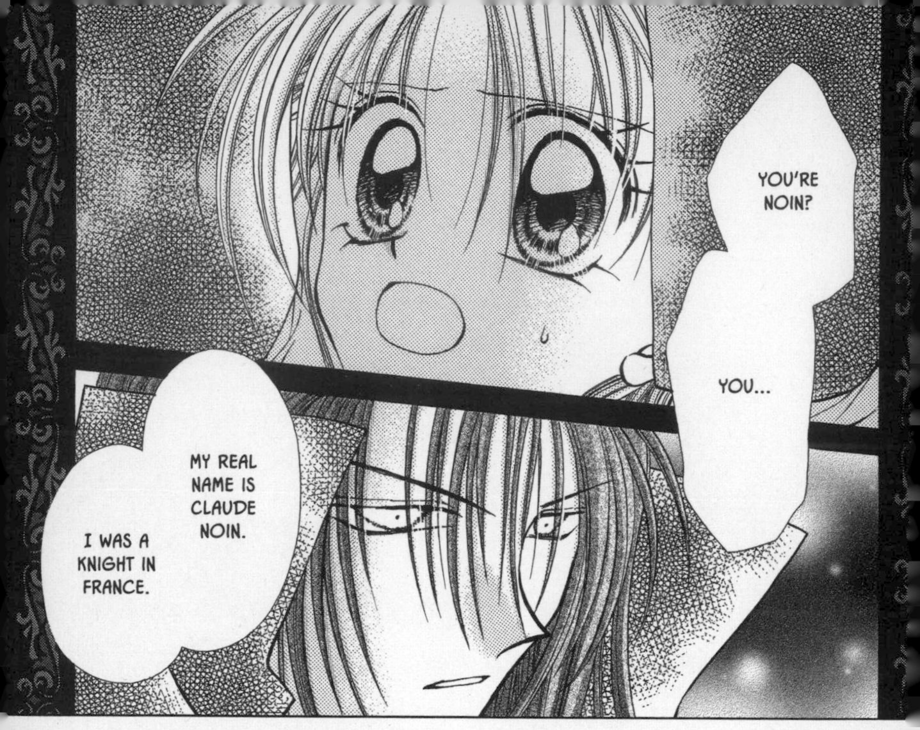
YOU'RE NOIN?
YOU...
MY REAL NAME IS CLAUDE NOIN.
I WAS A KNIGHT IN FRANCE.

PHANTOM THIEF JEANNE

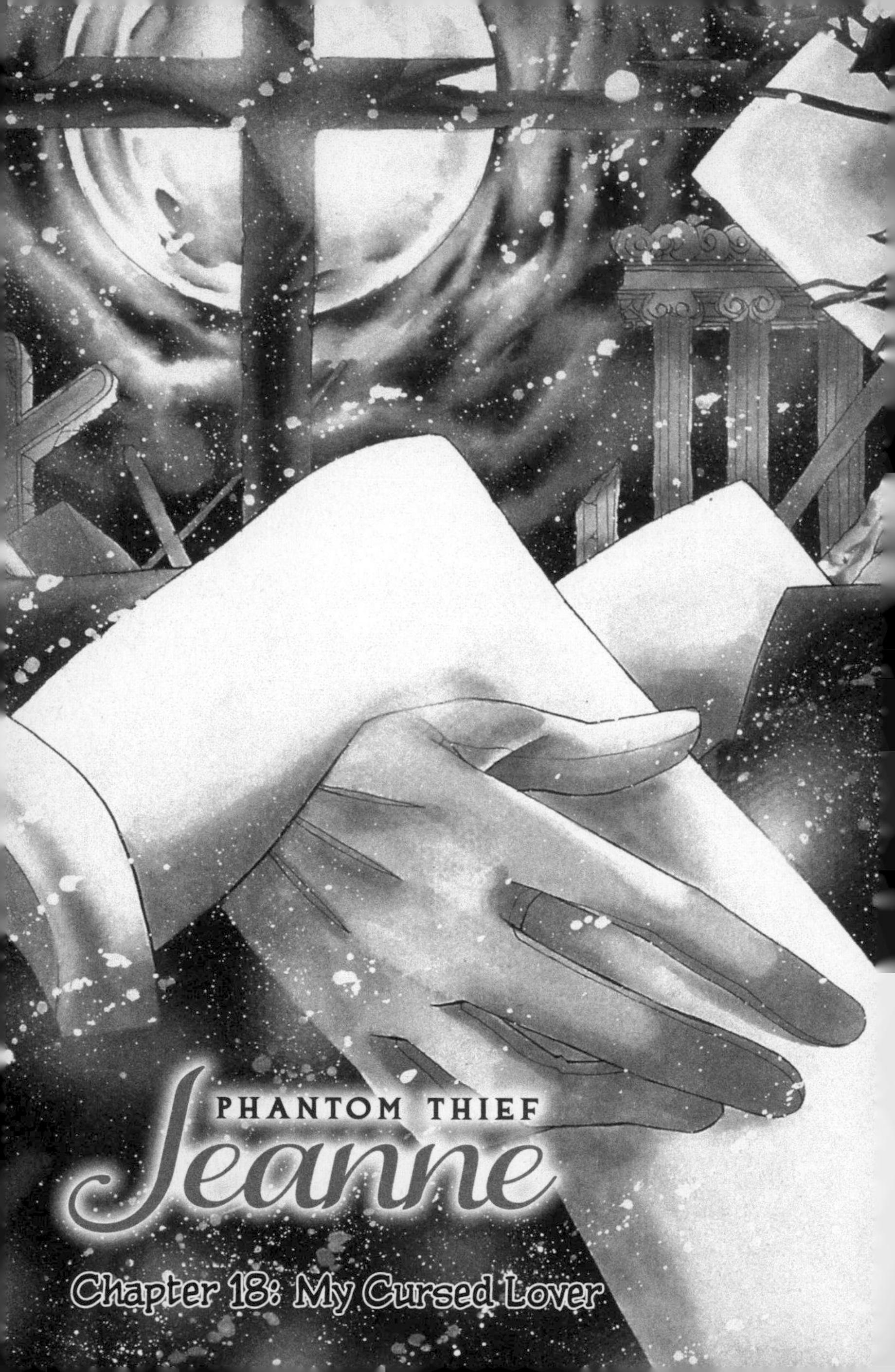
PHANTOM THIEF
Jeanne
Chapter 18: My Cursed Lover

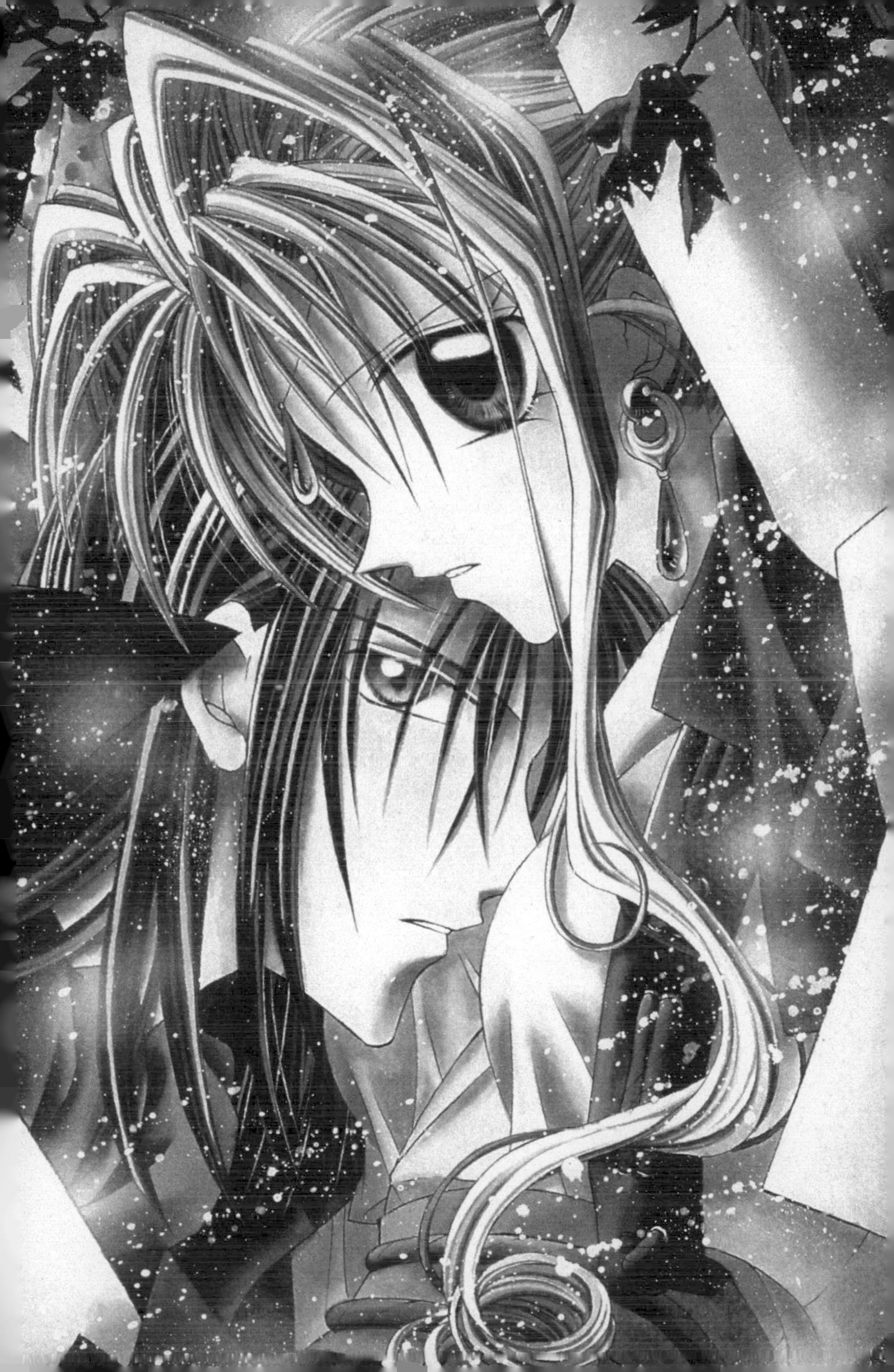

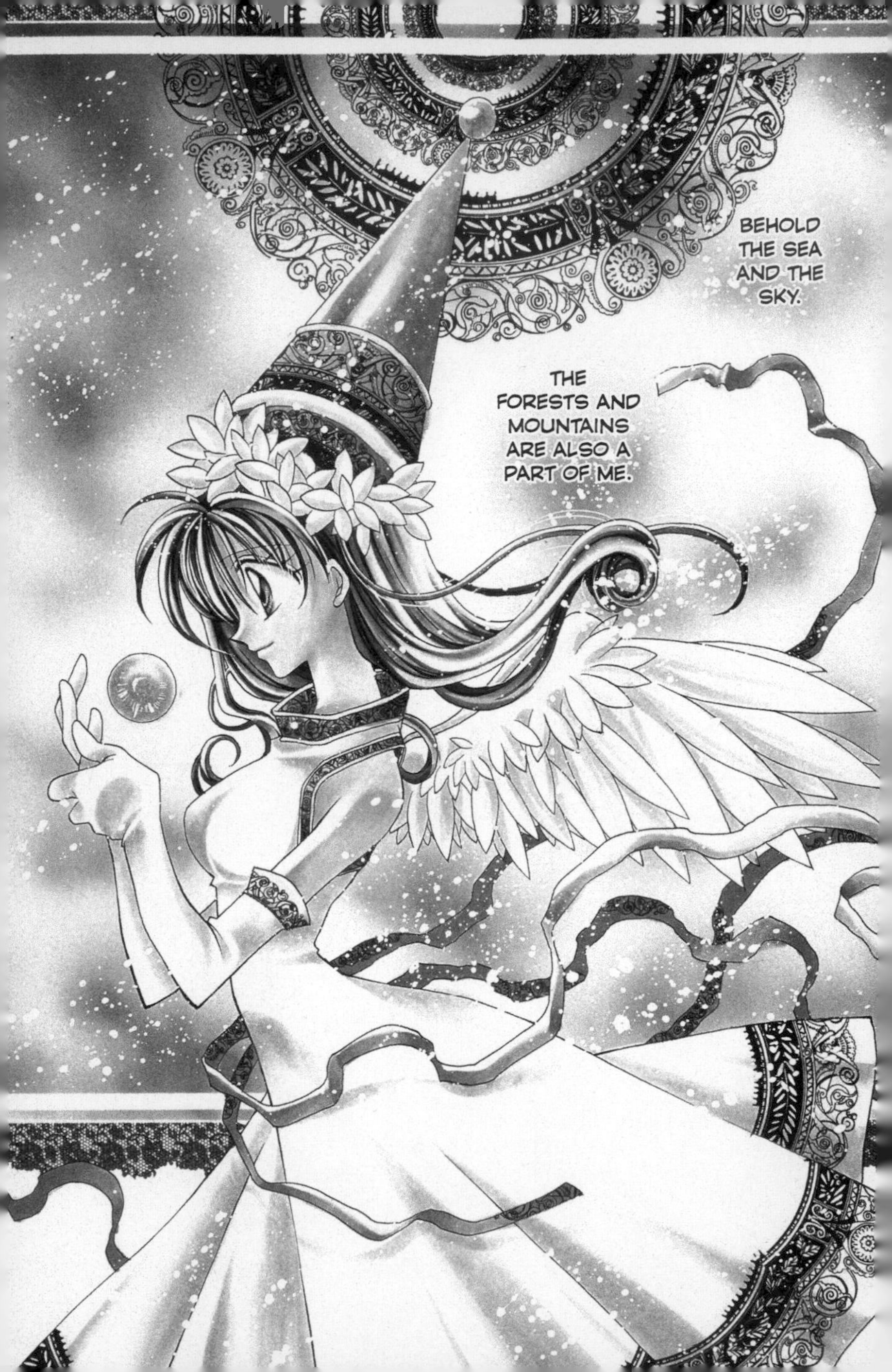
BEHOLD THE SEA AND THE SKY.
THE FORESTS AND MOUNTAINS ARE ALSO A PART OF ME.

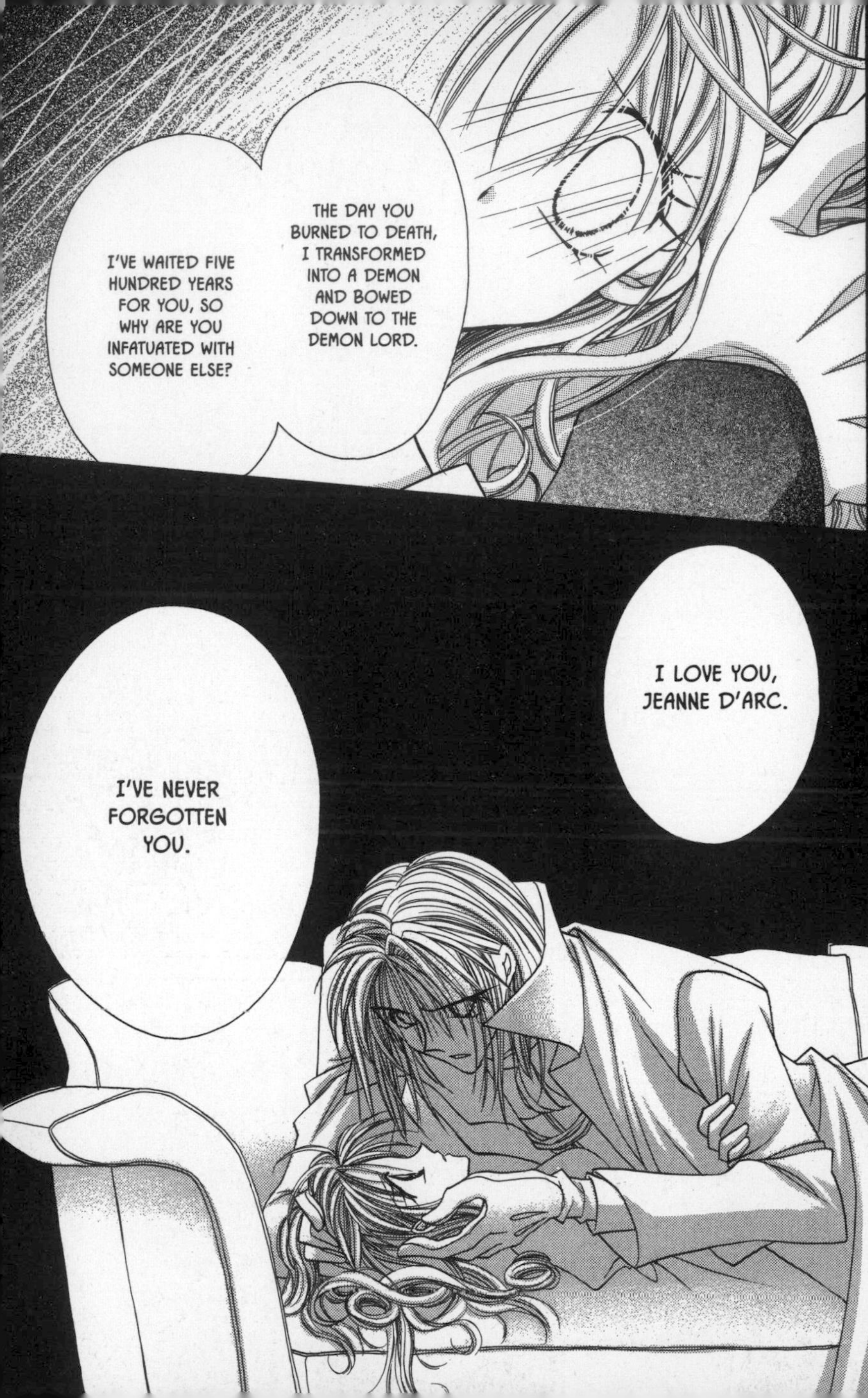
THE DAY YOU BURNED TO DEATH, I TRANSFORMED INTO A DEMON AND BOWED DOWN TO THE DEMON LORD.
I'VE WAITED FIVE HUNDRED YEARS FOR YOU, SO WHY ARE YOU INFATUATED WITH SOMEONE ELSE?
I LOVE YOU, JEANNE D'ARC.
I'VE NEVER FORGOTTEN YOU.

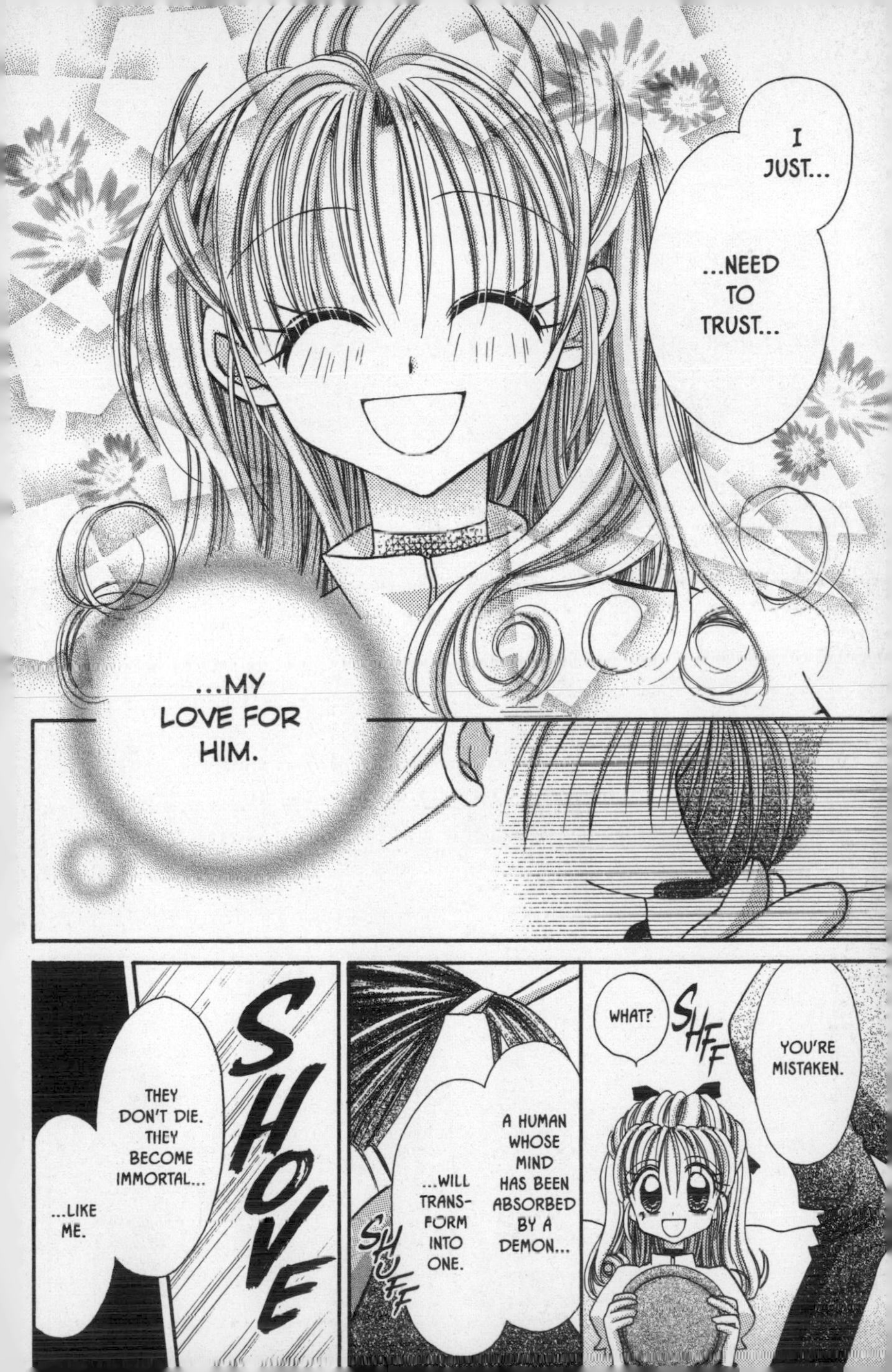
I JUST...
...NEED TO TRUST...
...MY LOVE FOR HIM.
YOU'RE MISTAKEN.
SHFF
WHAT?
A HUMAN WHOSE MIND HAS BEEN ABSORBED BY A DEMON...
...WILL TRANS-FORM INTO ONE.
SHUFF
SHOVE
THEY DON'T DIE. THEY BECOME IMMORTAL...
...LIKE ME.

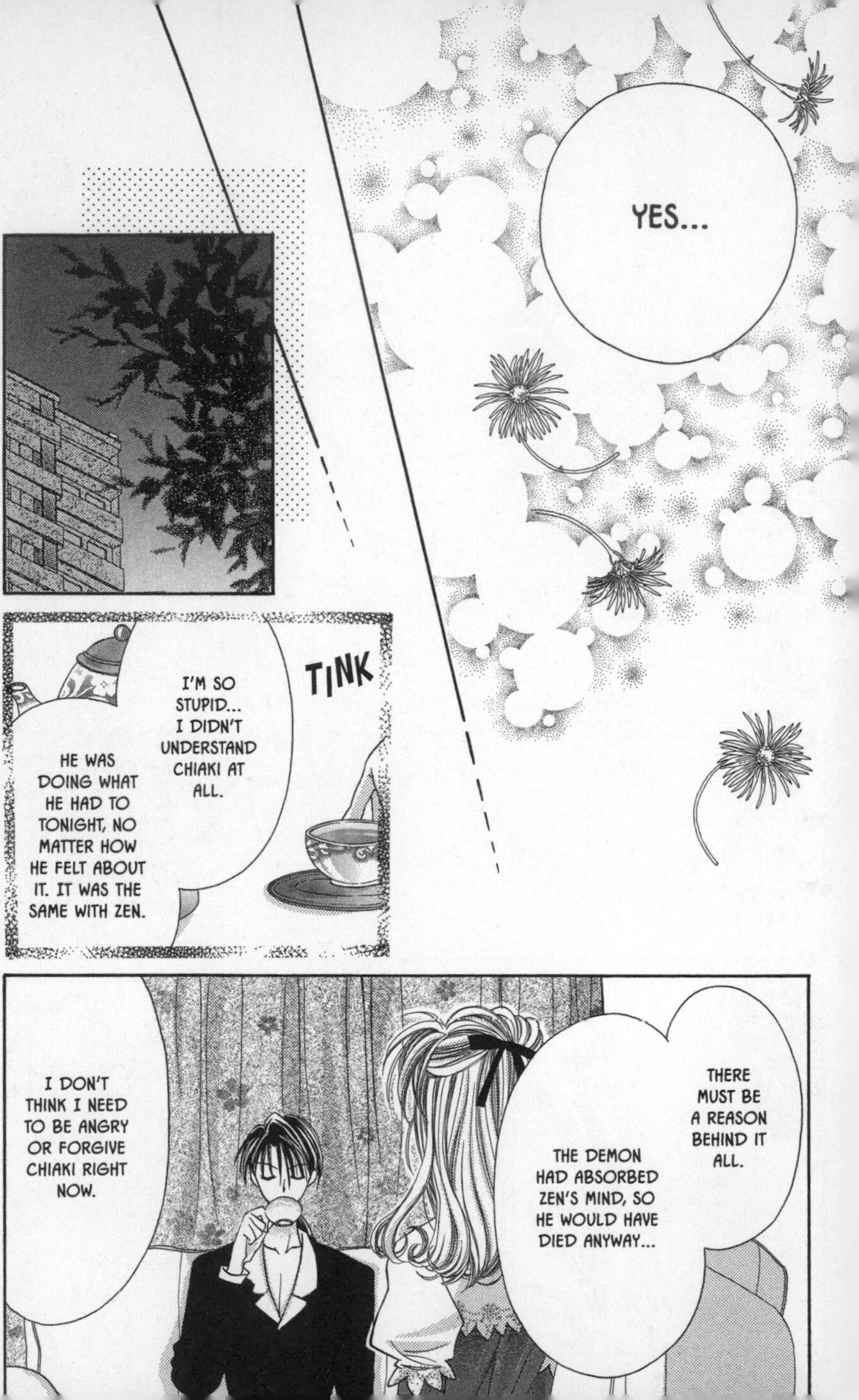
YES...
TINK
I'M SO STUPID... I DIDN'T UNDERSTAND CHIAKI AT ALL.
HE WAS DOING WHAT HE HAD TO TONIGHT, NO MATTER HOW HE FELT ABOUT IT. IT WAS THE SAME WITH ZEN.
THERE MUST BE A REASON BEHIND IT ALL.
THE DEMON HAD ABSORBED ZEN'S MIND, SO HE WOULD HAVE DIED ANYWAY...
I DON'T THINK I NEED TO BE ANGRY OR FORGIVE CHIAKI RIGHT NOW.

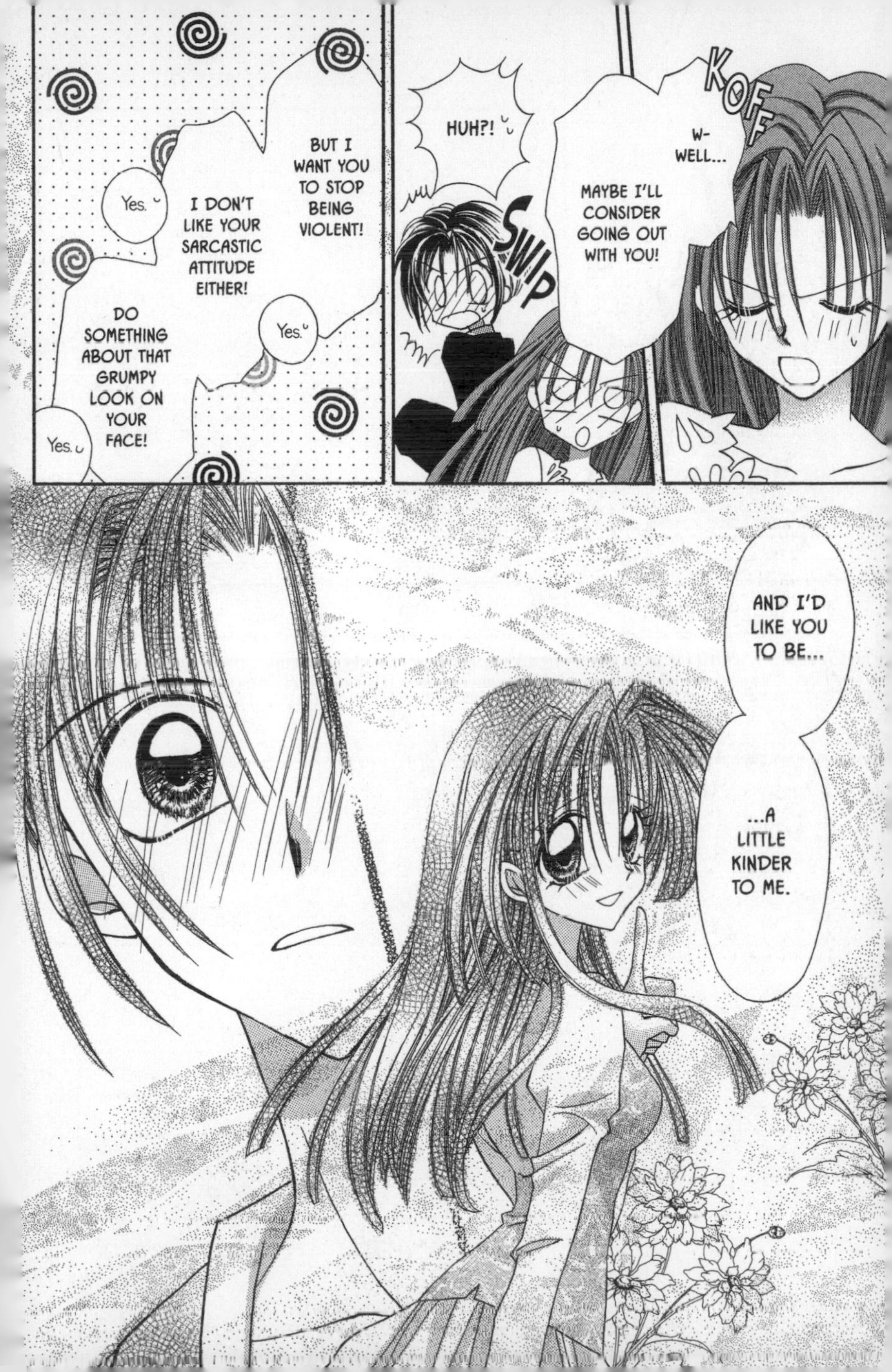
KOFF
W-
WELL...
MAYBE I'LL CONSIDER GOING OUT WITH YOU!
HUH?!
SWIP
BUT I WANT YOU TO STOP BEING VIOLENT!
Yes.
I DON'T LIKE YOUR SARCASTIC ATTITUDE EITHER!
Yes.
DO SOMETHING ABOUT THAT GRUMPY LOOK ON YOUR FACE!
Yes.
AND I'D LIKE YOU TO BE...
...A LITTLE KINDER TO ME.

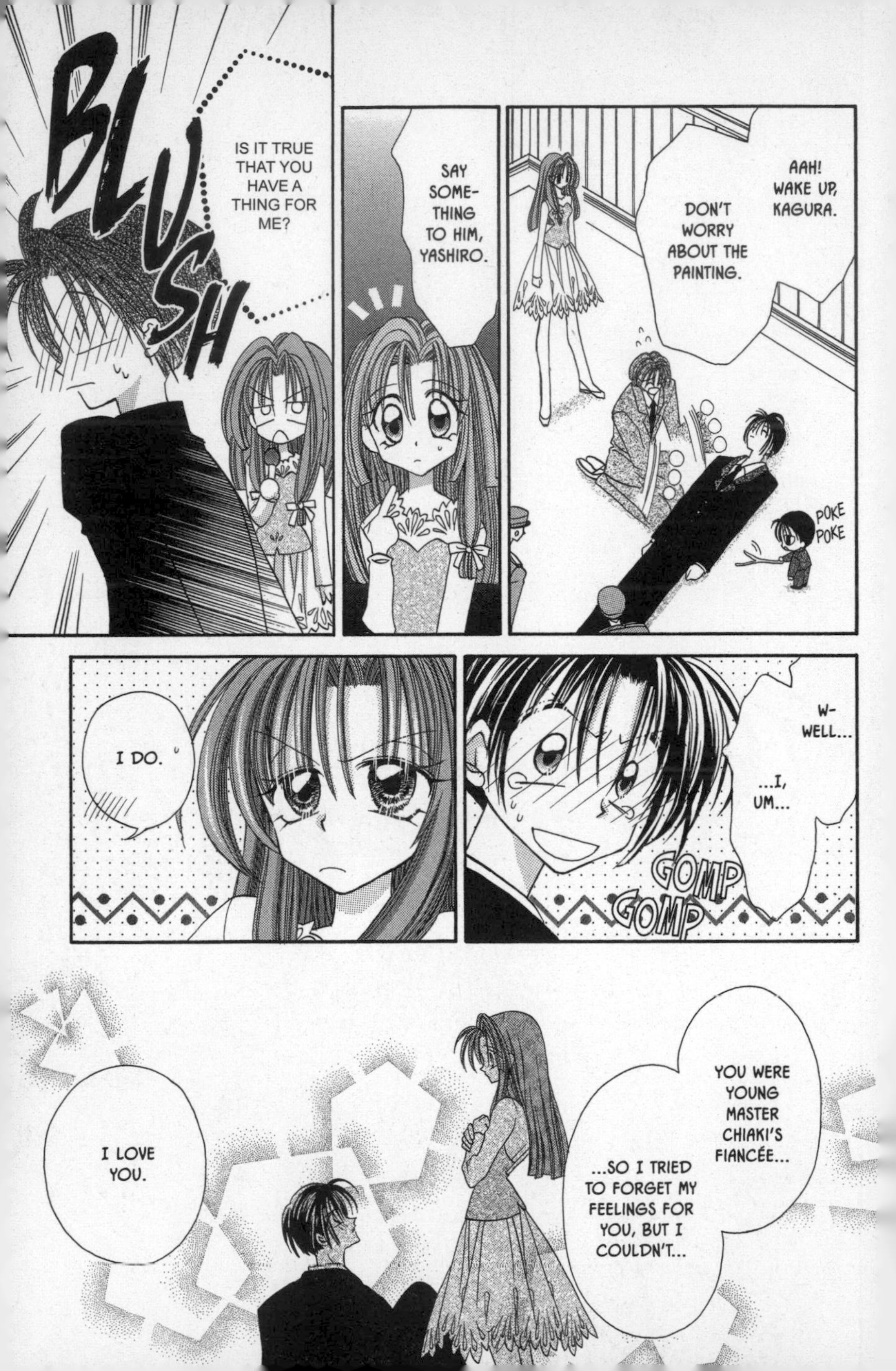
AAH! WAKE UP, KAGURA.
DON'T WORRY ABOUT THE PAINTING.
POKE POKE
SAY SOME-THING TO HIM, YASHIRO.
IS IT TRUE THAT YOU HAVE A THING FOR ME?
BLUSH
W-WELL...
...I, UM...
GOMP GOMP
I DO.
YOU WERE YOUNG MASTER CHIAKI'S FIANCÉE...
...SO I TRIED TO FORGET MY FEELINGS FOR YOU, BUT I COULDN'T...
I LOVE YOU.

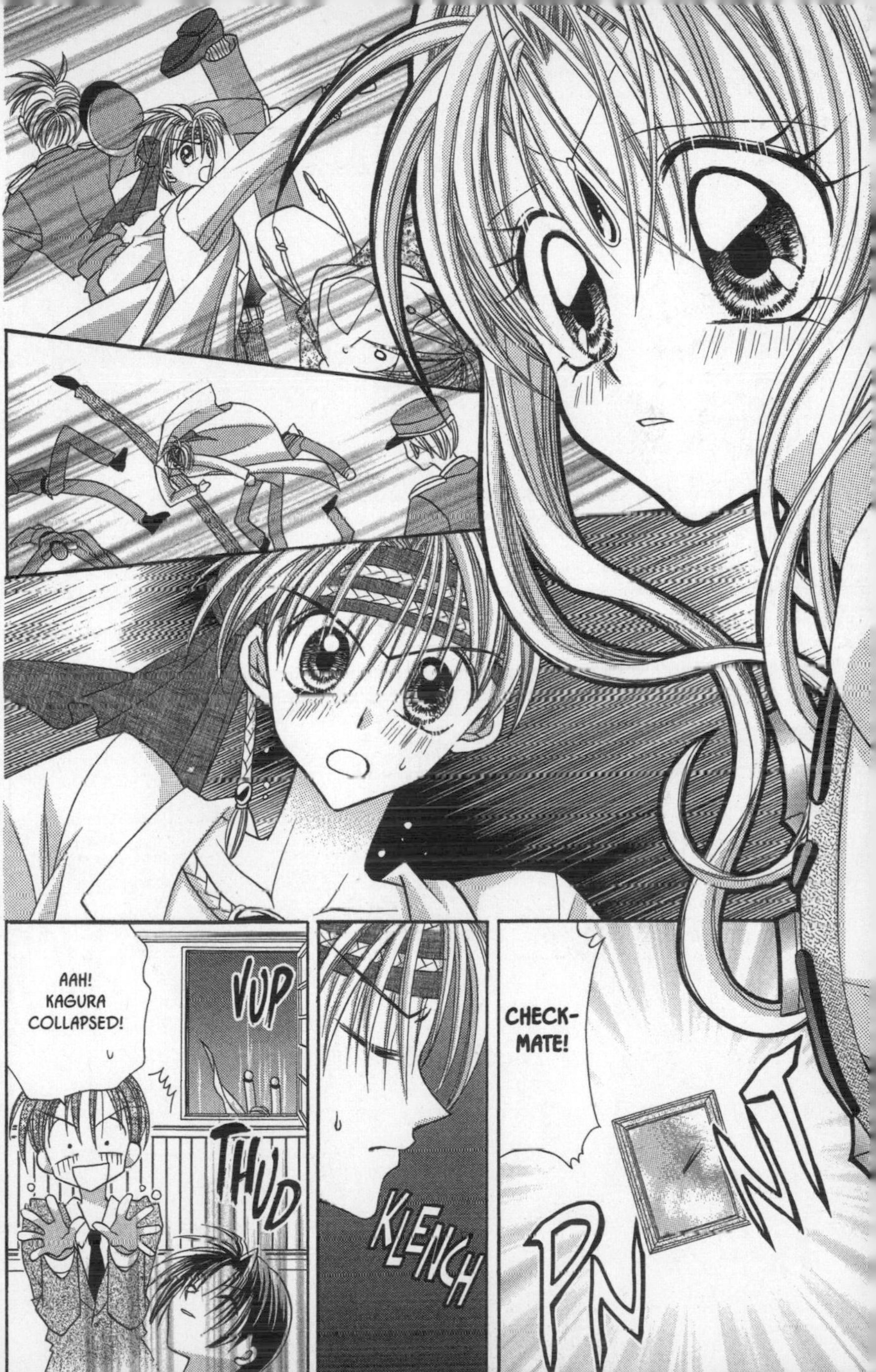
CHECK-MATE!
PNNT
KLENCH
VUP
AAH! KAGURA COLLAPSED!
THUD

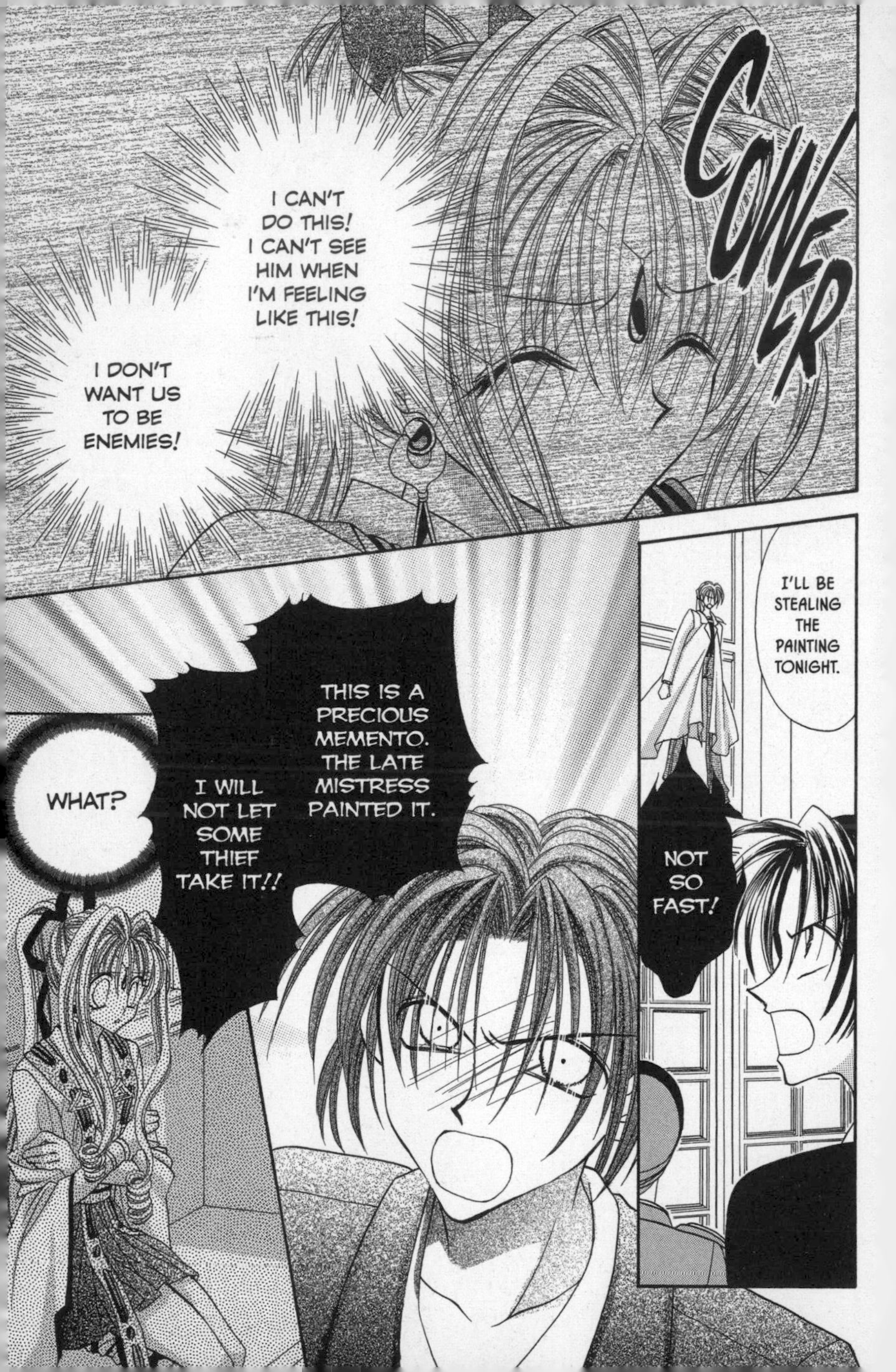
COVER
I CAN'T DO THIS! I CAN'T SEE HIM WHEN I'M FEELING LIKE THIS!
I DON'T WANT US TO BE ENEMIES!
I'LL BE STEALING THE PAINTING TONIGHT.
NOT SO FAST!
THIS IS A PRECIOUS MEMENTO. THE LATE MISTRESS PAINTED IT.
I WILL NOT LET SOME THIEF TAKE IT!!
WHAT?

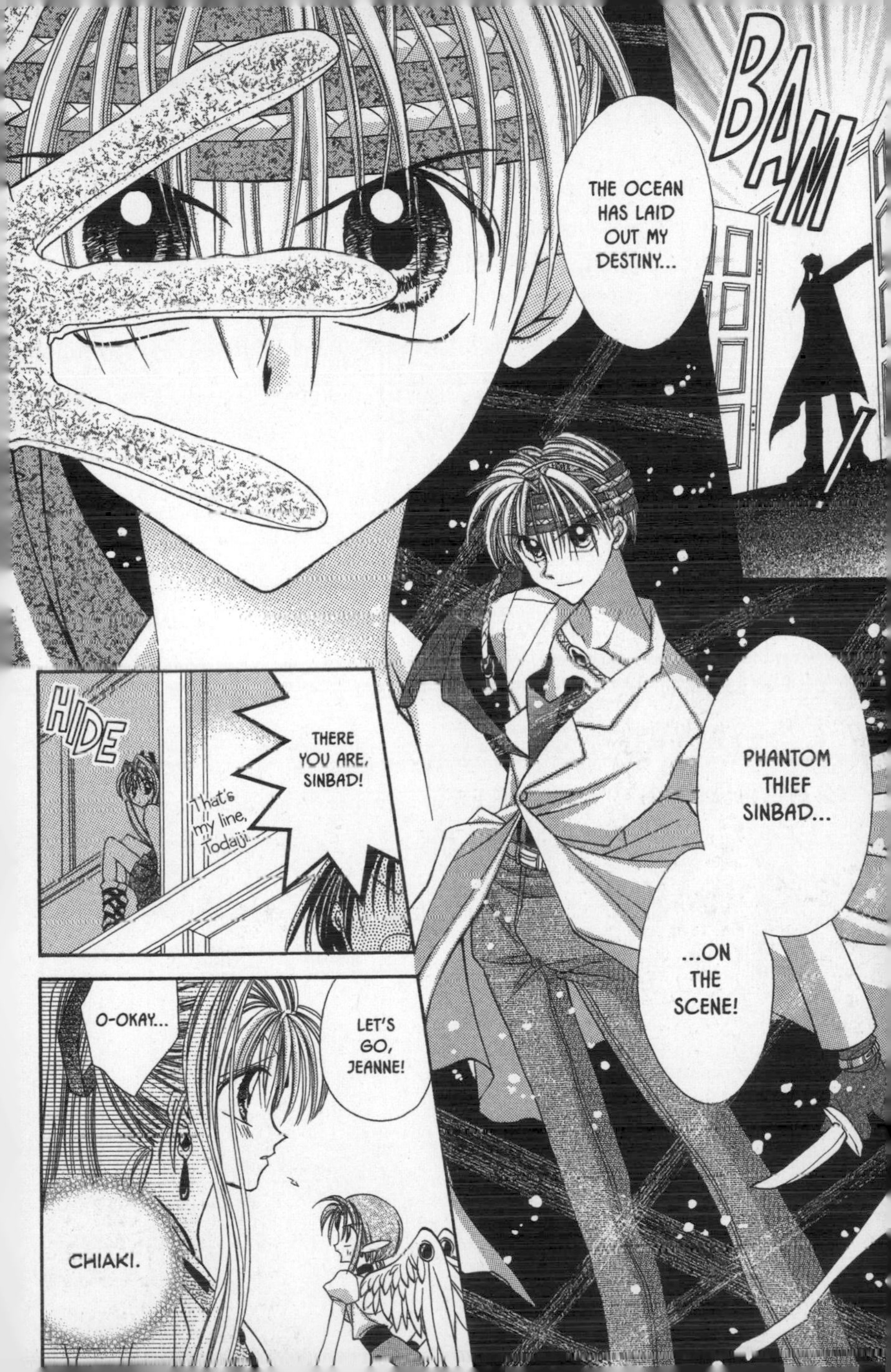
BAM
THE OCEAN HAS LAID OUT MY DESTINY...
PHANTOM THIEF SINBAD...
...ON THE SCENE!
THERE YOU ARE, SINBAD!
HIDE
That's my line, Todaiji.
LET'S GO, JEANNE!
O-OKAY...
CHIAKI.

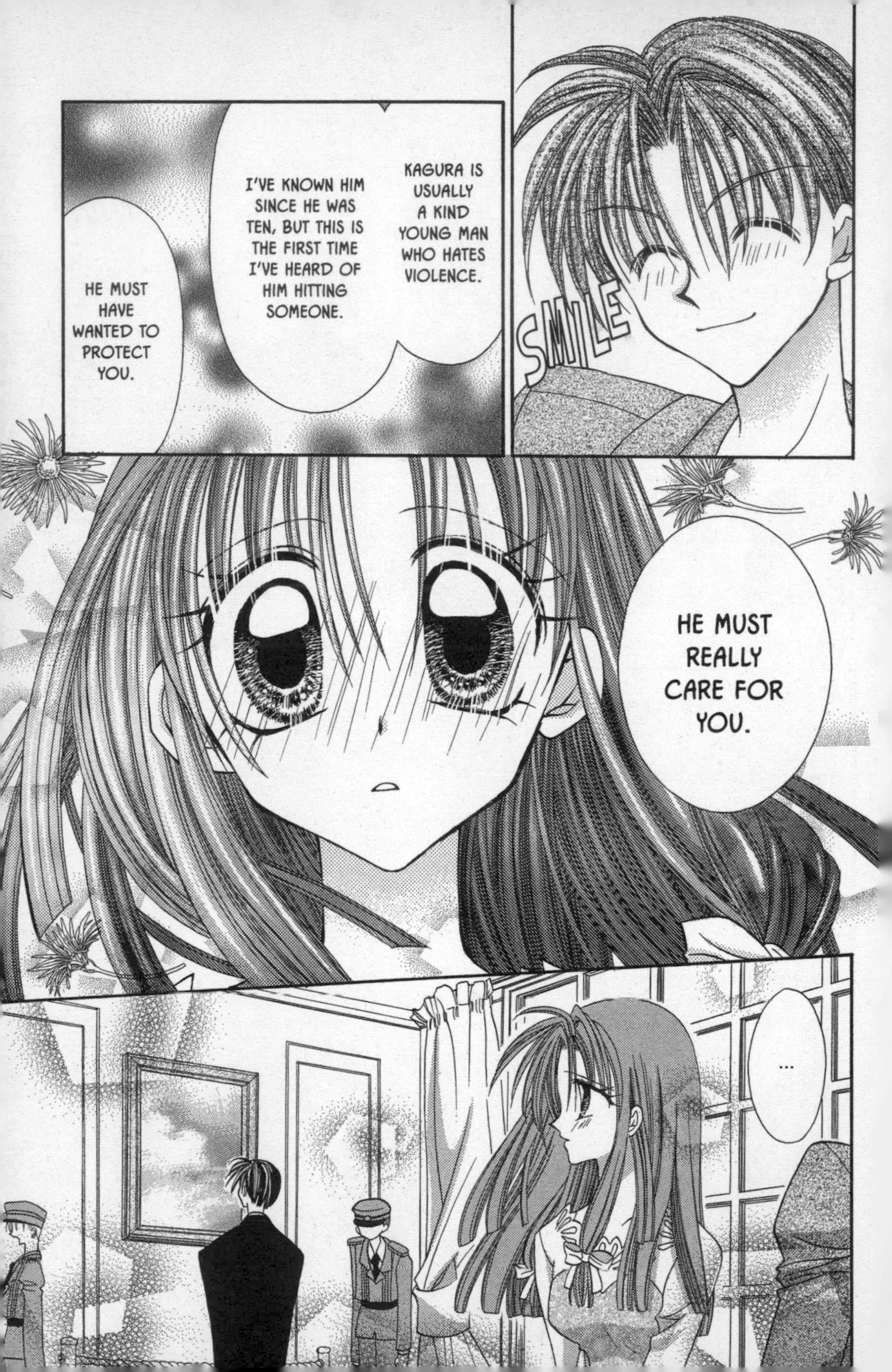
SMILE
KAGURA IS USUALLY A KIND YOUNG MAN WHO HATES VIOLENCE.
I'VE KNOWN HIM SINCE HE WAS TEN, BUT THIS IS THE FIRST TIME I'VE HEARD OF HIM HITTING SOMEONE.
HE MUST HAVE WANTED TO PROTECT YOU.
HE MUST REALLY CARE FOR YOU.
...

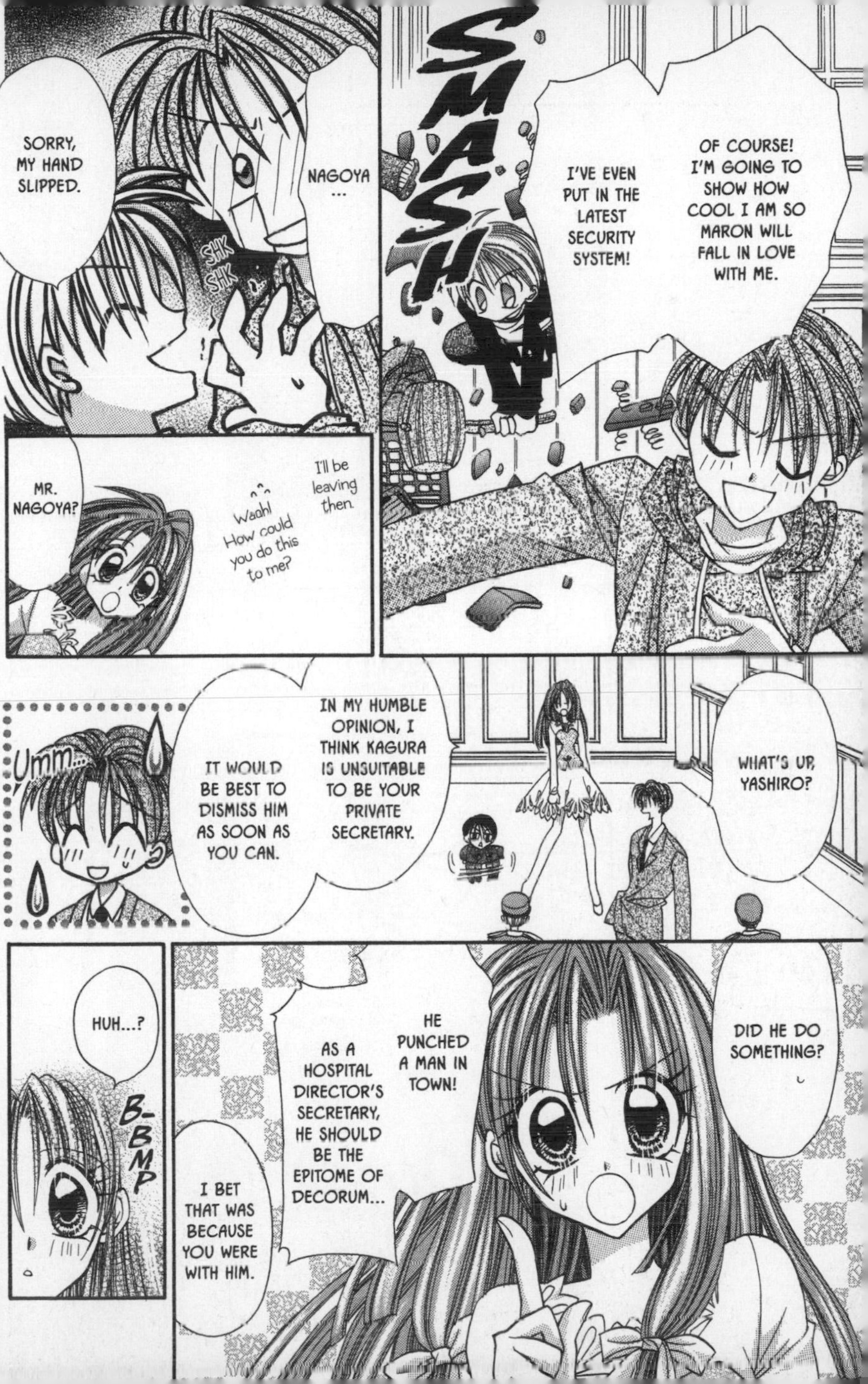
SMASH
OF COURSE! I'M GOING TO SHOW HOW COOL I AM SO MARON WILL FALL IN LOVE WITH ME.
I'VE EVEN PUT IN THE LATEST SECURITY SYSTEM!
NAGOYA ...
SORRY, MY HAND SLIPPED.
SHK SHK
MR. NAGOYA?
I'll be leaving then.
Waah! How could you do this to me?
WHAT'S UP, YASHIRO?
IN MY HUMBLE OPINION, I THINK KAGURA IS UNSUITABLE TO BE YOUR PRIVATE SECRETARY.
IT WOULD BE BEST TO DISMISS HIM AS SOON AS YOU CAN.
Umm...
DID HE DO SOMETHING?
HE PUNCHED A MAN IN TOWN!
AS A HOSPITAL DIRECTOR'S SECRETARY, HE SHOULD BE THE EPITOME OF DECORUM...
I BET THAT WAS BECAUSE YOU WERE WITH HIM.
HUH...?
B-BMP

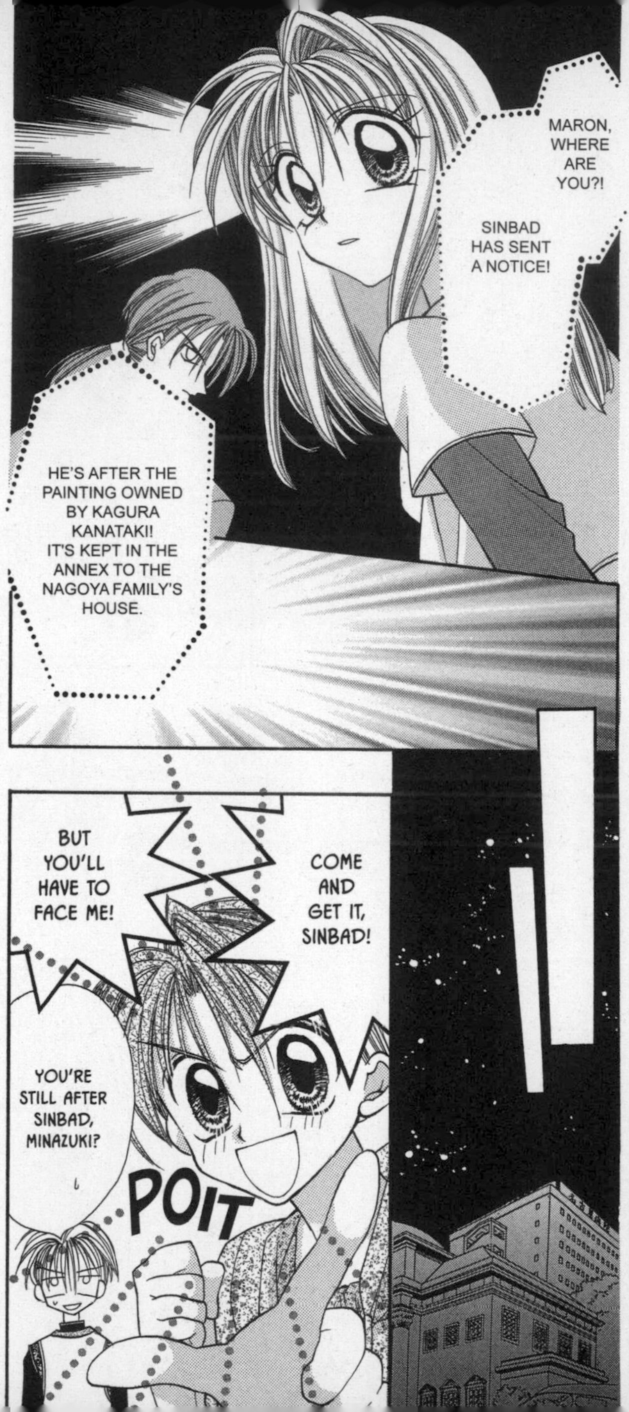
MARON, WHERE ARE YOU?!
SINBAD HAS SENT A NOTICE!
HE'S AFTER THE PAINTING OWNED BY KAGURA KANATAKI! IT'S KEPT IN THE ANNEX TO THE NAGOYA FAMILY'S HOUSE.
COME AND GET IT, SINBAD!
BUT YOU'LL HAVE TO FACE ME!
POIT
YOU'RE STILL AFTER SINBAD, MINAZUKI?

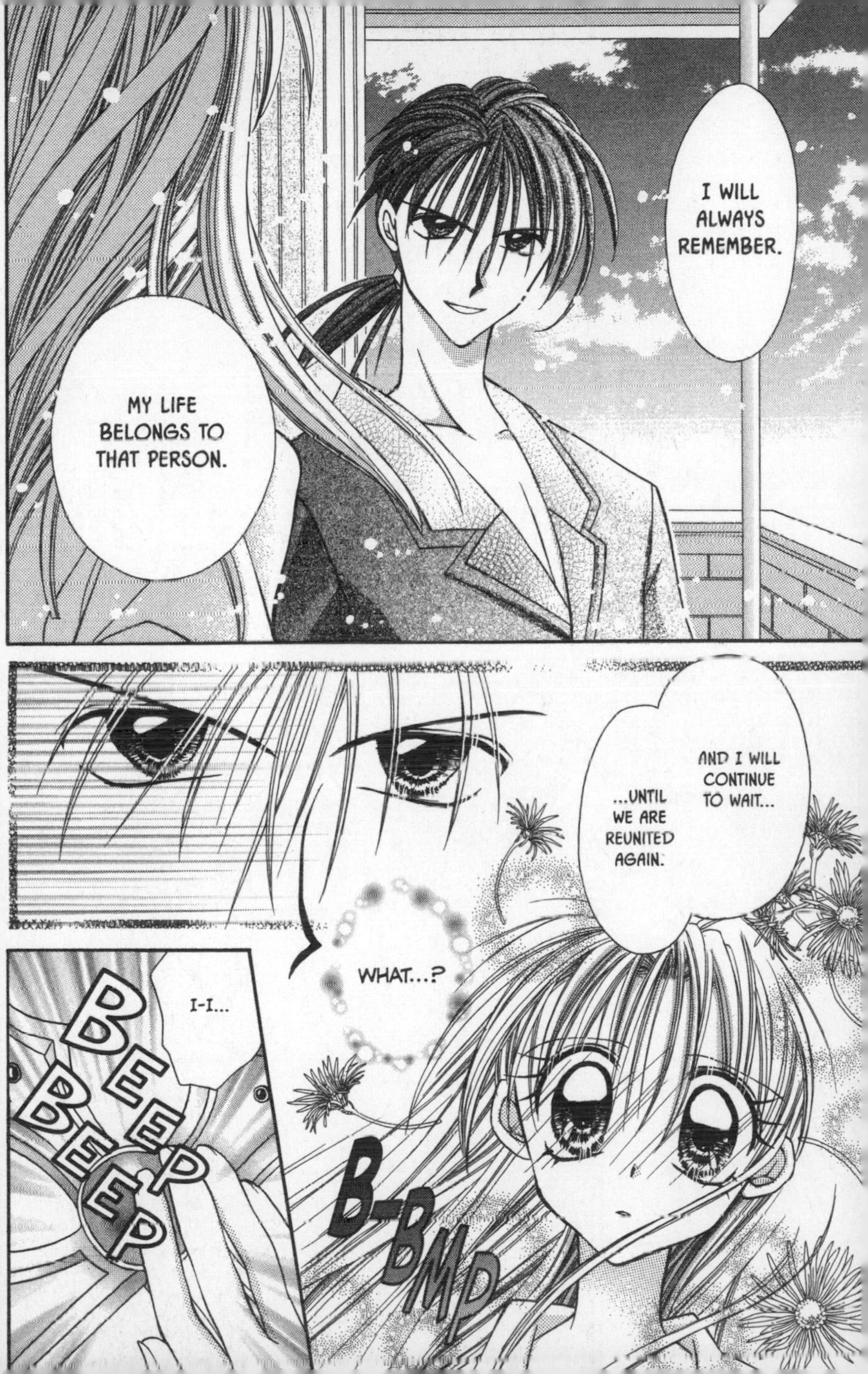
I WILL ALWAYS REMEMBER.
MY LIFE BELONGS TO THAT PERSON.
AND I WILL CONTINUE TO WAIT...
...UNTIL WE ARE REUNITED AGAIN.
WHAT...?
B-BMP
I-I...
BEEP BEEP

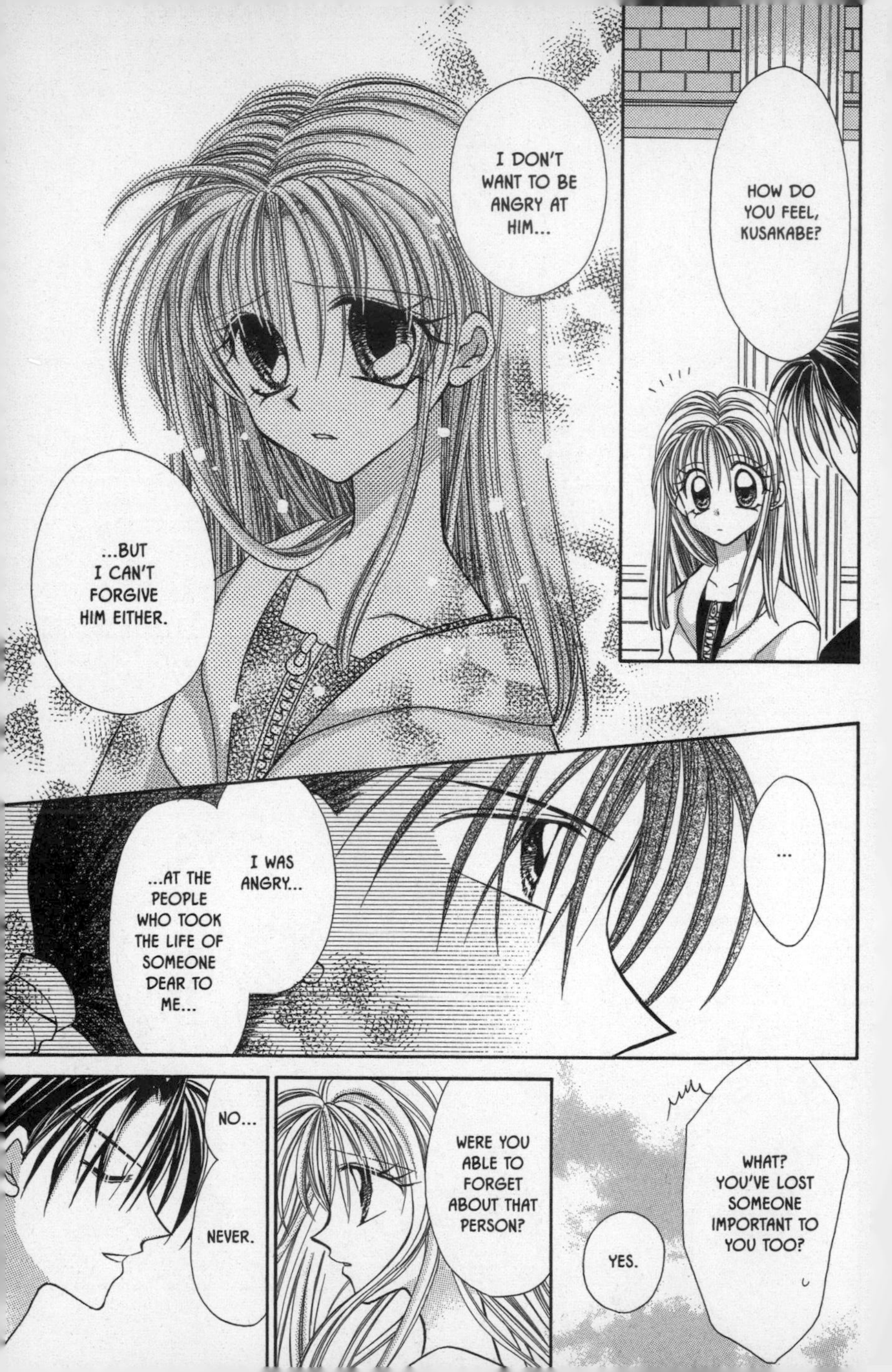
HOW DO YOU FEEL, KUSAKABE?
I DON'T WANT TO BE ANGRY AT HIM...
...BUT I CAN'T FORGIVE HIM EITHER.
...
I WAS ANGRY...
...AT THE PEOPLE WHO TOOK THE LIFE OF SOMEONE DEAR TO ME...
WHAT? YOU'VE LOST SOMEONE IMPORTANT TO YOU TOO?
YES.
WERE YOU ABLE TO FORGET ABOUT THAT PERSON?
NO...
NEVER.

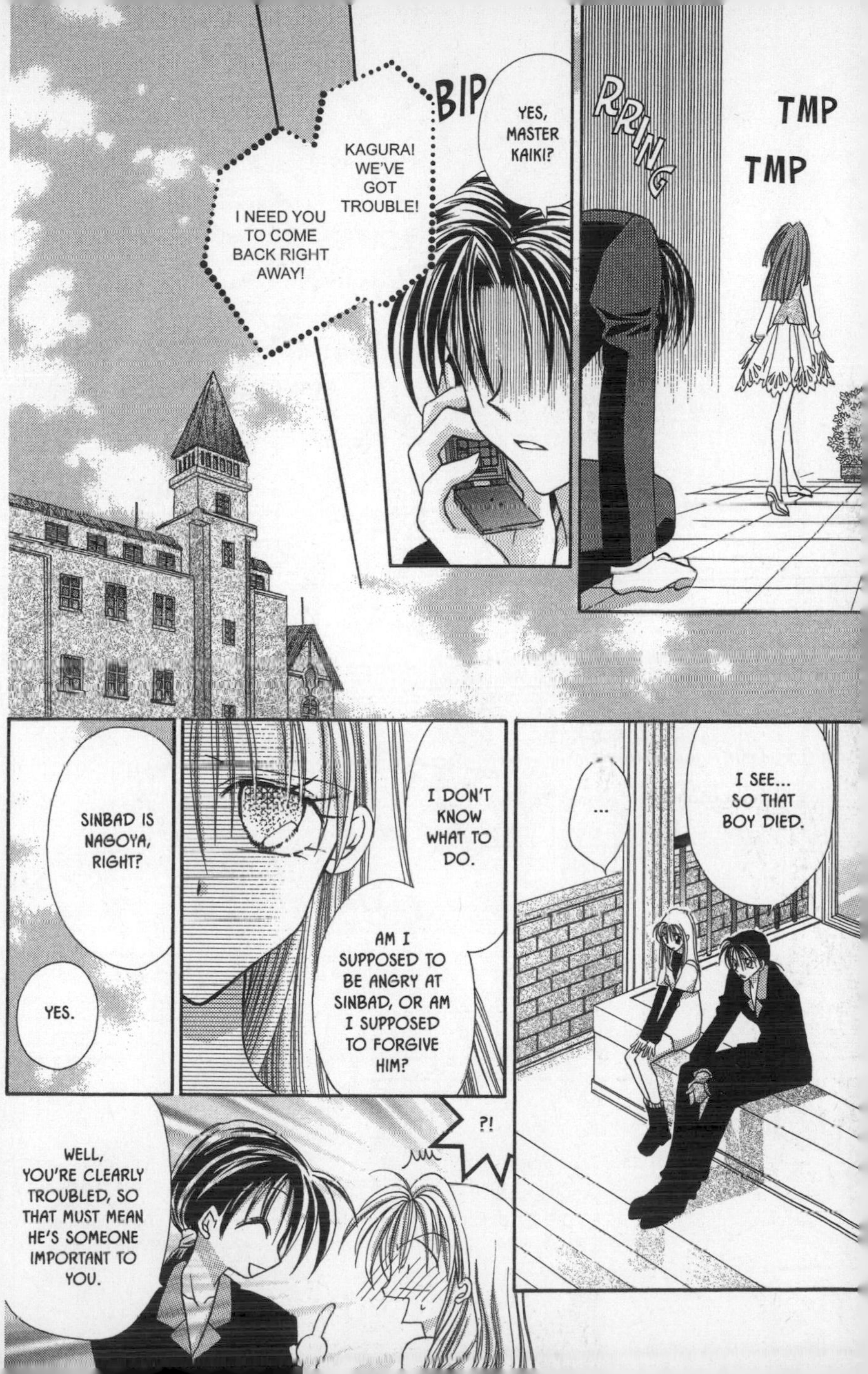
TMP
TMP
RRING
BIP
YES, MASTER KAIKI?
KAGURA! WE'VE GOT TROUBLE!
I NEED YOU TO COME BACK RIGHT AWAY!
I SEE... SO THAT BOY DIED.
...
I DON'T KNOW WHAT TO DO.
AM I SUPPOSED TO BE ANGRY AT SINBAD, OR AM I SUPPOSED TO FORGIVE HIM?
SINBAD IS NAGOYA, RIGHT?
YES.
?!
WELL, YOU'RE CLEARLY TROUBLED, SO THAT MUST MEAN HE'S SOMEONE IMPORTANT TO YOU.

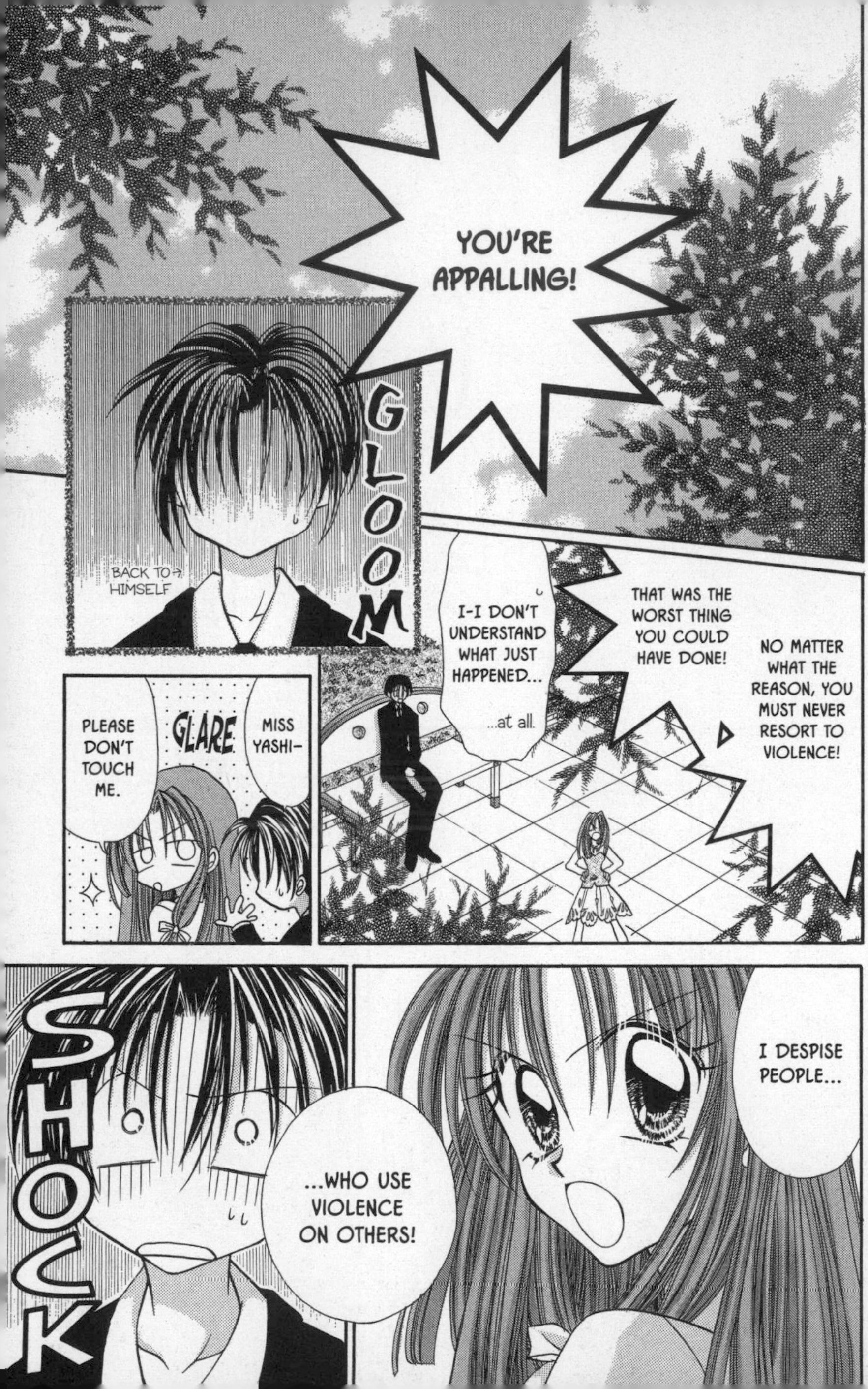
YOU'RE APPALLING!
GLOOM
BACK TO HIMSELF
THAT WAS THE WORST THING YOU COULD HAVE DONE!
NO MATTER WHAT THE REASON, YOU MUST NEVER RESORT TO VIOLENCE!
I-I DON'T UNDERSTAND WHAT JUST HAPPENED...
...at all.
MISS YASHI-
GLARE
PLEASE DON'T TOUCH ME.
I DESPISE PEOPLE...
...WHO USE VIOLENCE ON OTHERS!
SHOCK

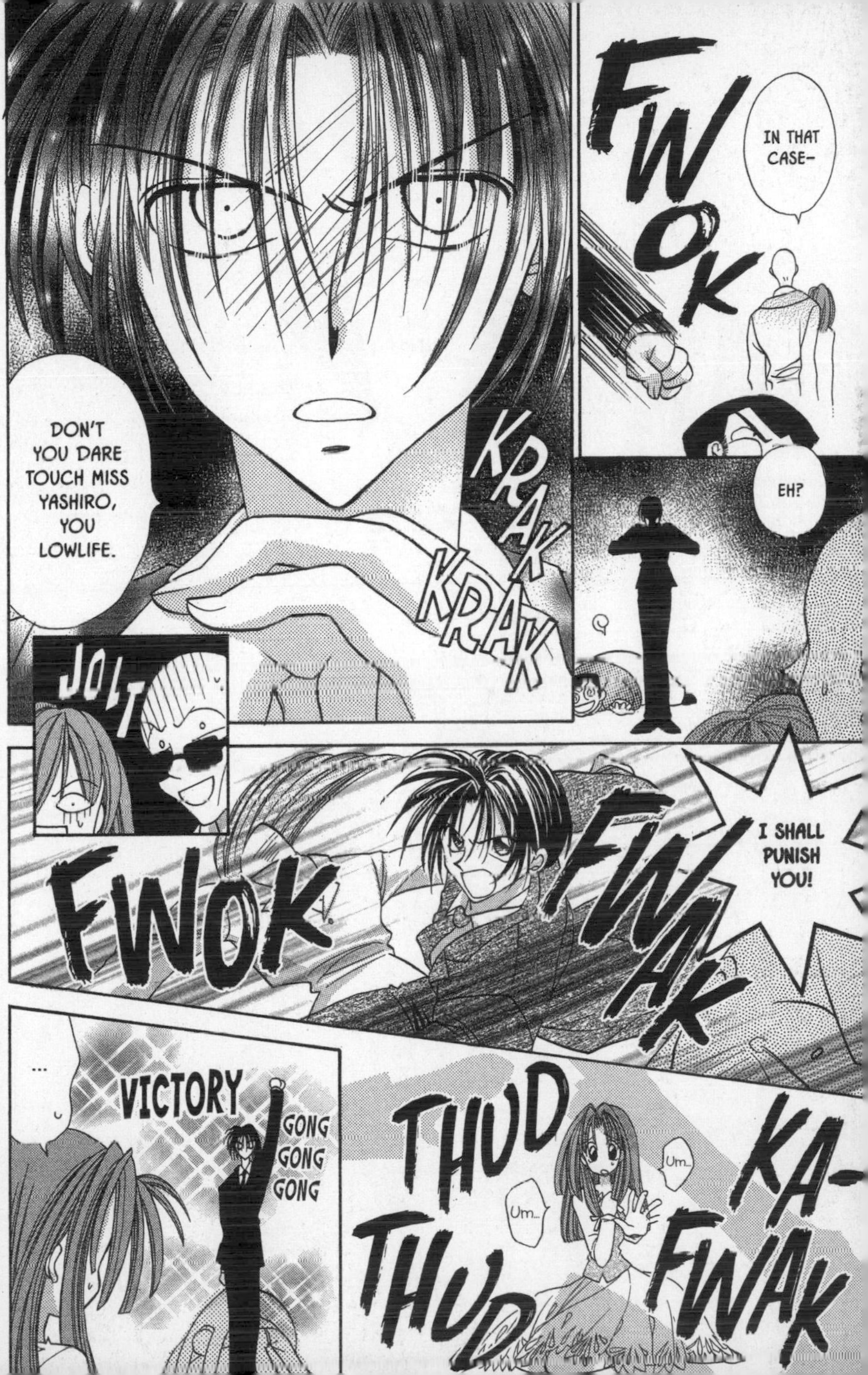
FWOK
IN THAT CASE–
EH?
KRAK KRAK
DON'T YOU DARE TOUCH MISS YASHIRO, YOU LOWLIFE.
JOLT
I SHALL PUNISH YOU!
FWAK
FWOK
KA-FWAK
Um...
Um...
THUD THUD
GONG GONG GONG
VICTORY
...

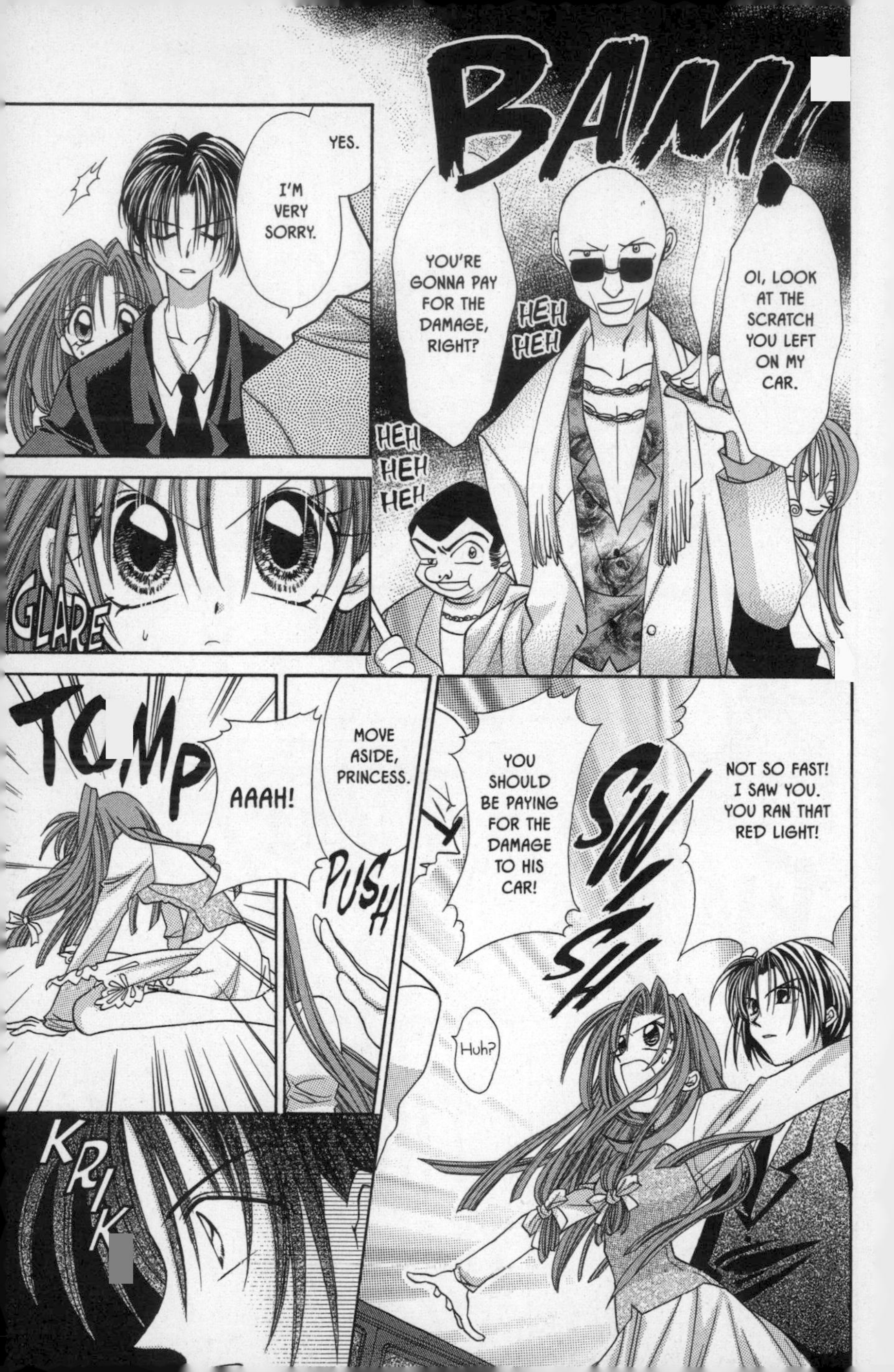
BAM!
OI, LOOK AT THE SCRATCH YOU LEFT ON MY CAR.
YOU'RE GONNA PAY FOR THE DAMAGE, RIGHT?
HEH HEH
HEH HEH HEH
YES.
I'M VERY SORRY.
GLARE
NOT SO FAST! I SAW YOU. YOU RAN THAT RED LIGHT!
YOU SHOULD BE PAYING FOR THE DAMAGE TO HIS CAR!
Huh?
MOVE ASIDE, PRINCESS.
PUSH
AAAH!
KRIK

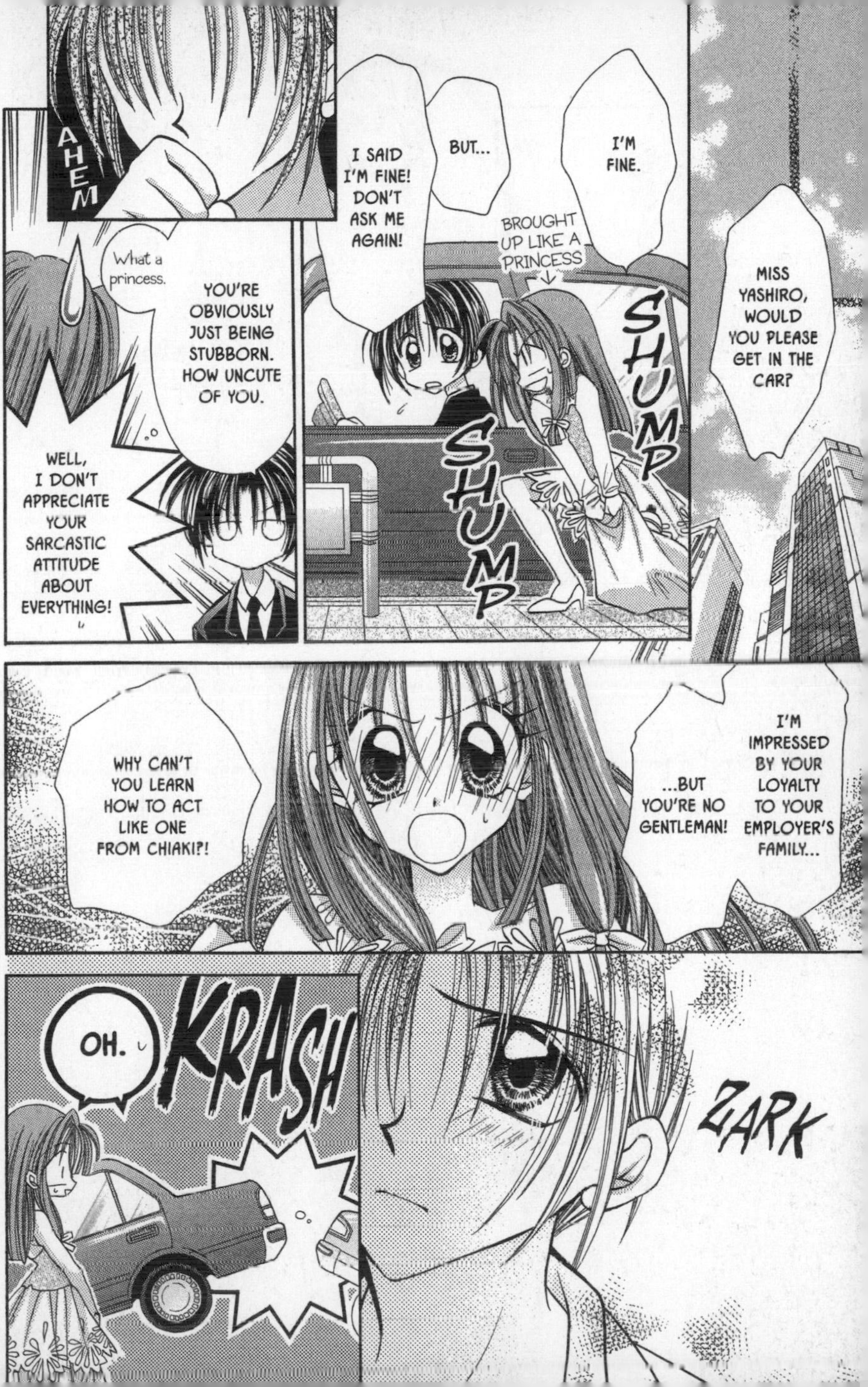

MISS YASHIRO, WOULD YOU PLEASE GET IN THE CAR?
I'M FINE.
BROUGHT UP LIKE A PRINCESS
BUT...
I SAID I'M FINE! DON'T ASK ME AGAIN!
SHUMP
SHUMP
AHEM
YOU'RE OBVIOUSLY JUST BEING STUBBORN. HOW UNCUTE OF YOU.
What a princess.
WELL, I DON'T APPRECIATE YOUR SARCASTIC ATTITUDE ABOUT EVERYTHING!
I'M IMPRESSED BY YOUR LOYALTY TO YOUR EMPLOYER'S FAMILY...
...BUT YOU'RE NO GENTLEMAN!
WHY CAN'T YOU LEARN HOW TO ACT LIKE ONE FROM CHIAKI?!
ZARK
KRASH
OH.

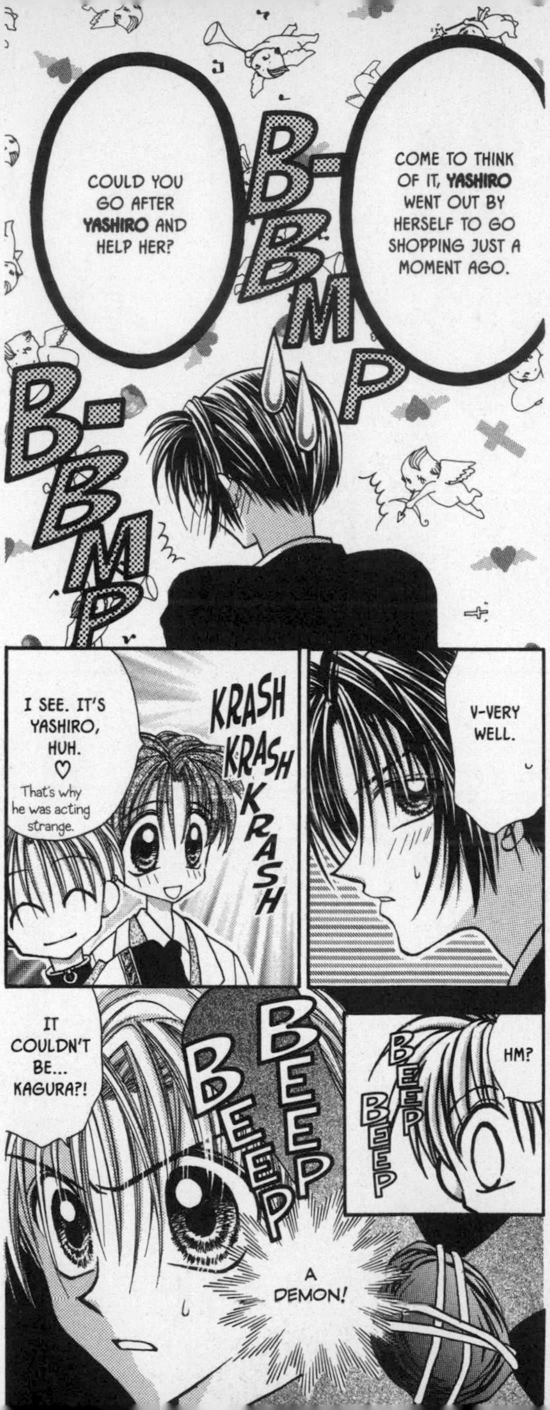
COME TO THINK OF IT, YASHIRO WENT OUT BY HERSELF TO GO SHOPPING JUST A MOMENT AGO.
B-BBMP
COULD YOU GO AFTER YASHIRO AND HELP HER?
B-BBMP
V-VERY WELL.
I SEE. IT'S YASHIRO, HUH. ♡
That's why he was acting strange.
KRASH KRASH KRASH
BEEP BEEP
HM?
IT COULDN'T BE... KAGURA?!
BEEP BEEP
A DEMON!

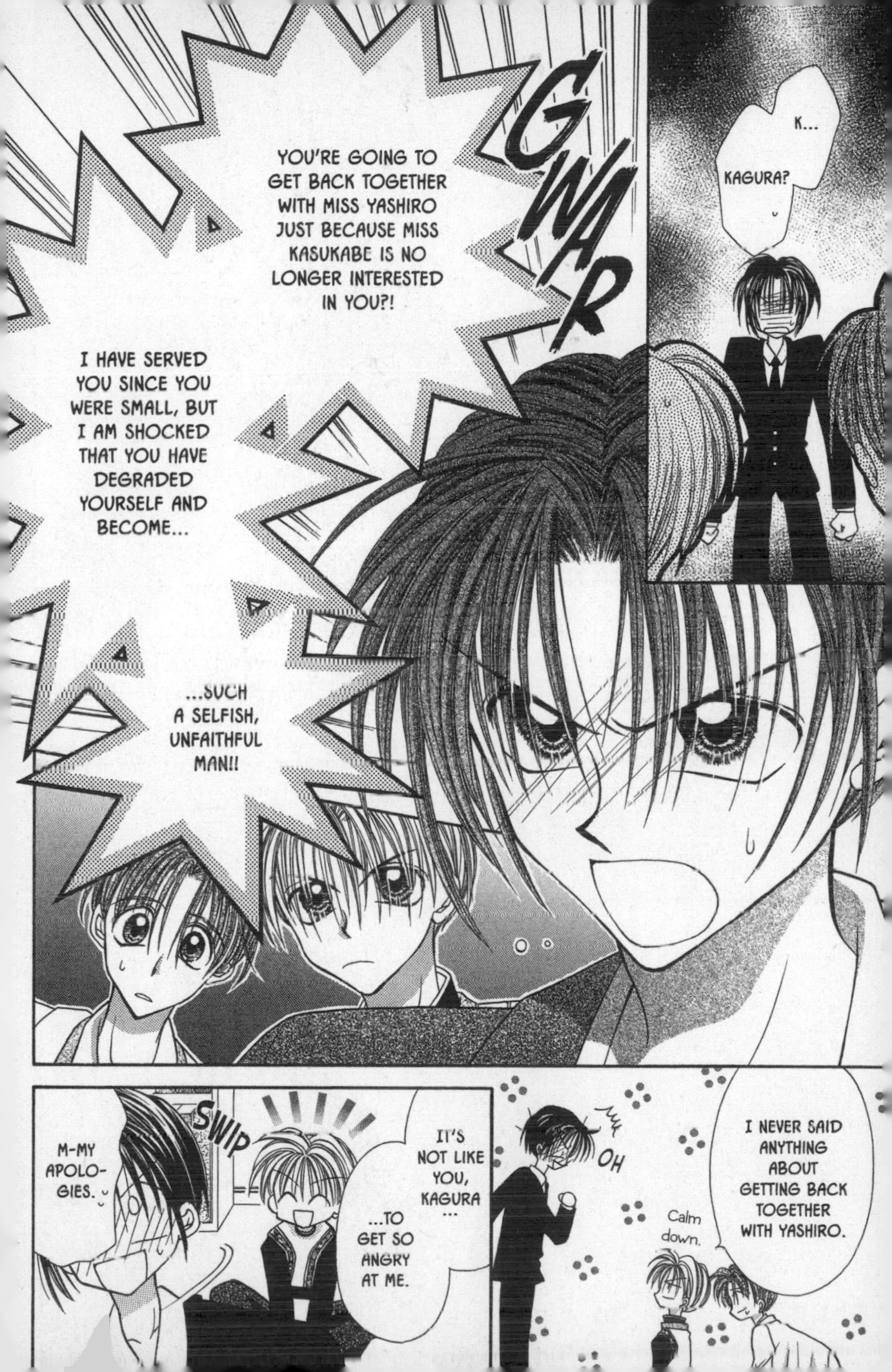

K...
KAGURA?
GWAR
YOU'RE GOING TO GET BACK TOGETHER WITH MISS YASHIRO JUST BECAUSE MISS KASUKABE IS NO LONGER INTERESTED IN YOU?!
I HAVE SERVED YOU SINCE YOU WERE SMALL, BUT I AM SHOCKED THAT YOU HAVE DEGRADED YOURSELF AND BECOME...
...SUCH A SELFISH, UNFAITHFUL MAN!!
I NEVER SAID ANYTHING ABOUT GETTING BACK TOGETHER WITH YASHIRO.
OH
Calm down.
IT'S NOT LIKE YOU, KAGURA...
...TO GET SO ANGRY AT ME.
SWIP
M-MY APOLOGIES.

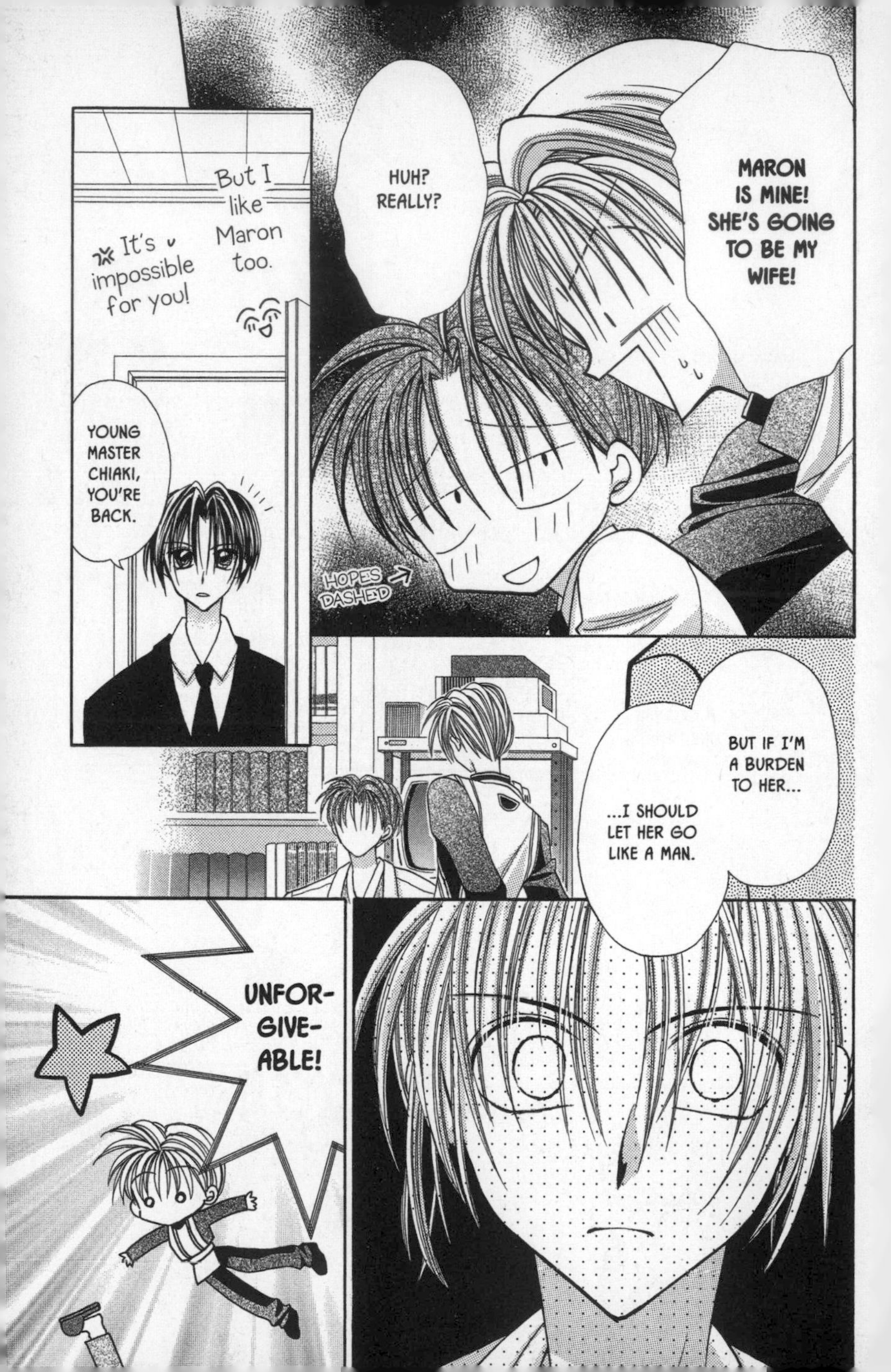
MARON IS MINE! SHE'S GOING TO BE MY WIFE!
HUH? REALLY?
HOPES DASHED
But I like Maron too.
It's impossible for you!
YOUNG MASTER CHIAKI, YOU'RE BACK.
BUT IF I'M A BURDEN TO HER...
...I SHOULD LET HER GO LIKE A MAN.
UNFOR-GIVE-ABLE!

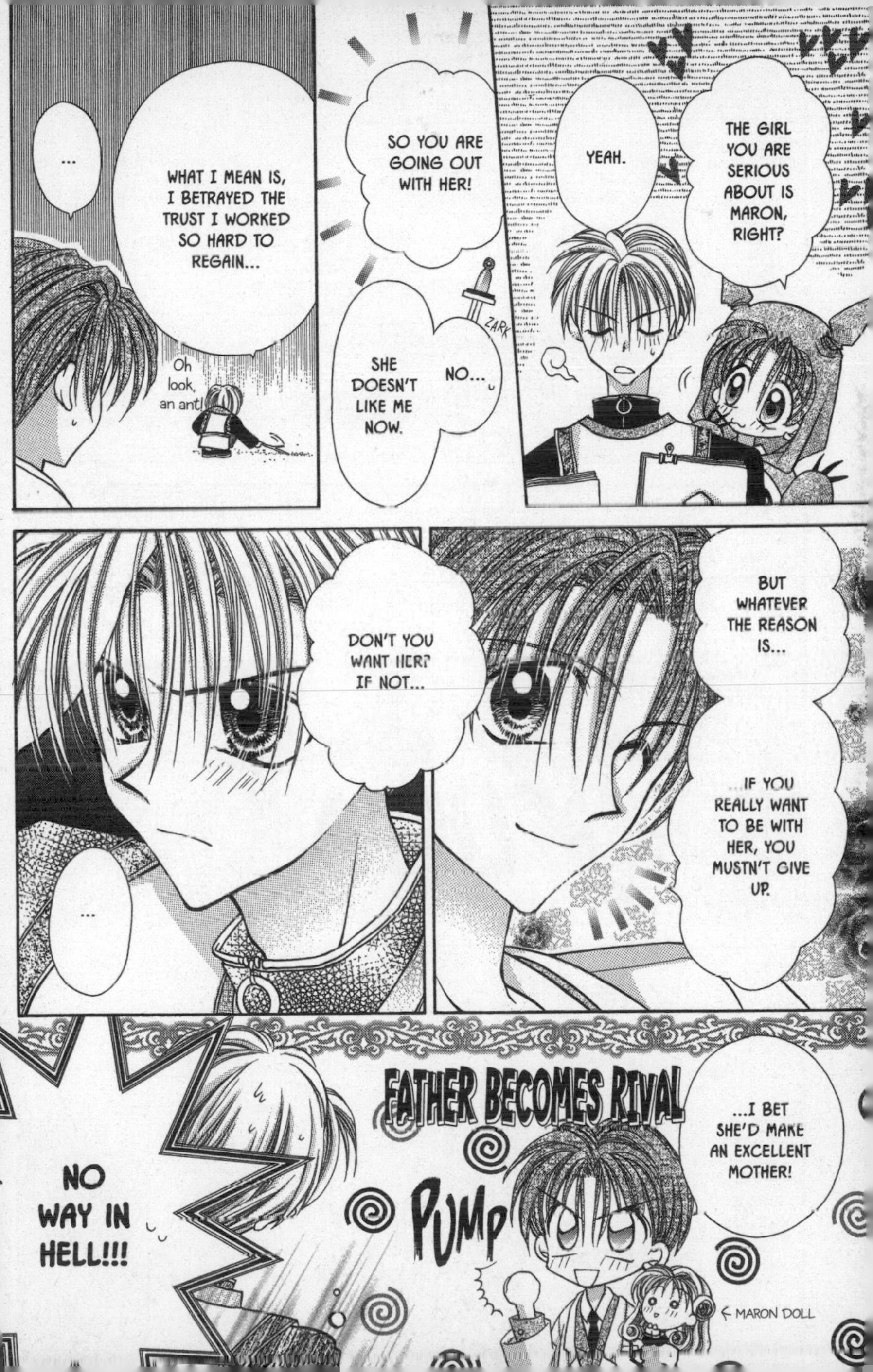
THE GIRL YOU ARE SERIOUS ABOUT IS MARON, RIGHT?
YEAH.
SO YOU ARE GOING OUT WITH HER!
NO...
ZARK
SHE DOESN'T LIKE ME NOW.
WHAT I MEAN IS, I BETRAYED THE TRUST I WORKED SO HARD TO REGAIN...
...
Oh look, an ant!
BUT WHATEVER THE REASON IS...
...IF YOU REALLY WANT TO BE WITH HER, YOU MUSTN'T GIVE UP.
DON'T YOU WANT HER? IF NOT...
...
...I BET SHE'D MAKE AN EXCELLENT MOTHER!
FATHER BECOMES RIVAL
PUMP
← MARON DOLL
NO WAY IN HELL!!!

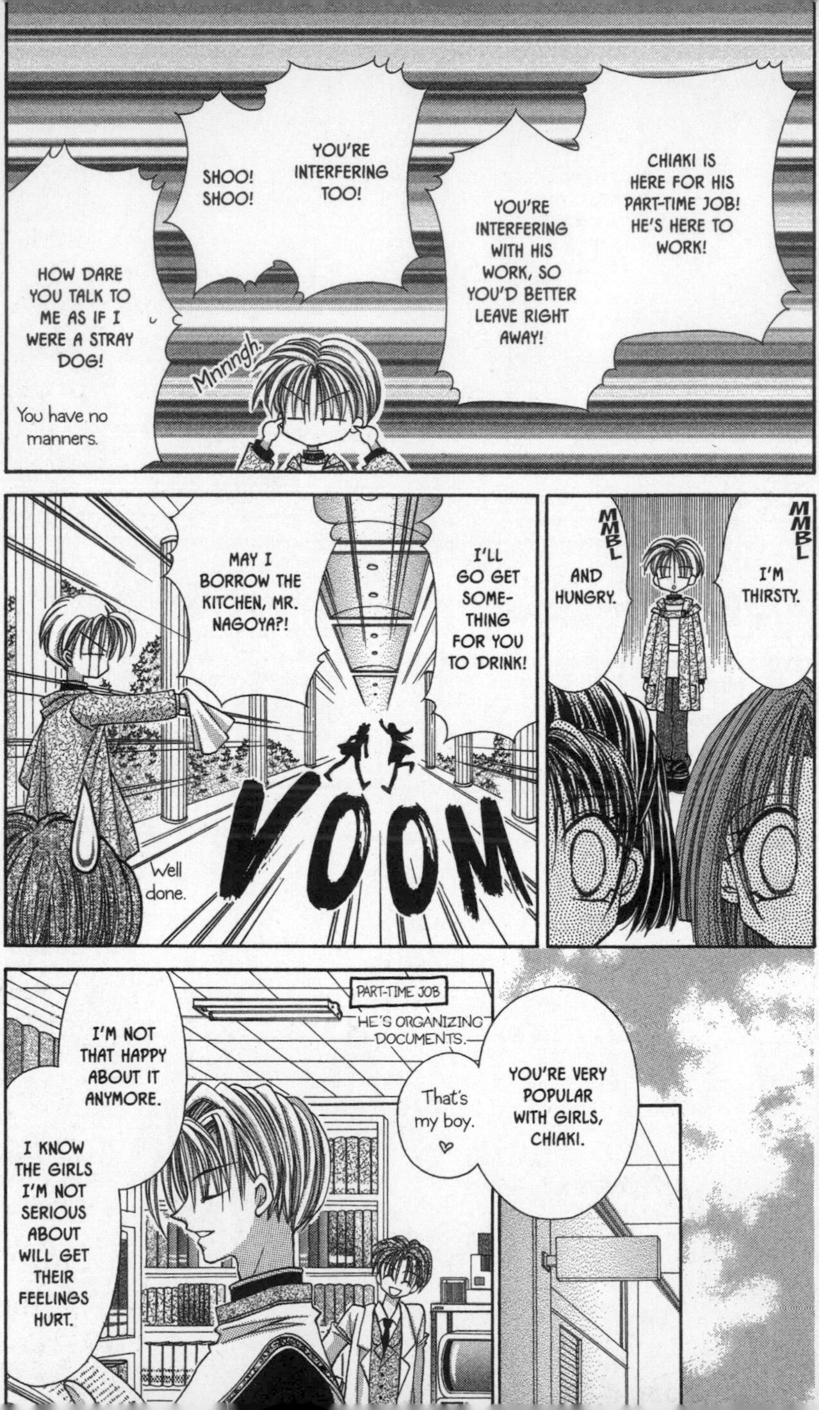
CHIAKI IS HERE FOR HIS PART-TIME JOB! HE'S HERE TO WORK!
YOU'RE INTERFERING WITH HIS WORK, SO YOU'D BETTER LEAVE RIGHT AWAY!
YOU'RE INTERFERING TOO!
SHOO! SHOO!
Mnnngh.
HOW DARE YOU TALK TO ME AS IF I WERE A STRAY DOG!
You have no manners.
MMBL
I'M THIRSTY.
MMBL
AND HUNGRY.
I'LL GO GET SOMETHING FOR YOU TO DRINK!
MAY I BORROW THE KITCHEN, MR. NAGOYA?!
VOOM
Well done.
PART-TIME JOB
HE'S ORGANIZING DOCUMENTS.
YOU'RE VERY POPULAR WITH GIRLS, CHIAKI.
That's my boy. ♡
I'M NOT THAT HAPPY ABOUT IT ANYMORE.
I KNOW THE GIRLS I'M NOT SERIOUS ABOUT WILL GET THEIR FEELINGS HURT.

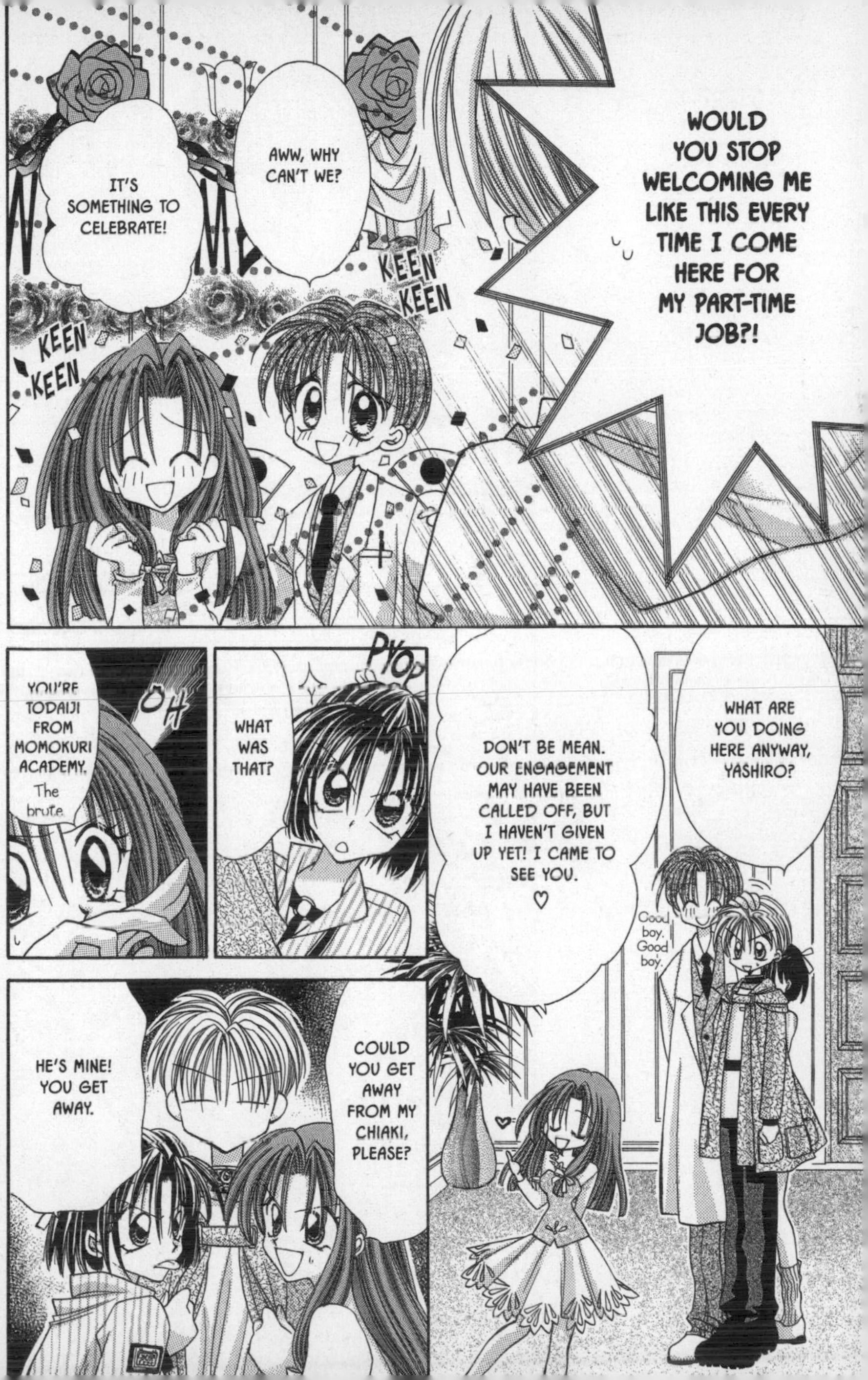
WOULD YOU STOP WELCOMING ME LIKE THIS EVERY TIME I COME HERE FOR MY PART-TIME JOB?!
KEEN KEEN
AWW, WHY CAN'T WE?
IT'S SOMETHING TO CELEBRATE!
KEEN KEEN
WHAT ARE YOU DOING HERE ANYWAY, YASHIRO?
DON'T BE MEAN. OUR ENGAGEMENT MAY HAVE BEEN CALLED OFF, BUT I HAVEN'T GIVEN UP YET! I CAME TO SEE YOU. ♡
Good boy. Good boy.
PYOP
WHAT WAS THAT?
OH
YOU'RE TODAIJI FROM MOMOKURI ACADEMY.
The brute.
COULD YOU GET AWAY FROM MY CHIAKI, PLEASE?
HE'S MINE! YOU GET AWAY.

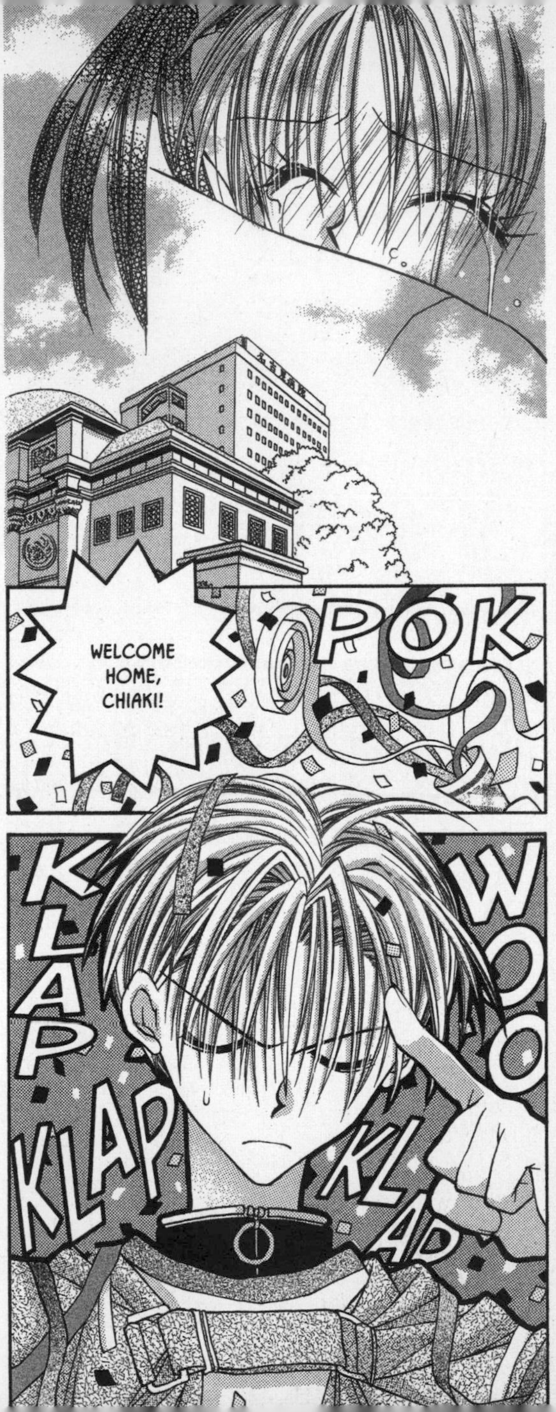
WELCOME HOME, CHIAKI!
POK
WOO
KLAP
KLAP
KLAP

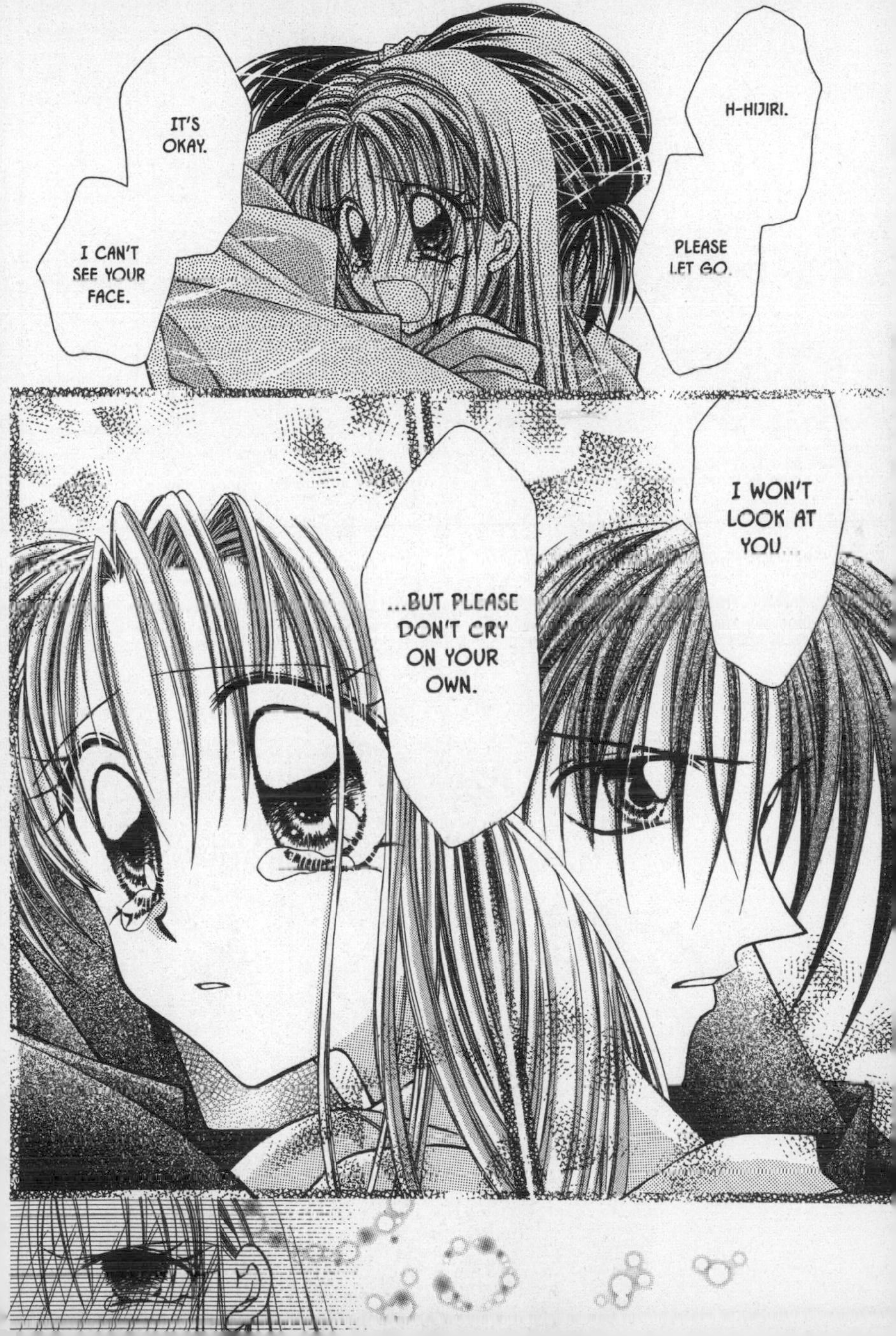
H-HIJIRI.
PLEASE LET GO.
IT'S OKAY.
I CAN'T SEE YOUR FACE.
I WON'T LOOK AT YOU...
...BUT PLEASE DON'T CRY ON YOUR OWN.

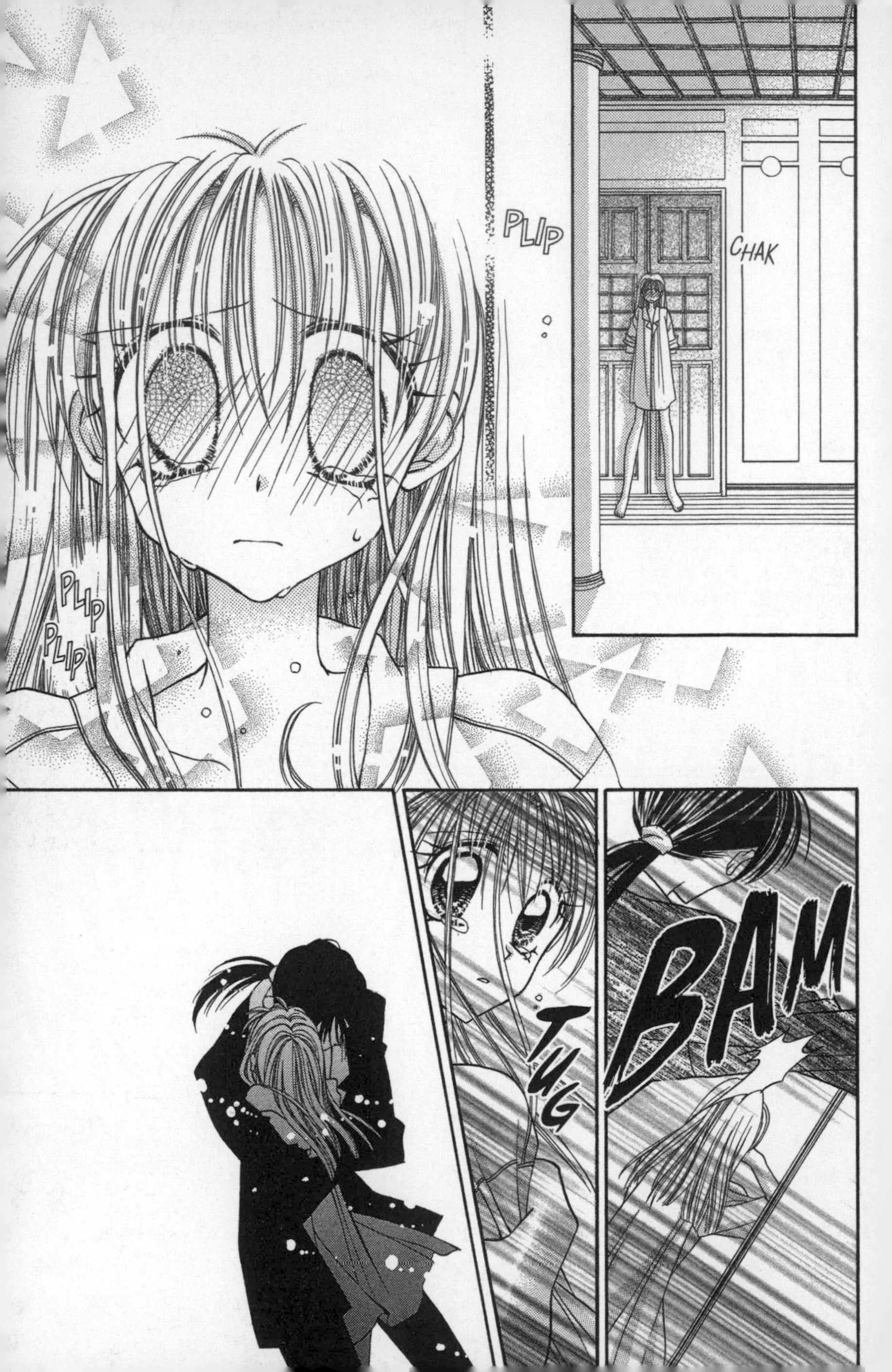
CHAK
PLIP
PLIP
PLIP
BAM
TUG

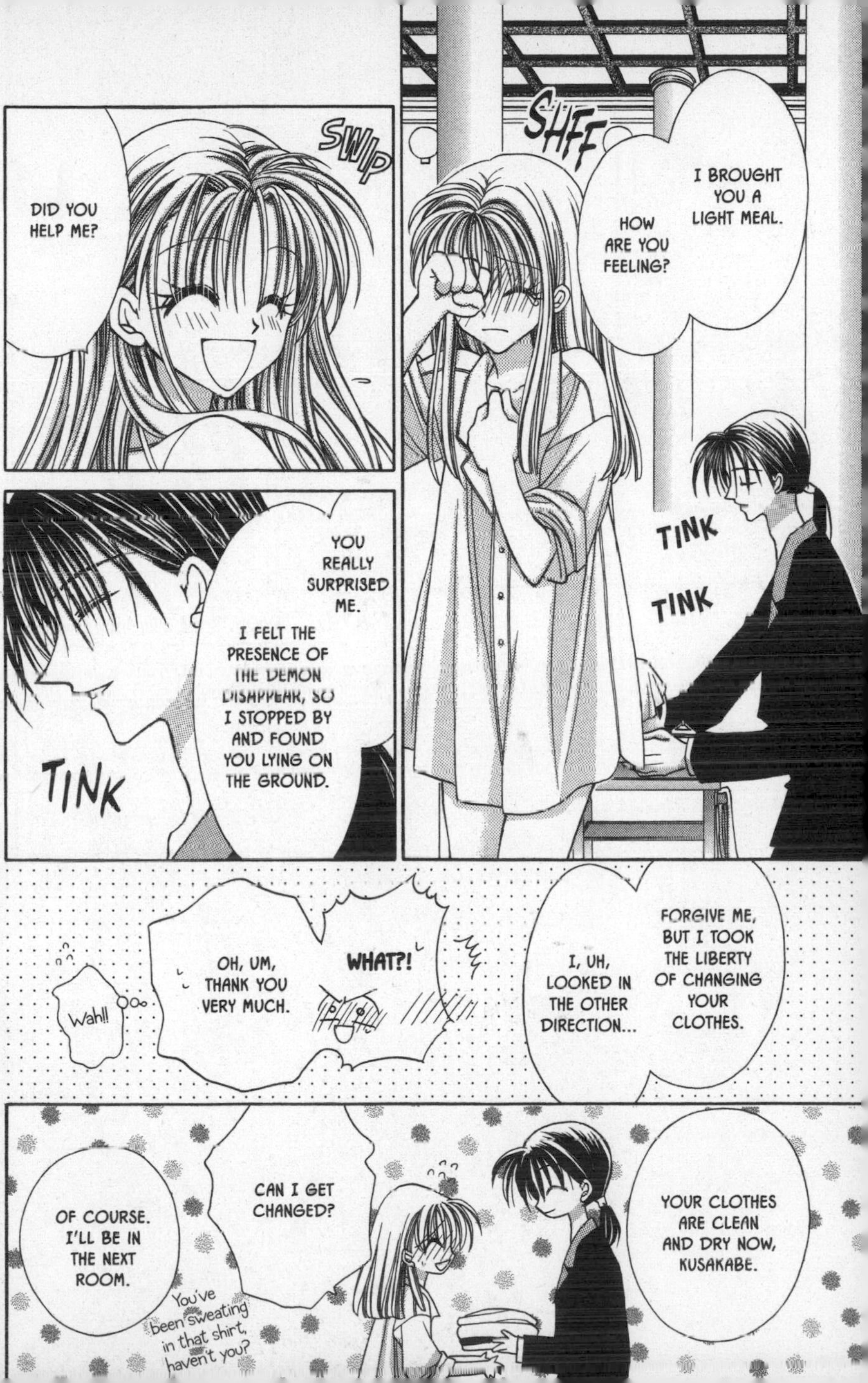
SHFF
I BROUGHT YOU A LIGHT MEAL.
HOW ARE YOU FEELING?
TINK
TINK
SWIP
DID YOU HELP ME?
YOU REALLY SURPRISED ME.
I FELT THE PRESENCE OF THE DEMON DISAPPEAR, SO I STOPPED BY AND FOUND YOU LYING ON THE GROUND.
TINK
FORGIVE ME, BUT I TOOK THE LIBERTY OF CHANGING YOUR CLOTHES.
I, UH, LOOKED IN THE OTHER DIRECTION...
WHAT?!
OH, UM, THANK YOU VERY MUCH.
Wah!!
YOUR CLOTHES ARE CLEAN AND DRY NOW, KUSAKABE.
CAN I GET CHANGED?
OF COURSE. I'LL BE IN THE NEXT ROOM.
You've been sweating in that shirt, haven't you?

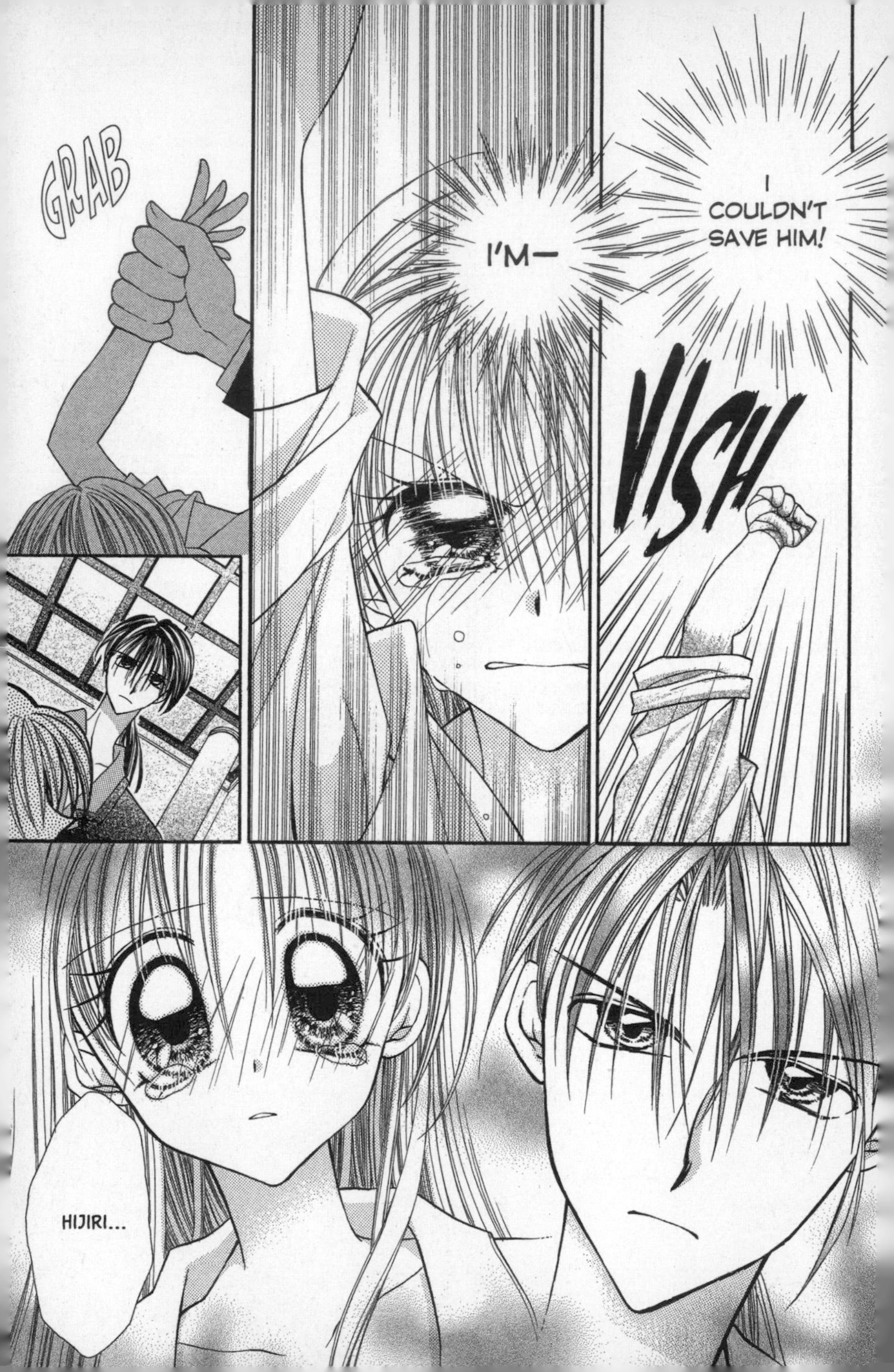
I COULDN'T SAVE HIM!
VISH
I'M—
GRAB
HIJIRI...

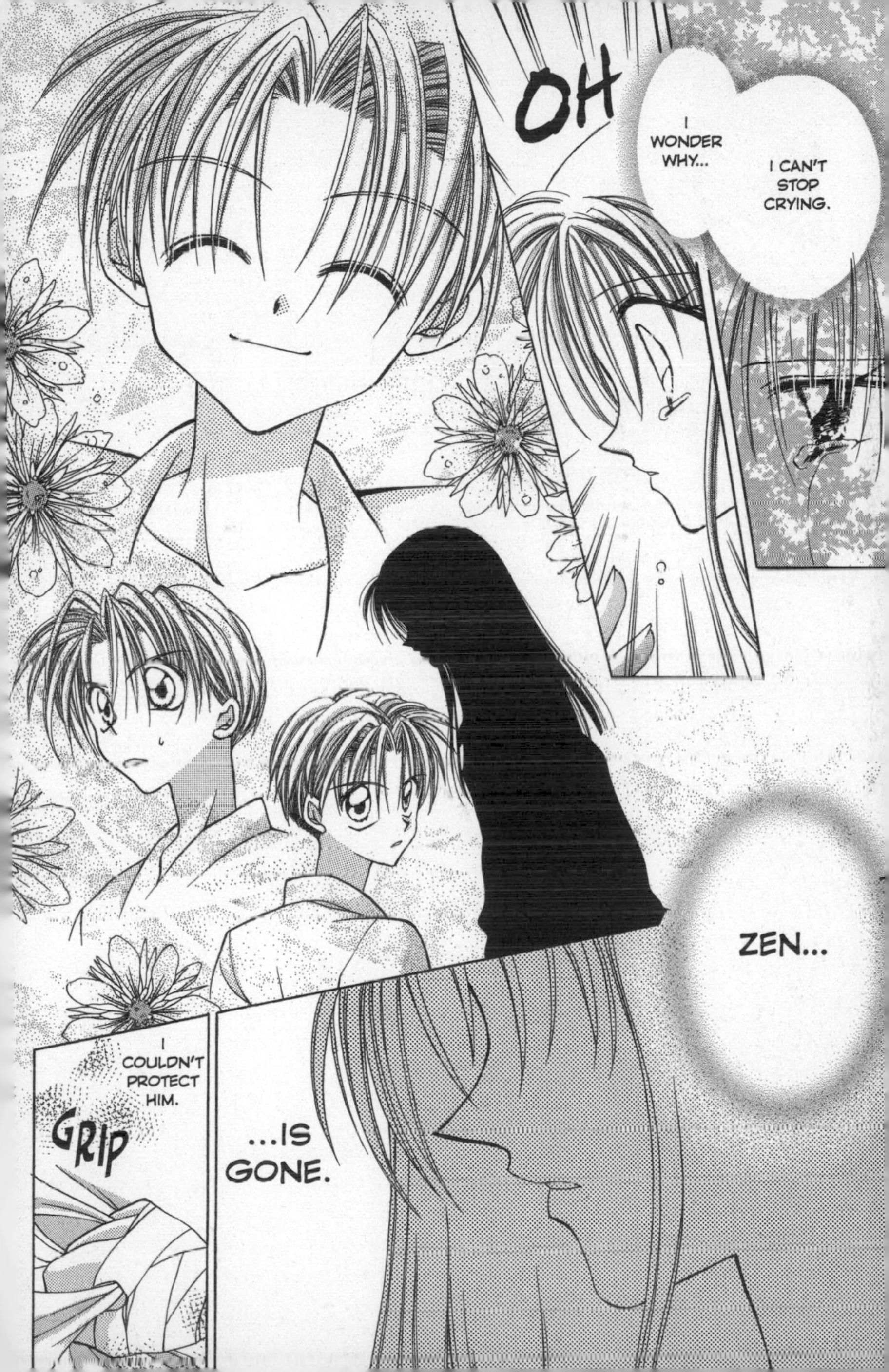
I WONDER WHY...
I CAN'T STOP CRYING.
OH
ZEN...
...IS GONE.
I COULDN'T PROTECT HIM.
GRIP

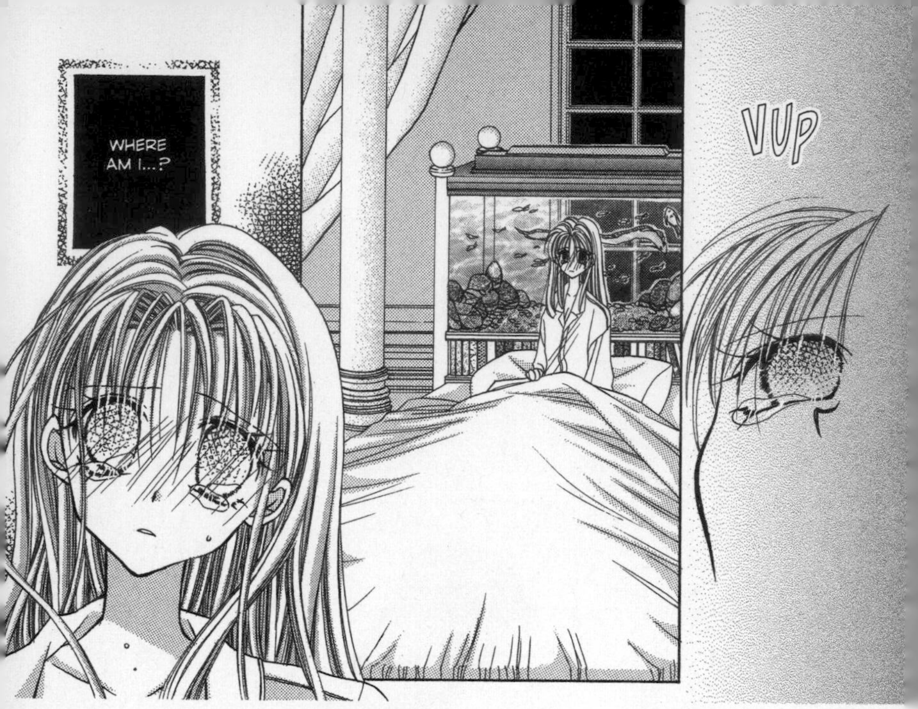
VUP
WHERE AM I...?

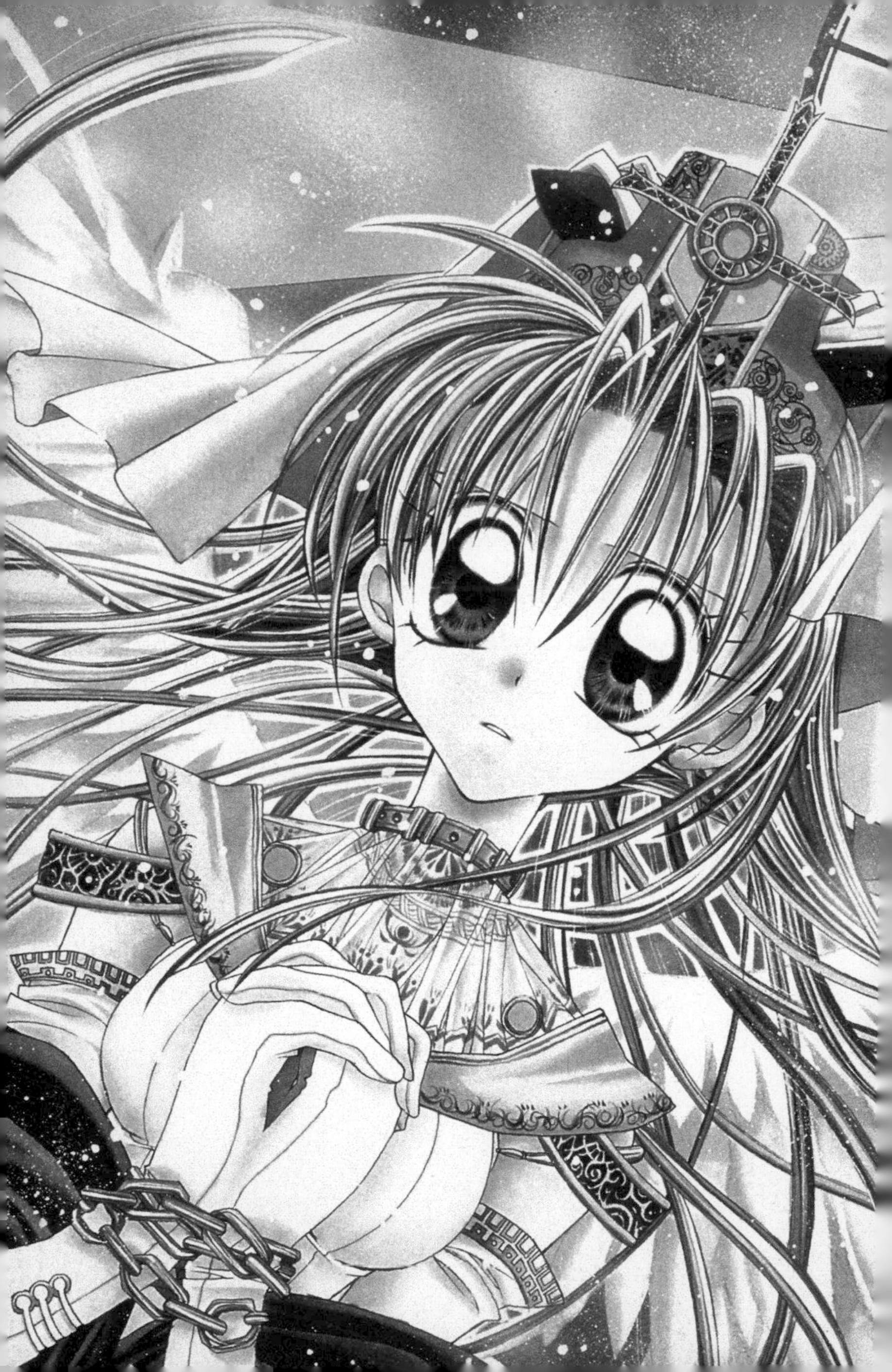

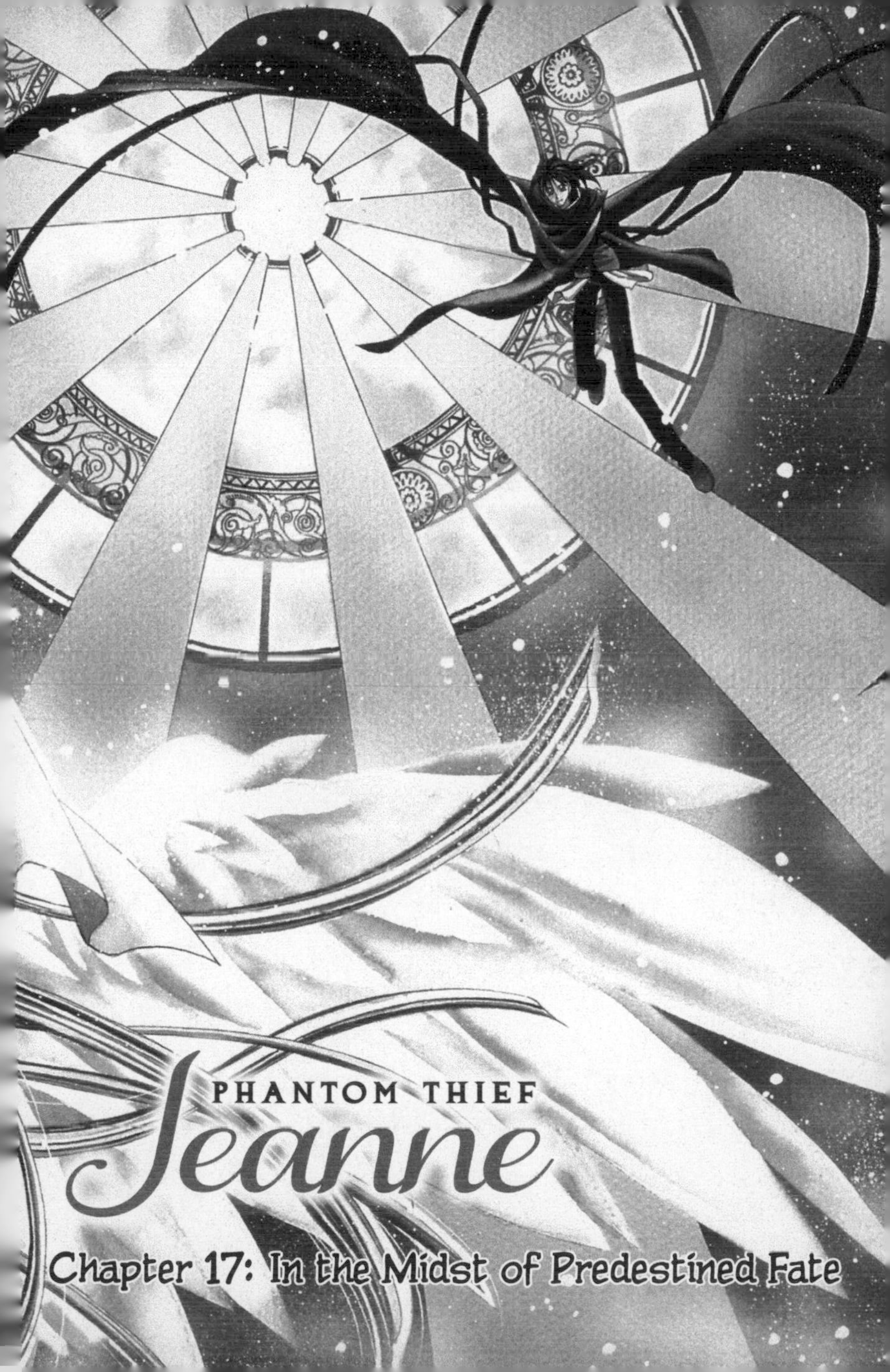
PHANTOM THIEF
Jeanne
Chapter 17: In the Midst of Predestined Fate

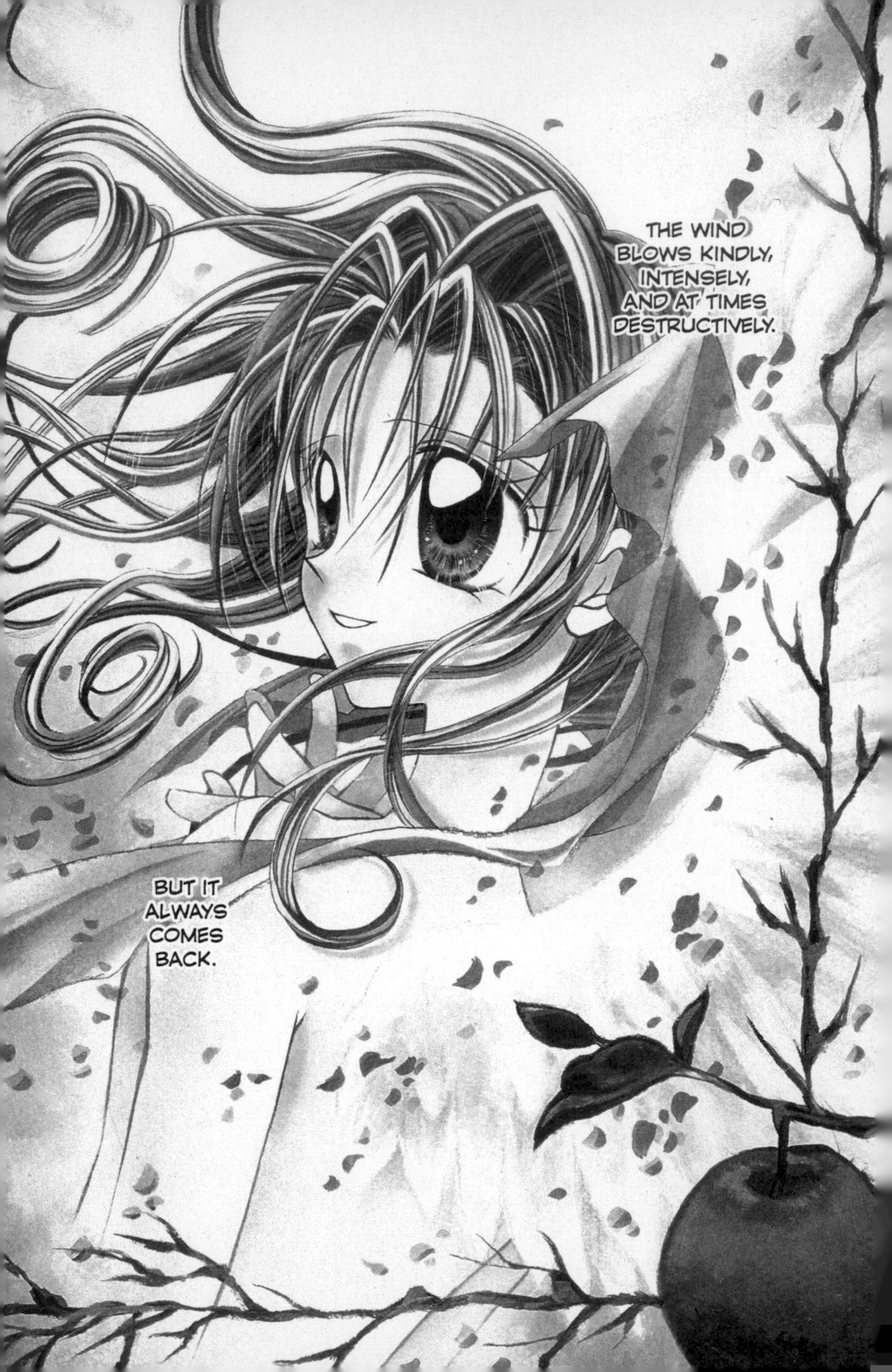
THE WIND BLOWS KINDLY, INTENSELY, AND AT TIMES DESTRUCTIVELY.
BUT IT ALWAYS COMES BACK.

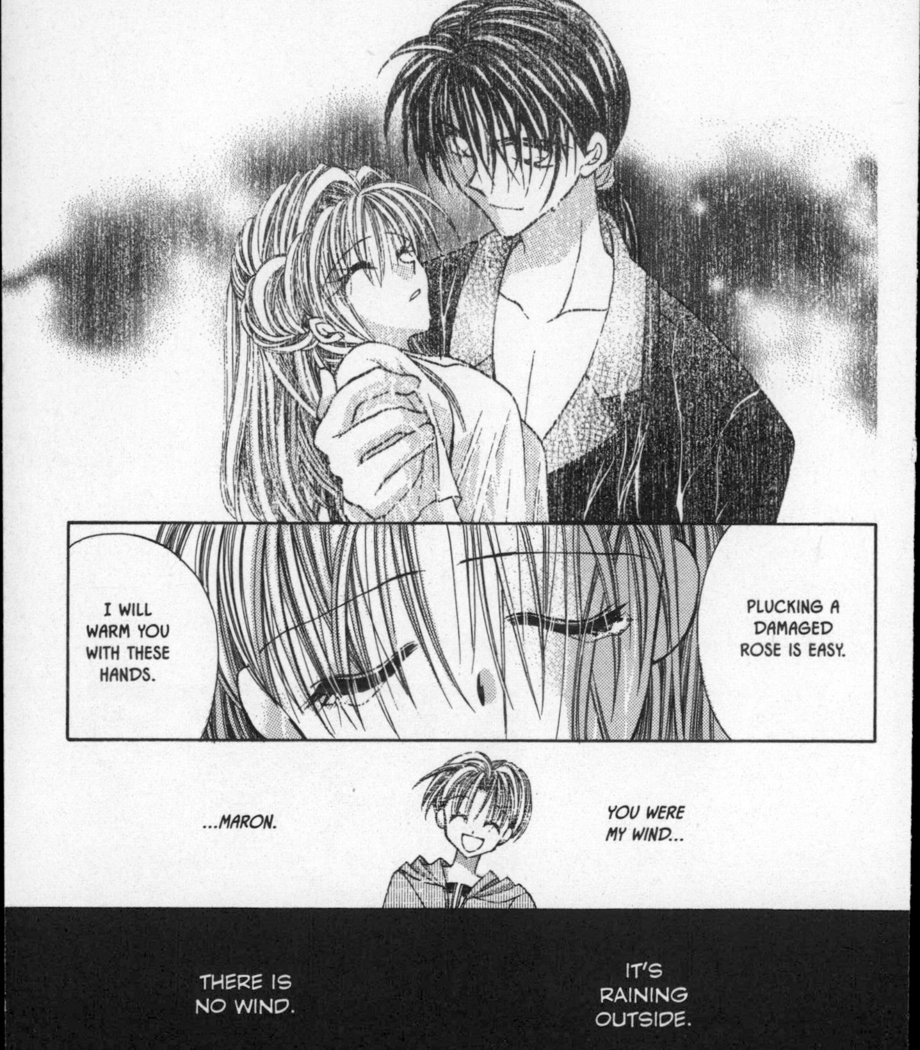
PLUCKING A DAMAGED ROSE IS EASY.
I WILL WARM YOU WITH THESE HANDS.
YOU WERE MY WIND...
...MARON.
IT'S RAINING OUTSIDE.
THERE IS NO WIND.

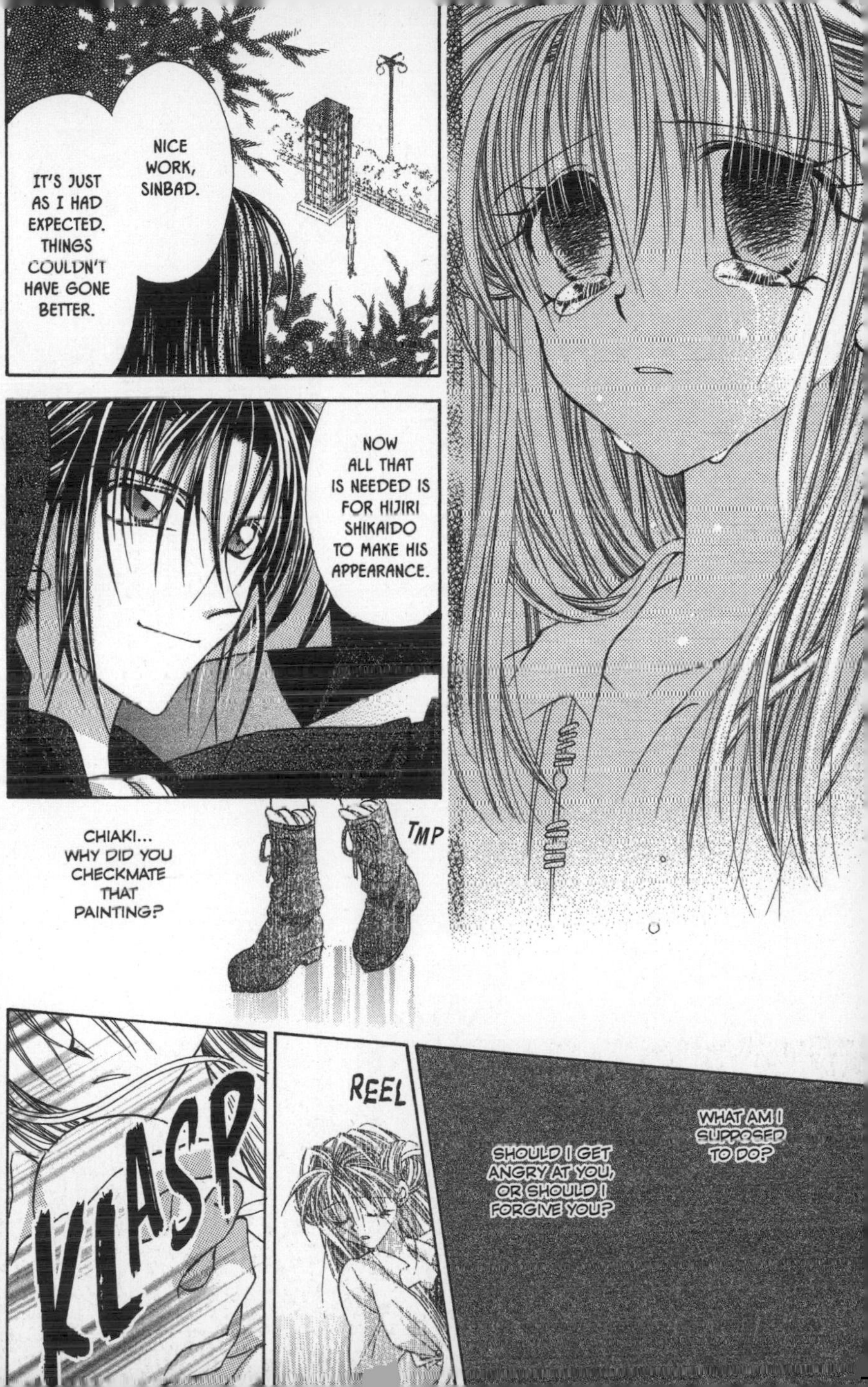
NICE WORK, SINBAD.
IT'S JUST AS I HAD EXPECTED. THINGS COULDN'T HAVE GONE BETTER.
NOW ALL THAT IS NEEDED IS FOR HIJIRI SHIKAIDO TO MAKE HIS APPEARANCE.
TMP
CHIAKI... WHY DID YOU CHECKMATE THAT PAINTING?
WHAT AM I SUPPOSED TO DO?
SHOULD I GET ANGRY AT YOU, OR SHOULD I FORGIVE YOU?
REEL
KLASP

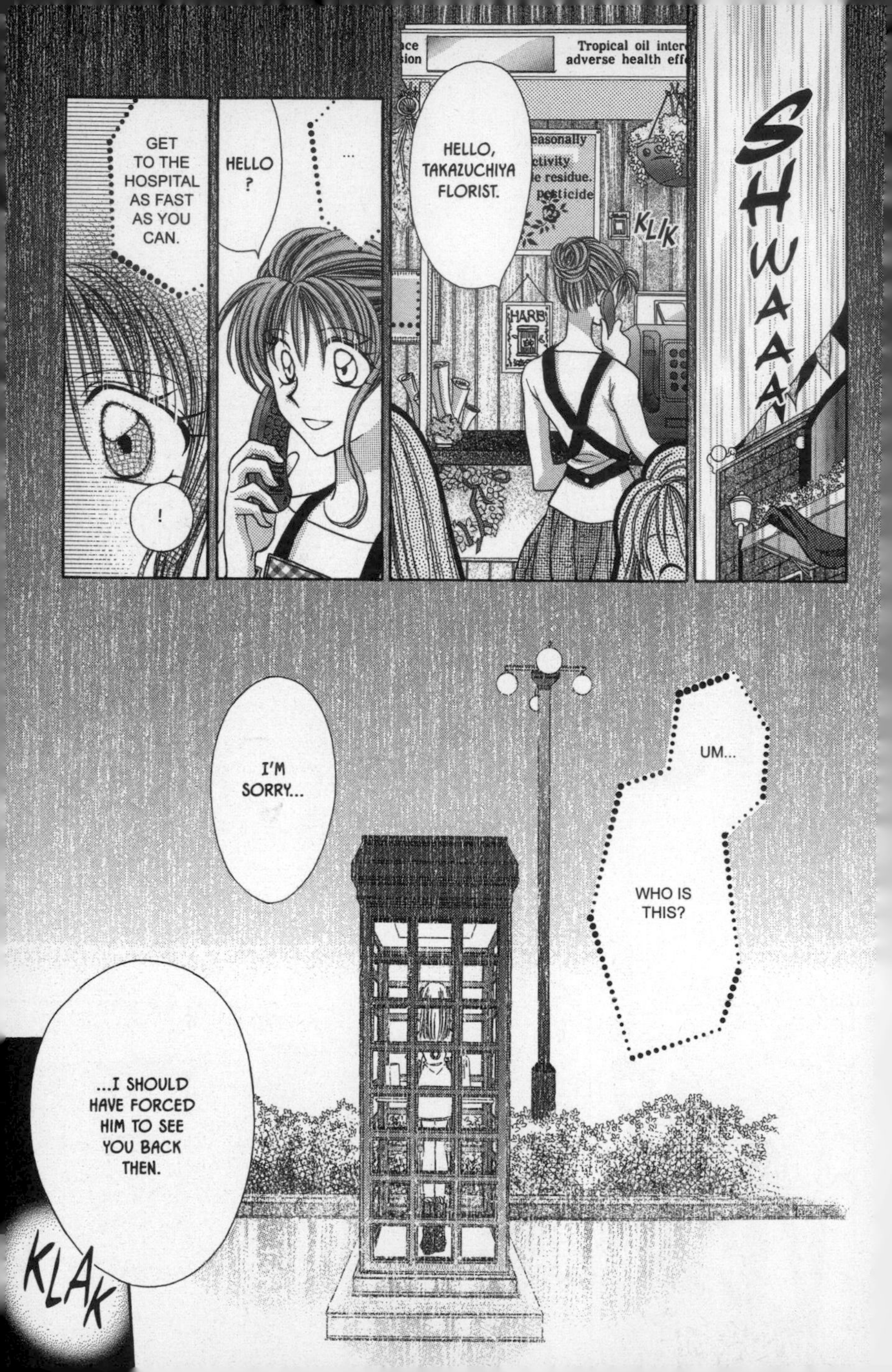
SHWAAA
HELLO, TAKAZUCHIYA FLORIST.
KLIK
HELLO ?
...
GET TO THE HOSPITAL AS FAST AS YOU CAN.
!
UM...
WHO IS THIS?
I'M SORRY...
...I SHOULD HAVE FORCED HIM TO SEE YOU BACK THEN.
KLAK

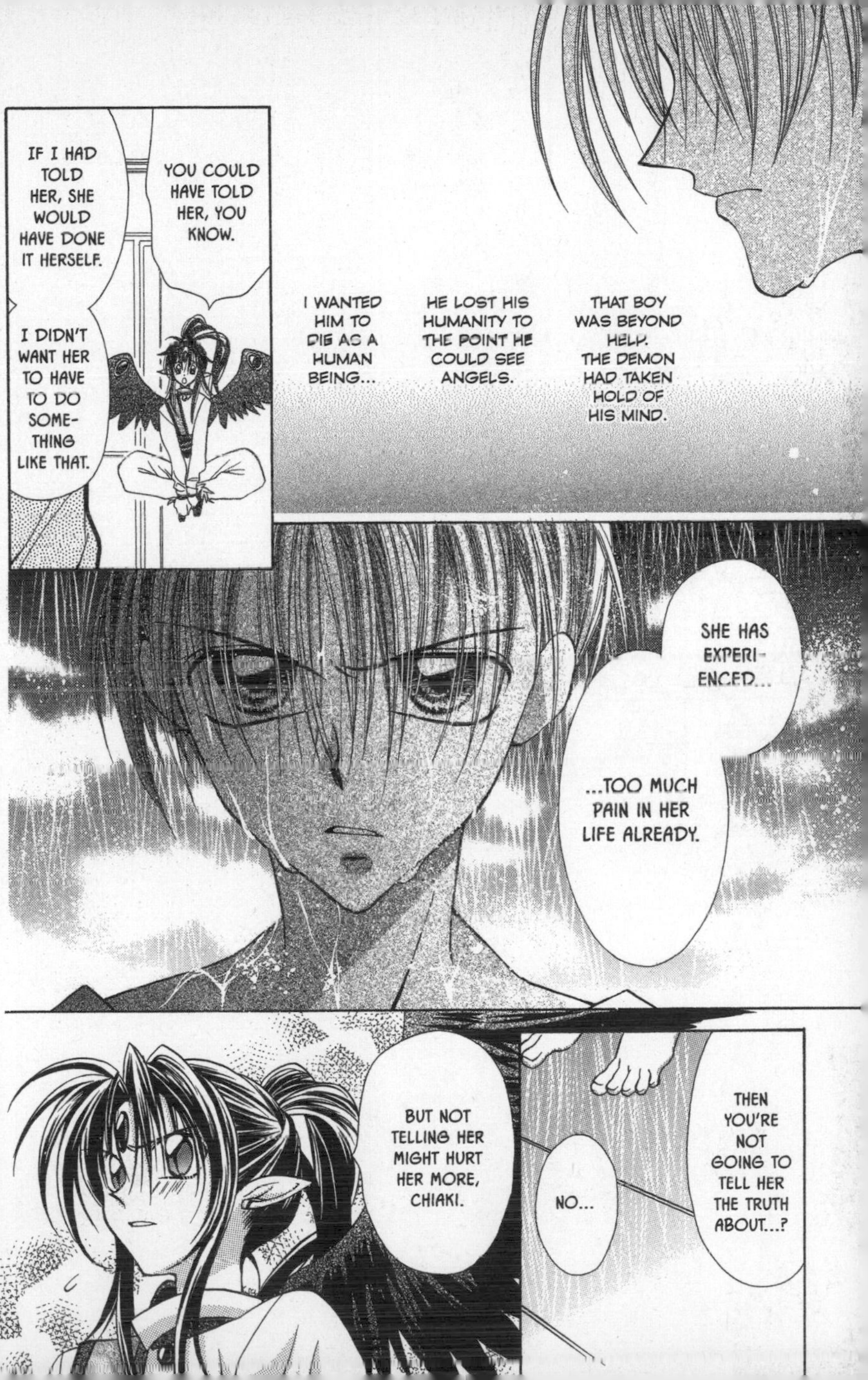
THAT BOY WAS BEYOND HELP. THE DEMON HAD TAKEN HOLD OF HIS MIND.
HE LOST HIS HUMANITY TO THE POINT HE COULD SEE ANGELS.
I WANTED HIM TO DIE AS A HUMAN BEING...
YOU COULD HAVE TOLD HER, YOU KNOW.
IF I HAD TOLD HER, SHE WOULD HAVE DONE IT HERSELF.
I DIDN'T WANT HER TO HAVE TO DO SOME-THING LIKE THAT.
SHE HAS EXPERI-ENCED...
...TOO MUCH PAIN IN HER LIFE ALREADY.
THEN YOU'RE NOT GOING TO TELL HER THE TRUTH ABOUT...?
NO...
BUT NOT TELLING HER MIGHT HURT HER MORE, CHIAKI.

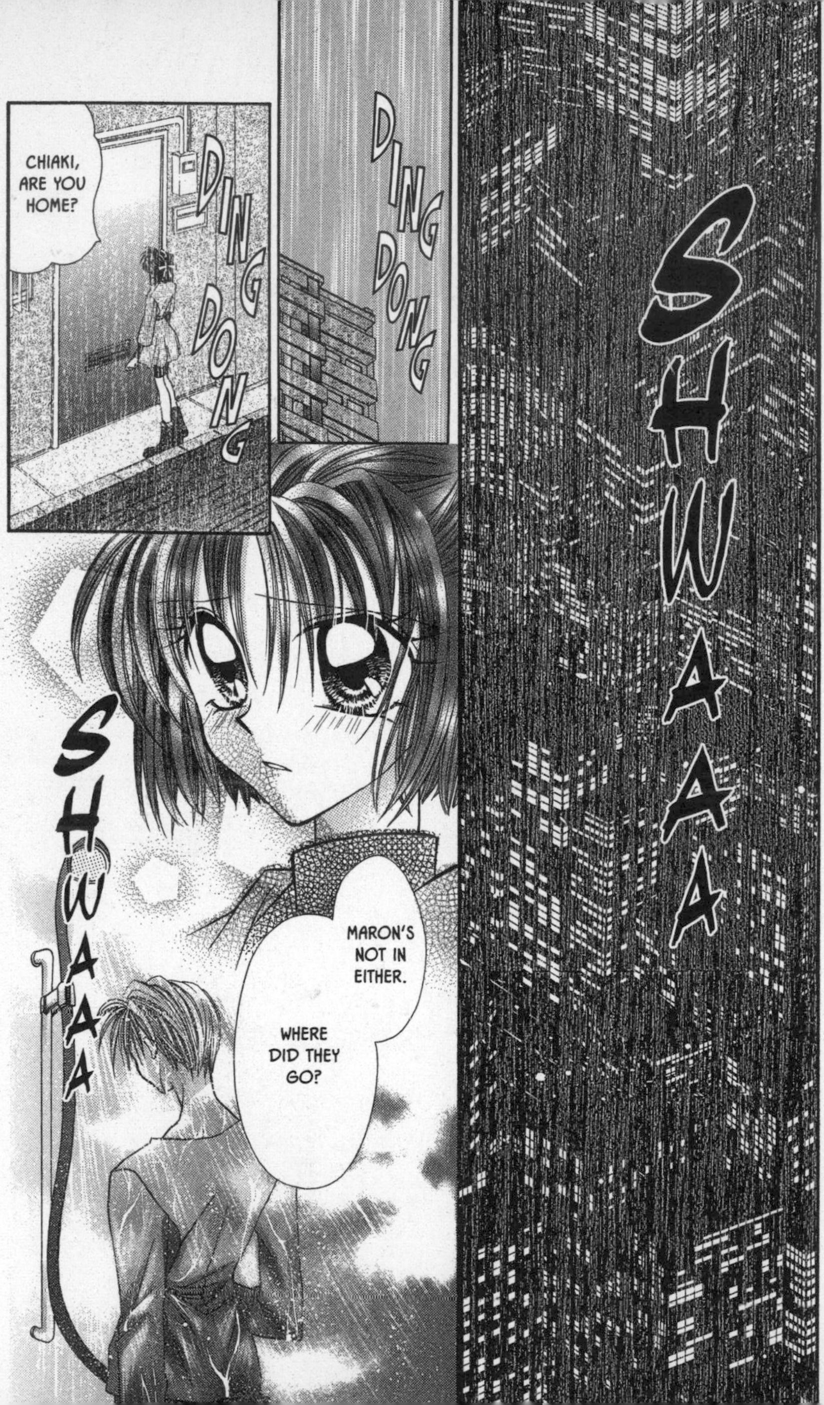
SHUWAAA
DING DONG
CHIAKI, ARE YOU HOME?
DING DONG
SHUWAAA
MARON'S NOT IN EITHER.
WHERE DID THEY GO?

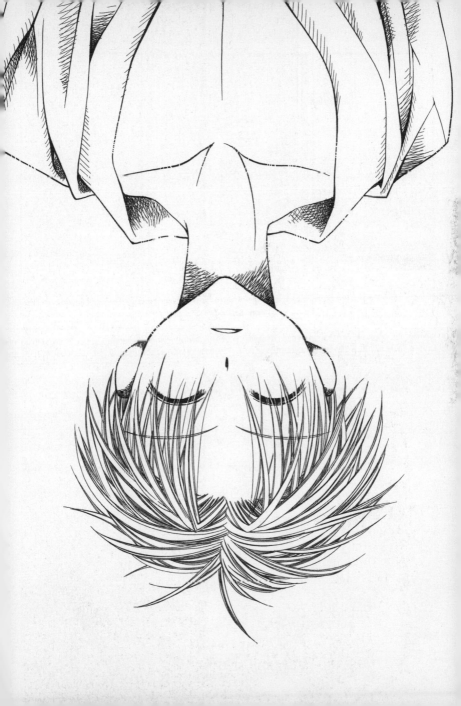

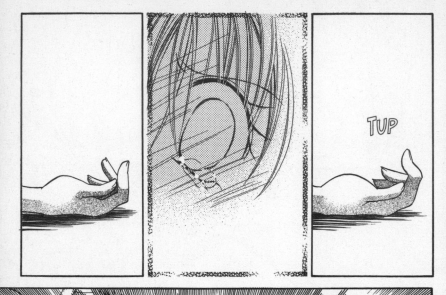

TUP

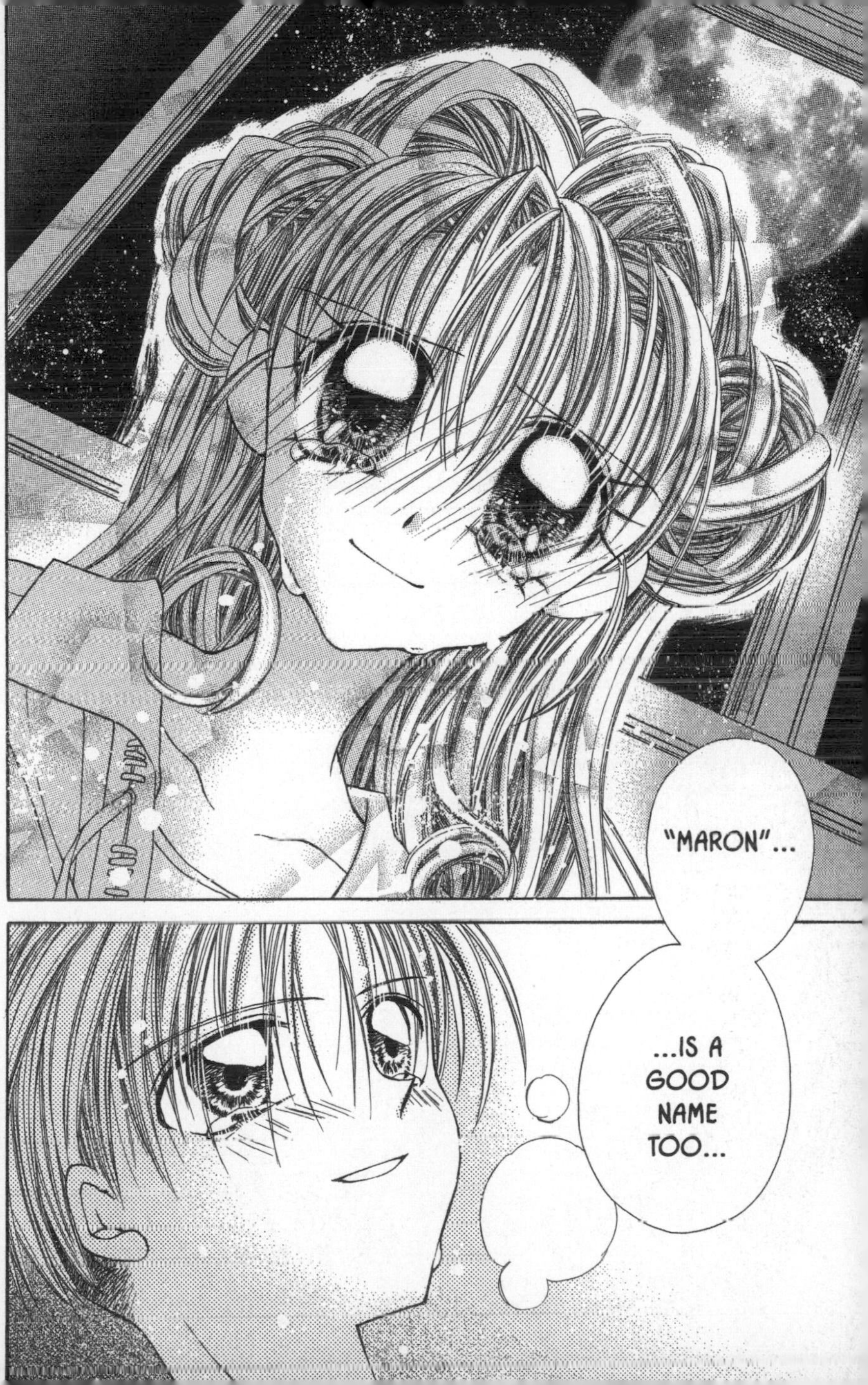
"MARON"...
...IS A GOOD NAME TOO...

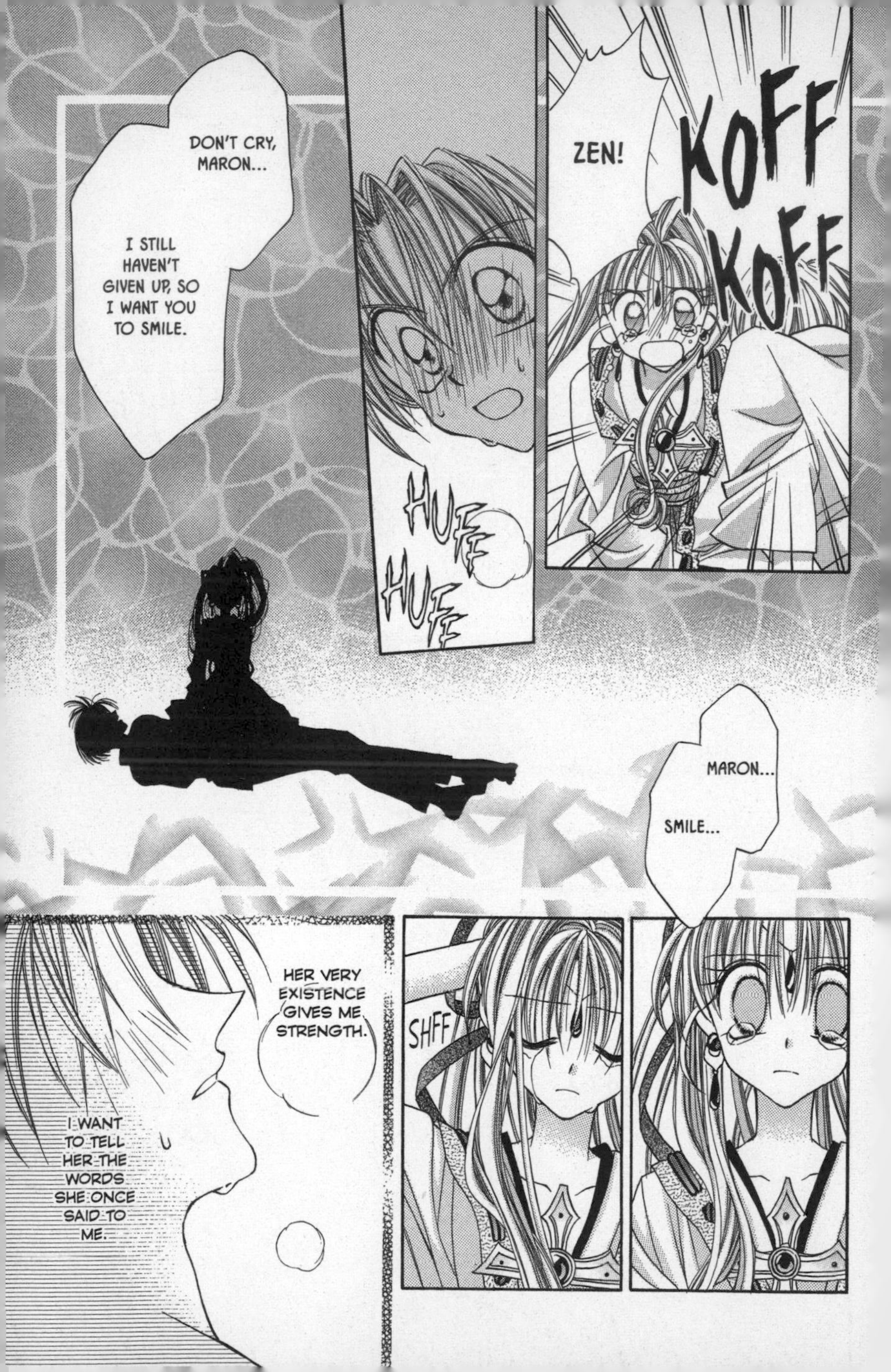
ZEN!
KOFF KOFF
HUFF HUFF
DON'T CRY, MARON...
I STILL HAVEN'T GIVEN UP, SO I WANT YOU TO SMILE.
MARON...
SMILE...
SHFF
HER VERY EXISTENCE GIVES ME STRENGTH.
I WANT TO TELL HER THE WORDS SHE ONCE SAID TO ME.

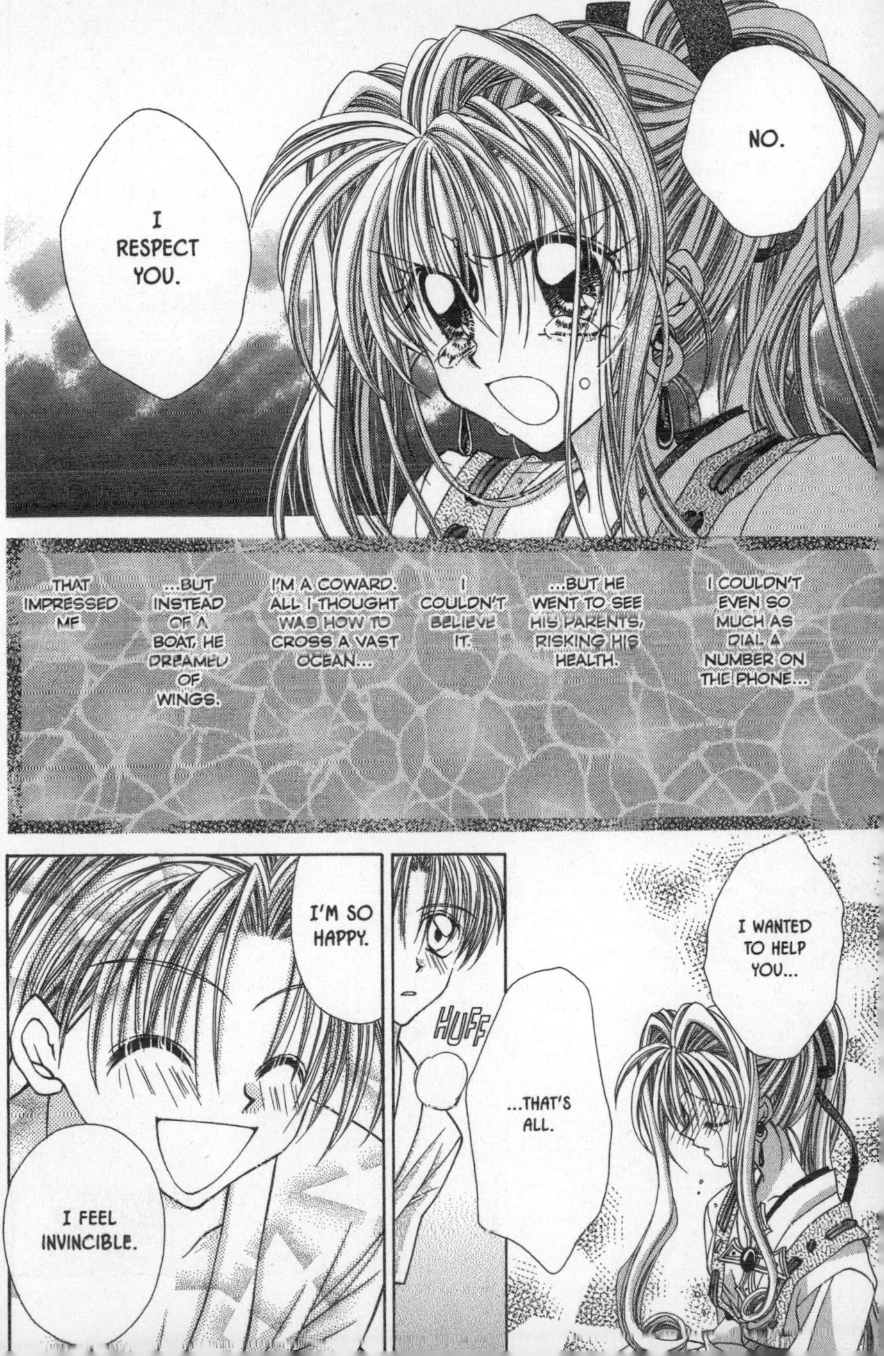
NO.
I RESPECT YOU.
I COULDN'T EVEN SO MUCH AS DIAL A NUMBER ON THE PHONE...
...BUT HE WENT TO SEE HIS PARENTS, RISKING HIS HEALTH.
I COULDN'T BELIEVE IT.
I'M A COWARD. ALL I THOUGHT WAS HOW TO CROSS A VAST OCEAN...
...BUT INSTEAD OF A BOAT, HE DREAMED OF WINGS.
THAT IMPRESSED ME.
I WANTED TO HELP YOU...
...THAT'S ALL.
HUFF
I'M SO HAPPY.
I FEEL INVINCIBLE.

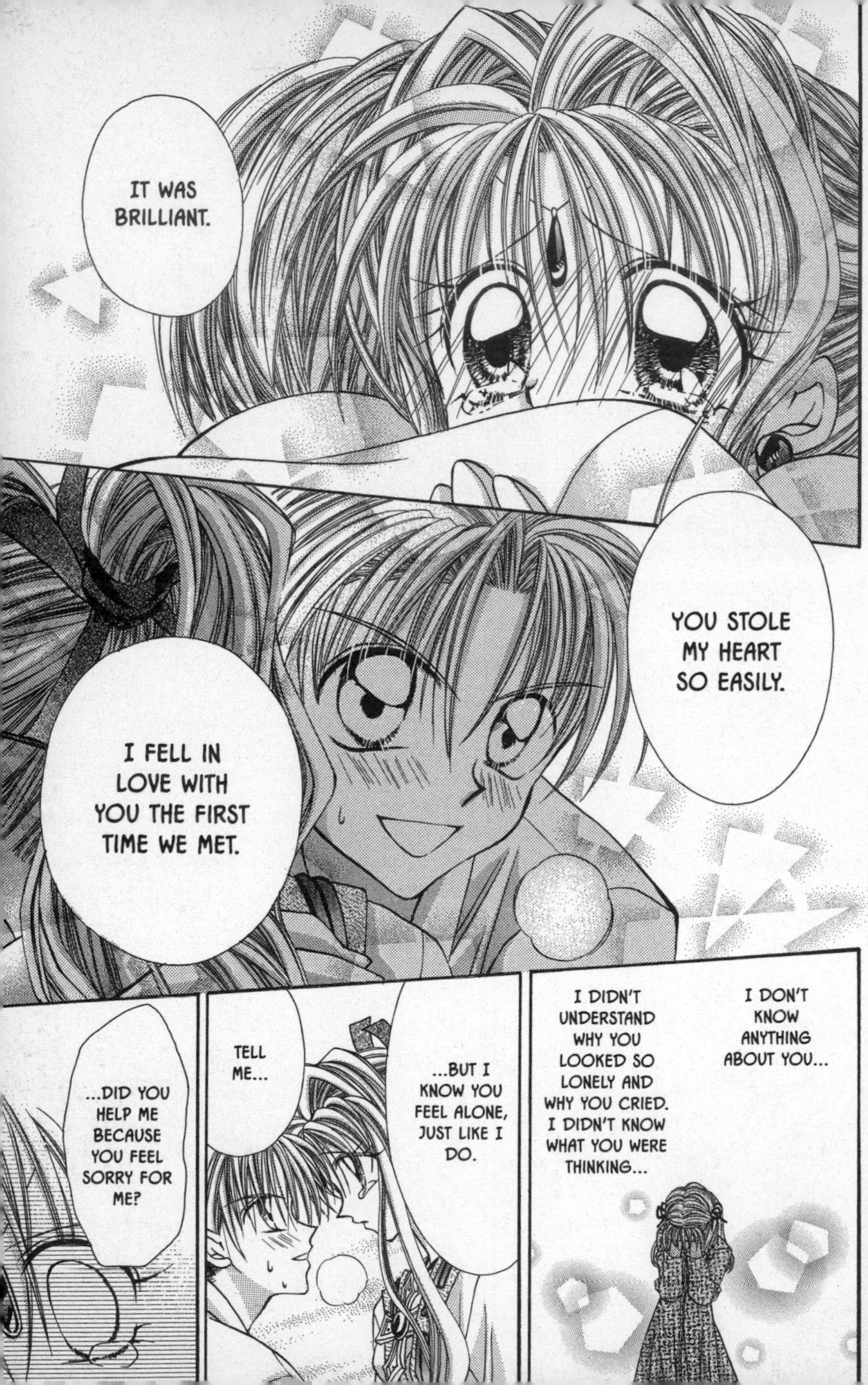
IT WAS BRILLIANT.
YOU STOLE MY HEART SO EASILY.
I FELL IN LOVE WITH YOU THE FIRST TIME WE MET.
I DON'T KNOW ANYTHING ABOUT YOU...
I DIDN'T UNDERSTAND WHY YOU LOOKED SO LONELY AND WHY YOU CRIED. I DIDN'T KNOW WHAT YOU WERE THINKING...
...BUT I KNOW YOU FEEL ALONE, JUST LIKE I DO.
TELL ME...
...DID YOU HELP ME BECAUSE YOU FEEL SORRY FOR ME?

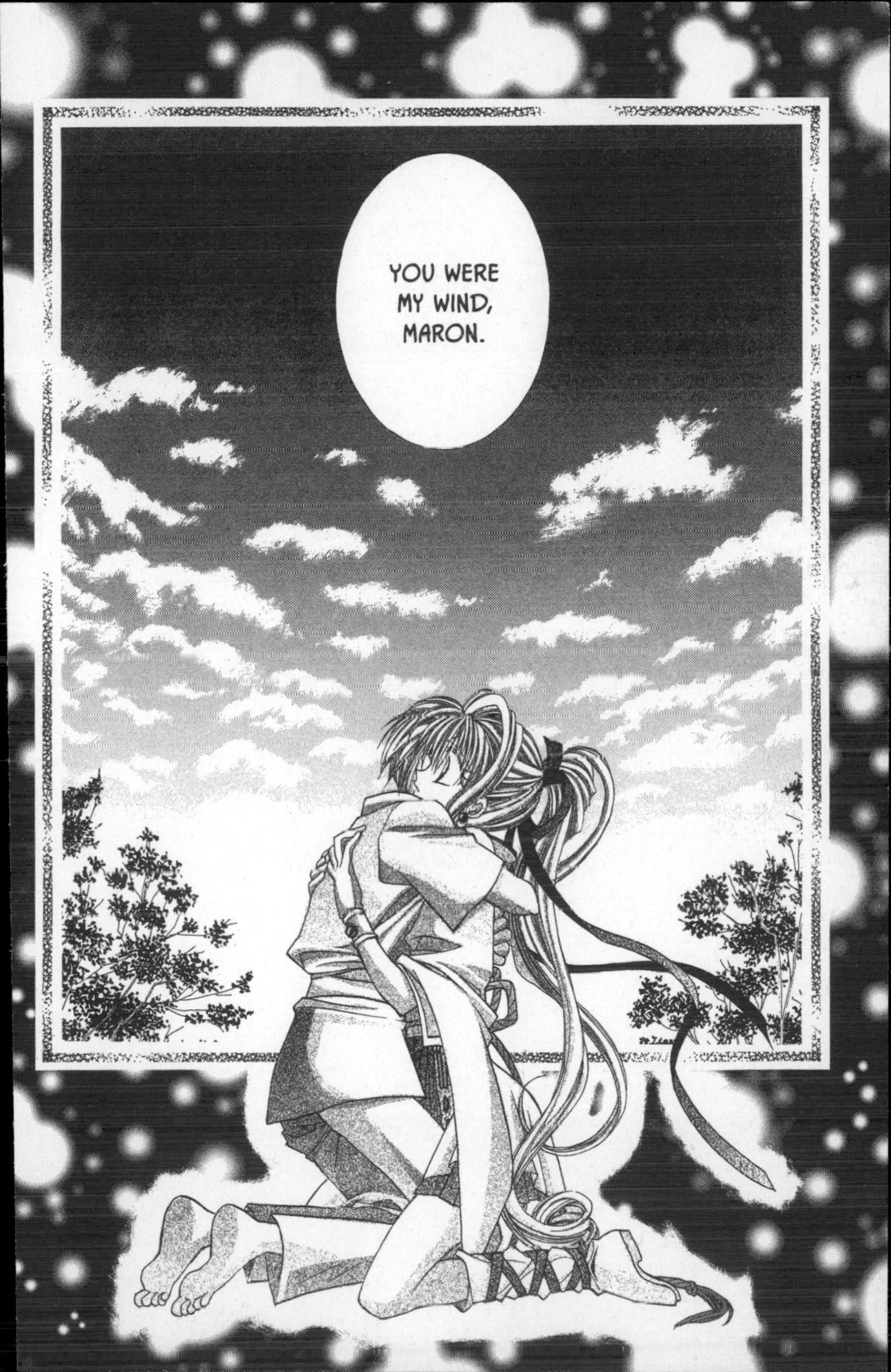
YOU WERE MY WIND, MARON.

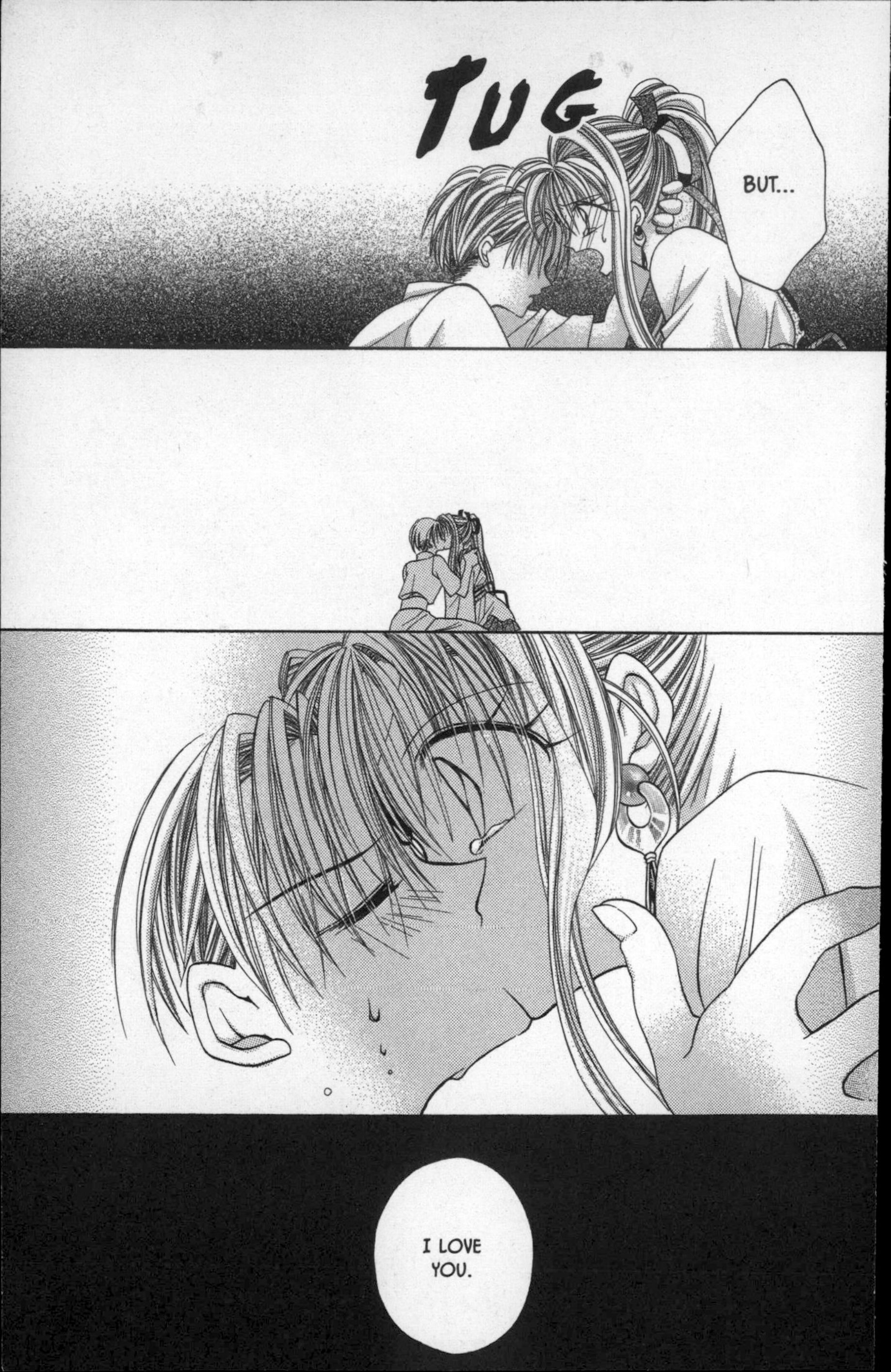
BUT...
TUG
I LOVE YOU.

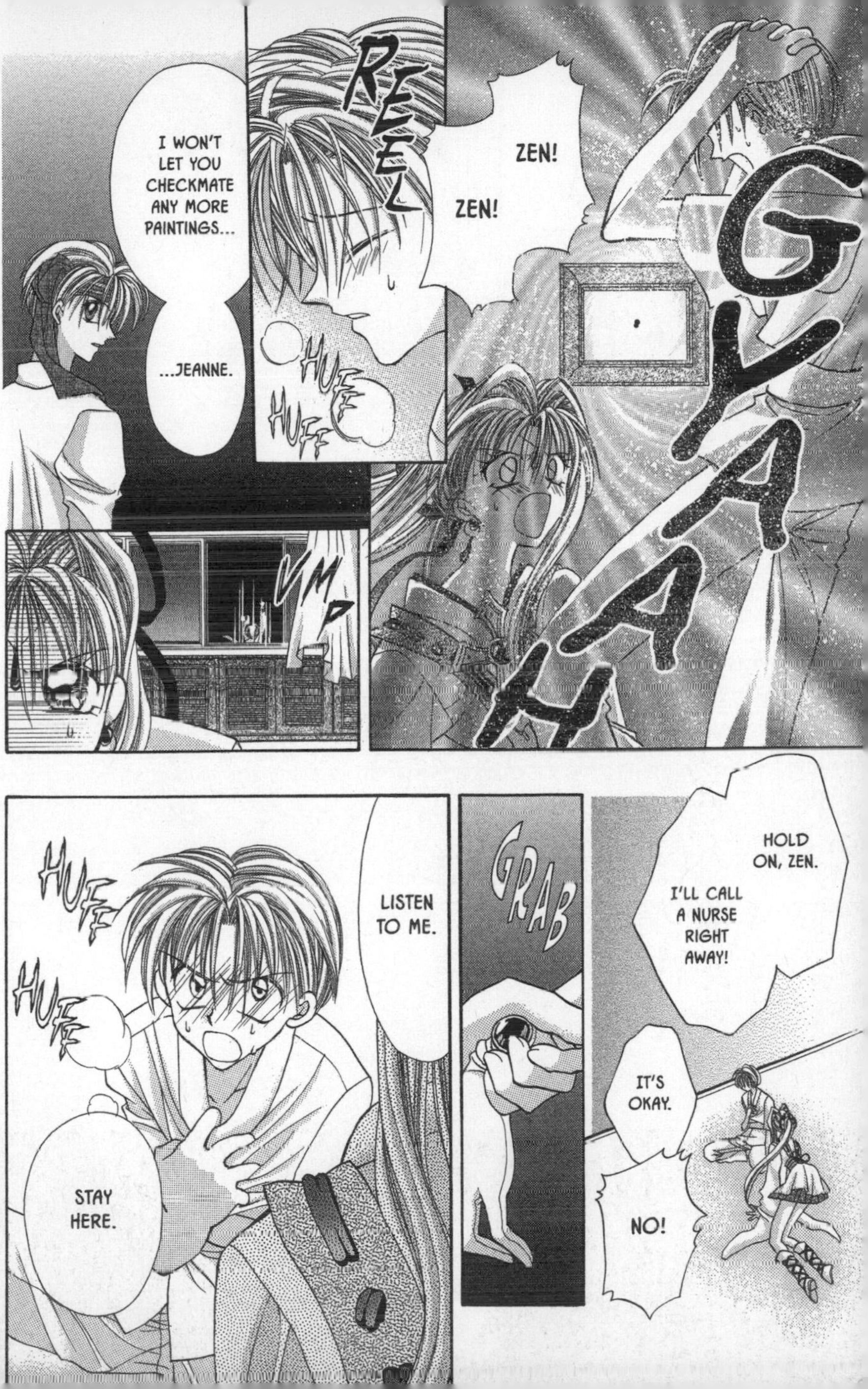
ZEN!
ZEN!
GYAAHH
REEL
HUFF HUFF
I WON'T LET YOU CHECKMATE ANY MORE PAINTINGS...
...JEANNE.
VMP
HOLD ON, ZEN.
I'LL CALL A NURSE RIGHT AWAY!
IT'S OKAY.
NO!
GRAB
LISTEN TO ME.
HUFF HUFF
STAY HERE.

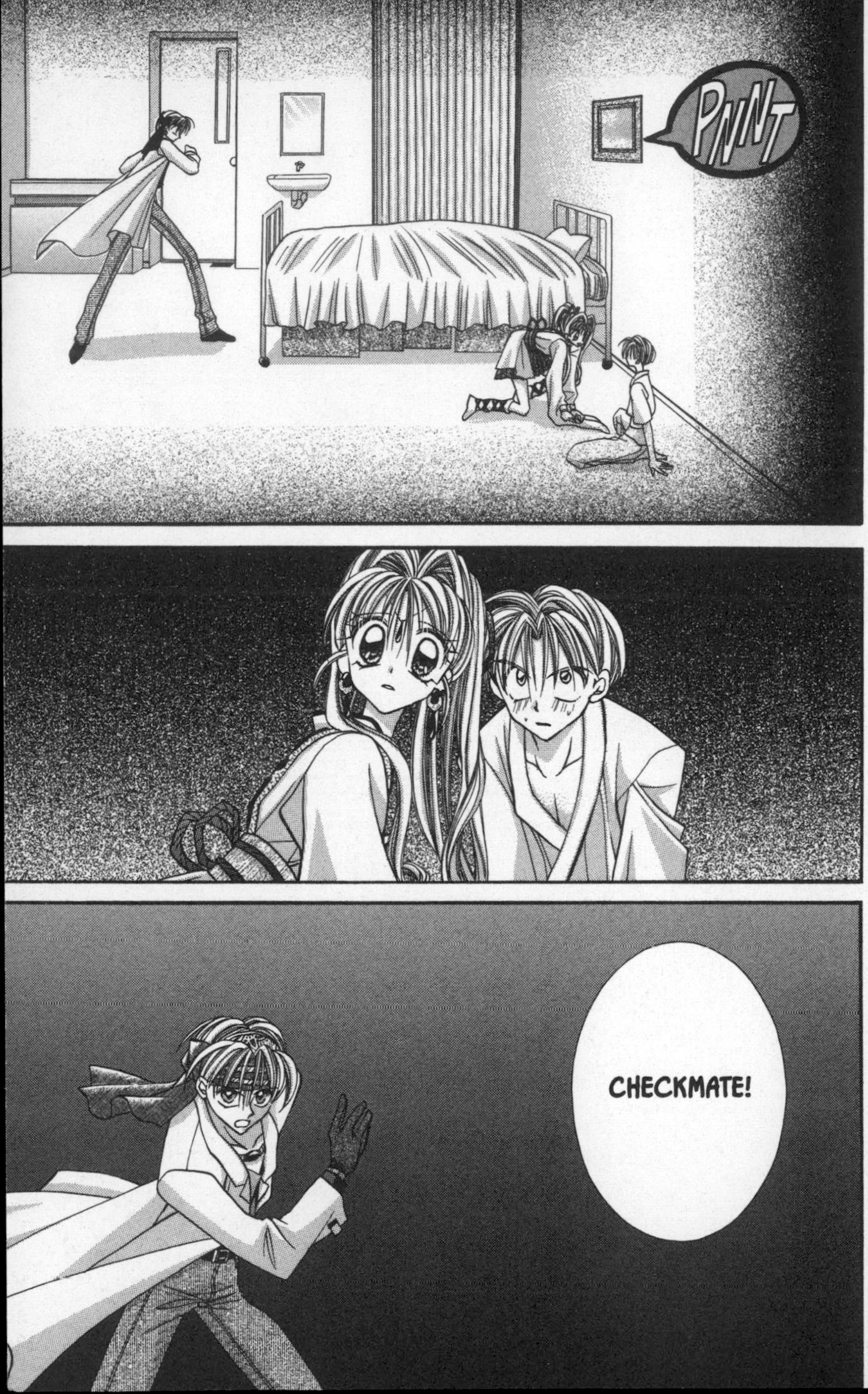
PNINT
CHECKMATE!

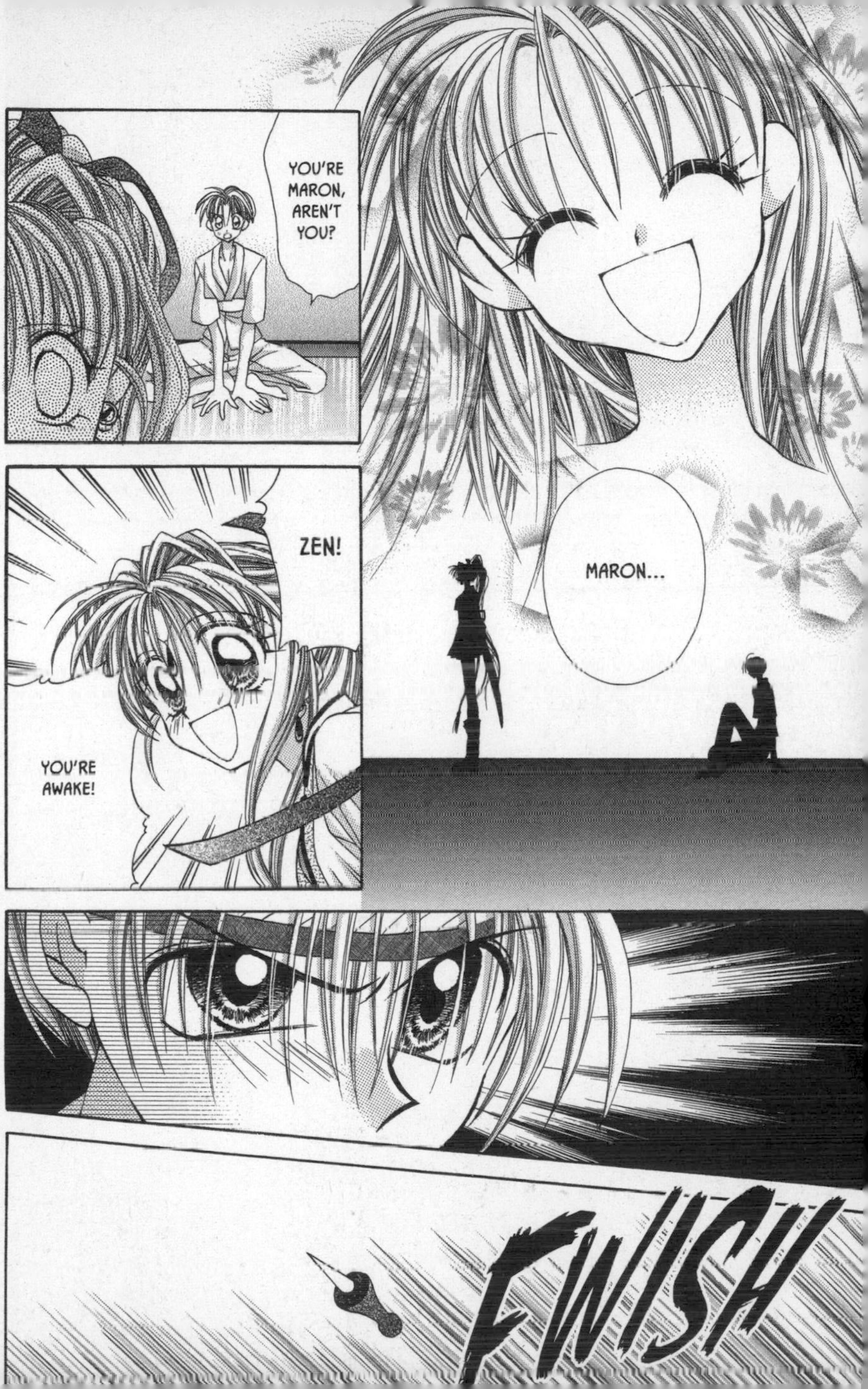
MARON...
YOU'RE MARON, AREN'T YOU?
ZEN!
YOU'RE AWAKE!
FWISH

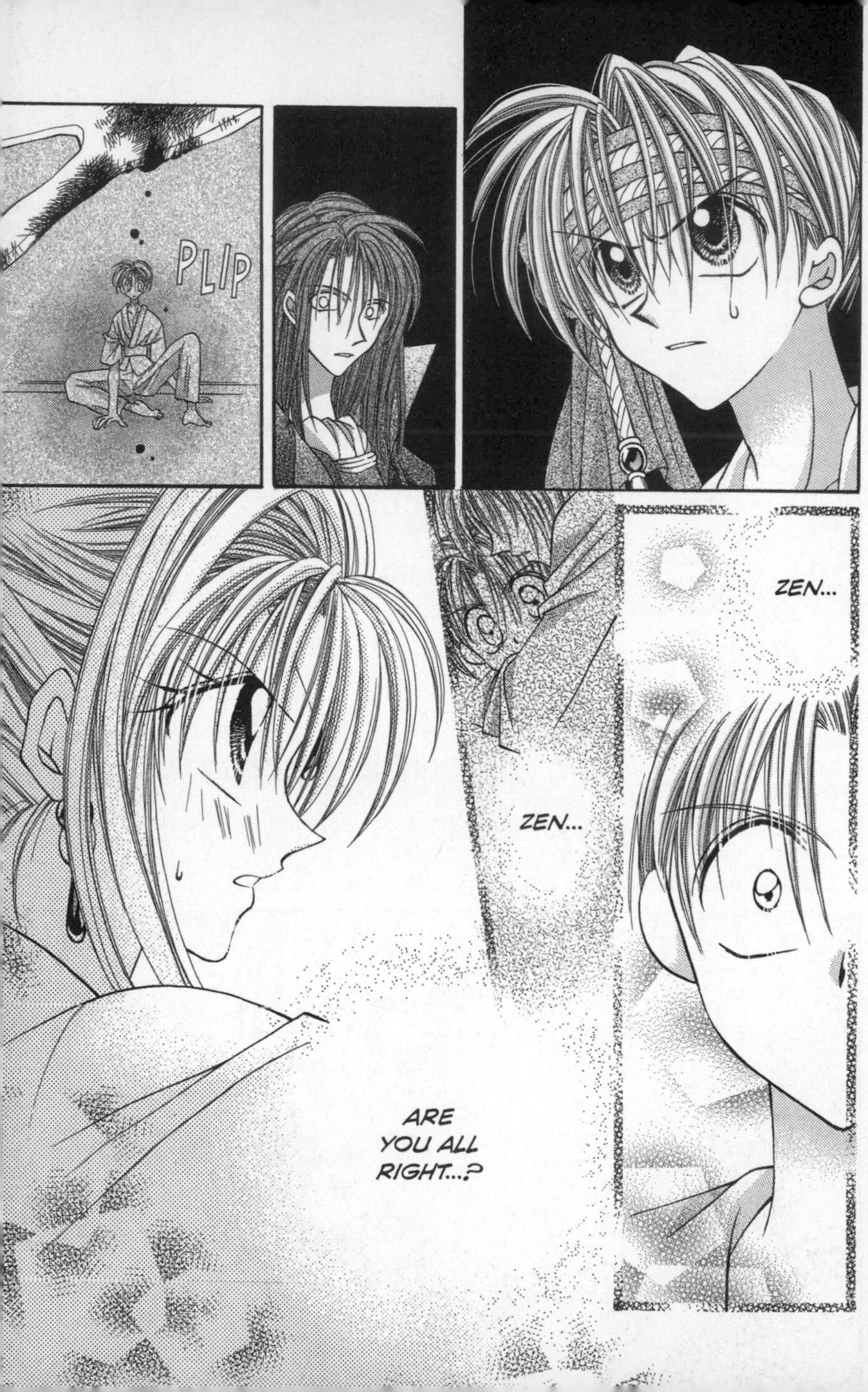
PLIP
ZEN...
ZEN...
ARE YOU ALL RIGHT...?

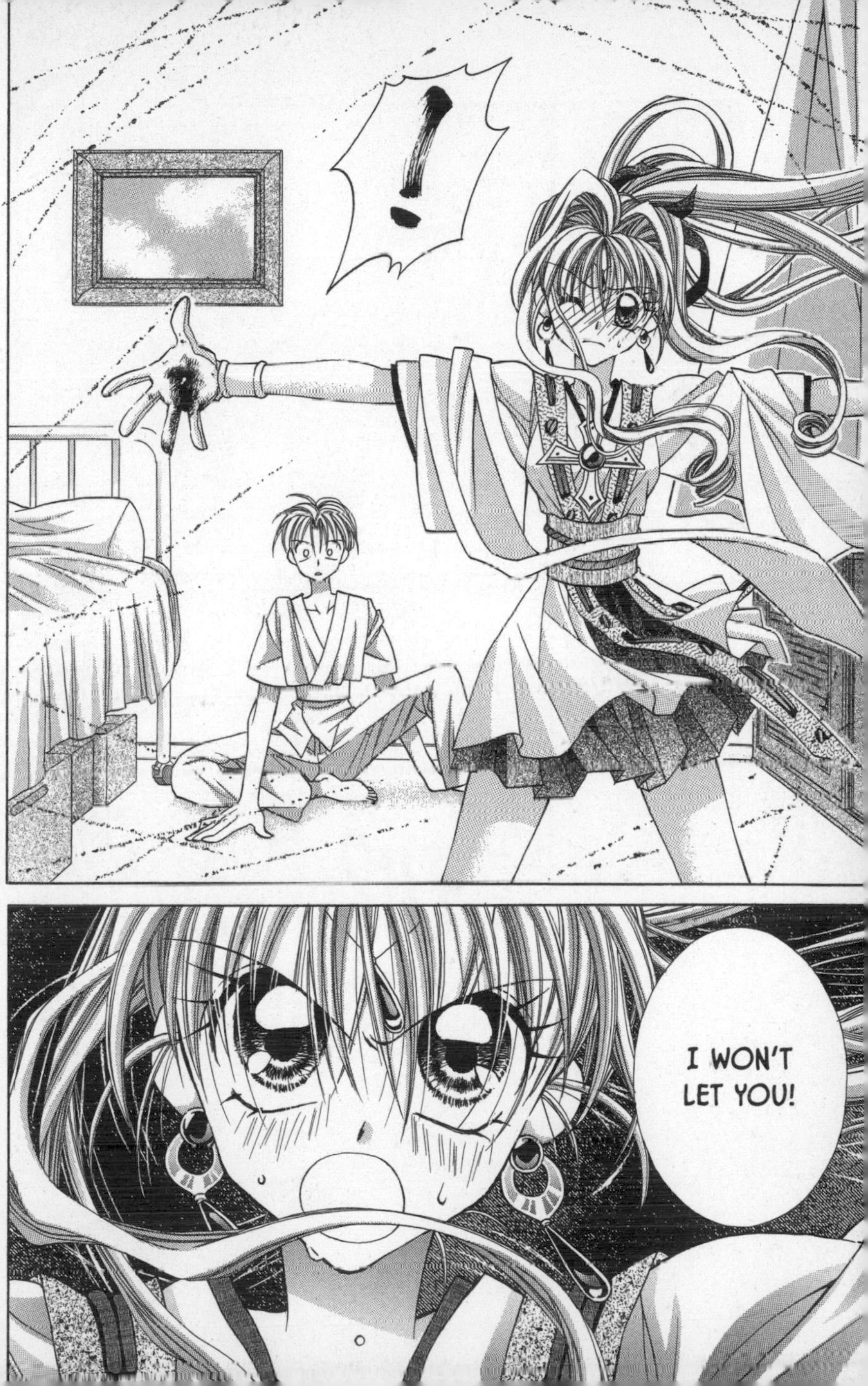
!
I WON'T LET YOU!

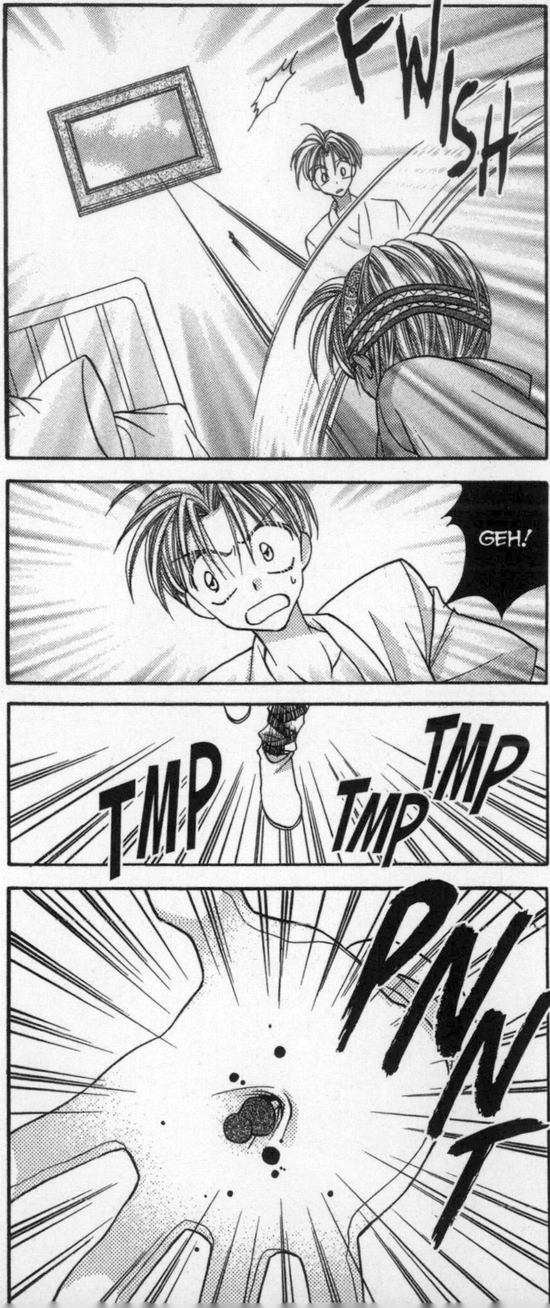
FWISH
GEH!
TMP
TMP
TMP
PNNT

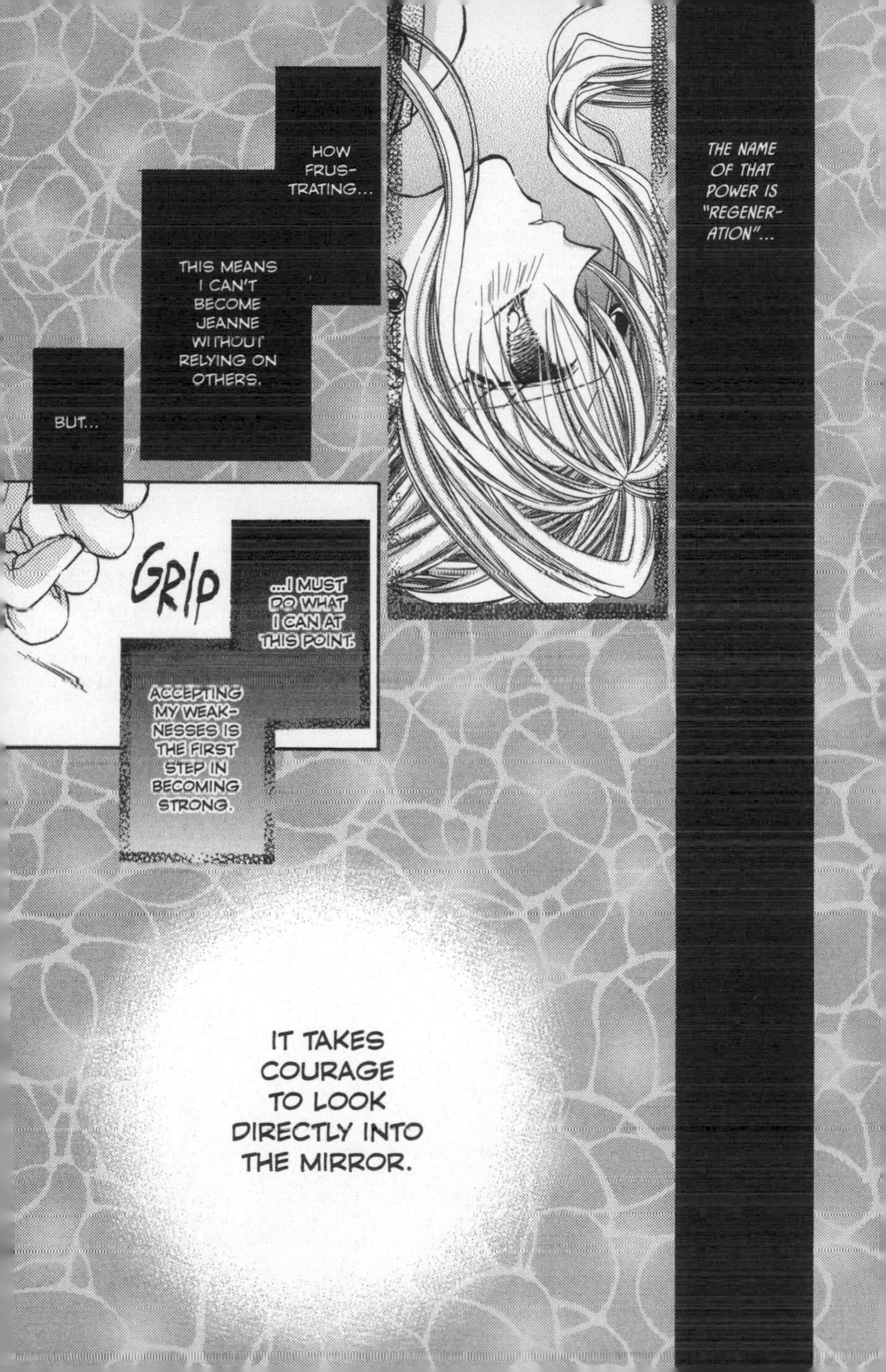
THE NAME OF THAT POWER IS "REGENERATION"...
HOW FRUSTRATING...
THIS MEANS I CAN'T BECOME JEANNE WITHOUT RELYING ON OTHERS.
BUT...
GRIP
...I MUST DO WHAT I CAN AT THIS POINT.
ACCEPTING MY WEAKNESSES IS THE FIRST STEP IN BECOMING STRONG.
IT TAKES COURAGE TO LOOK DIRECTLY INTO THE MIRROR.

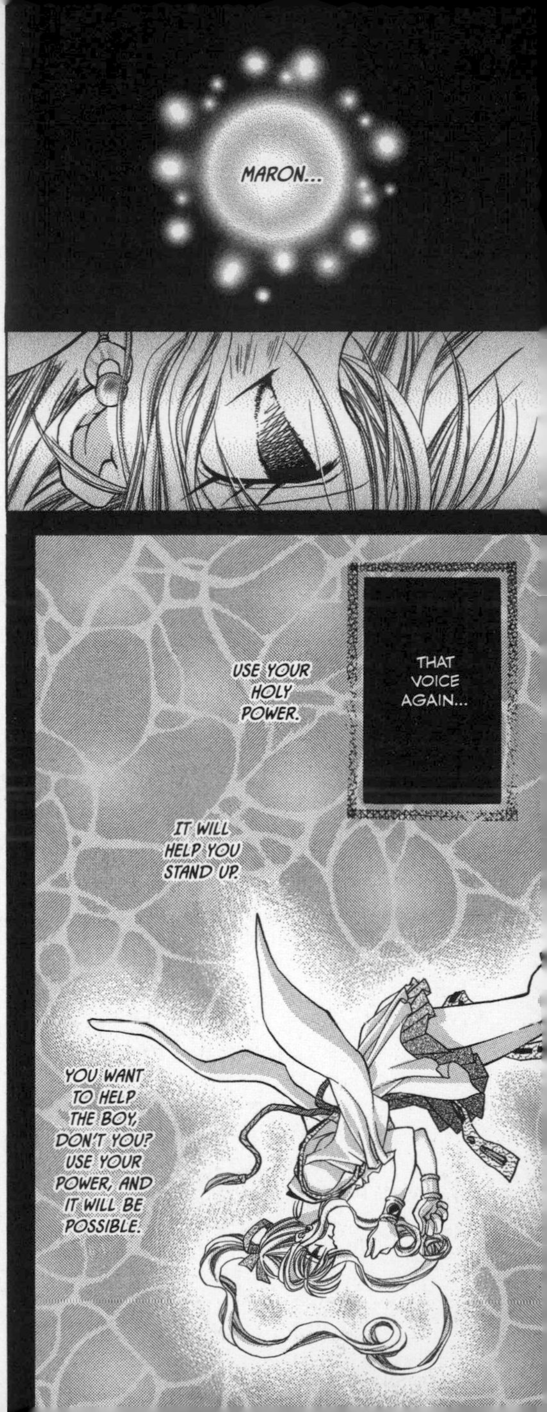
MARON...
THAT VOICE AGAIN...
USE YOUR HOLY POWER.
IT WILL HELP YOU STAND UP.
YOU WANT TO HELP THE BOY, DON'T YOU? USE YOUR POWER, AND IT WILL BE POSSIBLE.

PHANTOM THIEF JEANNE

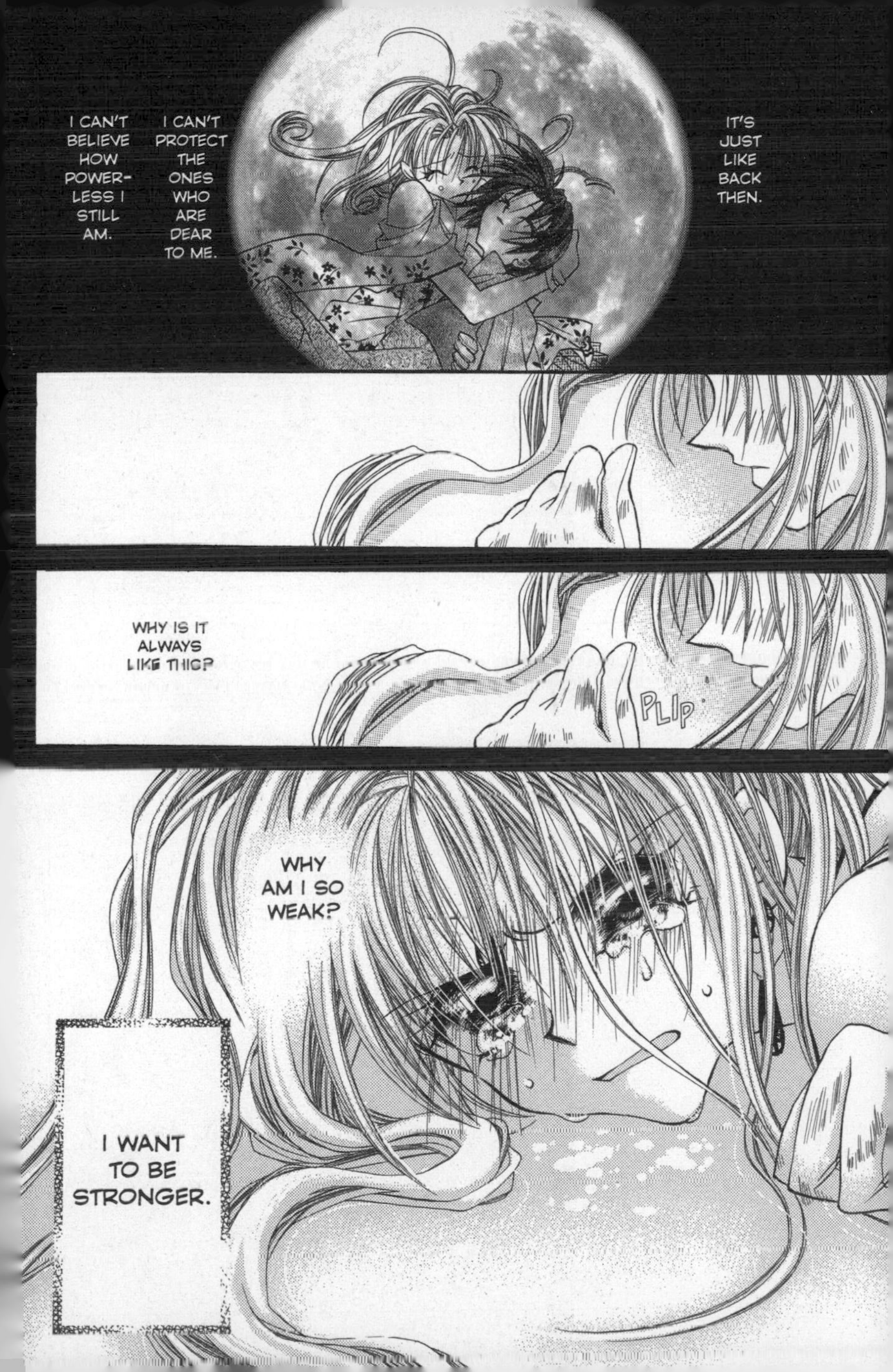
IT'S JUST LIKE BACK THEN.
I CAN'T PROTECT THE ONES WHO ARE DEAR TO ME.
I CAN'T BELIEVE HOW POWER-LESS I STILL AM.
PLIP
WHY IS IT ALWAYS LIKE THIS?
WHY AM I SO WEAK?
I WANT TO BE STRONGER.

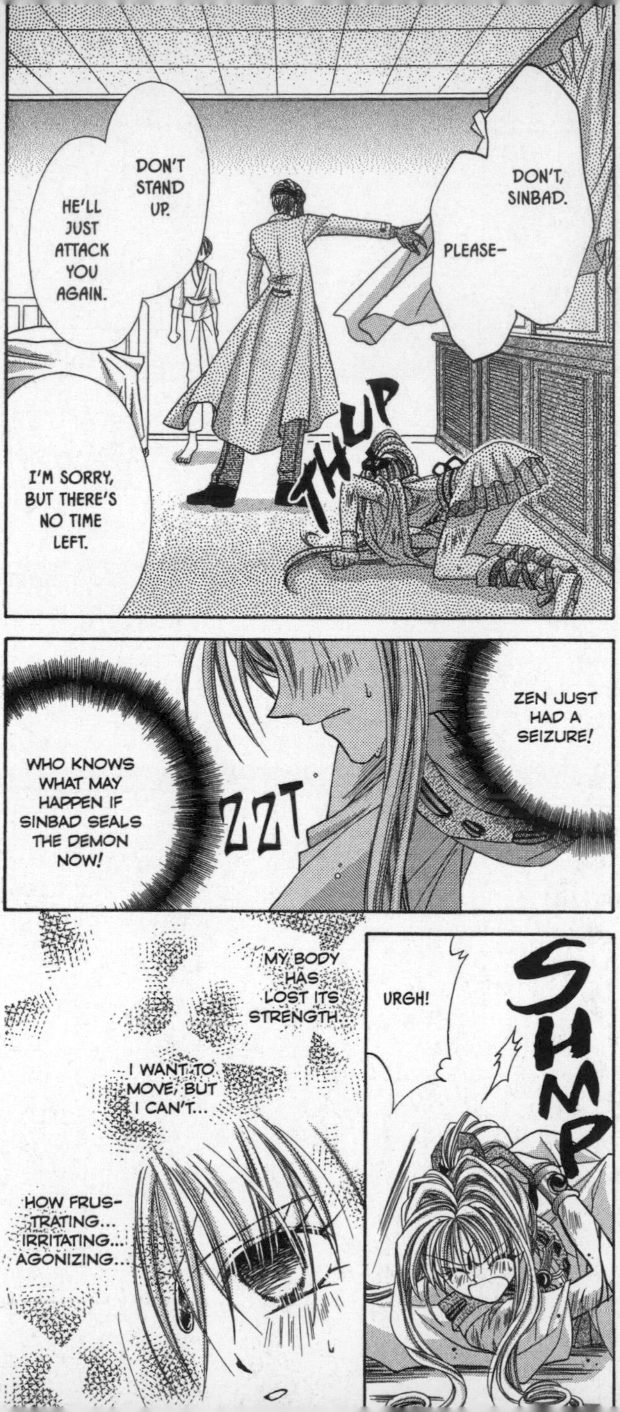
DON'T, SINBAD.
PLEASE–
DON'T STAND UP.
HE'LL JUST ATTACK YOU AGAIN.
THUP
I'M SORRY, BUT THERE'S NO TIME LEFT.
ZEN JUST HAD A SEIZURE!
ZZT
WHO KNOWS WHAT MAY HAPPEN IF SINBAD SEALS THE DEMON NOW!
SHMP
URGH!
MY BODY HAS LOST ITS STRENGTH.
I WANT TO MOVE, BUT I CAN'T...
HOW FRUS-TRATING... IRRITATING... AGONIZING...

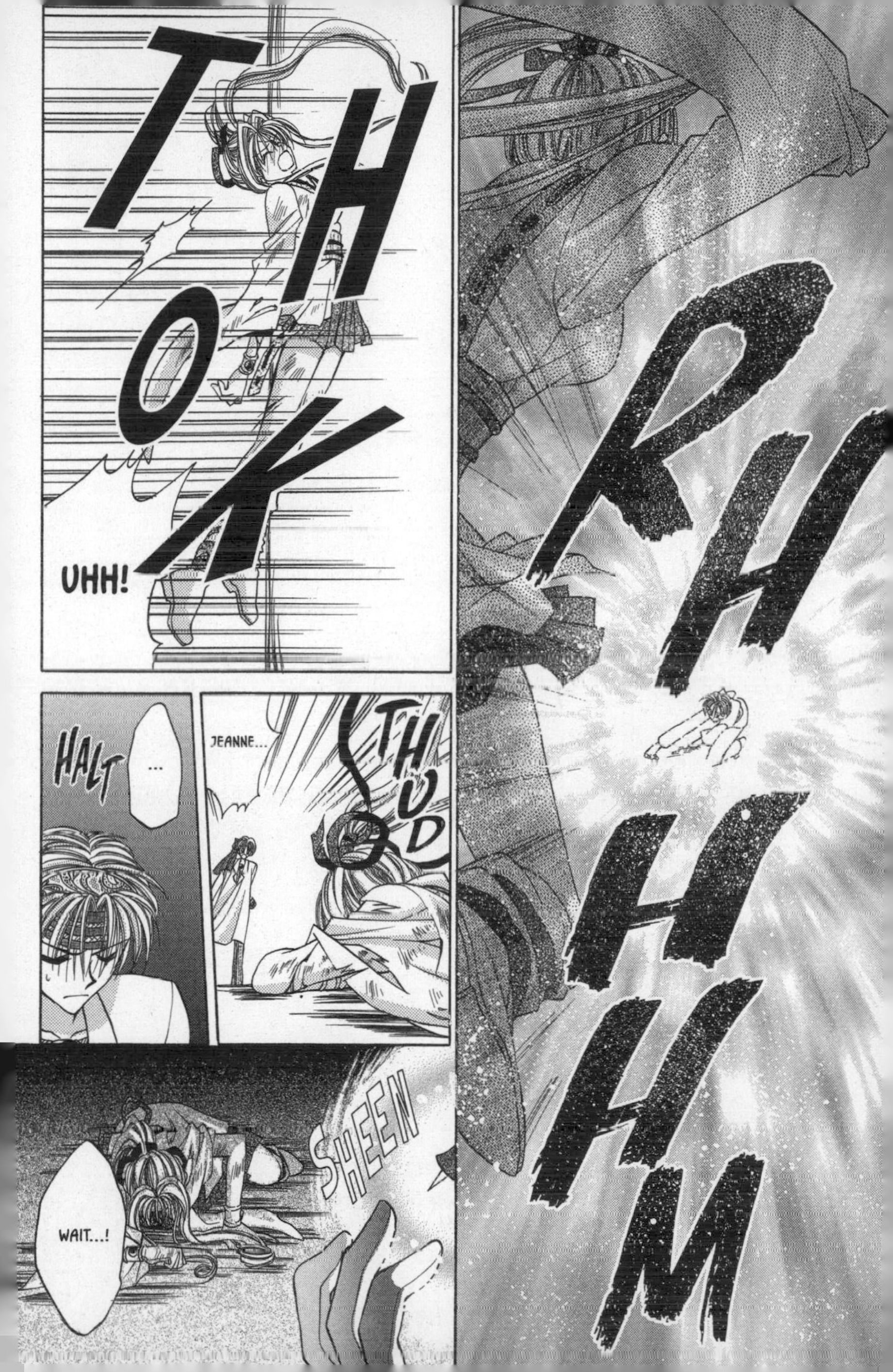
RHHHM
THOK
UHH!
JEANNE...
THUD
HALT
...
SHEEN
WAIT...!

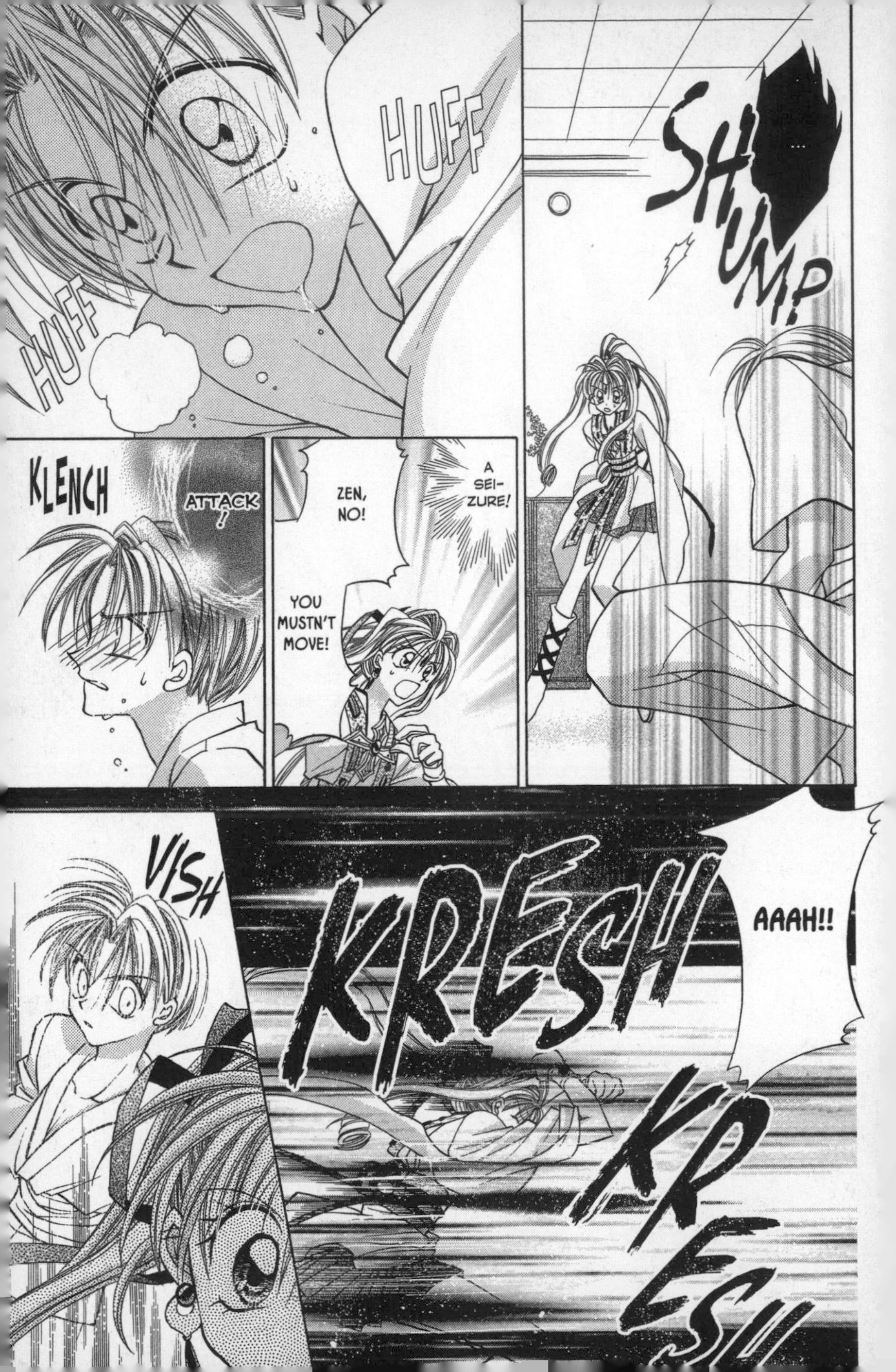

SHUMP
...
HUFF
HUFF
A SEI-ZURE!
ZEN, NO!
YOU MUSTN'T MOVE!
KLENCH
ATTACK!
AAAH!!
KRESH
KRESH
VISH

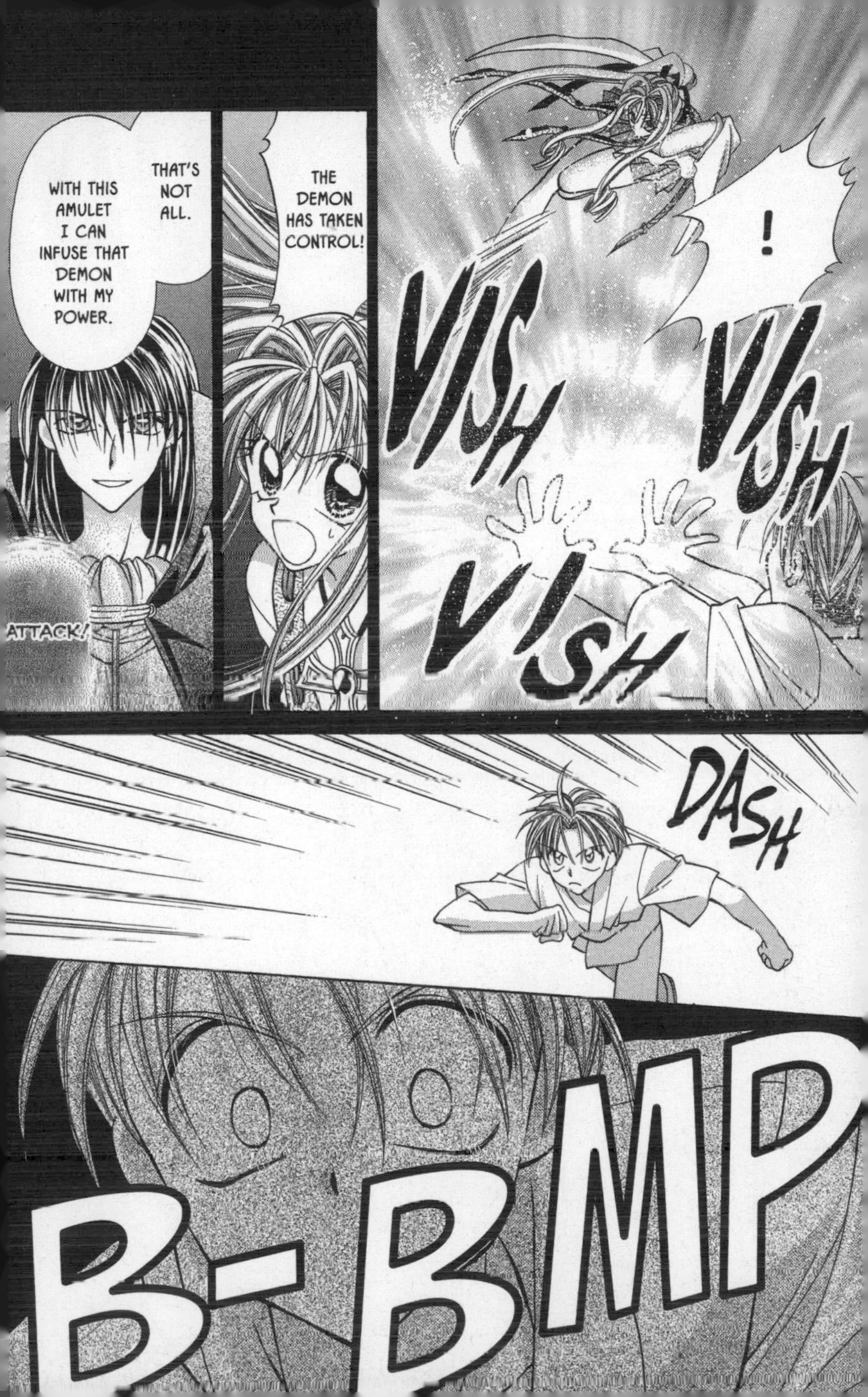
!
VISH
VISH
VISH
THE DEMON HAS TAKEN CONTROL!
THAT'S NOT ALL.
WITH THIS AMULET I CAN INFUSE THAT DEMON WITH MY POWER.
ATTACK!
DASH
B-BMP

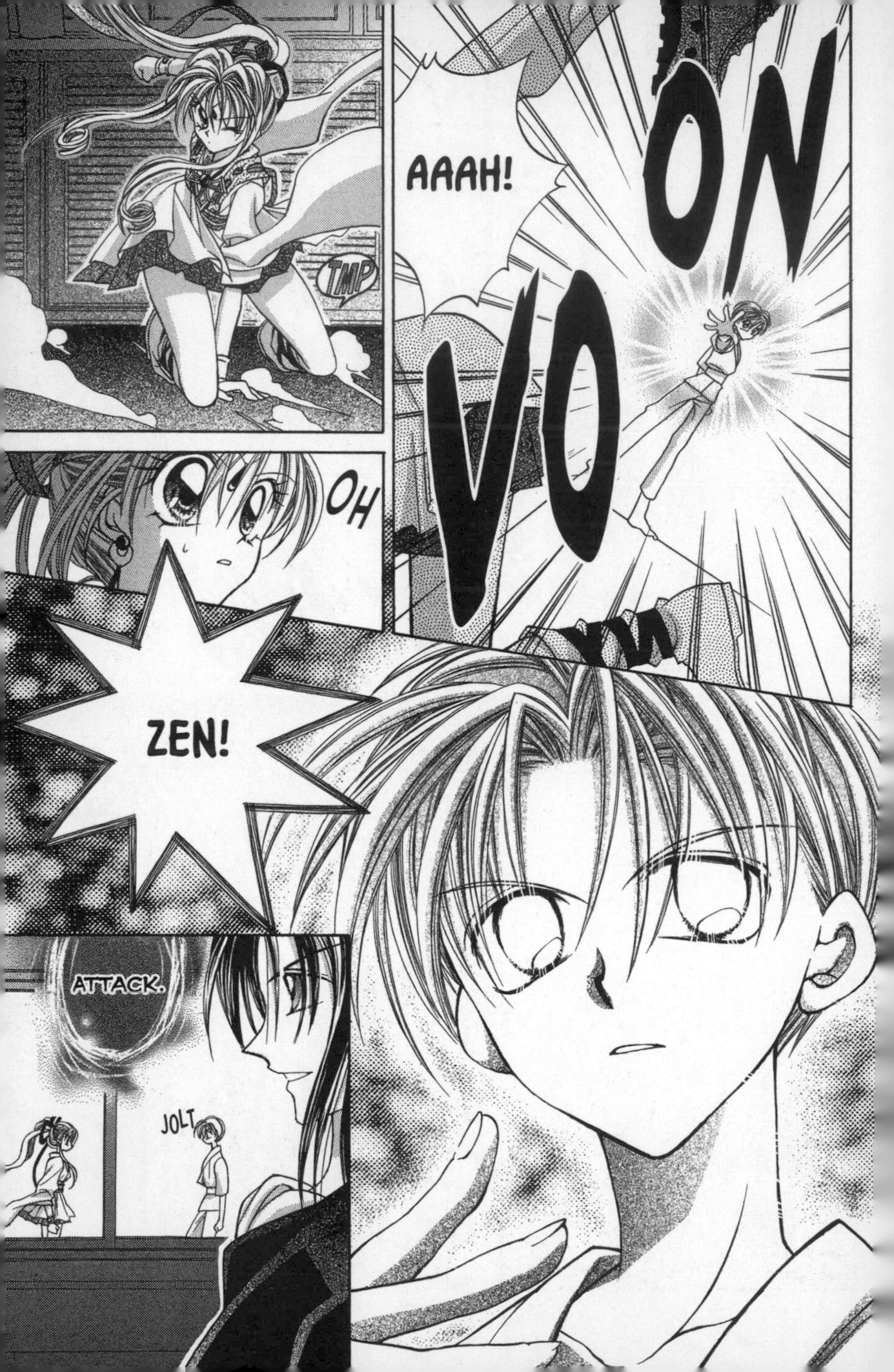
AAAH!
VOON
TMP
OH
ZEN!
ATTACK.
JOLT

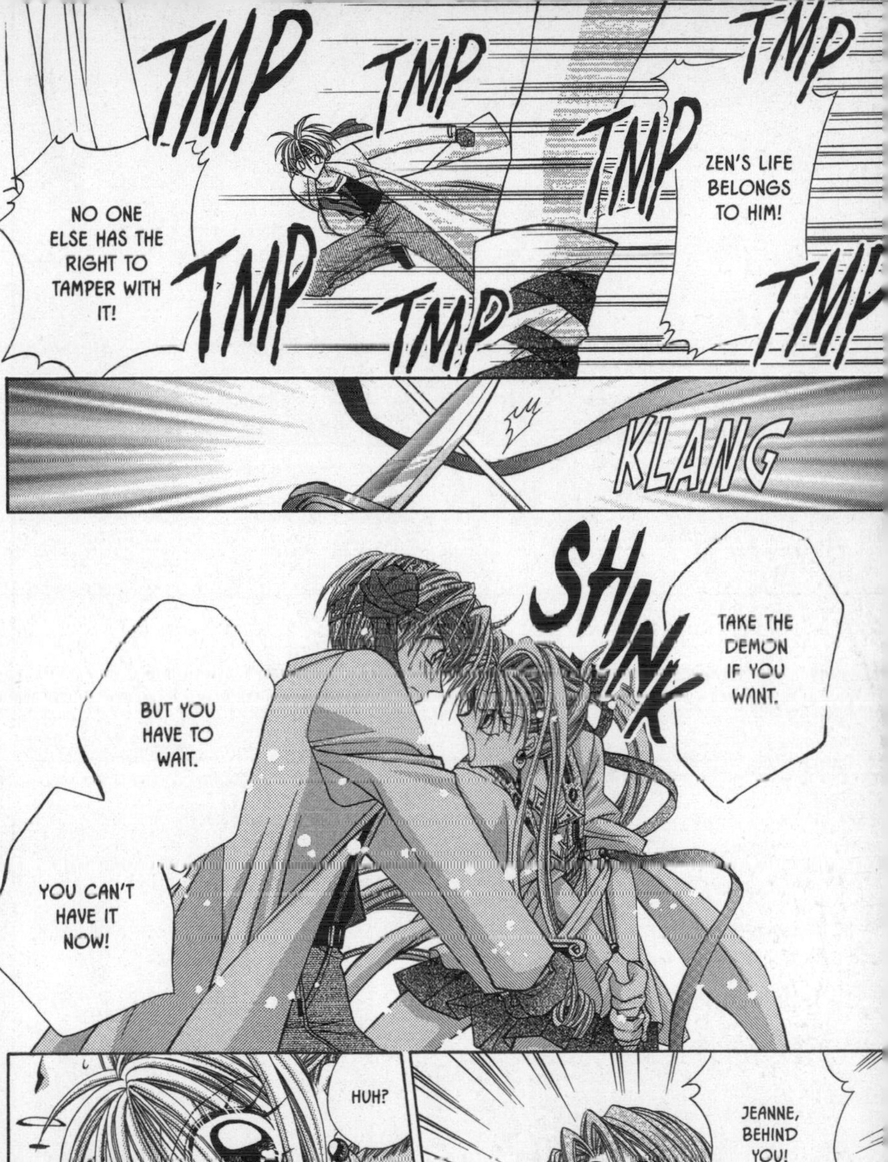
TMP
TMP
ZEN'S LIFE BELONGS TO HIM!
TMP
TMP
TMP
TMP
TMP
NO ONE ELSE HAS THE RIGHT TO TAMPER WITH IT!
KLANG
SHINK
TAKE THE DEMON IF YOU WANT.
BUT YOU HAVE TO WAIT.
YOU CAN'T HAVE IT NOW!
JEANNE, BEHIND YOU!
HUH?

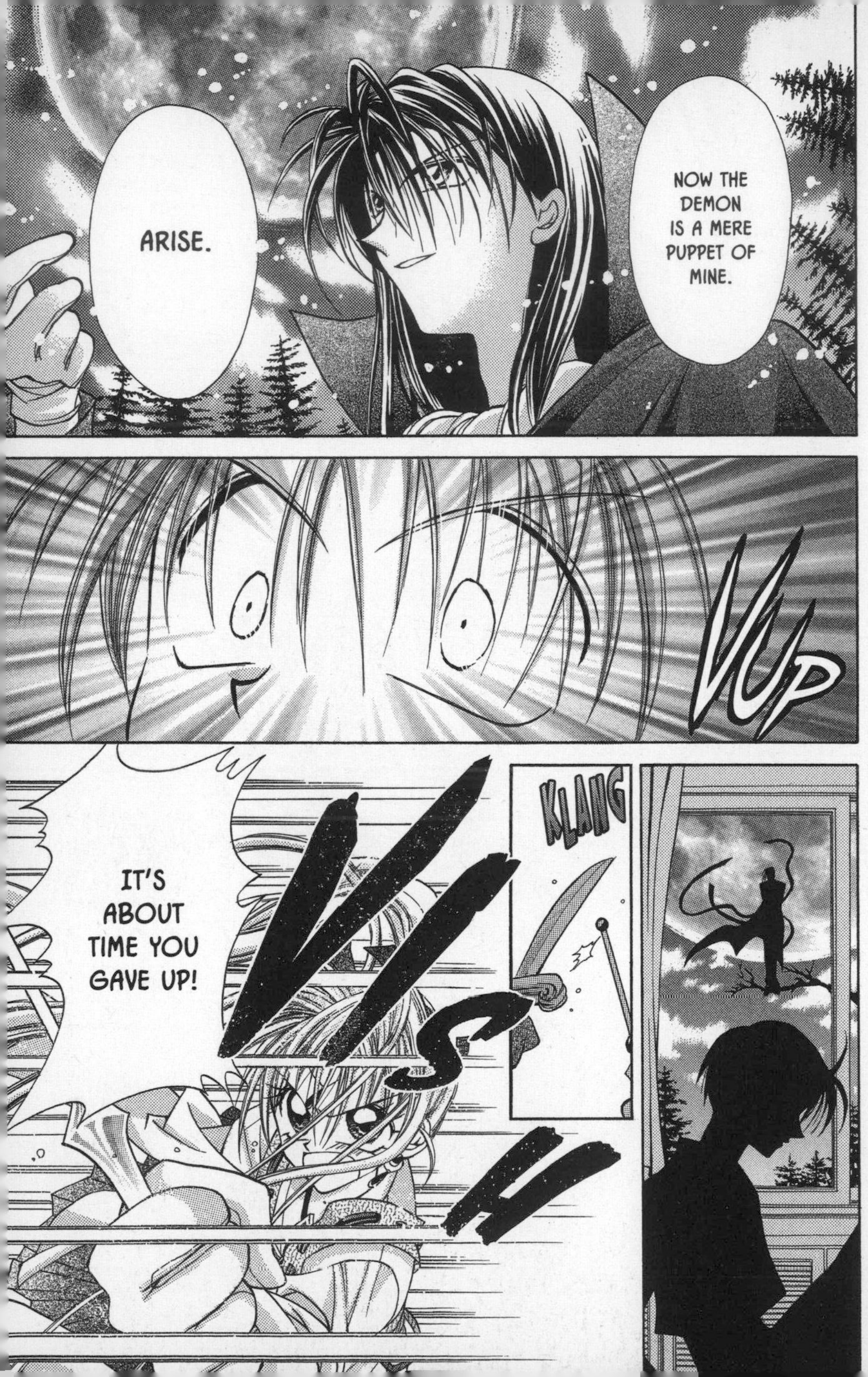
NOW THE DEMON IS A MERE PUPPET OF MINE.
ARISE.
VUP
KLANG
IT'S ABOUT TIME YOU GAVE UP!
WSH

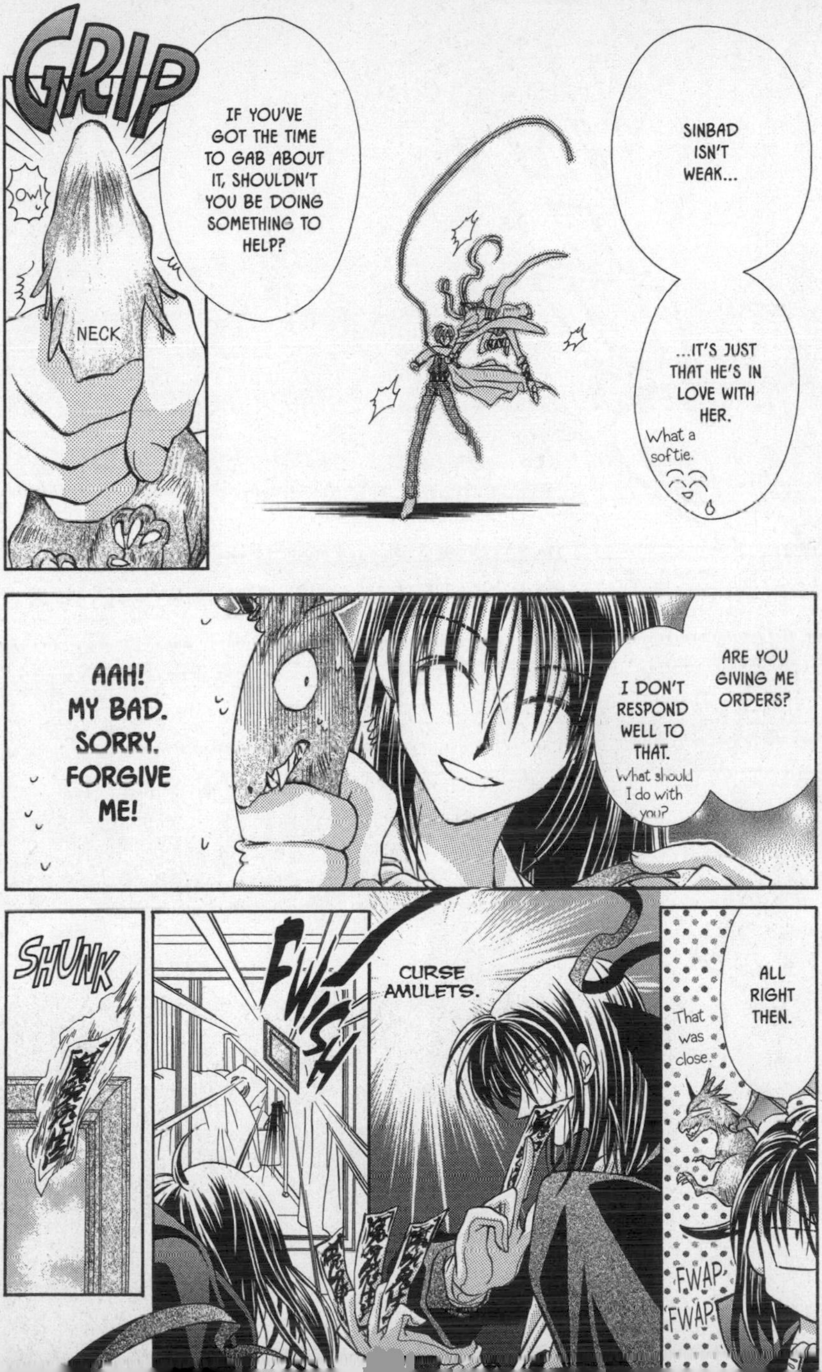
SINBAD ISN'T WEAK...
...IT'S JUST THAT HE'S IN LOVE WITH HER.
What a softie.
IF YOU'VE GOT THE TIME TO GAB ABOUT IT, SHOULDN'T YOU BE DOING SOMETHING TO HELP?
GRIP
Ow!
NECK
ARE YOU GIVING ME ORDERS?
I DON'T RESPOND WELL TO THAT.
What should I do with you?
AAH! MY BAD. SORRY. FORGIVE ME!
ALL RIGHT THEN.
That was close.
FWAP
FWAP
CURSE AMULETS.
FWISH
SHUNK

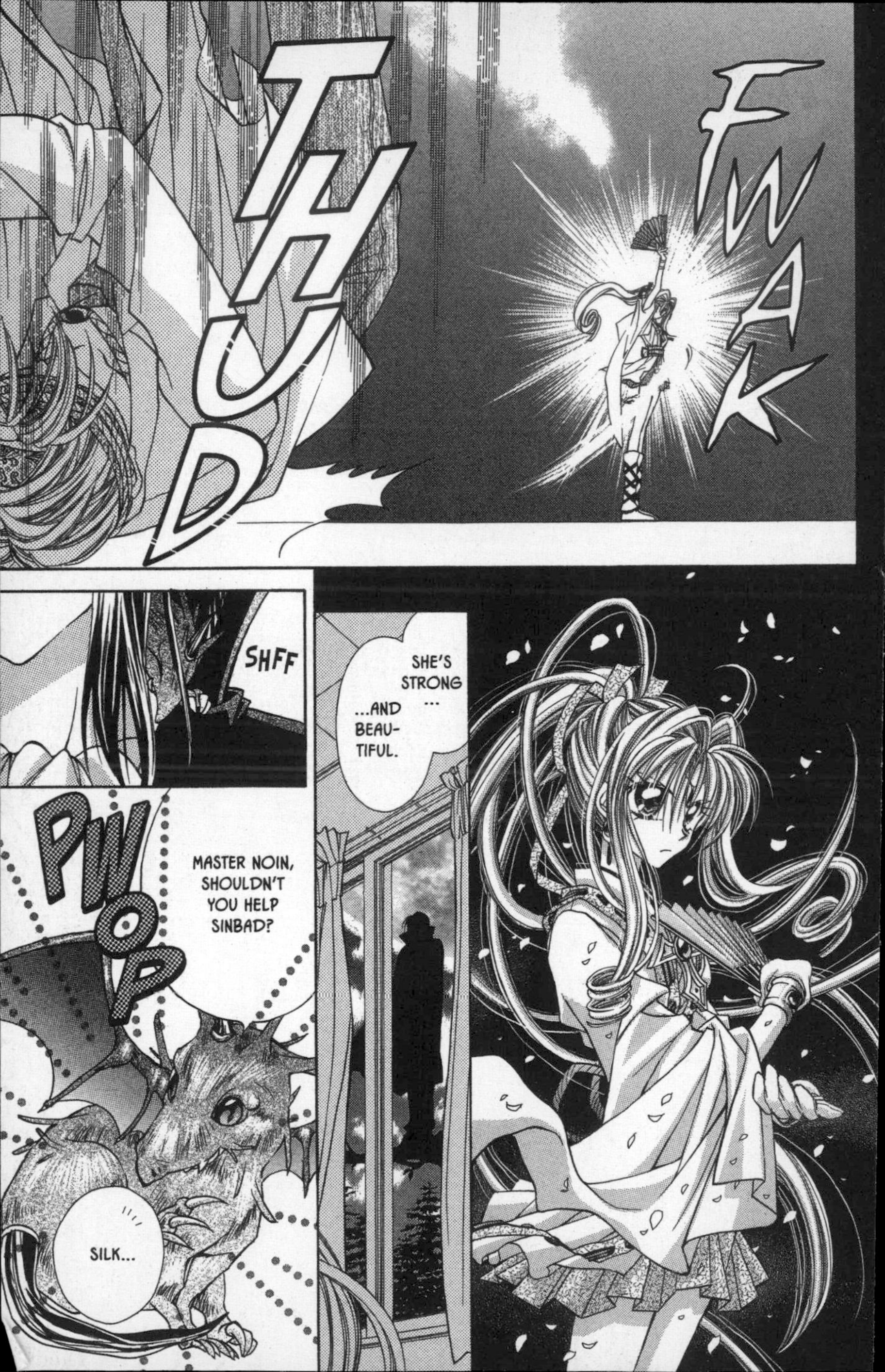
FWAK
THUD
SHE'S STRONG...
...AND BEAUTIFUL.
SHFF
PWOP
MASTER NOIN, SHOULDN'T YOU HELP SINBAD?
SILK...

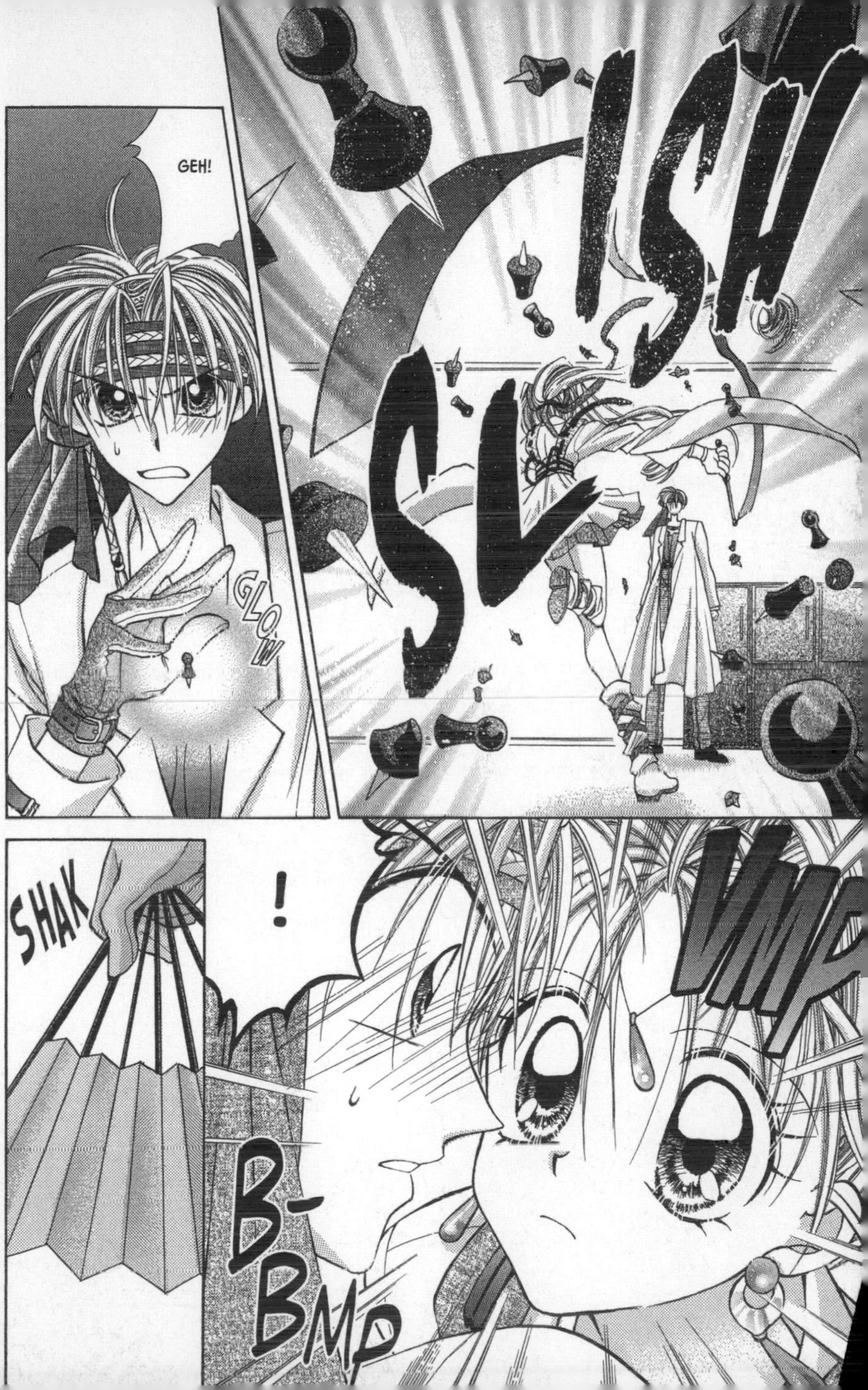
SLISH!
GEH!
GLOW
VWIP
!
B-BMP
SHAK

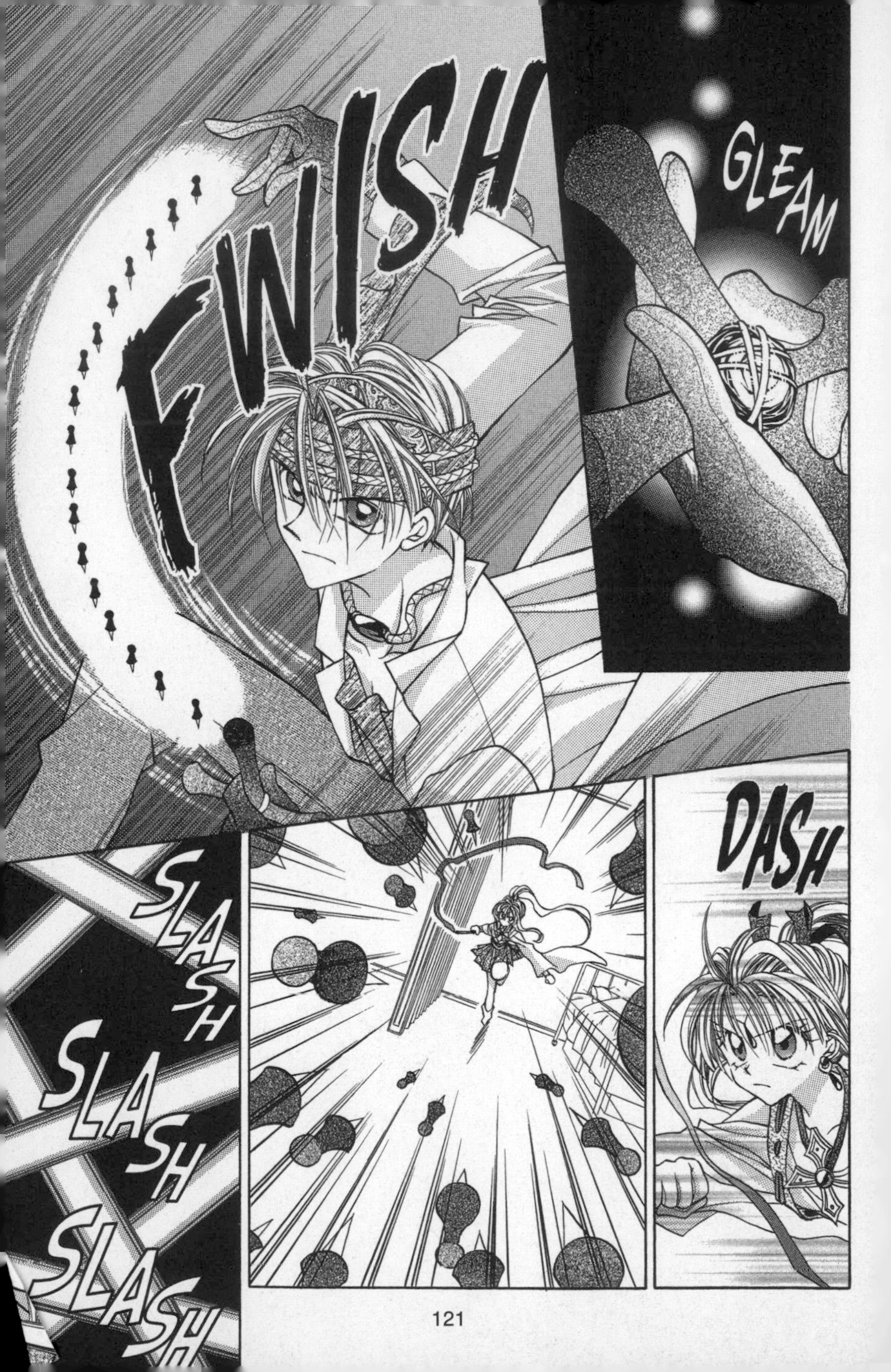
GLEAM
FWISH
DASH
SLASH
SLASH
SLASH
SLASH

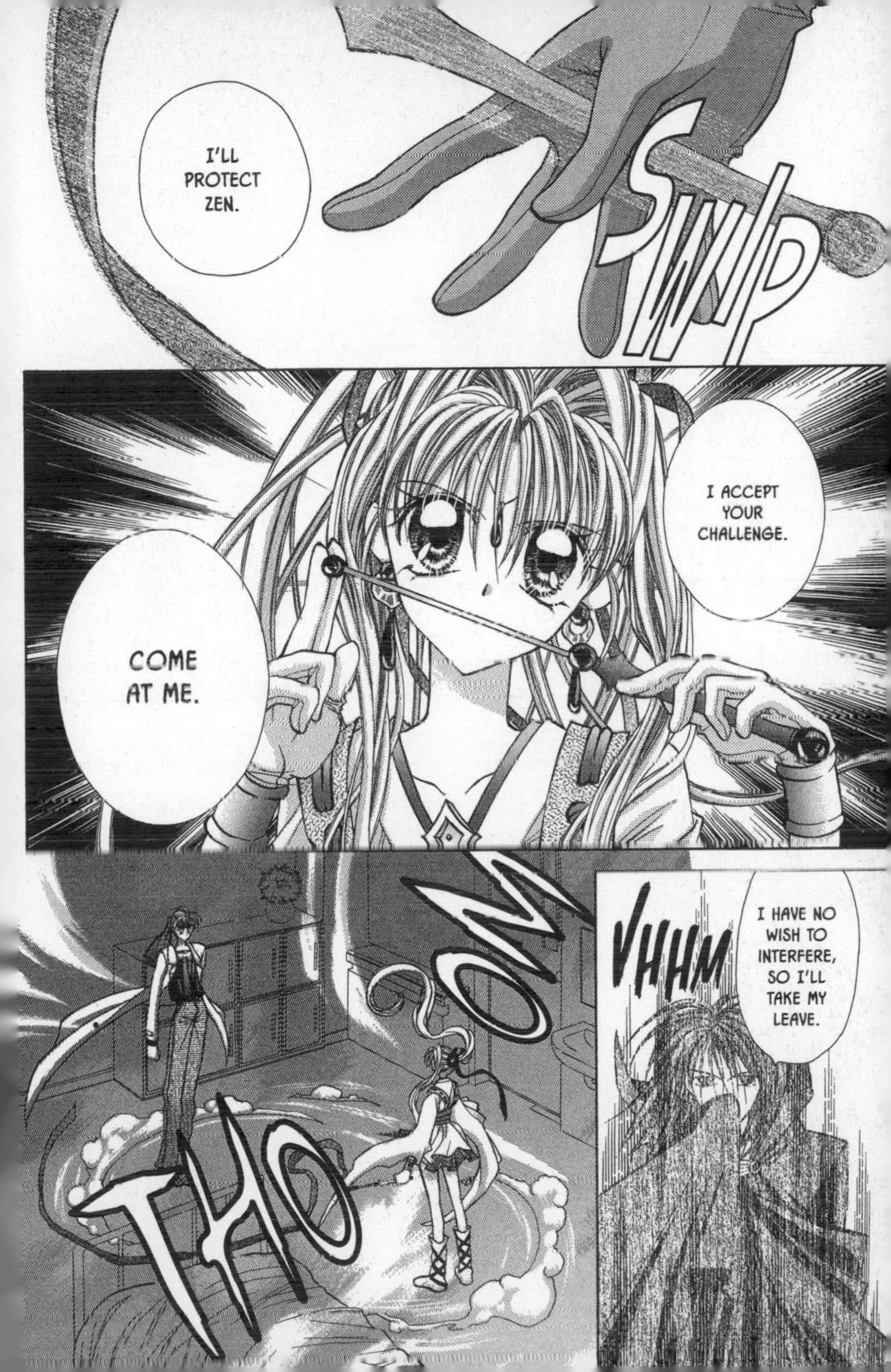
I'LL PROTECT ZEN.
SWIP
I ACCEPT YOUR CHALLENGE.
COME AT ME.
VHHM
I HAVE NO WISH TO INTERFERE, SO I'LL TAKE MY LEAVE.
THOOOM

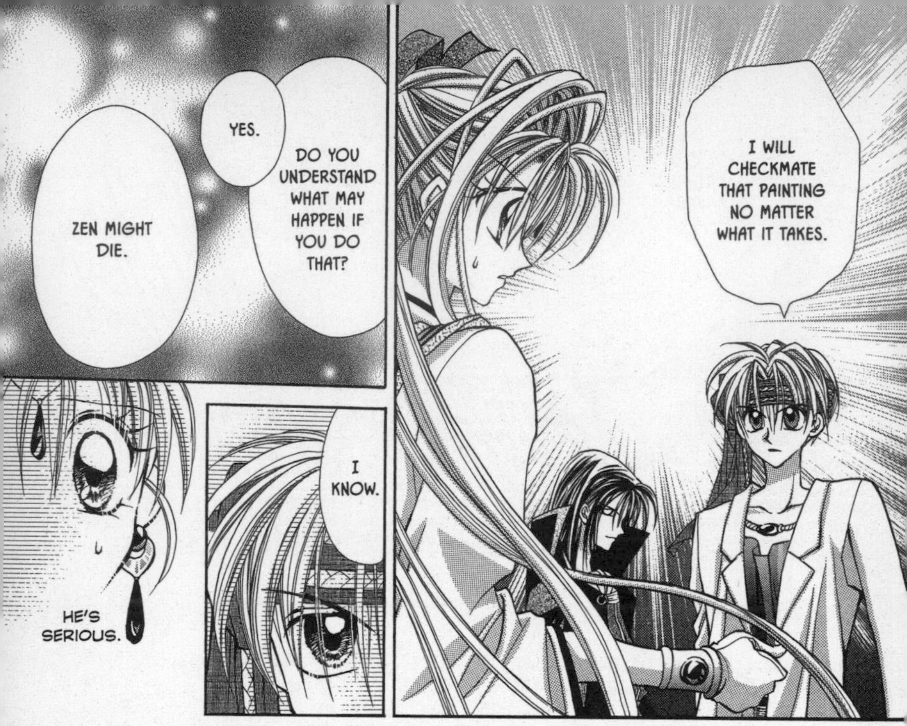
I WILL CHECKMATE THAT PAINTING NO MATTER WHAT IT TAKES.
DO YOU UNDERSTAND WHAT MAY HAPPEN IF YOU DO THAT?
YES.
ZEN MIGHT DIE.
I KNOW.
HE'S SERIOUS.

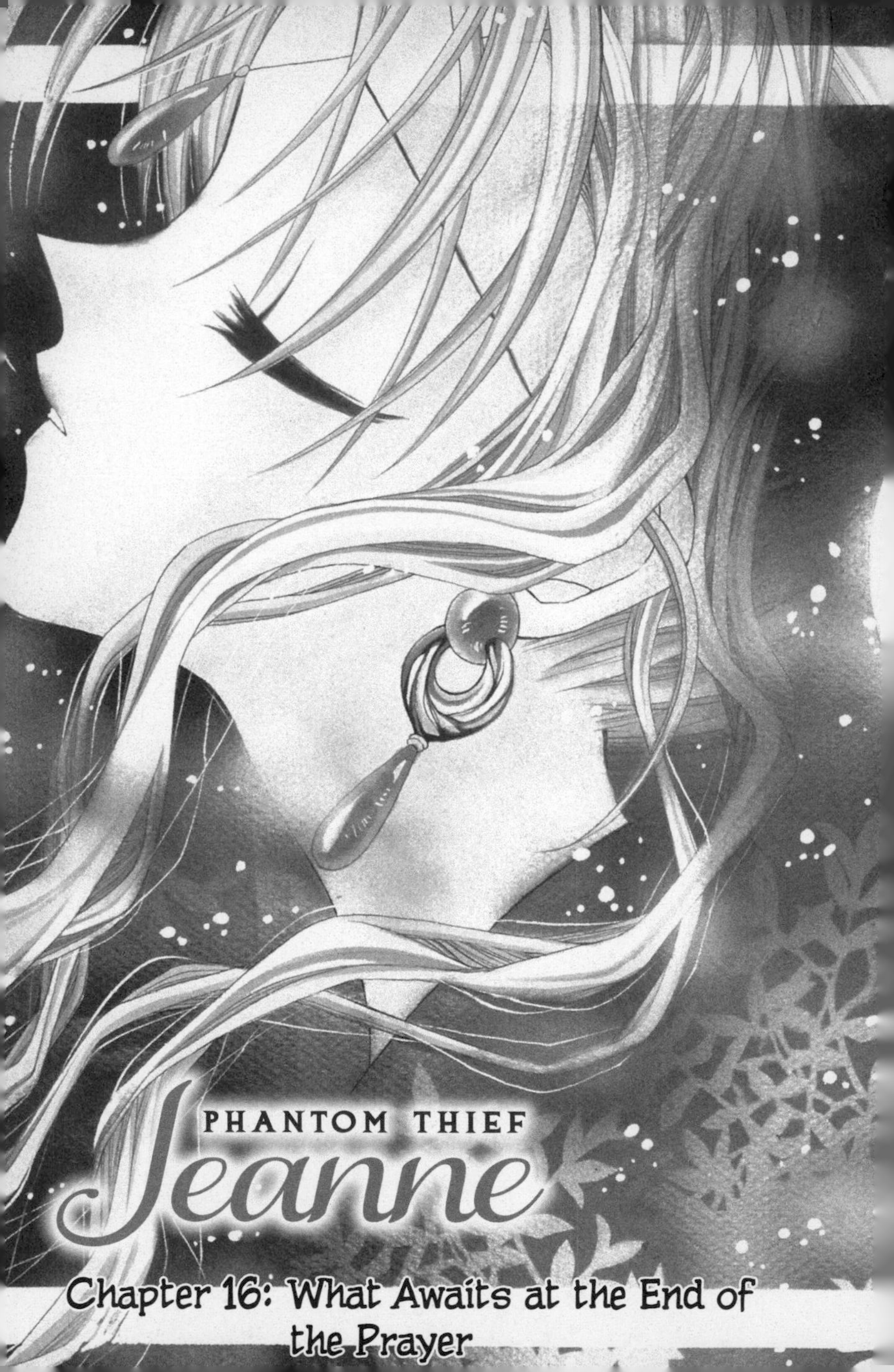
PHANTOM THIEF
Jeanne
Chapter 16: What Awaits at the End of the Prayer

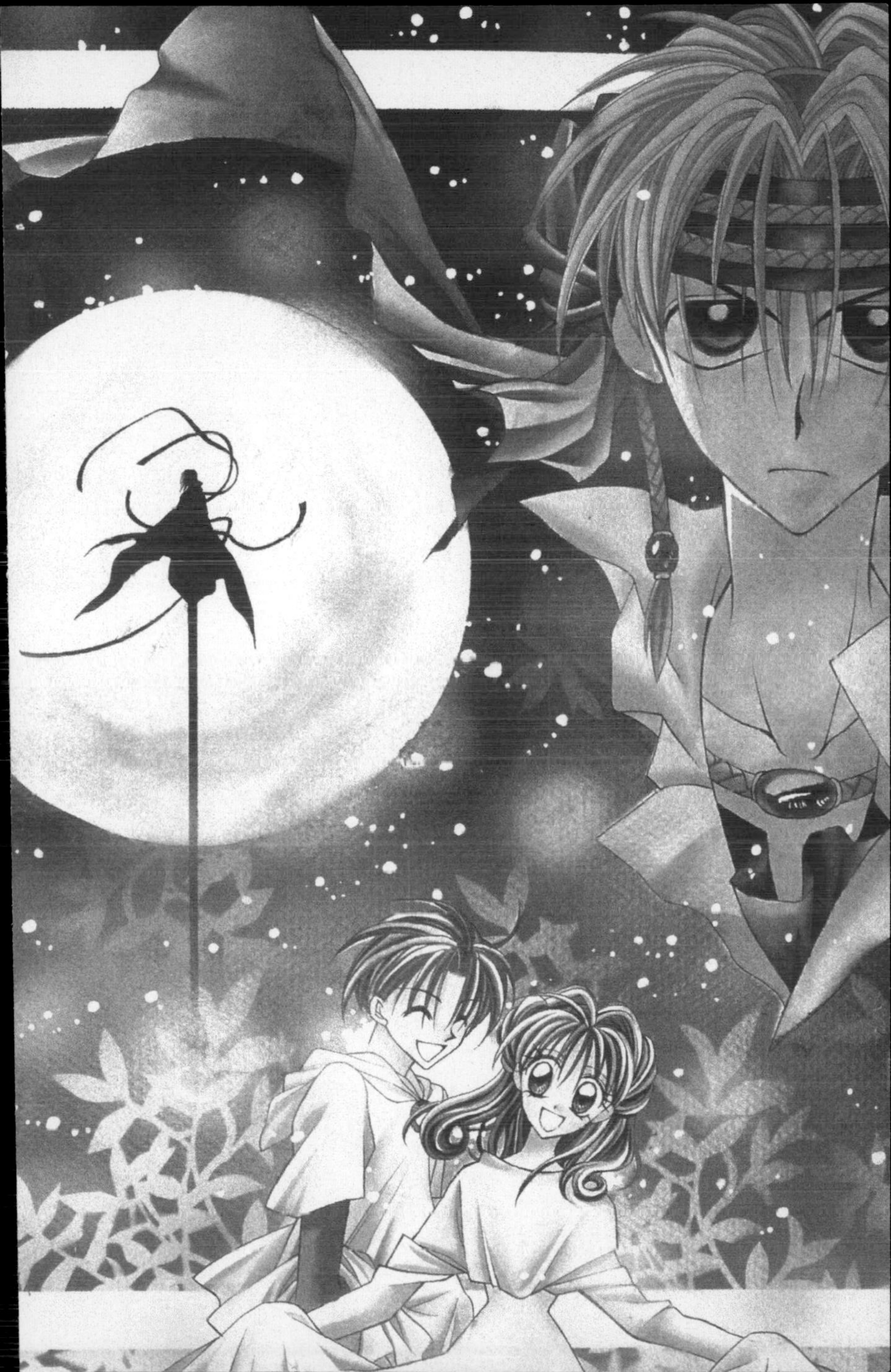

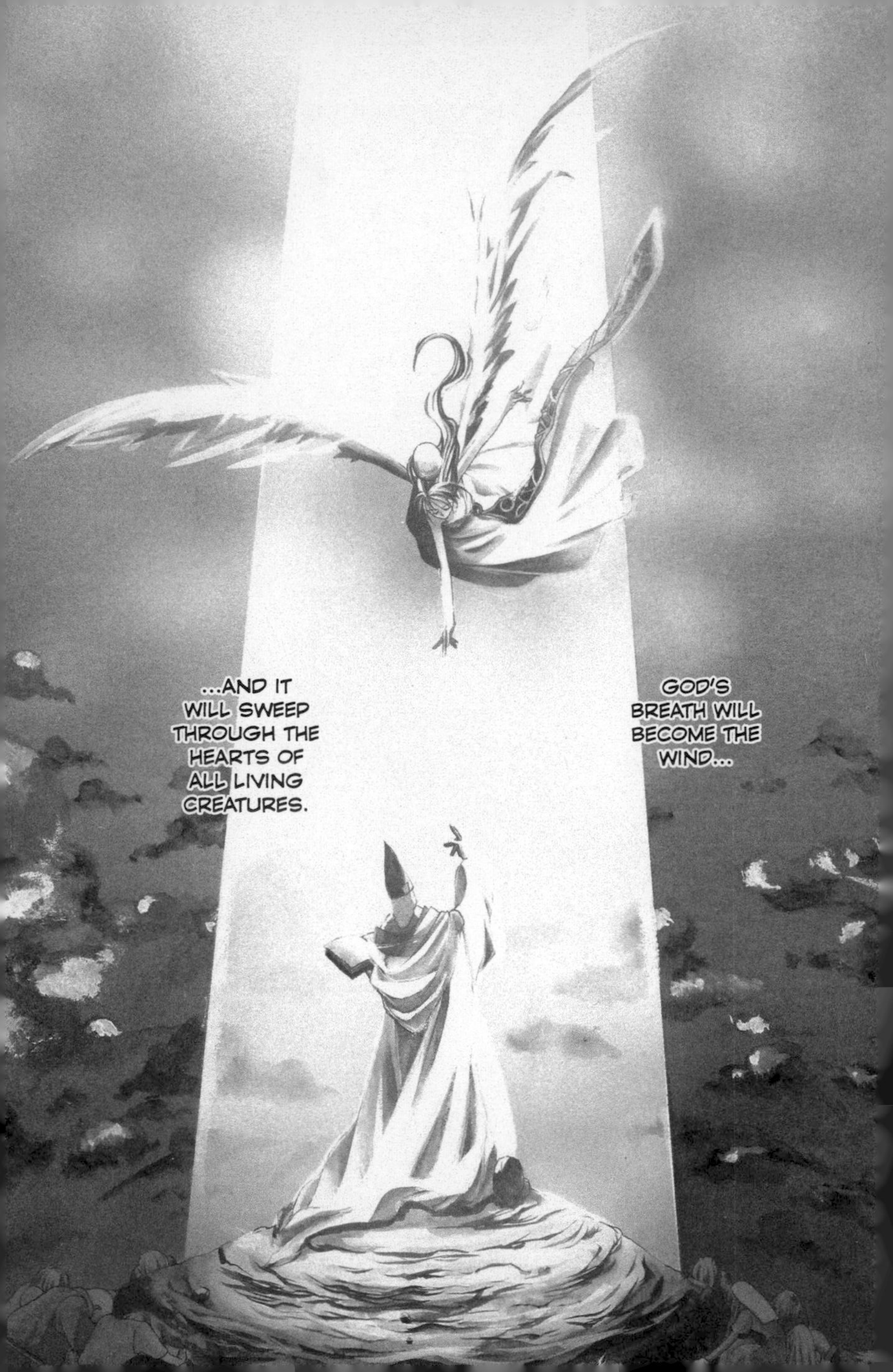
GOD'S BREATH WILL BECOME THE WIND...
...AND IT WILL SWEEP THROUGH THE HEARTS OF ALL LIVING CREATURES.

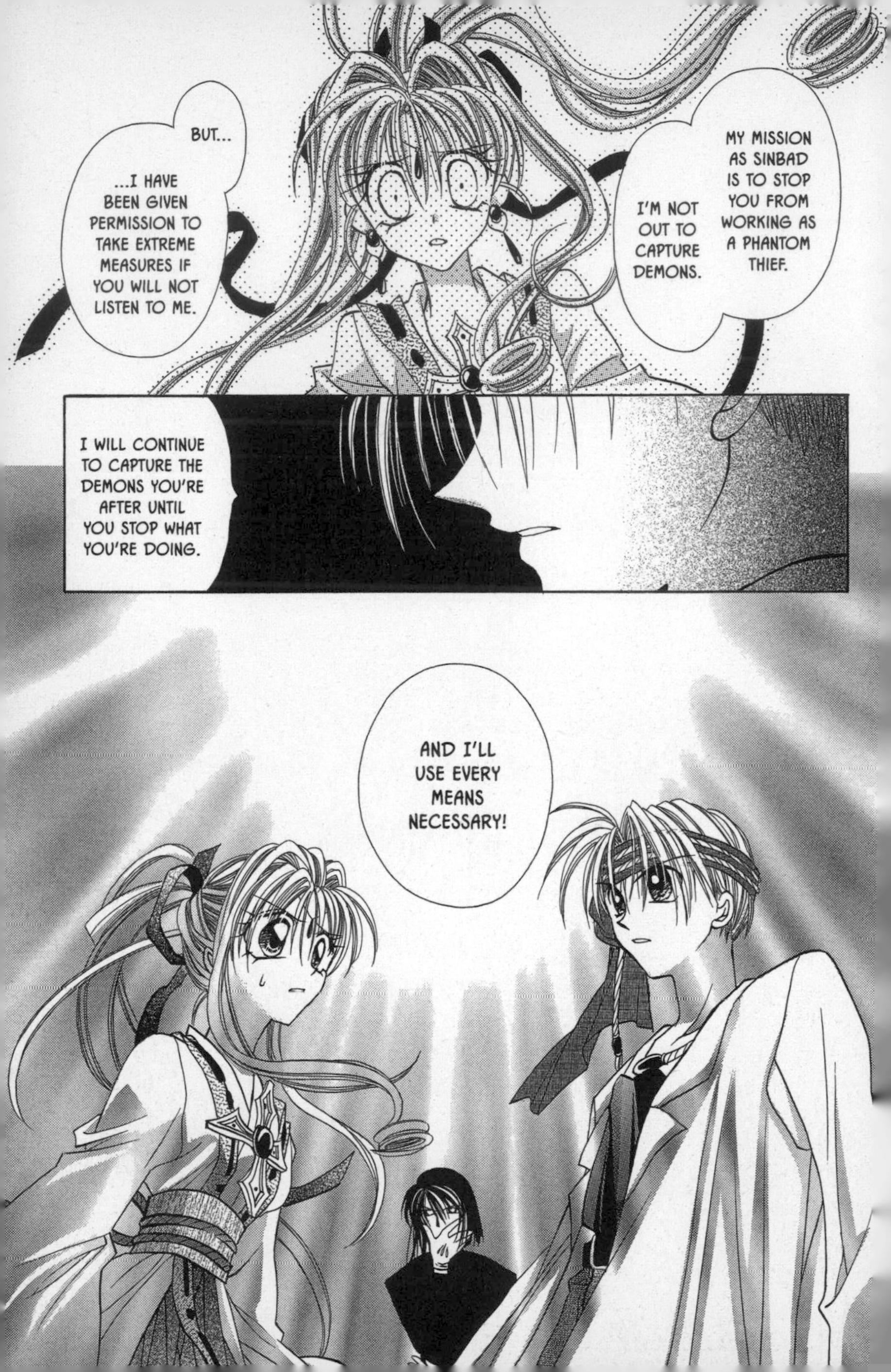
MY MISSION AS SINBAD IS TO STOP YOU FROM WORKING AS A PHANTOM THIEF.
I'M NOT OUT TO CAPTURE DEMONS.
BUT...
...I HAVE BEEN GIVEN PERMISSION TO TAKE EXTREME MEASURES IF YOU WILL NOT LISTEN TO ME.
I WILL CONTINUE TO CAPTURE THE DEMONS YOU'RE AFTER UNTIL YOU STOP WHAT YOU'RE DOING.
AND I'LL USE EVERY MEANS NECESSARY!

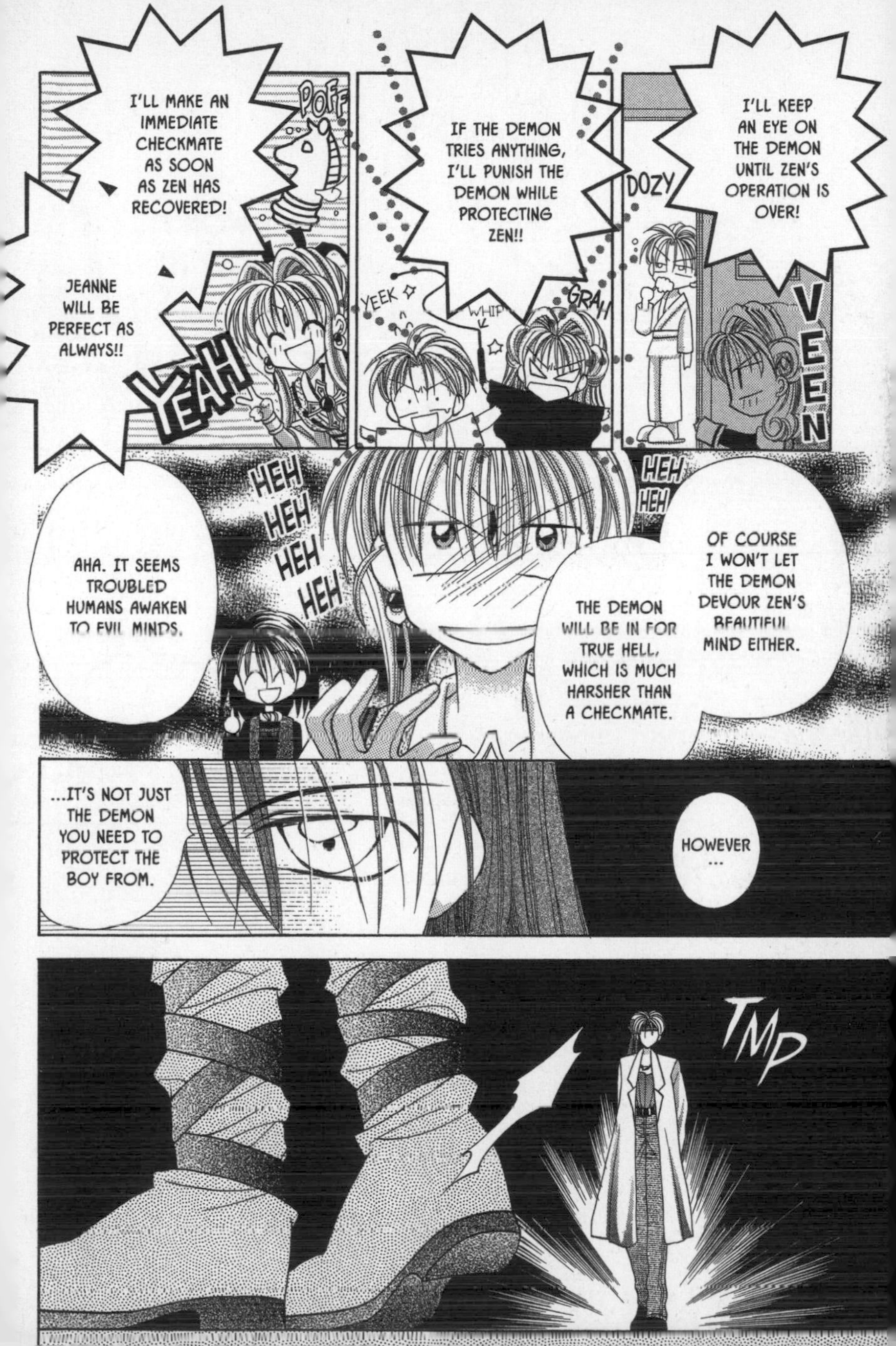
I'LL KEEP AN EYE ON THE DEMON UNTIL ZEN'S OPERATION IS OVER!
DOZY
VEEN
IF THE DEMON TRIES ANYTHING, I'LL PUNISH THE DEMON WHILE PROTECTING ZEN!!
GRAH
WHIP
YEEK
POFF
I'LL MAKE AN IMMEDIATE CHECKMATE AS SOON AS ZEN HAS RECOVERED!
JEANNE WILL BE PERFECT AS ALWAYS!!
YEAH
HEH HEH
OF COURSE I WON'T LET THE DEMON DEVOUR ZEN'S BEAUTIFUL MIND EITHER.
THE DEMON WILL BE IN FOR TRUE HELL, WHICH IS MUCH HARSHER THAN A CHECKMATE.
HEH HEH HEH HEH
AHA. IT SEEMS TROUBLED HUMANS AWAKEN TO EVIL MINDS.
HOWEVER...
...IT'S NOT JUST THE DEMON YOU NEED TO PROTECT THE BOY FROM.
TMP

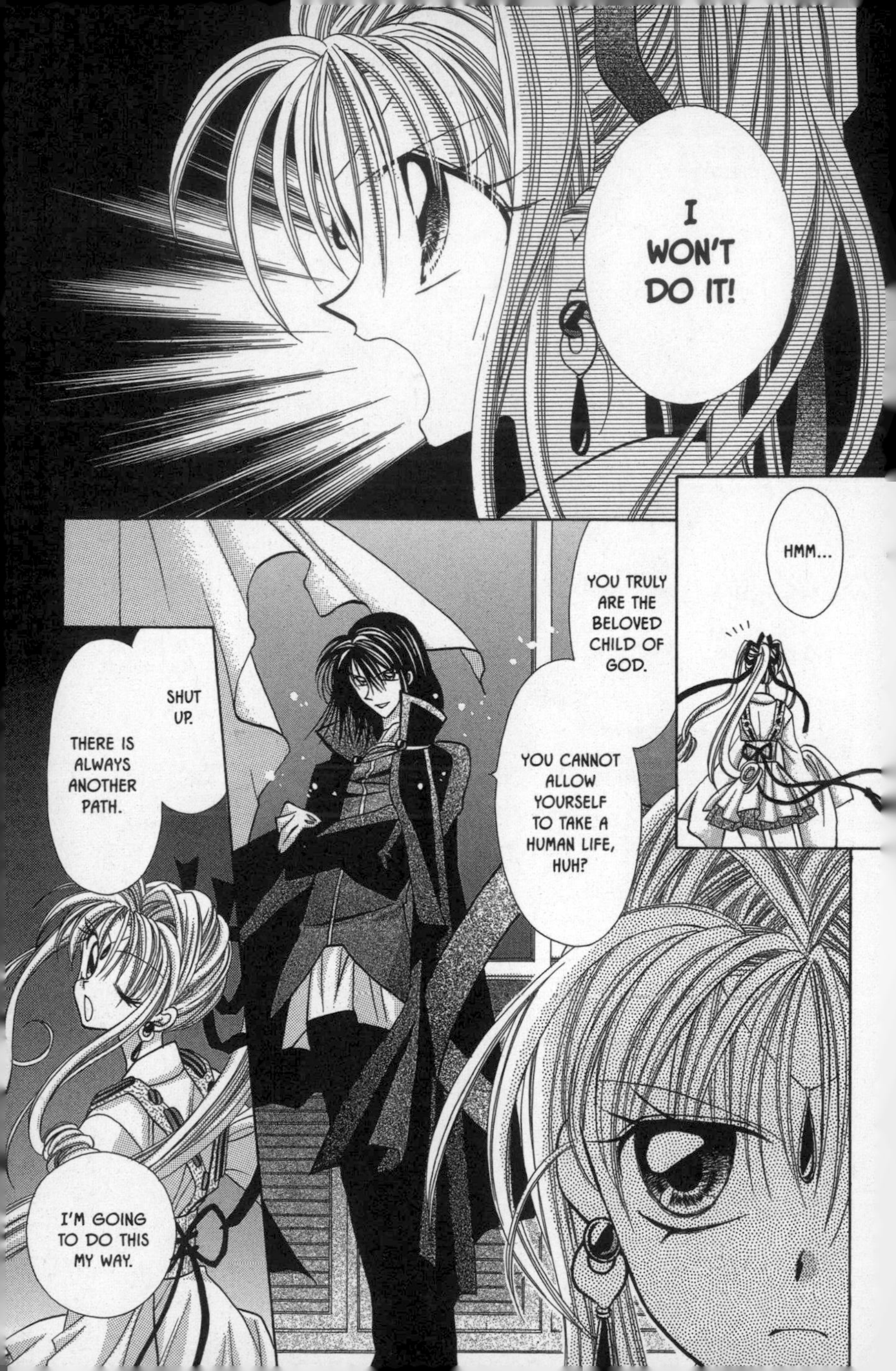
I WON'T DO IT!
HMM...
YOU TRULY ARE THE BELOVED CHILD OF GOD.
YOU CANNOT ALLOW YOURSELF TO TAKE A HUMAN LIFE, HUH?
SHUT UP.
THERE IS ALWAYS ANOTHER PATH.
I'M GOING TO DO THIS MY WAY.

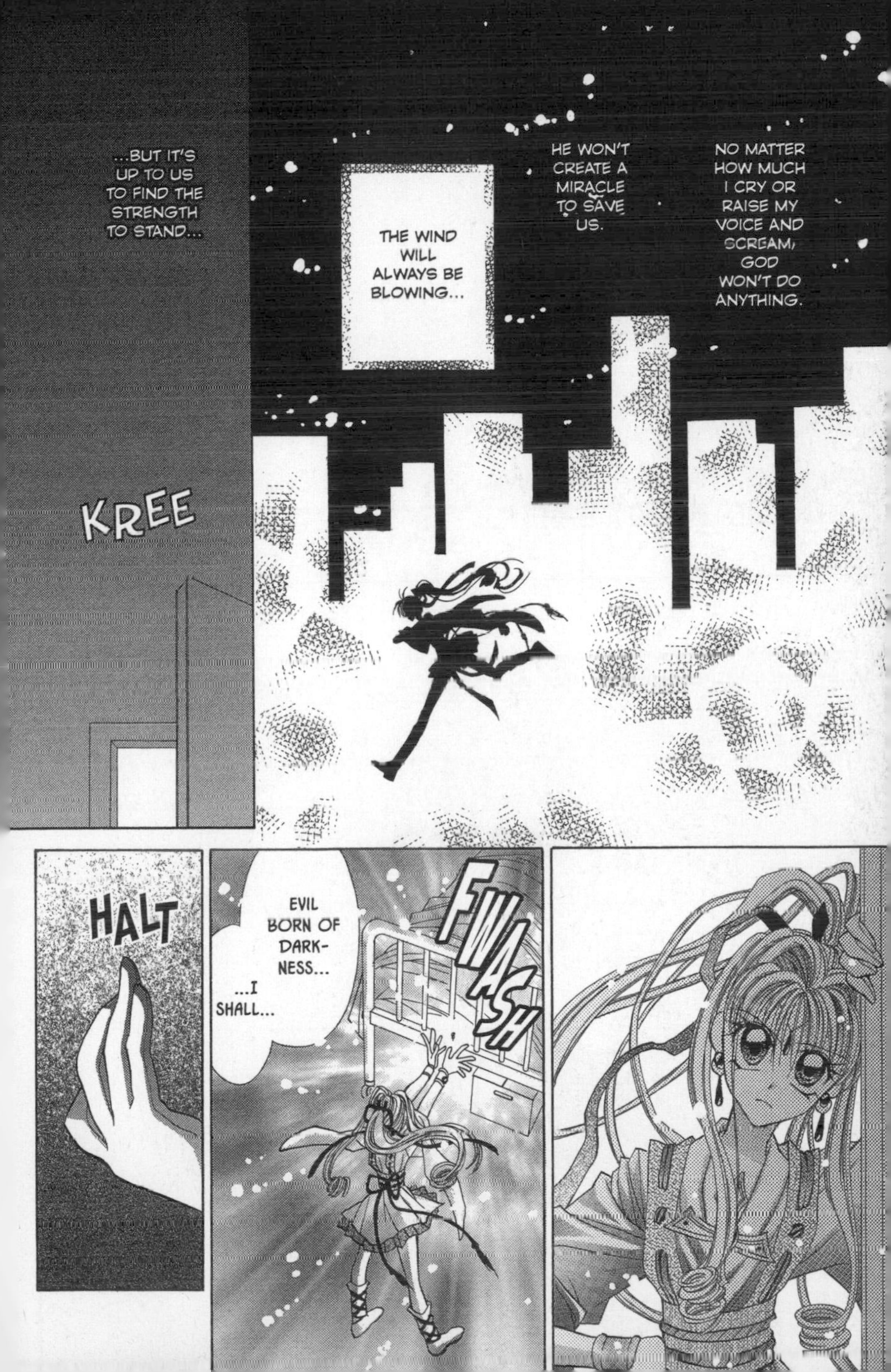
NO MATTER HOW MUCH I CRY OR RAISE MY VOICE AND SCREAM, GOD WON'T DO ANYTHING.
HE WON'T CREATE A MIRACLE TO SAVE US.
THE WIND WILL ALWAYS BE BLOWING...
...BUT IT'S UP TO US TO FIND THE STRENGTH TO STAND...
KREE
FWASH
EVIL BORN OF DARK-NESS...
...I SHALL...
HALT

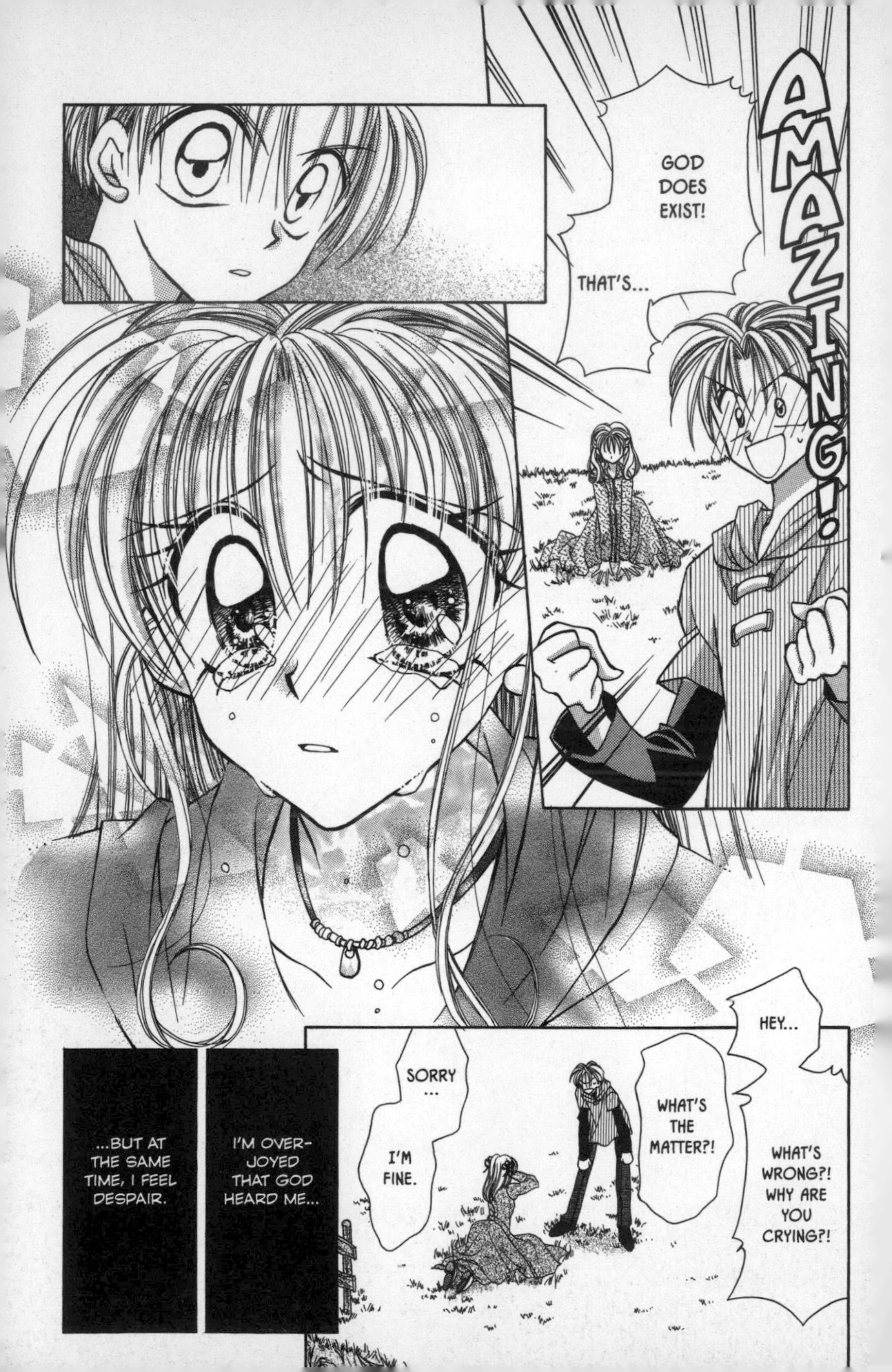
AMAZING!
GOD DOES EXIST!
THAT'S...
HEY...
WHAT'S WRONG?! WHY ARE YOU CRYING?!
WHAT'S THE MATTER?!
SORRY... I'M FINE.
I'M OVER-JOYED THAT GOD HEARD ME...
...BUT AT THE SAME TIME, I FEEL DESPAIR.

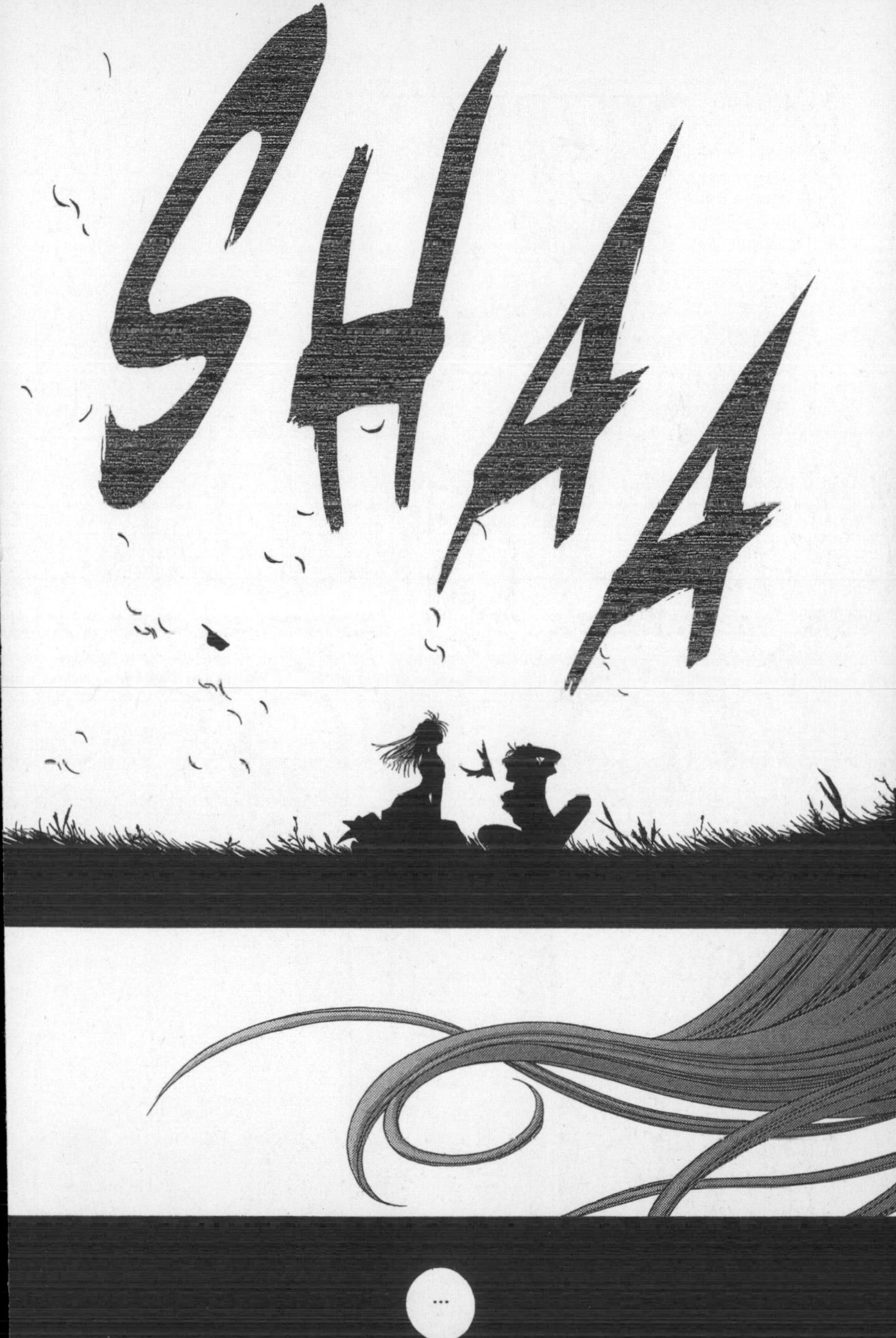
SHAA
...

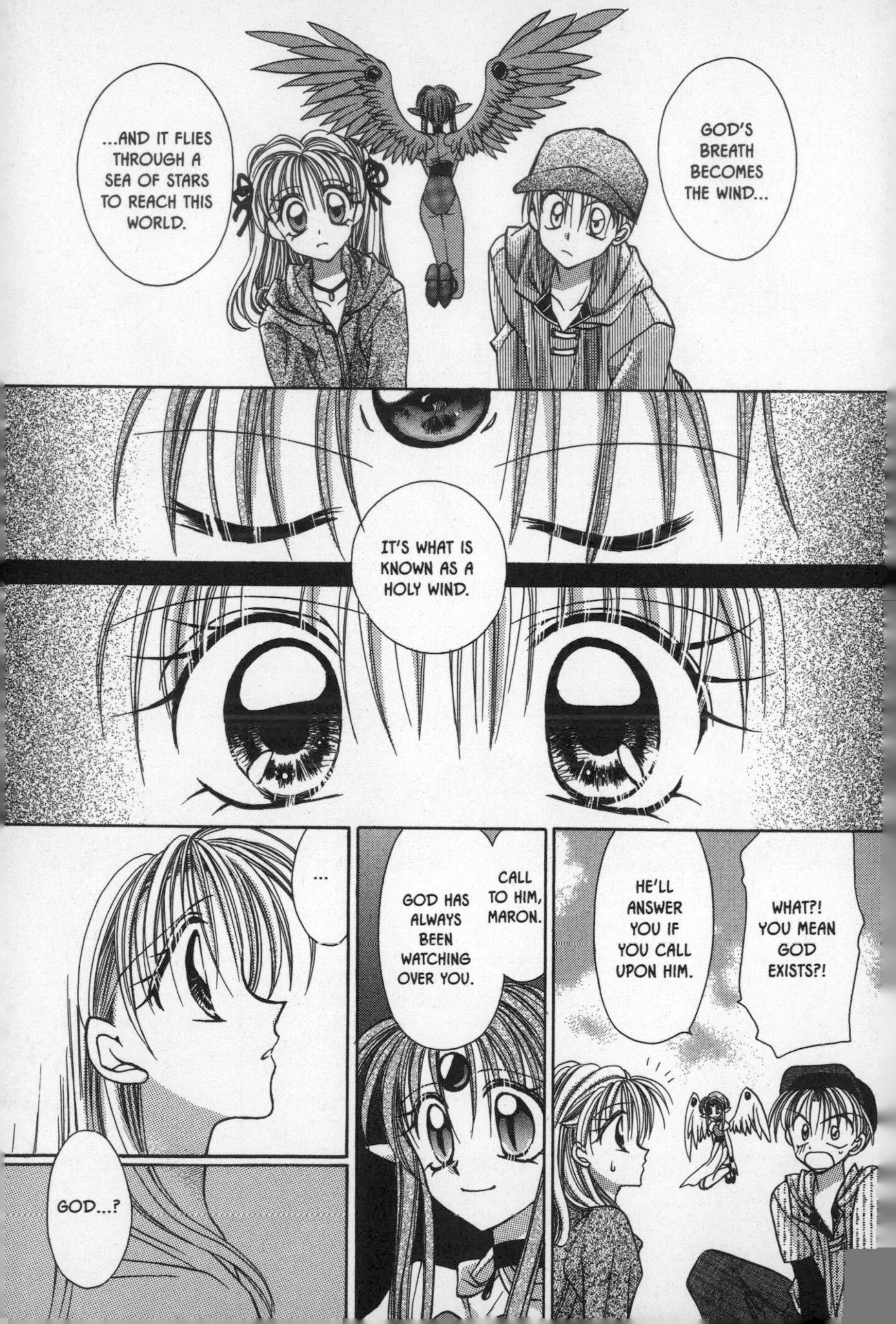
GOD'S BREATH BECOMES THE WIND...
...AND IT FLIES THROUGH A SEA OF STARS TO REACH THIS WORLD.
IT'S WHAT IS KNOWN AS A HOLY WIND.
WHAT?! YOU MEAN GOD EXISTS?!
HE'LL ANSWER YOU IF YOU CALL UPON HIM.
CALL TO HIM, MARON.
GOD HAS ALWAYS BEEN WATCHING OVER YOU.
...
GOD...?

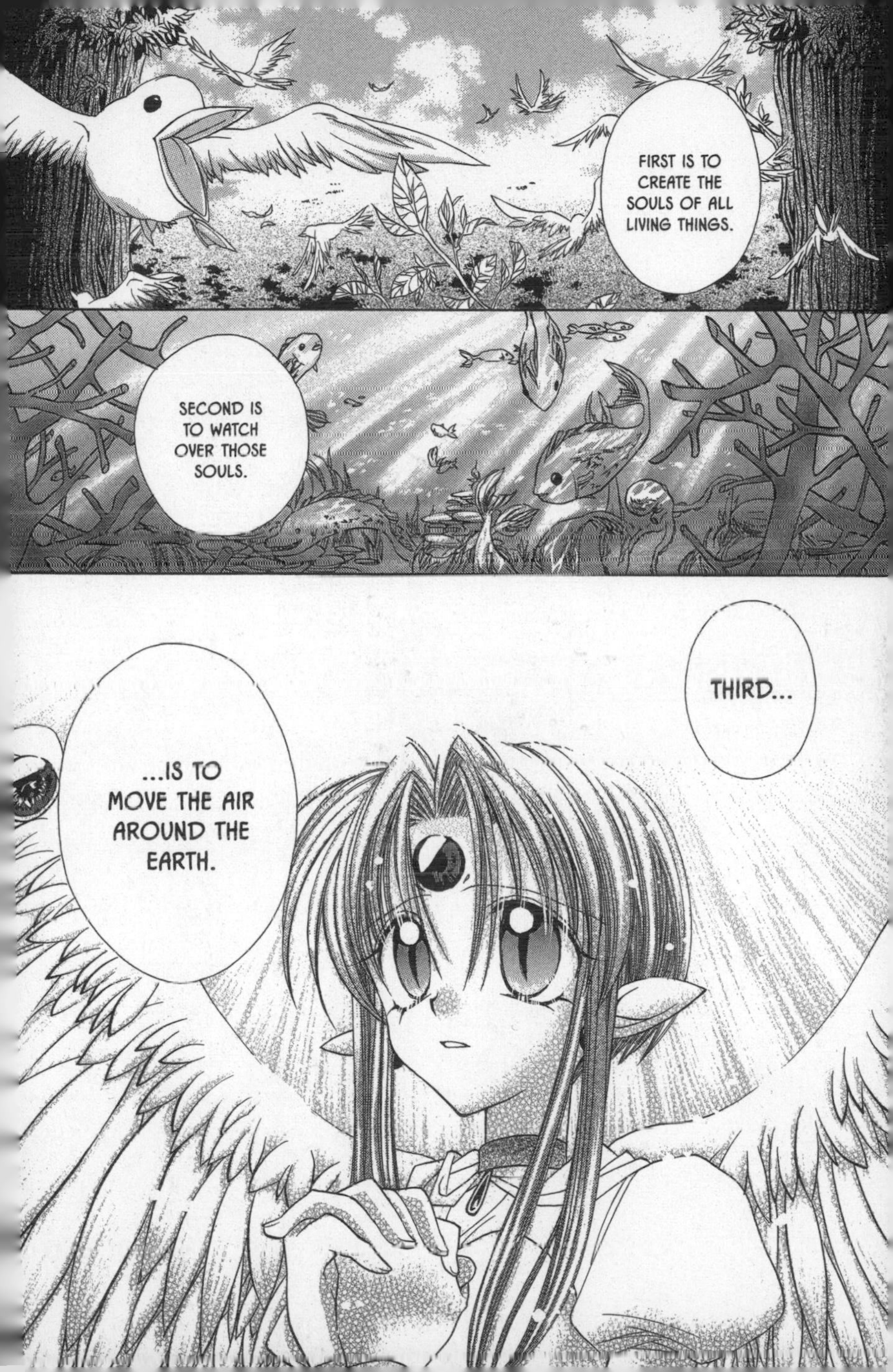
FIRST IS TO CREATE THE SOULS OF ALL LIVING THINGS.
SECOND IS TO WATCH OVER THOSE SOULS.
THIRD...
...IS TO MOVE THE AIR AROUND THE EARTH.

FINN!
I'VE BEEN LOOKING ALL OVER FOR YOU!
THE HOSPITAL IS IN CHAOS.
PWOP
HM, SHE LOOKS LIKE A FAIRY TO ME.
I THOUGHT SHE WAS A FAIRY TOO THE FIRST TIME I MET HER.
WHAT?!
WHAT?!
PSST
MARON... ARE YOU GOING TO CHECK-MATE THE PAINTING?
YOU'RE STILL WORRIED ABOUT THAT, FINN?
...
I'LL BE FINE. GOD IS ON MY SIDE.
IT'S NO GUAR-ANTEE, MARON...
THERE ARE ONLY THREE THINGS THAT GOD CAN DO FOR PEOPLE.

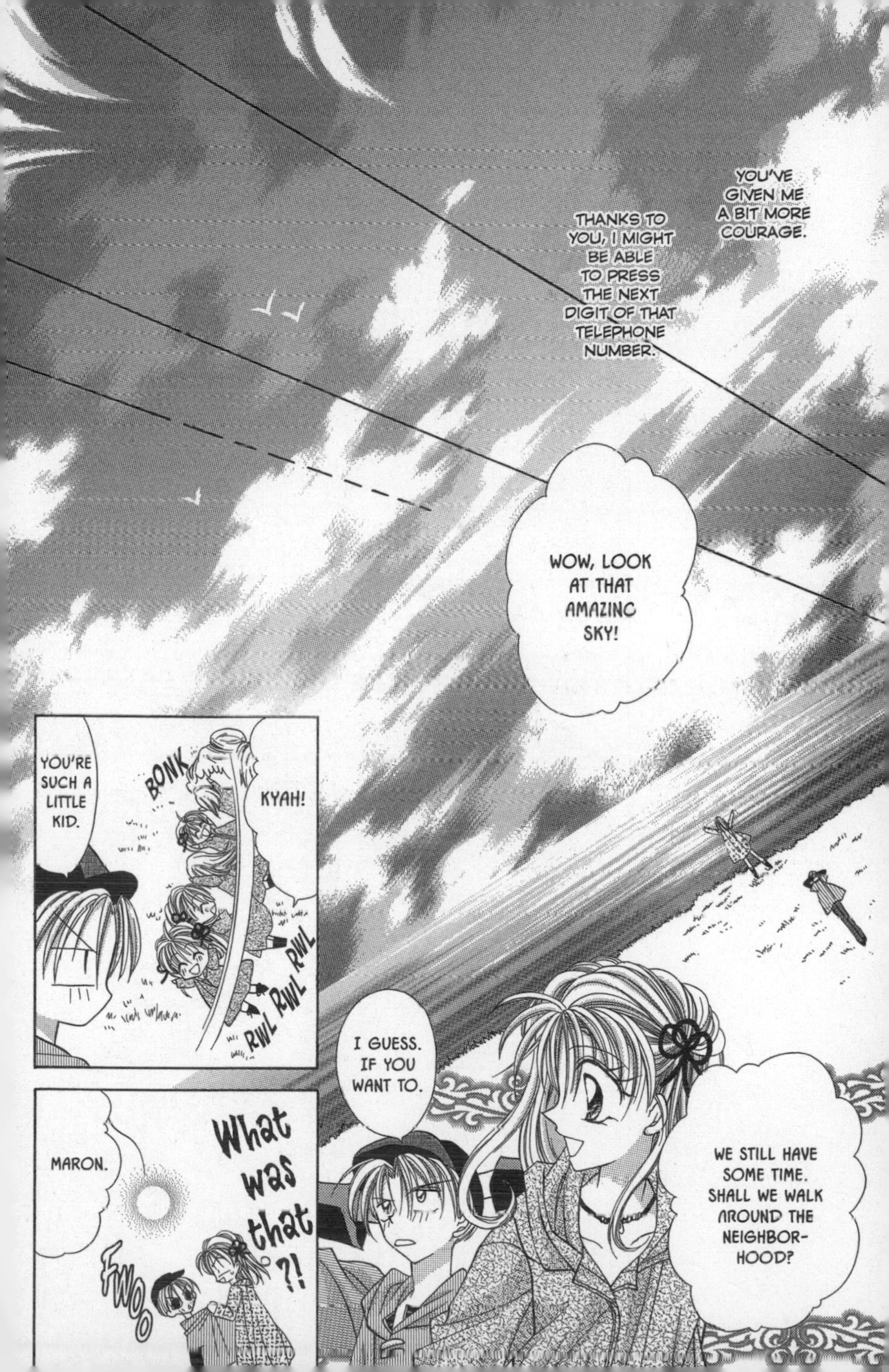
YOU'VE GIVEN ME A BIT MORE COURAGE.
THANKS TO YOU, I MIGHT BE ABLE TO PRESS THE NEXT DIGIT OF THAT TELEPHONE NUMBER.
WOW, LOOK AT THAT AMAZING SKY!
WE STILL HAVE SOME TIME. SHALL WE WALK AROUND THE NEIGHBOR-HOOD?
I GUESS. IF YOU WANT TO.
KYAH!
BONK
YOU'RE SUCH A LITTLE KID.
RWL RWL RWL
MARON.
What was that?!
FWOO

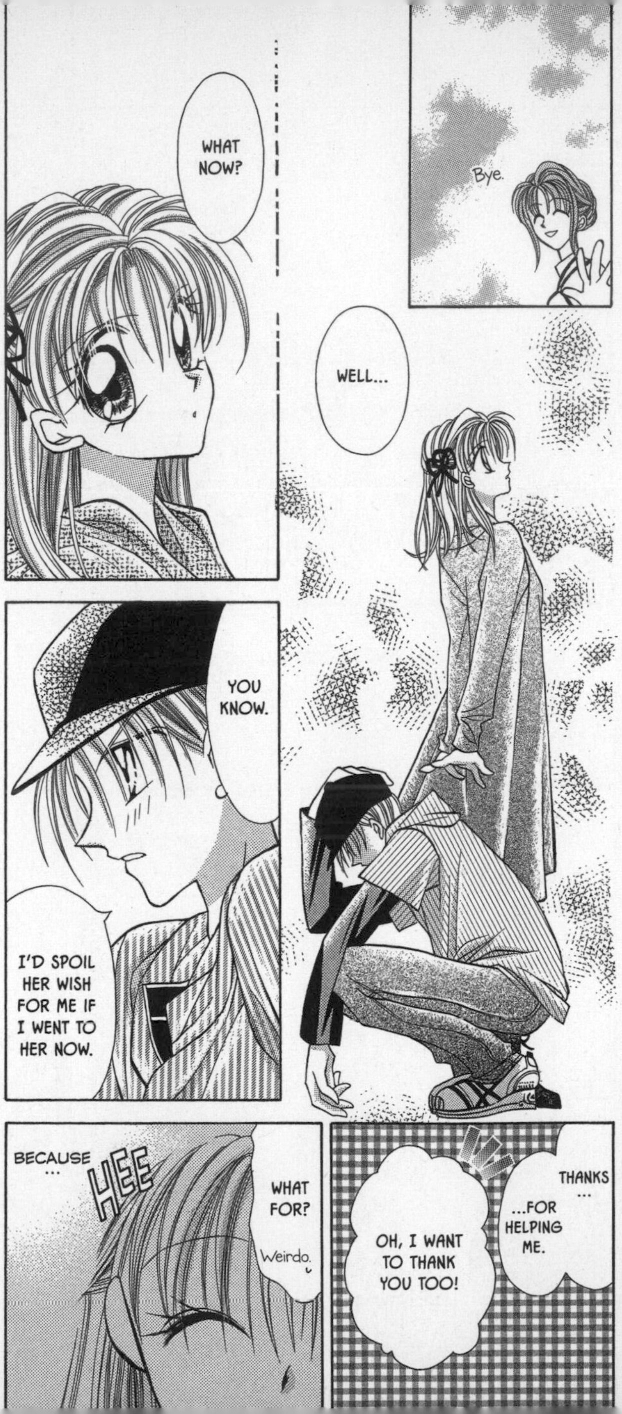
Bye.
WHAT NOW?
WELL...
YOU KNOW.
I'D SPOIL HER WISH FOR ME IF I WENT TO HER NOW.
THANKS...
...FOR HELPING ME.
OH, I WANT TO THANK YOU TOO!
WHAT FOR?
Weirdo.
HEE
BECAUSE...

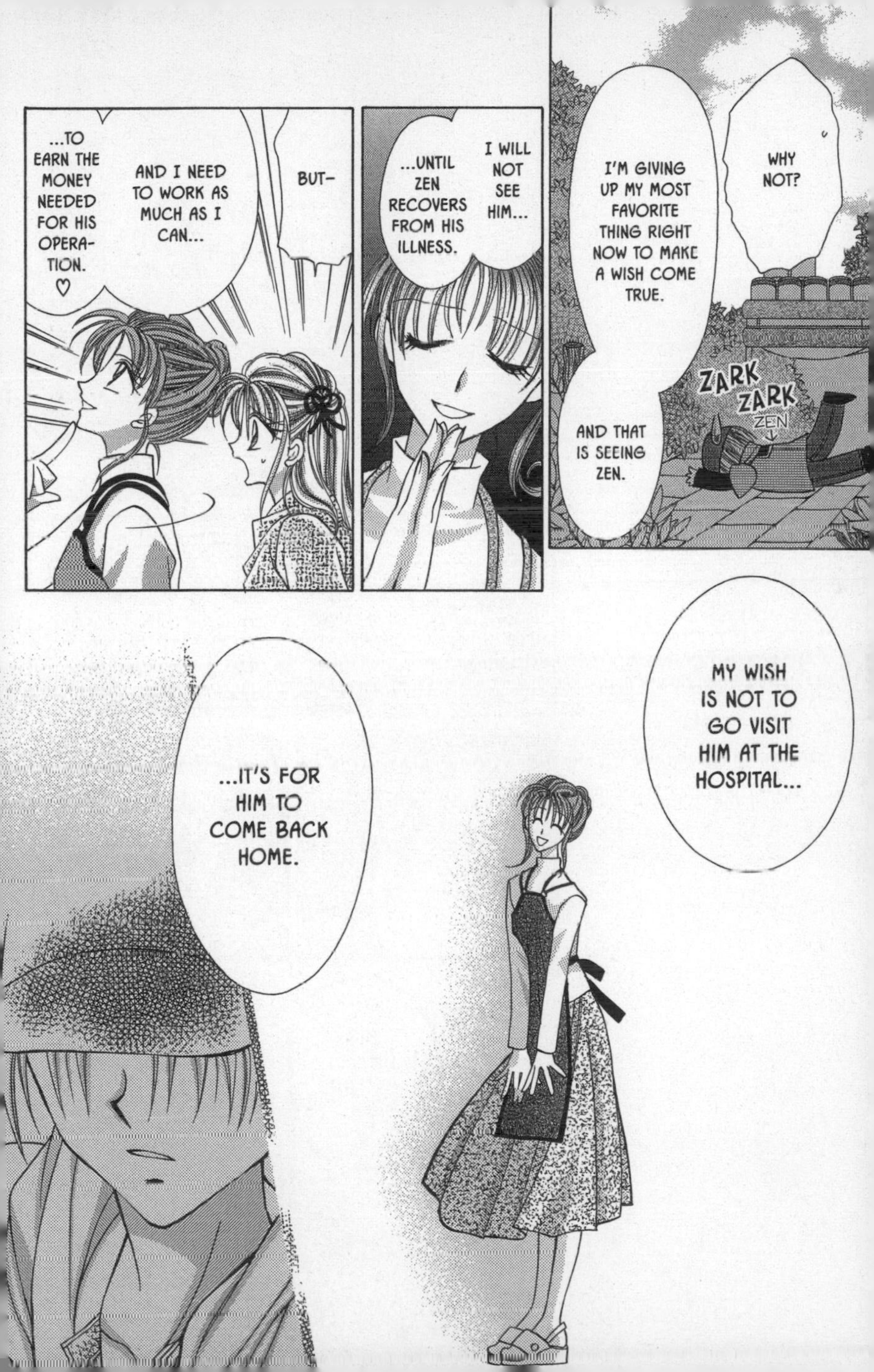
WHY NOT?
I'M GIVING UP MY MOST FAVORITE THING RIGHT NOW TO MAKE A WISH COME TRUE.
ZARK ZARK
ZEN
AND THAT IS SEEING ZEN.
I WILL NOT SEE HIM...
...UNTIL ZEN RECOVERS FROM HIS ILLNESS.
BUT–
AND I NEED TO WORK AS MUCH AS I CAN...
...TO EARN THE MONEY NEEDED FOR HIS OPERATION. ♡
MY WISH IS NOT TO GO VISIT HIM AT THE HOSPITAL...
...IT'S FOR HIM TO COME BACK HOME.

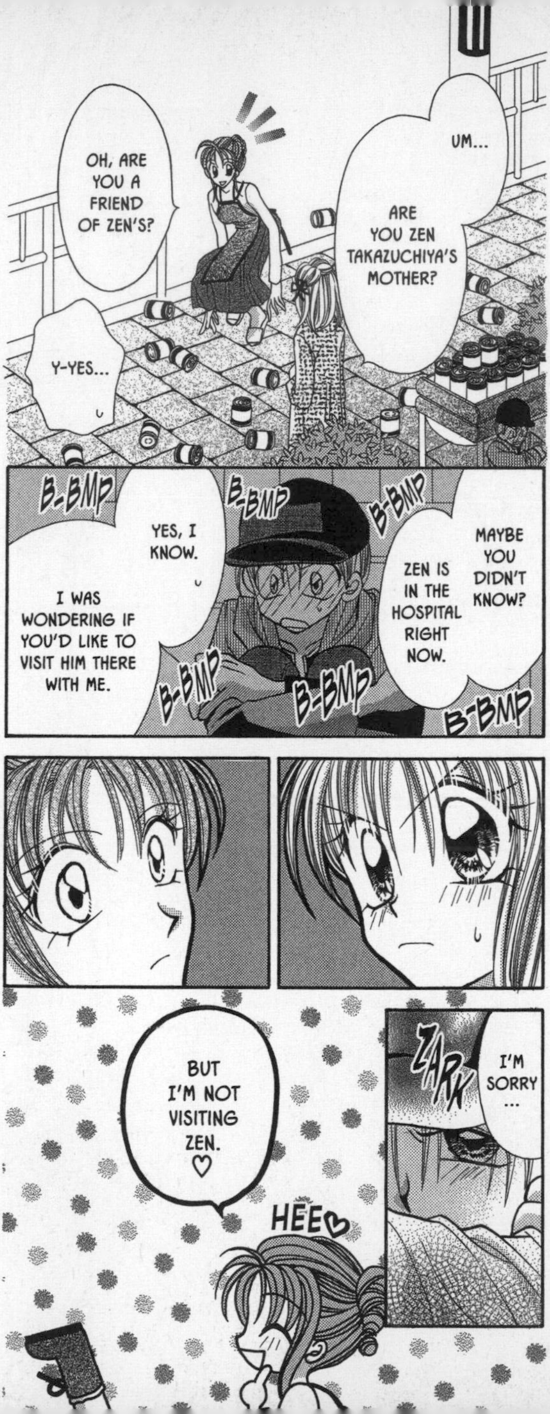
UM...
ARE YOU ZEN TAKAZUCHIYA'S MOTHER?
OH, ARE YOU A FRIEND OF ZEN'S?
Y-YES...
B-BMP
B-BMP
B-BMP
MAYBE YOU DIDN'T KNOW?
ZEN IS IN THE HOSPITAL RIGHT NOW.
YES, I KNOW.
I WAS WONDERING IF YOU'D LIKE TO VISIT HIM THERE WITH ME.
B-BMP
B-BMP
B-BMP
ZARK
I'M SORRY ...
BUT I'M NOT VISITING ZEN. ♡
HEE♡

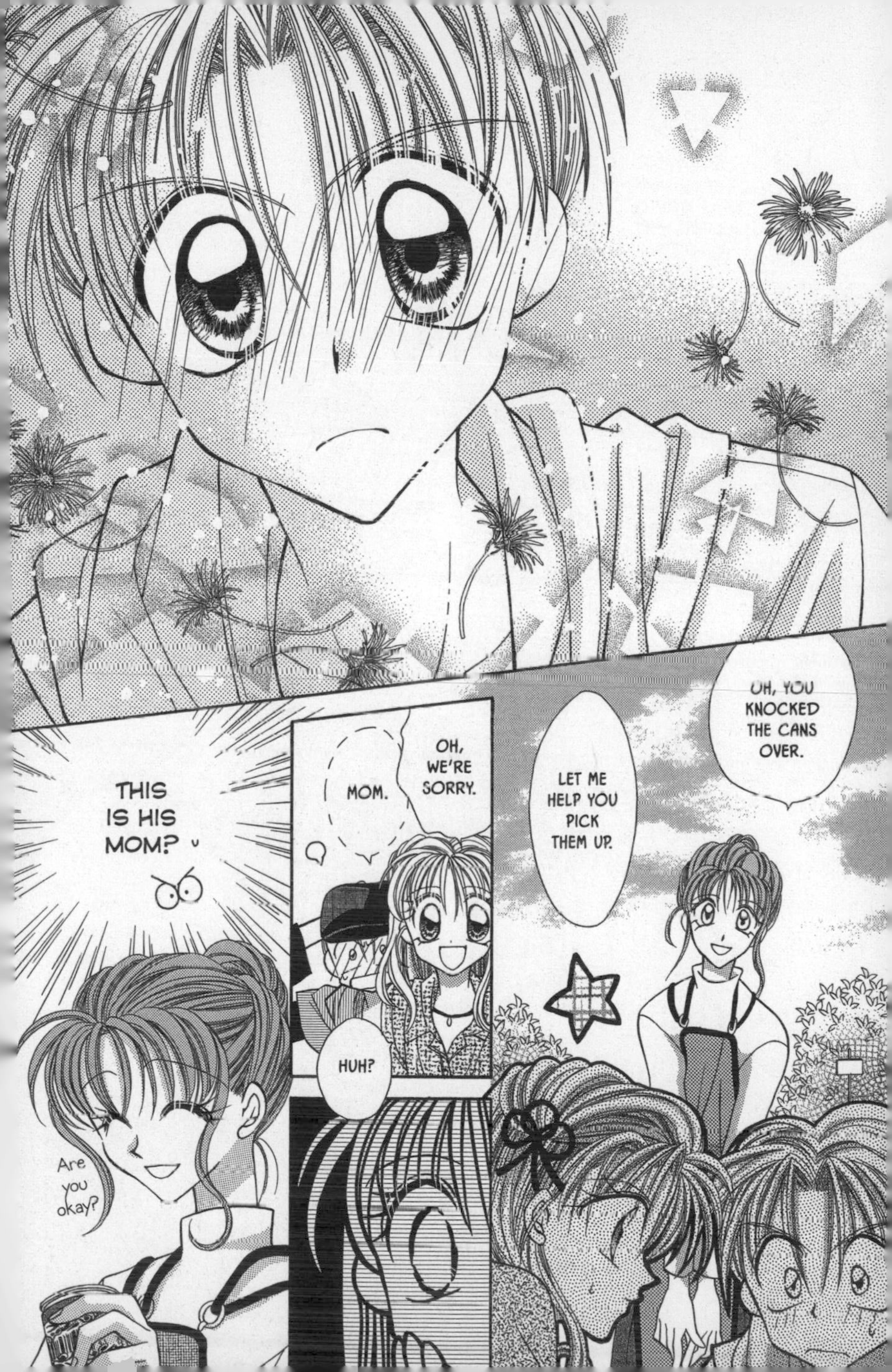
OH, YOU KNOCKED THE CANS OVER.
LET ME HELP YOU PICK THEM UP.
OH, WE'RE SORRY.
MOM.
HUH?
THIS IS HIS MOM?
Are you okay?

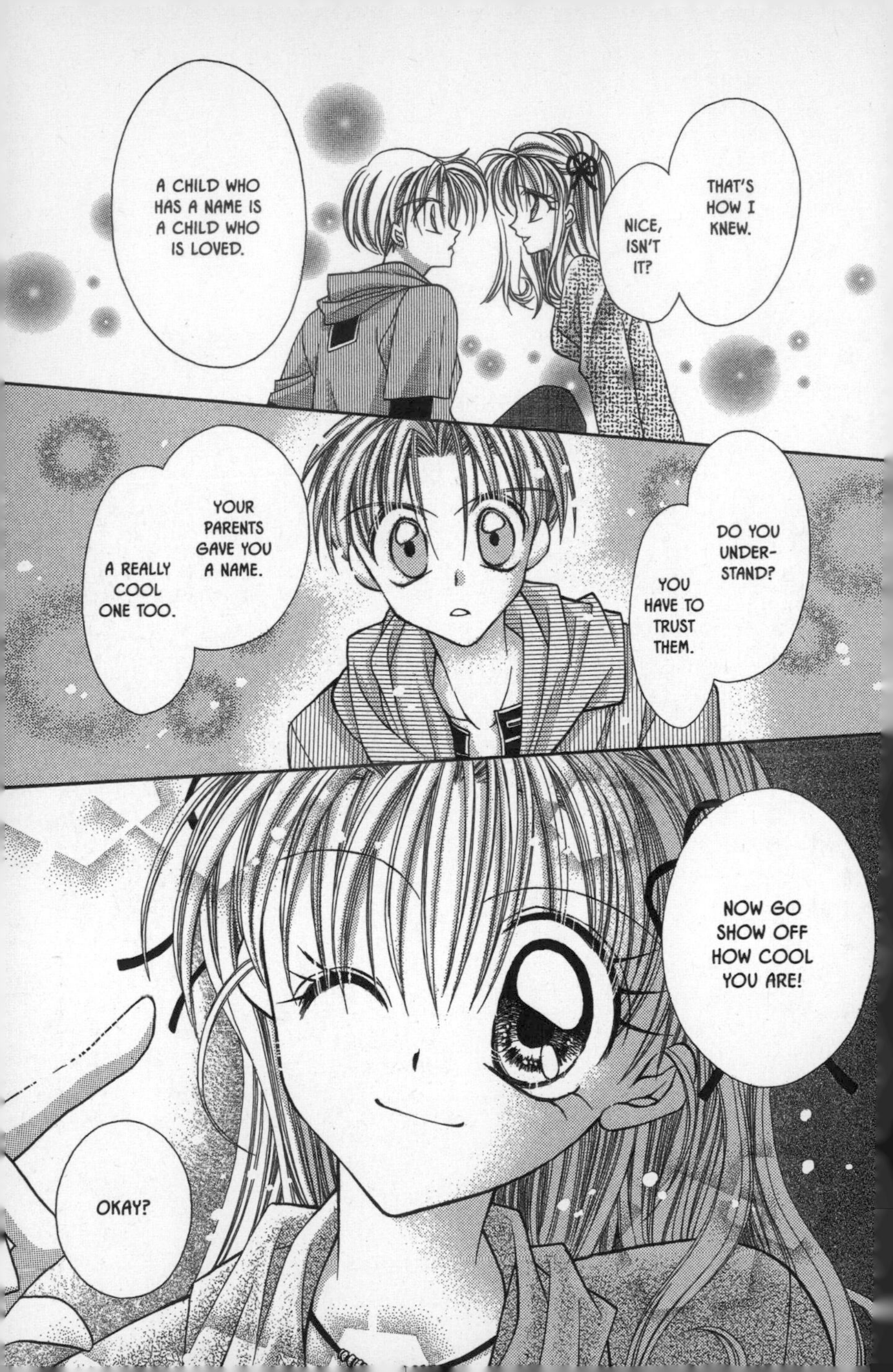
THAT'S HOW I KNEW.
NICE, ISN'T IT?
A CHILD WHO HAS A NAME IS A CHILD WHO IS LOVED.
DO YOU UNDER-STAND?
YOU HAVE TO TRUST THEM.
YOUR PARENTS GAVE YOU A NAME.
A REALLY COOL ONE TOO.
NOW GO SHOW OFF HOW COOL YOU ARE!
OKAY?

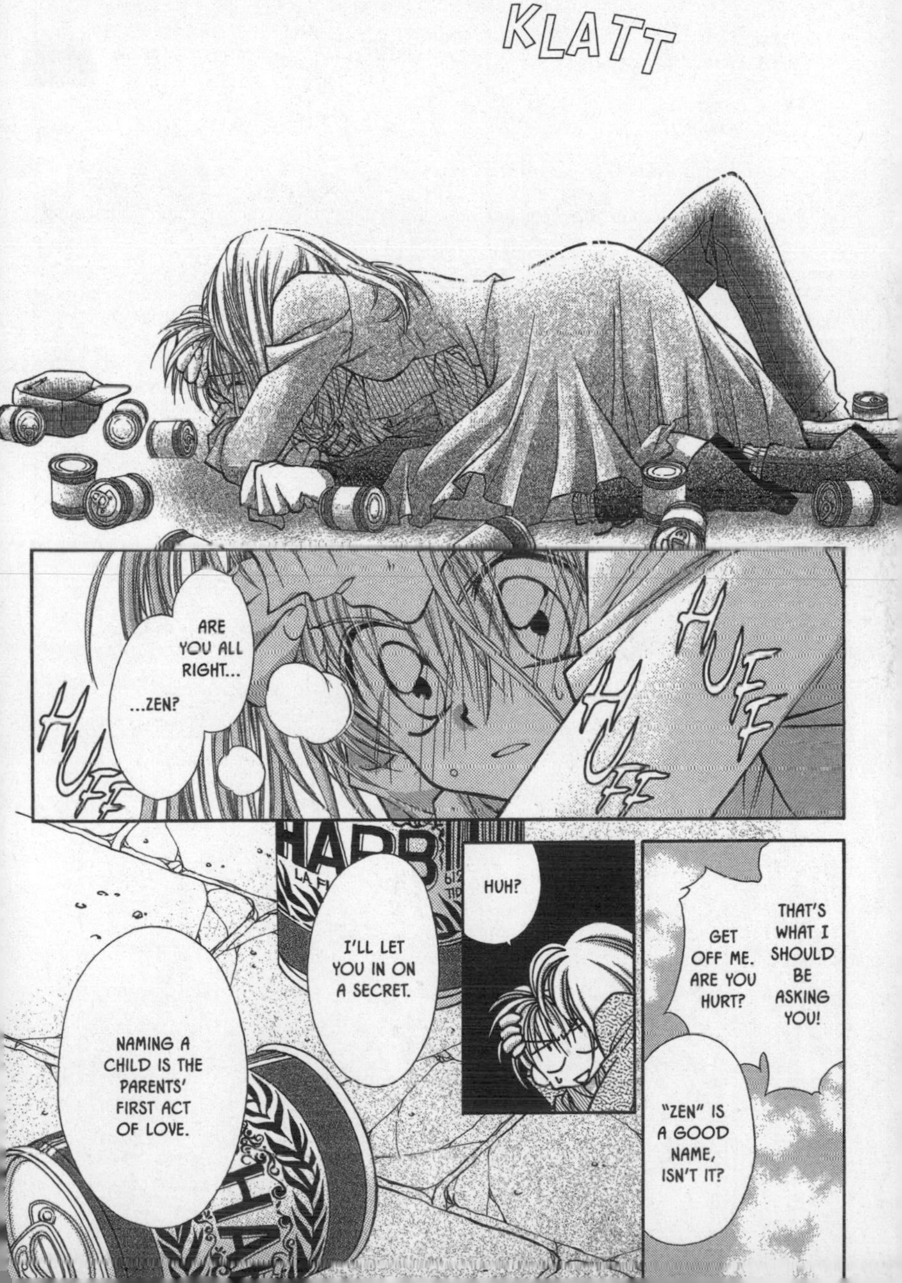
KLATT
HUFF HUFF
ARE YOU ALL RIGHT...
...ZEN?
HUFF
THAT'S WHAT I SHOULD BE ASKING YOU!
GET OFF ME. ARE YOU HURT?
"ZEN" IS A GOOD NAME, ISN'T IT?
HUH?
I'LL LET YOU IN ON A SECRET.
NAMING A CHILD IS THE PARENTS' FIRST ACT OF LOVE.

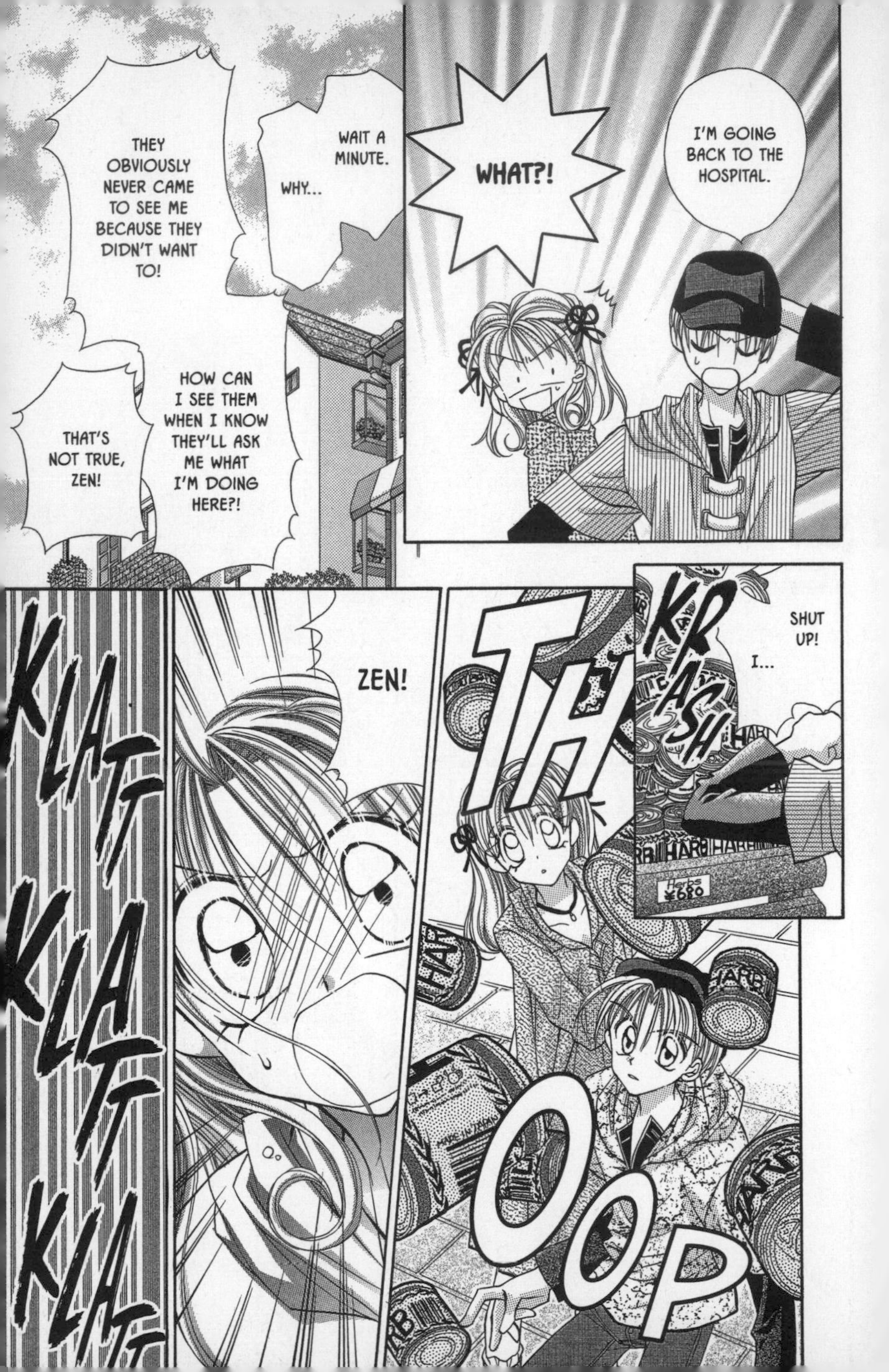
I'M GOING BACK TO THE HOSPITAL.
WHAT?!
WAIT A MINUTE.
WHY...
THEY OBVIOUSLY NEVER CAME TO SEE ME BECAUSE THEY DIDN'T WANT TO!
HOW CAN I SEE THEM WHEN I KNOW THEY'LL ASK ME WHAT I'M DOING HERE?!
THAT'S NOT TRUE, ZEN!
SHUT UP!
I...
KRASH
TH
OOP
ZEN!
KLATT
KLATT
KLATT

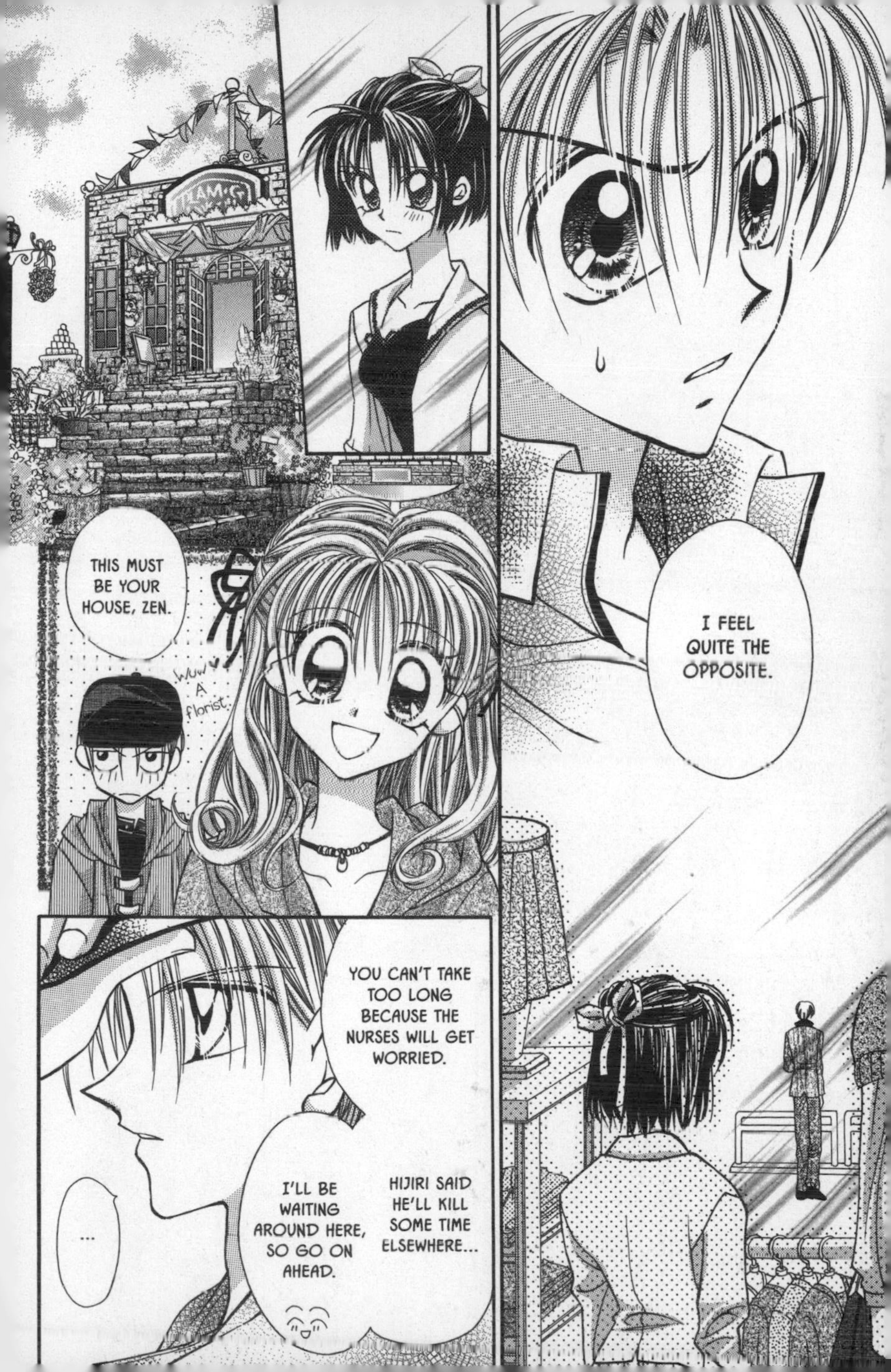
I FEEL QUITE THE OPPOSITE.
THIS MUST BE YOUR HOUSE, ZEN.
Wow♥ A florist.
YOU CAN'T TAKE TOO LONG BECAUSE THE NURSES WILL GET WORRIED.
HIJIRI SAID HE'LL KILL SOME TIME ELSEWHERE...
I'LL BE WAITING AROUND HERE, SO GO ON AHEAD.
...

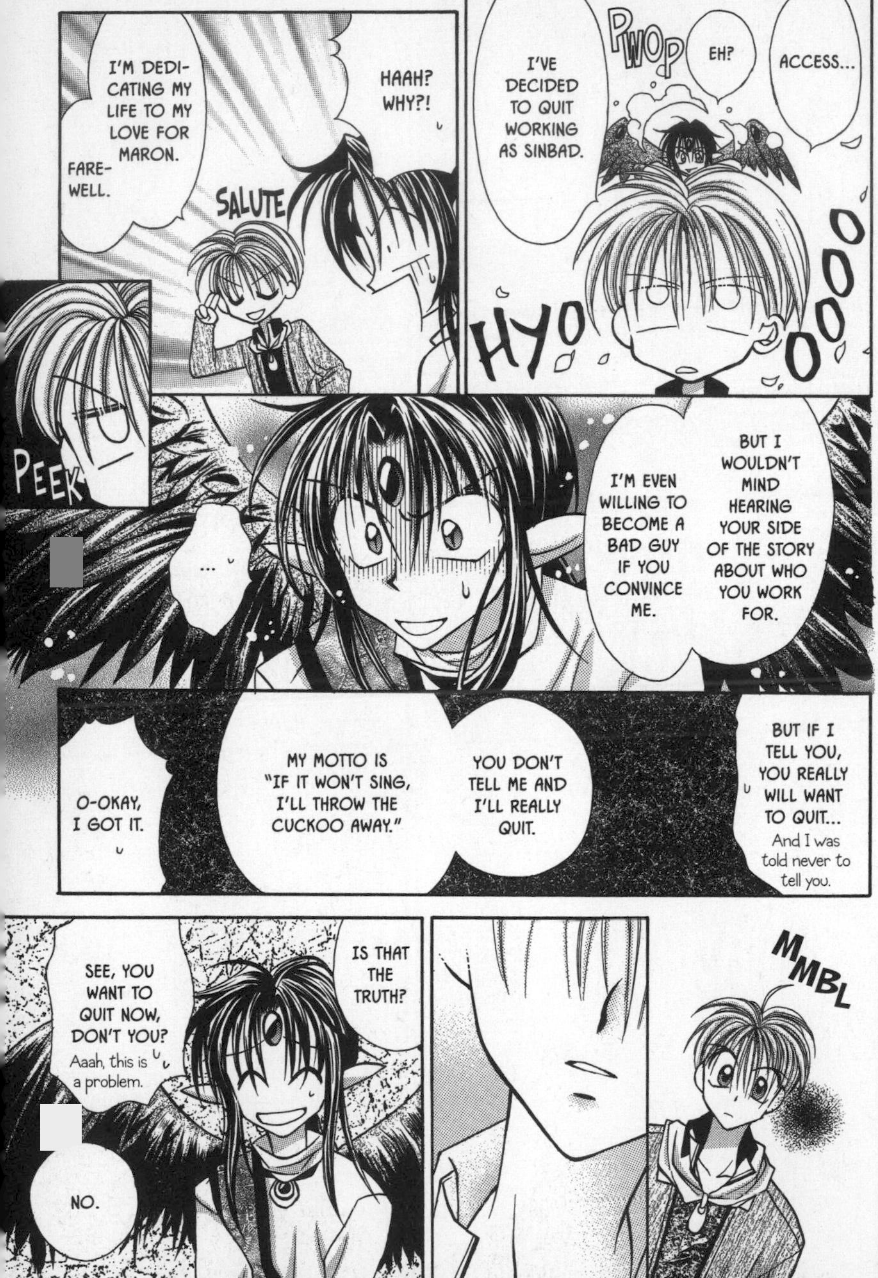
ACCESS...
EH?
PWOP
I'VE DECIDED TO QUIT WORKING AS SINBAD.
HYOOOOOO
HAAH? WHY?!
I'M DEDI-CATING MY LIFE TO MY LOVE FOR MARON.
FARE-WELL.
SALUTE
BUT I WOULDN'T MIND HEARING YOUR SIDE OF THE STORY ABOUT WHO YOU WORK FOR.
I'M EVEN WILLING TO BECOME A BAD GUY IF YOU CONVINCE ME.
...
PEEK
BUT IF I TELL YOU, YOU REALLY WILL WANT TO QUIT...
And I was told never to tell you.
YOU DON'T TELL ME AND I'LL REALLY QUIT.
MY MOTTO IS "IF IT WON'T SING, I'LL THROW THE CUCKOO AWAY."
O-OKAY, I GOT IT.
MMBL
IS THAT THE TRUTH?
SEE, YOU WANT TO QUIT NOW, DON'T YOU?
Aaah, this is a problem.
NO.

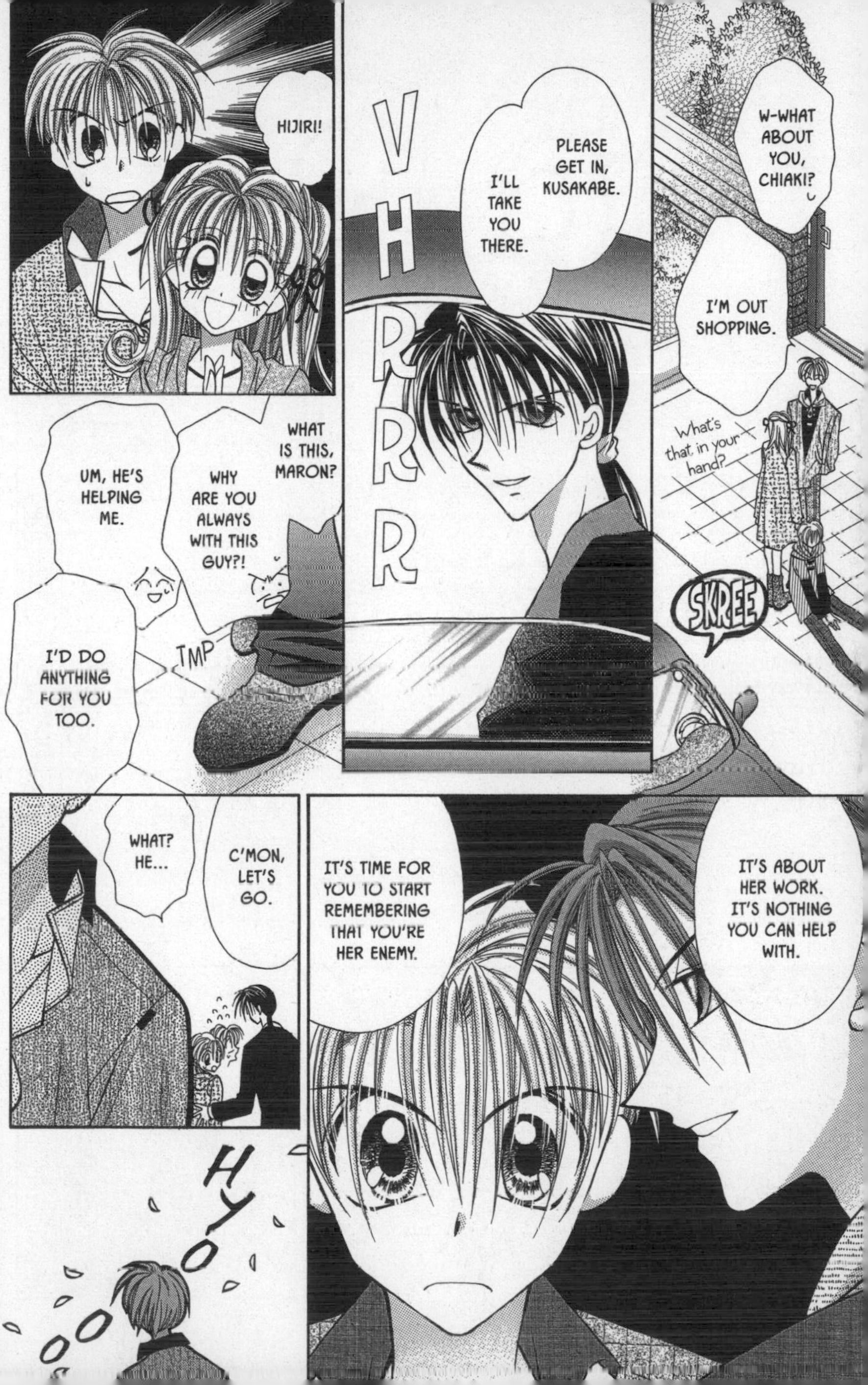
W-WHAT ABOUT YOU, CHIAKI?
I'M OUT SHOPPING.
What's that in your hand?
SKREE
PLEASE GET IN, KUSAKABE.
I'LL TAKE YOU THERE.
VHRRR
HIJIRI!
WHAT IS THIS, MARON?
WHY ARE YOU ALWAYS WITH THIS GUY?!
UM, HE'S HELPING ME.
I'D DO ANYTHING FOR YOU TOO.
TMP
IT'S ABOUT HER WORK. IT'S NOTHING YOU CAN HELP WITH.
IT'S TIME FOR YOU TO START REMEMBERING THAT YOU'RE HER ENEMY.
C'MON, LET'S GO.
WHAT? HE...
HYOOOO

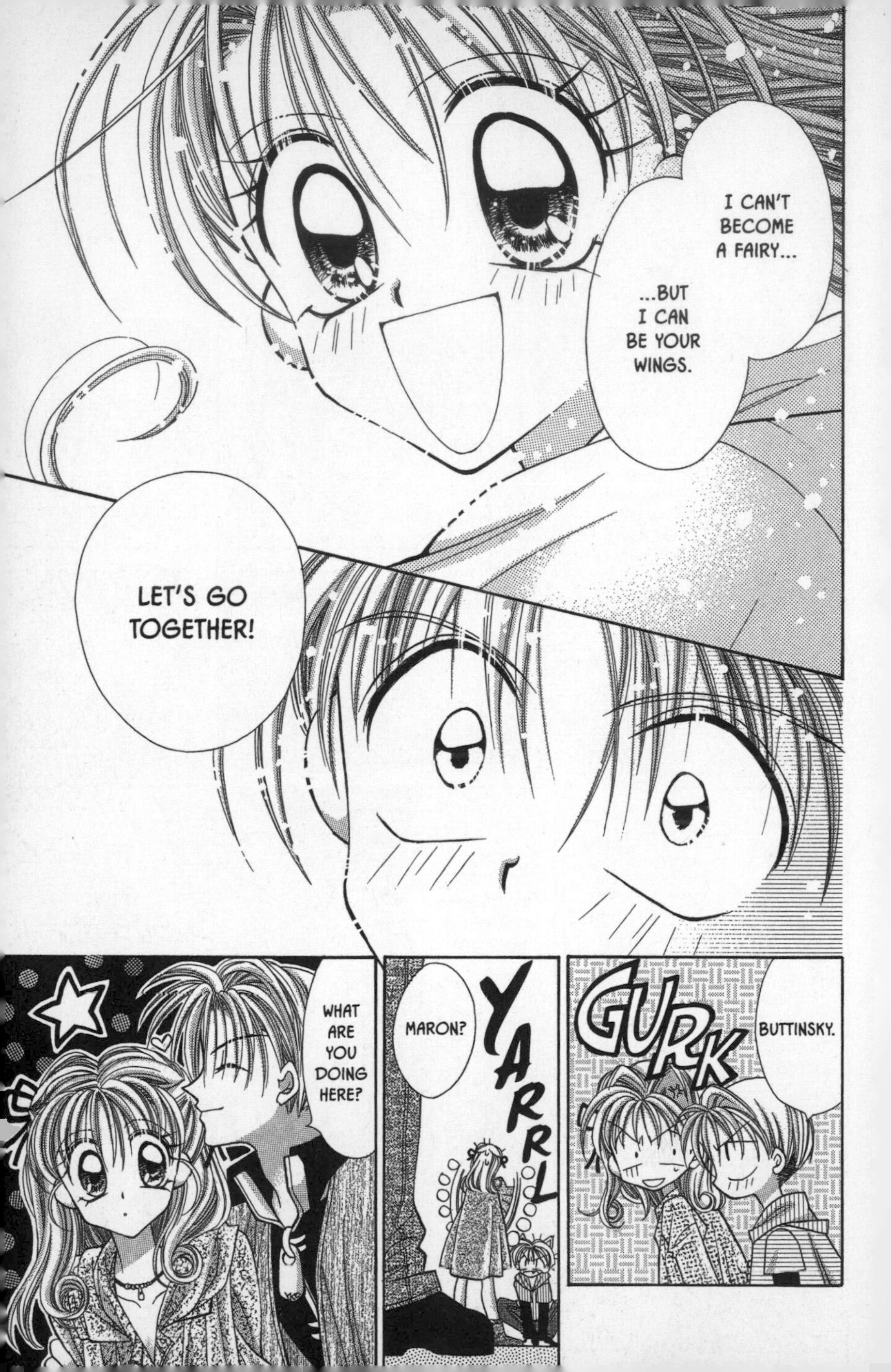
I CAN'T BECOME A FAIRY...
...BUT I CAN BE YOUR WINGS.
LET'S GO TOGETHER!
BUTTINSKY.
GURK
YARRL
MARON?
WHAT ARE YOU DOING HERE?

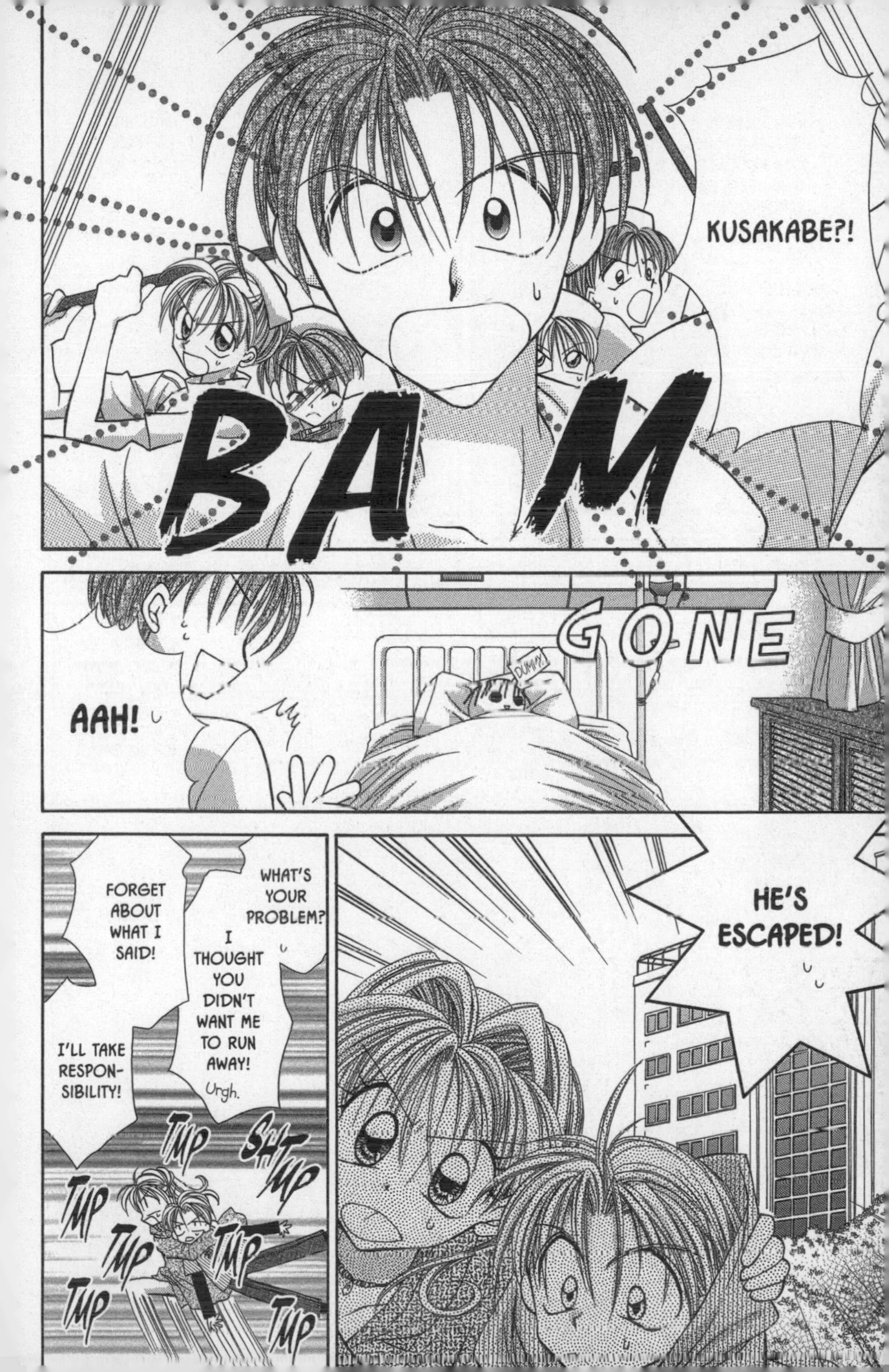
KUSAKABE?!
BAM
GONE
DUMMY
AAH!
HE'S ESCAPED!
WHAT'S YOUR PROBLEM?
I THOUGHT YOU DIDN'T WANT ME TO RUN AWAY!
Urgh.
FORGET ABOUT WHAT I SAID!
I'LL TAKE RESPON-SIBILITY!
SHTMP
TMP
TMP
TMP
TMP
TMP
TMP

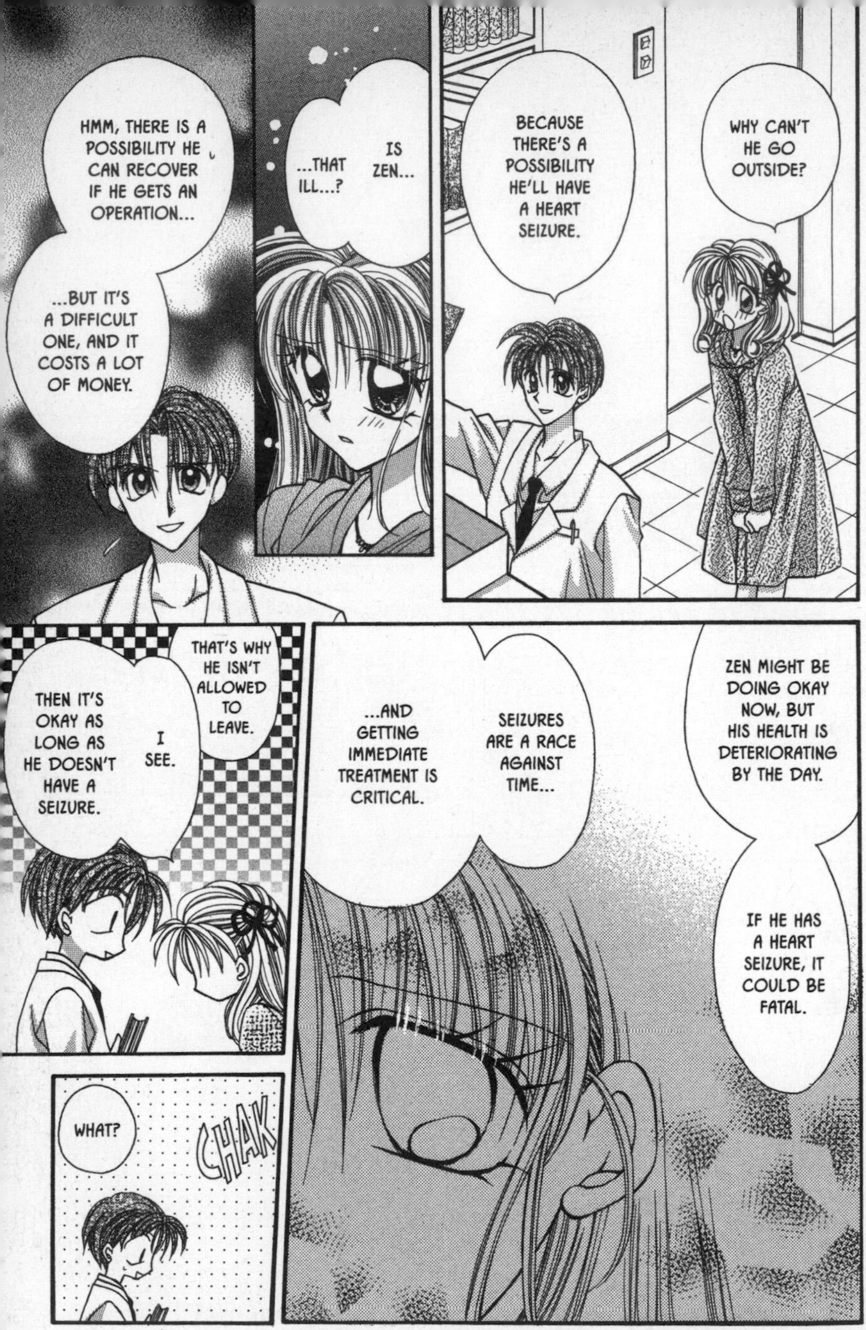
WHY CAN'T HE GO OUTSIDE?
BECAUSE THERE'S A POSSIBILITY HE'LL HAVE A HEART SEIZURE.
IS ZEN...
...THAT ILL...?
HMM, THERE IS A POSSIBILITY HE CAN RECOVER IF HE GETS AN OPERATION...
...BUT IT'S A DIFFICULT ONE, AND IT COSTS A LOT OF MONEY.
ZEN MIGHT BE DOING OKAY NOW, BUT HIS HEALTH IS DETERIORATING BY THE DAY.
IF HE HAS A HEART SEIZURE, IT COULD BE FATAL.
SEIZURES ARE A RACE AGAINST TIME...
...AND GETTING IMMEDIATE TREATMENT IS CRITICAL.
THAT'S WHY HE ISN'T ALLOWED TO LEAVE.
I SEE.
THEN IT'S OKAY AS LONG AS HE DOESN'T HAVE A SEIZURE.
CHAK
WHAT?

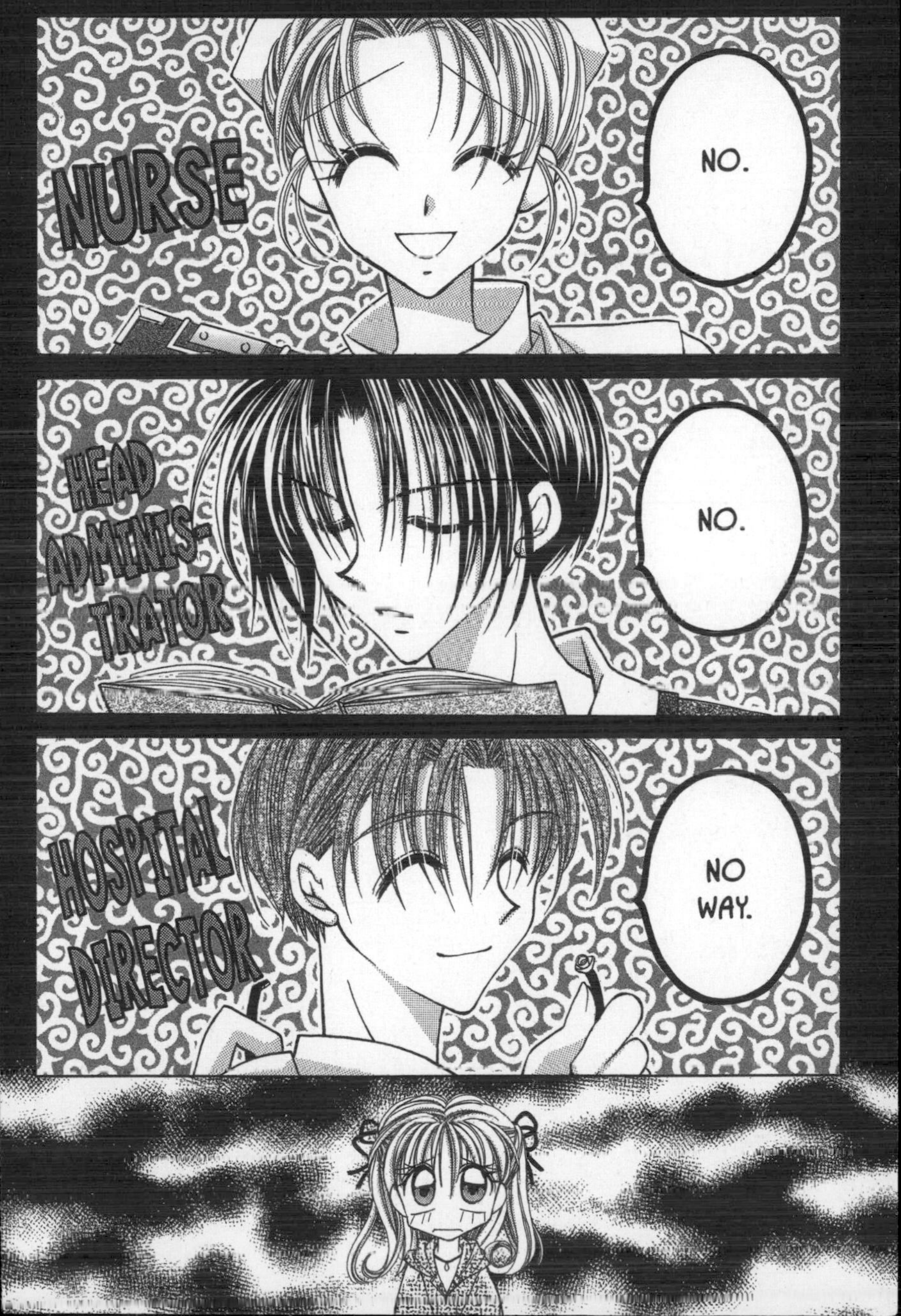
NURSE
NO.
HEAD ADMINIS-TRATOR
NO.
HOSPITAL DIRECTOR
NO WAY.

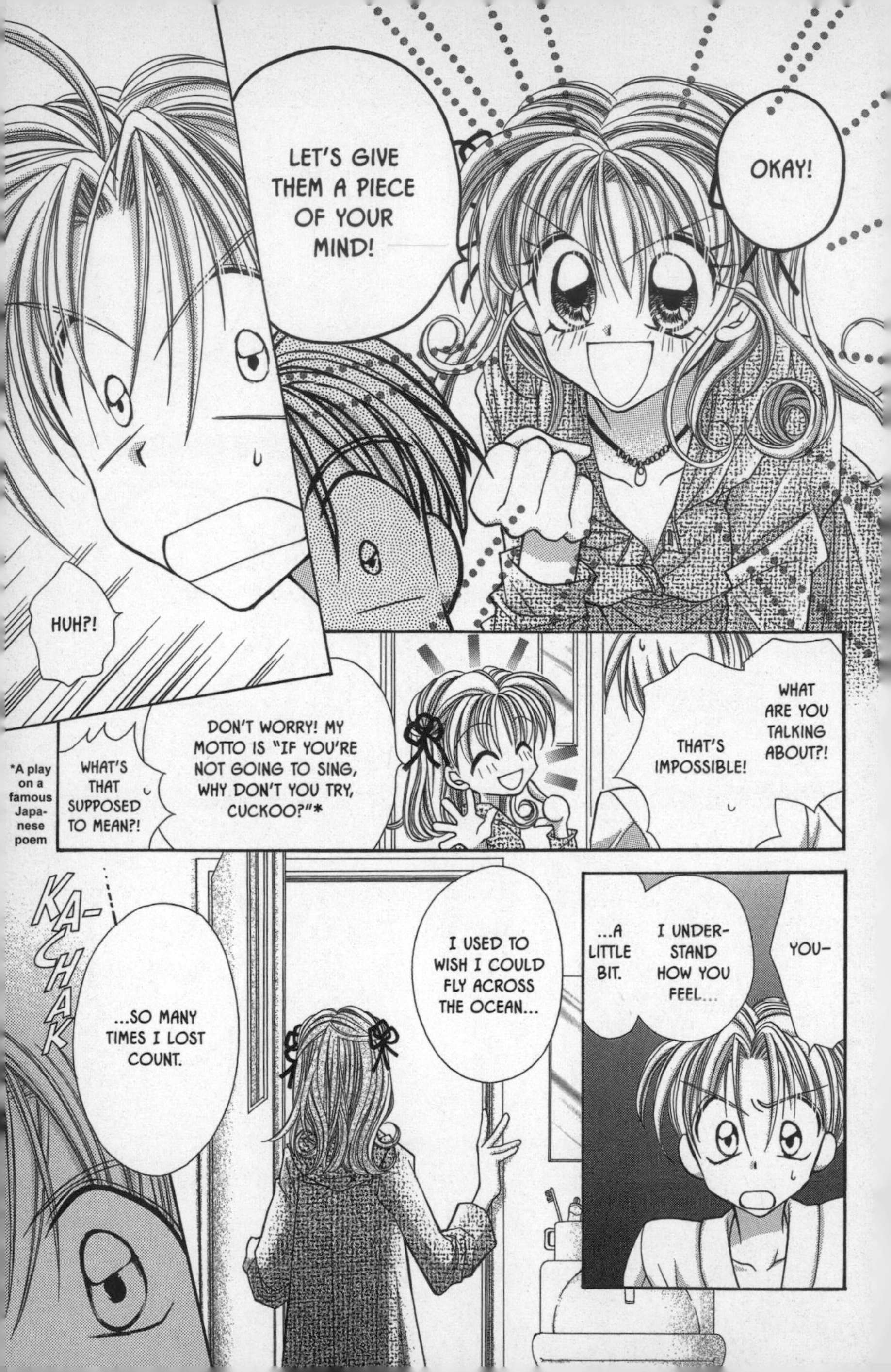
OKAY!
LET'S GIVE THEM A PIECE OF YOUR MIND!
HUH?!
WHAT ARE YOU TALKING ABOUT?!
THAT'S IMPOSSIBLE!
DON'T WORRY! MY MOTTO IS "IF YOU'RE NOT GOING TO SING, WHY DON'T YOU TRY, CUCKOO?"*
WHAT'S THAT SUPPOSED TO MEAN?!
YOU—
I UNDER-STAND HOW YOU FEEL...
...A LITTLE BIT.
I USED TO WISH I COULD FLY ACROSS THE OCEAN...
KA-CHAK
...SO MANY TIMES I LOST COUNT.

*A play on a famous Japanese poem

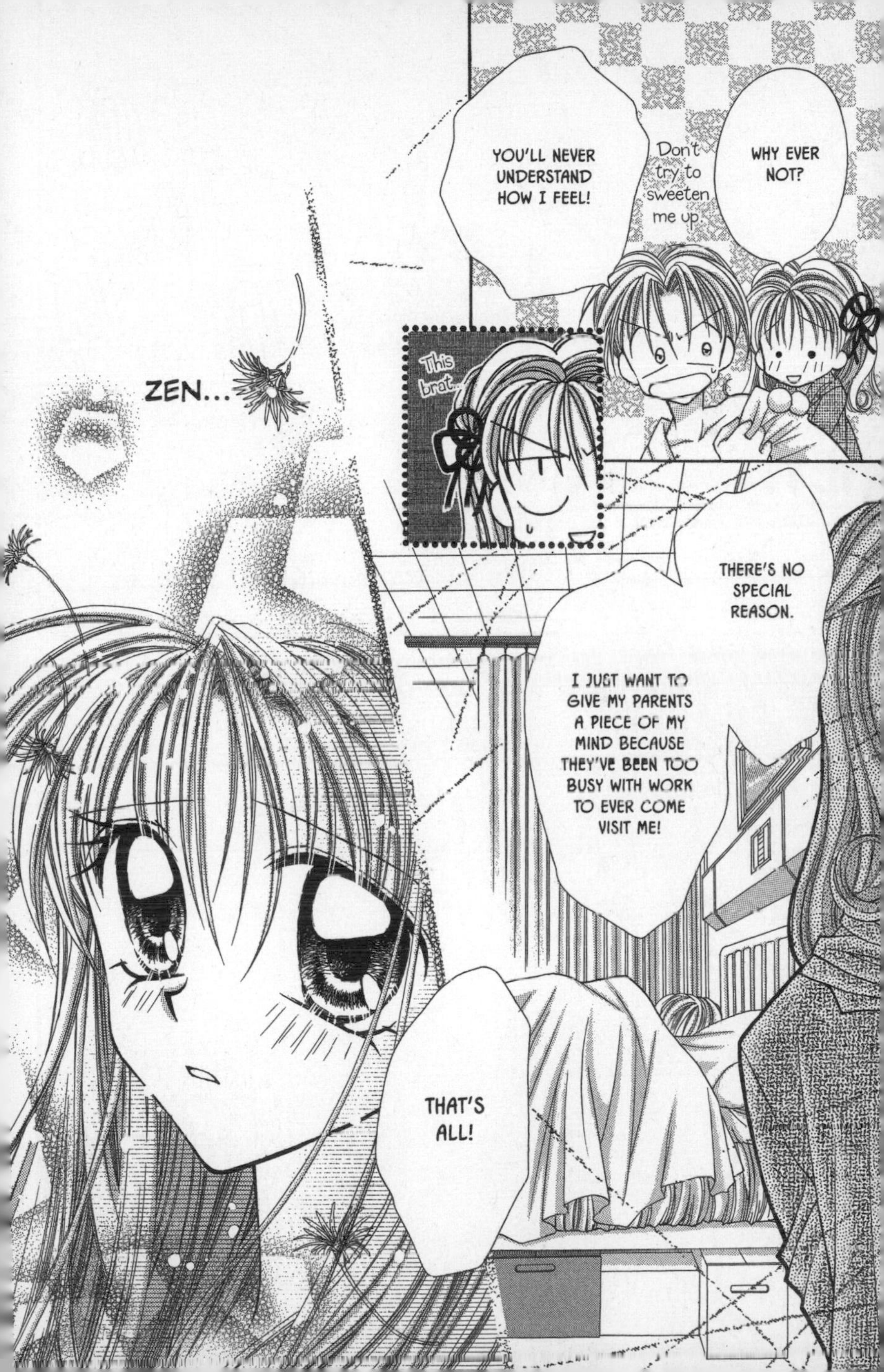
WHY EVER NOT?
Don't try to sweeten me up.
YOU'LL NEVER UNDERSTAND HOW I FEEL!
This brat...
ZEN...
THERE'S NO SPECIAL REASON.
I JUST WANT TO GIVE MY PARENTS A PIECE OF MY MIND BECAUSE THEY'VE BEEN TOO BUSY WITH WORK TO EVER COME VISIT ME!
THAT'S ALL!

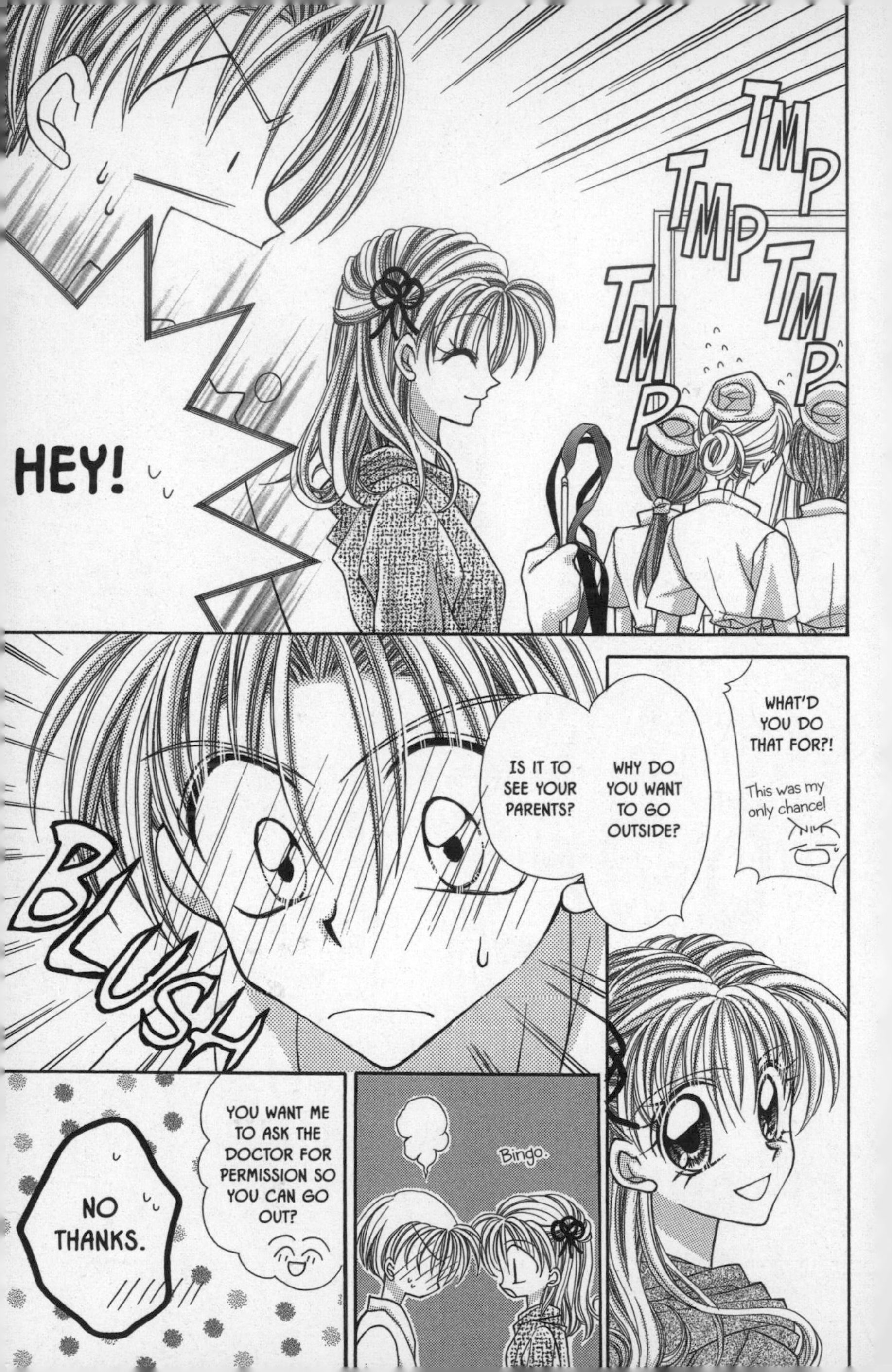
TMP TMP TMP TMP TMP
HEY!
WHAT'D YOU DO THAT FOR?!
This was my only chance!
WHY DO YOU WANT TO GO OUTSIDE?
IS IT TO SEE YOUR PARENTS?
BLUSH
Bingo.
YOU WANT ME TO ASK THE DOCTOR FOR PERMISSION SO YOU CAN GO OUT?
NO THANKS.

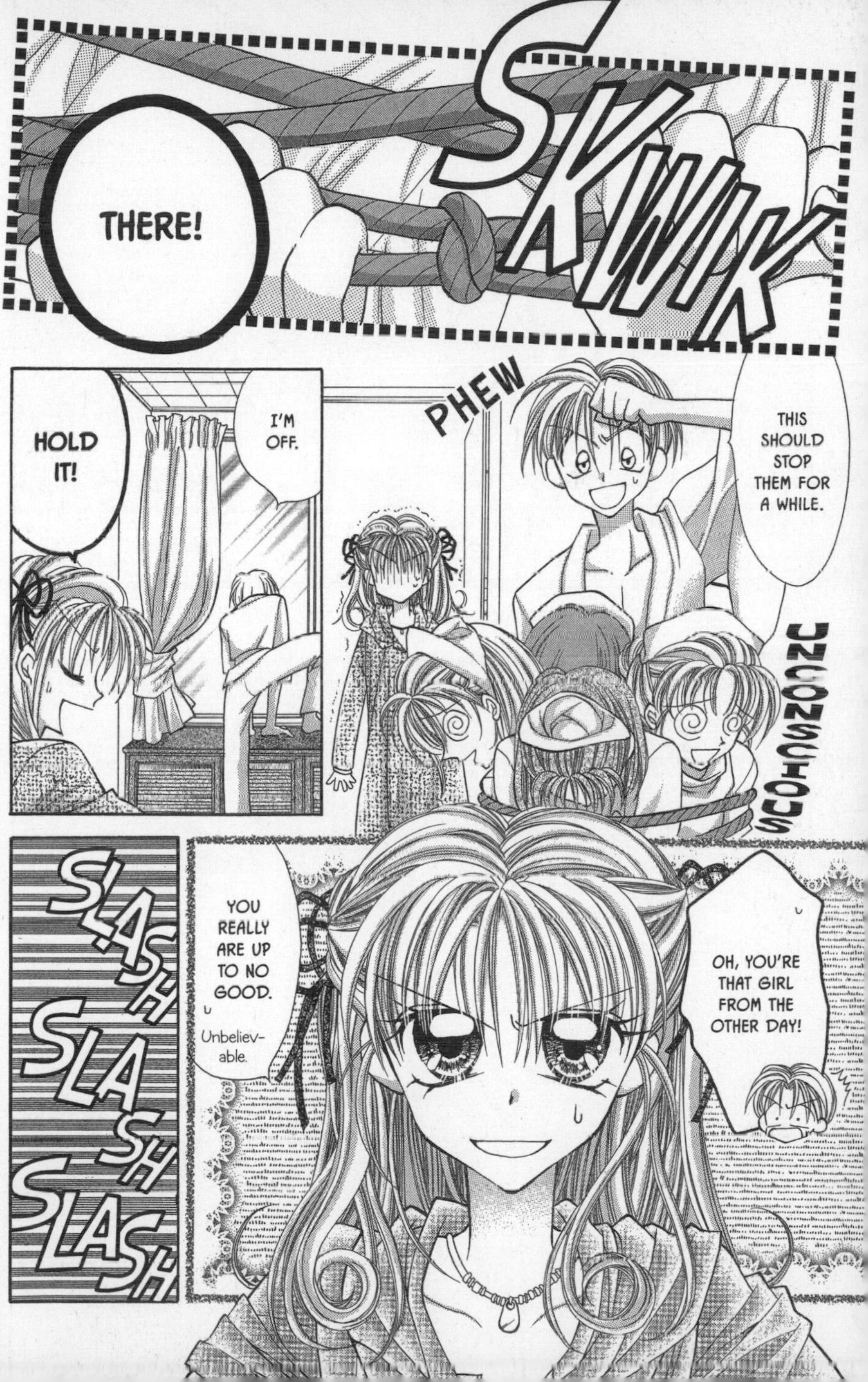
SKWNK
THERE!
THIS SHOULD STOP THEM FOR A WHILE.
PHEW
UNCONSCIOUS
I'M OFF.
HOLD IT!
OH, YOU'RE THAT GIRL FROM THE OTHER DAY!
YOU REALLY ARE UP TO NO GOOD.
Unbelievable.
SLASH SLASH SLASH

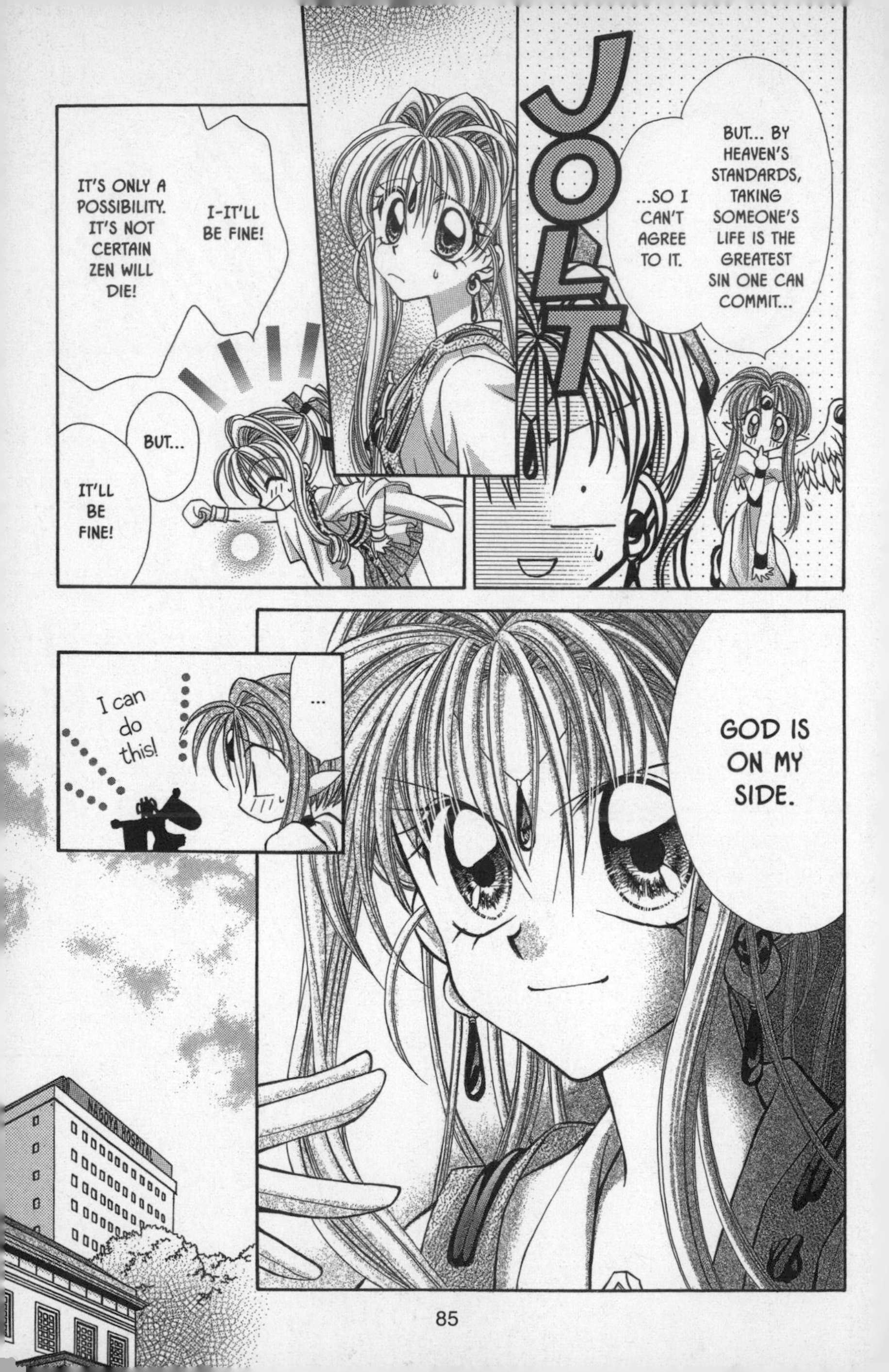
BUT... BY HEAVEN'S STANDARDS, TAKING SOMEONE'S LIFE IS THE GREATEST SIN ONE CAN COMMIT...
...SO I CAN'T AGREE TO IT.
JOLT
I-IT'LL BE FINE!
IT'S ONLY A POSSIBILITY. IT'S NOT CERTAIN ZEN WILL DIE!
BUT...
IT'LL BE FINE!
GOD IS ON MY SIDE.
...
I can do this!
NAGOYA HOSPITAL

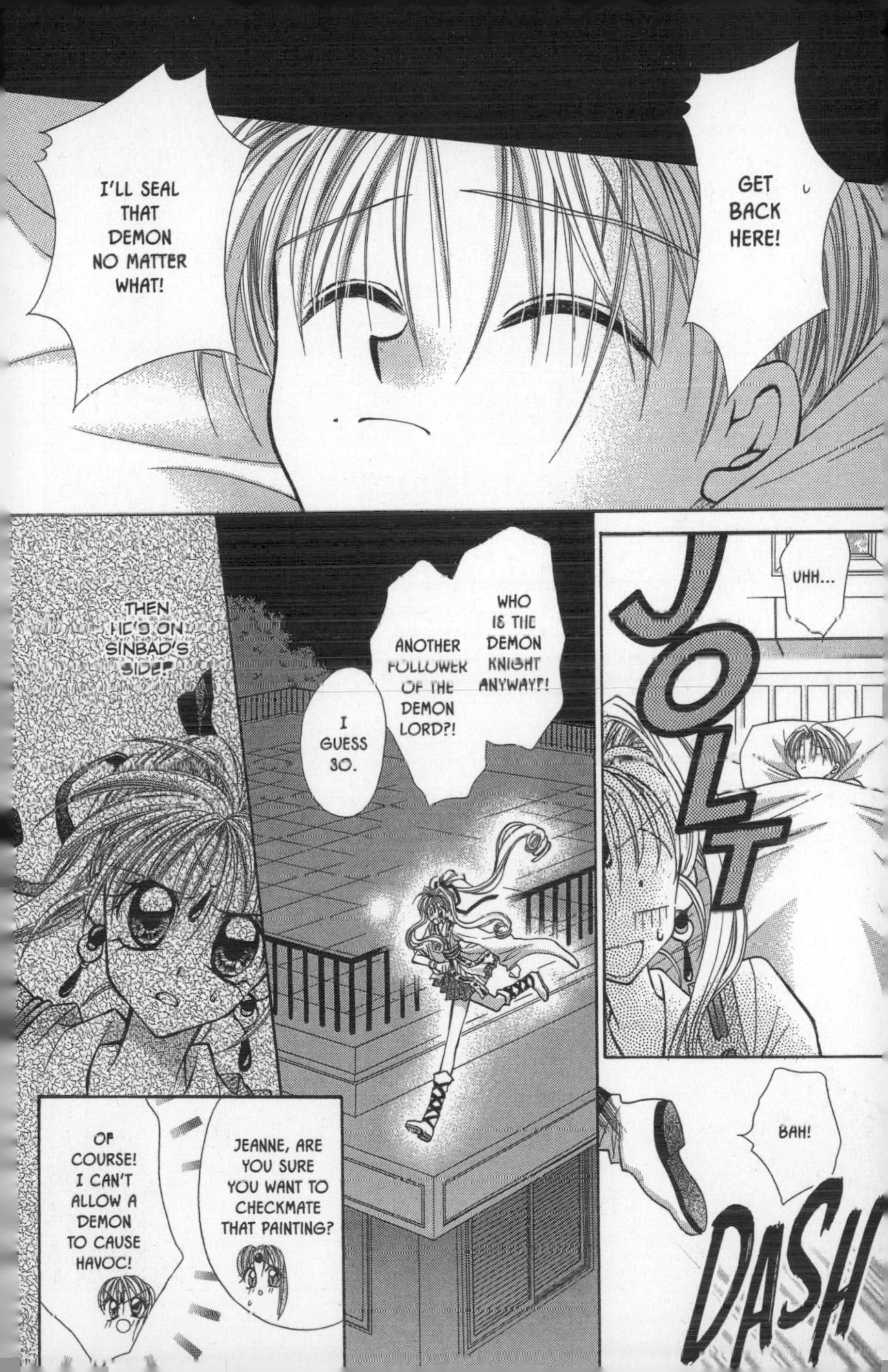
GET BACK HERE!
I'LL SEAL THAT DEMON NO MATTER WHAT!
UHH...
JOLT
BAH!
DASH
WHO IS THE DEMON KNIGHT ANYWAY?!
ANOTHER FOLLOWER OF THE DEMON LORD?!
I GUESS SO.
THEN HE'S ON SINBAD'S SIDE!?
JEANNE, ARE YOU SURE YOU WANT TO CHECKMATE THAT PAINTING?
OF COURSE! I CAN'T ALLOW A DEMON TO CAUSE HAVOC!

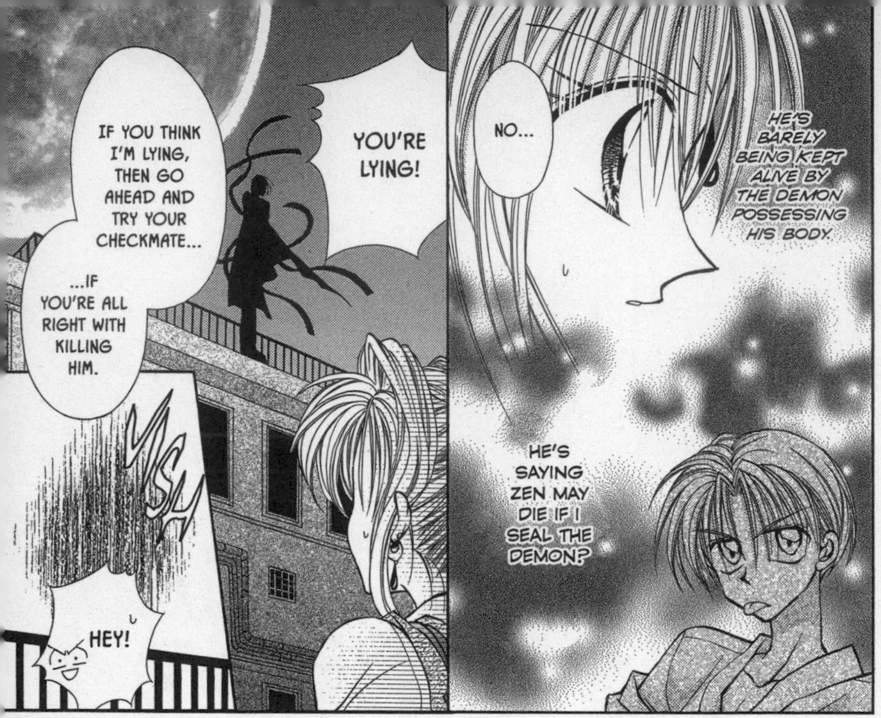
NO...
HE'S BARELY BEING KEPT ALIVE BY THE DEMON POSSESSING HIS BODY.
HE'S SAYING ZEN MAY DIE IF I SEAL THE DEMON?
YOU'RE LYING!
IF YOU THINK I'M LYING, THEN GO AHEAD AND TRY YOUR CHECKMATE...
...IF YOU'RE ALL RIGHT WITH KILLING HIM.
VISH
HEY!

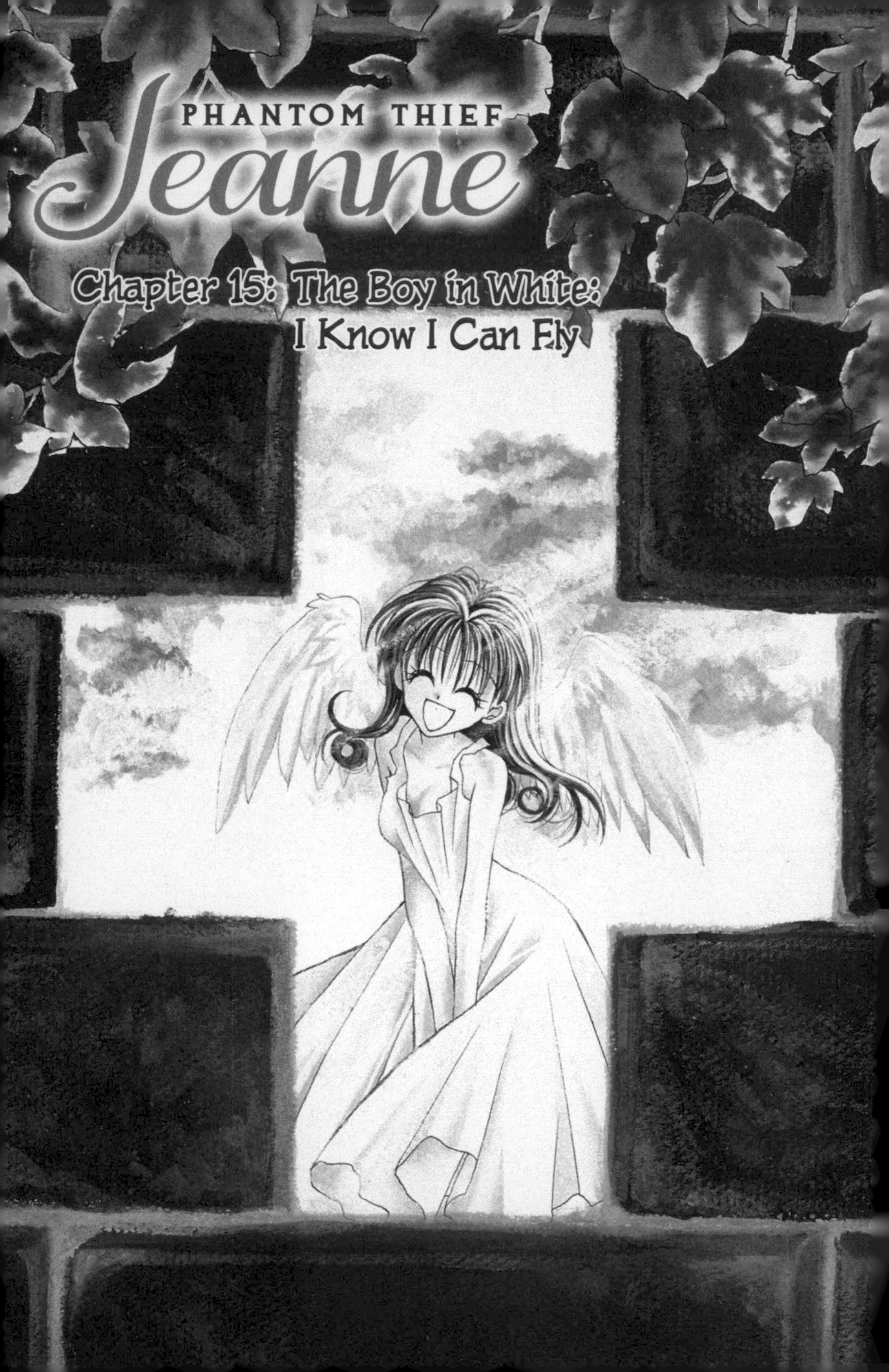
PHANTOM THIEF
Jeanne
Chapter 15: The Boy in White:
I Know I Can Fly

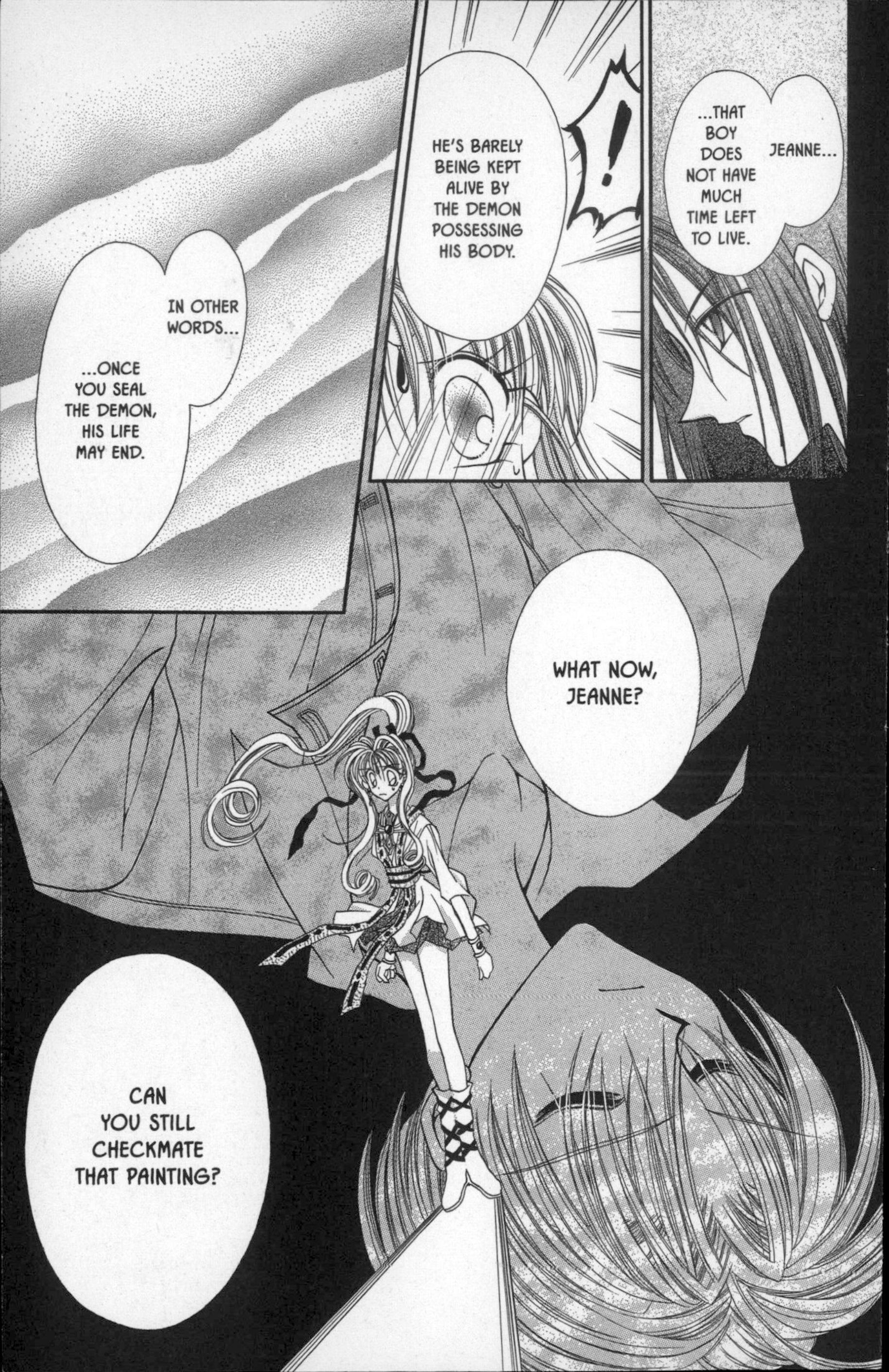
JEANNE...
...THAT BOY DOES NOT HAVE MUCH TIME LEFT TO LIVE.
!
HE'S BARELY BEING KEPT ALIVE BY THE DEMON POSSESSING HIS BODY.
IN OTHER WORDS...
...ONCE YOU SEAL THE DEMON, HIS LIFE MAY END.
WHAT NOW, JEANNE?
CAN YOU STILL CHECKMATE THAT PAINTING?

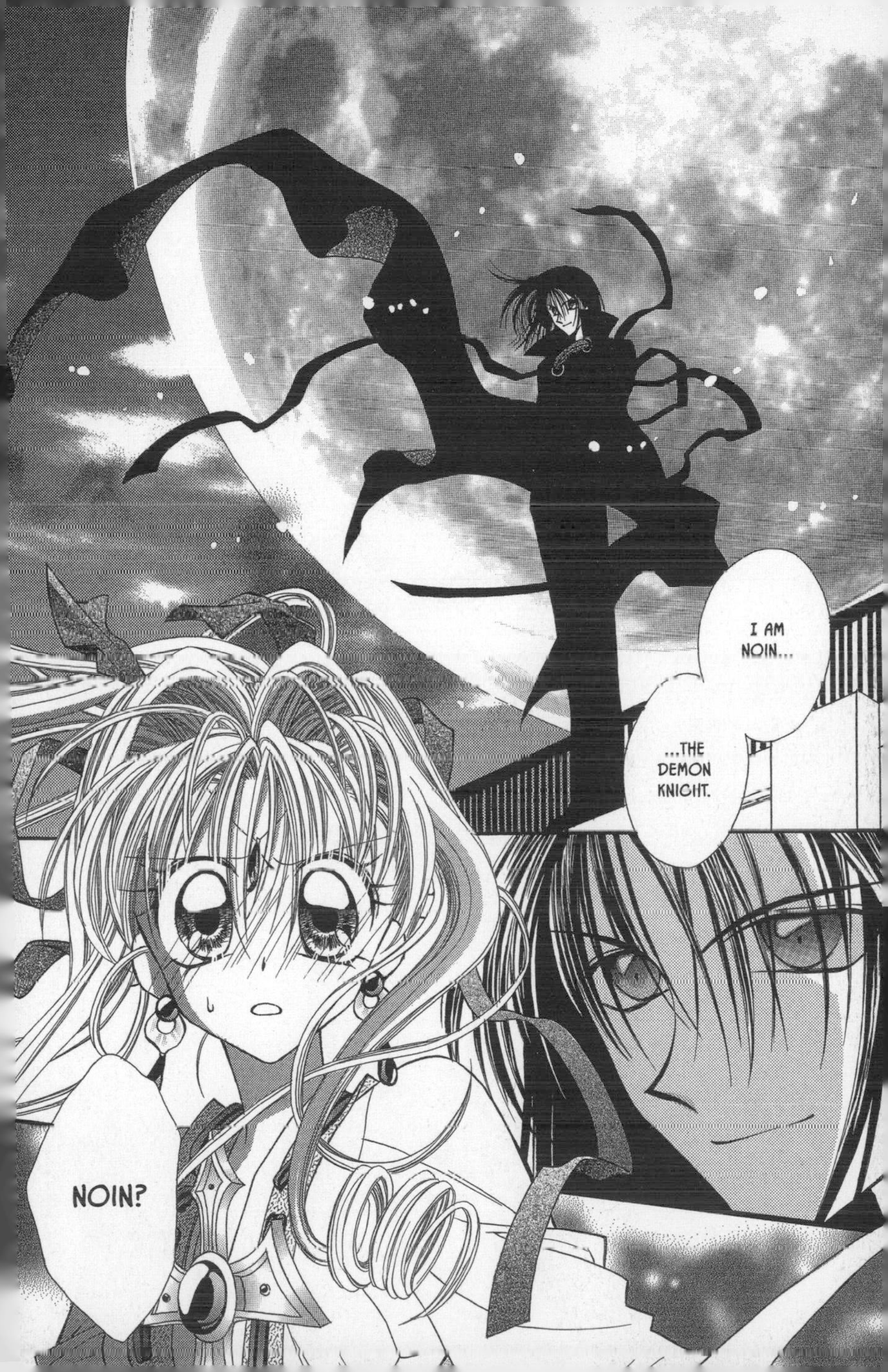
I AM NOIN...
...THE DEMON KNIGHT.
NOIN?

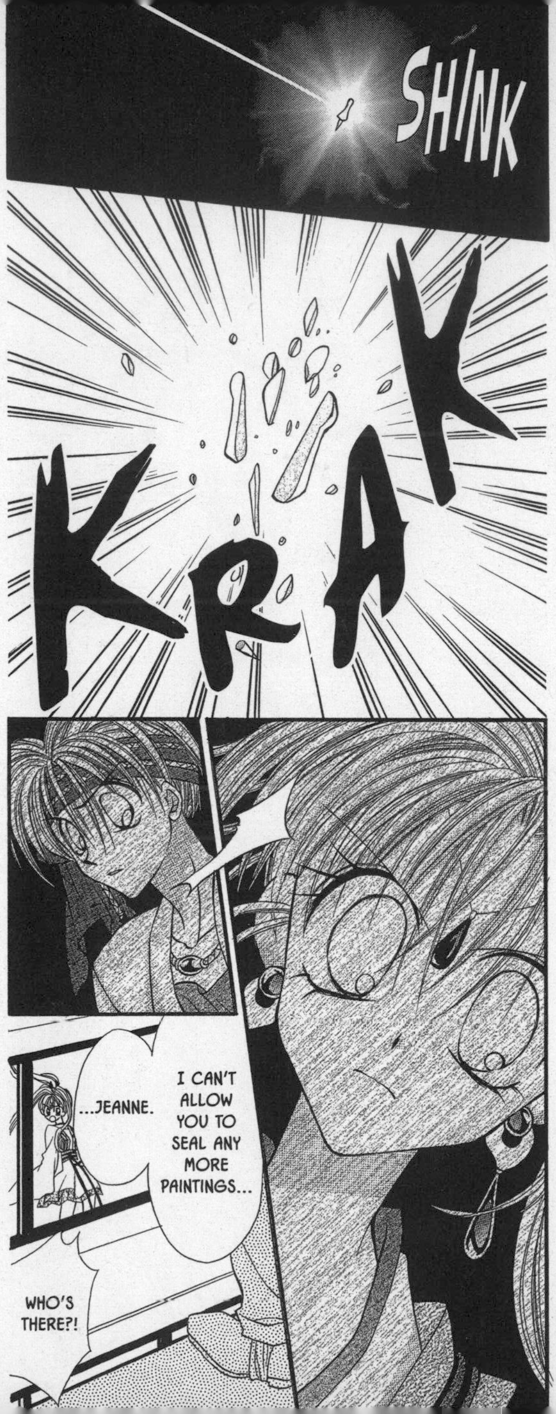
SHINK
KRAK
I CAN'T ALLOW YOU TO SEAL ANY MORE PAINTINGS...
...JEANNE.
WHO'S THERE?!

PHANTOM
THIEF
JEANNE

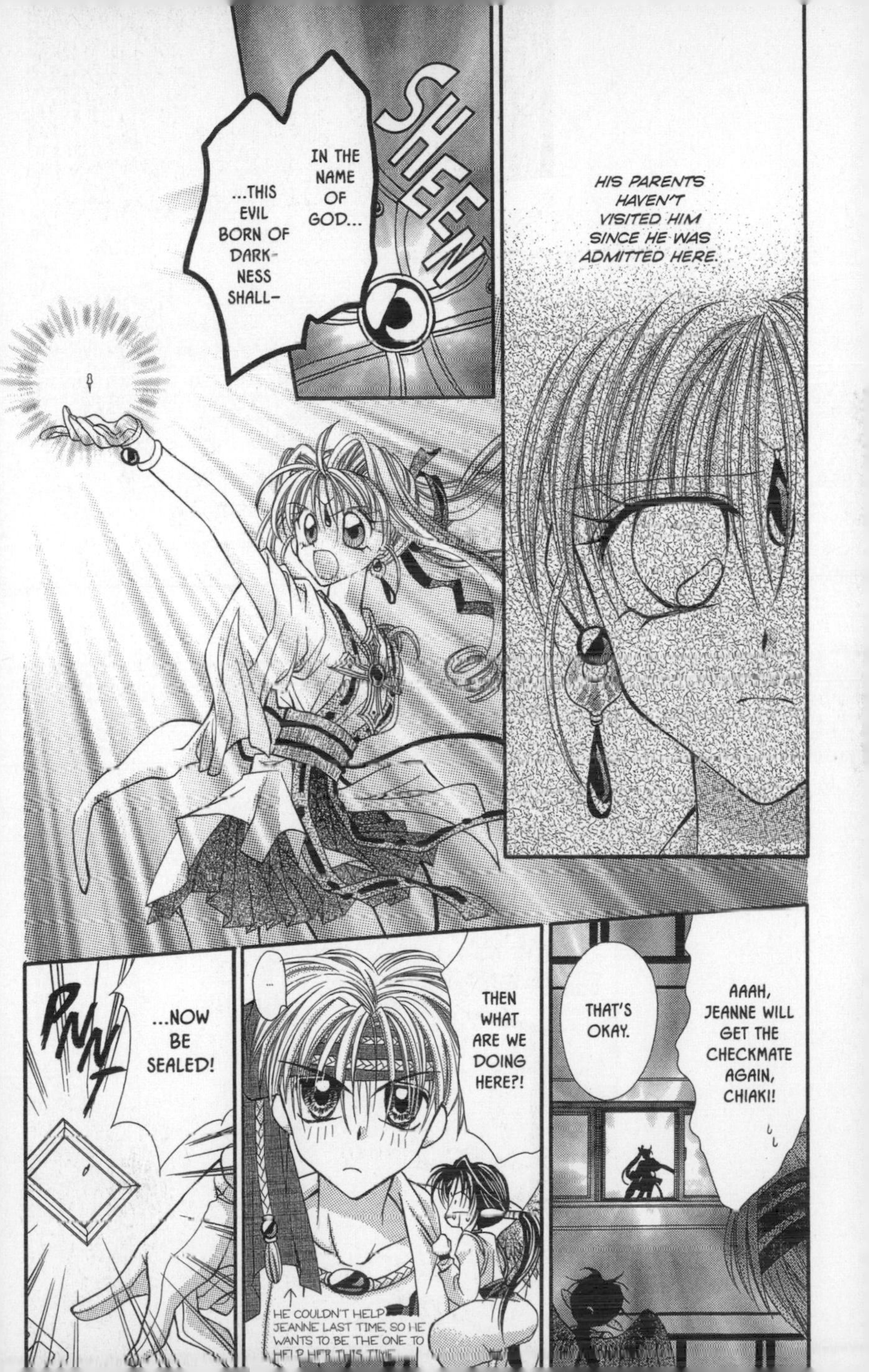
HIS PARENTS HAVEN'T VISITED HIM SINCE HE WAS ADMITTED HERE.
SHEEN
IN THE NAME OF GOD...
...THIS EVIL BORN OF DARKNESS SHALL—
AAAH, JEANNE WILL GET THE CHECKMATE AGAIN, CHIAKI!
THAT'S OKAY.
THEN WHAT ARE WE DOING HERE?!
...
HE COULDN'T HELP JEANNE LAST TIME, SO HE WANTS TO BE THE ONE TO HELP HER THIS TIME.
...NOW BE SEALED!
PWNT

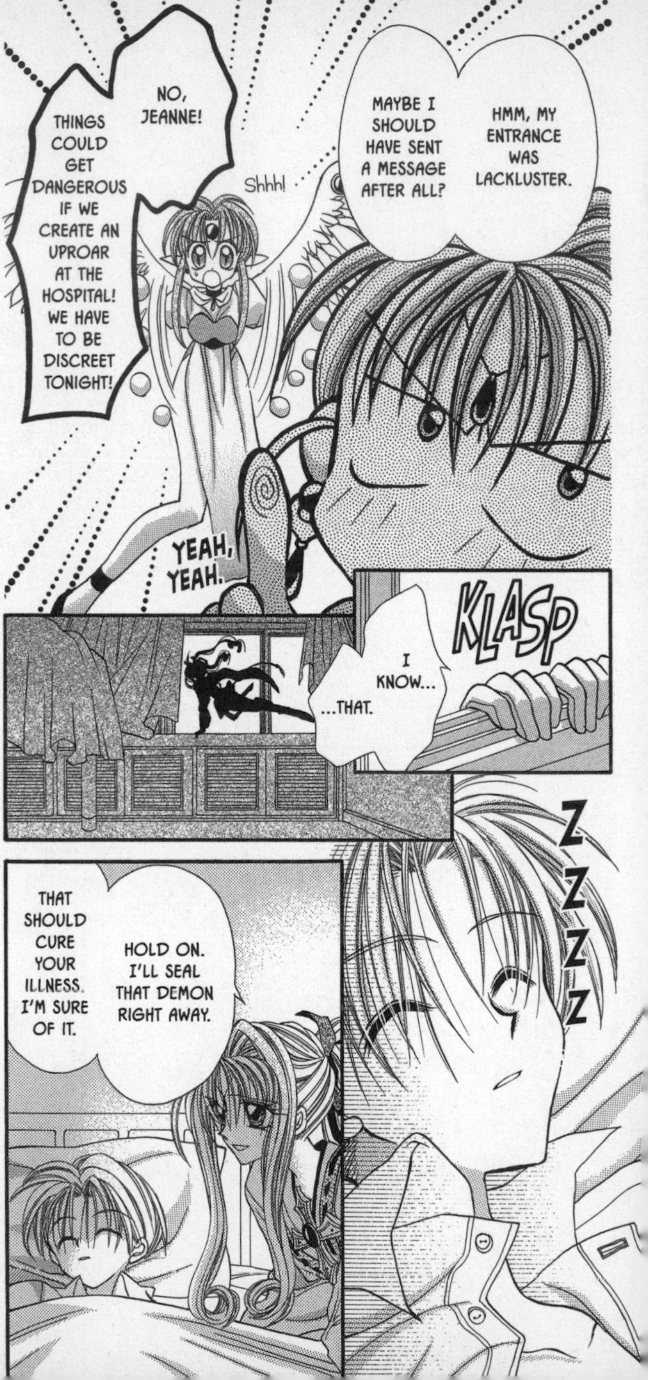
HMM, MY ENTRANCE WAS LACKLUSTER.
MAYBE I SHOULD HAVE SENT A MESSAGE AFTER ALL?
NO, JEANNE!
THINGS COULD GET DANGEROUS IF WE CREATE AN UPROAR AT THE HOSPITAL! WE HAVE TO BE DISCREET TONIGHT!
Shhh!
YEAH, YEAH.
KLASP
I KNOW...
...THAT.
ZZZZ
HOLD ON. I'LL SEAL THAT DEMON RIGHT AWAY.
THAT SHOULD CURE YOUR ILLNESS. I'M SURE OF IT.

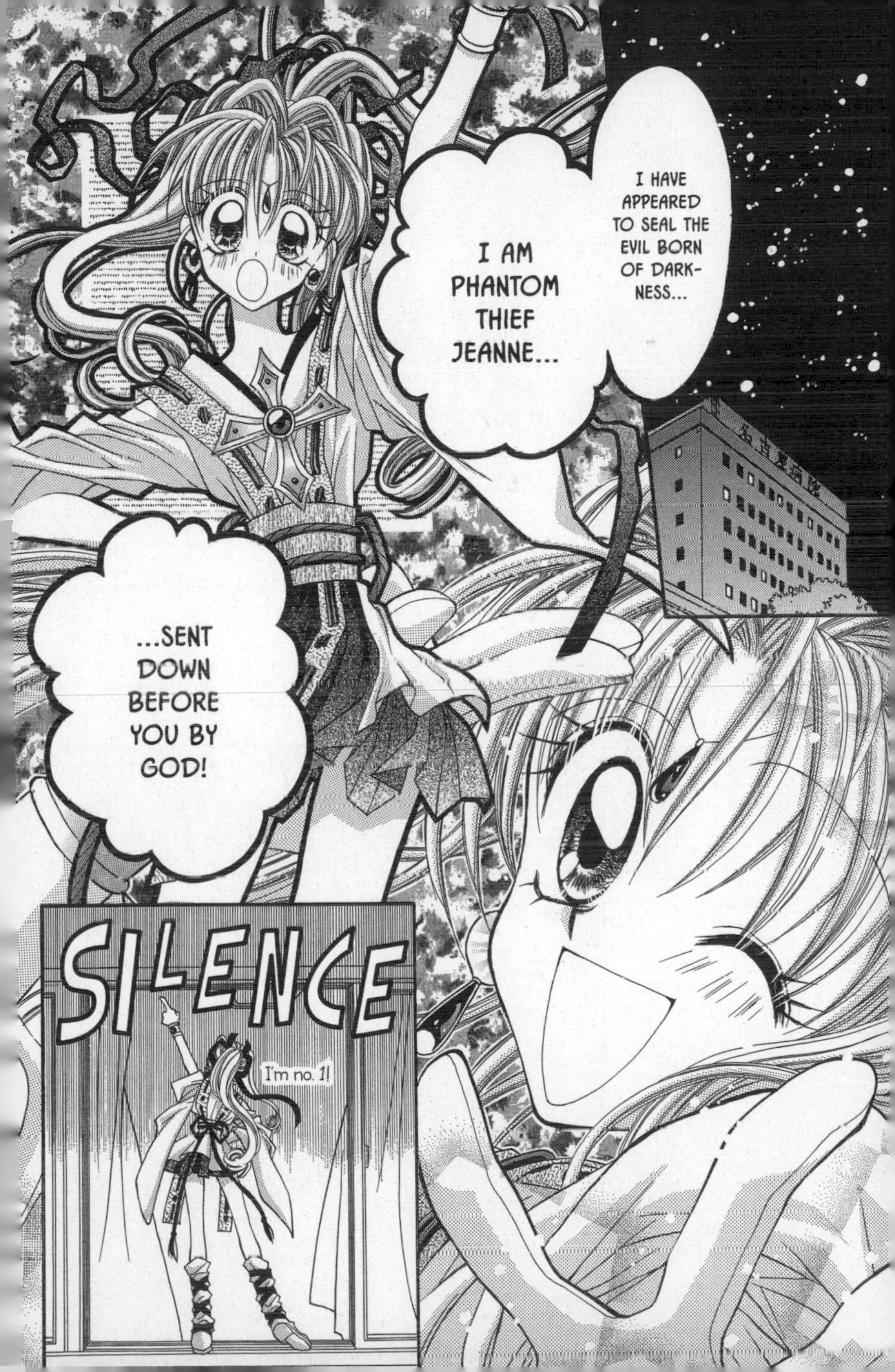
I AM PHANTOM THIEF JEANNE...
...SENT DOWN BEFORE YOU BY GOD!
I HAVE APPEARED TO SEAL THE EVIL BORN OF DARK-NESS...
SILENCE
I'm no. 1!

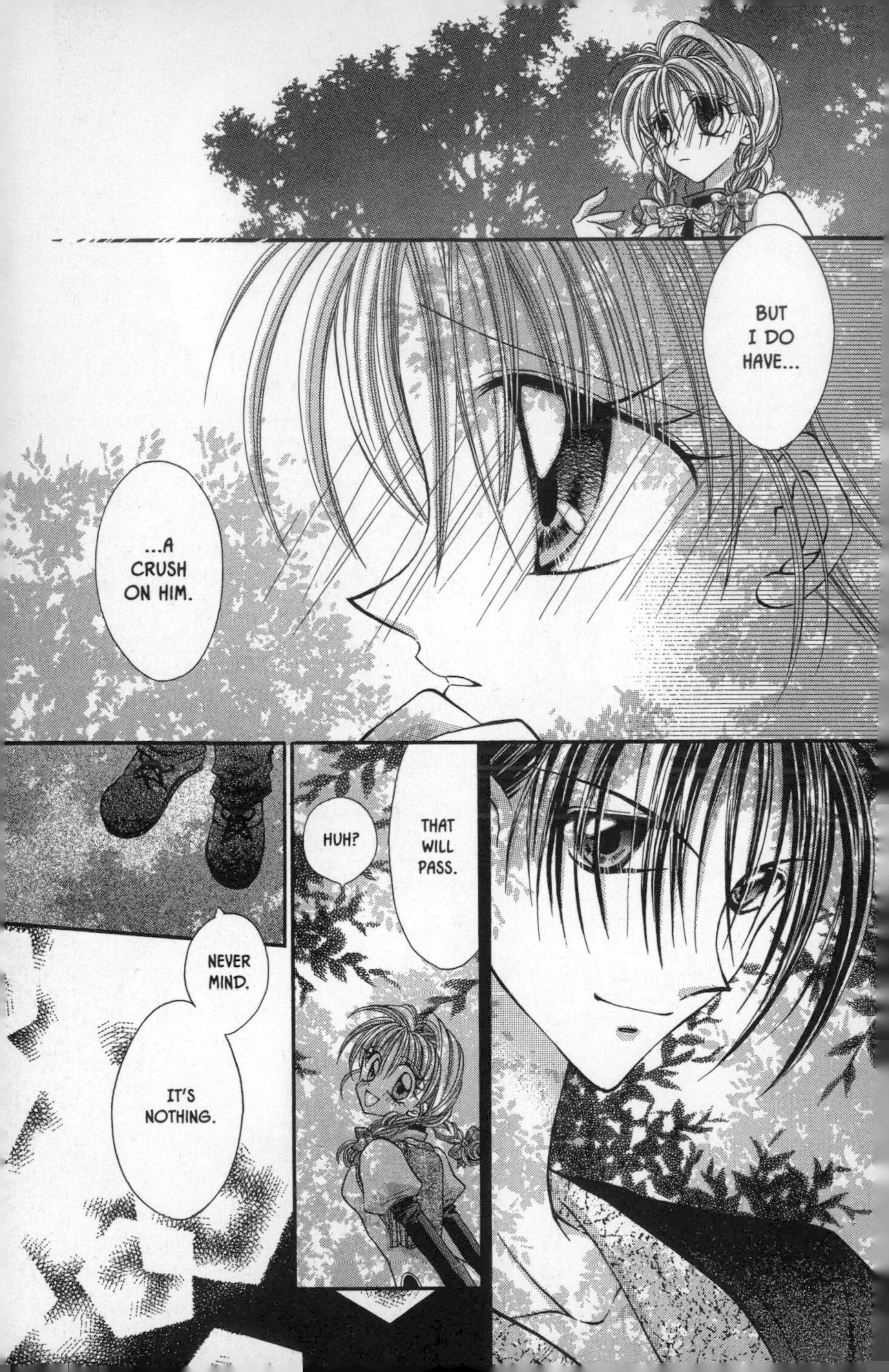
BUT I DO HAVE...
...A CRUSH ON HIM.
THAT WILL PASS.
HUH?
NEVER MIND.
IT'S NOTHING.

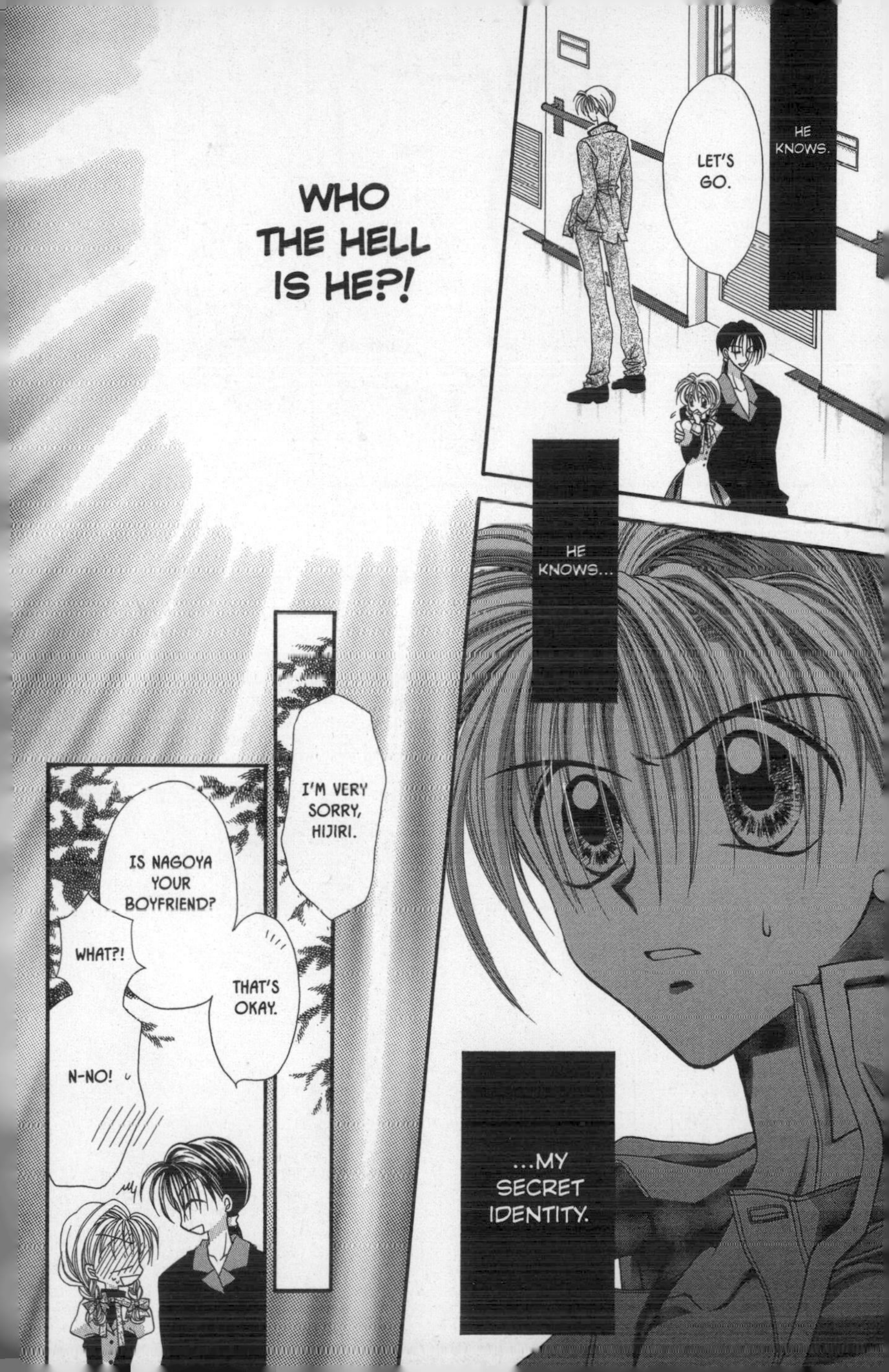
HE KNOWS.
LET'S GO.
HE KNOWS...
...MY SECRET IDENTITY.
WHO THE HELL IS HE?!
I'M VERY SORRY, HIJIRI.
THAT'S OKAY.
IS NAGOYA YOUR BOYFRIEND?
WHAT?!
N-NO!

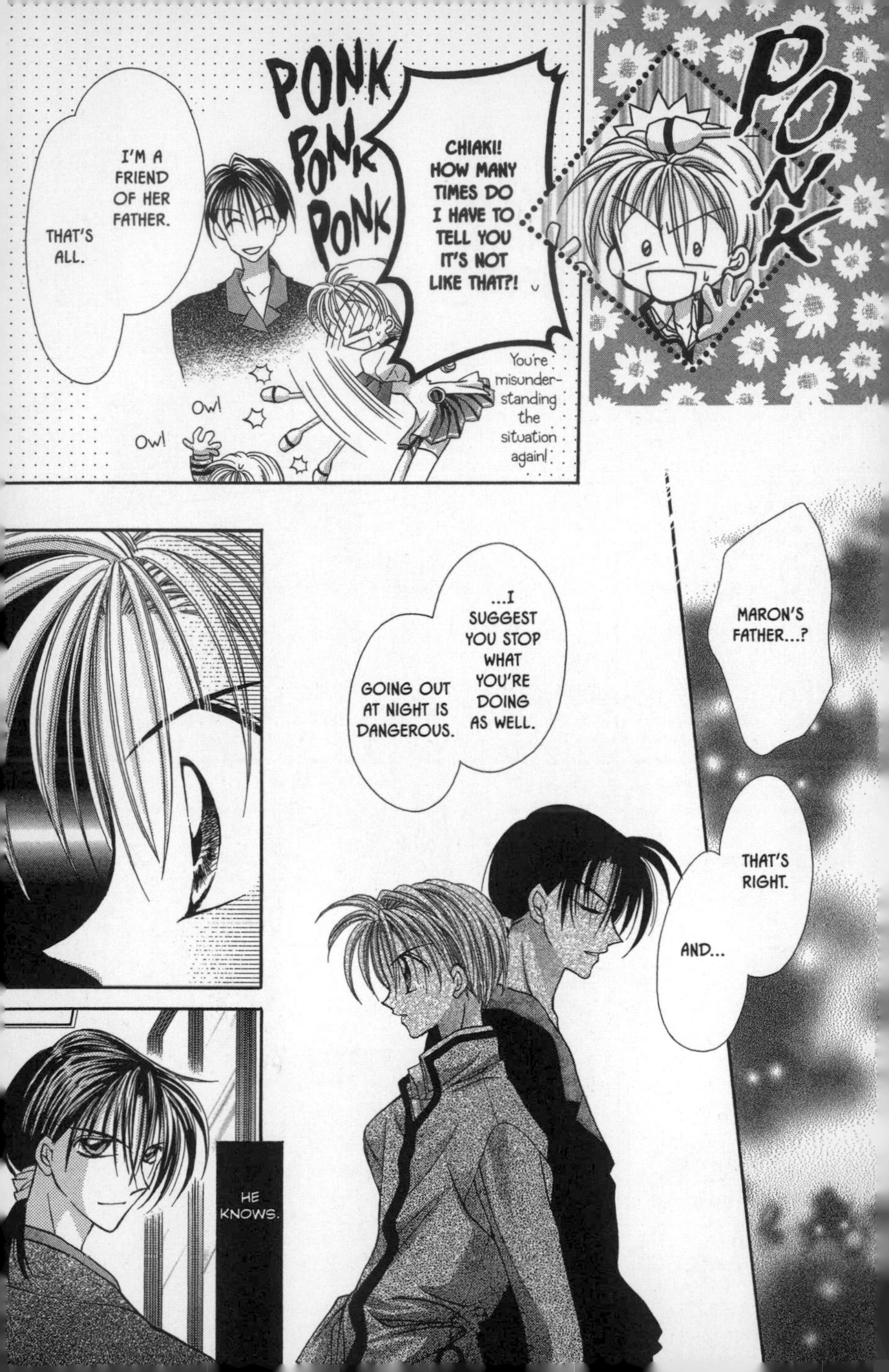
PONK
CHIAKI! HOW MANY TIMES DO I HAVE TO TELL YOU IT'S NOT LIKE THAT?!
PONK PONK PONK
You're misunderstanding the situation again!
I'M A FRIEND OF HER FATHER.
THAT'S ALL.
Ow!
Ow!
MARON'S FATHER...?
THAT'S RIGHT.
AND...
...I SUGGEST YOU STOP WHAT YOU'RE DOING AS WELL.
GOING OUT AT NIGHT IS DANGEROUS.
HE KNOWS.

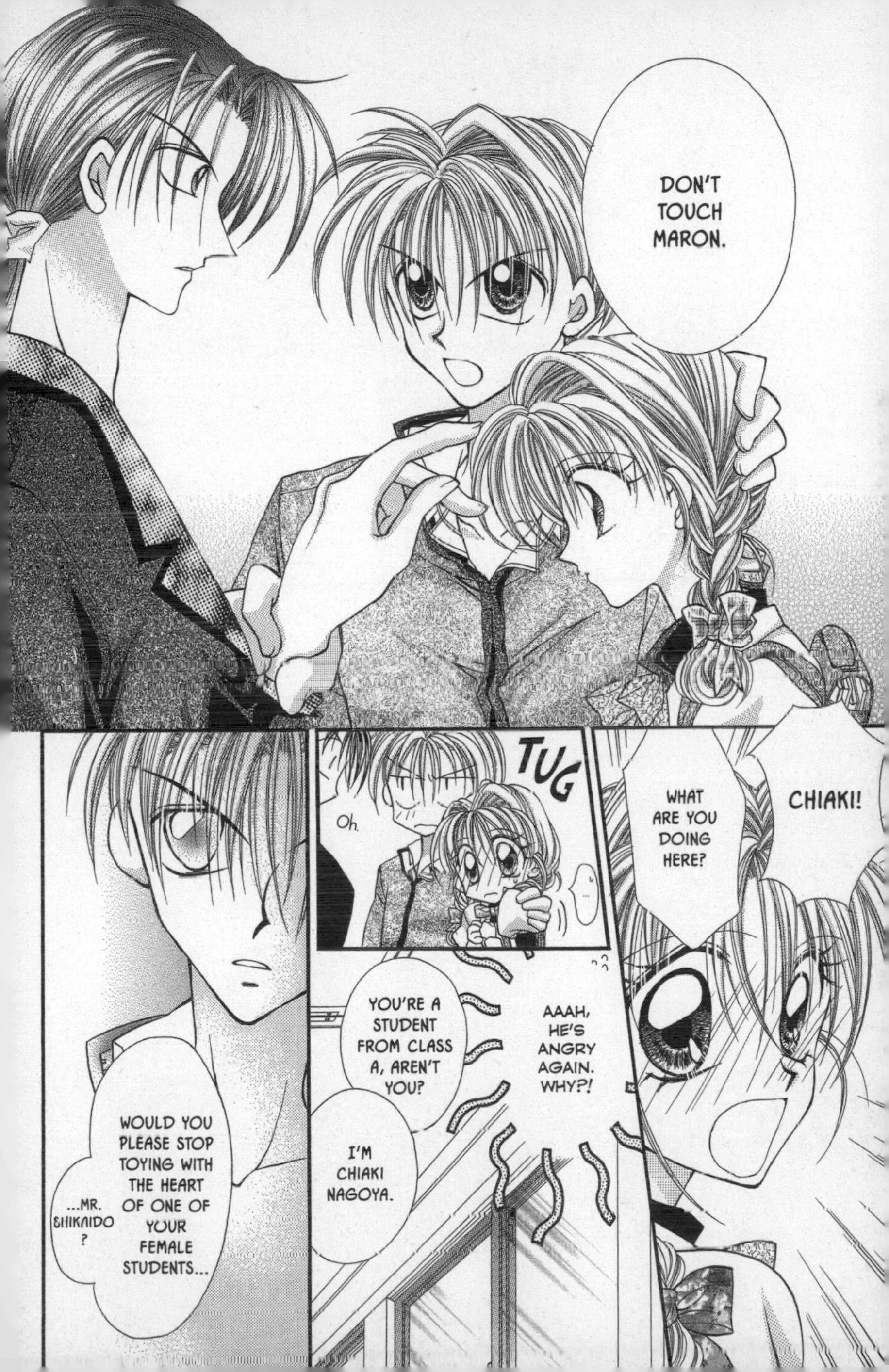
DON'T TOUCH MARON.
CHIAKI!
WHAT ARE YOU DOING HERE?
TUG
Oh.
...
AAAH, HE'S ANGRY AGAIN. WHY?!
YOU'RE A STUDENT FROM CLASS A, AREN'T YOU?
I'M CHIAKI NAGOYA.
WOULD YOU PLEASE STOP TOYING WITH THE HEART OF ONE OF YOUR FEMALE STUDENTS...
...MR. SHIKAIDO ?

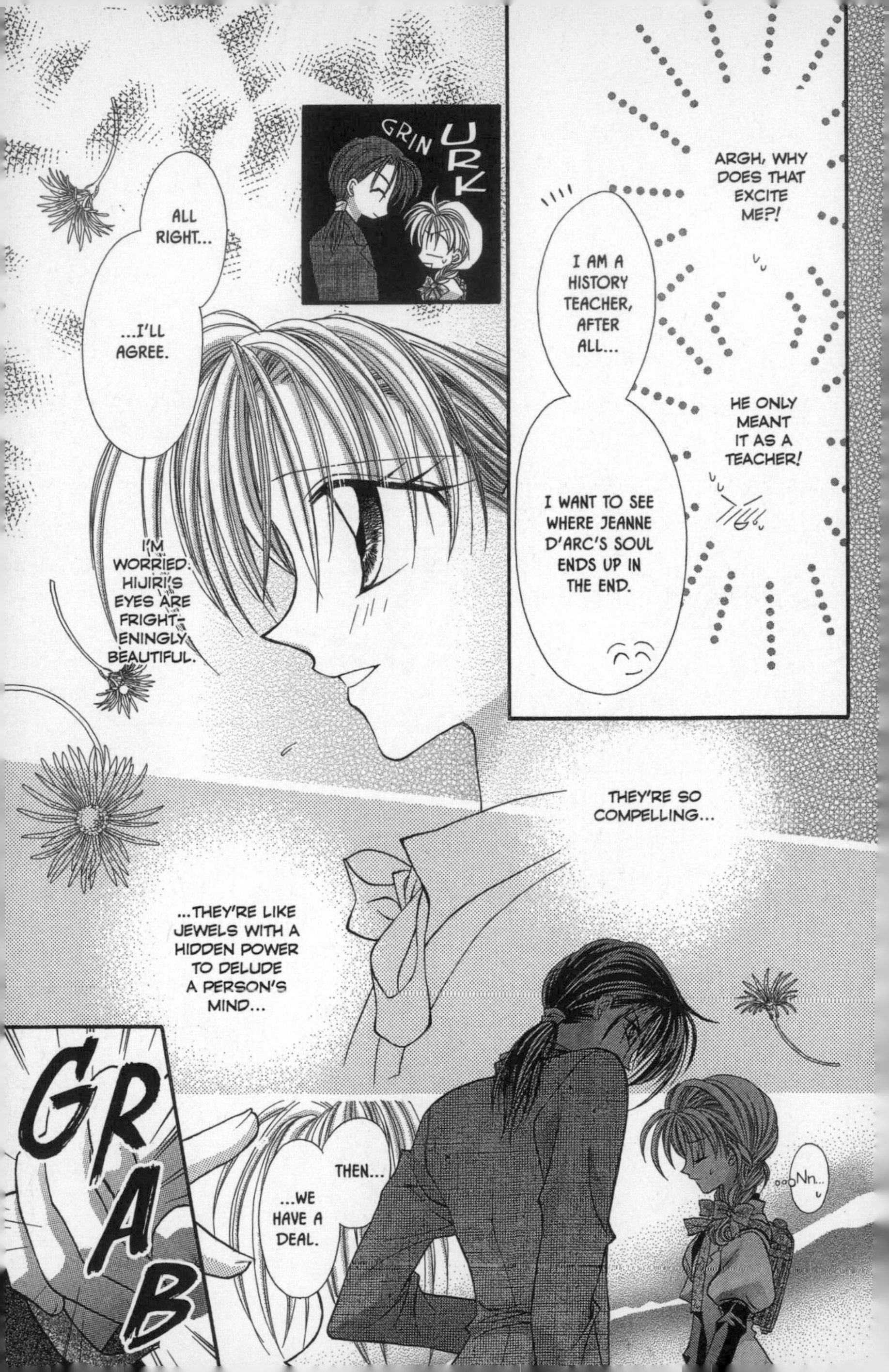
I AM A HISTORY TEACHER, AFTER ALL...
I WANT TO SEE WHERE JEANNE D'ARC'S SOUL ENDS UP IN THE END.
ARGH, WHY DOES THAT EXCITE ME?!
HE ONLY MEANT IT AS A TEACHER!
GRIN
URK
ALL RIGHT...
...I'LL AGREE.
I'M WORRIED. HIJIRI'S EYES ARE FRIGHTENINGLY BEAUTIFUL.
THEY'RE SO COMPELLING...
...THEY'RE LIKE JEWELS WITH A HIDDEN POWER TO DELUDE A PERSON'S MIND...
...Nn...
THEN...
...WE HAVE A DEAL.
GRAB

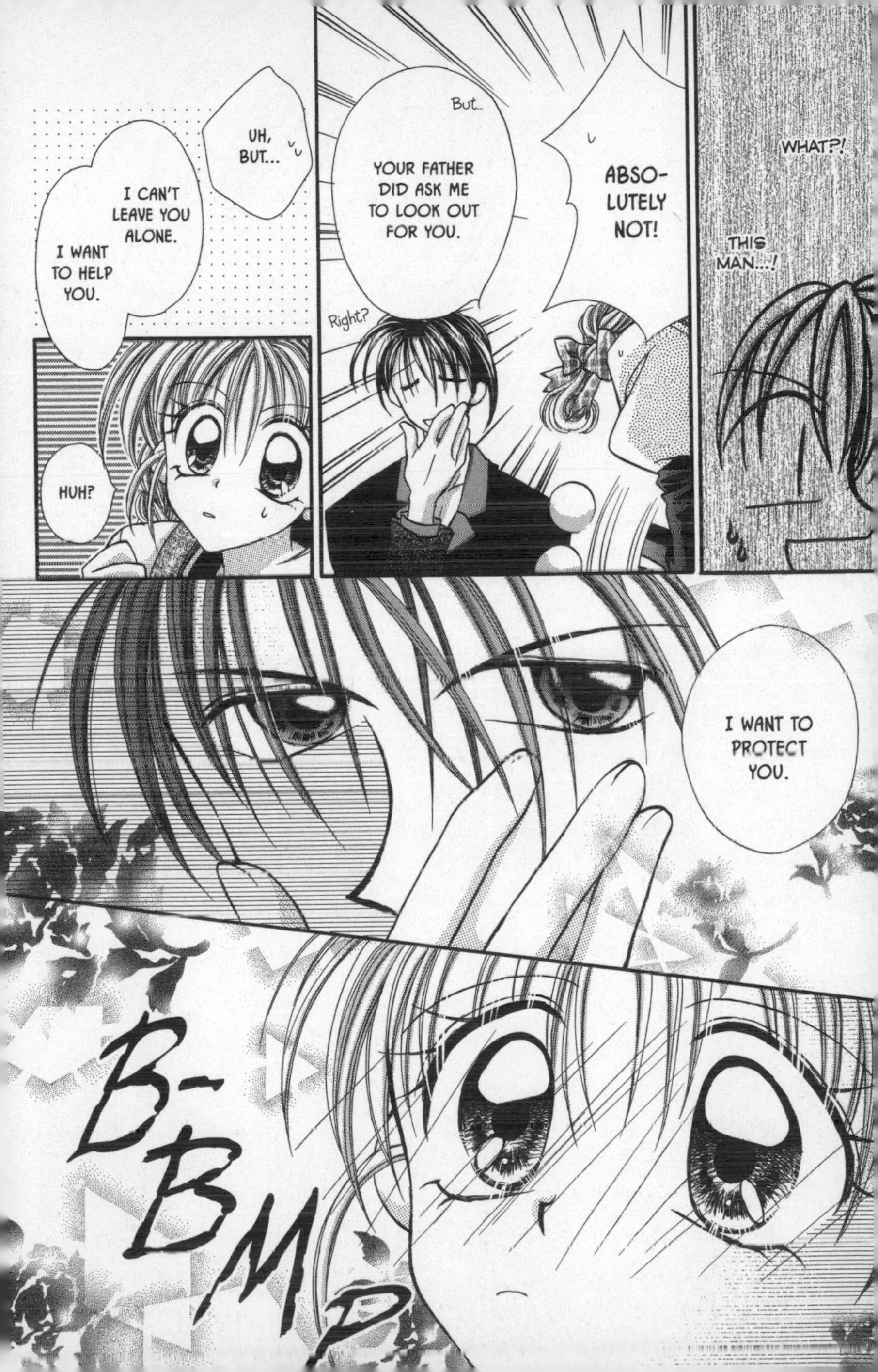
WHAT?!
THIS MAN...!
ABSO-LUTELY NOT!
But...
YOUR FATHER DID ASK ME TO LOOK OUT FOR YOU.
Right?
UH, BUT...
I CAN'T LEAVE YOU ALONE.
I WANT TO HELP YOU.
HUH?
I WANT TO PROTECT YOU.
B-BMP

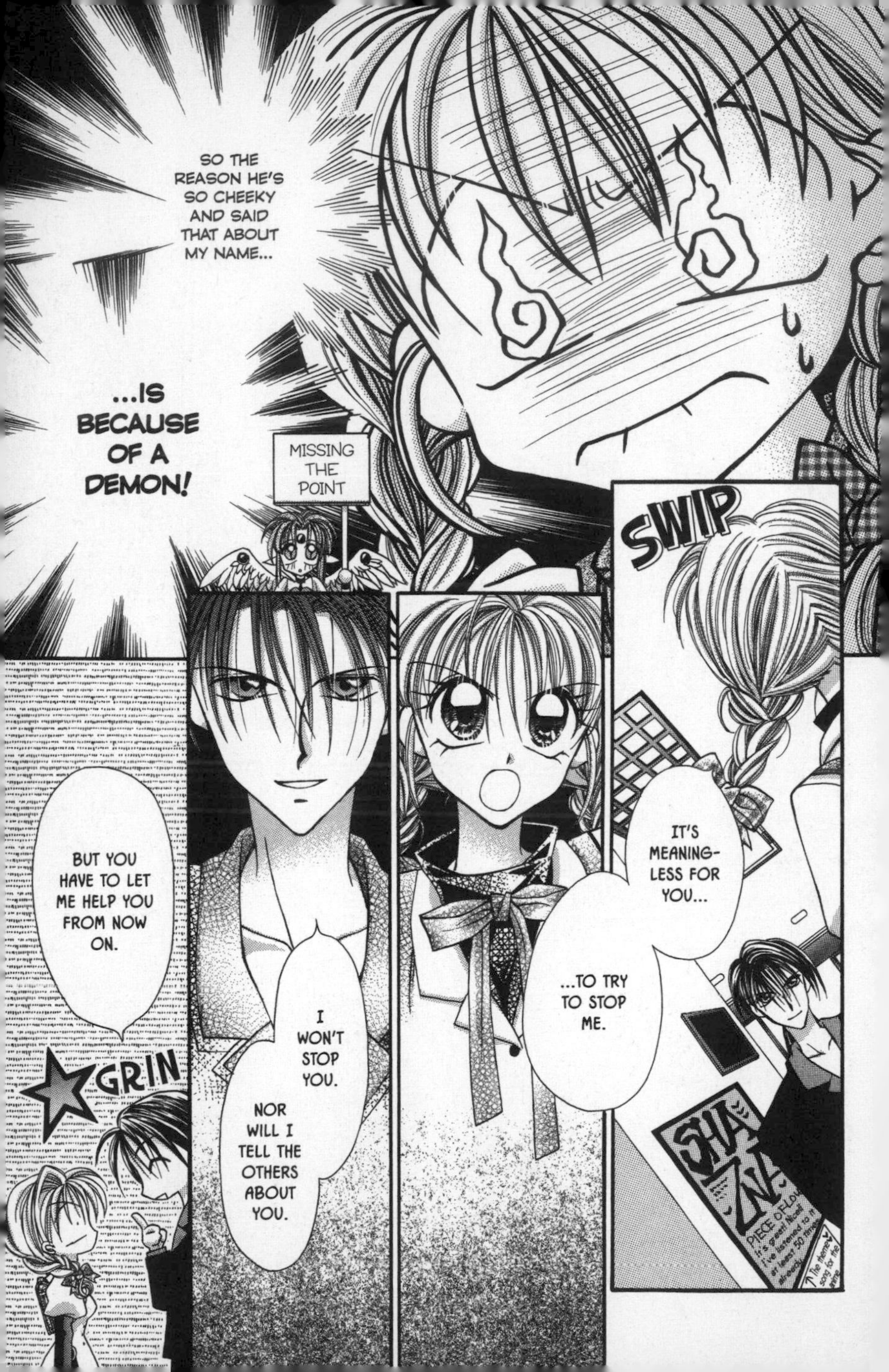
SO THE REASON HE'S SO CHEEKY AND SAID THAT ABOUT MY NAME...
...IS BECAUSE OF A DEMON!
MISSING THE POINT
SWIP
IT'S MEANING-LESS FOR YOU...
...TO TRY TO STOP ME.
I WON'T STOP YOU.
NOR WILL I TELL THE OTHERS ABOUT YOU.
BUT YOU HAVE TO LET ME HELP YOU FROM NOW ON.
GRIN

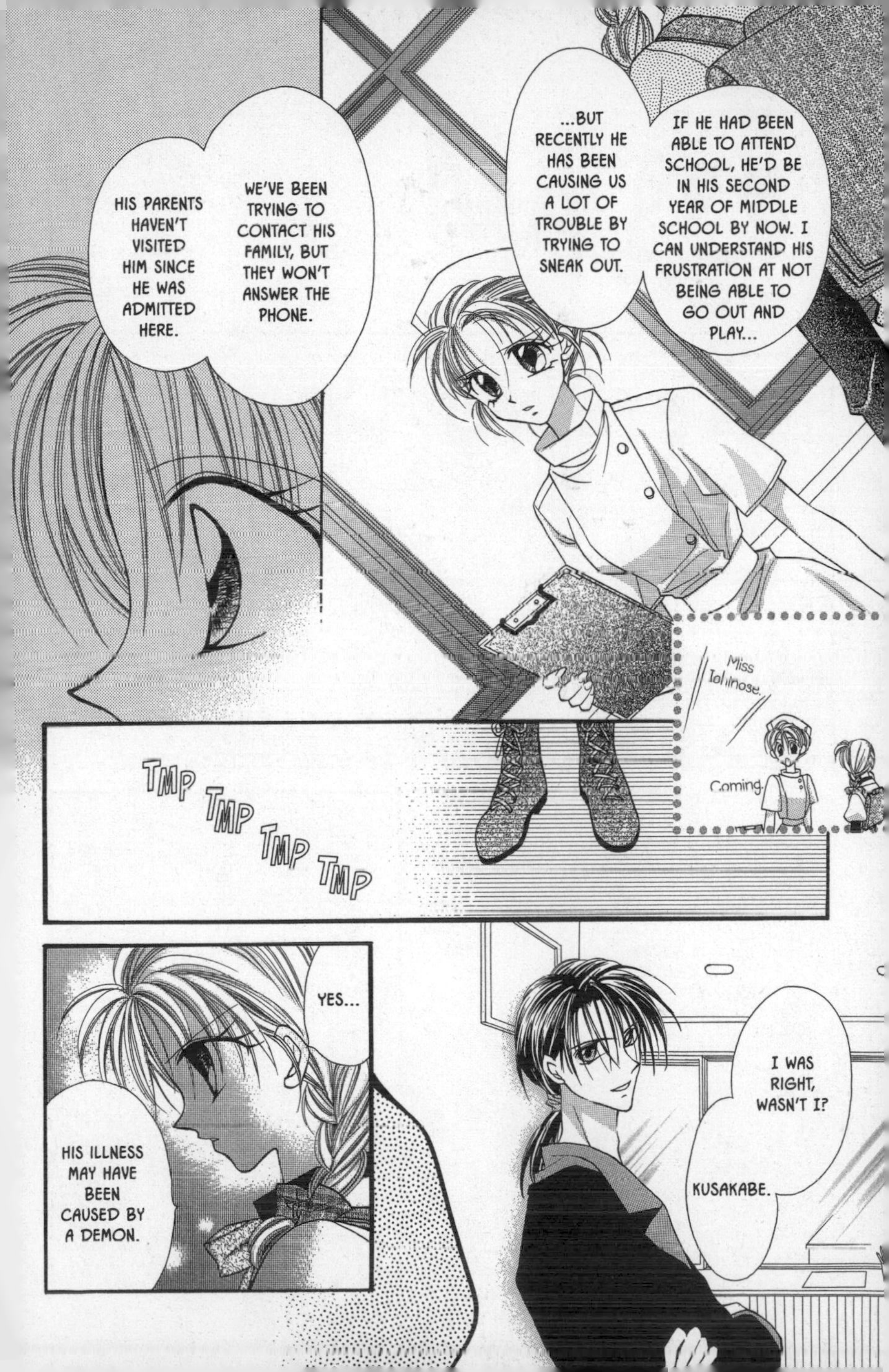
IF HE HAD BEEN ABLE TO ATTEND SCHOOL, HE'D BE IN HIS SECOND YEAR OF MIDDLE SCHOOL BY NOW. I CAN UNDERSTAND HIS FRUSTRATION AT NOT BEING ABLE TO GO OUT AND PLAY...
...BUT RECENTLY HE HAS BEEN CAUSING US A LOT OF TROUBLE BY TRYING TO SNEAK OUT.
WE'VE BEEN TRYING TO CONTACT HIS FAMILY, BUT THEY WON'T ANSWER THE PHONE.
HIS PARENTS HAVEN'T VISITED HIM SINCE HE WAS ADMITTED HERE.
Miss Ichinose.
Coming.
TMP TMP TMP TMP
I WAS RIGHT, WASN'T I?
KUSAKABE.
YES...
HIS ILLNESS MAY HAVE BEEN CAUSED BY A DEMON.

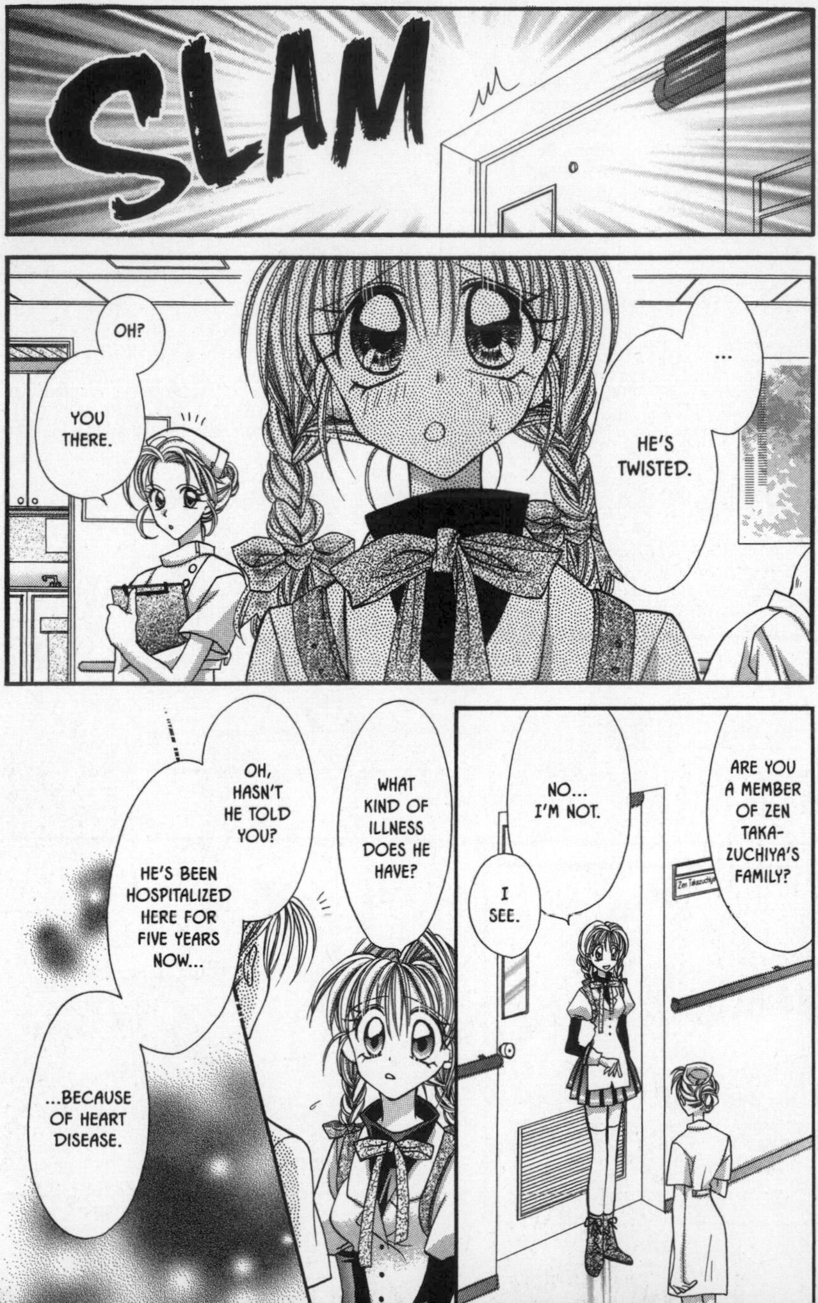
SLAM
...
HE'S TWISTED.
OH?
YOU THERE.
ARE YOU A MEMBER OF ZEN TAKA-ZUCHIYA'S FAMILY?
NO... I'M NOT.
I SEE.
WHAT KIND OF ILLNESS DOES HE HAVE?
OH, HASN'T HE TOLD YOU?
HE'S BEEN HOSPITALIZED HERE FOR FIVE YEARS NOW...
...BECAUSE OF HEART DISEASE.

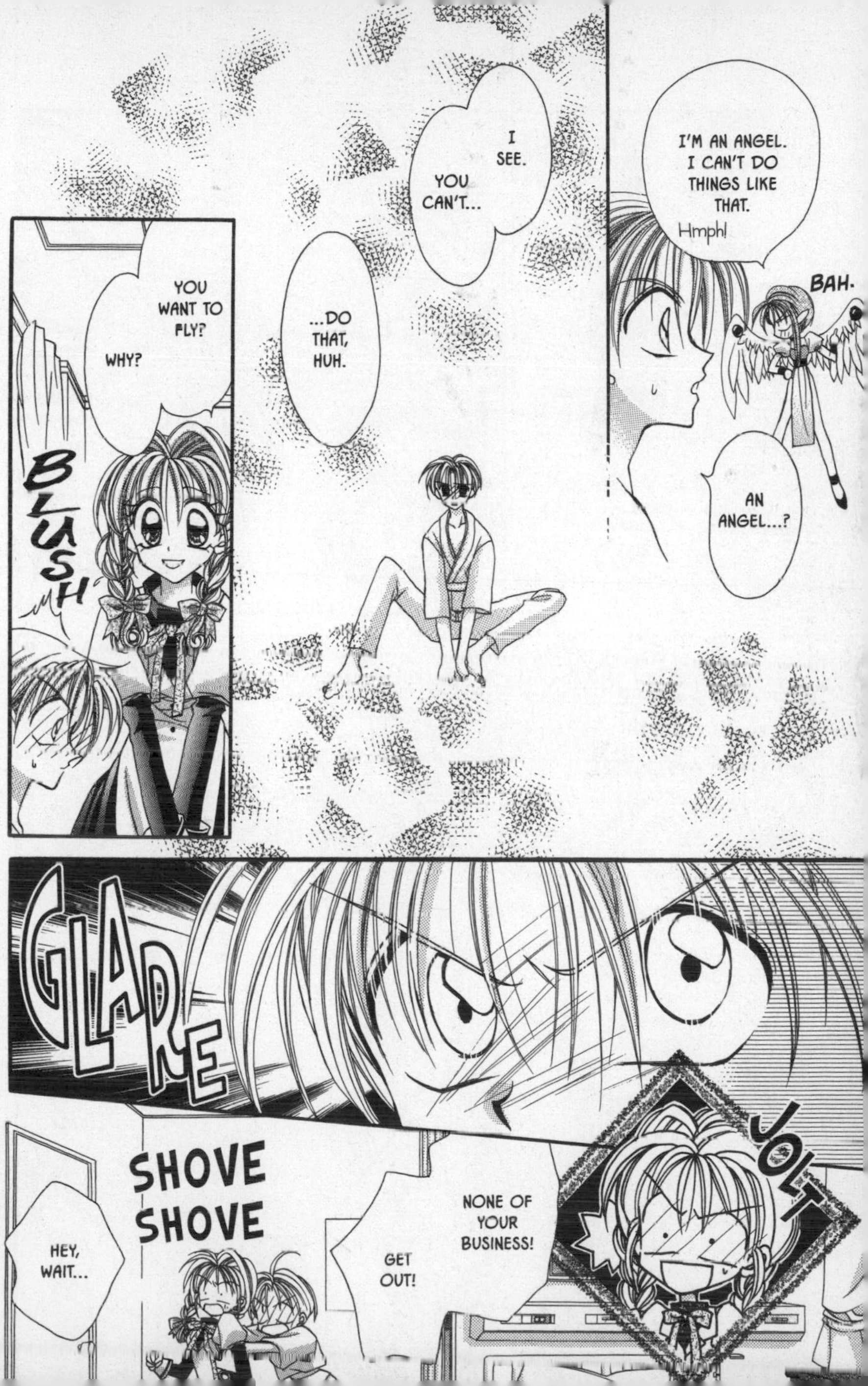

I'M AN ANGEL. I CAN'T DO THINGS LIKE THAT. Hmph!
BAH.
AN ANGEL...?
I SEE. YOU CAN'T...
...DO THAT, HUH.
YOU WANT TO FLY? WHY?
BLUSH
GLARE
JOLT
NONE OF YOUR BUSINESS!
GET OUT!
SHOVE SHOVE
HEY, WAIT...

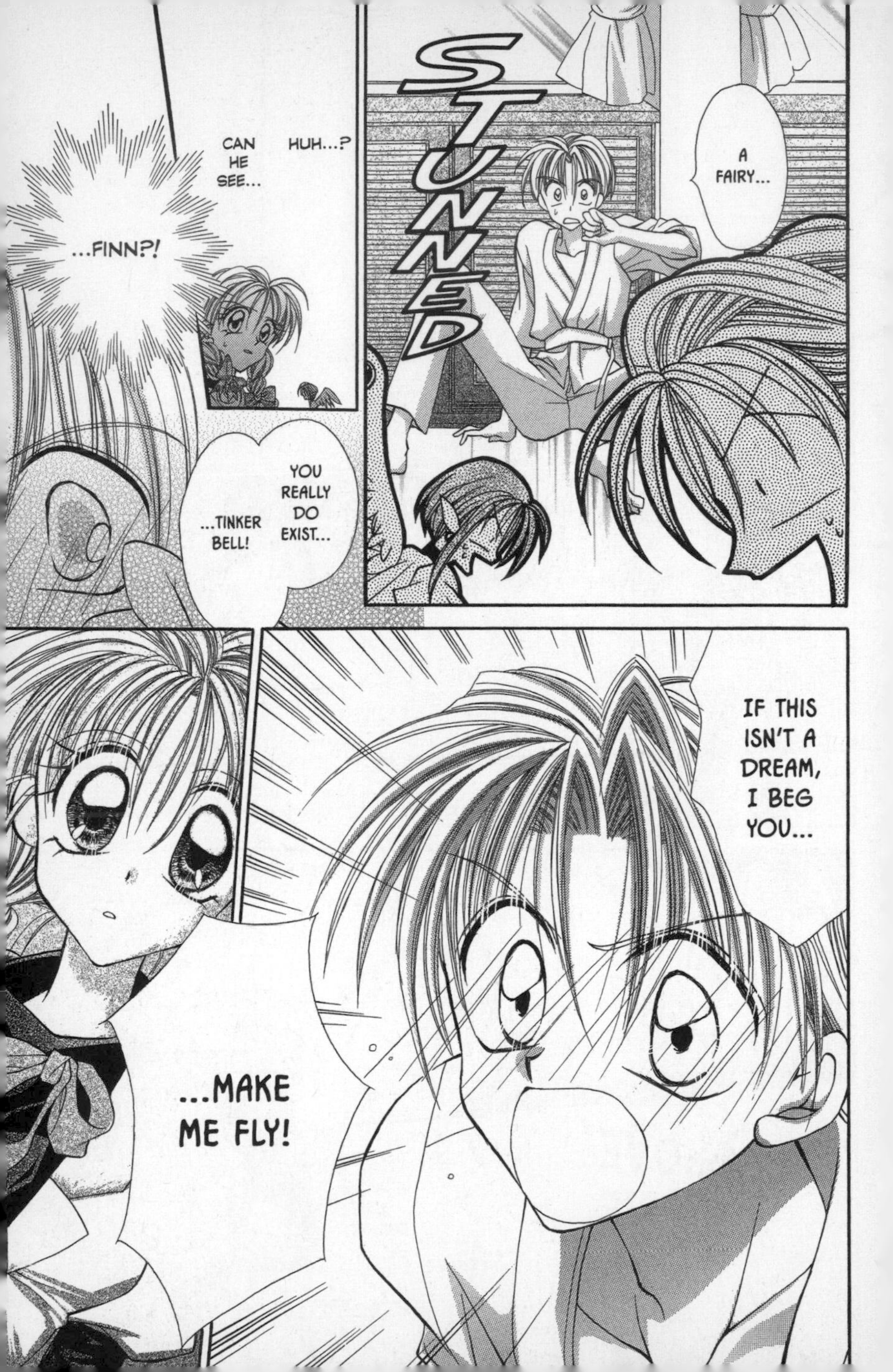
A FAIRY...
STUNNED
HUH...?
CAN HE SEE...
...FINN?!
YOU REALLY DO EXIST...
...TINKER BELL!
IF THIS ISN'T A DREAM, I BEG YOU...
...MAKE ME FLY!

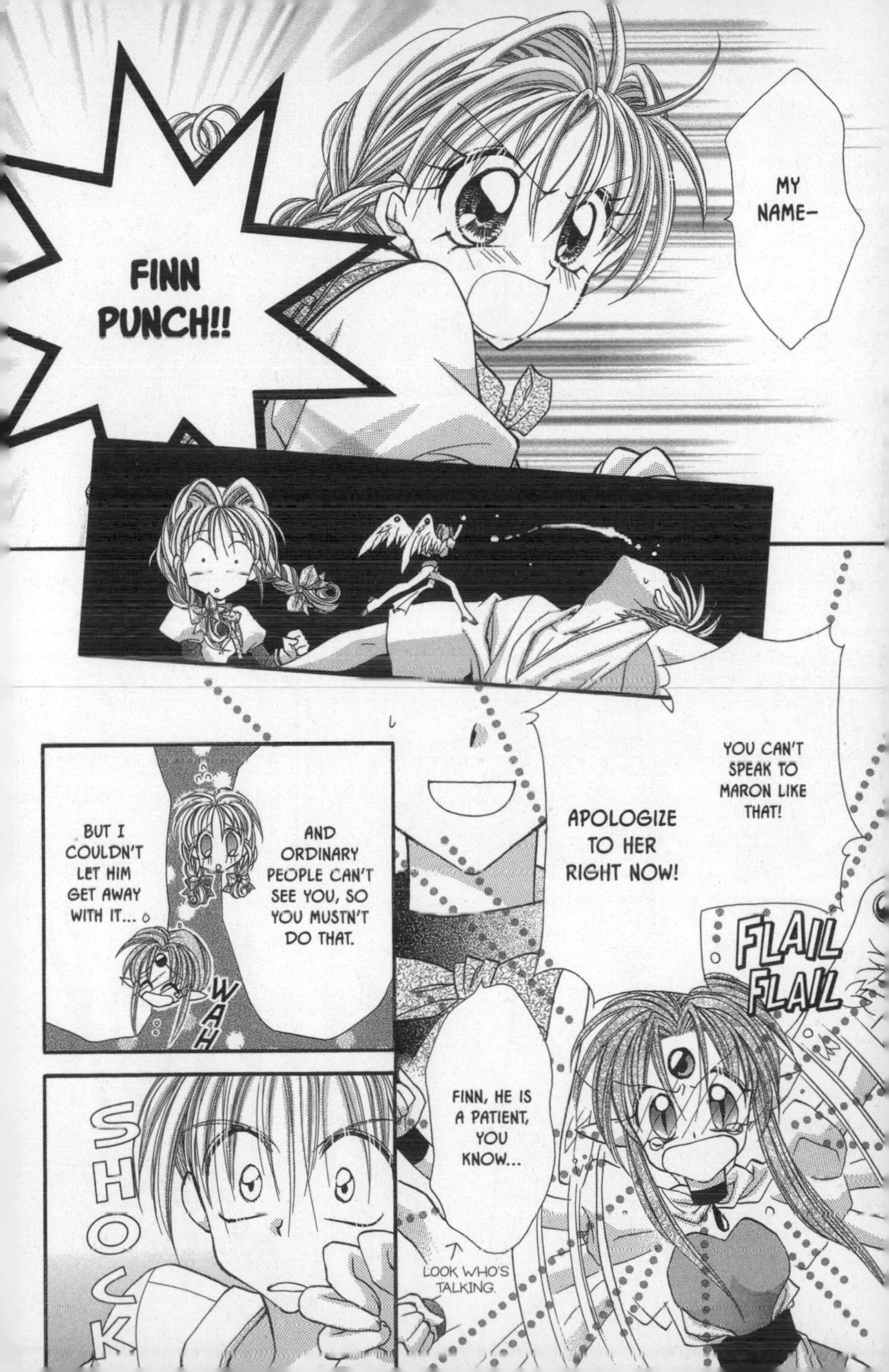
MY NAME—
FINN PUNCH!!
YOU CAN'T SPEAK TO MARON LIKE THAT!
APOLOGIZE TO HER RIGHT NOW!
FLAIL FLAIL
FINN, HE IS A PATIENT, YOU KNOW...
LOOK WHO'S TALKING.
AND ORDINARY PEOPLE CAN'T SEE YOU, SO YOU MUSTN'T DO THAT.
BUT I COULDN'T LET HIM GET AWAY WITH IT...
WAH
SHOCK

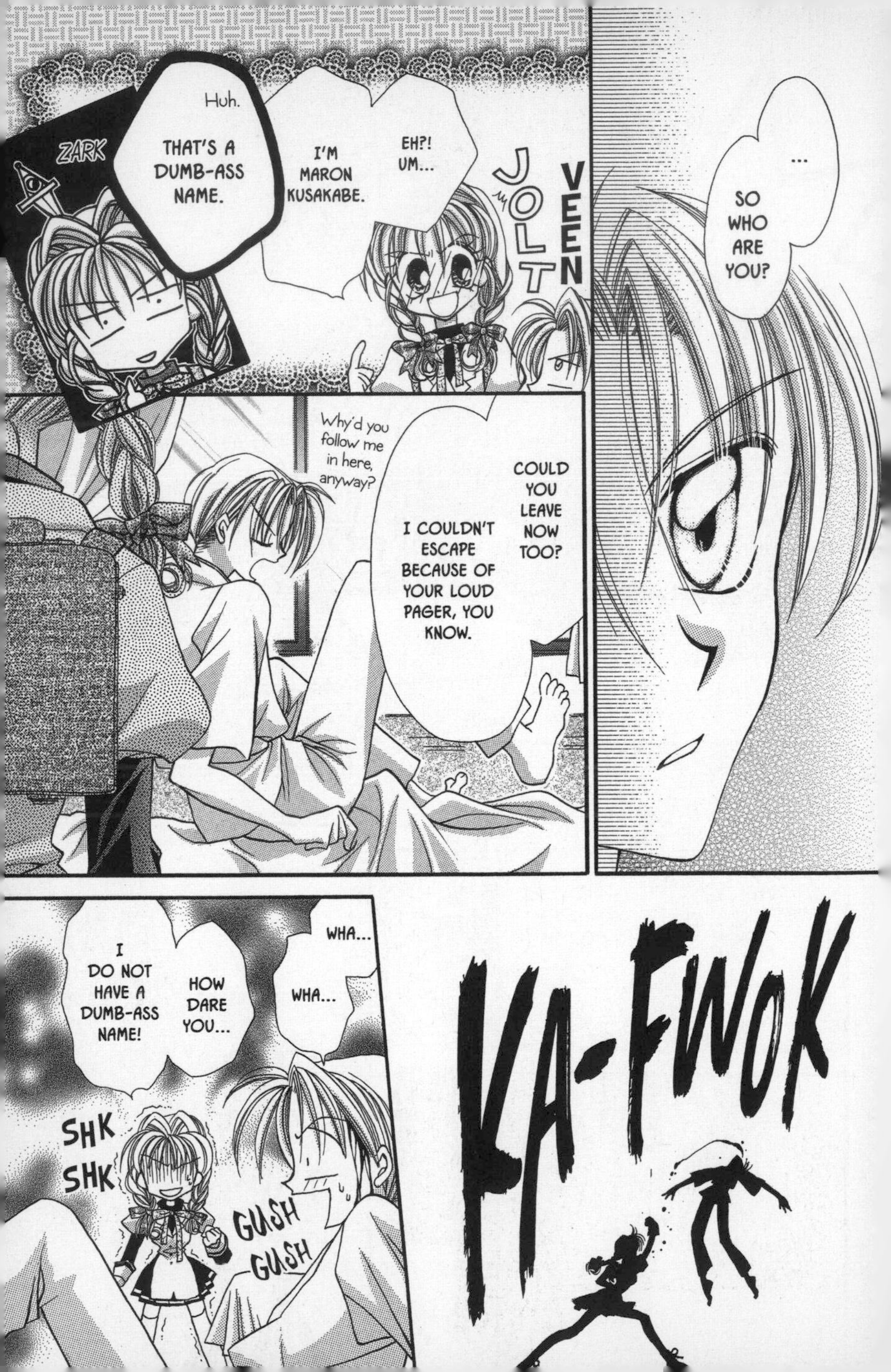
...
SO WHO ARE YOU?
VEEN
JOLT
EH?! UM...
I'M MARON KUSAKABE.
Huh.
THAT'S A DUMB-ASS NAME.
ZARK
COULD YOU LEAVE NOW TOO?
I COULDN'T ESCAPE BECAUSE OF YOUR LOUD PAGER, YOU KNOW.
Why'd you follow me in here, anyway?
KA-FWOK
WHA...
WHA...
HOW DARE YOU...
I DO NOT HAVE A DUMB-ASS NAME!
GUSH GUSH
SHK SHK

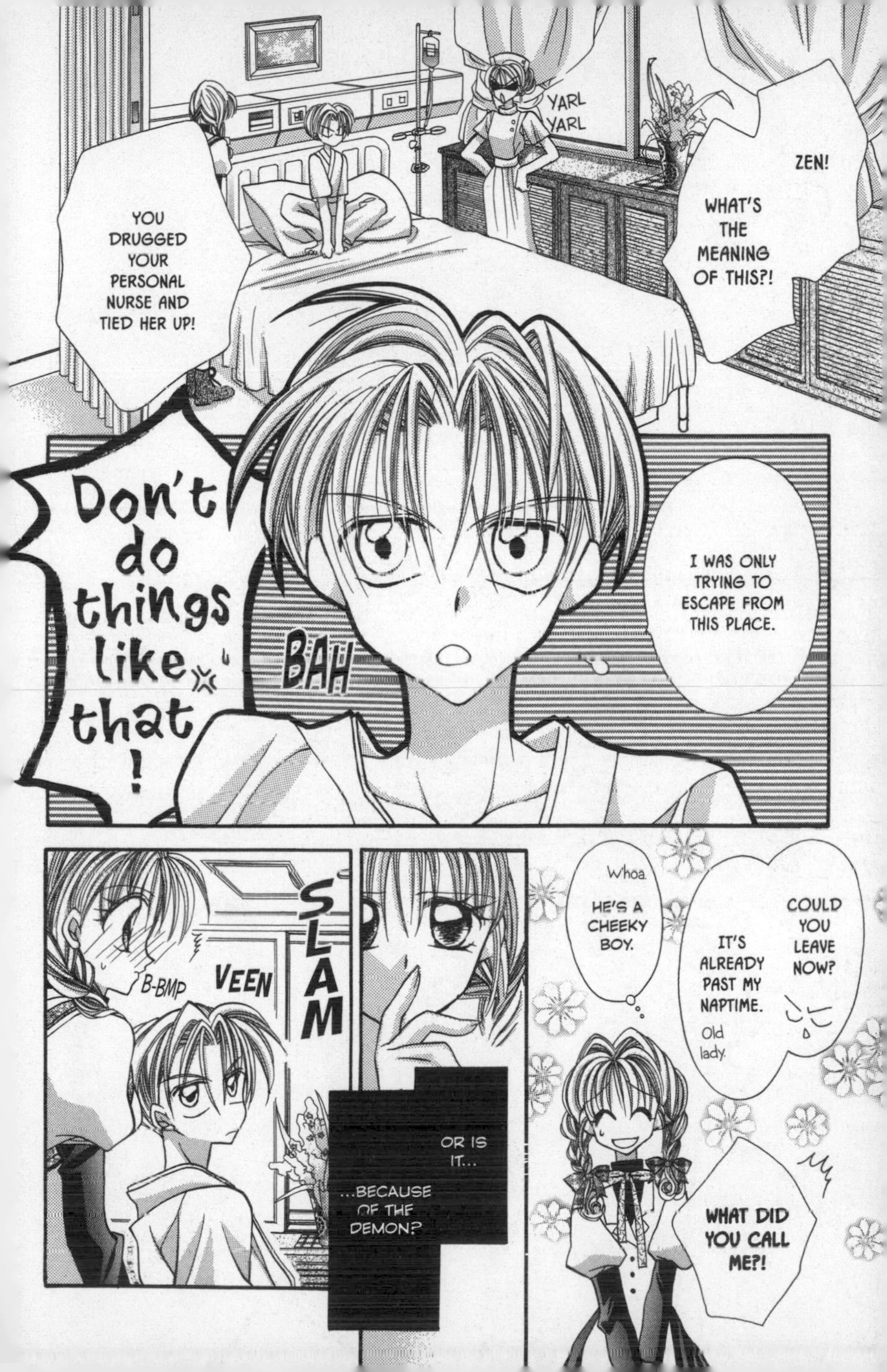
ZEN!
WHAT'S THE MEANING OF THIS?!
YARL YARL
YOU DRUGGED YOUR PERSONAL NURSE AND TIED HER UP!
I WAS ONLY TRYING TO ESCAPE FROM THIS PLACE.
BAH
Don't do things like that!
COULD YOU LEAVE NOW?
IT'S ALREADY PAST MY NAPTIME.
Old lady.
Whoa.
HE'S A CHEEKY BOY.
WHAT DID YOU CALL ME?!
SLAM
OR IS IT...
...BECAUSE OF THE DEMON?
VEEN
B-BMP

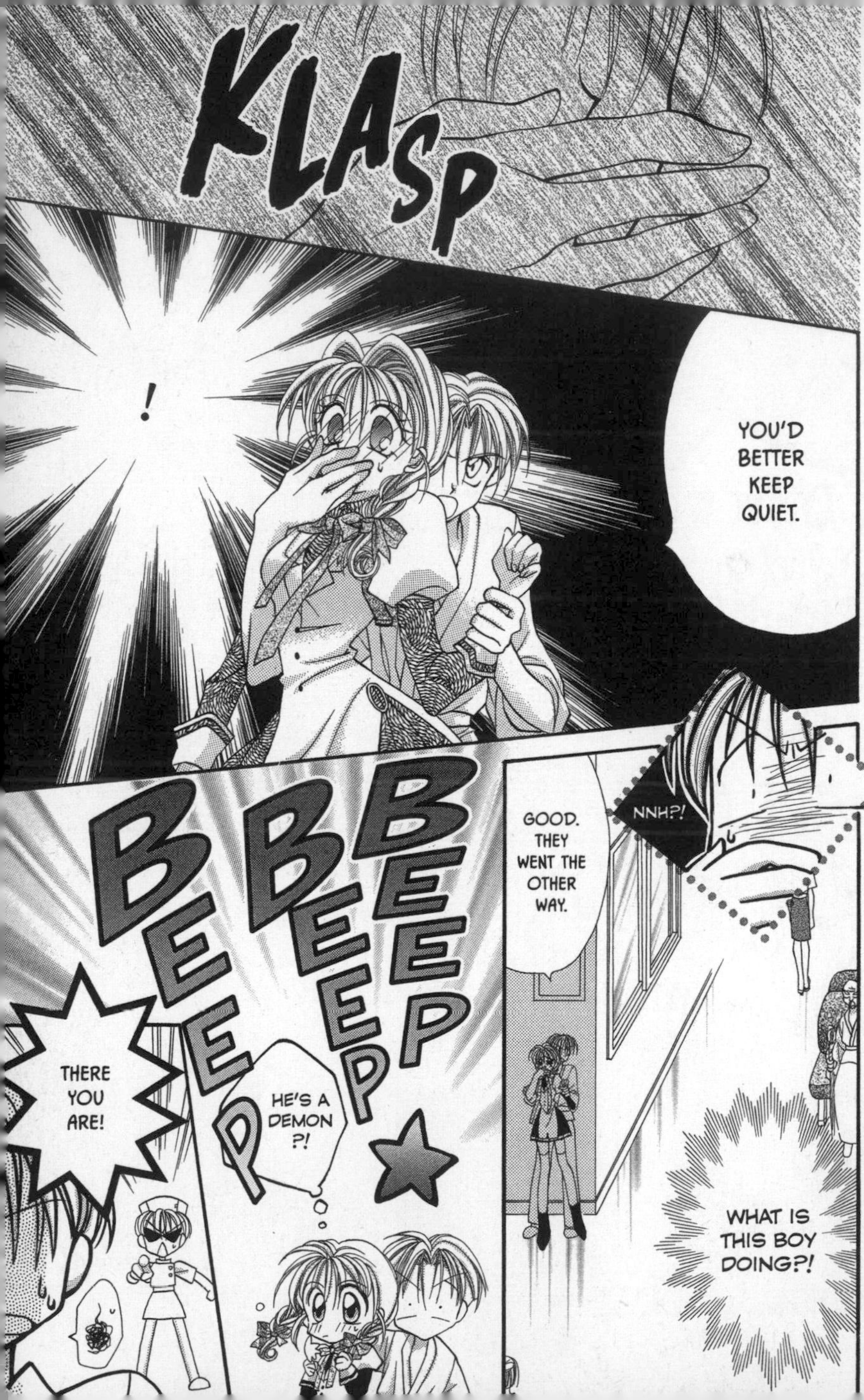
KLASP
YOU'D BETTER KEEP QUIET.
!
NNH?!
GOOD. THEY WENT THE OTHER WAY.
WHAT IS THIS BOY DOING?!
BEEEP BEEEP BEEEP
THERE YOU ARE!
HE'S A DEMON?!

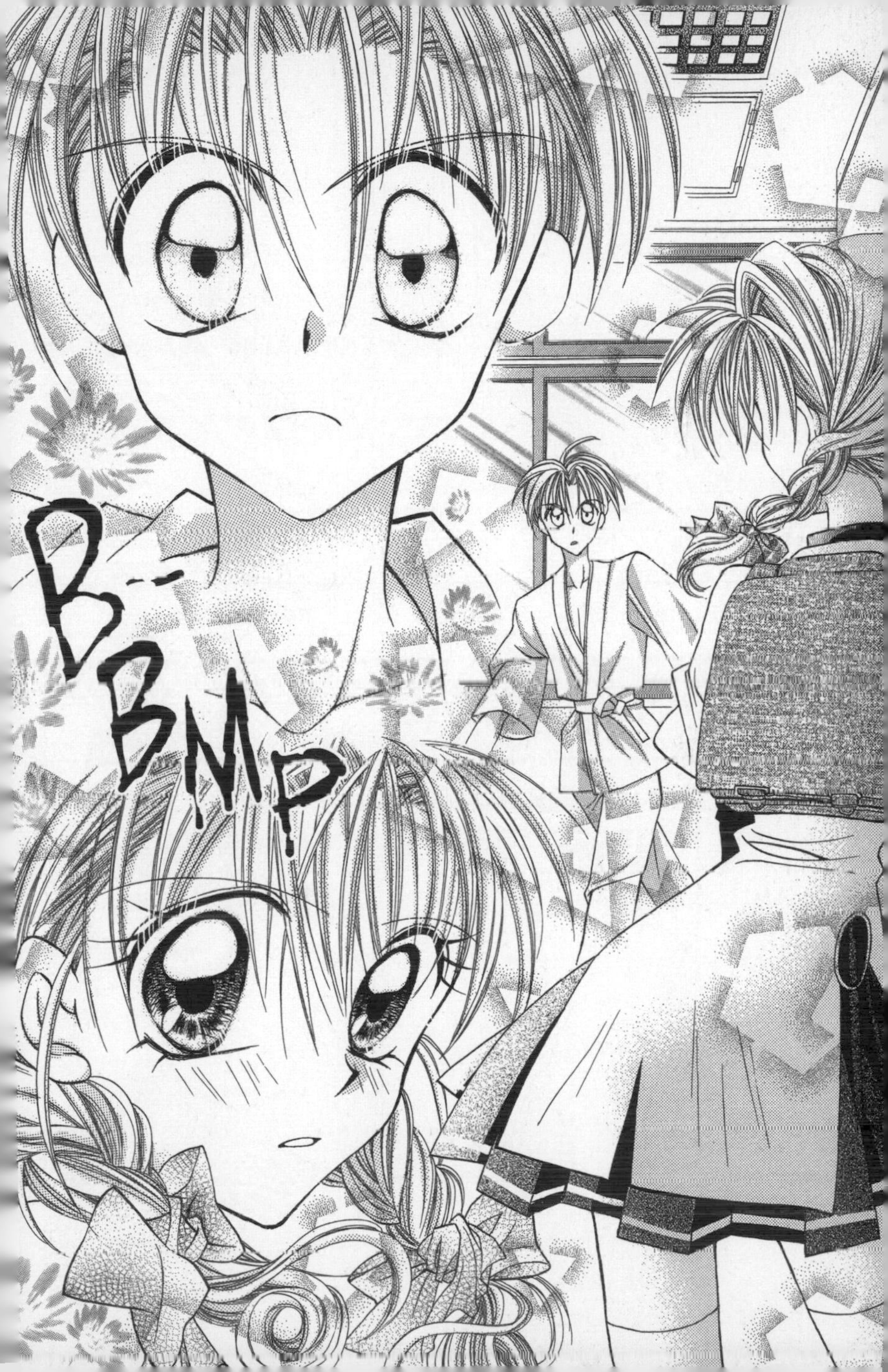
B-BMP

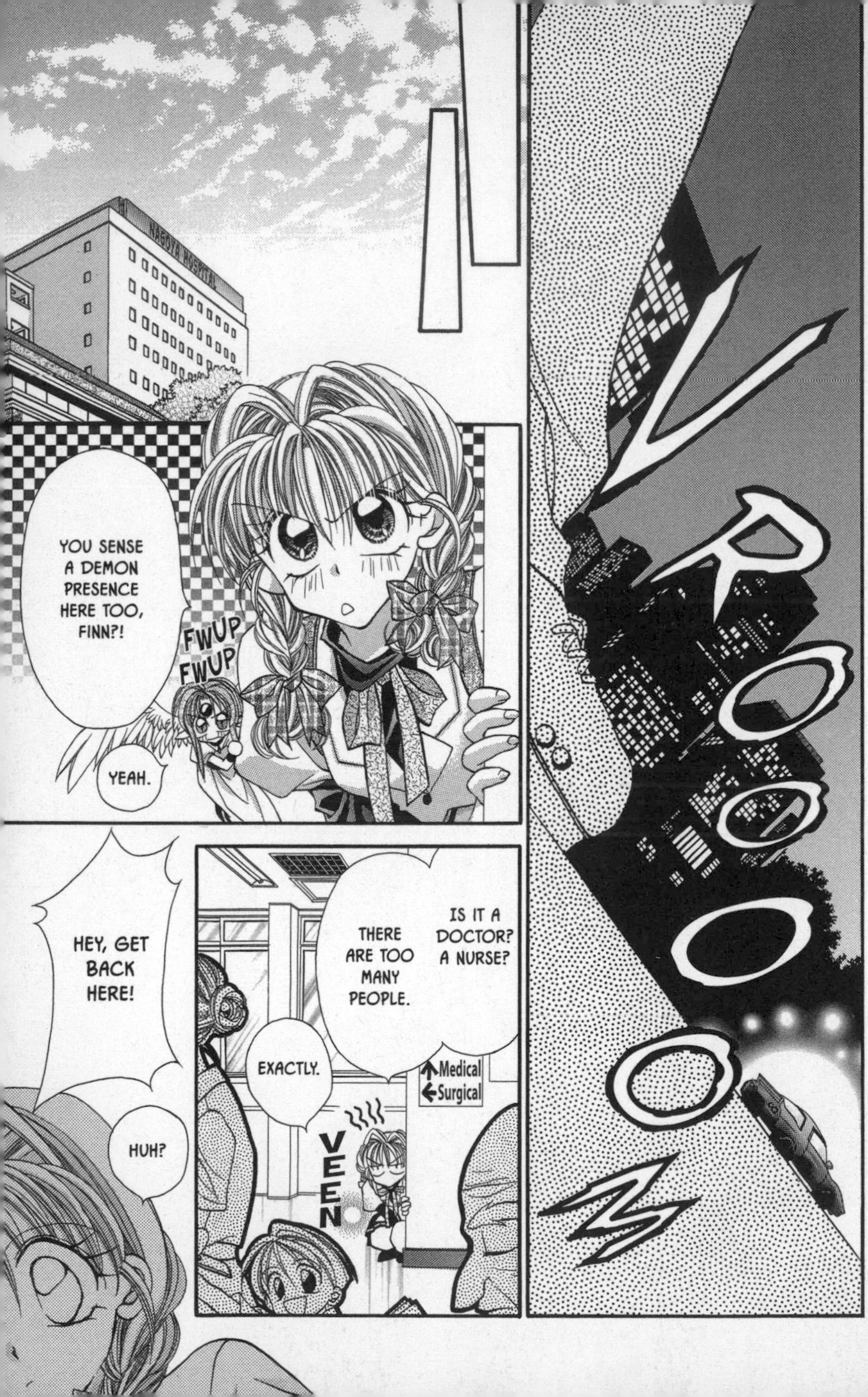
VROOOOM
NAGOYA HOSPITAL
YOU SENSE A DEMON PRESENCE HERE TOO, FINN?!
FWUP FWUP
YEAH.
IS IT A DOCTOR? A NURSE?
THERE ARE TOO MANY PEOPLE.
EXACTLY.
↑Medical
←Surgical
VEEN
HEY, GET BACK HERE!
HUH?

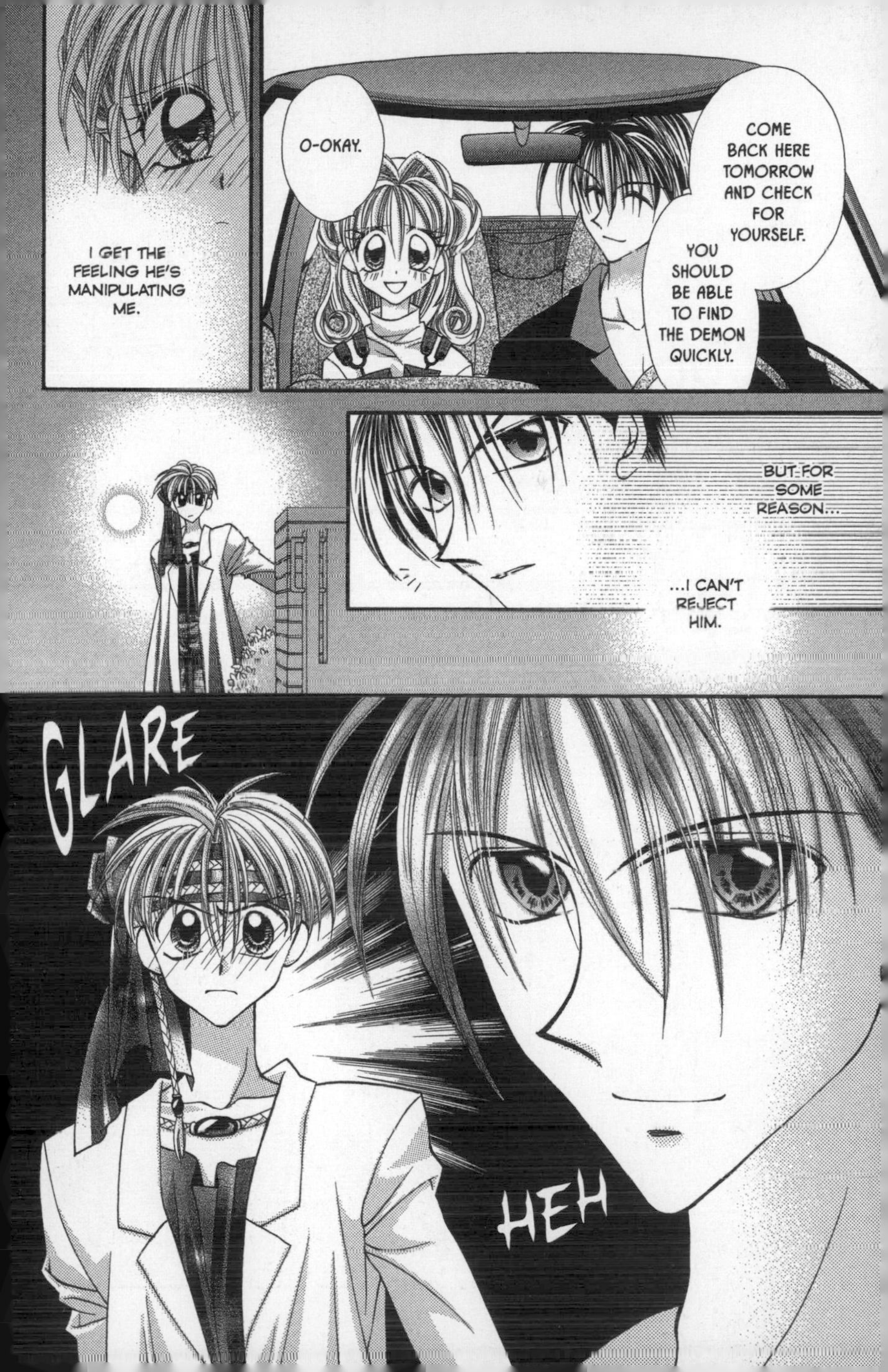
COME BACK HERE TOMORROW AND CHECK FOR YOURSELF.
YOU SHOULD BE ABLE TO FIND THE DEMON QUICKLY.
O-OKAY.
I GET THE FEELING HE'S MANIPULATING ME.
BUT FOR SOME REASON...
...I CAN'T REJECT HIM.
HEH
GLARE

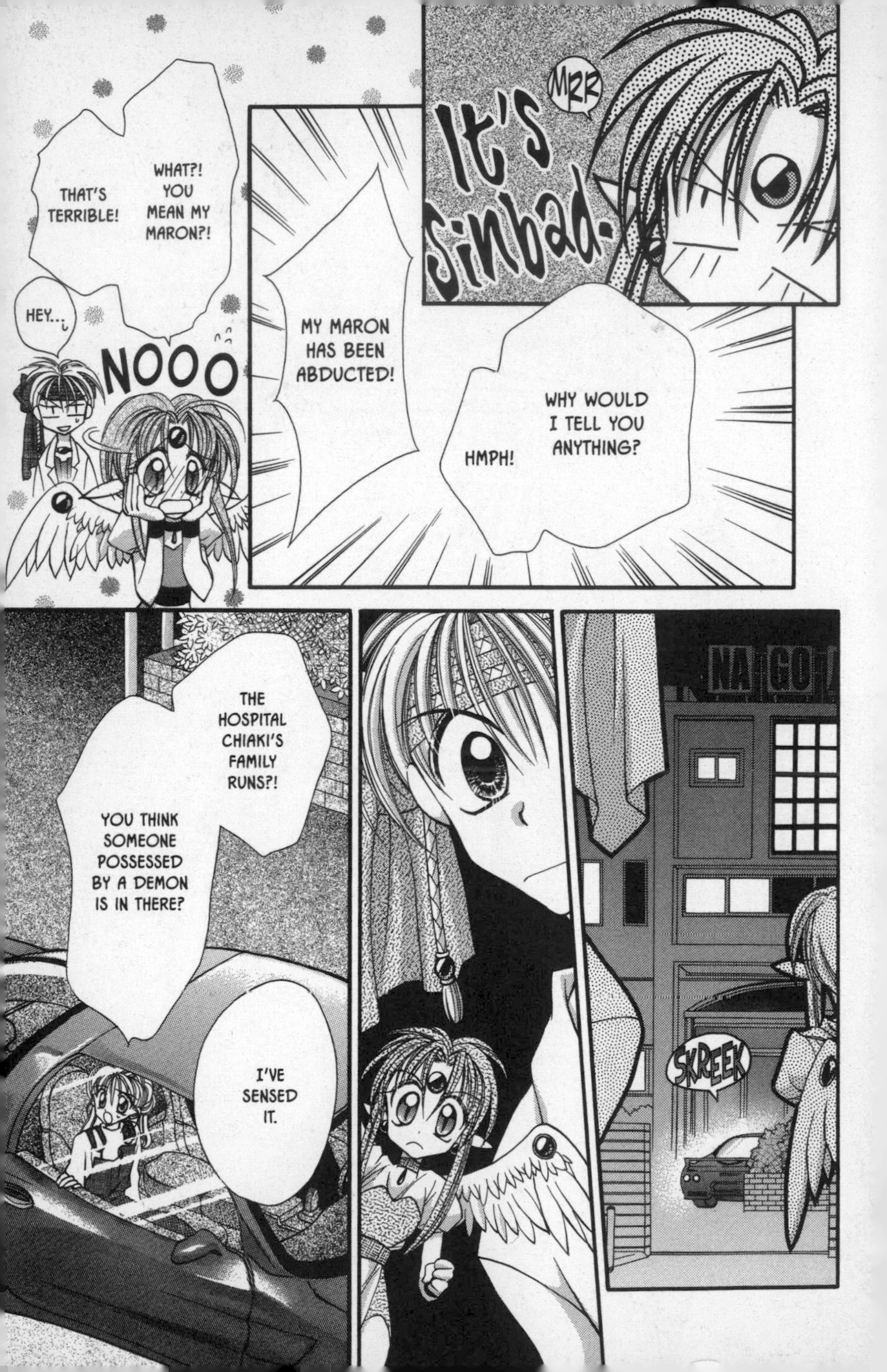

MRR
It's Sinbad.
WHY WOULD I TELL YOU ANYTHING?
HMPH!
MY MARON HAS BEEN ABDUCTED!
WHAT?! YOU MEAN MY MARON?!
THAT'S TERRIBLE!
HEY...
NOOO
NA GO
SKREEK
THE HOSPITAL CHIAKI'S FAMILY RUNS?!
YOU THINK SOMEONE POSSESSED BY A DEMON IS IN THERE?
I'VE SENSED IT.

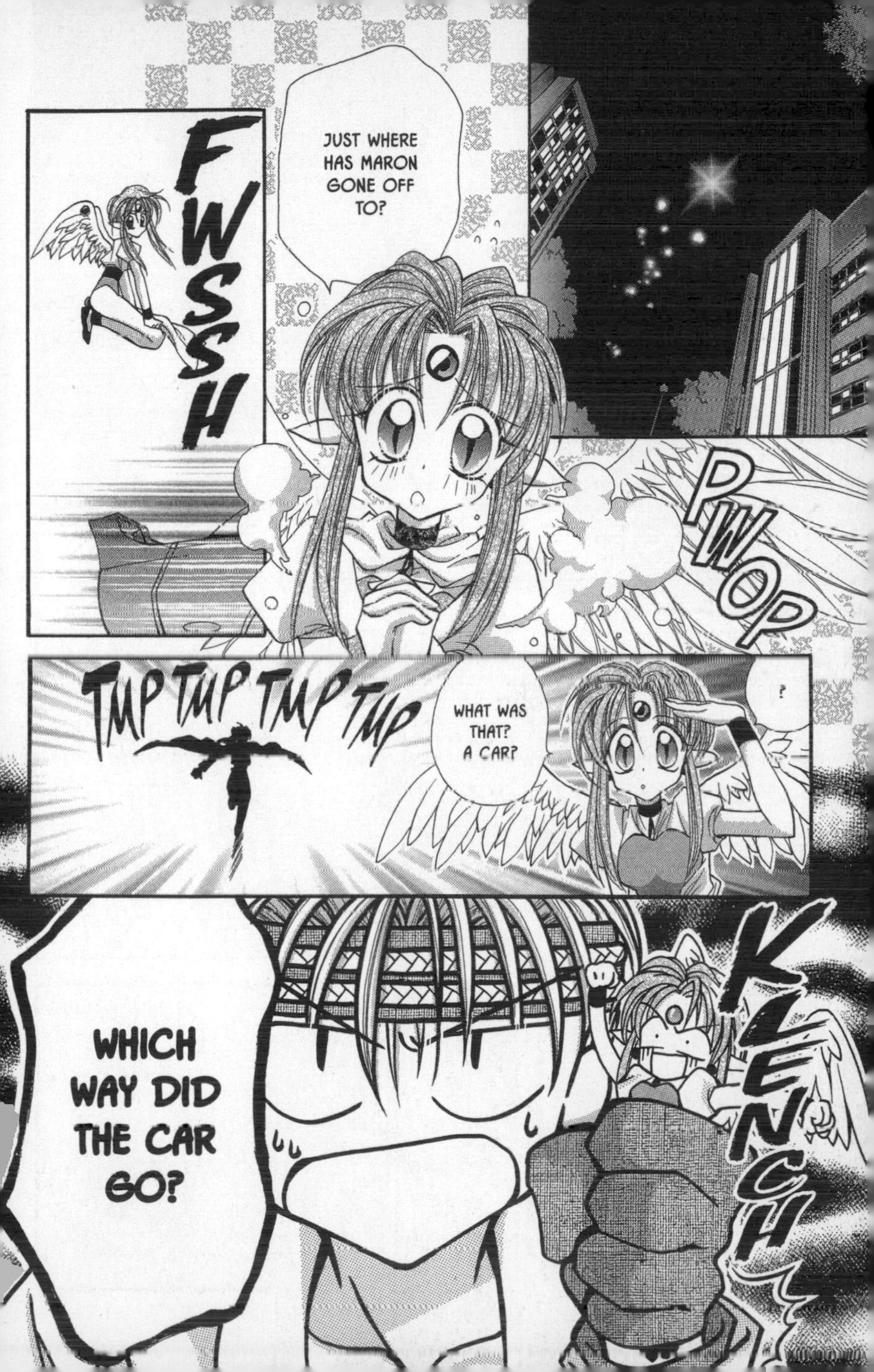
JUST WHERE HAS MARON GONE OFF TO?
PWOP
FWSSH
?
WHAT WAS THAT? A CAR?
TMP TMP TMP TMP
KLENCH
WHICH WAY DID THE CAR GO?

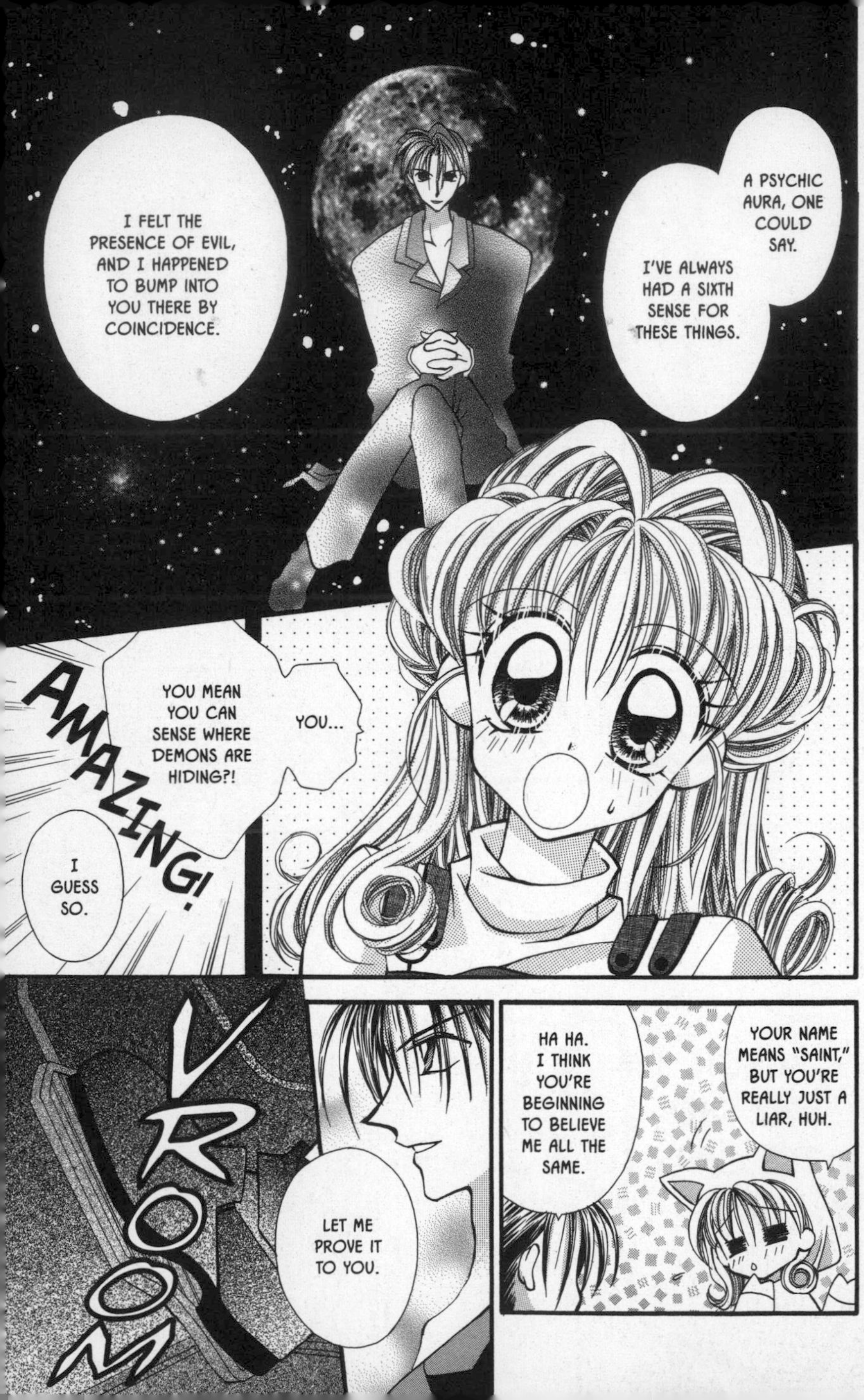

A PSYCHIC AURA, ONE COULD SAY.
I'VE ALWAYS HAD A SIXTH SENSE FOR THESE THINGS.
I FELT THE PRESENCE OF EVIL, AND I HAPPENED TO BUMP INTO YOU THERE BY COINCIDENCE.
YOU...
YOU MEAN YOU CAN SENSE WHERE DEMONS ARE HIDING?!
AMAZING!
I GUESS SO.
YOUR NAME MEANS "SAINT," BUT YOU'RE REALLY JUST A LIAR, HUH.
HA HA. I THINK YOU'RE BEGINNING TO BELIEVE ME ALL THE SAME.
LET ME PROVE IT TO YOU.
VROOOM

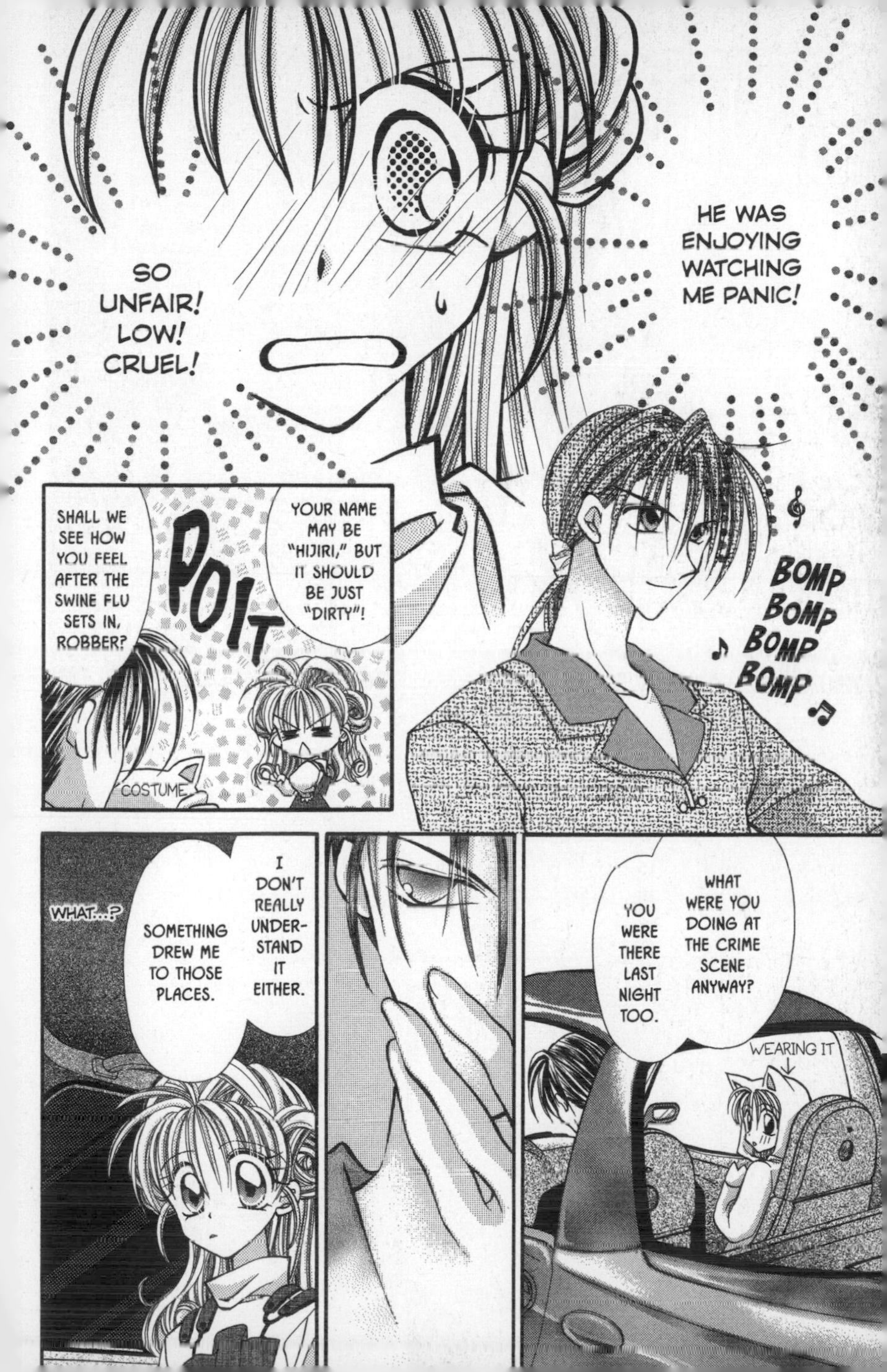
HE WAS ENJOYING WATCHING ME PANIC!
SO UNFAIR! LOW! CRUEL!
BOMP BOMP BOMP BOMP
YOUR NAME MAY BE "HIJIRI," BUT IT SHOULD BE JUST "DIRTY"!
POIT
SHALL WE SEE HOW YOU FEEL AFTER THE SWINE FLU SETS IN, ROBBER?
COSTUME
WHAT WERE YOU DOING AT THE CRIME SCENE ANYWAY?
YOU WERE THERE LAST NIGHT TOO.
WEARING IT
I DON'T REALLY UNDER-STAND IT EITHER.
SOMETHING DREW ME TO THOSE PLACES.
WHAT...?

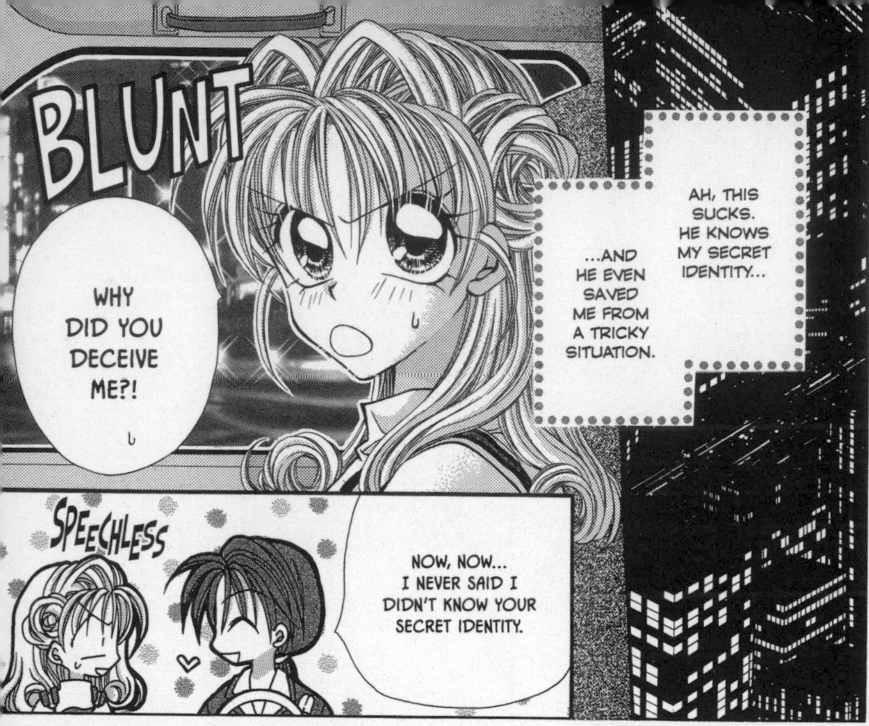
AH, THIS SUCKS. HE KNOWS MY SECRET IDENTITY...
...AND HE EVEN SAVED ME FROM A TRICKY SITUATION.
BLUNT
WHY DID YOU DECEIVE ME?!
NOW, NOW... I NEVER SAID I DIDN'T KNOW YOUR SECRET IDENTITY.
SPEECHLESS

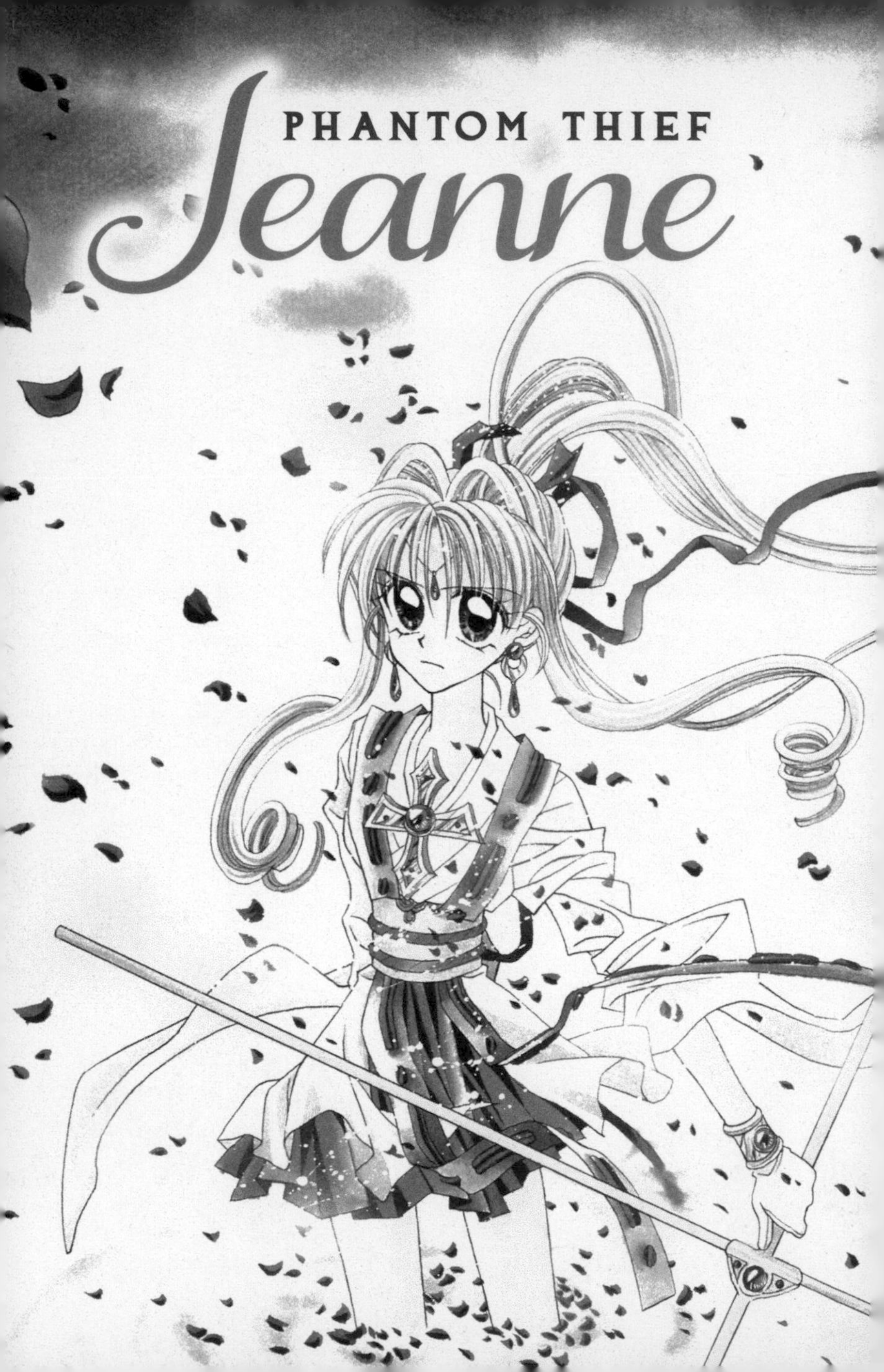
PHANTOM THIEF
Jeanne

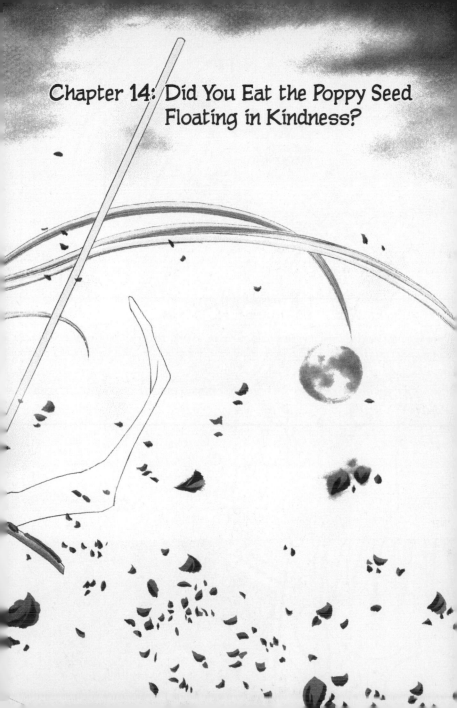

Chapter 14: Did You Eat the Poppy Seed
Floating in Kindness?

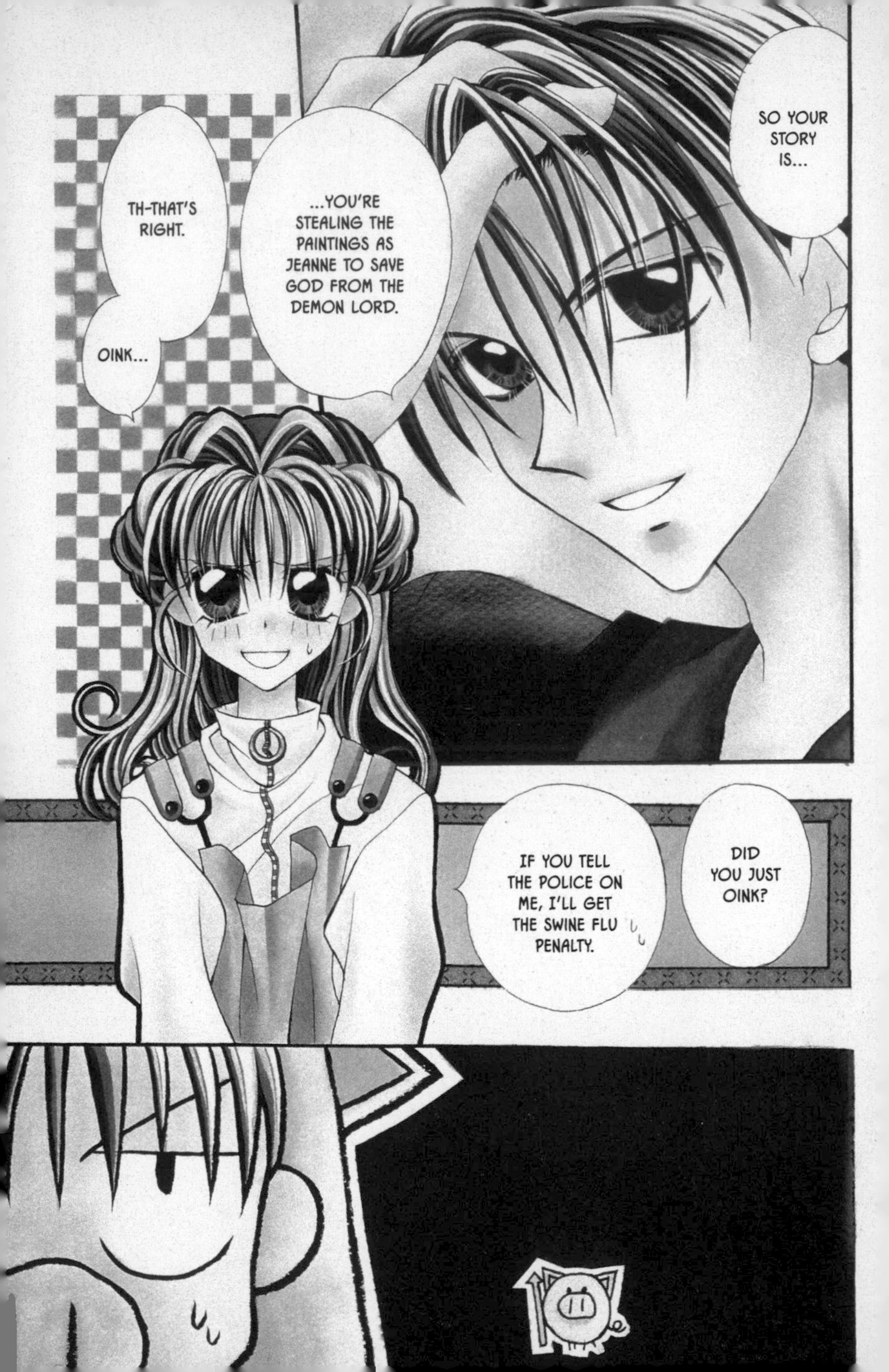
SO YOUR STORY IS...
...YOU'RE STEALING THE PAINTINGS AS JEANNE TO SAVE GOD FROM THE DEMON LORD.
TH-THAT'S RIGHT.
OINK...
DID YOU JUST OINK?
IF YOU TELL THE POLICE ON ME, I'LL GET THE SWINE FLU PENALTY.

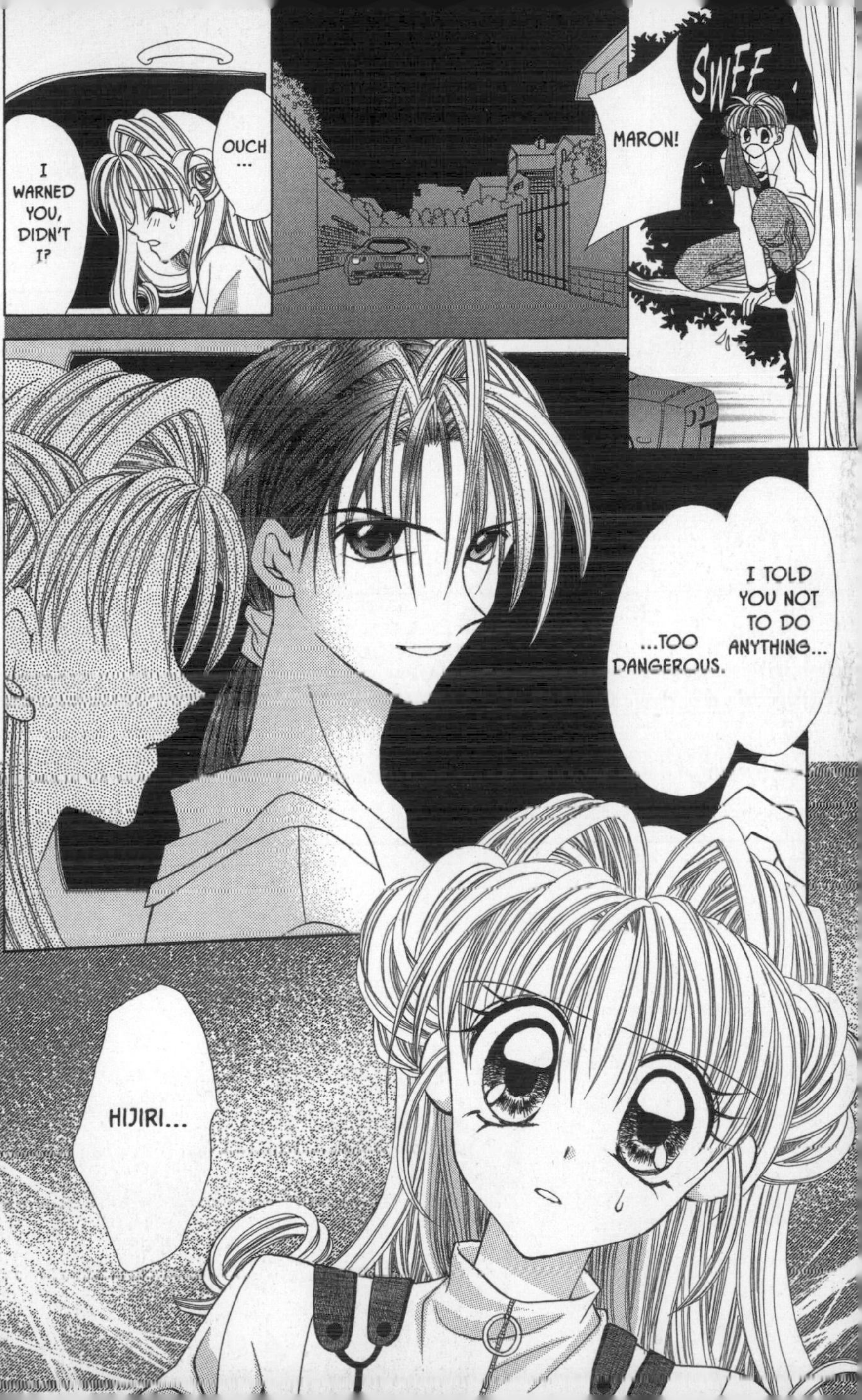
SWFF
MARON!
OUCH...
I WARNED YOU, DIDN'T I?
I TOLD YOU NOT TO DO ANYTHING...
...TOO DANGEROUS.
HIJIRI...

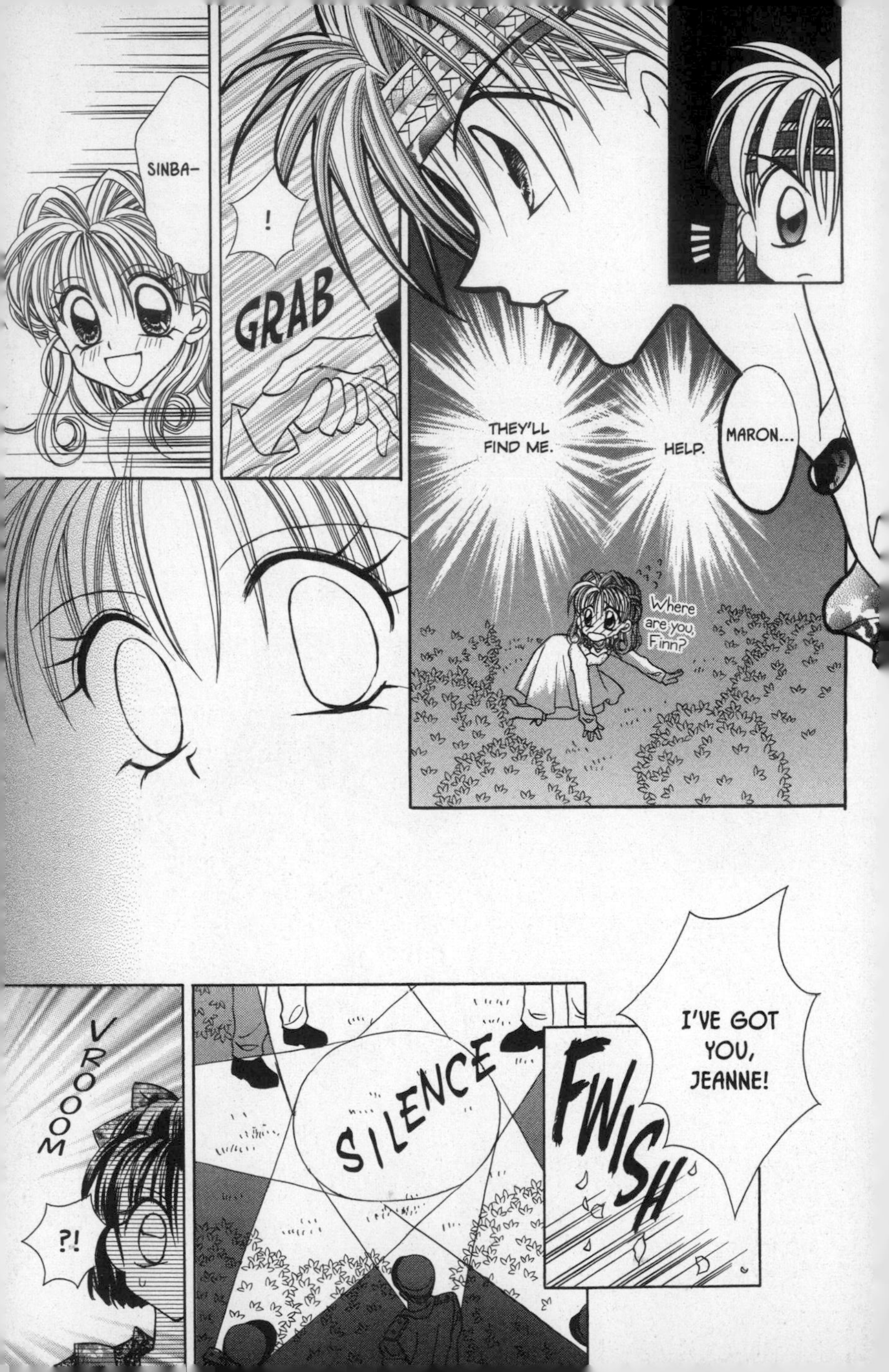

!
GRAB
SINBA-
MARON...
HELP.
THEY'LL FIND ME.
Where are you, Finn?
I'VE GOT YOU, JEANNE!
FWISH
SILENCE
VROOOOM
?!

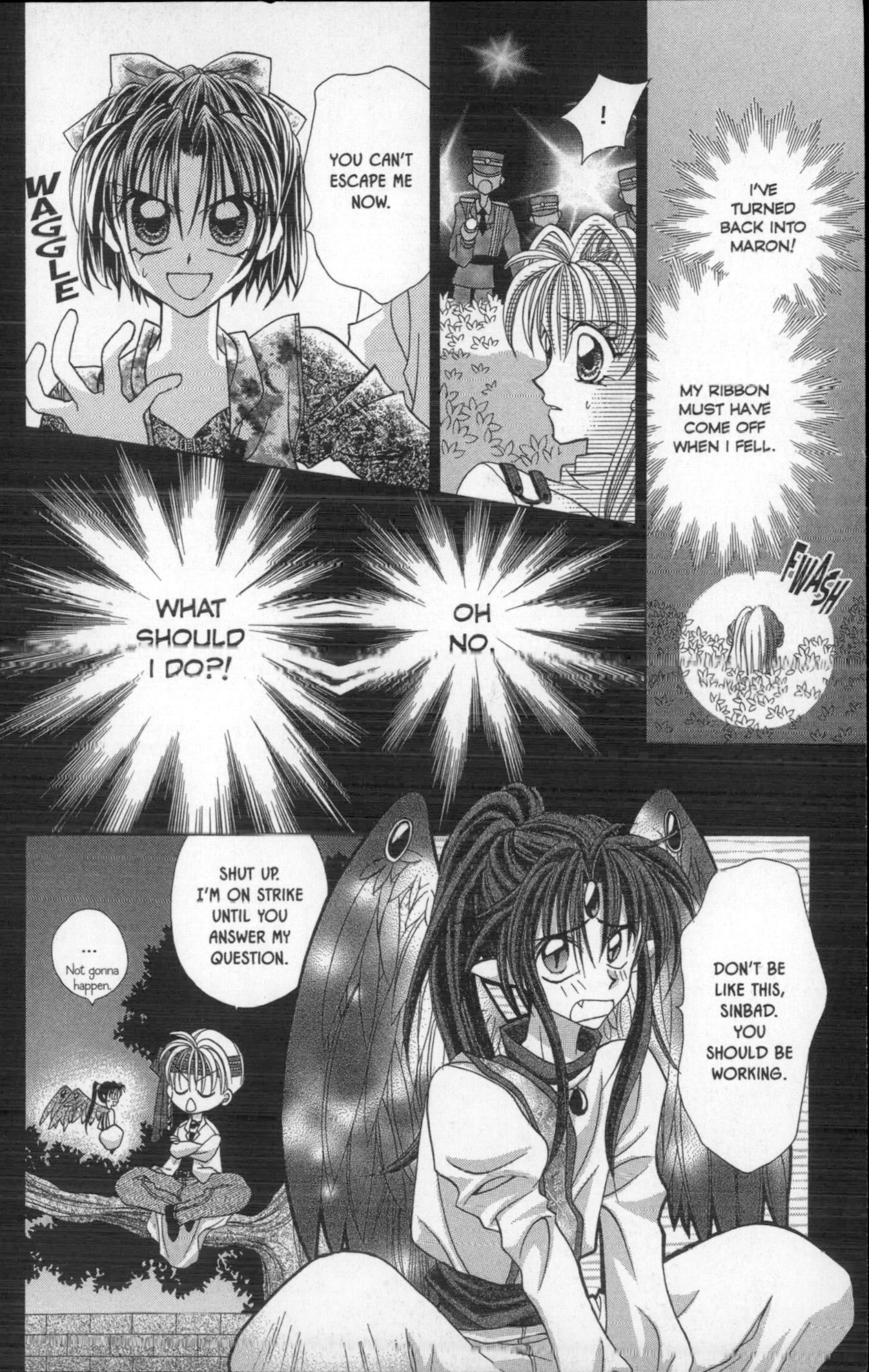
I'VE TURNED BACK INTO MARON!
MY RIBBON MUST HAVE COME OFF WHEN I FELL.
FWASH
!
YOU CAN'T ESCAPE ME NOW.
WAGGLE
OH NO.
WHAT SHOULD I DO?!
DON'T BE LIKE THIS, SINBAD. YOU SHOULD BE WORKING.
SHUT UP. I'M ON STRIKE UNTIL YOU ANSWER MY QUESTION.
... Not gonna happen.

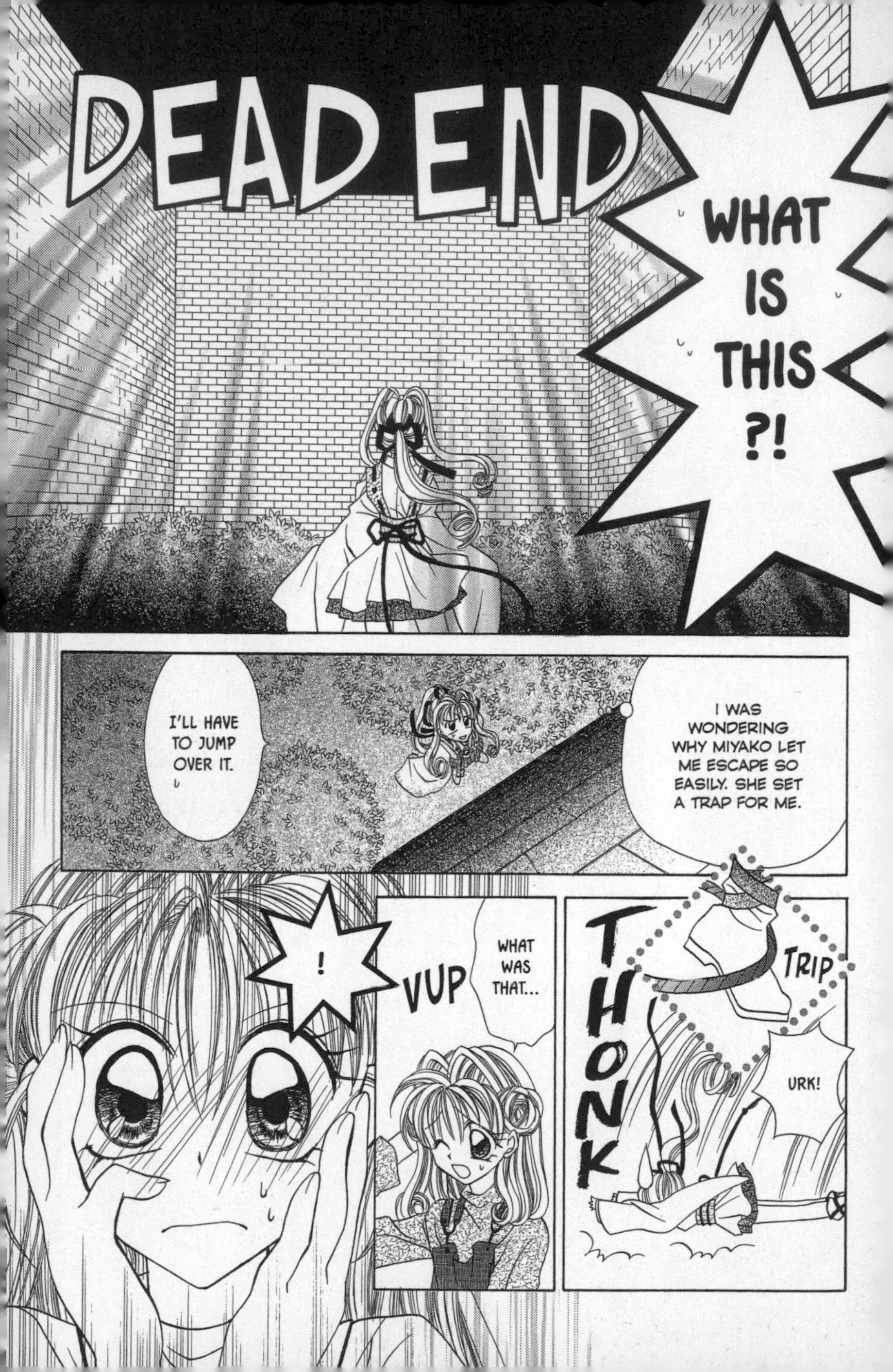
WHAT IS THIS ?!
DEAD END
I WAS WONDERING WHY MIYAKO LET ME ESCAPE SO EASILY. SHE SET A TRAP FOR ME.
I'LL HAVE TO JUMP OVER IT.
TRIP
THONK
URK!
WHAT WAS THAT...
VUP
!

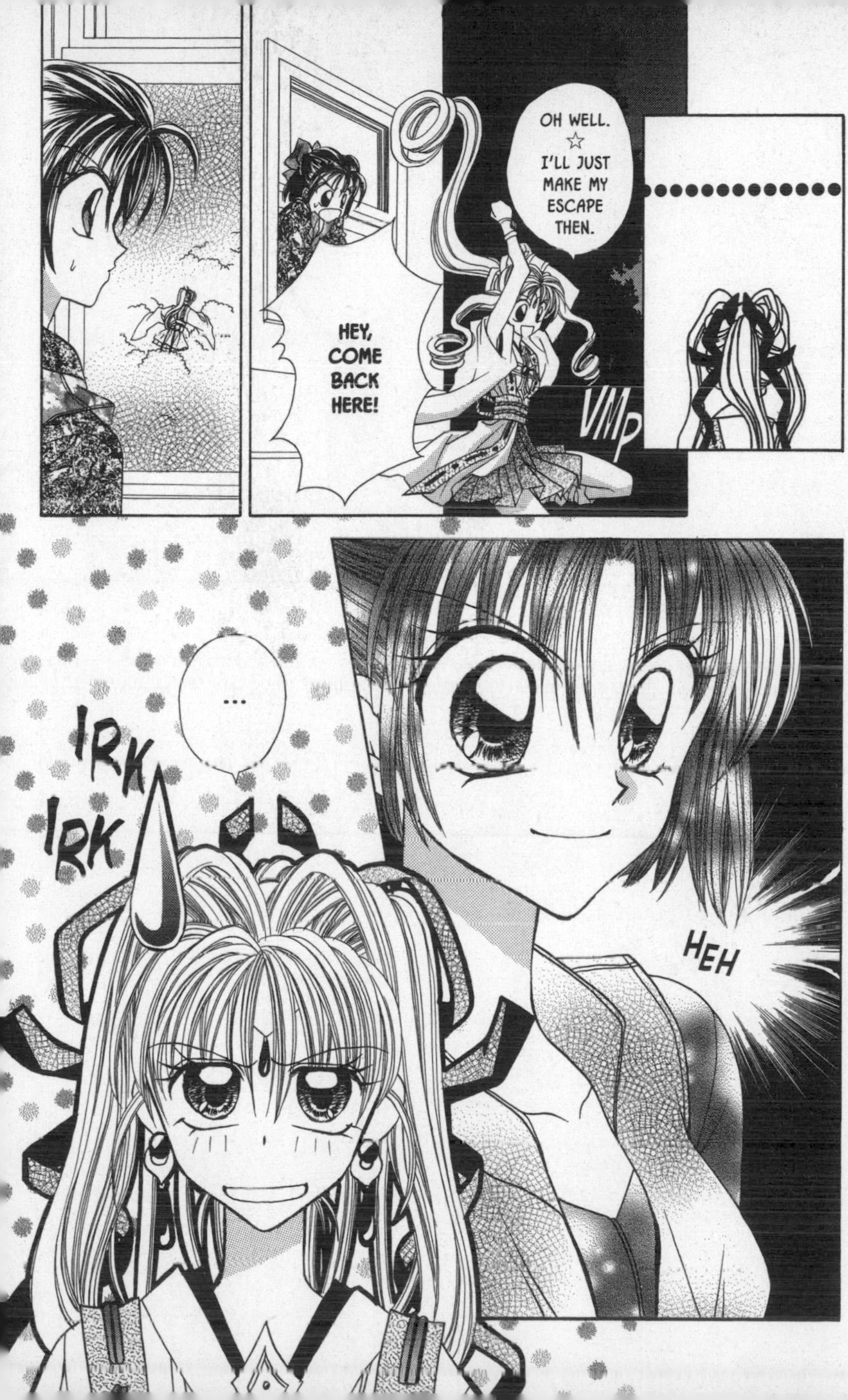
OH WELL. ☆ I'LL JUST MAKE MY ESCAPE THEN.
VMP
HEY, COME BACK HERE!
HEH
...
IRK IRK

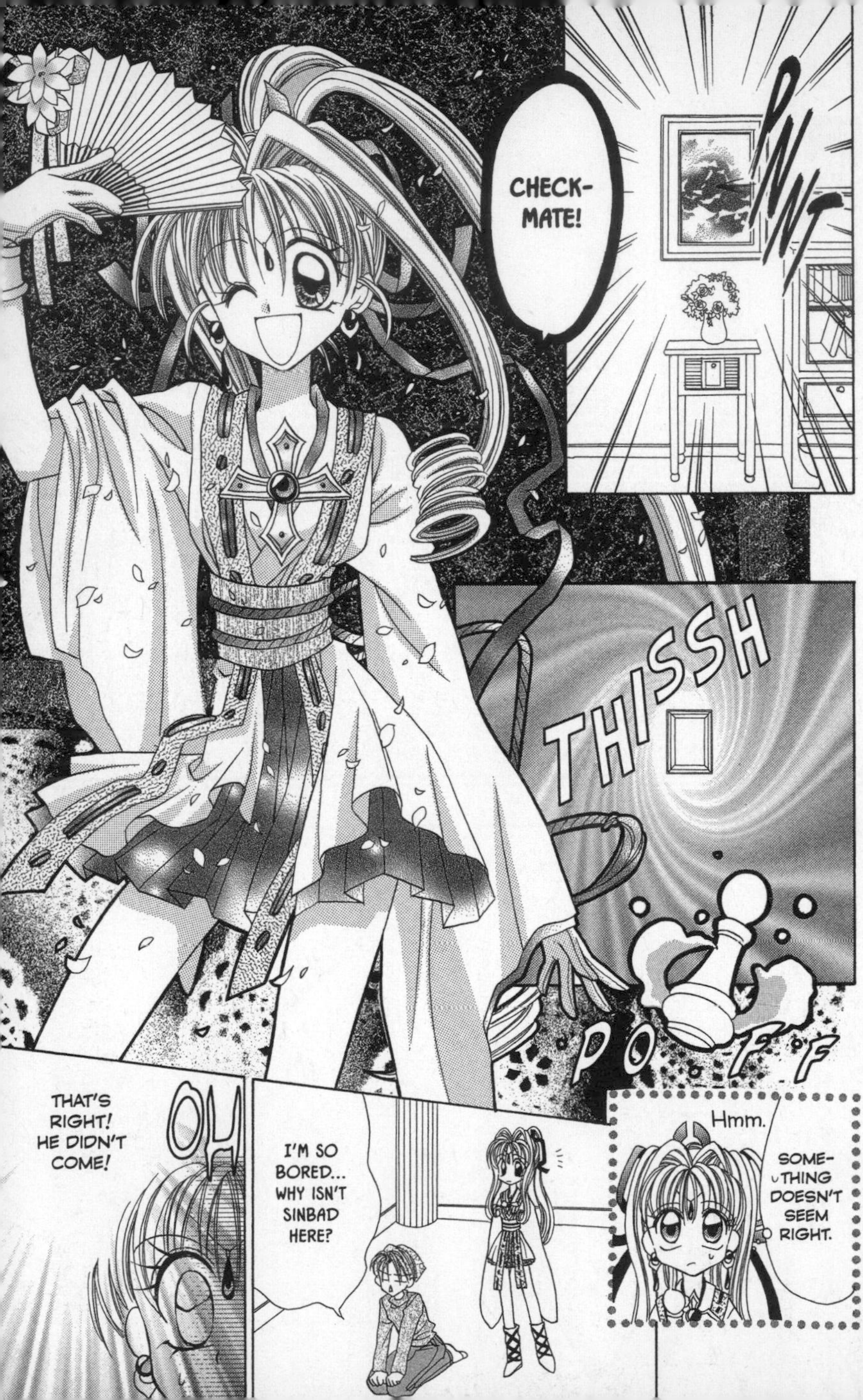
PNNT
CHECK-MATE!
THISSH
POFF
Hmm.
SOME-THING DOESN'T SEEM RIGHT.
I'M SO BORED... WHY ISN'T SINBAD HERE?
OH
THAT'S RIGHT! HE DIDN'T COME!

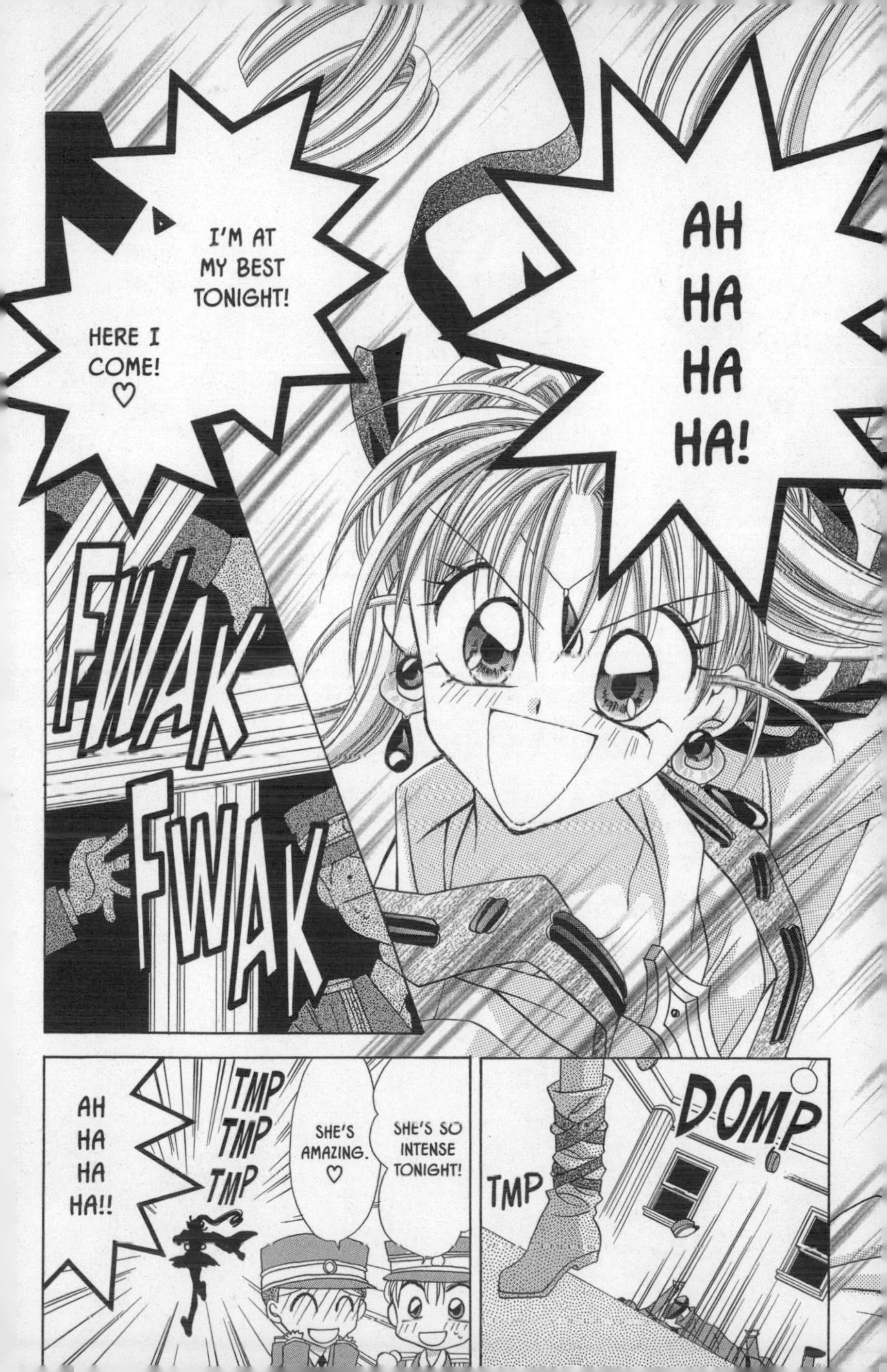
AH HA HA HA HA!
I'M AT MY BEST TONIGHT!
HERE I COME! ♡
FWAK
FWAK
DOMP
TMP
SHE'S SO INTENSE TONIGHT!
SHE'S AMAZING. ♡
TMP TMP TMP
AH HA HA HA!!

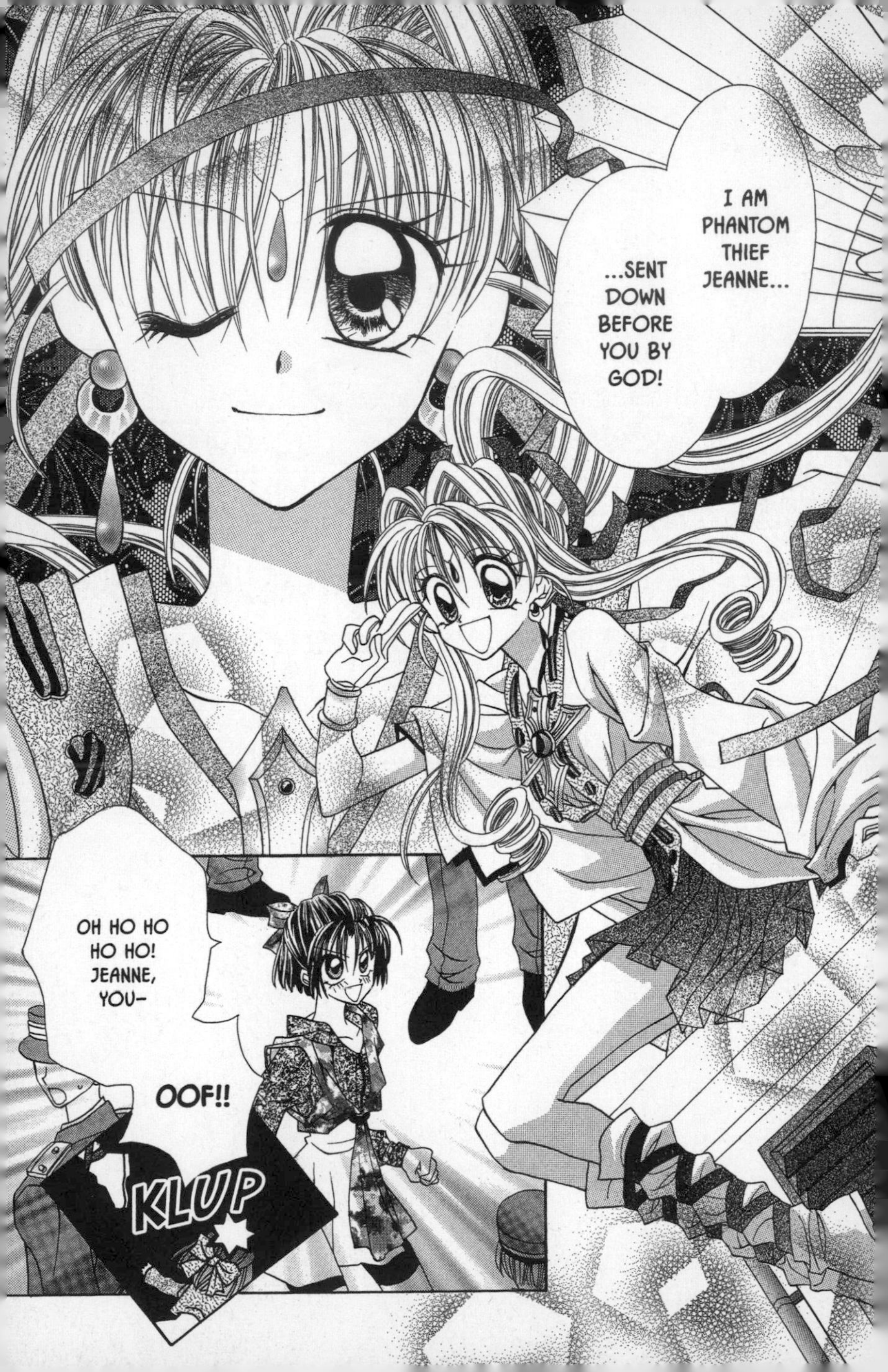
I AM PHANTOM THIEF JEANNE...
...SENT DOWN BEFORE YOU BY GOD!
OH HO HO HO HO! JEANNE, YOU–
OOF!!
KLUP

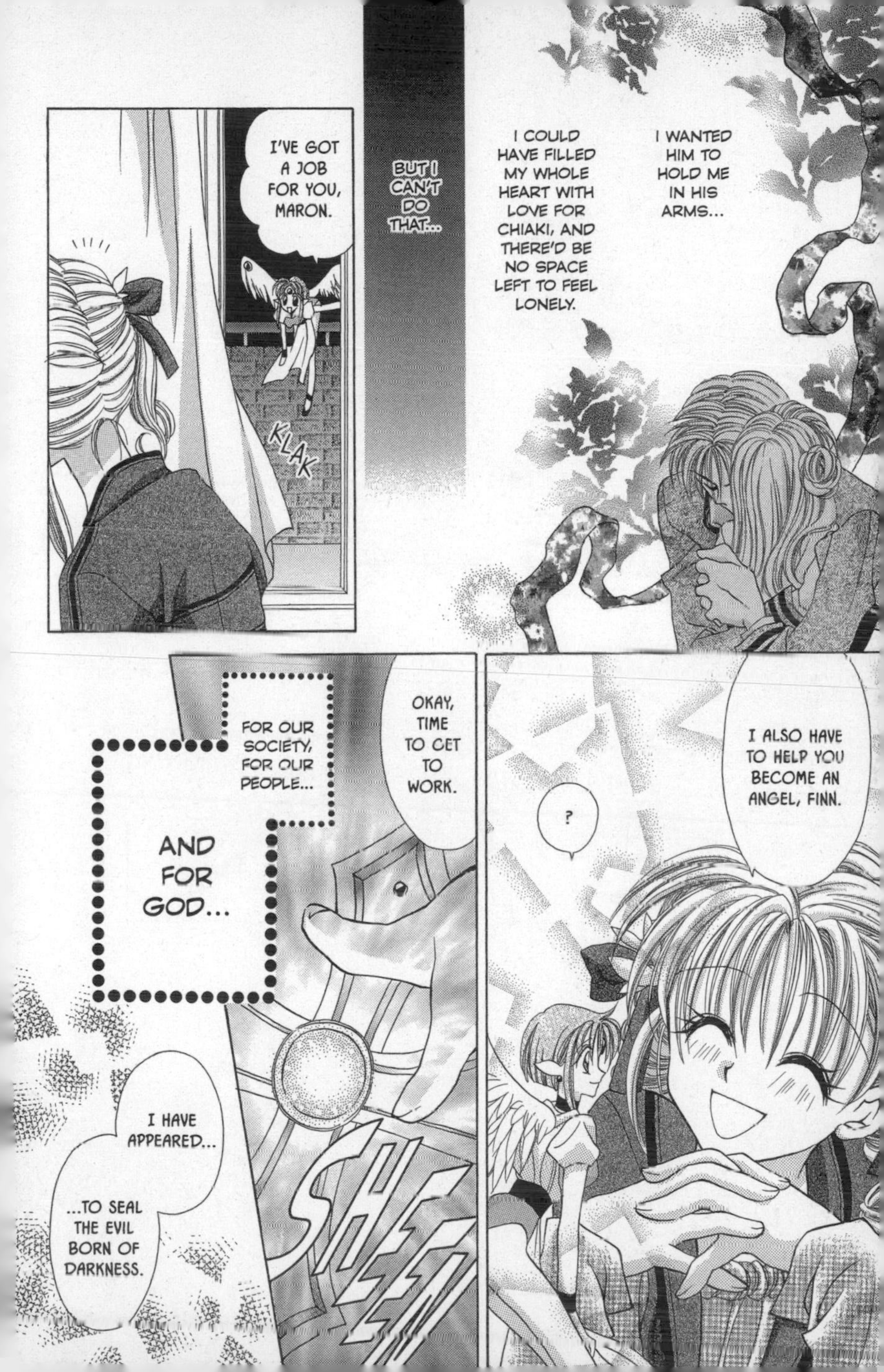
I WANTED HIM TO HOLD ME IN HIS ARMS...
I COULD HAVE FILLED MY WHOLE HEART WITH LOVE FOR CHIAKI, AND THERE'D BE NO SPACE LEFT TO FEEL LONELY.
BUT I CAN'T DO THAT...
I'VE GOT A JOB FOR YOU, MARON.
KLAK
I ALSO HAVE TO HELP YOU BECOME AN ANGEL, FINN.
?
OKAY, TIME TO GET TO WORK.
FOR OUR SOCIETY, FOR OUR PEOPLE...
AND FOR GOD...
I HAVE APPEARED...
...TO SEAL THE EVIL BORN OF DARKNESS.

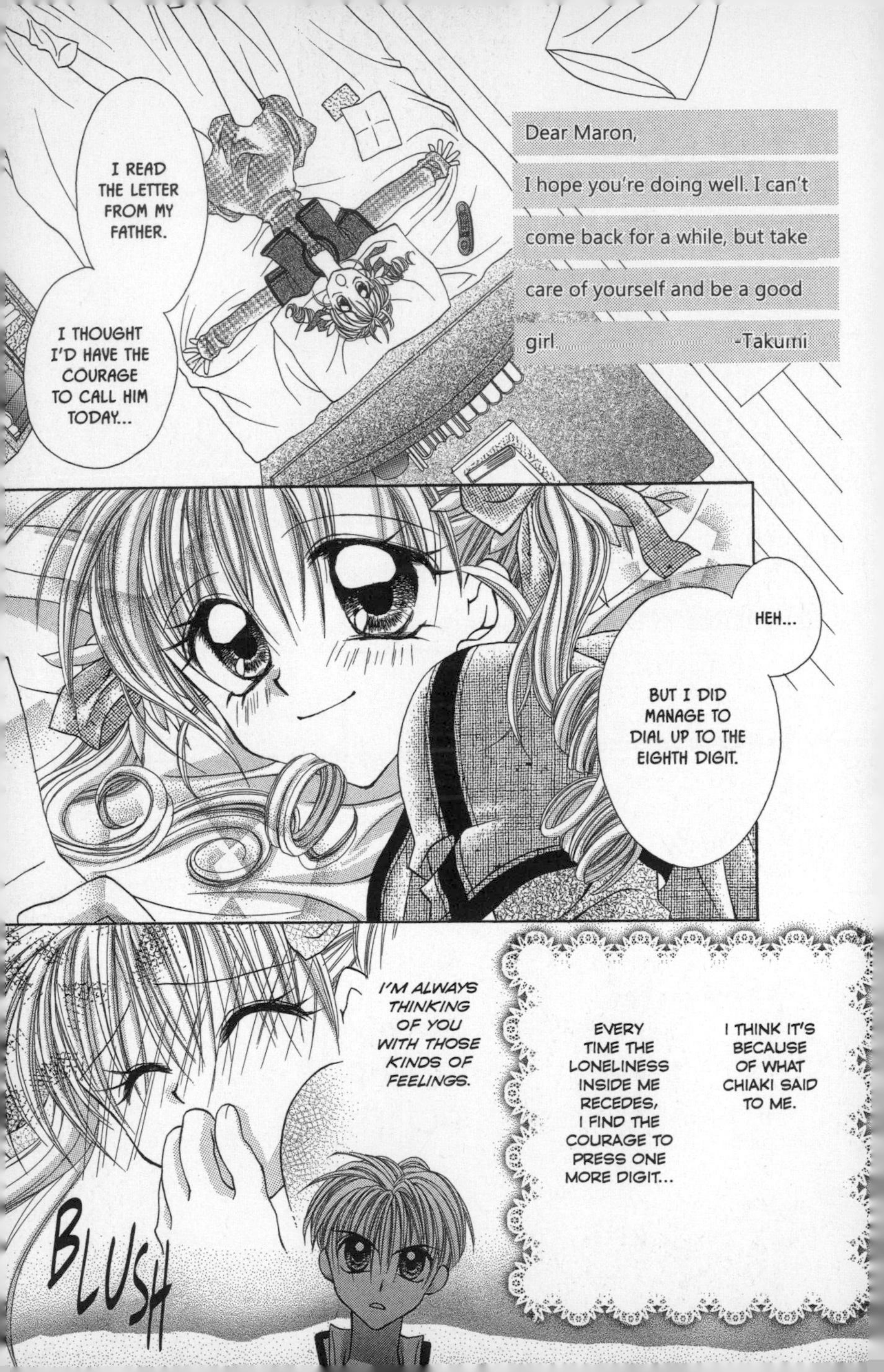
Dear Maron,
I hope you're doing well. I can't come back for a while, but take care of yourself and be a good girl. -Takumi
I READ THE LETTER FROM MY FATHER.
I THOUGHT I'D HAVE THE COURAGE TO CALL HIM TODAY...
HEH...
BUT I DID MANAGE TO DIAL UP TO THE EIGHTH DIGIT.
I THINK IT'S BECAUSE OF WHAT CHIAKI SAID TO ME.
EVERY TIME THE LONELINESS INSIDE ME RECEDES, I FIND THE COURAGE TO PRESS ONE MORE DIGIT...
I'M ALWAYS THINKING OF YOU WITH THOSE KINDS OF FEELINGS.
BLUSH

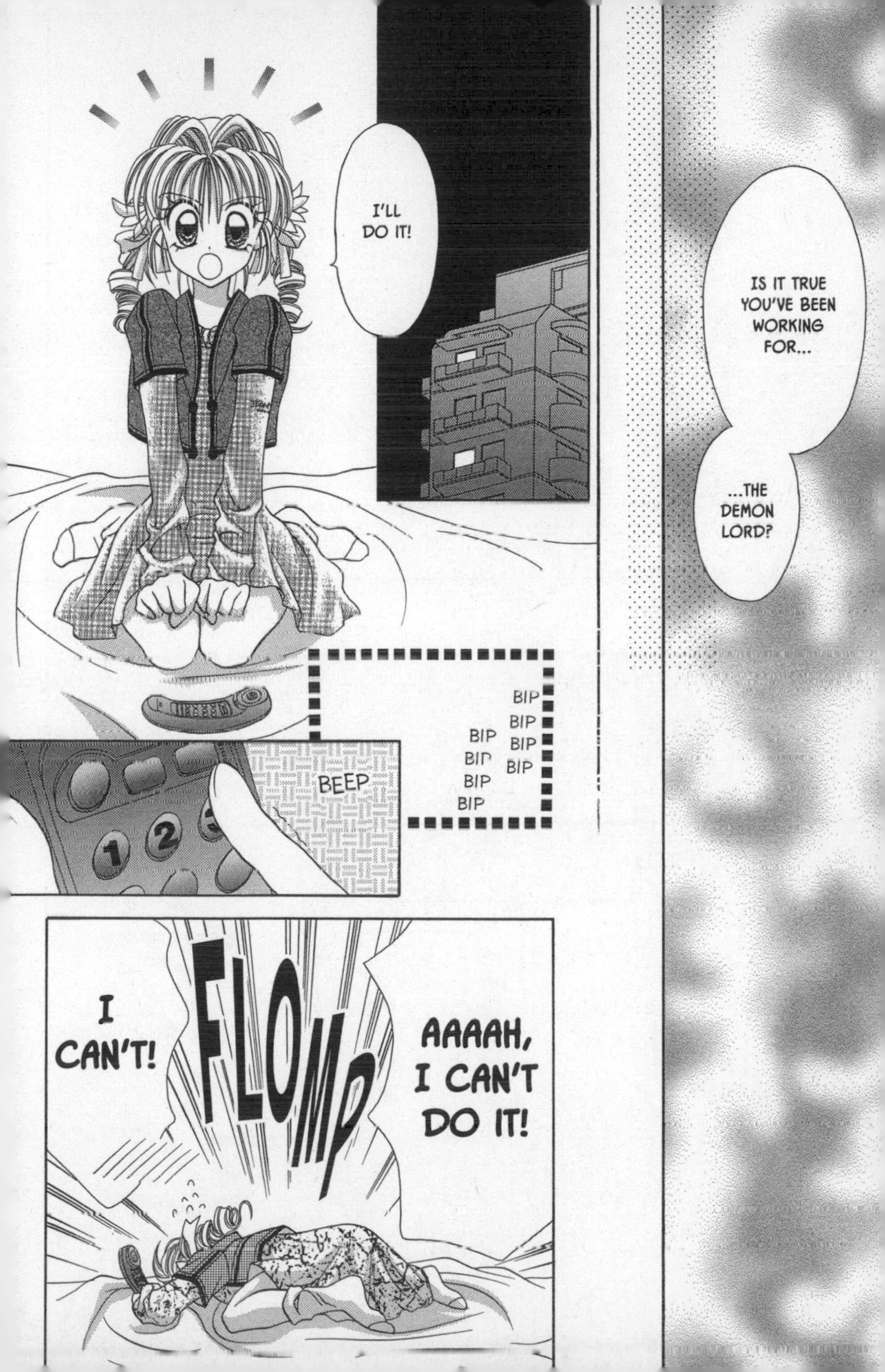
IS IT TRUE YOU'VE BEEN WORKING FOR...
...THE DEMON LORD?
I'LL DO IT!
BIP BIP BIP BIP BIP BIP BIP BIP
BEEP
AAAAH, I CAN'T DO IT!
FLOMP
I CAN'T!

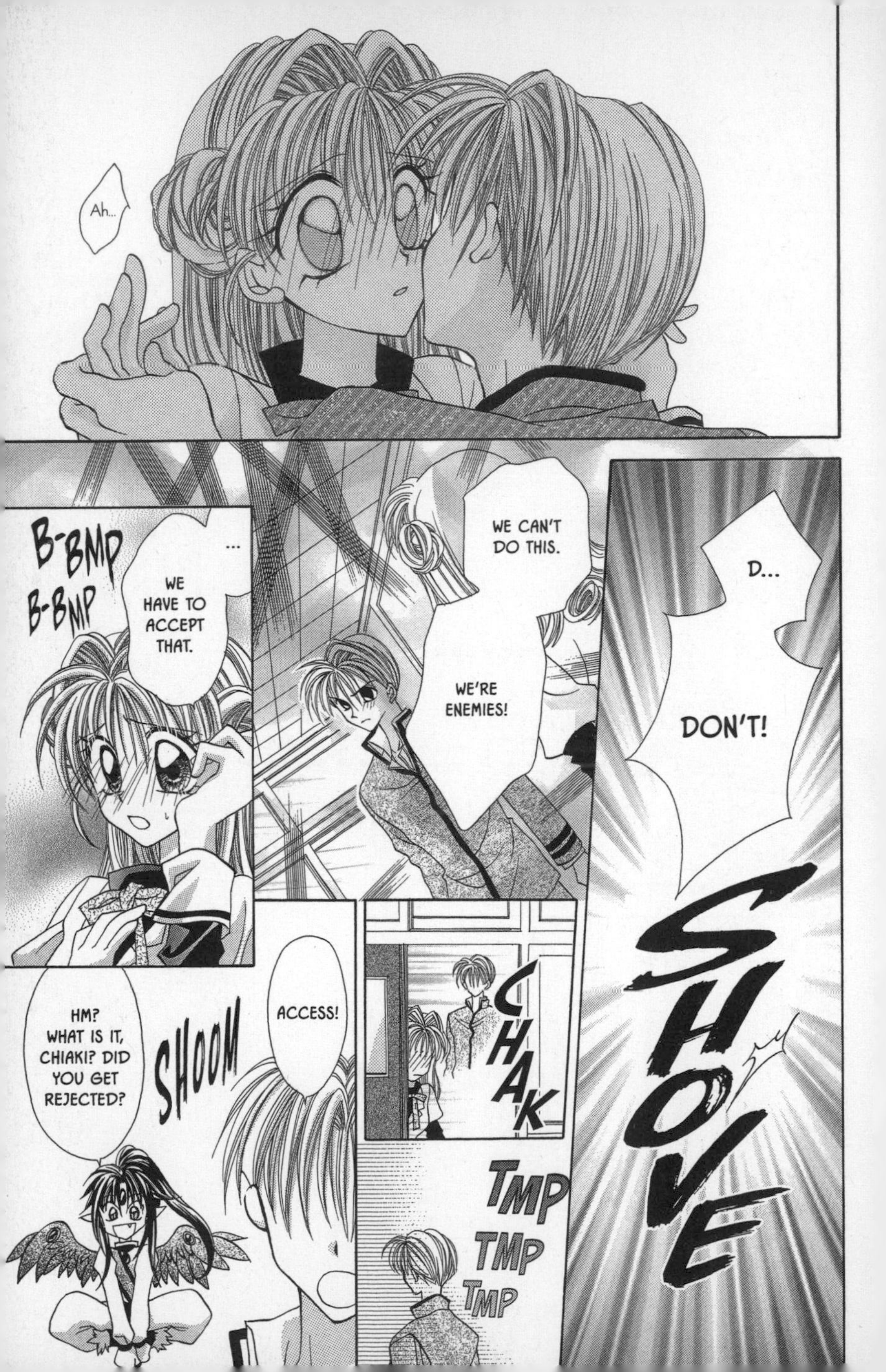
Ah...
D...
DON'T!
SHOVE
WE CAN'T DO THIS.
WE'RE ENEMIES!
B-BMP B-BMP
...
WE HAVE TO ACCEPT THAT.
CHAK
ACCESS!
TMP TMP TMP
HM? WHAT IS IT, CHIAKI? DID YOU GET REJECTED?
SHOOM

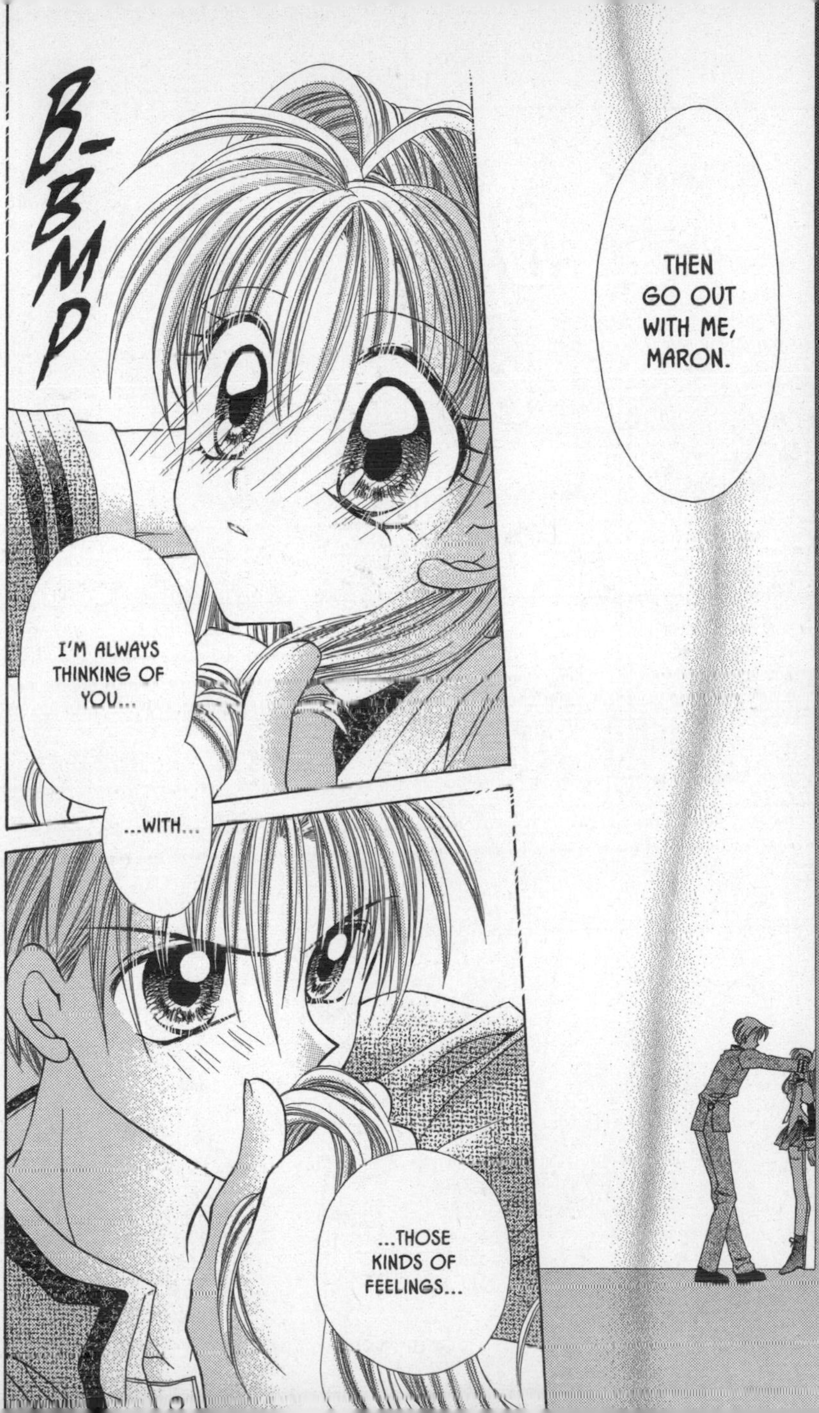
THEN GO OUT WITH ME, MARON.
B-BMP
I'M ALWAYS THINKING OF YOU...
...WITH...
...THOSE KINDS OF FEELINGS...

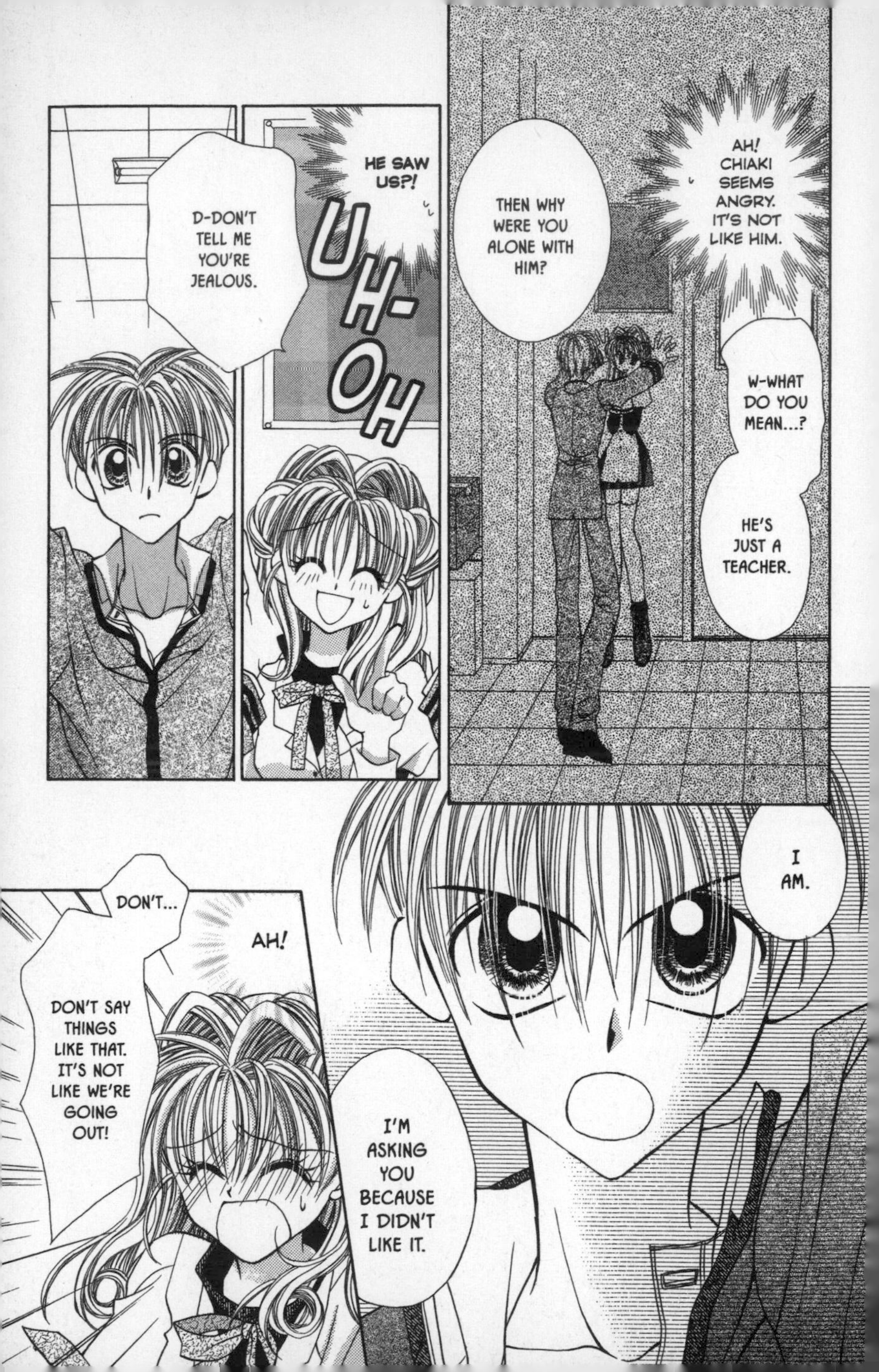
AH! CHIAKI SEEMS ANGRY. IT'S NOT LIKE HIM.
THEN WHY WERE YOU ALONE WITH HIM?
W-WHAT DO YOU MEAN...?
HE'S JUST A TEACHER.
HE SAW US?!
UH-OH
D-DON'T TELL ME YOU'RE JEALOUS.
I AM.
I'M ASKING YOU BECAUSE I DIDN'T LIKE IT.
DON'T...
AH!
DON'T SAY THINGS LIKE THAT. IT'S NOT LIKE WE'RE GOING OUT!

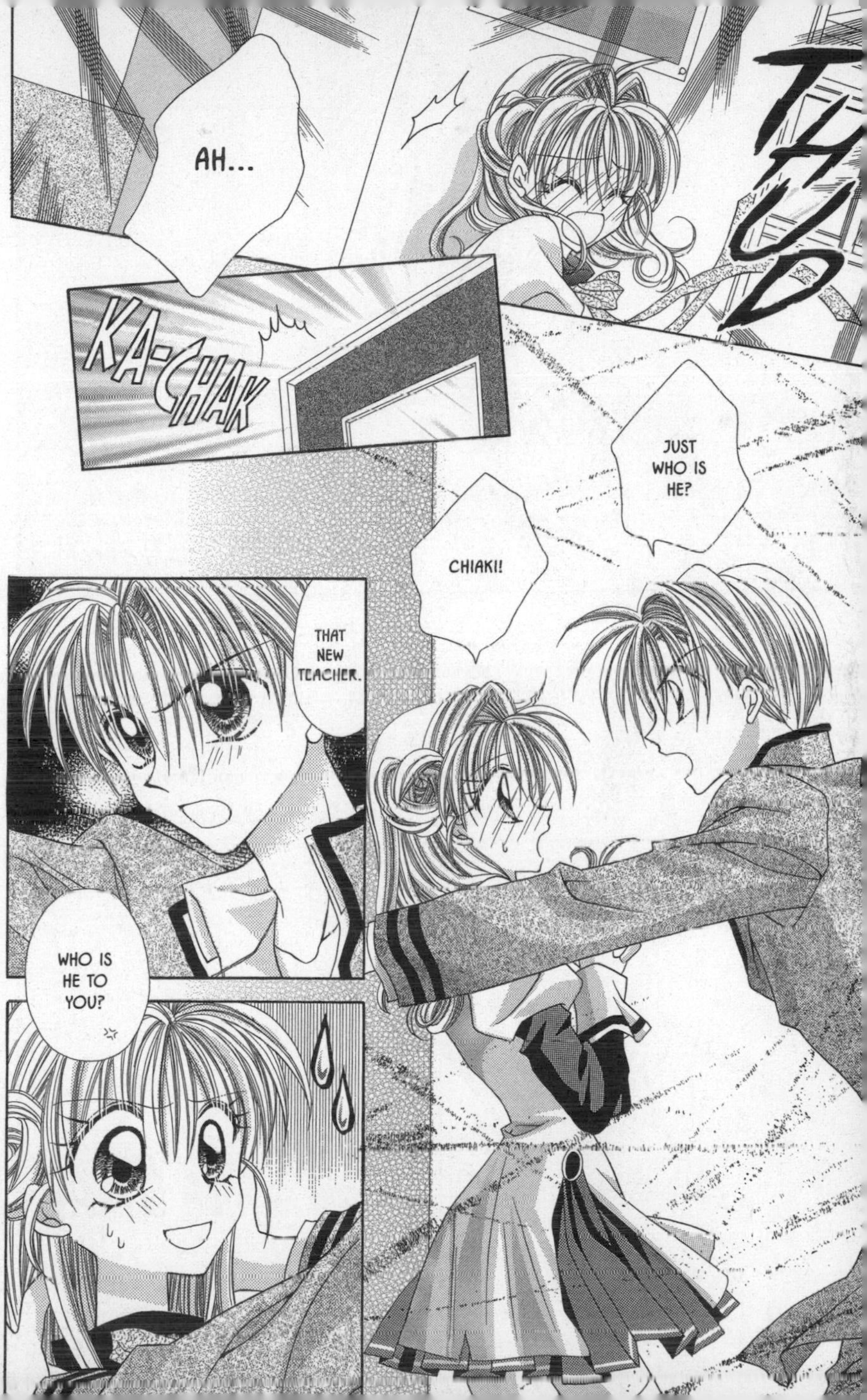
THUD
AH...
KA-CHAK
JUST WHO IS HE?
CHIAKI!
THAT NEW TEACHER.
WHO IS HE TO YOU?

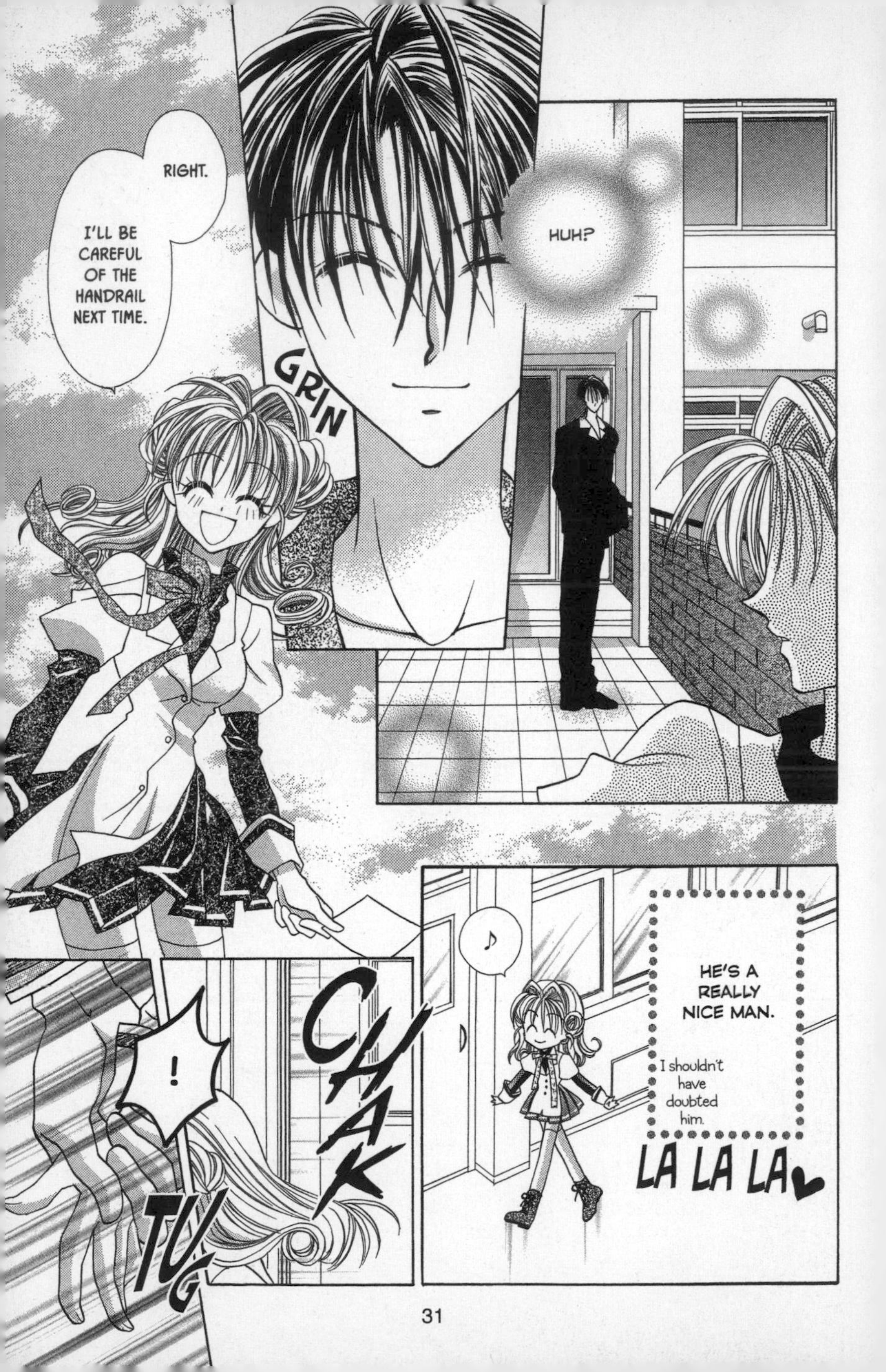
HUH?
GRIN
RIGHT.
I'LL BE CAREFUL OF THE HANDRAIL NEXT TIME.
♪
HE'S A REALLY NICE MAN.
I shouldn't have doubted him.
LA LA LA♥
CHAK
!
TUG

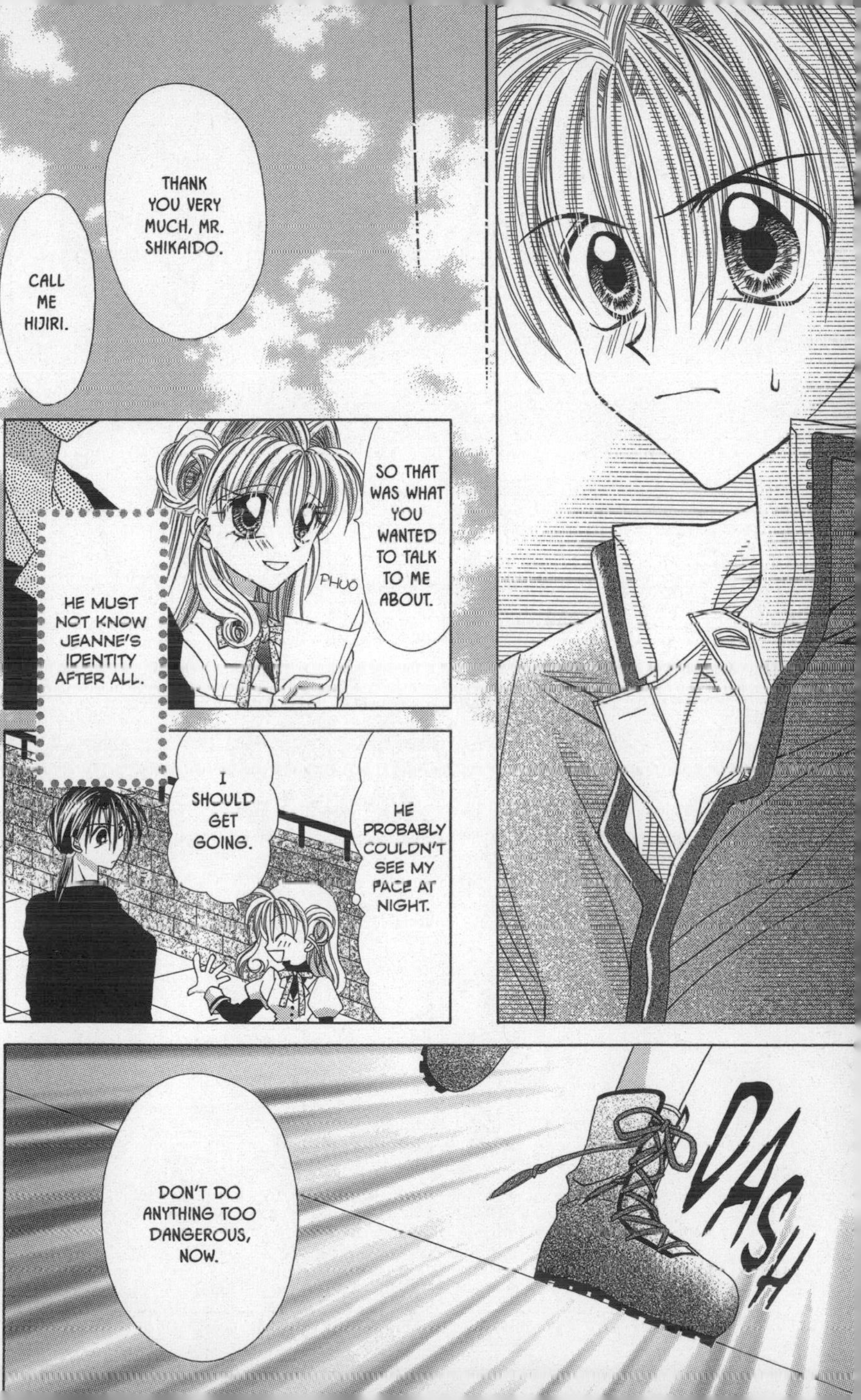
THANK YOU VERY MUCH, MR. SHIKAIDO.
CALL ME HIJIRI.
SO THAT WAS WHAT YOU WANTED TO TALK TO ME ABOUT.
PHUO
HE MUST NOT KNOW JEANNE'S IDENTITY AFTER ALL.
HE PROBABLY COULDN'T SEE MY FACE AT NIGHT.
I SHOULD GET GOING.
DASH
DON'T DO ANYTHING TOO DANGEROUS, NOW.

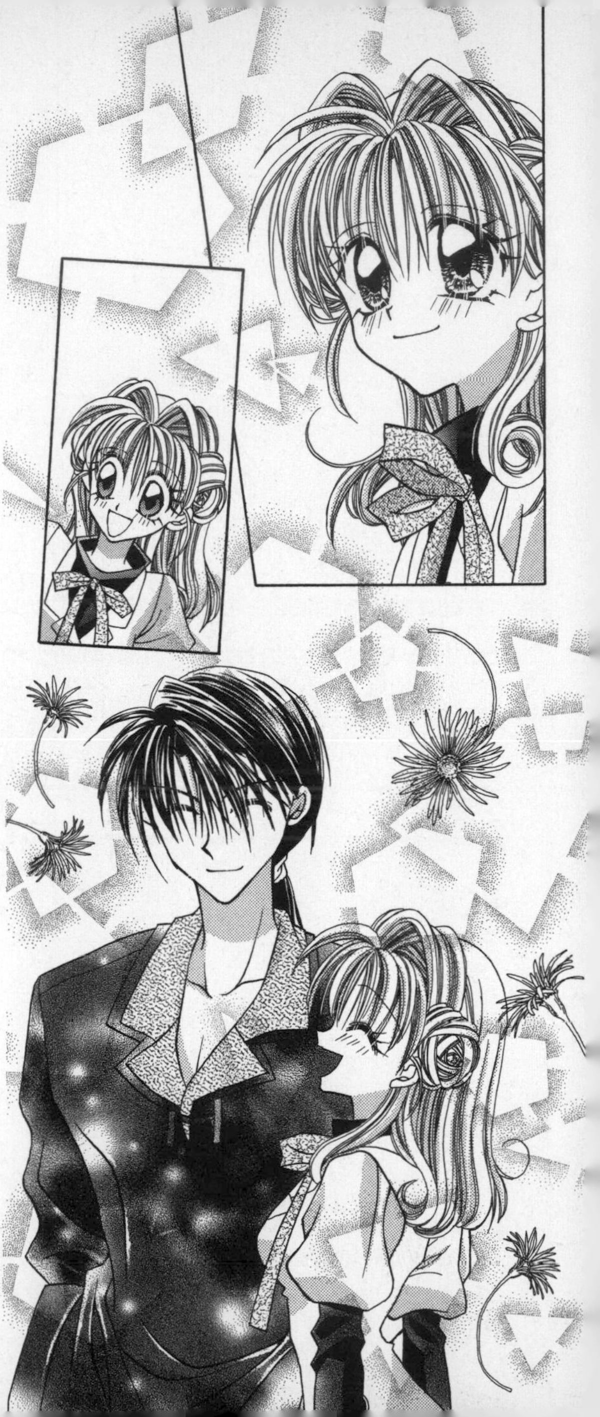

PHANTOM
THIEF
JEANNE

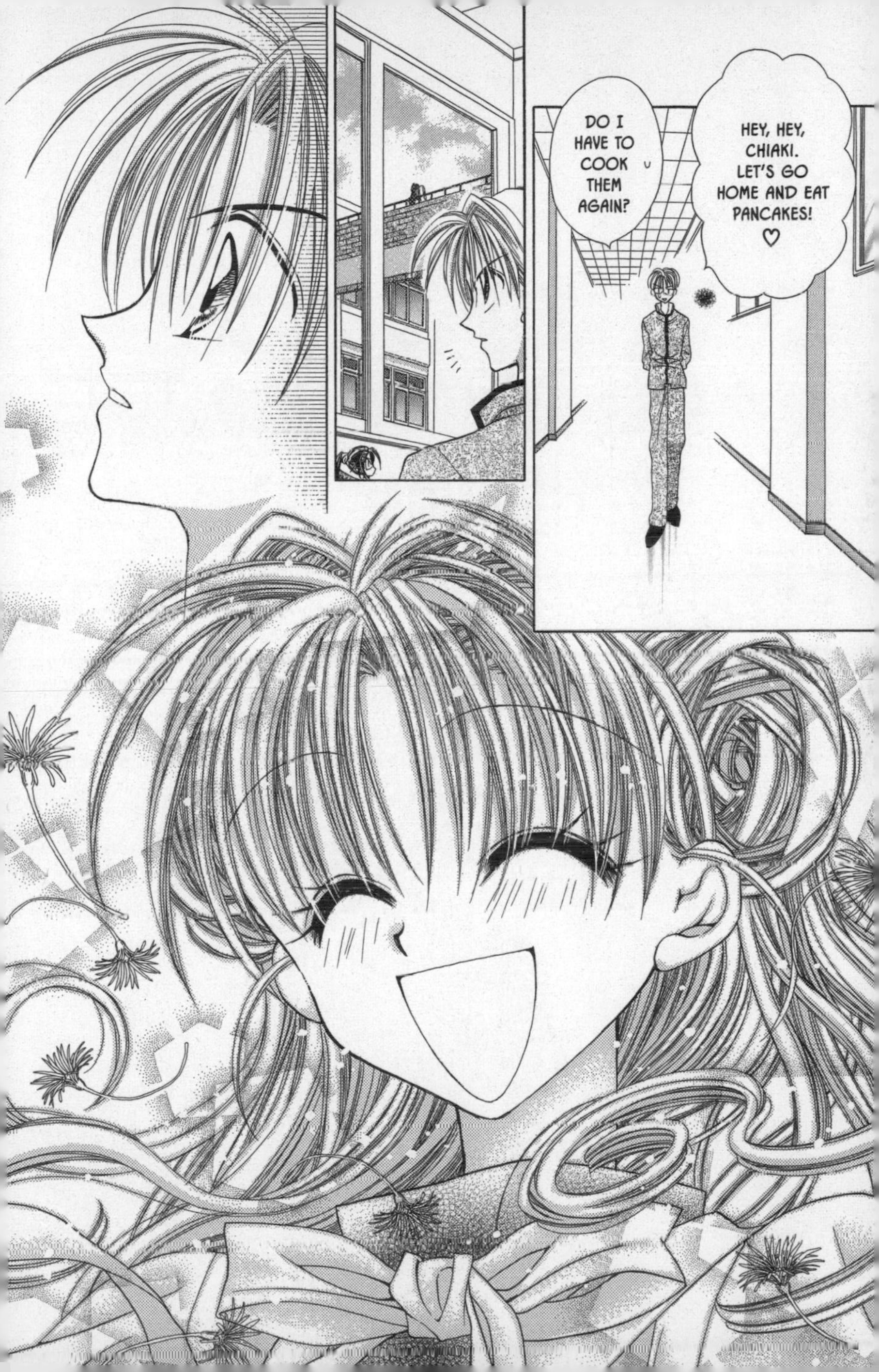
HEY, HEY, CHIAKI. LET'S GO HOME AND EAT PANCAKES! ♡
DO I HAVE TO COOK THEM AGAIN?

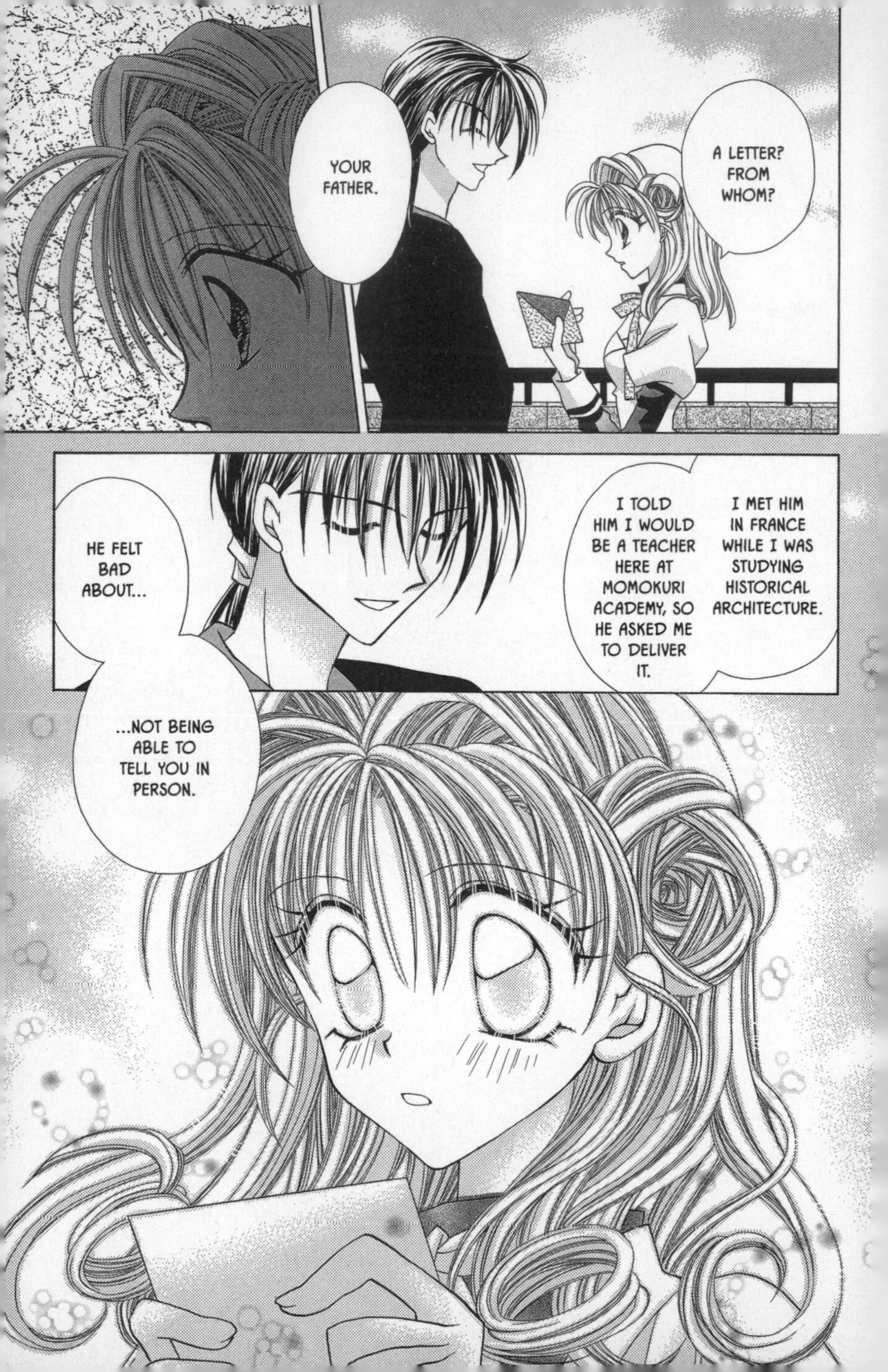
A LETTER? FROM WHOM?
YOUR FATHER.
I MET HIM IN FRANCE WHILE I WAS STUDYING HISTORICAL ARCHITECTURE.
I TOLD HIM I WOULD BE A TEACHER HERE AT MOMOKURI ACADEMY, SO HE ASKED ME TO DELIVER IT.
HE FELT BAD ABOUT...
...NOT BEING ABLE TO TELL YOU IN PERSON.

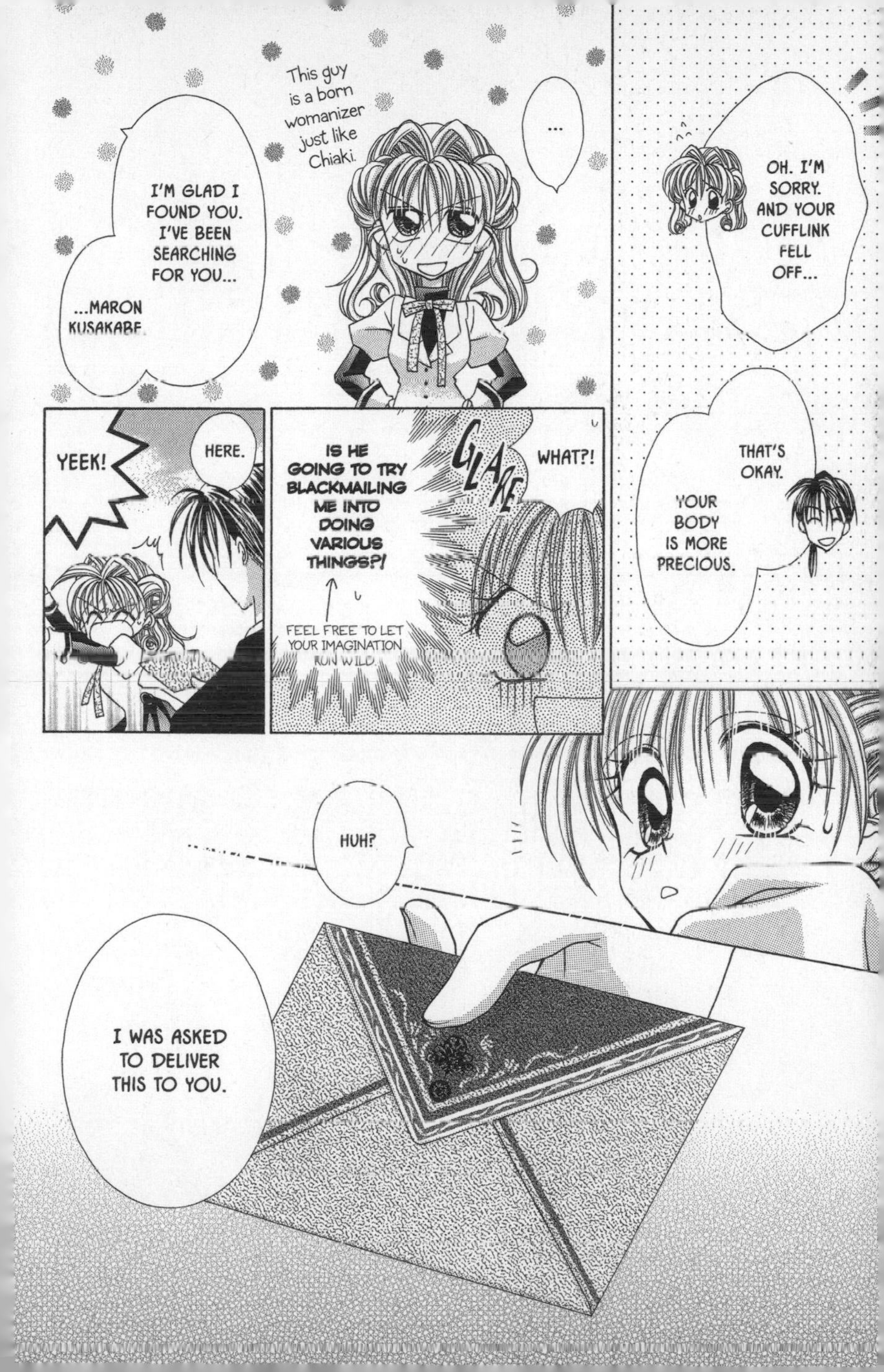
OH. I'M SORRY. AND YOUR CUFFLINK FELL OFF...
THAT'S OKAY.
YOUR BODY IS MORE PRECIOUS.
...
This guy is a born womanizer just like Chiaki.
I'M GLAD I FOUND YOU. I'VE BEEN SEARCHING FOR YOU...
...MARON KUSAKABE.
WHAT?!
GLARE
IS HE GOING TO TRY BLACKMAILING ME INTO DOING VARIOUS THINGS?!
FEEL FREE TO LET YOUR IMAGINATION RUN WILD.
HERE.
YEEK!
HUH?
I WAS ASKED TO DELIVER THIS TO YOU.

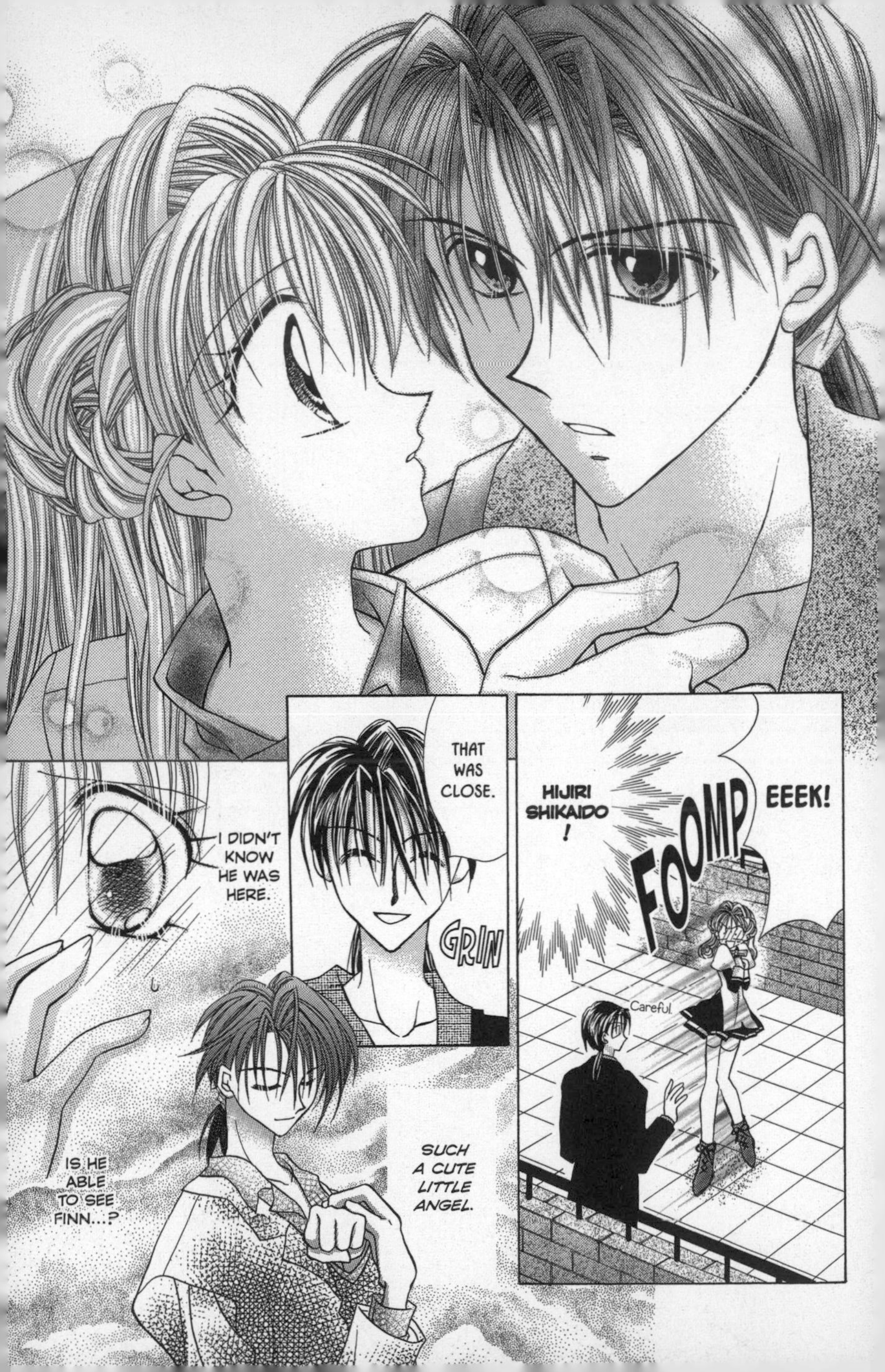
EEEK!
HIJIRI SHIKAIDO!
FOOMP
Careful.
THAT WAS CLOSE.
GRIN
I DIDN'T KNOW HE WAS HERE.
SUCH A CUTE LITTLE ANGEL.
IS HE ABLE TO SEE FINN...?

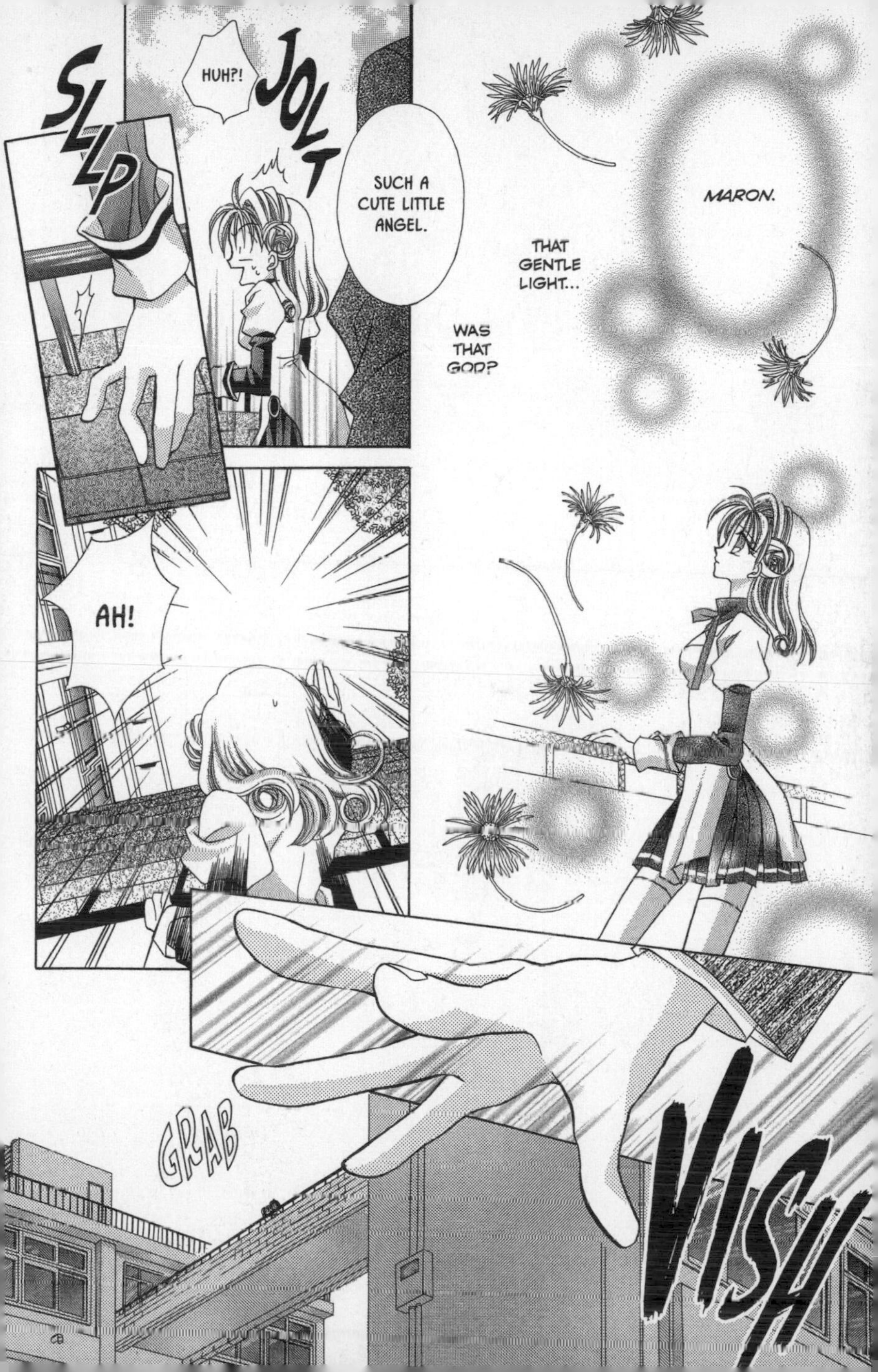
MARON.
THAT GENTLE LIGHT...
WAS THAT GOD?
SUCH A CUTE LITTLE ANGEL.
JOLT
HUH?!
SLLP
AH!
WISH
GRAB

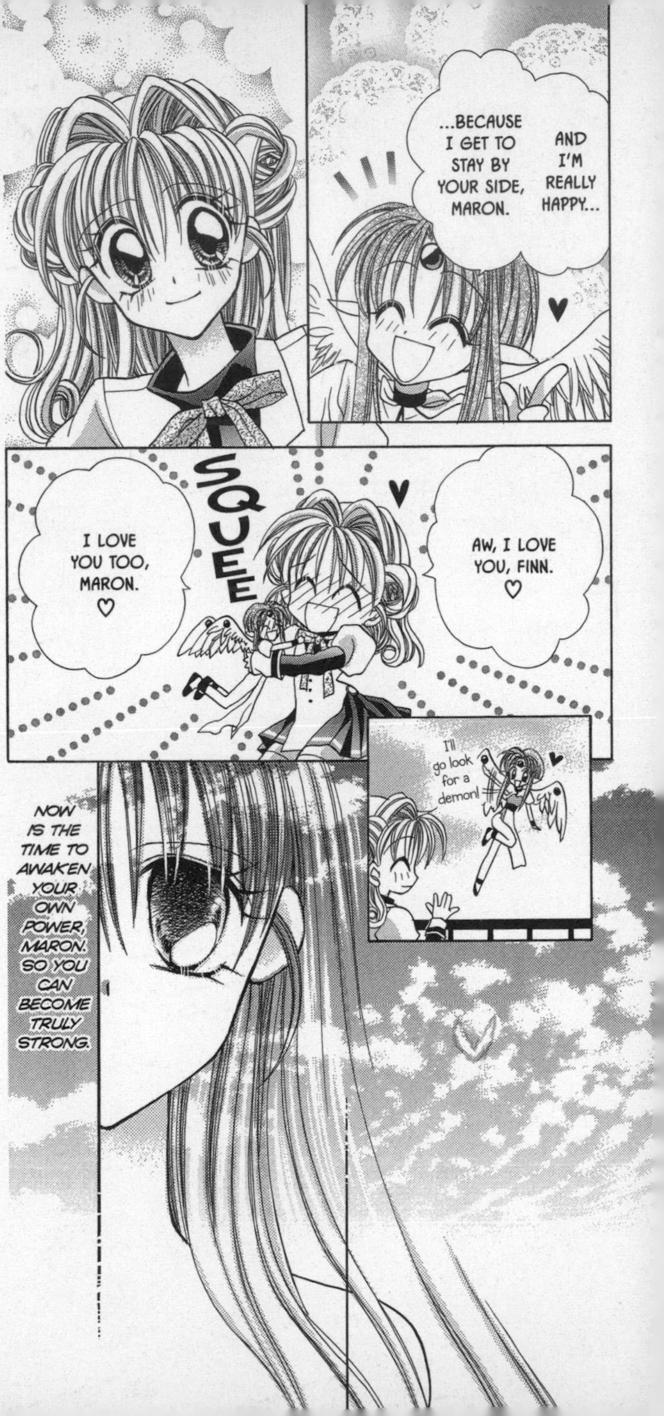
AND I'M REALLY HAPPY...
...BECAUSE I GET TO STAY BY YOUR SIDE, MARON.
AW, I LOVE YOU, FINN. ♡
SQUEEE
I LOVE YOU TOO, MARON. ♡
I'll go look for a demon!
NOW IS THE TIME TO AWAKEN YOUR OWN POWER, MARON. SO YOU CAN BECOME TRULY STRONG.

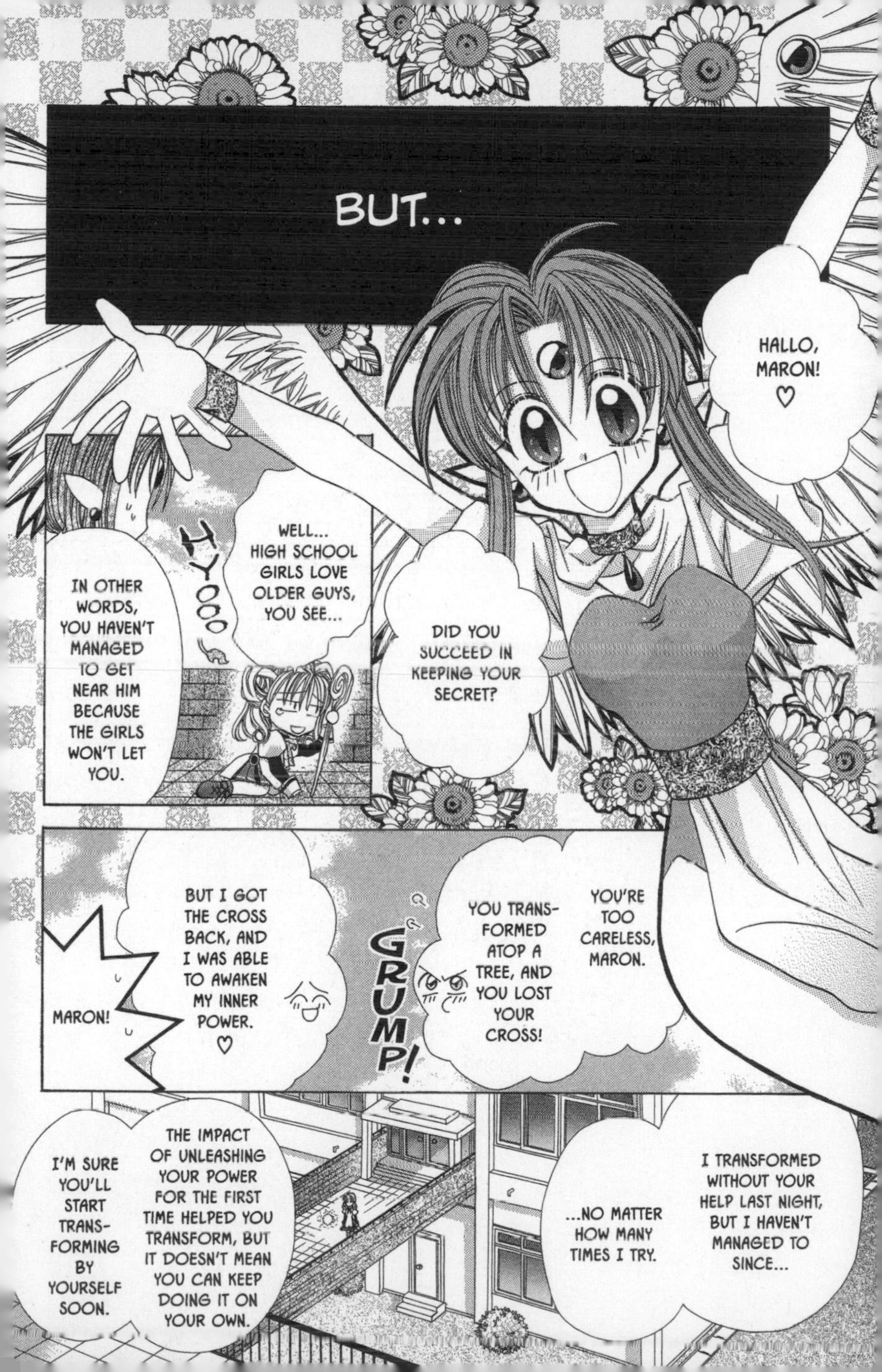
BUT...
HALLO, MARON! ♡
DID YOU SUCCEED IN KEEPING YOUR SECRET?
WELL... HIGH SCHOOL GIRLS LOVE OLDER GUYS, YOU SEE...
HYOOOO
IN OTHER WORDS, YOU HAVEN'T MANAGED TO GET NEAR HIM BECAUSE THE GIRLS WON'T LET YOU.
YOU'RE TOO CARELESS, MARON.
YOU TRANSFORMED ATOP A TREE, AND YOU LOST YOUR CROSS!
GRUMP!
BUT I GOT THE CROSS BACK, AND I WAS ABLE TO AWAKEN MY INNER POWER. ♡
MARON!
I TRANSFORMED WITHOUT YOUR HELP LAST NIGHT, BUT I HAVEN'T MANAGED TO SINCE...
...NO MATTER HOW MANY TIMES I TRY.
THE IMPACT OF UNLEASHING YOUR POWER FOR THE FIRST TIME HELPED YOU TRANSFORM, BUT IT DOESN'T MEAN YOU CAN KEEP DOING IT ON YOUR OWN.
I'M SURE YOU'LL START TRANSFORMING BY YOURSELF SOON.

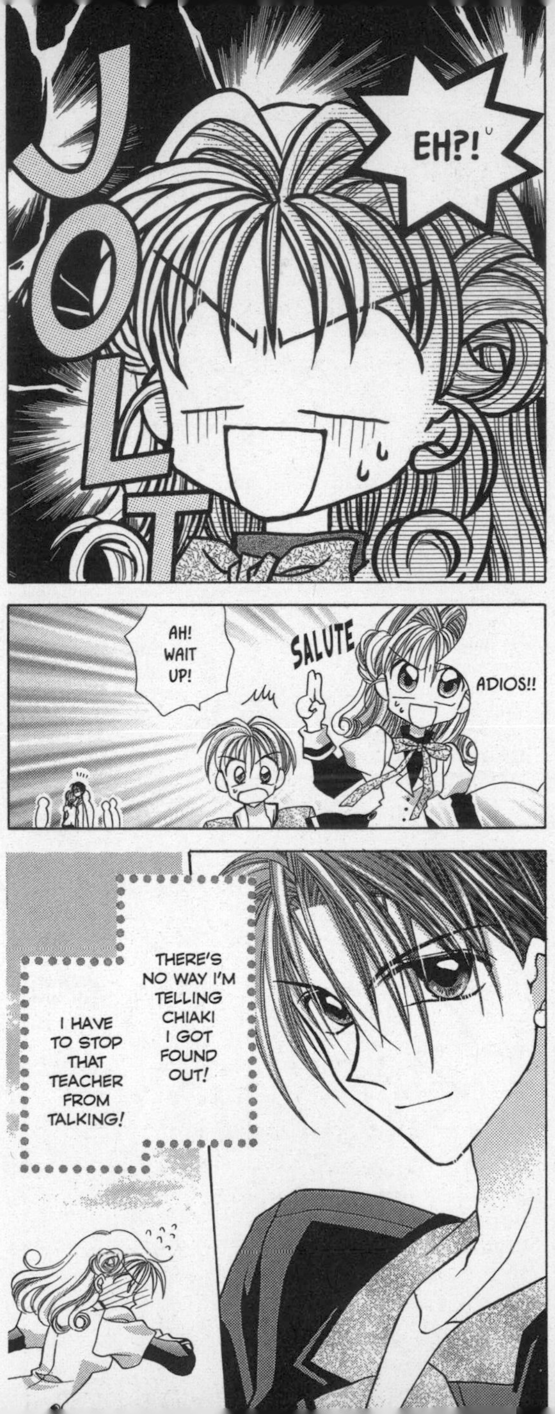
EH?!
JOLT
ADIOS!!
SALUTE
AH! WAIT UP!
THERE'S NO WAY I'M TELLING CHIAKI I GOT FOUND OUT!
I HAVE TO STOP THAT TEACHER FROM TALKING!

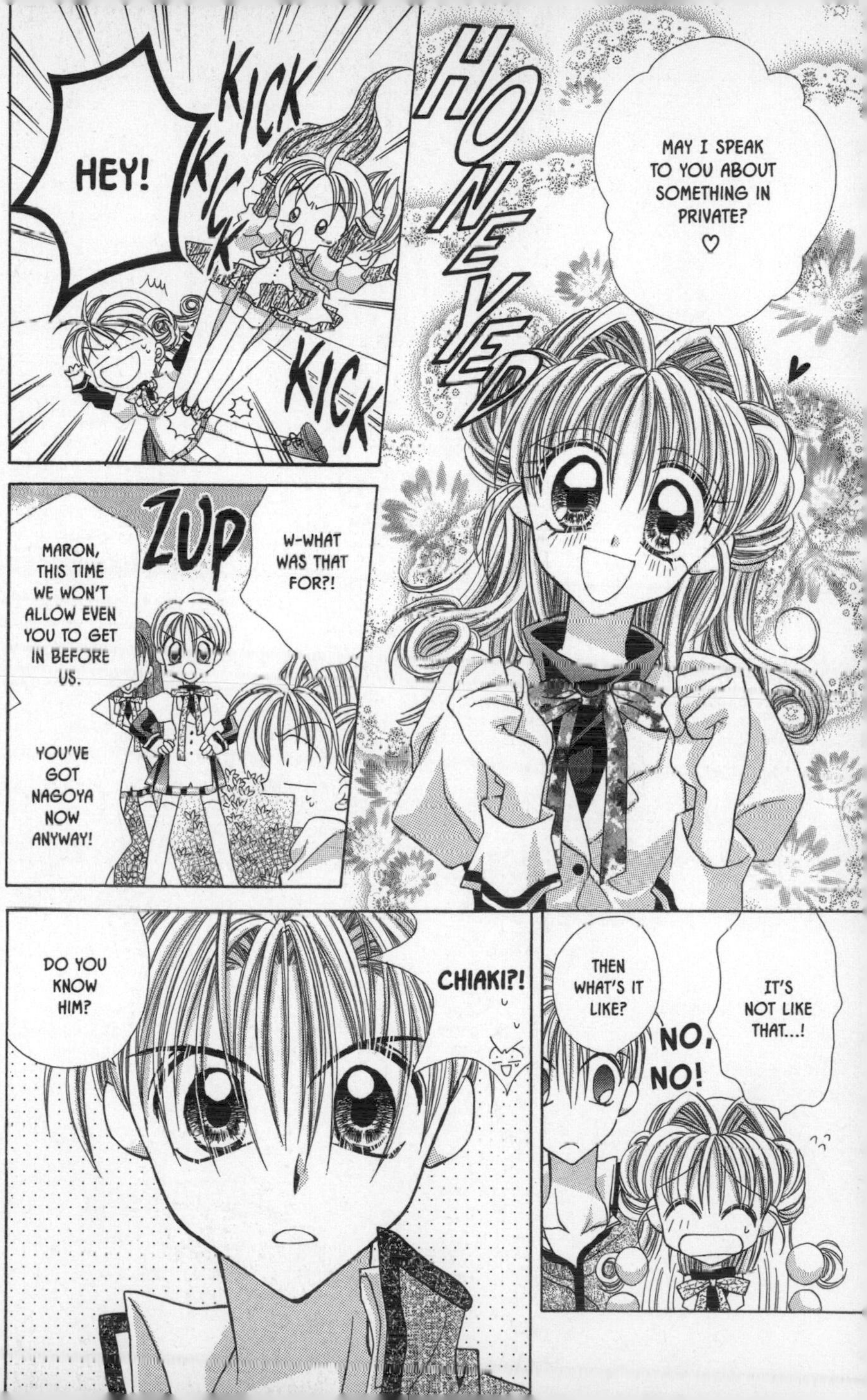
HONEYEYED
MAY I SPEAK TO YOU ABOUT SOMETHING IN PRIVATE? ♡
KICK
KICK
HEY!
KICK
W-WHAT WAS THAT FOR?!
ZUP
MARON, THIS TIME WE WON'T ALLOW EVEN YOU TO GET IN BEFORE US.
YOU'VE GOT NAGOYA NOW ANYWAY!
IT'S NOT LIKE THAT...!
NO, NO!
THEN WHAT'S IT LIKE?
CHIAKI?!
DO YOU KNOW HIM?

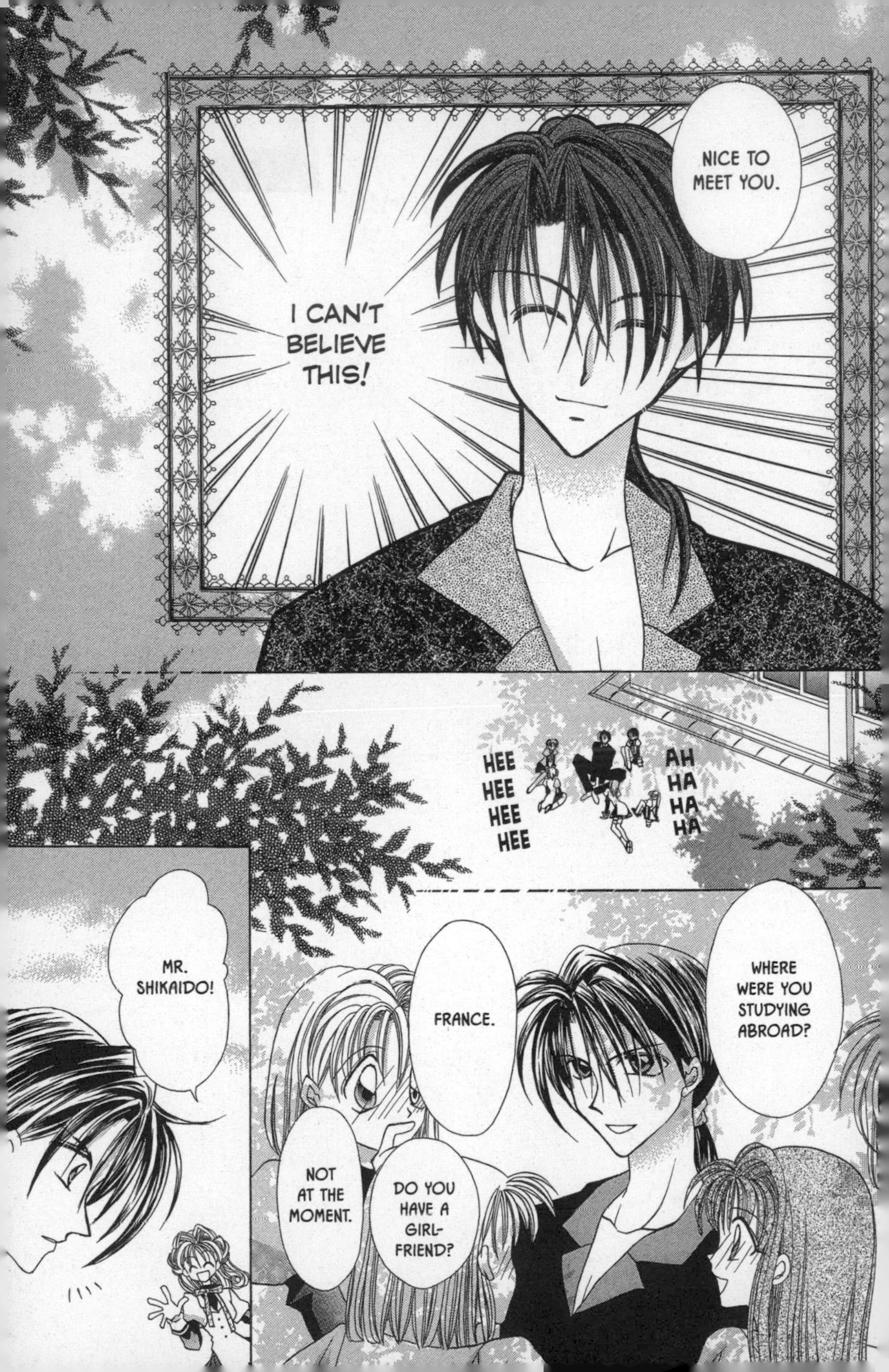
NICE TO MEET YOU.
I CAN'T BELIEVE THIS!
AH HA HA HA
HEE HEE HEE HEE
WHERE WERE YOU STUDYING ABROAD?
FRANCE.
DO YOU HAVE A GIRL-FRIEND?
NOT AT THE MOMENT.
MR. SHIKAIDO!

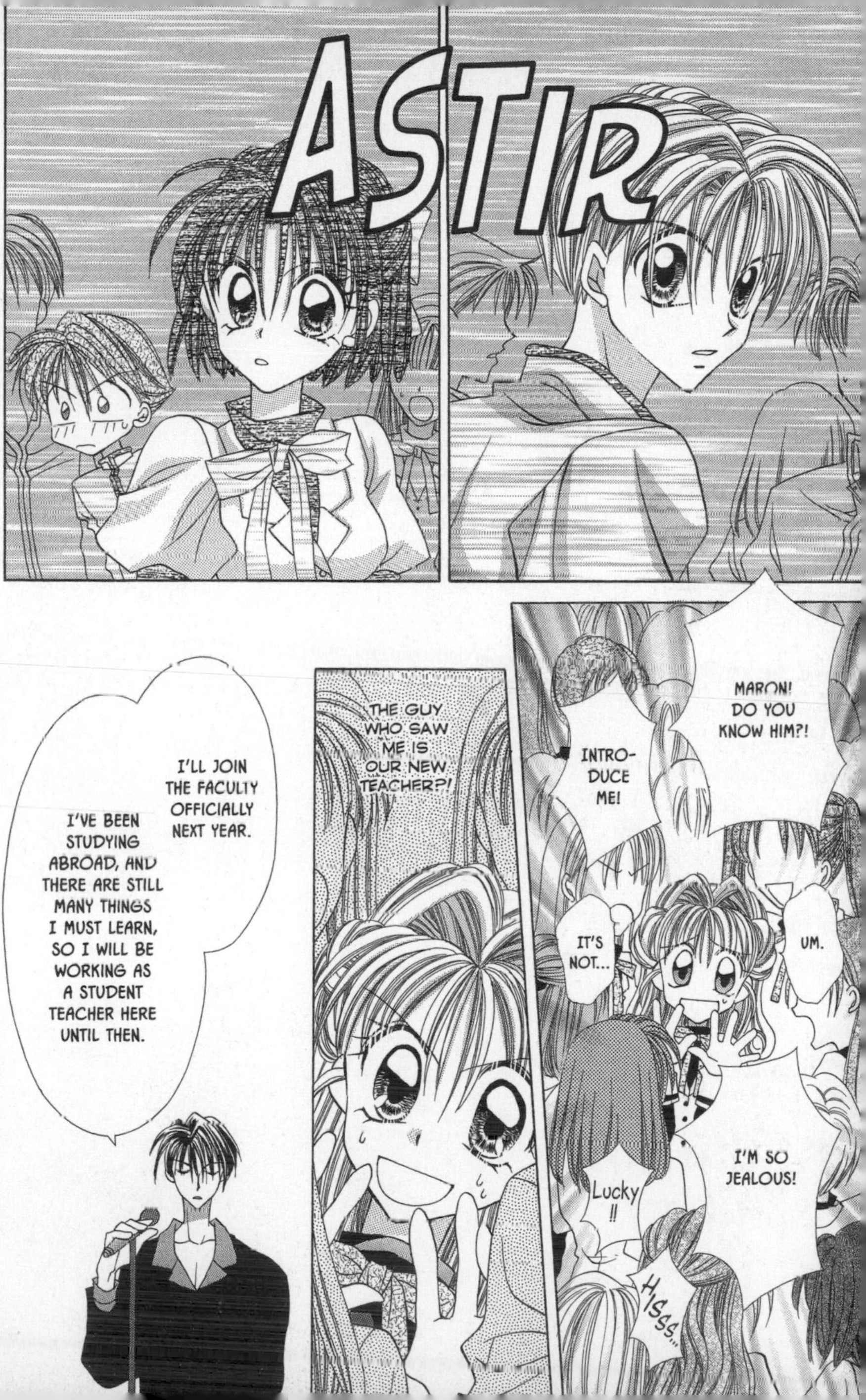
ASTIR
MARON! DO YOU KNOW HIM?!
INTRODUCE ME!
UM.
IT'S NOT...
I'M SO JEALOUS!
Lucky!!
HISSS...
THE GUY WHO SAW ME IS OUR NEW TEACHER?!
I'LL JOIN THE FACULTY OFFICIALLY NEXT YEAR.
I'VE BEEN STUDYING ABROAD, AND THERE ARE STILL MANY THINGS I MUST LEARN, SO I WILL BE WORKING AS A STUDENT TEACHER HERE UNTIL THEN.

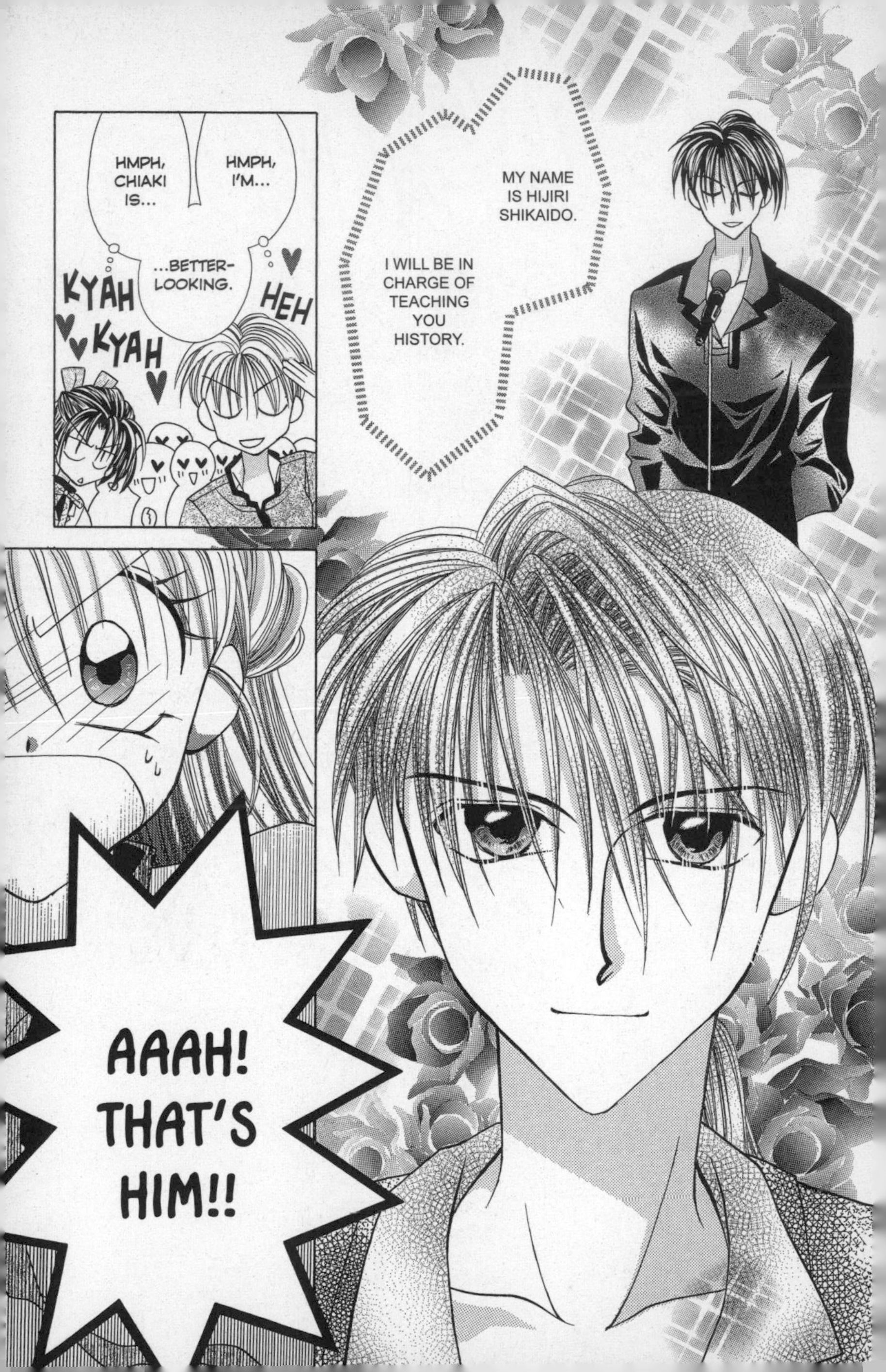
MY NAME IS HIJIRI SHIKAIDO.
I WILL BE IN CHARGE OF TEACHING YOU HISTORY.
HMPH, I'M...
HMPH, CHIAKI IS...
...BETTER-LOOKING.
HEH
KYAH
KYAH
AAAH! THAT'S HIM!!

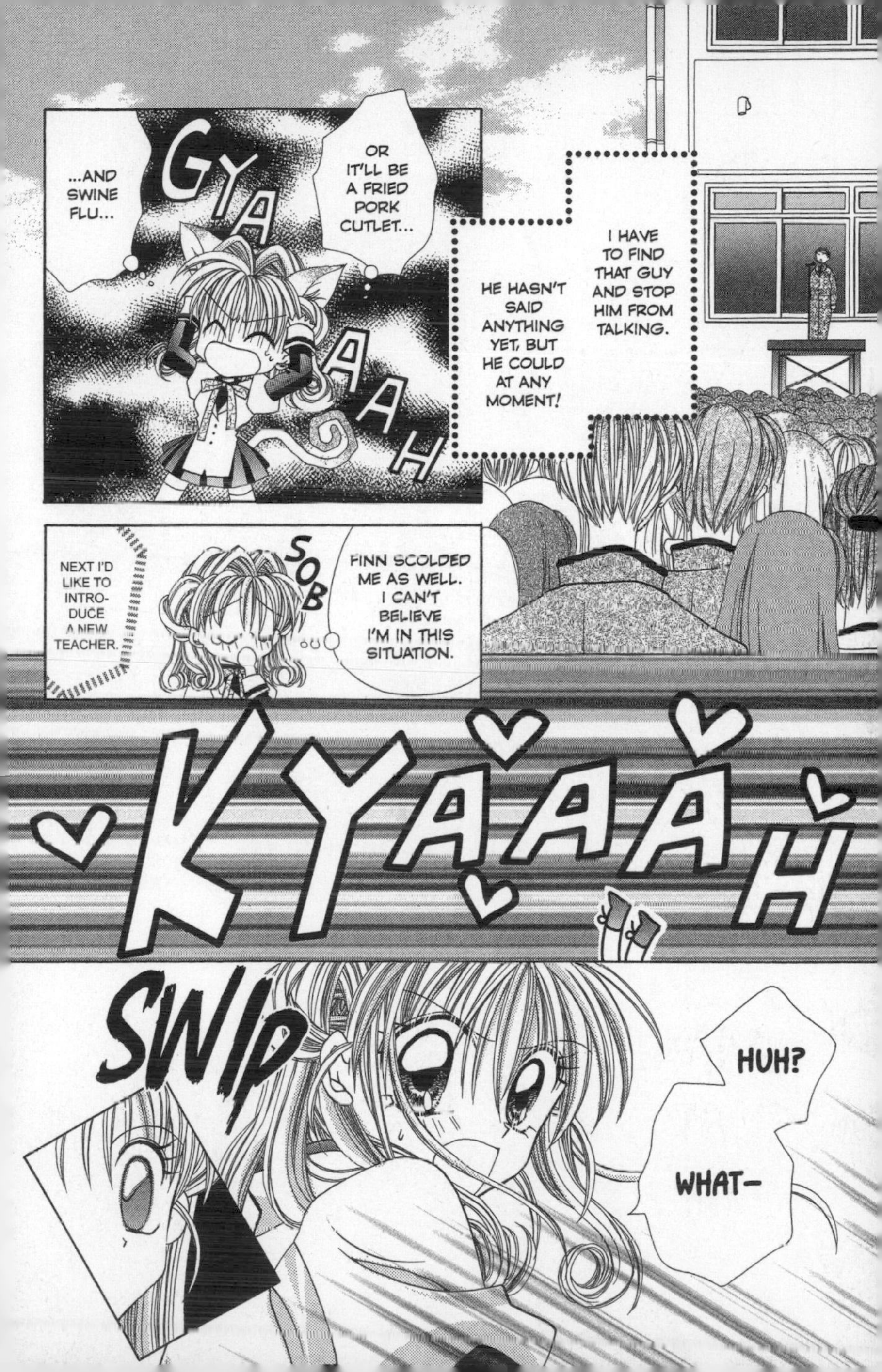
I HAVE TO FIND THAT GUY AND STOP HIM FROM TALKING.
HE HASN'T SAID ANYTHING YET, BUT HE COULD AT ANY MOMENT!
OR IT'LL BE A FRIED PORK CUTLET...
GYAAAAH
...AND SWINE FLU...
FINN SCOLDED ME AS WELL. I CAN'T BELIEVE I'M IN THIS SITUATION.
SOB
NEXT I'D LIKE TO INTRO-DUCE A NEW TEACHER.
KYAAAH
HUH?
WHAT-
SWIP

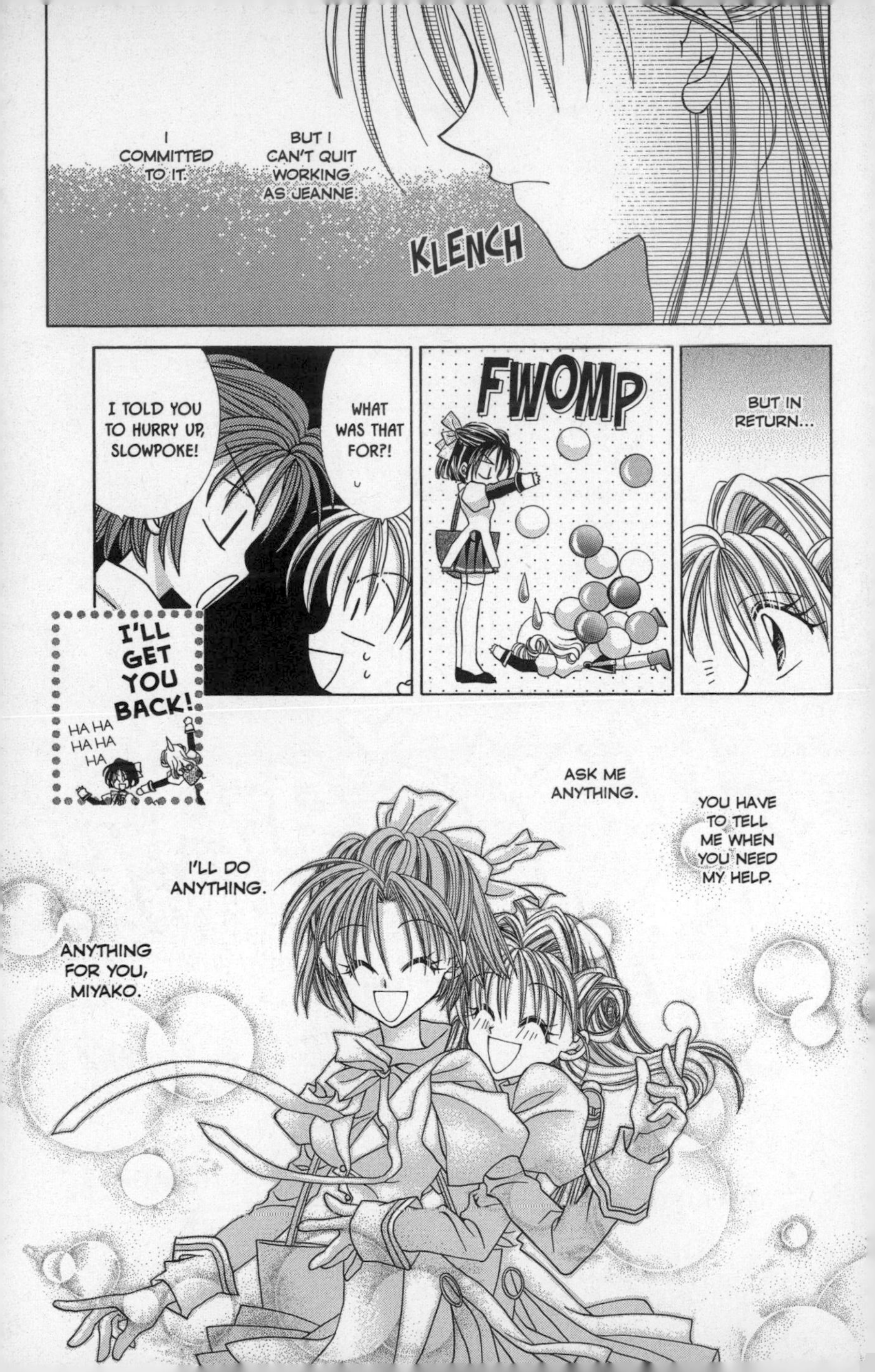
BUT I CAN'T QUIT WORKING AS JEANNE.
I COMMITTED TO IT.
KLENCH
BUT IN RETURN...
FWOMP
WHAT WAS THAT FOR?!
I TOLD YOU TO HURRY UP, SLOWPOKE!
I'LL GET YOU BACK!
HA HA HA HA HA
YOU HAVE TO TELL ME WHEN YOU NEED MY HELP.
ASK ME ANYTHING.
I'LL DO ANYTHING.
ANYTHING FOR YOU, MIYAKO.

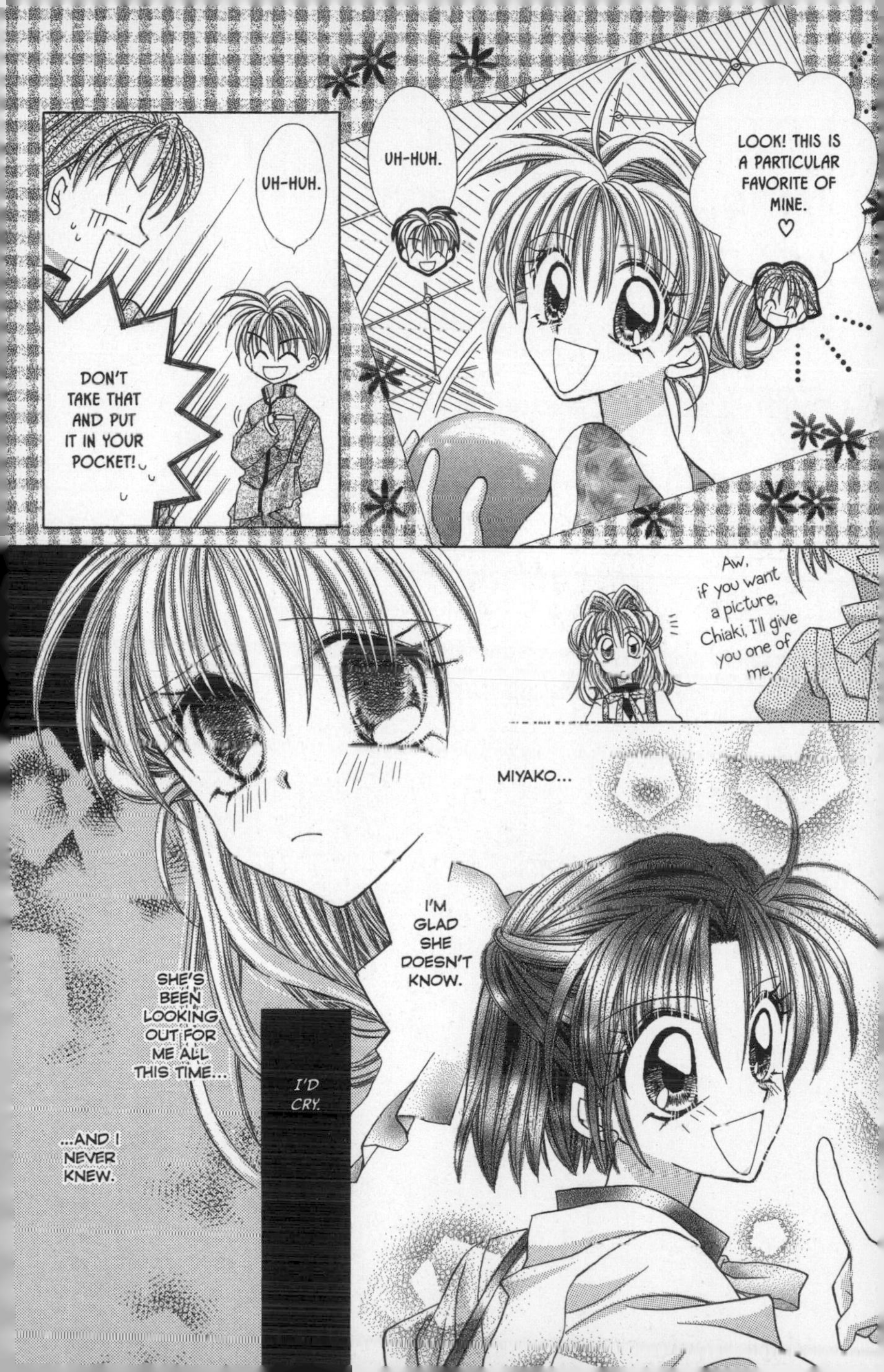
LOOK! THIS IS A PARTICULAR FAVORITE OF MINE. ♡
UH-HUH.
UH-HUH.
DON'T TAKE THAT AND PUT IT IN YOUR POCKET!
Aw, if you want a picture, Chiaki, I'll give you one of me.
MIYAKO...
I'M GLAD SHE DOESN'T KNOW.
SHE'S BEEN LOOKING OUT FOR ME ALL THIS TIME...
I'D CRY.
...AND I NEVER KNEW.

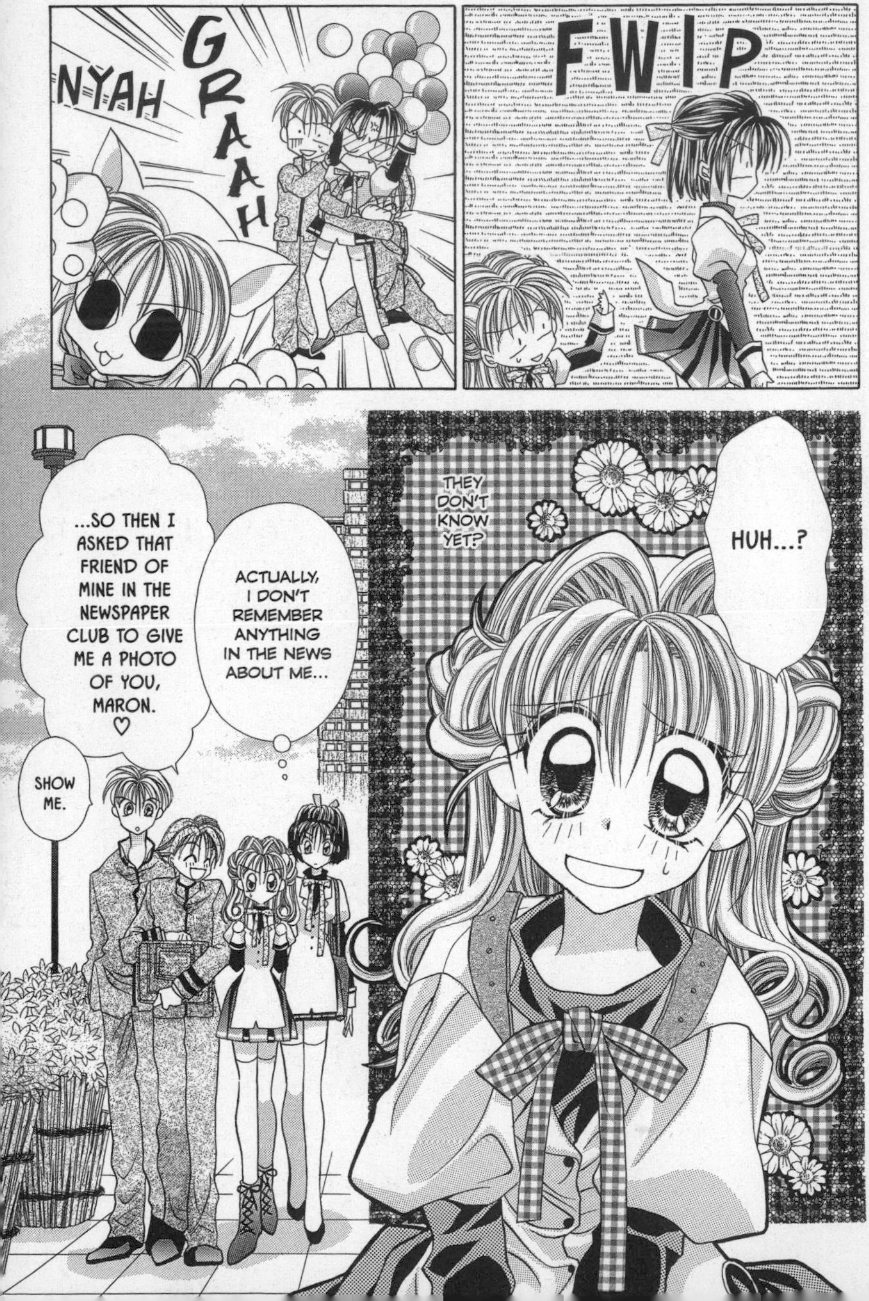
FWIP
GRAAH
NYAH
HUH...?
THEY DON'T KNOW YET?
...SO THEN I ASKED THAT FRIEND OF MINE IN THE NEWSPAPER CLUB TO GIVE ME A PHOTO OF YOU, MARON. ♡
ACTUALLY, I DON'T REMEMBER ANYTHING IN THE NEWS ABOUT ME...
SHOW ME.

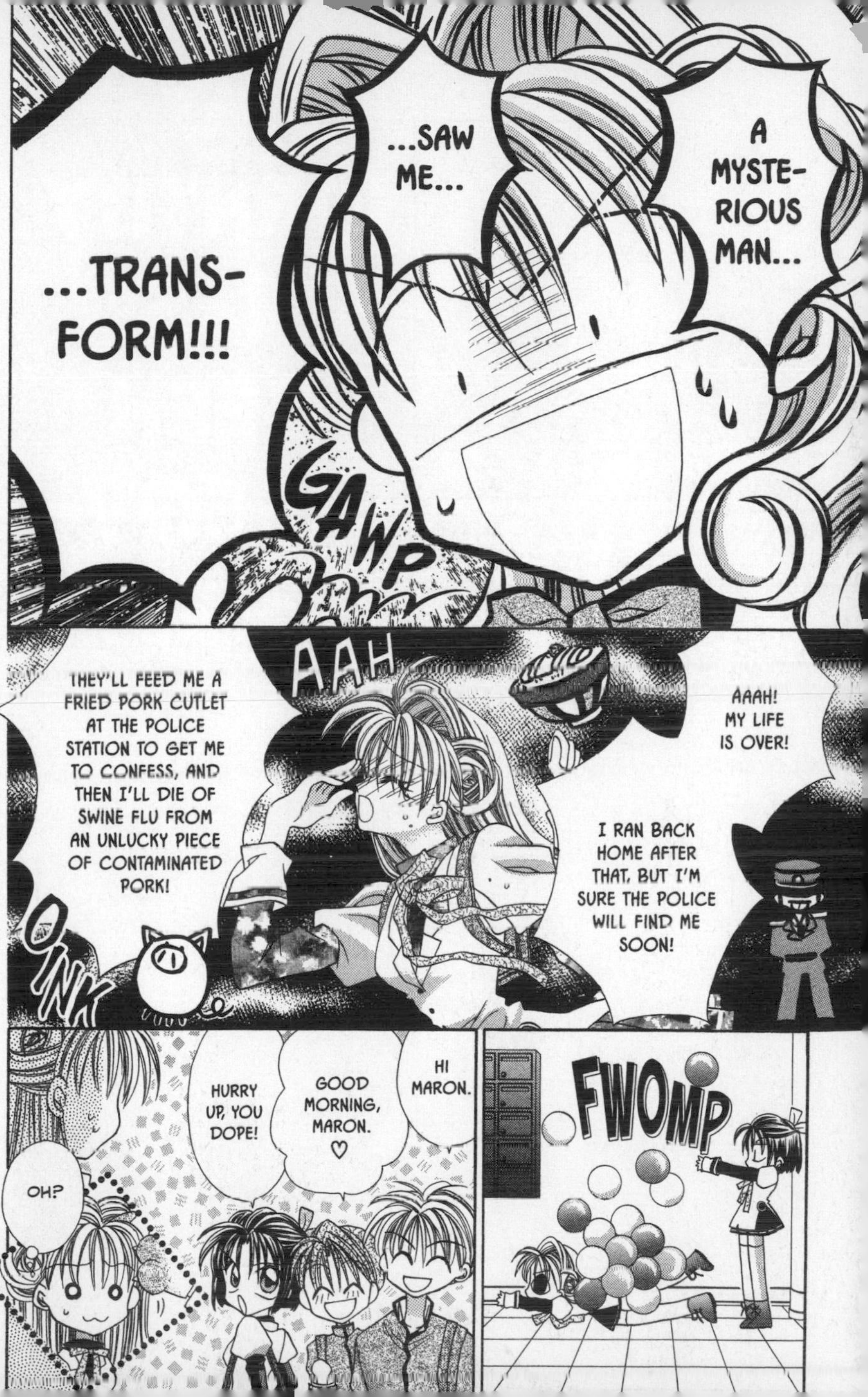
A MYSTE-RIOUS MAN...
...SAW ME...
...TRANS-FORM!!!
GAWP
AAAH! MY LIFE IS OVER!
I RAN BACK HOME AFTER THAT, BUT I'M SURE THE POLICE WILL FIND ME SOON!
AAH
THEY'LL FEED ME A FRIED PORK CUTLET AT THE POLICE STATION TO GET ME TO CONFESS, AND THEN I'LL DIE OF SWINE FLU FROM AN UNLUCKY PIECE OF CONTAMINATED PORK!
OINK
FWOMP
HI MARON.
GOOD MORNING, MARON. ♡
HURRY UP, YOU DOPE!
OH?

IDENTITY HAS BEEN DISCOV-ERED.

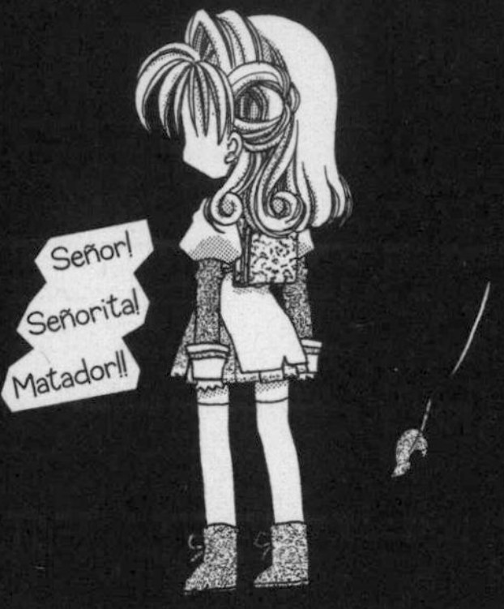
Señor!
Señorita!
Matador!!

PHANTOM
THIEF
JEANNE

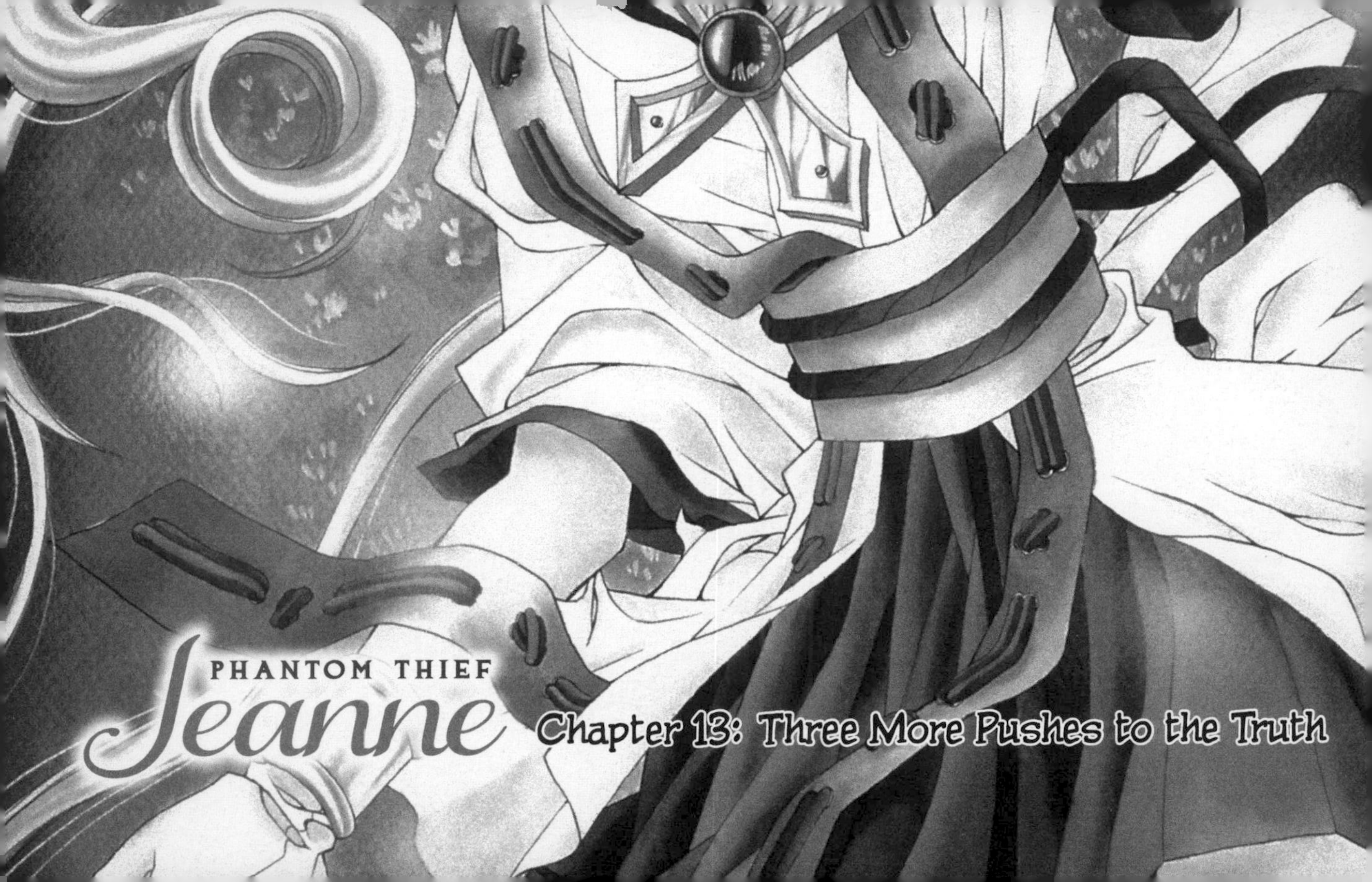
PHANTOM THIEF
Jeanne
Chapter 13: Three More Pushes to the Truth

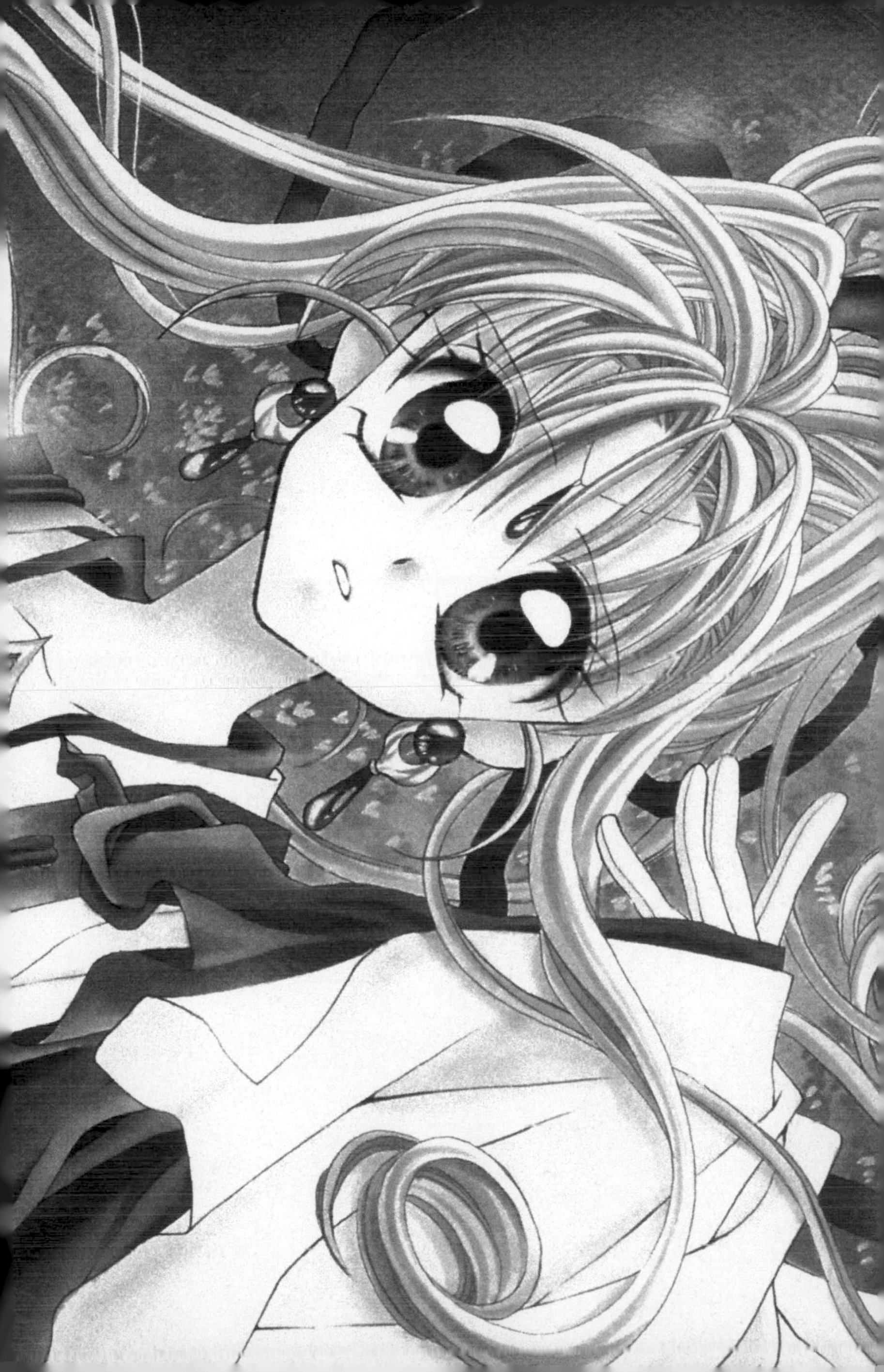

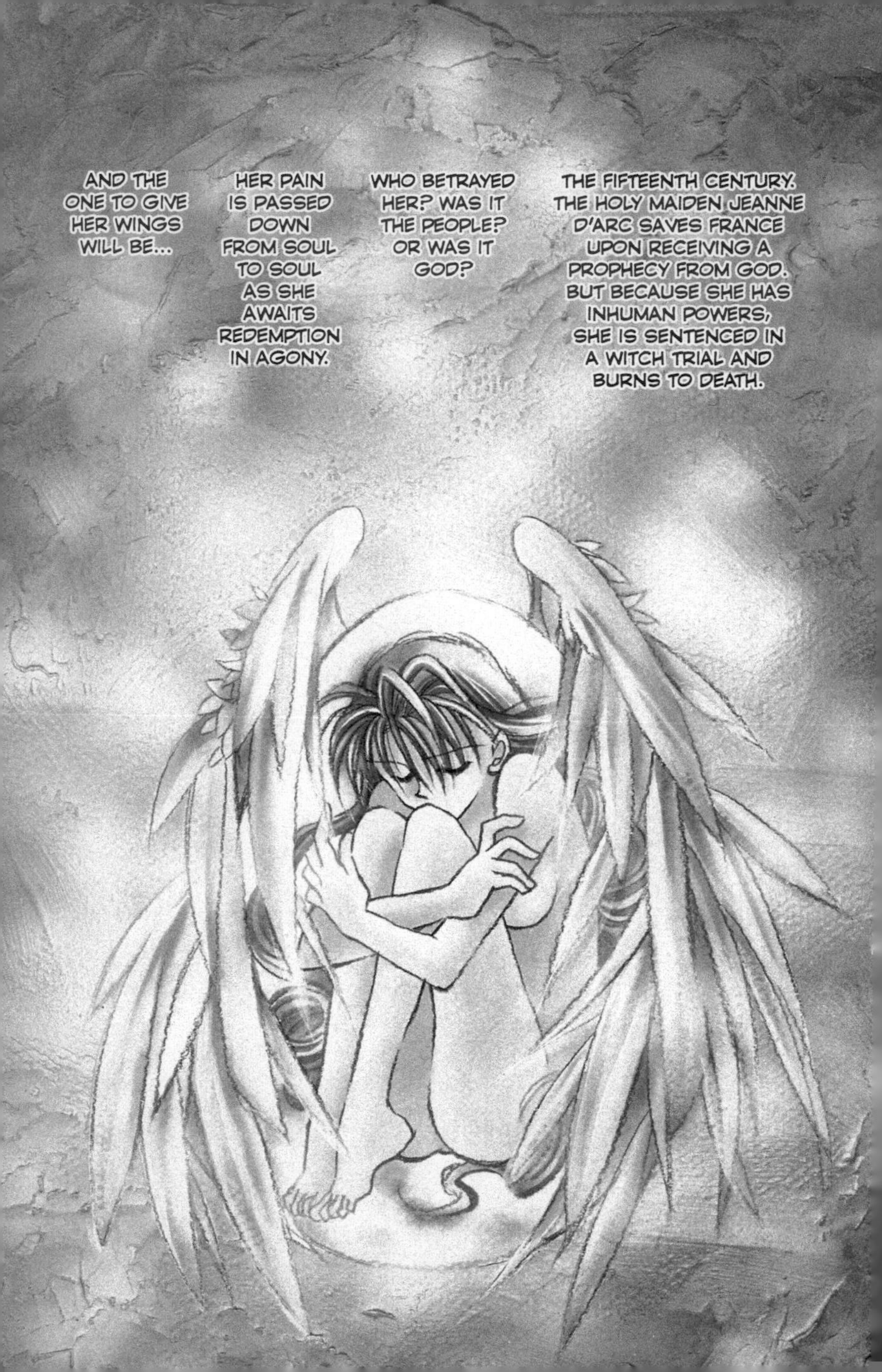
THE FIFTEENTH CENTURY. THE HOLY MAIDEN JEANNE D'ARC SAVES FRANCE UPON RECEIVING A PROPHECY FROM GOD. BUT BECAUSE SHE HAS INHUMAN POWERS, SHE IS SENTENCED IN A WITCH TRIAL AND BURNS TO DEATH.
WHO BETRAYED HER? WAS IT THE PEOPLE? OR WAS IT GOD?
HER PAIN IS PASSED DOWN FROM SOUL TO SOUL AS SHE AWAITS REDEMPTION IN AGONY.
AND THE ONE TO GIVE HER WINGS WILL BE...

PHANTOM THIEF

# Jeanne

# 3

STORY AND ART BY
## Arina Tanemura